Praise for *Manipulating*

"A fascinating study into the origins of t[e]
and fake news, and the creators who unleashed them on our world
out of misguided patriotism."

—**David Callaway**, former editor-in-chief of *USA Today*

"An instant classic. This stunning history of the origins of American
propaganda and the information state unveils the threat to self-government that's been with us since World War I. If you care about
democracy, this book belongs at the top of your reading list."

—**Thomas E. Patterson**, Bradlee Professor of Government
and the Press of Harvard University

"There are fewer more important obligations of government in a democracy than to keep citizens informed and to tell the truth. That
standard, sadly, has failed at crucial moments in our history, and
John Maxwell Hamilton's volume recalls the history of a seminal
failure. This book should open our eyes to shortcomings in what
we get as 'public information' and ask us all to demand better from
our nation's leaders."

—**Mike McCurry**, former White House and State Department
spokesman and director of the Center for Public Theology
at Wesley Theological Seminary

"George Creel and his Committee on Public Information, directed
by President Woodrow Wilson, represented a massive and successful effort during World War I to mold opinion in favor of American involvement in the war. Hamilton's book demonstrates that
distorted propaganda such as what we saw during the Vietnam War
and from today's White House is nothing new. His story is a mirror
into our own times."

—Former ambassador **Theodore Sedgwick**, commissioner of the
World War I Centennial Commission

"This highly readable, meticulously researched book examines the origins of modern US propaganda, as refined in the twentieth century. These practices, well-intended at first, have ended up harming this nation by undermining its democratic principles. Professor Hamilton rings a warning bell that all should hear about the dangers that propaganda, whether from abroad or within our own land, continues to hold for the future of America's open society."

—**Loch K. Johnson**, Regents Professor Emeritus of Public and International Affairs at the University of Georgia

"John Hamilton has written an outstanding, timely new book. A century ago, President Woodrow Wilson's Ministry of Public Information was America's first and only propagandistic Ministry of Information. Today, we have deteriorated to darker, diminished discourse with phrases such as 'fake news' by a president who has made tens of thousands of false or misleading public statements since his inauguration. All of this can be traced to the story Hamilton tells."

—**Charles Lewis**, founder of the Center for Public Integrity and the International Consortium of Investigative Journalists

"*Manipulating the Masses* brilliantly tells the story of President Woodrow Wilson's 1916 reelection campaign and how Wilson used the same techniques to shape public opinion when he took the country into World War I and created the Committee on Public Information. All public affairs offices in government today as well as the private sector's public relations industry owe their birth to Wilson's CPI and what was done there. It's quite a story."

—**Charlie Cook**, editor and publisher of *The Cook Political Report*

MANIPULATING THE MASSES

President Woodrow Wilson and George Creel, in step, as they stride a train station platform in France on the eve of peace treaty negotiations, 1919. (Getty Images)

MANIPULATING THE MASSES

Woodrow Wilson and the Birth of AMERICAN PROPAGANDA

John Maxwell Hamilton

Louisiana State University Press
Baton Rouge

Published with the assistance of the Noland Fund

Published with the assistance of the Borne Fund

Published by Louisiana State University Press
Copyright © 2020 by John Maxwell Hamilton
All rights reserved. Except in the case of brief quotations used in articles or reviews, no part of this publication may be reproduced or transmitted in any format or by any means without written permission of Louisiana State University Press.

Louisiana Paperback Edition, 2024

Designer: Laura Roubique Gleason
Typeface: Garamond Premier Pro

About the cover image: Joseph Pennell's famous poster depicting a direct German attack on New York, 1918, made the war in Europe seem an immediate threat to Americans at home, which it was not. The emotionally riveting poster, designed to promote Liberty Loans, did not have the CPI's name on it, but the CPI inspired it and helped produce it—and many more messages like it.

Library of Congress Cataloging-in-Publication Data

Names: Hamilton, John Maxwell, author.
Title: Manipulating the Masses : Woodrow Wilson and the Birth of American Propaganda / John Maxwell Hamilton.
Other titles: Woodrow Wilson and the birth of American propaganda
Description: Baton Rouge : Louisiana State University Press, [2020] | Includes bibliographical references and index.
Identifiers: LCCN 2020013943 (print) | LCCN 2020013944 (ebook) | ISBN 978-0-8071-7077-9 (cloth) | ISBN 978-0-8071-7417-3 (pdf) | ISBN 978-0-8071-7418-0 (epub) | ISBN 978-0-8071-8171-3 (paperback)
Subjects: LCSH: United States. Committee on Public Information. | Propaganda, American—History. | World War, 1914–1918—Public opinion. | World War, 1914–1918—Propaganda.
Classification: LCC D632 .H36 2020 (print) | LCC D632 (ebook) | DDC 940.3/73—dc23
LC record available at https://lccn.loc.gov/2020013943
LC ebook record available at https://lccn.loc.gov/2020013944

In memory of Michael H. B. Adler
and Mary Townsend Heathcote

I suspect the future historian will find that the thing which ultimately brought about the victory of the Allied forces on the western front was not wholly the strength of the arm of the soldier, nor wholly the number of guns of the Allied nations; it was rather the mental forces that were at work nerving those arms, and producing those guns, and producing in the civil populations and military populations alike of those countries that unconquerable determination that this work should have but one end, a righteous end. . . . The whole business of mobilizing the mind of the world so far as American participation in the war was concerned was in a sense the work of the Committee on Public Information.

—Newton D. Baker, Secretary of War, November 20, 1918

For five years there has been no free play of public opinion in the world. Confronted by the inexorable necessities of war, governments conscripted public opinion as they conscripted men and money and materials. Having conscripted it, they dealt with it as they dealt with other raw recruits. They mobilized it. They put it in charge of drill sergeants. They goose-stepped it. They taught it to stand at attention and salute. . . . Its ultimate function was to suppress all information that Government wished to suppress for any reason whatsoever.

—Frank I. Cobb, Editor, *New York World,* December 31, 1919

Contents

Illustrations

MANIPULATING
THE MASSES

Prologue
Building 406

In March 2003, when the United States was preparing to invade Iraq, hundreds of journalists arrived in Doha, the capital of Qatar, and made their way ten miles southwest to Camp As Sayliyah where the US Central Command's forward headquarters was located. Inside the camp, journalists were restricted to Building 406, a windowless, over-air-conditioned warehouse the color of the beige desert around it. The centerpiece of Building 406 was a glitzy, twenty-square-yard media center that had nothing in common with the government-issue feel of the rest of the camp.

The briefing room became the story for war correspondents desperate to write about something while they waited for the action to begin. They reported its cost, $1.5 million, and that it was created by George Allison, a Hollywood set designer who did the same for the game show *Who Wants to Be a Millionaire.* They described the five fifty-inch plasma screens and two seventy-inch projection screens, the clocks that ticked off time in half a dozen other parts of the world, the powder blue and white map of the world overlaid with Centcom's emblem. "We use the latest technology in our military operations," a Centcom public affairs officer said. "It's only fitting we use it here."[1]

After the invasion was launched, Centcom did not hold briefings for two days. Furious reporters stood around drinking coffee and watching the war on the media center's large television screens. When the briefing set was finally lit up on March 22, the 7:00 a.m. press conferences were heavily staged. The principal choreographer was Jim Wilkerson, the director of strategic communication for Centcom. An intense, competitive marathon runner in his early thirties, Wilkerson had earned his chops in the world of partisan messaging and tactics. He was one of the team of Republicans who fought against a recount of Florida ballots in the 2000 presidential election of George Bush. While serving as Bush's White House deputy communications director, he drafted a paper that made the case for the United States to invade Iraq. It carried a title that subsequent events rendered ironic: "A Decade of Deception and Defiance." His instructions in Doha were to push three news narratives: Iraqi jubilation over their liberation by American forces; US provision of humanitarian assistance; and the discovery of weapons of mass destruction. Detailed guidance came from Washington in a daily conference call.[2]

Every day a photogenic army general, Vincent Brooks, strode to the lectern to deliver an upbeat message. "Ladies and gentlemen," he said on April 28, "Operation Iraqi Freedom is now in the 28th day since coalition forces entered Iraq. Iraq is more stable today than yesterday." It was true that the swift, well-coordinated marine and army advance left the Iraqis little time to harden Baghdad's defenses. Nevertheless, the invasion did not conform to the script Washington called for. When it did not, Centcom tried its best to Wite-Out the discrepancies. Lieutenant General John Abizaid, Centcom's second in command, mounted the podium one day with Brooks and blew off the significance of "troops dressed in civilian clothes that appeared to welcome the forces and then ambushed them." These were, he said, "the actions of desperate people that are trying to save a doomed regime. . . . These moves are all dangerous to the troops in the field, but they're not dangerous to the success of the mission." As time would tell, the irregular forces whose importance the general dismissed were a harbinger of the difficulties that lay ahead in making Iraq a stable state—a task that remains to this day uncompleted.[3]

Correspondents had been told they would "get the big picture here from this podium," CBS's Tom Fenton complained one morning. "And instead we have been getting snapshot videos, vague generalities." When a correspondent asked for videos of unsuccessful attacks, Brooks answered, "I don't have images of unsuccessful attacks." That day he called the briefing room "a platform for truth."[4]

Building 406 was a landmark in government control of public opinion. Its most profound significance, however, did not reside in the new equipment. Nor did it reside in having Wilkinson, a civilian, hovering over field briefings, a development that the military public affairs officers in Doha considered unprecedented. The deeper meaning of Building 406 was its fundamental familiarity.[5]

Propaganda in all its manifestations—both the provision and the suppression of information—is a quotidian feature of American government. It comes in a daily flow of press releases, Facebook postings, Instagram messages, Snapchats, YouTube videos, live-streamed speeches, scripted press conferences, strategic leaks, background briefings, and Twitter feeds—whatever will project an administration's message.

Building 406 is one of a great many landmarks that trace the rise of the Information State. Enhanced techniques for managing news and opinion appear especially in wars. But innovation is constant, as more and more officials employ increasingly sophisticated equipment and increasingly refined persuasion techniques to win office and govern.

There was a time, however, when American government propaganda was truly new and unfamiliar. That time, too, saw an explosion of new communication technologies. While manipulation of information and minds was then a concern, it was a period of great faith that does not exist today. That faith held that government publicity would enrich public opinion and take democracy to new levels.

That time was during another military conflict, the Great War, more than a century ago. The epicenter of this revolutionary challenge to American democracy was a row of red brick townhouses as unprepossessing as Building 406. Here, on Lafayette Square, a few paces from the White House, stood the headquarters of the Committee on Public Information.

Introduction

This book is about the profound and enduring threat to American democracy that rose out of the Great War—the establishment of pervasive, systematic propaganda as an instrument of the state. That horrific conflict required the mobilization of entire nations, no less the United States than the countries of Europe. The government in Washington exercised unprecedented power to shape the views and attitudes of the citizens it was supposed to serve. Its agent for this was the Committee on Public Information, the first and only time the United States government had a ministry of propaganda. Nothing like it had existed before, and it would be dismantled at the end of the war. But the CPI endured as a blueprint for the Information State that exists today in peacetime as well as during war.[1]

Journalist Walter Lippmann went into the war an eager propagandist and left it disillusioned with the "manufacture of consent." He summed up the CPI's legacy in his classic book *Public Opinion,* published in 1922. "Persuasion," he wrote, "has become a self-conscious art and a regular organ of popular government."[2]

From the beginning of the American democratic experiment, political leaders were preoccupied with public opinion. "Dominion is founded in Opinion," Benjamin Franklin warned the British of the consequences of denying colonists fair treatment. In times of perceived crisis, presidents occasionally took direct action to curb unwanted news and views. The Sedition Acts, signed by President John Adams in 1798, aimed to silence Thomas Jefferson–led Republicans whose enthusiasm for the French Revolution, or so the Federalists alleged, would sweep the United States into a reign of terror. The acts criminalized any expression that brought the United States, the president, or Congress into "contempt or disrepute." During the Civil War, Abraham Lincoln authorized Secretary of War Edwin Stanton to take control of the telegraphs. Stanton stopped news stories, jailed reporters and editors, and issued news bulletins. "As false as a news bulletin" became a newsroom saying. President William McKinley, who introduced procedures to monitor the press closely in order to gauge public opinion, increased the number of White House news releases in the run-up to the Spanish-American War and embedded reporters in the White House after it began. His goal was not better news reporting but better management of it. One of McKinley's assistants triumphantly reported that few "authentic details of what is going on reach the public."[3]

Except for these short-lived bursts of suppression, however, the government did little to stifle political speech. The Sedition Act expired after three years. The use of government propaganda to shape opinion in times of peace was distasteful. In 1905 President Theodore Roosevelt hired a former journalist as secretary of the Panama Canal Commission. Part of his duties was to build public support for the endeavor. Congress pushed back so hard that Roosevelt caved. His secretary would do no more publicity work. In 1913 Congress passed legislation forbidding, without its expressed approval, the expenditure of appropriated funds on *publicity experts,* a term then gaining currency. "It does not seem to me," said Frederick Gillett, the author of the legislation and a future Speaker of the House, "that it is proper for any department of the Government to employ a person simply as a press agent."[4]

President Woodrow Wilson shattered these traditions when he established the Committee on Public Information on April 14, 1917, one week after the United States entered the war. Although it was not clear at that moment how sweeping this change would be, the priority given to the CPI's work *was* clear. It was created a month before passage of the conscription law to build a fighting force. The initial concern was to censor news that could compromise military action. Congress had not passed laws governing that; administrative rules and procedures had yet to be written. Nor had anyone spelled out what information the CPI would provide. Wilson merely created "a Committee on Public Information, to be composed of the Secretary of State, the Secretary of War, the Secretary of the Navy, and a civilian who shall be charged with the executive direction of the committee." George Creel was named the civilian chairman. Nothing more. In the absence of congressional hearings or authorization, the CPI could be anything Woodrow Wilson and George Creel wanted it to be.[5]

TOUCHING EVERY PART OF THE WAR MACHINERY

The nineteen months the United States was at war set in motion the expansion of government propaganda that has occurred relentlessly since. "There was no part of the great war machinery that we did not touch, no medium of appeal that we did not employ," Creel said. It was one of the few times the hyperbolic journalist made an understatement.[6]

The CPI shot propaganda through every capillary in the American bloodstream. It established a national newspaper, the *Official Bulletin,* and filled war-making agencies with news multipliers who cranked out press releases and guided reporters. The CPI spread its messages through articles, cartoons, and advertisements in newspapers and magazines; through textbooks and Sunday church sermons; through feature films, talks during intermission, and the ads it put on theater curtains; through posters plastered on buildings and displayed in storefront windows; through pamphlets distributed by the millions.

Overseas, the CPI was similarly energetic. It established a pioneering news service to transmit the American point of view to foreign audiences. It created the first public affairs offices in conjunction with embassies. It set up reading rooms, tested techniques for dropping leaflets in enemy territory by air, put up thousands of posters, and distributed movies. To a degree never before seen with presidential utterances, the CPI promoted Wilson's idealistic rhetoric abroad.

The scope of the battlefield in the Great War, the range of weapons, required an entirely new mindset. For the first time whole nations had to be geared to the war machine. "Everyone is a beginner at this new game," novelist H. G. Wells wrote. "Everyone is experimenting." Wells was one of those experimenters as head of British propaganda directed at the Germans, a position he left when he became disturbed by the intense German hatred created at home. The Germans felt the same pressure to invent. "Despite all preparations, the world confronted enemy propaganda with unexpected tasks during the Great War," observed Walter von Hofmann, perhaps the most thoughtful German propagandist of his time. "The immense dimensions it took on raised unforeseen problems on a national, military, political, economic, moral and spiritual level." "Step by step," a French historian wrote of his country, "proceeding by trial and error, the analysis of the nation's morale became a major preoccupation."[7]

Creel started with a blank page and sketched in the CPI on the fly. There was no planning, much improvisation. Reorganization was constant. A skilled manager would have found this a challenge, and Creel was not that. He was energetic and creative, impulsive and mercurial. In one of his greatest failures, he insisted the CPI should be in charge of field propaganda against enemy military forces and then failed to mount a serious effort, leaving a void that was filled by the American Expeditionary Forces. Edward Bernays, often considered the father of public relations, was an upstart when he worked for the CPI. He saw "it as a pioneer effort with trial and error, with much fumbling, and not as a well planned activity.... There never was a chart drawn in advance for the Committee on Public Information that I know of."[8]

Added to this was the CPI chairman's obstreperousness. "Brother Creel," observed Gus Karger, a Washington correspondent who often defended him, had "a delicious propensity for getting himself into trouble." With friends, Creel was "loveable and loving," wrote humor columnist Irwin S. Cobb, "but in his visible aspects as a publicist [he] is a professional hater. He takes in hating for a living." Creel needlessly provoked controversy and aggravated where a light touch would have saved him a lot of trouble, with Congress especially. As it was, legislators resented not having been consulted by Wilson in the creation of the CPI and, in the case of Republicans, regarded the CPI as his personal press agency and Creel as the "editor of the Court Chronicle."[9]

The CPI's propaganda was stunning in its extent and range. The *Official Bulletin* and other information vehicles were superb examples of government transparency. Creel was ahead of his time in hiring women for senior positions. The staff was high minded. Some deserve to be called heroic. Arthur Bullard, a foreign correspondent who helped conceptualize the CPI, produced some of the worthiest American propaganda during the war. Vira Whitehouse, a leader of the women's suffrage movement, overcame the American legation's opposition to create an outstanding publicity program in Bern. Josephine Roche, a social worker who reformed prostitutes in Denver, carried her progressive ideals into the Division of Work with the Foreign Born, which she headed. Ray Stannard Baker, who entered the story in a central way when Wilson negotiated the peace treaty in Paris, qualifies as the first American presidential press secretary and a model of how the job should be done. Among the many who toiled diligently and effectively at the local level was Tennessean Porter Dunlap, whom the reader will meet in the account of the Four Minute Men, who were organized to speak during movie intermissions.

The CPI's accomplishments are not its whole story, however. More than anything else, this book is a cautionary lesson about the intoxicating power of propaganda. John Adams recognized this in retirement, when he sought to rekindle friendship with the man whose party he had targeted with the Sedition Acts. "Power always thinks it has a great soul and vast views beyond the comprehension of the weak," he wrote to Thomas Jefferson, "and that it is doing God's service when it is violating all His laws." Walter von Hofmann on the German general staff put it more bluntly: "Following the principle that the end justifies the means, propaganda is not fussy about the latter."[10]

The CPI subverted the democratic ideals it espoused. It sanitized news, distorted facts, and was tendentious. It appealed to emotions of home and hearth, which was relatively benign, but aroused fear and hatred, which was not. It was not above shaming and coercion. At the same time that Creel insisted the CPI was always open, it worked through front organizations. Overseas it secretly subsidized news organs and bribed journalists. In its zeal to discredit the fledgling Bolshevik government in Russia, it was the conduit for forged documents that purported to show Vladimir Lenin and his comrades were German agents—and then it challenged the American loyalty of the few who dared question the documents' authenticity. It allied itself with some of the most vicious patriotic societies in the country. Working with federal intelligence agencies eager to sniff out subversives and stifle dissent, the CPI was an accomplice to the Wilson administration's trampling of civil liberties.

"Mr. Creel, public opinion can be informed both by the denial of information and by the supplying of information," a member of Congress pointedly remarked during a hearing on the CPI, "and it may be either accurately or inaccurately informed, according as that denial or supplying of information is honestly done." As it had come to pass, the CPI was not given direct legal authority to censor, but it acquired referred authorities to do so from the army, navy, and post office. The ostensible objective was to suppress information that jeopardized military pursuit of the war. "I am not a censor," Creel said repeatedly—and disingenuously. He used his official censorship authorities and enlarged on them informally by intimidating editors and reporters. He did not confine the CPI to protecting sensitive military subjects. He beat back opinion that challenged administration policies.[11]

THE NEED FOR CONTEXT

The CPI's story is a sprawling one. The few histories of it that have been written pass over congressional inquiries into its practices, its failures in field propaganda, its heavy-handed promotion of White Russian disinformation, and Creel's bizarre (there is no better word for it) end-of-war mission to central Europe, to name a few episodes. Not well understood or documented is the CPI's connection to intelligence agencies or its use of subterfuge. No attention has been given to the constitutional irregularity of Wilson's creation of the CPI by executive order rather than with congressional authorization, a lapse that put it on uncertain footing from the beginning.

The full story cannot be found in the CPI records in the National Archives.

The archives of organizations with which the CPI interacted, the personal papers of individuals whom it touched, and the records of other countries that waged propaganda at the same time contain invaluable information on what the CPI did to shape views and provide context for reconstructing the conditions that shaped it. Altogether I consulted some 150 collections. Those that I have cited are identified in "A Note on Sources" at the back of this book.

The activities of the CPI are taken up in detail in part II. Part I focuses on three of its antecedents, outlined below.

The Universality of Propaganda

The Committee on Public Information reflected the personalities of two individuals: Woodrow Wilson, who preferred to convey his idealistic messages magisterially to audiences of thousands rather than in give-and-take with small groups of politicians and journalists, and George Creel, whose bond with Wilson and outsized personality made him a powerful figure in wartime Washington. Washington pundits had not yet coined the term *spin*. Then the term was "creeling."[12]

Government propaganda, however, was inevitable no matter who was president—or German chancellor, or British prime minister, or French president. Politicians already had a heightened sensitivity to public opinion. One aspect of this was the increase in the number and quality of newspapers and magazines and in the number of people who could read them. More information led to greater accountability. But for every force there is a counterforce. Government officials used these same communication tools to move opinion in the direction they wanted it to move. The perfection of these manipulative techniques accelerated as a result of the unprecedented nature of the war. "The conditions of modern warfare" made propaganda essential, observed an official in the British Department of Information in 1917. "It is less a question of armies being arrayed against armies than of nations against nations—so that the civilian front is scarcely, if any, less important than the fighting front." It was "a war of the people in the fullest sense," said German quartermaster General Erich Ludendorff."[13]

The first chapter of this book recounts the origins of propaganda at the beginning of the war in 1914 and the steps that were immediately taken to control opinion at home and abroad. Special attention is accorded to belligerents' efforts to shape opinion in United States, either to keep it out of war (the goal of the Central Powers) or to get it in (the Allies' goal). The British were particularly effective in making inroads with the Wilson administration. Despite Creel's claim about the sui generis nature of American propaganda, the CPI learned from the British and worked closely, if sometimes unharmoniously, with them. The Germans' hapless propaganda subsequently made it easier for the CPI to portray them as sinister intriguers who posed an immediate threat to domestic security unless the American public got behind the Wilson administration's policies to win a war an ocean away.

Political Campaigning

It is often said that election campaigns have no bearing on what the victor does in office. But how one wins office determines how one governs in it. Barack Obama was the first social-media president, as John F. Kennedy was the first television president. Television helped Kennedy win election and govern. Obama harnessed social media in his ride to the presidency and, in office, created an Office of Digital Strategy to reach the public directly. In 2015, the office had fourteen staff members, two more people than were in George Bush's press office, which also carried on under Obama. In winning support for its nuclear pact with Iran, his administration created an "echo chamber" to channel its point of view through social media, journalists, and friendly interest groups. Obama advisor David Axelrod said that the White House staff "approached these major foreign-policy challenges as campaign challenges, and they've run campaigns, and those campaigns have been very sophisticated." [14]

Wilson's 1916 campaign for his second term in the White House—the subject of chapter 2—was the incubator for the Committee on Public Information. Wilson, by all rights, should have lost the election. A powerful factor in his victory was the Democratic National Committee's publicity bureau and Robert Woolley, the former journalist and political operative who ran it. Presidential campaigning had changed from being based on local party loyalty to requiring a national strategy to woo voters and enlist independent newspapers. Woolley adroitly used every form of communication available, targeted potential voters, and manufactured opportunities to embarrass Wilson's opponent, Charles Evans Hughes. His tactics reappeared in the CPI, as did his chief lieutenant, George Creel. In the future individuals would make similarly easy transitions from election campaigning to government propaganda—and back again. Each endeavor at persuasion would be a test kitchen for new techniques that would be employed and improved on later.

Progressivism

The CPI attracted prominent progressives. Many were muckrakers. Others came from the ranks of social work, the arts, the suffrage movement, universities, labor—anywhere that individuals sought to fashion a better nation. Progressives, the subject of chapter 3, spoke reverentially of "publicity," as they termed the purifying light they shed on social and political ills. Presenting himself as a progressive in his campaign for governor of New Jersey in 1910, Wilson said "pitiless publicity" would drive boss-run politics out of the state. Creel spoke in 1916 of digging "new wells of information that may be kept free from poison, filth and stagnancy." "It is hardly an exaggeration," historian Richard Hofstadter noted, "that the Progressive mind was characteristically a journalistic mind, and that its characteristic contribution was that of the socially responsible reporter-reformer."[15]

The CPI enlarged on publicity in a manner that resonated with another aspect of progressivism. This was the idea that experts, often working through government, could engineer solutions to society's problems. Before the war, publicity was a way to identify problems for the public. During the war, public attitudes became *the* problem that needed fixing, and publicity was a way to do it.

As we shall see, the CPI's attempt to shape the American mind was self-defeating as a progressive ideal. Progressives were correct that publicity led to greater accountability by every institution, from the corporation to city hall. But the federal government could not be accountable if it was to be the dominant source of fact and opinion. While a progressive might reasonably seek to clean up the slums, cleaning up minds was inherently undemocratic.

THE NEWS

A fourth factor, woven throughout the book and essential to understanding the CPI, is the attitude of journalists toward propaganda.

The CPI introduced a new dynamic into press-government relations. Journalists simultaneously resented and depended on the CPI. They resented that it stood between them and the news. They depended on it because the government's extensive wartime programs strained the resources of newspapers and magazines. They needed help to keep track of what the government was doing. This set a pattern that lasts up to the present.

In addition to shaping the news, propaganda became a subject of the news. Journalists treated this new element of governing as a "news beat," like covering city hall or major league baseball. Much of the reporting and commentary about Creel was negative; many suggestions were offered for reorganizing the CPI. But journalists were fascinated by the heightened attention that government gave to public opinion and embraced their role in it. Their suggestions on reforming censorship called for giving more authority to them to suppress the wrong kind of news.

Journalists amplified the CPI's messages, including some of the most emotionally charged. *Editor & Publisher,* a trade journal for the press, created a Gold Medal of Honor for the best editorial on behalf of a Liberty Loan drive at the end of the war. The winner was the *Wichita Beacon,* whose winning entry read, in part, "The Beast of the centuries, with his jaws dripping innocent blood, but with calculating eyes still watching for the slightest loop-hole for escape, is finally enveloped by the net of humanity. . . . Now, if ever, we must remember the acts of the Huns. . . . They are still ravishers of women and butchers of babies."[16]

One of the journalists who made propaganda a specialty, privately advised the administration on the subject, and welcomed direct guidance from it was Carl Ackerman. "In the war for Democracy, the press must lead," he wrote in one of his frequent letters to Wilson's closest advisor, Colonel Edward House. Ackerman's comment was emblematic of widespread hopefulness at the beginning of the war that public opinion, shaped by the government and the press, was a new positive factor that would make the world a better place. By war's end, this view had changed. The beginning of press cynicism about official Washington is often linked to government officials' deception and manipulation of the news during the Vietnam War, but its roots were in the Great War.[17]

LASTING SIGNIFICANCE

When the war ended, the Committee on Public Information's offices on Lafayette Square were put to other government uses. Like many of its files, the CPI disappeared from the government bureaucracy. But its lasting effects were felt in two contradictory ways: its absence when Wilson needed it immediately after the war, and the persistence of its techniques as a method of governing. The final two chapters of the book are devoted to these dual legacies.

Wilson took America into war with a promise to make the world "safe for democracy." In the coming months he called for a just peace and an association of nations to guarantee "political independence and territorial integrity." These statements elevated Wilson's image at home and abroad. He was, a British journalist said, "the greatest propagandist the modern world has known, displaying extraordinary skill and dexterity."[18]

Wilson's pronouncements, however, were vague and not easily realized. Achieving the grand peace that he had articulated required sustained propaganda after the last shot of the war was fired. Wilson had to manage public opinion in Paris during the treaty negotiations, where Allied leaders sought a vengeful peace, and at home, if he was to win Senate approval in a war-weary country with a long tradition of isolationism. The CPI never had greater potential value than at this time. But its heavy-handedness and partisanship during the war hastened its demise.

Physically unwell, beleaguered by the trying negotiations, and deluded in his conviction that the Senate and the public would stand with him, Wilson did not adjust. He did not develop a new publicity apparatus suited to the normal give-and-take of peacetime democracy. "In making plans for the new enduring peace," historian Thomas Bailey was to say, "he lost sight of the American people." Wilson's failure to secure Senate ratification of the treaty and the League of Nations Covenant was a tragic close to one of the boldest presidencies in history. It was tragic, too, for the CPI. Had it continued for a little while longer, it could have redeemed itself for the undemocratic methods it had employed during the war.[19]

The mind-set and techniques used by the CPI are written indelibly on contemporary America. Every element of the Information State has antecedents in the CPI. As the concluding chapter chronicles, it is a vehicle for understanding propaganda and its methods of operation, the imperial presidency, and the threat these pose to democracy.

The Committee on Public Information propelled mass persuasion into a profession. Improved propaganda techniques during the Great War left the public at a disadvantage that became more lopsided with each passing year. The number of government propagandists has grown relentlessly; their power is enhanced by powerful information technologies and science-based understanding of the way people process information. The ceaseless search for new ways to manipulate the masses has increased public cynicism about government, a poison to democracy.

The quest for more effective propaganda—and the danger to democracy—

intensifies when a nation is at war. This is the case today. We are in a state of prolonged war against global terrorism—what a George W. Bush administration lawyer termed an "undefined war with a limitless battlefield." Additionally, we face threats from authoritarian states that employ disruptive information practices against democratic opponents. "It has become increasingly clear that information is one element, and perhaps the most important, of state power," historian Walter Russell Mead writes. "Given the increasing importance of signals intelligence, cyberwar, and 'big data,' the power that information will give to states is only going to grow. This raises fundamental questions of sovereignty, security, and of course of civil liberties that will need to be answered."[20]

I
ORIGINS

1

A Sector of the Battle Front

The present European war, unique in the number of nations involved and
the enormous number of combatants, in the employment of flying machines
to drop bombs on towns and camps and spy upon the movements of the
enemy, and in the use of many death-dealing contrivances of recent invention,
deserves to be distinguished in history as "the first press agents' war."

—*New York Times,* September 9, 1917

The prelude to the Great War in the summer of 1914 is often told as a tale of two
assassinations. One deserved extensive news coverage that it did not receive.
The other received enormous coverage it did not deserve.

The less well-covered assassination occurred on a sunny Sunday morning,
June 28. The heir to the Austro-Hungarian throne, Archduke Franz Ferdinand,
was making a short visit to Sarajevo, Bosnia, which his country had annexed
six years before. Driving along the Miljäcke River in the heart of the city, the
archduke's chauffeur took a wrong turn and stopped the automobile, whose
roof was rolled down. In that moment of stasis, an irredentist Serb nationalist,
Gavrilo Princip, stepped out of the crowd and shot twice, hitting the archduke
in the jugular vein and his wife in the abdomen. The archduke's wife slumped
into his lap; Franz Ferdinand's feather-plumed helmet slipped off his head.
Within minutes both were dead. With the archduke's death, the Dual Monarchy lost one of its strongest proponents for settling international disputes by
diplomacy instead of guns.[1]

The other assassination was in Paris. On the evening of March 16, a woman
dressed elegantly in a fur coat and gown entered the office of the editor of *Le
Figaro.* For three months, Gaston Calmette's newspaper had attacked her husband, Joseph Caillaux, the finance minister. Henriette Caillaux feared the editor was about to publish spicy love letters her husband wrote to her when they

were married to others. Madame Caillaux pulled a small Browning pistol from her fur muff and fired six times. Four bullets hit Calmette, who died shortly after. When *Le Figaro* staff rushed into the room, she ordered them not to touch her: "Je suis une dame!"[2]

One hundred and forty reporters covered Madame Caillaux's eight-day trial in July 1914. They jostled with Parisian celebrities, who treated the event like opening night at the opera and paid as much as $400 for a seat. The defendant, one French reporter wrote, wore a "modest black suit, barely brightened by the mauve of her blouse"; the outline of her blond hair appeared beneath her simple plumed hat. She fainted when her husband's love letters were read in court.[3]

French newspapers covered the trial lavishly, devoting far less space to the smoldering conflict following the archduke's assassination. United Press instructed its Paris correspondent to "down hold warscare and upplay Caillaux." The *Chicago Daily News,* arguably the best American newspaper on foreign news coverage at the time, carried stories related to the archduke's assassination on only four days from July 6, when it ran an article on his funeral, to July 24, when Austria-Hungary delivered an ultimatum to Serbia. Not until July 26 did the first British journalist leave London for Vienna. On July 28, Austria-Hungary declared war on Serbia. The next day, *Le Temps,* one of France's better papers, gave twice as much attention to Madame Caillaux's nearly unanimous acquittal, for her *crime passionnel,* as it did to the impending war.[4]

In the decades afterward, the juxtaposition of the two assassinations stood out as a blatant example of errant journalism. By focusing on the sensational, the press ill-prepared readers for a defining event of the twentieth century. But true as that might be, the Caillaux trial was not a simple drama about love letters and murder. The proceedings in the stifling hot courtroom that July were just as much about the machinations to manipulate public opinion in the run-up to the war. It serves as a point of departure for understanding the rapid development of propaganda once the war began.

In tracing that development, this chapter pays special attention to propaganda directed at the United States. "American public opinion," said journalist Mark Sullivan, "constituted a sector of the battle-front rather more important to capture than Mons or Verdun." The skill with which British propagandists made inroads with American opinion leaders and the contrasting blundering by German propagandists continued to matter after the United States entered the war.[5]

THE IRRESISTIBLE POWER OF PUBLIC OPINION

When talking about this war as "the first press agents' war," the *New York Times* observed, "Frederick the Great and Napoleon were as little versed in ways to create sentiment favorable to their cause in foreign countries as Hannibal and Caesar." Before the war, the tools for shaping public opinion had been as crude as trepanning for the treatment of brain ailments. The techniques of manipulating minds flowered when the fighting started.[6]

This press agents' war was the culmination of a century-old realization by the governing classes that the public's opinion mattered. During the reign of Louis XVI, *opinion publique* was a frequent topic of conversation in the Palace of Versailles's lavish halls, often expressed with remarkable sanguinity. "Public opinion now has, in Europe, a preponderant power against which one cannot resist," said French writer and keen observer of the Paris scene Louis-Sébastien Mercier. "In estimating the progress of enlightenment and the change it must produce, one can thus reasonably hope that it will bring the greatest good to the world and that tyrants of all kinds will tremble before the universal cry that reverberates through, fills, and awakens Europe." Shortly before his coronation, Louis XVI said, "I must always consult public opinion; it is never wrong." He soon found that public opinion, this new factor in governing, would not wait upon his decisions.[7]

Previously, monarchs were dethroned chiefly by their relatives. Now it was the people they had to fear. The decapitation of royal power led to the institutionalization of public opinion in the form of elected governments. "What was called the *public* last year is called the *Nation* today," said a French statesman in 1788, five years before Louis was executed. In stages, France became a nation of citizens, not subjects. Even kaiser-led Germany had its word for public opinion, *öffentliche Meinung,* and had been practicing democracy for decades. From its founding in 1871, the Second Empire enjoyed universal manhood suffrage. German newspapers expressed a variety of viewpoints. Communist and socialist papers reached a large number of voters. Weak though it was during the war, the Reichstag debated war issues including censorship.[8]

Democratizing forces pushed each other along like streams feeding into a swelling river. The market society led to booming cities filled with people who were more economically autonomous than their forebears and lived in shouting distance of their local and national governments. They had the time and money to sit in Parisian cafés and London alehouses, which numbered in the thousands and served as news stock exchanges. An eighteenth-century German prince recognized that the proliferation of cafés was a stimulant to revolution and sought to restrict coffee drinking to the upper class. The courtly theater gave way to the commercial public theater, where sociopolitical themes acted out on the stage stirred talk in the street. In an average year before the French Revolution, 165,000 people attended the Comédie Française in Paris. By the beginning of the nineteenth century nearly every substantial German town had a lending library. Reading clubs sprang up.

Local conversation was a "formative agent" of opinion, argued French intellectual Gabriel Tarde, one of a new class of nineteenth-century intellectuals called sociologists. But public opinion, he argued, was impossible without the communication revolution that knit together the thoughts of people sitting in hundreds of cafés. At one time only kings and popes sent and received what might be called mail. By 1851, Britain's post office was the largest civilian organization in the country. Authorities began to put numbers on houses to facilitate mail delivery—and surveillance, a sign of the fear that would always reside in public opinion in even the most hopeful nations. The number of letters in France rose from 63 million in 1830 to 773 million in 1892, Tarde pointed out; the number of telegrams rose from 32 million in 1858 to 463 million in 1892. In so many ways the local became the national. The telephone was a national coffeehouse without walls. People poured into movie theaters to see films that simultaneously flickered on screens hundreds of miles apart. They huddled around gramophones to listen to identical music created by unseen orchestras. These developments operated on the same principle as the distant and unifying voice of propaganda would.

The press counted more than any other factor. "The work of journalism," Tarde wrote, "has been to nationalize more and more, and even to internationalize, the public mind." The steam-powered press, invented in Germany and perfected in England, permitted the mass production of cheap newspapers, magazines, and books. At the time of the Caillaux trial, Paris had fifty-seven newspapers, and virtually every French adult could afford to put down a sou to buy one. Germany had more than forty-two hundred daily and weekly newspapers, more than two and a half times the number that existed half a century before. In Britain, where literacy approached one hundred percent, members of Parliament worried the press would displace them as the voice of the people. "One pen," Tarde said, "suffices to set off a million tongues."[9]

Officials came to see the press as a tool for assessing what the public thought and for changing those thoughts. French newspapers employed a new journalistic technique, the *enquête,* or investigation, in which they surveyed the public on timely issues. In Germany, Kaiser Wilhelm II studied press clippings for clues to popular views. Government officials responsible for foreign affairs interacted with reporters in hopes of manipulating news. Russian diplomats and journalists drew so close that one journalist thought the ministry of foreign affairs in St. Petersburg "seemed like a mere branch office of the *Novoye Vremya,*" a local newspaper. In France the line between politician and journalist scarcely existed. Almost half of the Third Republic's foreign ministers had been writers or journalists.[10]

The absence of standards made these nascent press systems ripe for crude propaganda. The Germans bribed French, British, and Russian journalists. The French bought Italian journalists. The Russians, who wanted French support in case of war, bribed French journalists. In the middle of the July crisis Germans took false hope from an article in the influential *Westminster Gazette* that was sympathetic to the Austrian attitude toward Serbia. Berlin believed the article had been planted by British officials as a signal they would not go to war. Actually, the inspiration for the article came from the Austrian ambassador in London. Officials combined the planting of self-serving assertions with the suppression of disadvantageous facts. As a British diplomat observed before the war, "We have had to suppress the truth and resort to subterfuge at times to meet public opinion."[11]

Gaston Calmette's murder was a product of the political tussling that lay behind the news. Joseph Caillaux had generated sensational headlines for years. He was a brilliant, rich, smartly dressed "bald don Juan" who took pleasure in openly traveling with a mistress. He authored bold reforms as finance minister. His long-standing preference for peaceful Franco-German relations led to the attacks on him by *Le Figaro,* which was acting as the mouthpiece of the ruthless and punctilious French president Raymond Poincaré. Poincaré's view of German-French relations was formed in 1870, when the Germans marched into his hometown during the Franco-Prussian War. He preferred building alliances against the Germans rather than bridges to work with them.[12]

Henriette Caillaux's time in the dock was blatant political theater. Her attorney had participated in one of the most notorious political trials of the last century when he defended Alfred Dreyfus, the Jewish army captain wrongly convicted of treason for passing secret information to the Germans. When

Le Petit Journal

ADMINISTRATION
61, RUE LAFAYETTE, 61

Les manuscrits ne sont pas rendus

On s'abonne sans frais
dans tous les bureaux de poste

5 CENT. SUPPLÉMENT ILLUSTRÉ **5** CENT.

25ᵐᵉ Année ———— 66 ———— Numéro 1.219

DIMANCHE 29 MARS 1914

ABONNEMENTS

SEINE et SEINE-ET-OISE.
DÉPARTEMENTS
ÉTRANGER

Tragique épilogue d'une querelle politique

Mᵐᵉ CAILLAUX, FEMME DU MINISTRE DES FINANCES, TUE A COUPS DE REVOLVER
M. GASTON CALMETTE DIRECTEUR DU " FIGARO "

Henriette Caillaux's sensational murder of *Le Figaro* editor Gaston Calmette (*illustrated to the left*) was a product of the political tussling that shaped front-page news on the eve of the Great War. When her day in court came, Mme. Caillaux's haughty husband Joseph (*above*) was as much on trial as she was. (Library of Congress)

Joseph Caillaux took the stand on the second day, *La Lanterne* reported, "The courtroom was brusquely transformed into a political meeting hall." The French press refracted simple facts, such as whether the defendant sobbed when testifying, through a partisan lens (*Le Figaro* said she did not shed a tear). For the first time a French president testified in a trial (by deposition, as Poincaré was at the time in St. Petersburg strengthening the Franco-Russian alliance against Germany). Haughty and commanding, Caillaux testified eleven times. He alleged that *Le Figaro*'s editor amassed his large fortune with money from foreign interests, a charge that was probably true. The existence of secret documents collected by Caillaux's rivals in the foreign ministry—and slipped to Calmette by Poincaré—were revealed to suggest that he was traitorous in his efforts to head off a Franco-German crisis a few years before. In his final statement, Henriette Caillaux's attorney called for "an acquittal. May we save our wrath for our enemies beyond the borders. Let us stand always united and determined against the perils that advance upon us!"[13]

Earlier in the year it seemed quite possible Caillaux would become prime minister in a coalition with the party of Jean Jaurès, a socialist leader who shared his views on war. By the time the trial was over, Caillaux's appointment was out of the question. He could not lead France when it was fighting an enemy with whom he sought détente. Jaurès suffered a worse fate. A deranged French nationalist shot him dead in a Parisian café on July 31. The *New York Times*'s Wythe Williams, who covered the Caillaux trial, concluded, "Had [Calmette] not died, had Caillaux remained in power, the subsequent history of Europe might have been far different."[14]

"The July Crisis of 1914," Christopher Clark observed in his brilliant history on events leading to the war, "became the most complex and opaque political crisis of modern times." The war would be opaque as well. One of the French minister of war's first acts was to set up a press bureau in the Hôtel des Invalides, formerly a hospital and retirement home for veterans. On August 4 a telegram went to all prefects. No military news could be published without the bureau's permission. Wanting no open discussion about the possibility of finding a peaceful solution with the Central Powers, the ministry forbade journals from mentioning Joseph Caillaux's name.[15]

THE FIRST INFORMATION BATTLES

One country after another followed Austria-Hungary's declaration of war against Serbia. Germany declared war on Russia on August 1, France on Germany two days later, Turkey on the Allies on November 11, and so on. (Honduras, the last, declared war on Germany on July 19, 1918.) Each belligerent issued a report justifying its actions and shifting the blame to others. The reports, aimed especially at neutral countries, were known by the rainbow of colors on their covers—the German "White Book" on August 4, the British "Blue Book" on August 6, the Russian "Orange Book" on August 16, and the French "Yellow Book" on December 1, which egregiously omitted important facts and falsified others.[16]

A more clever ploy in this information war occurred a few hours after German troops marched into Belgium on August 4. At eleven o'clock that night the British declared war on Germany. Shortly after midnight their cable ship *Alert* hove out of the Dover docks into the English Channel. Under heavy rain and wind, the *Alert*'s hatchet-wielding crew severed Germany's five most important Atlantic cables.[17]

This was a premeditated stroke of propaganda genius. In the previous century the British had begun to think of their communications network as a military asset. They controlled more than 60 percent of the world's cables and held sway over much of the rest. In the event of war, the planners concluded in 1898, "We ought to cut the enemy's cables." In 1911, they focused on Germany, which was doing more than any other country to establish cable independence from Britain. The British simultaneously worked out "an organized system of censorship" over cables that was implemented two days before the *Alert* set out. The chief cable censor was delighted at the "completeness" with which the measures were put into operation."[18]

The *Alert*'s actions left Berlin with less convenient, indirect cable communications via neutral countries as well as newer, but iffy, wireless communication from three stations in Germany, only one of which, at Nauen, reached North America. The British sought to disrupt these as well. Because the Spanish were slow to block German use of its cable network to the Canaries, the British severed the line. A royal marine officer sabotaged a German wireless station in Mexico by stealing its vacuum tube and acquiring all the spares in the country. When a German team headed for the Mexican coast in hopes of putting a smaller radio set to work there, the British officer spread the word their crystal detectors were diamonds. The team disappeared.[19]

With equal vigor the British turned their attention to stymying German communications in the United States. Also on August 4, it requested that the Wilson administration forbid the Germans from using the wireless stations in Sayville, New York, and Tuckerton, New Jersey, for purposes that would "prejudice" British interests. The next day President Wilson barred all wireless stations on American soil from rendering "any unneutral service" to belligerents on either side. When news reports alleged that the German stations were receiving and sending coded military messages, Wilson put navy censors in wireless stations and required that they have German codebooks. The Germans' wireless communication to the United States became more effective as time passed but still was hampered by atmospheric interference of its signal, which in any case could be intercepted by skilled British code breakers who worked at the Admiralty's Old Building in an office cryptically known as Room 40. The Germans enjoyed limited use of neutral Sweden's cables, but the line to Washington touched Britain and its diligent Room 40.[20]

To counter the communications blockade, the Germans cut Allied cables in the North and Baltic Seas. In one case they affixed a rheostat to the severed cable that gave false readings to British repair crews. A note attached to the device said, "No more Reuter war-lies on this line! Kindest regards from a 'Hun' and a 'Sea-Pirate.'" This amounted to little more than harassment. When the Germans cut cables linking Britain and France with Russia, the Allies used an alternative line via Siberia. Repair to cable lines was easier for the British. They had greater control of the seas.[21]

British censors delayed or killed cable dispatches from the dozen or so American correspondents in Berlin and scrubbed out information that reflected well on the Germans. A *New York World* correspondent complained that only twenty-one of his seventy-two dispatches in July 1916 reached his newspaper. According to one study, 70 percent of page-one war stories in US newspapers during the first year of the conflict came from Entente countries; those from Germany did not exceed 4 percent. "German news is at a premium here," the United Press's general manager informed Carl Ackerman, a young correspondent sent to Berlin in April 1915. The simple act of sending mail home was a problem. "We are sending you at least one and many times two or three letters every week," Ackerman wrote his father. "We cannot tell what ones may go to you and there is no way to keep account." In 1916, the British Foreign Office triumphantly reported that the volume of German securities mailed to the United States had almost reached "the vanishing point."[22]

"We are cut off from the largest parts of the outside world, especially with the United States," German secretary of state Arthur Zimmermann complained. "Our enemies use the cable, the mails and the spoken word, to plead their cause before the world." The complaint became a refrain. A German envoy in Washington told Berlin, "The correction of false press releases is exceedingly hindered by the lack of direct links with Germany."[23]

This battle of words in the United States was not confined to sending and blocking news over the high seas. Much of it took place on American soil, the prime focus being Washington, where the decisions would be made to keep the United States out of the war or take it in on the side of the Allies. For each side this was an urgent matter. Other countries might come into the war, but none would count as much in the outcome as the United States.

This contest for American public opinion fascinated Carl Ackerman. In the first days of the war in 1914, he was one of four reporters who patrolled the public opinion battle line along Washington's embassy row. Only a year before he had been in the first cohort of students to graduate from Columbia's new journalism school. He previously dabbled in a nascent field of professional public opinion molding, that of advertising. While trolling through the embassies for news, Ackerman made notes for a book on the diplomatic revolution he believed he was witnessing. It was, he jotted down, "the first time any foreign power ever attempted through its official representatives to fight for the good will—the public opinion—of this nation." Ackerman was as hopeful about public opinion as Louis-Sébastien Mercier had been. "The opinion of the world," he wrote, "may then be a stronger international force than large individual armies and navies." Calling on some embassies as often as three times a day, he felt like "an agent of public opinion."[24]

THE GERMANS

Four days before invading Belgium, the German government announced a wartime law whose title had propaganda value. The Imperial Law of the State of Siege suggested Germany was a victim in the conflict. To meet this threat to national security, the law put the military outside the control of civilian government and gave it extraordinary power over domestic affairs, including the principal levers of propaganda and censorship, a sharp contrast with Britain and France. The day the law was promulgated every newspaper publisher received a secret memorandum with detailed instructions. One of them forbade discussion of censorship.

Regulations governing news, which grew in number, built on a tradition of news management dating to Chancellor Otto von Bismarck. The government-subsidized Wolff Telegraph Bureau operated with the understanding that it exclusively carried official news and avoided "politically sensitive material." News on food shortages, casualties, and peace demonstrations was *verboten*. In a fit of patriotism, a military commander suppressed a newspaper for giving inadequate attention to the empress's birthday. A memorandum to the press said journalists should "give thanks to the War Command when the latter informs it as to what publications would be injurious to the Fatherland."[25]

Within a few weeks some two dozen German agencies conducted foreign propaganda. The priority given to shaping American minds is indicated by the opening of an information bureau in New York on August 14, less than two weeks after the war started. When German ambassador Count Johann Heinrich von Bernstorff returned to Washington from a European vacation later in August, he had with him two men who would become involved with propaganda. Dr. Bernhard Dernburg, formerly head of the German Colonial Office, represented the German Red Cross. Dr. Heinrich Albert, a tall blond previously in the German Imperial Ministry of the Interior, represented a German purchasing company.[26]

Bernstorff could take some comfort from the state of public opinion. On November 6, Wilson issued ten proclamations outlining norms that would preserve neutrality. This resonated with national sentiment. A *Literary Digest* survey of newspapers editors shortly after the fighting began found 105 sided with the Allies and 20 with the Germans. As lopsided as this was, a more significant statistic was that 242 were neutral.[27]

Nearly one in five Americans—twenty million in all—were of German descent in 1914. More than eight million had been born in Germany or had a parent who was. German-Americans tended to be hardworking, well educated, and proud of their heritage. German-language papers in the United States totaled 564 in 1914. (French-language newspapers numbered 43.) The Germans had natural alliances with millions of other hyphenated Americans: the Irish, who opposed British rule; Swedes and Poles, who disliked Russia; and Jews, who were anti-Russian and pro-German, or both.[28]

Dernburg took charge of the new German Information Service, which shared space with the German Red Cross at 1123 Broadway in New York City. He was considered adept "at cleaning things up." He came from a newspaper family, his father having been editor of the *Berliner Tageblatt.* The service generated newspaper stories, pamphlets, books, and newsreels designed to work on American thinking. Additionally, the Germans kept the *New Yorker Staats-Zeitung* alive and subsidized other foreign-language papers with advertising. Bernstorff failed in an apparent attempt to acquire the *Washington Post,* one of the few English-language newspapers that favored the Germans, but in 1916 the Germans did buy, through a third party, the *New York Evening Mail,* which was singular in the city for its pro-German stance. The Germans also purchased the *International Monthly* and a Jewish newspaper, maintained an Irish news service, and enlisted William Bayard Hale to edit their daily news bulletin at a handsome salary. Hale was married to a German and fluent in the language. And he had a standing. In journalism, he had reported for the *New York Times, Cosmopolitan,* and the *New York World*. In politics, he worked on Wilson's first presidential campaign, at the end helping put together a book of his speeches.[29]

Behind the scenes, Hale helped organize two national movements with German money, the American Embargo Conference and the Organization of American Women for Strict Neutrality. Other groups, such as the National

German-American Alliance, which claimed two million members, raised large sums for imperial war bonds and pressured political leaders. At a January 1915 meeting in Washington, its leaders exhorted members to "bring their adopted country, misled and misrepresented by its newspapers, back to authentic Americanism." Local German-American organizations were urged to recruit speakers to "counteract the influence of the English press."[30]

Another prominent pro-German voice belonged to George Sylvester Viereck, whose complex personality cried out for psychoanalysis, which Sigmund Freud eventually provided. Born in Munich in 1884 and brought to New York twelve years later, Viereck obsessively boasted that his often absent father was the illegitimate offspring of Kaiser Wilhelm I. He kept up his father's traditions of political agitation (Friedrich Engels attended his father's wedding) and sexual promiscuity. Viereck's early success at poetry led the *Saturday Evening Post* to write, "Not in a decade, perhaps, has any young person been so unanimously accused of being a genius." Viereck, the magazine added, "does not object to acting as his own press agent." His *Confessions of a Barbarian* extolled Germany and denigrated America. In 1912, in what some saw as a search for a father figure, he worked in Theodore Roosevelt's presidential campaign. Ready to do his part for Germany in 1914, he started a weekly. Heavily subsidized by the Germans, the *Fatherland* inveighed against American press bias and borrowed muckrakers' techniques to attack the "Munitions Trust" and Wall Street financiers supporting the Allies. By October the *Fatherland* had a circulation of 100,000.[31]

Much smoother was Ambassador Count Bernstorff, the son of a one-time royal Prussian foreign minister. Trim and broad-shouldered, well dressed, the tips of his mustaches curved upward at attention, he was a picture-book Prussian who nevertheless mixed easily in American bourgeois and Jewish society. Bernstorff spent ten boyhood years in Britain when his father was ambassador to the Court of St. James and married a German-American. While in Washington, he had as a mistress Cissy Paterson, whose family owned the *Chicago Tribune*. He accumulated honors from universities including Wilson's Princeton.

Germany posted him in Washington in 1908 with ample funds "to inform the American public about the peaceful and friendly intentions of German foreign policy." When Dernburg and Albert arrived at the start of the war, Bernstorff shrewdly "disconnected himself from . . . the propaganda Cabinet," as Viereck put it. Carl Ackerman and other reporters found Bernstorff more con-

George Sylvester Viereck's *The Fatherland* was representative of the heavy-handed German propaganda that worked against their interests in the United States. Ambassador Count von Bernstorff, who sought a defter approach to keeping the United States out of the war, considered *The Fatherland* so over the top he wanted "to get rid" of it. (Roe Studios of New York and *World's Work.*)

genial than the tightly wound British ambassador, Cecil Spring-Rice, who was put off by Ackerman's German name.[32]

In 1915, following the German sinking of the *Lusitania,* Bernstorff persuaded Wilson to make a concession in the interests of speeding up the resolution of such crises. Wilson agreed the Germans could transmit messages over State Department lines using a cipher it did not have to divulge. Not that this did Berlin much good. Room 40 deciphered German messages (as well as eavesdropped on American diplomatic communications). The German-American situation, one British code breaker quipped, "was our daily bread."[33]

Germany targeted legislators with large German constituencies. In the very first months of the war, its propagandists raised public consciousness that war guilt was shared by both sides, and they fed the Anglophobia and distaste for Russian despotism that resided in sectors of the American population. As the Germans improved wireless communication, more of its news made its way into German-language and mainstream American newspapers. By October 1916, news from Transocean, effectively an agency of the German foreign ministry, reached two thousand newspapers, which often published the stories under the anodyne tag "Overseas News Agency."[34]

Even with improved wireless communication, however, the total amount of news sent by the Germans was far less than that by the Allies. Much of the content, for instance emphasis on the birthdays of German nobility, was ill-suited to the American audience. Furthermore, the Germans consistently found themselves embarrassed in the court of public opinion. Some of this can be laid at the feet of their clumsy propagandists. Some came about because the British tripped them.

THE BRITISH

America was neutral in principle, but the principle worked in the favor of the British, as their maritime blockade illustrates. The United States proposed a relatively loose arrangement for control of the seas embodied in the 1909 Declaration of London, which allowed Americans to trade widely. The British, determined to use their mighty navy to the fullest advantage, claimed the declaration never entered the canon of sea law. Even so, their blockade—a term they avoided—was of dubious legality under the old rules. It covered an entire sea, not just ports and sections of coastline, and stopped food as well as military supplies. Because imports accounted for one-quarter of German grain needs at the start of the war and 40 percent of its fats, the cordon contributed to malnutrition and some 300,000 deaths, according to conservative estimates. To reinforce the power of the blockade, the British navy boarded neutral vessels deemed to have cargo bound for the Central Powers. After much diplomatic wrangling, the Wilson administration acquiesced to this. The British further tightened the blockade by mining the North Sea. Neutral ships needed a British escort to make safe passage. This required them to put into British ports where cargo could be more easily inspected. American trade with the Allies in munitions, food, and other commodities flourished. It was negligible with the Central Powers.[35]

Secretary of State William Jennings Bryan stood for balanced neutrality. When a German submarine sank the British liner *Lusitania* in May 1915, killing 128 Americans, he wanted to challenge both Germany and Britain, whose blockade prevented "food from reaching non-combatant enemies." In a cabinet meeting, he erupted, "You people are not neutral. You are taking sides!"

Although Wilson chided him, Bryan was correct. Wilson's wish to steer a truly neutral course inevitably ran up on the shoals of his biases. His mother was born in Britain. As a boy he hung a picture of Prime Minister William Gladstone over his desk. At the start of the war, Wilson's confidant, Edward House, observed in his diary that the president thought "German philosophy was essentially selfish and lacking in spirituality." House's father was born in Britain, and House did a stint of schooling in Bath.[36]

A common language and shared ideas about law and liberty forged an Anglo-American bond. The imperial Central Powers presented a contrastingly illiberal image. It was inconceivable the United States would fight on their side. When Bryan resigned over the handling of the *Lusitania* sinking, the State Department counselor, Robert Lansing, replaced him. "Germany must not be permitted to win this war," Lansing wrote in his diary. "American public opinion must be prepared for the time, which may come, when we will have to cast aside our neutrality and become one of the champions of democracy."[37]

Britain's interception of American mail on ships and its blacklist of American firms that traded with the Central Powers provoked strong complaints from American business as well as Wilson and Congress.* But the harsh British blockade, which earned Germany some sympathy in America, was more than offset by the kaiser's submarine warfare, a new form of fighting that did not exist at the time of the Declaration of London. The Wilson administration acknowledged the legitimacy of sinking warships, but German torpedoes seemed more barbaric than the British blockade when they sank neutral vessels with women and children on board, a maneuver that achieved little militarily. Americans, as Dernburg observed, could not visualize thousands of "German children starving by slow degrees as a result of the British blockade, but they can visualize the pitiful face of a little child drowning amidst the wreckage caused by a German torpedo."[38]

In other ways, too, German leaders seemed determined to help their adversary tarnish their image. The German government preposterously claimed their invasion of neutral Belgium was an act of self-defense. In October 1915 they legitimately, but needlessly, executed by firing squad a British nurse, Edith Cavell, who had helped Allied prisoners of war escape Belgium. A German patriotic poem, "Hymn of Hate against England," grated in foreign ears: "Come,

* The blacklist focused not only on individuals who financially supported Germany but also those who used secret codes over cable lines or propagandized for the Central Powers.

hear the word, repeat the word / Throughout the Fatherland make it heard. / We will never forego our hate." The poet, Ernest Lissauer, came to regret that he had not written "A Hymn of Love for Germany." The German government, however, awarded him the Order of the Red Eagle.[39]

This ham-handedness was born out of arrogance. The leaders who strode Berlin's magnificent Unter den Linden boulevard considered Washington, where President William Taft's dairy cow had grazed in sight of the White House, an uncultured backwater. "A hostile America was not to be feared," the war minister said. Hard as he tried, Bernstorff could not convince his superiors that this was not so and that they should not encourage speakers in the United States to use the aggressive tone employed in Germany. Officials like Dernburg were not ideally suited for subtle forms of propaganda. Viereck remembered the cigar-smoking propagandist as diligent and possessing superb English but also heavy and unkempt, occasionally rude and bumptious. As for Viereck, Bernstorff considered his *Fatherland* so over the top he wanted "to get rid" of it.[40]

German spies and saboteurs further tarnished the German image. Two of the most controversial were military attaché Captain Franz von Papen and naval attaché Captain Karl Boy-Ed, both attached to Bernstorff's embassy. Boy-Ed's "astute propaganda for naval expansion" was credited with creating the modern German navy. Seeking to disrupt manufacturing and shipping that benefited the Allies, they and other agents provoked strikes, crafted financial deals to corner the market on strategic materials, and planted bombs. They used the United States as a launching pad for disrupting the British as far afield as India, Egypt, and Ireland. One of the more fantastic plots was to invade Canada at three or four spots with a force recruited from German-American associations. It never came off, and neither did a scheme of bombing five Canadian bridges. (Not surprisingly, von Papen was unable to recruit adequate personnel.) In July 1916, a devastating explosion occurred at the Black Tom munitions depot in Jersey City. Shrapnel spewed as far as the Statue of Liberty, which had to be closed to visitors. Another blast occurred at the Kingsland Assembly Plant in New Jersey the following January. German guilt was not established conclusively, but under the circumstances it was widely believed. In May 1915, Germans were arrested for destroying a cargo of explosives. Among those found guilty was the German consul in San Francisco. The British Foreign Office told its consul general there to forward details of the trial so as "to make use of it for propaganda purposes."[41]

Spying and sabotage, remarked a sensible diplomat in the German embassy, "poisoned public opinion and were a hindrance everywhere to the real public relations work." For many Americans an impression took shape of all-subversive Germans, torpedoing passenger liners at sea and hatching plots on American soil. The United States, Wilson thought, "was honeycombed with German intrigue and infested with spies." He ordered the monitoring of German propagandists and spies.[42]

As a sign of how badly they were beaten in propaganda, the Germans' image became simultaneously one of ruthless Teutonic efficiency and hapless bungling of the sort found in comic book characters. Wilson's comment on spy infestation came on the heels of a German blunder that led to an exposé in the anti-German *New York World*. On a Saturday afternoon in July 1915, Dernburg's lieutenant, Heinrich Albert, left a meeting with Viereck. The pair boarded a New York elevated train. Viereck was followed by two Secret Service agents; the oblique dueling scars on Albert's face marked him as German of rank and worthy of shadowing as well. Albert was carrying a briefcase full of papers marked "*streng vertraulich*"—"strictly private." He became so engrossed in reading after Viereck disembarked that he did not realize he had reached his stop. Albert came to his senses as the train doors were about to close and bolted from the car, leaving his portfolio behind. By the time he realized his mistake, a Secret Service agent had run off with his papers.[43]

After huddling in his New York apartment with Lansing, Treasury Secretary William Gibbs McAdoo, the agent's boss, gave the documents to Frank I. Cobb, the pro-Wilson editor of the *New York World,* on the condition that he tell no one whence they came. The *World* splashed the contents of Albert's briefcase across its pages for five days starting on a Sunday in mid-August. Facsimiles of the documents plus related stories revealed no illegal activities, but insinuated a slew of them and hinted that Viereck was a sexual deviant because he "proudly exhibits it to all visitors to his interesting apartments" a framed violet from Oscar Wilde's grave. "There is a German side and there is an American side," the *World* editorial page declared, "and the American who now furthers the German paid propaganda is guilty of moral treason toward the Republic."[44]

McAdoo would later claim that he gave the Albert story to the *World* so it could "throw a reverberating scare into the whole swarm of propagandists—British and French as well as German." This is dubious, to say the least. His Secret Service agents did not shadow British or French envoys. The same bias pervaded the administration. House, who received copies of the Albert documents from Wilson, welcomed the *World* exposé, as he hoped it would stymie

German propaganda. He expressed no concerns about British propaganda. He condoned it.[45]

BRITISH SECRECY

On September 2, 1914, Charles F. G. Masterman, chairman of the National Insurance Commission, convened a meeting in his offices at Wellington House in London. Tall, slightly stooped, looking like a pensive cleric, Masterman was an accomplished writer and social reformer. He had risen rapidly in politics, attaining cabinet rank in Prime Minister Herbert Asquith's government. The meeting was called because Asquith asked him to create a propaganda bureau to counter German propaganda with foreign audiences. Arthur Conan Doyle, G. K. Chesterton, John Galsworthy, Thomas Hardy, H. G. Wells, and other literary lights attended.[46]

They gathered around a large blue table. The sun, shining in from the dusty street, cast a foreboding light on the meeting, as Hardy recalled. When he left London that night, the streets were "hot and sad, and bustling with soldiers and recruits." The writers agreed to respond collectively to a manifesto by German writers justifying the invasion of Belgium. Their letter, with fifty-two signatures, appeared in the *Times* of London and called for maintaining "the free and law-abiding ideals of Western Europe against the rule of 'Blood and Iron.'"[47]

This was a leap for the British. Public officials used commercial advertising techniques to win office. They maintained personal contacts with journalists. But unlike in Berlin and other major European capitals, the government had virtually no formal mechanisms to manage press relations or shape public opinion.[48]

Wellington House was an ideal base for the fledgling propaganda bureau the British had in mind. It was out of the way, near a block of residential flats at Buckingham Gate, better enabling the government to keep it secret. All that Asquith told Parliament, when pressed, was that Masterman was involved in "highly confidential" work. The National Insurance Commission had been the setting for one of the government's few publicity campaigns, organized in large measure by Masterman, to win support for national health and unemployment insurance. Masterman drew on assistants who helped in that trailblazing effort at social engineering.[49]

Wellington House reported to the Foreign Office, dominated by well-educated and titled men who considered diplomacy an elite undertaking best

done largely out of public view. A reporter visiting the Foreign Office, as one recalled, was "ushered into a chilly waiting room by a still more chilly attendant"
only to be told there was no news. Foreign Office men approved of the secrecy
surrounding Wellington House, and they appreciated Masterman's reliance on
literary figures to make their case with neutral nations and his preference for
facts, at least the facts as those London officials saw them.[50]

This is not to say Wellington House was a sleepy literary bureau caught in a
Foreign Office time warp. Very quickly, it was turning out articles, pamphlets,
and books by the hundreds of thousands. It distributed these to more than five
hundred newspapers in the United States alone. It pioneered the use of artists to
illustrate the war and produced posters, postcards, cartoons, cigarette stiffeners,
shop-window exhibitions, films, and lantern slides. Ferris Greenslet, a director
at publisher Houghton Mifflin, went to England at the outbreak of the war for
book ideas and authors. He planned to present both sides of the war, but he
ended up tilting heavily toward the Allies. Wellington House, whose mission
was not a secret to him or to others whom it could use, was a prolific source of
books on the "causes, conduct, and aims of the war."[51]

The Foreign Office eventually created a news department and posted staff in
its embassies for publicity work. In 1916, the government silently took over the
financially failing Reuters. It put seemingly independent third parties in control and made the news service a conduit for propaganda. Reuters, an internal
government report observed, was an independent news agency "with propaganda secretly infused." By the end of 1916 it sent a million words by cable each
month.[52]

A liberal member of Parliament, Masterman cared about uplifting "the Mul-
titude," which, like a good American progressive, he believed needed help arriving at sound views. Accordingly, the prime targets for Wellington House were
"the creators of public opinion—editors, financiers, lawyers, doctors, clergy,
engineers, and so on. . . . Each of these fans out the literature in the shape of editorial, reviews, lectures, addresses, speeches, sermons and so forth to audiences
all over the States."[53]

The United States constituted the greatest part of Wellington House's portfolio. The man in charge was Sir Gilbert Parker, a successful, if second-rate, Canadian novelist who was well known in the United States, married to a wealthy
American, and held a seat in Parliament. Based near Victoria Station, Parker's
staff grew from nine to fifty-four and amassed a mailing list of thirteen thousand prominent Americans. These individuals received materials under Park-

er's name or that of another distinguished individual so as to mask the real source. Parker maintained voluminous personal correspondence, which gave him intelligence on American thinking as well as an opportunity to plant British ideas.*[54]

"My dear Sir Gilbert," began a letter from Willard Straight, a prominent New York investment banker and cofounder of the *New Republic.* "You have probably thought me unmindful of my promise to write you a weekly letter." Straight made up for the lapse with five pages about American attitudes toward the British in light of the upcoming 1916 presidential election. His letter was circulated at the Foreign Office. Parker helped American journalists in London secure interviews and courted Walter Hines Page, the Anglophile US ambassador.[55]

The British had counterparts in the United States to Dernburg, von Papen, and Boy-Ed. The *Times* of London correspondent Arthur Willert came to Washington with the conviction that what he wrote, and did not write, should be a function of British interests. When the war began, he effortlessly slipped into the collateral role of de facto press attaché to Ambassador Spring-Rice. The arrangement was sanctioned by his boss Lord Northcliffe, whose editors at the *Times* had similar relations with officials at home. Sir William Wiseman, 10th baronet of Canfield Hall, headed British intelligence in the United States. Willert considered him the T. E. Lawrence on the American front, although Wiseman was not advertised the way Lawrence was on the Eastern Front. His success lay in operating quietly. A banker and military officer gassed in Flanders, Wiseman was nominally a member of the Purchasing Commission of the Ministry of Munitions. He paid considerable attention to propaganda and, through House, became a liaison with Wilson. Wiseman plumbed Wilson's mind and did what he could to shape it to British ends. A second intelligence officer had a name and personality worthy of a James Bond thriller. This was naval attaché Captain Guy Gaunt, a swashbuckler who was initially considered a good choice

* The French did not reach the level of propagandizing in the United States that the British did, partly due to the same factors that held back the Germans, language differences and their dismissiveness of American culture. Like the British and the Germans, the French relied heavily on unofficial organizations. The Sorbonne in Paris worked through American universities. Before the end of 1914, a French committee supported by Catholic elites distributed 320,000 pamphlets. Chad R. Fulwider, *German Propaganda and U.S. Neutrality in World War I* (Columbia: University of Missouri Press, 2016), 26. Andre J. Allentuck, "A Study of French Propaganda in North America in World War I" (master's thesis, Marquette University, 1966), 18–20.

for interlocuter with Wilson but in their first meeting annoyed the president by pressing him to go to war right away. His "propaganda-cum-intelligence" operation included passing information to Theodore Roosevelt, who spoke out loudly for war.[56]

These three men, and talented colleagues, developed close ties to the administration that the Germans did not enjoy. In late 1916 Wiseman revealed himself to Frank Polk, Lansing's deputy, as Britain's chief of spies. Polk put him in touch with American agents, with whom Wiseman conducted combined operations. What distinguished the British from their German rivals was caution. "Dignity and reticence is our chief card," Willert told his editor. "I have, however, been very busy." The effort "to avoid the appearance of organization" included Gaunt. He was "not looked upon by the American newspaper men as running a propaganda bureau," an internal British report gloated. "He does not circulate any matter himself."[57]

Memoranda, minutes, and reports in the British National Archives brim with statements of "pride" over lagging behind "every Foreign Ministry on the Continent" in propaganda. As will be seen throughout this book, propagandists readily deceive themselves that what they are doing is wholly different from what the enemy does, and this was such a case. The British had a long acquaintance with two potent propagandistic arts, surveillance and censorship. In a rare lapse the curtain was pulled back in 1844, when it became known that the "Inner Room" of the post office opened the mail of Giuseppe Mazzini, an Italian revolutionary living in London, and passed the contents to his foreign adversaries. A parliamentary inquiry discovered that the practice of opening envoys' mail extended back many years and had recently expanded to the invasion of the mail of Members of Parliament. Despite public outcry, the home secretary, who claimed "respect for public opinion," refused to state how often he opened mail or on what basis. The "Inner Room" was quietly abolished without the passage of any laws to prevent something similar from being reconstituted.[58]

As much as possible the British government avoided statutes limiting secrecy and surveillance, whose enactment required public debate and afterward accountability, and instead used measures that were flexible and unadvertised. When the Great War began, the government had no stated policy on censorship until an errant censor's form showed up in an MP's envelope. The censorship staff, which grew to almost five thousand, aimed to intercept every letter and telegram coming into or going out of the country.[59]

Measures to deal with the press began with secrecy. On August 5, the first full day of war for Great Britain, Lord Kitchener, war minister, and Winston Churchill, first lord of the admiralty, set the process in motion for an Official Press Bureau, whose work "was improvised in a hurry." Although its existence was not as camouflaged as Wellington House, it was not mentioned in any act or regulation until April 22, 1916. In the early stages, the general attitude was summed up by Kitchener's comment: "Whenever there is any doubt, we do not hesitate to prevent publication." Journalists dubbed the Press Bureau the "Suppress Bureau."[60]

"Inexorable, systematized" British censorship was a constant torment, an Associated Press (AP) executive complained. "There has been and still is no certainty when dispatches, no matter how important they may be, will be delivered, if delivered at all." The censors refused to entertain inquiries about the fate of cables. Frederic William Wile, an American correspondent who worked for the *London Daily Mail,* was staunchly pro-British but fumed over British press policy. Press relations in Germany, where he had been based, were better. Carl Ackerman, who had spoken German at home thanks to his four immigrant grandparents, was able to develop his own sources in Berlin, which worried officials. Karl Boy-Ed considered him a spy. Still, he and other American reporters were allowed to go to the front. An American reporter asking for "bread in England," Wile said, "received a stone." The British kept American correspondents, as well as their own, far away from the fighting and issued bland communiqués from an "official eye-witness," Major Frank Swinton.[61]

Eventually the Foreign Office became more forthcoming, and the military allowed reporters to go to the front and visit the fleet. This marked a change of strategy, however, not a change in the underlying belief that information should be suppressed. Unlike the Germans, who commanded their journalists as if they were rank-and-file soldiers, the British adopted a more complex view of managing the press that, on the one hand, accorded considerable, if not total, respect for their liberal press tradition and, on the other, assumed that journalists' patriotic instincts would result in self-policing. In line with this cooperative spirit, leading journalists assumed government posts overseeing propaganda and censorship, and many of them acquired titles and honors. This, too, was different from German practice.[62]

The Official Press Bureau's only direct news censorship was of cable and telegraph transmissions. It let editors decide what they might publish, but they were liable for prosecution for running anything, even inadvertently, prohibited under the sweeping Defence of the Realm Act of 1914. DORA forbade pub-

lication of "any information of such a nature as is calculated to be or might be
directly or indirectly useful to the enemy." The way out was for editors to show
stories to the Press Bureau ahead of publication. The bureau published instructions, which its co-director, distinguished former journalist Edward Cook, described as "hints and elucidations." These were not binding but had the same
effect. The instructions, totaling 509 by the end of 1916, could not to be revealed
to the general public. They ranged from the obvious (no disclosure of military
movements) to matters far from the battlefield (orders not to print a story by
one C. H. Norman, who called for "immediate stoppage" of the war, or to make
mention of "arrangements for propaganda which now exist or to any proposed
alterations"). The government did not like to prosecute transgressions, for that
drew attention to news it was trying to suppress. But it did not have to worry
much about transgressions. The bureau supplied "a steady stream of trustworthy
information," as Churchill put it, and journalists used it. The press, Cook said,
"did all that it possibly could, and often more than from a strictly journalistic
point of view might reasonably have been expected."[63]

The British monitored American correspondents' mail as well as their dispatches. Journalists' letters provided clues on how they bypassed censors and
useful gossip on editors and reporters. Excerpts of intercepted letters were circulated among government officials. The British could be street fighters. To
them, newspaper publisher William Randolph Hearst was a "yellow dog, who
has no code of honour, or decency of any sort, his word is of no use, further,
morally, he is as bad as they make them in all ways." Hearst's offenses piled up.
He appealed for a peace settlement. He condemned the British blockade as well
as German sinking of the *Lusitania*. He sent William Bayard Hale to Berlin
"to get the German side of the war." Hearst's editors in New York rewrote dispatches after they were cleaned by censors in London. British authorities were
furious over coverage of what Hearst papers called their "overwhelming defeat"
in the Battle of Jutland in the summer of 1916, a sea battle whose outcome was
arguably a British loss.[64]

By fall 1916, Lord Robert Cecil, the parliamentary under secretary of state
for foreign affairs, concluded Hearst had "definitely declared war." Masterman
argued against seeming to bully a neutral country's newspaper syndicate. Besides, he noted, Hearst published "practically every first-class British writer"
and mailed "a vast number of copies of [Wellington House] pamphlets to individuals." But the Foreign Office was worried about making a "confession of

impotence." It barred Hearst's International News Service from British cable and mail facilities and induced similar steps by Canada, France, Italy, Australia, and South Africa. The latter two countries went so far as to ban Hearst's magazine *Motor Boating*.[65]

Despite the high emotions over Hearst, the British were calculated in their relations with the American press. When American correspondents in Berlin howled about increasing British censorship of their cables in mid-1916, the Foreign Office eased off for fear of "giving the American public any unnecessary sense of grievance." As one official commented, "It is entirely a question of what pays us best." In most cases the British realized they could count on American journalists to endure quite a lot without much cost. In April 1917, AP general manager Melville Stone told his London bureau chief he was "incensed" over the British dictating "to us what we should receive and print respecting the news of Germany and of Russia." He considered distributing a story about it to all of the AP's client papers but did not want to be responsible for raising "such a storm in this country." The British opened the gratifying letter and sent a copy to the Foreign Office. The friendship of the American press "forms a fund upon which we can draw," Lord Robert Cecil wrote in a cabinet note. "It might astonish some outside observers if they knew how much we have succeeded in stopping what might have been disadvantageous to us in the press of the United States."[66]

BRITISH PROPAGANDA JUJITSU

For all their claims to being ingenues in the arts of propaganda, the British had the cunning of jujitsu fighters who employ their opponent's energy against them. One of the most notable cases followed a German blunder after the sinking of the *Lusitania*.[67]

A commercial artisan in Munich produced a medal commemorating the event. This was a private endeavor but to many it appeared to be a government celebration of brutality. (Carl Ackerman thought the German navy created the medal.) The Germans produced five hundred medals; Wellington House made fifty thousand copies. Pictures of the medal were distributed to newspapers and magazines inside and outside Britain. At the suggestion of the Foreign Office, department store magnate Harry Gordon Selfridge manufactured more, selling them around the world and donating the proceeds to the Red Cross. The keeper of the Department of Coins and Medals in the British Museum wrote a book describing other German commemorative medals, which Wellington House sent to its American opinion leaders. German propaganda, one official said, "sometimes defeats itself, for his methods are not seldom clumsy and crude.... His communications are limited."[68]

Wellington House similarly used an inquiry on German atrocities in Belgium to cement the image of German barbarity. Respected jurist and former ambassador to the United States Viscount James Bryce led the inquiry. Although in some respects nuanced, the Bryce report contained lurid, uncorroborated testimony of German sadism that, as historians note, "exceeded any possible reality." Five days after the *Lusitania*'s sinking, Wellington House released the report simultaneously in Britain and in America, where forty-one thousand copies were distributed. A Wellington House survey of editorials showed the report and the *Lusitania*'s sinking blended together in American thinking. The report appeared in more than thirty languages.[69]

As much as the British decried William Bayard Hale's apologetics for the German side, they had American press champions of their own and in far greater numbers. Edward Price Bell of the *Chicago Daily News* and dean of the American press corps in London lionized British leaders such as the foreign secretary. "To interview Sir Edward Grey, one need hardly say, is a unique privilege and honour," he wrote in an article that appeared in a book of war propaganda essays by Bryce, Asquith, and other British statesmen. The book was brought out by the publishing house owned by the American ambassador, Walter Page.[70]

Frederic William Wile treated propaganda as a beat and an avocation. Like Carl Ackerman, Wile was an Indiana Hoosier of German-American stock. He started overseas with Bell's *Chicago Daily News* and later became Berlin correspondent for Lord Northcliffe's *London Daily Mail*. After the war broke out, the Germans ransacked Wile's office and expelled him. Back in London, Northcliffe gave Wile a column, "Germany Day by Day," in which the reporter made British propaganda out of German propaganda by combing the German press to report how it portrayed the war "with clumsy fabrications." Wile said his experience in Germany trained him "to read between the lines of German papers." Notwithstanding this supposed skill, he gave credence to one of the more outrageous pieces of war propaganda, that the Germans rendered the bodies of dead soldiers for oil, fertilizer, and pig fodder. As evidence, Wile cited a statement he found in a German paper: "The theory on which our Army works is that nothing must be allowed to go unused."* Charles Masterman at Wellington House refused to circulate the incredible story.[71]

Wile's search for German propaganda took him to the United States for a six-week fact-finding trip. The result was *The German-American Plot,* an account published in 1915 of the "diabolical comprehensiveness and steam-roller methods" of the Germans in America. The Germans, Wile noted, mailed free copies of Viereck's *Fatherland* "to everybody with an address accessible by mail." German waiters eavesdropped on Washington conversations. It was all part of a "System." The German press referred to Wile as one of the "fire spewing craters of the English press."[72]

The ability to intercept German messages, coupled with their tapping of German phone lines in the United States, allowed the British to collect information that could be passed to newspapers. Guy Gaunt shined at this. When a story needed to be circulated, a British cabinet memo noted, Gaunt "was the man on the spot." A favored outlet was the *Providence Journal,* edited by John Rathom, a fellow Australian. Gaunt first encountered the cigar-chewing Rathom impatiently seeking an audience at the British embassy. The two men found they both hailed from Melbourne and shared an interest in embarrassing the Germans. Rathom, a 270-pound giant with a booming voice, was not troubled by fidelity to fact in the sensational stories he ran about "the German spy system." These "exposés" were widely published by other newspapers.[73]

The *New York World's* August 17, 1915, edition shows the advantage held by the British. An article, reprinted from the *Providence Journal,* reported an investigation of leaks by state and treasury officials to German diplomats. Nearby were the breathless stories that the newspaper had concocted from the contents of Albert's briefcase. None of these stories acknowledged that the secretary of the treasury—or anyone else in government—had leaked those documents to the newspaper. The origin of the Albert documents was a "well-kept" secret from the press. Years later Washington journalists were still guessing where they came from.[74]

---

* In a note tucked into his papers—made up mostly of newspaper clippings—at the Library of Congress, Wile wrote: "We could believe anything about a military organization that had shot Edith Cavell, torpedoed the Lusitania, used poison gas, bombed sleeping civial [*sic*] communities with Zeppelins at night, enslaved into degaradation [*sic*] the women and girls of Lille—why doubt they would defile their own exploded Kanonenfutter for army uses?" (box 1, FWW).

CAMOUFLAGE OF THE RIGHT KIND

The day after the sinking of the *Lusitania,* Dernburg gave a speech in Cleveland. The attack, he said, was "retaliation" for the British blockade that starved innocent German women and children. Another justification for the sinking, he added, was that the ship was carrying munitions to Britain. This was true, but categorically denied by the British, who sounded more reasonable than Dernburg, whose statements were intemperate. High officials in the administration let it be known that he might be expelled and that the Justice Department was contemplating the use of obscenity laws to impose fines on a few newspapers whose editorials took the same line as he did. Bernstorff sent him home before the administration could. "The clarifying purposes of our propaganda in the United States," the ambassador said, "essentially came to an end."[75]

Others followed Dernburg out of the country. Von Papen had been warmly welcomed to Washington when he arrived in early January 1914. He was admitted to the Metropolitan Club, a few steps from the White House and a gathering place for senior officials, "as an agreeable and desirable member," in the words of an army lawyer who wrote a recommendation letter. Boy-Ed had been friends with Gaunt and gave him a loving cup as a gift shortly before the war. Both German attachés were expelled at the end of 1915 after the appearance of highly publicized news stories based on documents acquired by the British. The purloined papers, which also led to the expulsion of the Austro-Hungarian ambassador, contained plans to foment strikes and contained unflattering comments about Wilson. "We Germans," Boy-Ed said upon his expulsion, "do not understand what you call your 'free press.'" Back in Berlin, he resumed his old job as chief of the Admiralty News Division. "No attack has been made upon us in any quarter of the United States," Sir Gilbert Parker wrote in one of his periodic reports, adding, "in the eyes of the American people the quiet and subterranean nature of our work has the appearance of purely private patriotism and enterprise."[76]

British propaganda expanded in the coming months. John Buchan, a politically well-connected and popular author, took charge of a new Department of Information that subsumed Wellington House, which Masterman henceforth ran with diminished authority. Buchan had a previous brush with propaganda as an officer in the Intelligence Corps, where he wrote press summaries of the fighting. In his plan for the new department, Buchan argued that propaganda "resembles an election campaign, where seed must be sown broadcast. . . . It consequently involves many acts." The expansion he envisioned, however, did not include jettisoning all the ways of Wellington House. "*Camouflage* of the right kind is a vital necessity."[77]

British caution carried on during an actual election campaign, the 1916 presidential race. Dependence on American food, raw materials for munitions, and financing was "vital and complete in every respect," Foreign Secretary Edward Grey commented in an internal memorandum. It was essential for the British to keep a low profile, lest they alienate Wilson or his opponent, Charles Evans Hughes. As a solution, Grey and his colleagues adopted their own neutrality policy. In one of its "strictly confidential" instructions to journalists, the Official Press Bureau cautioned that "nothing in the presidential campaign . . . calls for any comment in our Press."[78]

The Germans were unable to emulate this low-key approach.

2

He Kept Us Out of War

Aside from the sheer joy that the campaign held for me,
it also had definite educational values.

—George Creel

As the race for president approached, Democrats were worried. In early 1916, financier Henry Morgenthau, who chaired the campaign finance committee in Wilson's 1912 campaign, returned to the United States from Turkey, where he had been ambassador. The gloomy predictions he heard from other Wilson appointees shocked him. Nobody expressed "the slightest hope that President Wilson would be reelected."[1]

Among the Democrat hand-wringers, none worked harder to improve the odds than Robert W. Woolley. For him, Wilson's 1912 race for the presidency never ended. In that campaign the elfin former journalist was deputy to North Carolina newspaperman Josephus Daniels, who headed the Democratic National Committee's publicity bureau. Woolley's reward was the directorship of the US Mint. He was so active on Wilson's reelection that House said in April 1916 that he was "the only man who is doing any political work of value."[2]

Woolley was a regular at the liberal Doughnut Cabinet's daily gathering at the Willard Hotel and president of the Common Counsel, a weekly lunch group of members of Congress and administration officials in the basement of the old Shoreham Hotel. An offshoot of the Common Counsel was the Inter-Departmental Committee on Information. Conceived in August 1915 and chaired by Woolley, its members wanted to ensure "everything worth while done anywhere in the Departments between now and November, 1916, receives the widest possible publicity." In articles sent to newspapers, the committee boasted of the administration's public works projects and American neutrality in the war. The committee planned meetings in "cheap lunch places" across the country. Woolley asked Richard Linthicum, on the *New York World* editorial page, to pen a campaign song called "America First." "The newspaper correspondents here are greatly pleased with the first articles sent to them," Woolley told House. But he realized much more needed to be done.[3]

Since the Civil War, only one Democrat besides Wilson had won the presidency. Although Grover Cleveland was elected twice, his terms were split by a loss to Benjamin Harrison. Andrew Jackson was the last Democrat to win successive terms. Wilson's 1912 victory was an anomaly, a four-way race with incumbent William Howard Taft, Theodore Roosevelt at the head of a splinter Progressive Party, and socialist Eugene Debs, whose showing was the largest ever for his party. Wilson won with less than 42 percent of the popular vote and received 100,000 fewer votes than Democratic candidate William Jennings Bryan had in 1908. "Cold reasoning" based on recent elections, a reporter said, made it certain Wilson would lose.[4]

Not only did history work against reelection. "Mr. Wilson's unpopularity," another reporter commented, "seems to be growing." The president had to his credit antitrust legislation, creation of the Federal Trade Commission, and other progressive reforms. But he did nothing to help the Tammany machine, which he needed to win New York. He alienated African-Americans with policies that increased segregation among government workers. He mismanaged policy toward Mexico, which was undergoing a revolution that imperiled American lives and American financial interests. Critics thought a punitive expedition under General John Pershing was too mild a response. Wilson's support of the reform government of anticlerical Venustiano Carranza angered American Catholics.[5]

With respect to the war in Europe, Wilson awkwardly straddled antagonistic domestic forces symbolized by the resignations from his cabinet of pacifist Bryan and Secretary of War Lindley Garrison, who was frustrated by the president's unwillingness to embrace compulsory military service. For progressives, the steps Wilson took toward preparedness were a distraction from domestic reform; for immigrants, they were a step toward war with their homelands; for war-minded critics, they were too little, too late. Wilson's statement after the sinking of the *Lusitania,* "There is such a thing as a man being too proud to fight," was "meat for the Republicans," Woolley said. German torpedoes had killed American women and children. A "disgusted" Roosevelt pawed the ground. Woolley considered Roosevelt "the shrewdest politician in the country" and dreaded the prospect of his making another run for the White House.[6]

When Roosevelt took himself out of the race, Woolley had another candidate to worry about. Since late 1915 he had been getting fretful news of "Hughes propaganda." By this, he meant a drive to orchestrate the nomination of Charles Evans Hughes, once the New York governor and currently a Supreme Court justice. "Wealthy Republicans who are bent upon restoring harmony in the ranks of the G.O.P., but who have succeeded in concealing their identity, have financed a campaign on Justice Hughes' behalf," Woolley reported to House. They had "the friendly aid of many newspaper men." When Hughes was nominated in June, both Roosevelt and Taft endorsed his candidacy. This time around, the Republican leaders were intent on not repeating their mistake of splitting the party.[7]

For many years Hughes had seemed destined for the White House. When he was governor of New York, journalists jovially roasted him at the Fifth Avenue Hotel. One journalist shouted out, "The next President of the United States." The rest roared approval. That the 1916 election did not turn out that way was stunning, although the wonderment was eclipsed by a more earth-shaking turn of events, Wilson's decision to go to war a month after his inauguration.[8]

The tendency to take Wilson's reelection for granted has obscured how easily Wilson could have lost the race. Woolley receives scant attention in histories of presidential campaigning. He deserves a chapter unto himself for his realization of the new kind of campaigning that was required.[9]

By 1916, candidates could no longer depend on steadfast party loyalty buttressed by brass bands and free beer. Voters, who cast their ballots secretly, away from the prying eyes of party agents, had to be wooed through nationally orchestrated campaigns. This meant preparing educational pamphlets, providing compelling news matter to the independent press, and selling an image of the candidate that would motivate a voter to pull the right lever on election day. As British propagandist John Buchan had said, in election campaigns, as in war, the "seed must be sown broadcast." Woolley elevated election propaganda to its highest level up to that time. This helped keep Wilson in the White House and was a training ground for those who would carry out the American war propaganda that followed his election.[10]

CHARLES EVANS HUGHES

Hughes's entry into politics was as sudden as Wilson's, who made the jump from president of Princeton University to governor of New Jersey in 1910. The catapult for Hughes, a Wall Street lawyer, was a surprise call (he was not the first choice) to head an investigation in 1905 of the inflated rates set by gas and electricity trusts in New York. On the strength of that sensational success, he was asked to investigate insurance companies, whose executives enriched themselves at the expense of policyholders and used policyholders' money to support politicians. Blessed with a near photographic memory and enormous power of concentration, Hughes mastered the complex financial dealings involved and relentlessly grilled witnesses. Although powerful Republicans advised him not to go too far, he revealed large insurance company contributions to Roosevelt's presidential campaign fund. Hughes gave "one of the most brilliant performances in the history of American law," thought Henry Morgenthau, whose Midas touch in New York investments did not blind him to the evils of trusts.[11]

A new bright star in the Republican firmament, Hughes was elected governor of New York in 1906 and 1908 (terms ran two years then). He was an able administrator, did not truckle to the old guard Republicans, championed progressive legislation that helped labor, and created public service commissions that became national models. "Charles Evans Hughes," wrote muckraker Ida Tarbell, "is engaged in a passionate effort to vindicate the American system of government." In 1910, President Taft nominated him for the Supreme Court, where he remained progressive in restraining laissez-faire capitalism and enlarging government regulatory powers.[12]

Confident that he would prevail and preferring Olympian detachment to the gritty business of politics, Charles Evans Hughes lost his race for the presidency in 1916. It was his only setback as a public man. (Library of Congress)

Hughes was Jovian with his deep-set, penetrating blue eyes and formidable, carefully groomed whiskers. Preferring Olympian detachment to the gritty business of politics and constrained by the fact he was a sitting justice, Hughes professed indifference to the nomination. When the news arrived on Saturday, June 10, that the Republican convention in Chicago had chosen him, he stepped out of his grand, four-story red brick home on Sixteenth Street, a thoroughfare that ran toward the front door of the White House. He greeted reporters with tears in his eyes. In his written acceptance, he recognized "that it is your right to summon and that it is my paramount duty to respond."[13]

Hughes left by train for New York on Sunday evening. He arrived at dawn the next day and went immediately to just-rented campaign offices at the Astor Hotel, overlooking Broadway. Like Hughes, the place glowed with positive energy. "It is the most cheerfully cocksure and confident headquarters from which a campaign was ever directed," a *New York Times* reporter wrote. "The casual visitor would think that it was all over except the inauguration. . . . [The staff] had a candidate whom they have canonized, his virtues have been remembered in all details, if not magnified; his faults, if he had any, have been forgotten." The gossip in this heady atmosphere was that William Willcox, whom Hughes made head of the Republican National Committee, would be ambassador to Berlin or London.[14]

Hughes had worked happily in the half-light of the Supreme Court. He did not speak publicly on political issues or return to New York to vote in elections. As a presidential candidate, he could start afresh building bridges to Roosevelt's Progressive Party members and Republicans as well as voters dissatisfied with Wilson. Six members of the Progressive National Committee joined the Republican National Committee to assist his campaign. One of them was James R. Garfield, the son of the twentieth US president. The graying Ohio lawyer had been one of Roosevelt's favorite young men at the White House. Garfield's investigations as commissioner of corporations led to the breakup of Standard Oil. The progressives, Garfield told a party colleague, would give "Hughes the strength that he needs in the contest against Mr. Wilson."[15]

WOOLLEY'S PUBLICITY BUREAU

The Democrats nominated Wilson a few days later in St. Louis. Woolley described the convention as "a jollification and ratification." The biggest surprise was Martin H. Glynn's keynote address. In the middle of his stem-winder, the former New York governor listed instances when the United States had avoided war. As if an electric shock coursed through the hall, delegates shouted "go on" and "say it again." Glynn obliged by reciting one historical example after another in which a national crisis was averted. So rousing was the speech that other orators picked up the theme. Pacifist Bryan wept. Before the convention was over the platform had a plank—exactly who put it in no one remembered— that commended Wilson for preserving "the vital interests of our government and its citizens, and [having] kept us out of war."[16]

The next step was to revamp the Democratic National Committee, another worry for Woolley. The party apparatus was rusty, if not broken. This had given urgency to Woolley's work on the Inter-Departmental Committee and led him to propose the creation of the Wilson League, which was done in the spring through *Collier's* editor Norman Hapgood and Morgenthau. At House's suggestion, Woolley approached Frederic William Wile, the *London Daily Mail's* specialist on German propaganda, about using his talents on behalf of the Democratic National Committee. When House was in London in early 1916, Wile had ingratiated himself by offering, as House recalled, "to be my man Friday" during the visit. Wile was initially enthusiastic about Woolley's offer. But it came to nothing, possibly because he could not leave the *Daily Mail* soon enough and possibly because he wanted too much money.[17]

Of overriding concern was replacing the chairman, William F. McCombs. In 1912, he had not coped well with the pressures of the campaign. At one point William McAdoo, his deputy, took over while McCombs retreated to a sanitarium. All sorts of names were considered as replacements. With no ideal candidate at hand, Wilson concluded, "If not Vance McCormick, who?" McCormick, an All-American football legend at Yale, belonged to a wealthy Pennsylvania family, owned two newspapers, and had been a superb mayor of Harrisburg. He was not a political warhorse, and his speaking skills tended toward gridiron metaphors. But he was a principled progressive. During his unsuccessful run for governor, Roosevelt campaigned for him. McCormick put Morgenthau in his old post over the campaign finance committee and Woolley over the publicity bureau.[18]

Five foot six, pudgy, with a cherubic face and a fondness for well-pressed three-piece suits, Bob Woolley had the look of a sedentary editor, although the forty-five-year-old journalist had been anything but stationary. At the turn of the century, journalists with an itch to travel found jobs wherever they lighted. For Woolley it was Kentucky, Illinois, New York, Washington, DC, Texas, and

Lake Charles, Louisiana, where he acquired a small crusading newspaper. He worked for *Munsey's* and *Country Life,* the latter inspired by a progressive Roosevelt commission to enhance rural living. Raised in a Kentucky family that "gave no quarter to the party of Abe Lincoln," Woolley quite naturally took a turn into politics. Democrat reformer Augustus Stanley from Kentucky chaired a House committee looking into US Steel. In 1911, Woolley became Stanley's chief investigator.[19]

From his experience in the 1912 presidential race, Woolley had clear ideas how to organize his publicity bureau. Against the vehement objections of President Wilson's secretary, Joseph Tumulty, he transferred all publicity efforts

By 1916 presidential candidates could no longer depend on steadfast party loyalty buttressed by brass bands and free beer. Robert Woolley, the elf-like man in the center of this *New York World* photograph taken at the Democratic National Committee headquarters, perfected techniques for the new kind of nationally orchestrated campaigns needed to win elections— and for propagandizing citizens when Wilson subsequently took the country into war.

from Washington to his New York office and convinced McCormick to give him control of the campaign mail office. With his many years toiling in newsrooms and tireless political networking, Woolley owned as good an address book a single man was likely to acquire and used it to assemble his staff. To a former Washington correspondent for the *St. Louis Globe,* who oversaw Post Office publicity, he gave responsibility for the campaign textbook, "the *vade mecum* of journalists, platform speakers, and party revivalists." A *Nashville Tennessean* editor handled the *Bulletin,* a weekly with news and editorial ideas sent to eighty-five hundred newspapers and all Washington correspondents. A *New York World* staffer ran the literary department. A Washington correspondent for the *Atlanta Constitution* wrote a daily article signed by Vance McCormick for the Hearst newspapers (Hearst tepidly endorsed Wilson). Another reporter serviced the pro-Wilson Newspaper Enterprise Association owned by Scripps Newspapers. The editor of a farm magazine prepared material for that constituency, and a woman with close ties to labor supervised appeals in that direction. Other departments handled daily news releases, advertisements, and motion pictures. Staff clipped cartoons from the press and distributed them in press-ready form to more than a thousand newspapers.[20]

Woolley ran his bureau along the lines of a metropolitan daily. "All articles," he said in his plan, "should be tabloids—as full of meat as the Sermon on the Mount." Said one man in the bureau, "Our office is just like a newspaper shop, only we are as busy every day as the newspapers were when the Lusitania was sunk." Structure and routine gave discipline to the operation, but he also wanted the bureau "to investigate and expose corrupt alliances between 'big business' and politics, and other forms of political fraud." Among the specialists he recruited were a journalist with expertise in religion, muckraker Lincoln Steffens, to help with the textbook, and Dr. George Dorsey, an anthropologist and sometimes *Chicago Tribune* correspondent who studied immigrants. His "chief special writer" was George Creel, a journalist who dubbed himself the "original Woodrow Wilson man."[21]

In 1905 Creel had suggested Wilson for president in the Kansas City weekly he owned. In 1912, while a writer on the *Rocky Mountain News,* he plumped for Wilson as the best Democratic nominee for president after William Jennings Bryan. When Wilson prevailed, Creel wrote, "Not since the days of Calhoun, Webster, and Clay—those splendid times when men of rare ability looked upon public service as a career—has anyone come forward with such pre-eminent qualifications for the high position to which he aspires." By 1914, he was trumpeting President Wilson's "record of amazing achievement." Ida Tarbell, who wrote a highly favorable article on Wilson, and Frederic Howe thought the Democrats needed "a good publicity man more than anything else in the world" and suggested Creel, an idea that made its way to Wilson.[22]

Woolley's bureau had the committee's largest budget, but that understated the money and energy that went into publicity. Homer Cummings, a large man with a commensurate presence, was McCormick's deputy and managed the speakers' bureau, which had offices in Chicago and, for the first time in any campaign, San Francisco. Daniel Roper, a fellow member of the Common Counsel, was in charge of organization, where he used his national connections as first assistant postmaster general. The question he "mulled over every night and tried to act on every day was how to convey [campaign] messages most effectively to the party organization throughout the country." He used his experience with the Census Bureau to devise a scheme for measuring public opinion at ten-day intervals.[23]

Campaign organization meant little without a campaign strategy. A shrewd approach came from William McAdoo. "It is most important, in my opinion, that we should make the first move and not permit our opponents to define the lines along which the campaign will be carried," he advised McCormick in early July. Hughes, he said, displayed a tendency to "pussyfoot" to avoid alienating any of his many prospective voters. The Democrats, McAdoo stressed, must make Hughes be specific. McCormick passed the suggestion to Woolley.[24]

Woolley had Creel draft a letter designed to put Hughes on the spot. On July 29 he assembled a group of notable writers at the New York Biltmore Hotel to secure their endorsement of it. The letter posed ten awkward questions. Among them: Would Hughes have protested the German invasion of Belgium and backed that up with the navy? Would he have broken relations with Germany after the sinking of the *Lusitania*? Would he have asked Congress to stop munition shipments to the Allies?[25]

On July 31 Hughes delivered his formal nomination acceptance speech in New York's Carnegie Hall. The candidate, reported the *New Republic*, "fell into pious words and utter vagueness" about what he would do. His sole issue seemed to be "anti-Wilsonism." Two days later Woolley released Creel's letter, with thirty-seven signatures. The ten questions appeared in the coming weeks in quarter-page newspaper advertisements that greeted Hughes wherever he campaigned. The headline on the ad was "'Yes!' or 'No!' Mr. Hughes." On cue, hecklers shouted "What would you do?"[26]

HUGHES'S MISSTEPS

On August 5, "feeling quite confident," a reporter noted, Hughes began the first of three major campaign swings, this one to the West. His wife, Antoinette, accompanied him, the first time a candidate's spouse made an extended campaign tour with her husband. As the "Hughes Special" cut across North Dakota and Montana, the *New York Times* reported that the candidate "at first acted as if he were a bit out of element, but the restraint soon was overcome." Cowboys dashing about on horses and shooting in the air, bands playing and flags waving, crowds cheering—all seemed to invigorate Hughes, who shook hands enthusiastically and swapped stories with cattlemen.[27]

That swing to the West, however, showed weaknesses in Hughes's campaign. Although Hughes could stir audiences, the first impression was always his imposing facade. In a letter to a friend that summer Roosevelt flippantly called him "the bearded iceberg." The supposed advantage of having been out of the political arena seemed to be a disadvantage. He was, James Garfield said, "out of practice." Hughes had themes: a constitutional amendment for women's suffrage, which he personally added to the Republican platform; reform of political appointments to the diplomatic service; support for the tariff. He criticized Wilson's bad appointments and his Mexico policy. But he tiptoed around the issue looming over the campaign, the war in Europe.[28]

As governor, Hughes had worked well with the press, often meeting with them twice a day. But he was not as effective in the national campaign. He did not hand out advance copies of his remarks for fear of giving an advantage to the Democrats. This made it difficult for editors to write timely editorials in support of his candidacy. On the hustings, he typically spoke off the cuff, with the result that reporters could only produce short stories if they wanted to get something in the paper the next day. Hughes's speech in Peoria, a reporter wrote his editor, "was an excellent one, but none of the men, even those representing news associations, could do it justice." Associated Press general manager Melville Stone met with Hughes to explain how he could help himself and reporters by handing out well-prepared speeches a week in advance. Robert McCormick, the Republican owner of the *Chicago Tribune,* offered similar advice: "Our opponents are the most capable fighters at hitting below the belt that have appeared in the political arena for many years. It will take the most complete campaign to discredit them." Hughes did not change his approach.[29]

Hughes's staff had respected veterans. His publicity director, David Barry,

was, like Woolley, an old hand at journalism and politics. Once he was simultaneously a reporter and a confidential secretary to a senator. Also like Woolley,
he was known for running his operation along newspaper lines. But the overall
campaign strategy and tactics were to play it safe, which meant avoiding controversy that might impede victory. The director of publicity in the Chicago
headquarters told a sympathetic editor that the strategy was "to explode the
Wilson Myth," a statement that carried with it no sense of what that myth was
or how to blow it up. While Wilson's campaign reached the masses with its
messages, Hughes was sent into small communities with small audiences and
where it was difficult to reach him when an urgent issue arose. "How could we
possibly get in touch with a man who was making speeches every few hundred
miles in a train," complained Frederick Tanner, state chair of the Republican
Party in New York.[30]

Work at the precinct level had "rarely been more ineptly conducted." Harold Ickes, a Roosevelt man who joined the Republican National Committee,
received reports that Colorado Republicans diverted money from Hughes's
campaign to reelect the governor. In Oklahoma, Ickes told William Willcox,
the Republican organization froze out Roosevelt Progressives "on the theory
that Hughes will win anyway," and they could keep the spoils for themselves.[31]

Willcox's appointment was a cause of "wonderment and amazement," said
Tanner, who warned Hughes against it. A personal friend of Hughes and Roosevelt, Willcox was respected for his integrity, kindliness, and distaste for factional fights. As president of the New York City Board of Education, he was
short on the political experience needed in a national campaign, especially one
that demanded shrewd judgment and a firm hand to unite Roosevelt's people and traditional Republicans. In the West, Garfield told Roosevelt, "the old
guard Republicans have acted very badly toward the Progressives."[32]

Hughes's visit to California was a political disaster for just that reason. California governor Hiram Johnson, Roosevelt's vice-presidential running mate in
1912, had just won the Progressive nomination for an open US Senate seat. Republican leaders were fighting a losing battle to keep him from receiving their
party's nomination as well. Willcox and Hughes ignored advice to call off a visit
to the state until these disputes were settled. In telegrams to both sides, Willcox insisted that senatorial nominations were strictly a state issue having nothing to do with the presidential contest and "that every effort should be made
to harmonize all differences" when it came to staging Hughes's visit. This was
akin to asking a scorpion and a tarantula to dance cheek to cheek. The Repub-

licans sought to sideline Johnson from events; Johnson and his loyal followers fought back.[33]

The denouement came on what was supposed to be a Sunday rest for Hughes in Los Angeles. The candidate took an impromptu trip over a bumpy road that stopped at the Hotel Virginia in Long Beach. Unbeknown to him, Hiram Johnson subsequently arrived at the hotel for a rest of his own. Sensitive that it might look as though he came to the hotel to make Hughes recognize him, Johnson went to his room, leaving the first move to Hughes. Johnson's hand was not among the hundreds Hughes shook that evening. Learning of this on his return to Los Angeles, Hughes tried to make amends, but the damage had been done. Johnson was popular in the state and possessed an outsized vanity that Hughes had tweaked. "Instead of a hundred thousand majority for Mr. Hughes in California, you may look at a mighty close vote," Johnson wrote to Garfield in July. "I confess that I will not stand side by side upon the same platform with the men who are demanding the destruction of those who have fought so faithfully with me." Johnson supported Hughes but never attacked Wilson.[34]

The Democrats did everything they could to sunder Republican unity. The day after Hughes's Carnegie Hall speech, Woolley asked Democratic state chairs for lists of "prominent progressives, independents and republicans in your state who have come out for Wilson following delivery of Hughes speech of acceptance." Whenever Wilson won a convert, Woolley told "the world they had joined the March to victory." Bainbridge Colby was a big catch. Colby was furious with Roosevelt for abandoning his Progressive Party. At Homer Cummings's request, he agreed to a speaking tour. A persuasive orator with a keener eye for publicity than the Republicans who managed Hughes's trips, Colby wanted to visit locales where news of his talks would have the widest distribution.[35]

Others chimed in. Republican Henry Ford endorsed Wilson in an interview with the Scripps-McRae Syndicate. Woolley mailed several million copies. Creel interviewed Republican Thomas A. Edison, another convert to Wilson, for an article that had a circulation of ten million. The Republicans aggressively criticized Wilson for appointing Josephus Daniels secretary of the navy. The North Carolinian's down-home manner and progressive reforms (such as eliminating alcohol from the officers' mess) lent themselves to facile criticism that he was not up to the job of running the navy. "A Vote for Wilson is a Vote for Daniels," declared Republican billboards. From beloved Admiral George Dewey, Creel secured a spirited defense of Daniels.[36]

The Democrats benefited from Republican mistakes as surely as the British did from the Germans' pratfalls. "We were to be kept busy playing the cards they persistently dealt us," Woolley said. One card was the Republicans' "Billionaire Special," as the Democrats called it. Women in eleven western states and Illinois had the right to vote for president. To carry the message of Hughes's sympathy for their suffrage, a group of East Coast women organized a transcontinental train journey. Accomplished individuals were among the passengers, but Mrs. Cornelius Vanderbilt, Mrs. Payne Whitney, and the wives of other tycoons had the look of dilettantes. Republican National Committee staff in Chicago and New York tried to scotch the idea, but again Willcox did not listen. Frederick Tanner considered it symptomatic of him to want to please people even when they had an awful idea. The women personified eastern arrogance in presuming to tell western women how to vote when they themselves could not cast ballots.[37]

Woolley did not want to win sympathy for the women by heaping scorn on them. Before the eight-car train pulled out of Grand Central Station on October 2, he issued a strictly factual story. It contained sketches of the women, one of whom, it was noted, adorned her dog with a diamond collar. The story was easy to embellish, and that is what local newspapers did to greet the train when it rolled into their cities. The locomotive had not left the state of New York before the heckling began. In Chicago, working women held up "Go Back to Wall Street" signs. One Billionaire Special passenger yelled back, "You are all ignorant." Woolley was not sure how it happened, but someone leaked an advertisement—the headline was "Fuss, Feathers and Femininity"—that he had nixed as too frivolous. At no expense to the national campaign, it ran widely. "We formally disapproved," Woolley said, "but were helpless and hugely amused." Afterward, someone asked a Republican leader how much the train cost. "About half a million votes," he replied.[38]

HUGHES, CANDIDATE OF THE KAISER

The Republicans saw the war in Europe as a winning theme. Wilson would be caught in a vise between those who wanted to fight and those who did not. Glynn's rousing keynote speech at St. Louis, however, pointed a decisive way out of the dilemma. The slogan "He Kept Us Out of War" was one of the most powerful in any presidential campaign, ever. The six monosyllabic words were catchy, they fit easily into advertisements, and they hit a political sweet spot—

the yearning of the great mass of Americans for continued peace, whether with Mexico or in staying out of the European war.

Agents of the campaign plastered the slogan on billboards, used it in campaign songs, and proclaimed it in speeches. Wilson did not like it, complaining he could not guarantee peace. He came to the campaign quarters to scold the staff about it. At least this is what Creel recalled. Woolley admitted that the idea of exploiting "the fact that President Wilson kept us out of war occurred to me after listening to the keynote speech" at the convention. His phrasing was "with honor he has kept us out of war." (Wilson used "honor" in making the case for military preparedness while remaining neutral.) Woolley insisted he did not put the punchier slogan on anything his department produced because "I always had in mind that we would eventually get into the war." In other ways, though, Woolley hammered on the peace theme. The message found its way into almost every major piece of campaign literature. Billboards carried the double message of peace and prosperity: "He has protected me and mine." The Democratic National Committee's *Workers' Manual* said, "President Wilson has kept the United States out of the most terrible war in the history of the world!" Woolley's bureau distributed five million copies of Glynn's speech. Others on the campaign did the same. Senator Thomas J. Walsh, who headed the party's Chicago headquarters, ordered speakers in his western region to make the slogan's theme their chief one, probably with Wilson's approval, for whatever Wilson's reservations about the slogan, he used his own versions of it. The Republicans would radically change foreign policy, he said. "There is only one choice as against peace, and that is war."[39]

With this strategy Hughes, not Wilson, was the candidate in a vise, a vise that was more uncomfortable because in addition to placating competing interests, he had to distinguish himself from Wilson when their positions on the war were similar. "With regard to foreign policies," wrote Cecil Spring-Rice, the British ambassador in Washington, in a report to the Foreign Office, "there is no difference whatever between the two candidates as to the prime necessity of preserving peace." For the British this made it all the more imperative to stay on the sidelines of the campaign, although pro-Allied propaganda continued. Wellington House distributed copious photographs and employed the new technique of movies and newsreels, while French speakers fanned out across the country.[40]

Hughes had no surcease from his vocal and mutually antagonistic supporters. "I need hardly tell you," Roosevelt wrote to Garfield, "that it has been no

You Are Working;
—Not Fighting!

Alive and Happy;
—Not Cannon Fodder!

Wilson and Peace with Honor?

or

Hughes with Roosevelt and War?

Roosevelt says we should hang our heads in shame because we are not at war with Germany in behalf of Belgium!

Roosevelt says that following the sinking of the Lusitania he would have foregone diplomacy and seized every ship in our ports flying the German Flag. That would have meant *war!*

Hughes Says
He and Roosevelt are in
Complete Accord!

Senator Fall, who has vast interests in Mexico and is Candidate Hughes' advisor as to Mexican Affairs declares "a Hughes *war* would be preferable to a Wilson peace."

Read the published list of Heavy Subscribers to the Republican campaign fund, then look up the list of Americans with enormous interests in Mexico and learn why those who place the almighty dollar ahead of human life would not hesitate to plunge this country into an ignoble war of conquest — would not stop at sacrificing thousands and thousands of American lives in their greed for oil and gold.

Look again at this list. Then you will see why the "Old Guard" appeals frantically for a protective tariff—

That breeder of strikes, of starvation wages, and of every panic that ever cursed this country—

And which made billions for organized wealth by putting honest competition out of business.

You will see why in sheer desperation and bereft of all decency the Republican "Old Guard" is capitalizing the lamentable incidents in Mexico and trying to discredit your President for sparing you the horrors that would come with intervention.

Read the list still again. Note the names of men heavily intrenched financially in the protective tariff system and in vicious special privilege.

Read and see why millions are being spent to re-enact the Payne-Aldrich tariff—to wipe out the Federal Reserve System—to repeal the Eight Hour law and other progressive laws—to undo the Wilson Record of unparalleled achievement.

Then understand why Candidate Hughes said in his Milwaukee speech: "The whole list of Democratic accomplishment must be wiped off the books for the good of the country."

Mr. Hughes "Would Name a STRONG Cabinet."

The Lesson is Plain:

If You Want WAR, Vote for HUGHES!

If You Want Peace With Honor

VOTE FOR WILSON!

and Continued Prosperity

The Tumult and the Shouting Die!   It is Up to You and Your Conscience!

Wilson Business Men's National League

"He Kept Us Out of War" became one of the most potent campaign slogans of all time. President Wilson did not like the slogan as it implied a promise that he might not be able to keep. Robert Woolley insisted he never used quite those words. But over and over Wilson and Woolley said more or less the same thing. This campaign advertisement appeared in the *New York Times* on November 4, 1916, three days before the election.

light task for me in my speeches to avoid seeming to clash with Hughes." Roosevelt railed at "hyphenism," by which he referred to immigrant groups who retained loyalties to their countries of origin. Democrats suggested Hughes would appoint Roosevelt secretary of war. At the same time Democrats portrayed Hughes as a tool of German-American leaders and their newspapers, which endorsed him well before the convention and continued to pound away afterward. Ambassador Bernstorff sorrowfully informed Berlin that Hughes was considered "the German candidate." He feared German-American criticism of Wilson would antagonize the president, whom he favored on the grounds Wilson was more likely to keep the United States out of the war. Despite Bernstorff's best efforts to dampen the attacks on Wilson, German-Americans persisted. In the process they did what they did not want to do, help Wilson.[41]

The vise tightened for Hughes following a private meeting he had in mid-September with Irish-American leader Jeremiah A. O'Leary and representatives of the American Independence Conference and other groups with German financial support. They wanted "to secure from Mr. Hughes a definite statement for the benefit of a broad and liberal Americanism that has been offended by the British propaganda." Hughes assured them he was for neutrality and followed up a few days later with a public statement that he would not "tolerate any improper interference with American commerce or with American mails." "There was nothing sinister in the transaction," George Sylvester Viereck said correctly. Hughes's speeches on neutrality were aligned with Wilson's views, who was furious when the British published their blacklist that July of American firms suspected of trading with the Central Powers. Nor was it inappropriate for Hughes to meet with immigrant constituencies. As the American Independence Conference noted in an internal communication on the meeting, "German-Americans and other loyal Americans have as much right, being Americans, to ask Mr. Hughes questions . . . as had Democrats who have been trying to embarrass the Republican candidate with questions."[42]

That Hughes did not advertise the meeting was understandable. He had to contend with Roosevelt and his truculent supporters on the Republican National Committee, who watched closely for deviations from their war agenda. But the secrecy made the meeting look all the worse when Woolley revealed it had taken place. The information came from what he breezily called his "bureau of intelligence," specifically a German-American named Hans Rieg who acquired internal documents of the American Independence Conference. Woolley released the documents on October 23 to expose "the secret racial organization under which Jeremiah O'Leary and his associates have been masking their furtive and nation-wide campaign in the interests of Charles Evans Hughes." Woolley dribbled out his exposé in six installments suitable for serialization in newspapers. The coverage was reminiscent of the way the *World* splashed revelations of Dr. Albert's suitcase across its pages. Norman Hapgood of *Collier's* added to this narrative of Hughes as a tool of subversive elements at a dinner given at the University Club of New York, when he dramatically brandished a letter he received from a "western senator." The senator said a German-American editor bragged of writing a Hughes speech against the blacklist.[43]

"I have made no private agreements and have engaged in no intrigues," Hughes insisted. Although he didn't "want the support of any one to whom the interest of this nation is not supreme," his statements seemed too late and too tepid. "We all wish Hughes would make a stronger fight on the Americanism issue," Garfield wrote in his diary. *World's Work* editorialized, "No nation has ever been called upon to suffer so seditious a press as that published in the United States in the German language. A few sharp, definite words from Mr. Hughes would have laid this ghost." The *Nation,* with some apparent nudging from Hughes's people, explained his conduct as that of the judge who refused comment on a pending case: "He expects to be elected President. As President he would have to conduct our relations with Germany."[44]

On the surface, the contrast with Wilson was sharp. In a blistering note to O'Leary, Wilson wrote, "I would feel deeply mortified to have you and anybody like you vote for me. Since you have access to many disloyal Americans and I have not, I will ask you to convey this message to them." Woolley claimed that he adopted the same attitude. Except for a few Jewish dailies in New York, he did not "patronize a single daily, weekly or monthly foreign language publication." But if Wilson's statement marked a difference with Hughes, his actions did not. When Roosevelt's martial speeches made it seem possible to acquire more of the hyphenate vote, Wilson tempered his comments. The Democrats had bureaus to work with the foreign-born in New York and in Chicago; the Wisconsin Democratic Committee had a German Publicity Bureau. It published materials in German, Hebrew, and Spanish as well as Scandinavian and Slavic languages. All of Homer Cummings's speakers worked for free, except for those who orated in foreign languages. The committee paid these individuals "a substantial amount." At the suggestion of Norman Hapgood, the Chicago headquarters urged newspapers to goad Roosevelt into making intemperate speeches about Germany when he was visiting the city.[45]

Democrats had their own private meetings with German-Americans. Breck-enridge Long, a wealthy young attorney, Princeton graduate, and president of the St. Louis Wilson Club, claimed to have convinced a German-American newspaper to support Wilson. In New York, Philadelphia, Chicago, and St. Louis, congressional leaders sought to convince German-Americans that Wilson was a better bet than Hughes insofar as staying out of the war was concerned. Martin Glynn struck up a conversation with O'Leary in the smoking car of a train between Albany and New York. Postmaster General Albert Burleson, a former Texas congressman whom Wilson called "my political ambassador," met with Viereck in McCormick's office at the Democratic National Committee. These meetings agitated Woolley, who rebuked Burleson. But they were no more sinister than Hughes's meeting and as sensible, considering the close race. In any event, when news about the meetings leaked out, the Republicans were unable to turn the tables. The difference was, first, Wilson's bold statement made him look decisive and principled, and, second, Woolley's press management was better than anything Republicans could muster. In Woolley's expert hands the simple image triumphed over complex reality.[46]

The Republicans were not above mischief. They used their influence with the owners of movie theaters to keep out the Democrats' campaign films. In an exposé of their own, they revealed that Texas Democrats illegally squeezed money out of local federal office holders. (Woolley wisely took the edge off this by quickly repudiating the Texan initiative.) They paid for news and editorials. In 1908, James Williams, Washington bureau chief of the prestigious and conservative *Boston Evening Transcript*, had taken a leave from his paper to work on Taft's campaign. In 1916, when he was the paper's editor, he remained at the *Transcript* while drawing $100 a week from the Republican Party. One of his assignments was to denigrate the slogan "He Kept Us Out of War." When he failed to alert his Republican bosses that the *Transcript* was running a Democratic advertisement aimed at religious audiences, the director of publicity, David Barry, treated Williams like the employee he was: "Wake up please, and try to stay awake for two weeks more, and it will be all over."[47]

The Democrats wrung their hands over a Republican whispering campaign about Wilson's illicit relationship with Mary Ellen Peck while he was married to his first wife, Ellen (a charge that may have had truth to it in view of the passionate letters he wrote to Peck while he was president of Princeton). Because Wilson considered it "utterly out of the question" to cooperate for a counter-story on his happy home life, McCormick, House, and Woolley arranged for one by Stockton Axson, Ellen's brother. *New York Times* editors liked it so much they made it into a Sunday magazine story.[48]

Democrats used mean ad hominem attacks themselves. Breckenridge Long laid out an elaborate argument that Hughes was ineligible to be president. At the date of Hughes's birth, Long claimed, his father was an English subject and thus the infant Hughes was not a citizen of the United States. Long spuriously argued that the Fourteenth Amendment, which gave natural-born citizenship to all persons born on US soil, did not cover Hughes because he was born before the amendment was enacted. At the time of his birth, Long ludicrously claimed, Hughes did not give "sole allegiance" to the United States.[49]

To disguise its origins, Woolley sometimes mailed campaign materials in blank envelopes. The Democrats had their equivalent of Boston editor James Williams working for them behind the scenes. *Baltimore Sun* Washington bureau chief Fred Essary told Woolley he was "on the job," arranging articles by cabinet members on the "constructive work" of the administration. Progressive E. W. Scripps, who had newspapers strung out across the West and Midwest as well as news services, established a phantom campaign headquarters in Cleveland. A trusted lieutenant ensured a steady flow of pro-Wilson stories and editorials.[50]

Creel's pen, furiously at work, produced a slim, vituperative book, *Wilson and the Issues,* that the Century Company published as the campaign heated up. Creel called Wilson's critics unpatriotic, undemocratic, unthinking, rapacious, stupid, and hypocritical. "Secret masters," he claimed, selected Hughes and sought "the elimination of a President who has stood in their way." Hughes, he wrote, "is a candidate of the Kaiser; he is the candidate of Toryism and reaction. It is millions drawn from these sources that will finance his campaign; it is the votes of these sinister forces that he will receive; it is their interests that will dominate in event of his election."[51]

Woolley serialized chapters from the book for use by the press and produced a paperback version with an introduction by Secretary of War Newton D. Baker. The book was sent to state committees and people who spoke on Wilson's behalf. Creel gave his royalties to the Democratic National Committee. Wilson reportedly was "mighty pleased" with the book.[52]

HUGHES FAVORED

At the beginning of the race, the Democratic campaign staff endured a two-hour Wilson lecture at the White House. Although Morgenthau, Roper, and

Woolley fell asleep in the sweltering August heat, they left keenly aware of what Wilson would and would not do in his reelection fight. One "would not" was Wilson's refusal to mount rostrums around the country to ply his oratorical skills, as he had done in 1912. He preferred the veranda of Shadow Lawn, the New Jersey home he rented during the campaign. His first major address did not come until September 23.[53]

McCormick had "thorough conversations" with Wilson weekly, often staying overnight in the White House. Wilson wrote to him on details, once enclosing a poem that had "so much swing and punch in it that I cannot help thinking it would make a rattling campaign document." But Wilson was not much engaged in the publicity side of the campaign, preferring instead to use the power of his office to advertise himself. He showed strength when he gave Germany an ultimatum that led it to suspend unrestricted submarine warfare. Henceforth, the Germans would adhere to traditional visit-and-search rules before sinking merchant vessels. Wilson added to his progressive credentials by naming the "People's Lawyer," Louis Brandeis, to the Supreme Court and successfully passing laws on workmen's compensation, rural credits, and protection of child labor. Woolley capitalized on Wilson's presidential actions. He advised him to sign two pieces of legislation separately so as "to get double the amount of immediate publicity; furthermore, the pictures taken could be used to advantage in appealing to separate groups, whereas the one picture might prove of doubtful value."[54]

Still, victory was far from assured. Lansing's Thursday luncheons with Democratic colleagues at the Metropolitan Club became "pretty gloomy affairs." Tumulty received reports of anti-Catholic feeling in the Midwest. Hughes regained momentum in late August when Wilson supported eight-hour-day legislation for railway workers in order to head off their strike. "I am certainly receiving 'a frost' from most of the bankers and cotton mill men," a Democratic fundraiser in North Carolina wrote to Josephus Daniels. The Republicans, he said, were telling all employers the Democrats were intent on enforcing "a universal eight hour day law," including for farms.[55]

Hughes got in the rhythm of campaigning. "Mr. Hughes is a kind of campaigner that every Republican ought to be proud of," wrote the *New York Evening Post*'s David Lawrence. His speeches were so powerful that Democrats in a Lincoln, Nebraska, audience were compelled to clap. Hughes visited Maine prior to its September elections, which turned out to be a great Republican victory. The result, James Garfield declared, "means better results in November than we thought two weeks ago." Republicans captured every federal and state seat on the ballot, despite Democrats pouring in money from their meager coffers. "The chances of Mr. Hughes have greatly increased," British ambassador Spring-Rice reported to the Foreign Office. Hughes resisted pleas to replace Willcox as his campaign chair but agreed that a friend of his could urge Willcox to focus on grassroots organization and sharpen strategy. Willcox laughed off the advice; all was going well.[56]

The Republican National Committee was on its way to spending more than twice as much as in the 1912 presidential contest, nearly $2.5 million. From time to time the Democrats received a financial boost. Young Breckenridge Long came in at a crucial moment with a $5,000 check and a $30,000 loan. But the Democrats spent 40 percent less than the Republicans, not counting expenditures by the separate Hughes Alliance. The Republicans also felt strong winds at their backs thanks to the base they built up over many years among the farming, business, and professional classes everywhere but in the South. "My trip west gives me more hope of Hughes election," Garfield scribbled in his diary in mid-October, when he was stumping for Hughes. "The press reports of conditions east are likewise more favorable." Two weeks later, back in the Republicans' Chicago office, Garfield concluded, "We will win unless our reports are woefully wrong."[57]

As the race came to a close, the demand by both parties for campaign buttons caused a shortage of celluloid used in their production and limited the supply. Homer Cummings reported that Republicans in his state, Connecticut, were "buying pages in all of the Democratic papers as well as their own, and their billboard advertising is greater than I have ever seen it in this State." It seemed to be the same everywhere. No longer could Wilson hang back from campaigning. He made four speeches on a single day in Cincinnati. Wilson was angry House arranged for him to speak at Madison Square Garden, but he did it.[58]

Woolley, who worked far into the night, seven days a week, accelerated his efforts. He added staff to the Literary Department. He hired a cartoonist to produce a daily feature and convinced famed cartoonist C. R. Macauley of the *New York World* to contribute ten more. In one of his targeted mailings, he sent colored pictures of Wilson to almost every woman in states where they could vote. At its high point his bureau had twenty-four clerical staff.[59]

Posters were plastered everywhere. Woolley personally supervised placements on billboards, street cars, and electric signs. He desperately shoveled ads into newspapers, sending the Democrats deep into debt. Cash strapped, he had not scheduled the ads far in advance at more favorable rates, as the Republicans had. One full-page advertisement three days before voting declared, "If You want War, vote for HUGHES!" On the eve of the election, a display ad in newspapers exposed the Republicans for using fake labor endorsements in their advertisements. The details had been uncovered by a labor leader Woolley hired late in the contest. The same day Willcox charged Democrats with distributing cartoons that misquoted Hughes.[60]

Word spread that Tammany was out to knife Wilson in New York. This was deadly, for it might become a self-fulfilling prophecy. Why should Democrats vote if Wilson was bound to lose? The Democrats responded by insisting Wilson was sure to win in New York, even though their count showed he could not. To back up "our magnificent bluff," as Woolley put it, the committee dug into its oversubscribed treasury to give money to the New York state committee. Creel, who began the campaign as an optimist, was worried. Martin Glynn worried they were being beaten by cartoons heavily financed by Republicans. In a Harvard straw poll, Hughes beat Wilson 1,140 to 627. Hughes was no longer a two-to-one favorite in the betting on Wall Street, but the ten-to-seven odds were heavily in his favor. As fiercely loyal as she was, Wilson's new wife, Edith, was convinced Hughes was going to win.[61]

WE ARE NOT LICKED

On November 7, James Garfield woke up in Cleveland to "a glorious day. The sun rose a brilliant red." Garfield took the train to Chicago, where he watched the returns at the campaign office. At midnight he thought Hughes's "election secured certain."[62]

The Hughes family dined at the Hotel Astor. Supporters burst in from time to time with positive reports that were driving up the odds for Hughes. When news of his victory was flashed in Times Square, throngs gathered outside the hotel shouting "Hughes!" "Gentlemen of the press," Hughes's son said to reporters, "I present to you the President-elect of the United States!" Not far away at the Biltmore Hotel, Democratic campaign staff also had a dinner, courtesy of Morgenthau. It began with hope, but as the election results came in, they lost their appetites. McCormick and Woolley excused themselves and returned to headquarters, passing a newsboy selling extras of the *New York Times* and the *World* proclaiming a Hughes victory.* [63]

* The German press also called Hughes the winner. Bernhard Dernburg, the German propagandist expelled from the United States the year before, exulted, "So, Hughes! So the election-mathematicians were right." *Berliner Tageblatt Und Handles-Zeitung,* November 8, 1916.

"Vance," Woolley told McCormick, "we are not licked." The danger, he counseled, was in acting as though they had been beaten. That would discourage their voters in the West from going to the polls, which was what the Republicans encouraged by wiring news reports of a Hughes victory to western states. (Woolley believed this tactic explained Hughes's victory in Oregon.) Unable to get the straitlaced McCormick to mislead the press by saying their calculations showed Wilson had the race in the bag, Woolley did so himself.[64]

Nerves frayed. Woolley overheard McCormick and Morgenthau whisper that he had lost the race for them while at the same time spending them deep into debt. When news came that wagers on the outcome were being taken at a hotel across the street, Creel "swung into action, his eyes batting and his arms gesticulating." He borrowed money to get a piece of the action.[65]

An hour later Creel's prospects improved. Word came in that California was heading toward the Wilson column. Around three o'clock, McCormick announced he had notified Wilson that he was likely to win. Tin horns were blown, rebel yells shouted, speeches given from desktops. When a rush of people tried to hoist the chairman on their shoulders, he directed them to Woolley.[66]

By the afternoon of the next day the betting odds favored Wilson. "Rain all day," Garfield jotted in his diary. "Tears for the country if Wilson is elected." The count was not final until November 22. Wilson lost his own state, New Jersey. Had Hughes not lost California by 3,773 votes, he would have been president. Wilson's electoral vote margin was 277 to 254. When the votes for socialist and prohibition candidates were counted, he had 49.24 percent of the popular vote, once again less than a clear majority.[67]

A NEAR EXACT SCIENCE

Californian Hiram Johnson won his Senate seat by 300,000 votes. A handshake at the Hotel Virginia probably would have swept Hughes to victory on his coattails, although this and much else were debated in autopsies of the campaign. Hughes's old-fashioned beard might have made a difference, some speculated. He was the last major presidential candidate to have one. Garfield blamed old guard Republicans for ignoring "Progressive sentiment throughout the country. These leaders entertained the foolish notion that anyone could beat Wilson." Several New York Democrats who supported Hughes blamed Roosevelt and his belligerent speeches. "You made Wilson a million votes," they said in an angry telegram to the former president. George Sylvester Viereck blamed "the crosscurrents of war propaganda." Burleson, Brandeis, and House said E. W. Scripps carried the day. Scripps's papers hammered hard in Ohio, a state Hughes lost despite its tradition of voting Republican and a large immigrant population. A victory there also would have given Hughes the presidency.[68]

Before the election, Hughes had leapt from one summit of success to another. When a version of Creel's ten questions was flung at him in his second gubernatorial race, his reply was decisive and put his opponent on the defensive. He did not rise to the challenge this time, journalist Walter Lippmann argued, because he was sure to win and played it safe. Hughes's anodyne slogan "The Man of the Hour" was no match for "He Kept Us Out of War," which Hughes, like many others, considered a major factor in his loss. "As a political tactician he did not measure up," Harold Ickes concluded in a postelection summary of the campaign. "He had the defects of his qualities."[69]

It could also be said, as indeed it was, that Woolley's publicity bureau was a decisive factor. It did not completely account for Wilson's victory, to be sure, but victory would not have been possible without it. McCormick, who had reversed recent Democratic campaign history by being a far better manager than his Republican counterpart, attributed the victory to two factors: their success attracting Progressive and independent voters and "the strongest publicity organization that they ever had." The first factor would not have been in play without the second. The publicity machine had many working parts: Cummings's speaker program, the most ambitious to date; Roper's tracking of public opinion; Senator Walsh's emphasis in the party's Chicago headquarters on message discipline. "As a matter of fact," campaign treasurer Wilbur W. Marsh commented on modern presidential elections, "the whole campaign is publicity." But McCormick singled out Woolley and the help he had from Creel.[70]

So did others. Roosevelt credited Woolley with "the most brilliant achievement in the history of American politics." Gifford Pinchot, a member of Roosevelt's inner circle along with Garfield, spoke with authority when he, too, lavished praise on Woolley. As head of the US Forest Service under Roosevelt, Pinchot surpassed any publicity previously generated by a federal official to promote a department. He was the first government official to show how much could be achieved with a press release. The Democrats, he wrote in a postmortem on the election, pulled off the best publicity campaign in history. It was "a masterful realization of 'a systematic publicity plan.'" "Publicity," Pinchot said, "has become a near exact science."[71]

"You are certainly the great little rallier," Frank Polk, Lansing's deputy as

State Department counselor, told Woolley. "Aside from keeping your nerve, which was some triumph, you must be gratified with all the approval that your work has received." Woolley's campaign colleagues celebrated his achievement at the Yale Club. Creel presented him with a platinum watch chain and a gold-handled knife.[72]

Behind this victory was the recognition that parties did not matter to voters as they had before. Roosevelt, who created the renegade Bull Moose Party in 1912, won more votes than the Republican candidate Taft. A number of factors changed the political equation. Civil service reforms broke the back of patronage. Ballot reforms permitted split-ticket voting. With more leisure time and money, voters no longer needed party rallies for entertainment. Discovering they could profit handsomely by catering to the masses and selling advertising rather than depending on party handouts, newspapers became increasingly independent, even if reporters like Fred Essary and James Williams were not. In recognition of this, the Democrats had replaced their stodgy Literary Bureau in 1908 with a Press Bureau and later a Publicity Bureau. "If there is one thing the election has said which should sink into all men's minds," the *Wall Street Journal* commented about the 1916 race, "it is that we should approach the voter—not the mob—by the most modern methods of publicity."[73]

Woolley's achievement of making the case for Wilson to the great mass of voters was less a matter of invention than of perfection. He worked "carefully, methodically, and wisely." Advertising was coming to the fore as a way to reach the masses, and Woolley's were compelling and ubiquitous. Posters, with bold color and large images of Wilson, were arresting. Woolley's bureau generated more printed material than any previous Democratic campaign. Mailings reached an unprecedented volume. When Robert Linthicum of the *New York World* wrote *Wit and Wisdom of Woodrow Wilson,* Woolley sent copies to twenty thousand editors and libraries. Exploiting the new medium of film, which the Democrats used for a cartoon feature in the 1912 election, the campaign produced *The President and His Cabinet in Action.* The "propaganda features" of the film, which humanized the smiling president, were "so insidious," Woolley said, that he had no trouble distributing it widely despite Republican efforts to keep it out of theaters. Woolley met the needs of newspapers by sending crisply written copy well in advance. Editors sent him a phenomenal number of letters and telegrams with profuse praise. "For the first time in my experience as a newspaper man extending back nearly twenty-five years, I find campaign publicity which is not a joke," wrote the managing editor of the *St.*

Louis Republic. "The stories which you so far sent us are real news stuff; the illustrations are pertinent, and available for immediate use."[74]

Woolley started work well before the official campaign began, something Pinchot emphasized as an important lesson for Republicans. His advance planning and disciplined execution were a realization of the progressive dream of expert management of the apparatus of government, in this case the apparatus of getting elected. Woolley contributed to the emergence of the "permanent campaign," the nonstop preparation for the next election by professionals with narrow specializations: voter identification and analysis; direct mailing; targeted messaging; polling; opposition research and attack ads—and image creation such as made Hughes, a man of utter integrity and independence, seem to be a cat's paw of both antiwar hyphenates and pro-war Roosevelt. "There is interposed between the voter and his final judgments the whole mechanism of modern publicity," the *New Republic* noted after the election. "The final vote is not the result of direct acquaintance; it is the result of the news reports, the advertising, the oratory, the elusive rumors which are the modern substitute for direct acquaintance."[75]

THE SAME SORT OF CAMPAIGN OF PUBLICITY FOR THE WAR

It did not take until the next presidential election for the discipline, energy, and creative opportunism of Woolley's bureau to be manifested again in American politics. The drive for a government publicity organization began almost immediately.

McCormick thought the "He Kept Us Out of War" slogan was "the keynote of the Wilson campaign." The election was "a referendum" on going to war in Europe, and the verdict was to avoid it. The feeling among his staff, however, had been that "Peace was hopeless," as Daniel Roper recalled. With war looming ever larger, it became clear that steps should be taken to reorient American thinking. One of many such suggestions came from Woolley in February 1917, a month before inauguration. He advised Frank Polk and Edward House on the "importance of establishing in the State Department, once war is declared, a real bureau of information" with responsibility for censorship and publicity. "Of course, it would not do to talk too much about censorship in announcing the creation of this bureau because of the effect it might have on the public mind." He said the Treasury Department needed a similar bureau.[76]

This sense of urgency was bipartisan. Shortly after the United States entered the war in April, a more ambitious recommendation than Woolley's came from a committee made up of Willcox, McCormick, Morgenthau, former Progressive Party leader George Perkins, and Charles Evans Hughes himself. The Committee on Public Information had only recently been established, and it was unclear what it would do apart from censorship and news releases. The bipartisan committee made up of Willcox, McCormick, and the others wanted something much larger. "There is urgent need," it said, "for exactly the same sort of campaign of publicity under Government direction as was promulgated by the English Government when that country was suddenly faced with the same crisis that now confronts this country." It was imperative "to unify the nation quickly and make the people as a whole understand their individual responsibilities in the progressive phases of this country's participation of war on a big scale as they do not at all understand those responsibilities now." The proposal suggested harnessing the national and local organizations of all parties for this purpose. They would develop alliances with leagues, societies, and chambers around the country.[77]

Wilson dismissed the scheme. He would be steadfast in support of Creel and had no intention of cooperating with Hughes, Willcox, "or any of their tribe." This disinterest in bipartisanship foreshadowed a central factor in his tragic failure to sell his peace treaty after the war.[78]

Nevertheless, the proposal was significant in reflecting the consensus among political leaders that the tools for campaign persuasion were suitable for governing. Creel, Woolley's student, would show how that could be done through a top-down, national structure like the Democratic National Committee's. The CPI would use all the strategies Woolley did. It perpetuated images of sinister German-Americans to make the country feel as though the enemy were right on its own shores. It used informants, surrogates, and sleight of hand. It was not averse to emotional appeals. Creel defended the mantra "He Kept Us Out of War." "People do not read," he said. "They are governed by slogans."[79]

3

A Matured Public Opinion

Politically, democracy means the sovereignty, not of the average man—
who is a rather narrow, short-sighted, muddle-headed creature—but
of a matured public opinion, a very different thing. . . . In the forming of
this opinion the sage has a million times the weight of the field hand. With
modern facilities for mind influencing mind, democracy, at its best,
substitutes the direction of the recognized moral and intellectual *élite*
for the rule of the strong, the rich, or the privileged.

—Edward Alsworth Ross, *Changing America*, 1912

The atmosphere was "arid and sterile" when Arthur Sweetser became an occupant in July 1916 of Room 246 ½, a tiny space set aside for the Associated Press
in the State, War, and Navy Building. Following the sinking of the *Lusitania* a
year before, President Wilson had suspended his weekly press conferences. He
said he was too busy with foreign affairs to spare the time. He held only one
press conference during the presidential campaign, in which he cagily avoided
saying much. He urged the State Department to "confine itself as much as possible to routine matters."[1]

The day the war broke out in 1914, the young reporter Sweetser quit his job
in Boston and caught a boat to Paris. Once there, he rode a bicycle to the other
side of the German lines. His experience, recounted in *Roadside Glimpses of the
Great War,* led him to doubt propaganda about German atrocities. A short stint
at the fledgling *New Republic* on his return home was unsatisfying, as he was
confined to the business side. In Room 246 ½ Sweetser hoped to be in the thick
of news. Instead reporters wandered the halls, played poker, and did "a whole
lot of gossiping and imagining."[2]

Then, suddenly, with the election decided, Sweetser got his wish: News!
Buoyed by the electorate's endorsement of his peace platform, Wilson directed
his energies at engineering an end to the war. "The President expects to deal

with all foreign questions without embarrassment," Sweetser reported. At the urging of his secretary, Joseph Tumulty, Wilson resumed news conferences.

Sweetser would have a ringside seat to a minidrama over the next days that revealed a lot about Wilson's complex approach to public opinion.[3]

WILSON'S PEACE PLAN AND THE NEWS

Many Republicans considered Wilson cynical or worse for his implied promise to avoid war. Roosevelt, whose hatred for Wilson was visceral, derided "He Kept Us Out of War" as "an utterly misleading phrase, the phrase of a coward." Frederick Tanner, the Republican chair in New York, thought it an "exaggerated illustration of deception." Lansing, too, complained about the slogan. The country, he admonished Vance McCormick, might be forced into war at any moment, and Wilson was saying that was not possible. Wilson privately admitted that the variations of the phrase he used promised too much. "I can't keep the country out of war," he lamented to Josephus Daniels. "They talk of me as though I were a god. Any little German lieutenant can put us into the war at any time by some calculated outrage."[4]

Wilson's desire for peace, however, was genuine. It dated from the first shots of the war. In August 1914, he informed the belligerent countries, "I should welcome an opportunity to act in the interests of European peace, either now or at any other time that might be thought more suitable." This departure from the tradition of American isolationism burst forth in his May 1916 speech to two thousand dignitaries assembled by the League to Enforce Peace. Wilson called for an international body with the power to "prevent any war begun either contrary to treaty covenants or without warning and full submission of the causes to the opinion of the world."[5]

Wilson put his aspirations for peace in concrete form a week after the election. Between other duties and a bout of illness that put him in bed, he worked long hours in his study on a proposal "to assist, if I may, in bringing the war to an end before it is too late to remedy what it has done." He called for a conference of belligerent and neutral nations to "define the terms upon which a settlement of the issues of war may be expected." This, he hoped, would pave the way for a postwar organization charged with maintaining peace. The proposal, he told his wife, "may prove the greatest piece of work in my life." Wilson finished a draft on November 25. While he pondered the timing of his proposal, two events clouded his initiative.[6]

Lansing inspired one of them. When rumors bubbled up that the administration was considering a peace plan, Sweetser privately asked him for confirmation. Lansing, who was pressing Wilson to go into the war, petulantly denied that a peace proposal was forthcoming. This Sweetser duly reported in a news story that Lansing read approvingly in draft. The story, Sweetser wrote in notes of his conversation with Lansing, was "a source of deep gratification to the Sec."[7]

On December 12, the day after Sweetser's story appeared, the second event occurred. This was the startling news of a German peace proposal. Germany had recent battlefield successes, but victory was far from assured. Dire food shortages caused by the blockade, United Press's Carl Ackerman observed, made Germany look "like a grocery store after a closing out sale." Despite government attempts to suppress discussion of shortages, food riots broke out. Many senior German military officers thought the resumption of submarine warfare would bring the war to a swift conclusion, but Chancellor Theobald von Bethmann-Hollweg calculated that Germans would be more supportive of continued war if attempts at peace were tried first.[8]

The German peace démarche deprived Wilson of the initiative, but his enthusiasm to lead the world to peace was unabated. He returned to his study to revise his plan. On Sunday, December 17, he sent a final draft to Lansing. Given his desire to keep his plan secret, this was not the time to resume press conferences, where the subject was sure to come up, but he did. To preempt any discussion of what he had in mind, he began the off-the-record session by stating, "Since the Government of the United States is doing nothing, I think perhaps it is best not to discuss whether it is going to do anything or not." Wilson's misleading statement left reporters with a clear understanding that, as Sweetser noted, "The United States had not and would not inject itself into the peace situation." While reporters wrote stories of the "newsless" meeting, the president directed Lansing to encode his peace note and send it "with the utmost privacy."[9]

Editing suggestions from House and Lansing diluted Wilson's plea for a conference of belligerent and neutral nations to end the fighting. They feared angering the Allies, who might see themselves at a disadvantage if forced to the negotiating table at that moment. Wilson's revised proposal merely sought elucidation of each nation's war aims so "that we may learn, the neutral nations with the belligerent, how near the haven of peace we may be." Wilson's desire for mediated peace could be discerned, along with his call for "a permanent concord" of nations, but ambiguities permitted unintended inferences. Had Wilson waited until Wednesday to hold his press conference, he could have guided reporters to his true intent. Because he did not, Lansing disastrously assumed that interpretive role.[10]

That Wednesday morning, December 20, the secretary of state informed reporters that a diplomatic note had been sent. He said the note did "not suggest peace." When the Dow Jones ticker reported the note *was* a peace proposal, Sweetser rushed to Lansing's office and, out of breath, asked for clarification. "What peace story?" said Lansing, yanking his pipe from his mouth and flashing anger. When a copy of it was put in front of him, Lansing put his finger on the word "peace." "See how inaccurate these people are," he said. "Boys," Sweetser said to reporters outside Lansing's office, "The Secretary has assured me this report is incorrect; that this note has nothing to do with peace." When Wilson's note was released that afternoon, the reporters were furious.[11]

Lansing was not finished. When asked about his prevarication at a news conference the next morning, he slowly recited a statement focusing on a passage in Wilson's proposal that said neutrality might become "intolerable." The United States, Lansing said, was "drawing nearer the verge of war." When Sweetser phoned this dramatic statement to the AP, his editor ordered him to double check it. Querying Lansing privately, Sweetser hotly related journalists' bitterness over the misleading statements he and the president had made. "I still say it's not a peace note," Lansing insisted. "Rather it's a war note."[12]

The AP's White House reporter showed Lansing's "verge of war" comment to Tumulty, who showed it to Wilson. As Sweetser learned from colleagues, Wilson telephoned "wildly for Lansing who was at lunch and for Polk, who went chasing after Lansing." Then he called the AP president. No, Frank Noyes said, he could not stop the story. It had been on the wire for half an hour. When Lansing was located eating lunch with Democratic colleagues, Wilson summoned him to the phone. They met afterward. Lansing's dismissal seemed imminent, although this rumor also proved false. Lansing met with the press that afternoon to say the administration was not altering its neutrality policy. "The whole tone and language of the note to the belligerents show the purpose without further comment on my part."[13]

"If our people only realized the insatiable greed of those German autocrats at Berlin and their sinister purpose to dominate the world," Lansing wrote in his diary, "we would be at war today." Although Bernstorff strove to win Berlin's support for Wilson's proposal, Lansing considered everything about him "sinister," including his thin lips. He confided to Sweetser that he made his "verge of war" comment to reassure the Allies that the United States was not abandoning them. In private meetings with Allied envoys, he suggested they respond to Wilson's peace overture by proposing terms the Germans would not accept. Both Lansing and House led European leaders to suspect Wilson was setting up a scenario to justify entering the war. The British Foreign Office warned its press to be restrained in criticizing Wilson's proposal.[14]

Wilson's quest for peace was a steep climb. The colossal loss of life. The mistrust and hatred fomented by the belligerents' propaganda. The possibility each side saw for victory. The war had momentum. It was unlikely the United States could avoid being drawn into the conflict. Americans were heavily committed in loans as well as in sympathy for the Allies.

The badly plotted peace note added to Wilson's difficulties achieving his peace goal. The fundamental error was rooted in his disdain for journalists. He wanted them to keep their pens in their pockets until he told them when it was time to write. His efforts to control the message this way produced exactly the opposite of what he wanted. By taking the press into his confidence, even if on background, he could have avoided confusion about his peace proposal. Instead, he handed Lansing and House the opportunity to put their own spin on it and alienated journalists unnecessarily, when many would have helped him sell it at home and abroad.

The episode revealed a fundamental aspect of Wilson's thinking about the presidency: the great faith he put in leading the public with soaring appeals through diplomatic notes and speeches from behind a lectern. This concept of leadership, which sprang from his thinking about government as a professor, was informed by progressive belief in the need to engineer citizens' opinions. That reasoning lay behind his creation of the Committee on Public Information when, within the next few weeks, the country went to war.

A GREAT NEW DISCOVERY IN SOCIOLOGY

During the 1894 Christmas recess, a young economics professor sat in a Stanford University library alcove. Dissatisfied with what he considered a bloodless discipline, Edward Alsworth Ross jotted down a list of the "linchpins which hold society together." "I have a great new discovery in Sociology," he wrote to his uncle-in-law, Lester F. Ward, a paleobotanist whose similarly wandering interests led him to teach, at Yale, the first sociology course in an American

university. "Fact is I am planning to bring out a book eventually." The publication of *Social Control: A Survey of the Foundations of Order* in 1901 marked a
rare instance when a new book instantly became a seminal scholarly work and a
popular success. It helped establish sociology as a distinct academic discipline.
The phrase "social control" became a progressive touchstone.[15]

Previously Americans lived in tightly knit, self-regulating communities. In
this "natural order," which Ross experienced as an Iowa farm boy, "nearly every
moral problem resolved itself into a question between man and man." Now, at
the end of the nineteenth century, *community* had given way to *society,* an amal-
gam of interdependent strangers. In these impersonal associations, Ross argued,
"the mean man finds it easier to prey and inflict damage upon the others, and
the individual reaction is less able to hold him in check. The development of
mutual aid and higher forms of organization, therefore, necessarily thrust upon
society the problem of controlling the delinquent class."[16]

Ross favored a wide range of controls—prohibition of liquor, eugenics, restriction on immigration, laws protecting children, public service commissions
to set fair prices for electrical power, settlement houses to shelter and uplift the
unfortunate, and "restraint . . . exercised through public opinion." This latter
was tied to publicity, abetted by "the abundance of communication," which ensured that far-flung citizens had the grains of information needed to produce
collectively the right-minded loaf of opinion. "This form of coercion," he argued, "is suited to the type of man created by modern life."[17]

In his eighteenth-century essay "Of Publicity," political thinker Jeremy Bentham argued for making government deliberations known to ordinary citizens:
"The public is placed in a situation to form an enlightened opinion, and the
course of the opinion is easily marked." Thinkers like Ross advanced a far more
ambitious conception of publicity. Just as experts should engineer solutions to
uncompetitive business practices and tuberculosis in slums, so should they engineer public opinion on a broad range of economic, social, and political issues.
Untutored public opinion, Ross argued, was "far from being a wise disciplinar-
ian, [it] meddles when it ought to abstain, and blesses when it ought to curse."[18]

Supreme Court Justice Oliver Wendell Holmes recommended *Social Control* to Roosevelt, who became a warm correspondent with Ross. "You insist,"
Roosevelt wrote, "as all healthy-minded patriots should insist, that public opinion, if only sufficiently enlightened and aroused, is equal to necessary regener-
ative tasks and can yet dominate the future." James Garfield called the Bureau
of Corporations, which he headed, a "publicity bureau" to correct corporate

abuses. Louis Brandeis systemically surveyed newspapers from around the country to measure attitudes and was in contact with a network of editors to shape them. The more an issue was "canvassed and discussed," he said, the better. "It is only ignorance and dark dealing that we must fear." In a 1913 article for *Harper's Weekly,* "What Publicity Can Do," he used the sanitation terms that came easily to social reformers: "Sunlight is said to be the best of disinfectants."[19]

Communication advances similar to those that made public opinion salient in Europe occurred in the United States: profitable markets for independent dailies; telegraph lines shooting news across the country; subsidized second-class mailing privileges, which enabled newspapers, magazines, and books to reach rural audiences. In 1917, Congressman Claude Kitchin complained, "The Government hauled, handled, and distributed 1,202,470,676 pounds of news-papers, magazines, and other periodicals," entailing a subsidy of $89 million for publishers. Knowledge, said a populist lecturer, "is cheaper than coal and more common than pork and beans." Between 1860 and 1900, when the national population doubled, the number of daily newspapers grew from 387 to 2,190 and doubled again by 1915. The number of magazines increased from seven hundred in 1865 to six thousand in 1905. Half joking, William Allen White, a progressive Kansas newspaperman who became a national figure by writing for these periodicals, spoke of "Government by Magazine."[20]

Muckraking, whose practitioners frankly described their sanitization work as "publicity," thrived. It is impossible to fix the date when muckraking began or pin down its precise meaning. The term did not come into use until 1906, well after the fact, as was the case with *progressivism,* which was uncommon until the end of the decade. Although he encouraged many reform-minded journalists, Roosevelt coined *muckraking* as a pejorative. He was piqued by what he considered journalists' excessive search for evils needing reform. Muckraking could be sober or as sensational as the yellow journalism of Joseph Pulitzer and William Randolph Hearst. *Everybody's* was bombastic; the *Saturday Evening Post* was conservative; *Life* was lighthearted. In 1894, 168 publications were dedicated to temperance. Reform literature included novels and books of nonfiction, poetry, and reports on urban conditions by the likes of social activist Jane Addams. Ross asserted cartoons were "to red ink and capitals what the arc-light is to the tallow dip."[21]

Mark Sullivan said he was the first muckraker on account of his 1901 *Atlantic* article, "The Ills of Pennsylvania." Although George Creel made no such claim, he exposed police bullying of voters in his crusading Kansas City weekly, the *Independent,* the year before, and other journalists were also tilting their pens at political, social, and economic wrongs. The signal moment for muck-raking came in January 1903, when *McClure's* published a triptych of articles: Lincoln Steffens's "The Shame of Minneapolis" on municipal corruption; an installment of Ida Tarbell's series on Standard Oil's lust for economic power; and Ray Stannard Baker's report that unions, seeking their own sort of trust, prevented nonunion men from working. Sensing the whole was more than the sum of these three parts, S. S. McClure proclaimed in an accompanying edi-torial that the articles constituted "an arraignment of American character as should make every one of us stop and think."[22]

"Publicity" was not the sole province of muckrakers. The forces muckrakers battled had an entirely different concept of publicity. Special interests bought advertising space and sometimes the newspaper itself; their publicists sought to convince journalists to write favorable stories. The reformers believed the redress to this perverse publicity was more publicity. Ross inveighed against newspaper dependence on advertising "tied into the business-control System." A long list of journalists muckraked the press. Ross's Stanford student Will Irwin wrote a memorable series on newspapers for *Collier's.* Robert Park, an-other pioneering sociologist, who began as a journalist, attacked the "giant Press Bureau" that cloaked Belgian king Leopold's exploitation of the Congo. Creel exposed fraudulent ads for patent medicine. "The more true publicity there is the better," Baker wrote in a *McClure's* exposé on the railroad publicity machine, "for the public mind should not only be made up, but made up right."[23]

The corollary to this credo was that "true publicity" was a benign form of so-cial control and democratic. By a hidden law of political physics, citizens would of their own free will gravitate toward the right facts. Communication was the "integrating and socializing principle," Park believed. "The very clamor of news-paper publicity was like an embodied public conscience pronouncing condem-nation, every headline an officer," wrote *New York Evening Post* editor Rollo Ogden. Perhaps the yellow press cared about newspaper sales first and democ-racy second, but journalists the likes of Baker, as well as academics the likes of Ross, had a near religious faith in the power of true publicity. Ross thought it worked "as if by magic." Baker believed that "to an extent that approaches mys-ticism—as in our faith in democracy—that there is a curious mystic something in the united action of men which infallibly reaches the right conclusions."[24]

Educators, whether trained in law, soil conservation, or philosophy, were well equipped for this tutorial task. For the first time they assumed large public profiles. Ross radiated authority. His 250 well-muscled pounds on a six-foot-five frame commanded attention. He delivered pungent thoughts in a booming voice. "I wouldn't give the snap of my finger for the 'pussyfooting' sociologist," he said. The day he received a publishing contract for *Social Control,* he made public his dismissal from Stanford. His criticism of the railroad practice of hiring cheap Japanese labor and his support for "free silver" had disturbed the widow of Leland Stanford, the railway tycoon who created the university. Seven fellow professors resigned in protest. In the first inquiry by American professors into subversion of academic freedom, the American Economic Association exonerated Ross. Ross, who found a new home at the University of Wisconsin, wrote voluminously in popular magazines. His *Sins and Society: An Analysis of Latter-Day Iniquity* was as much a muckraking volume as anything Lincoln Steffens wrote. "The mob lynches the red-handed slayer," he wrote, "when it ought to keep a gallows Haman-high for the venal mine inspector, the seller of infected milk, the maintainer of a fire-trap theater."[25]

Woodrow Wilson was an expert-activist focused on the burning issue of governing. Reforming zeal was spreading from city halls and statehouses to Washington, which was acquiring extensive and continuous responsibilities for society's smooth operation. Needed were leaders who understood government as a science. "It is getting harder to *run* a constitution than to frame one," wrote Wilson, who helped establish the new discipline of public administration. Eager to put his hands on the levers of government, he entered the race for governor of New Jersey in 1910. His speech accepting his party's nomination called for "reorganization and economy" in government, control of corporations, conservation of natural resources, and a commission to regulate utility and transportation rates.[26]

In an 1887 essay on government administration, Wilson sounded like Ross and Ray Stannard Baker: "Whoever would effect a change in a modern constitutional government . . . must make public opinion willing to listen and then see to it that it listens to the right things." In his campaign for governor he pledged to curtail sharp corporate business practices and the old political machine through "pitiless publicity," a phrase he borrowed from Ralph Waldo Emerson: "As gaslight is found to be the best nocturnal police, so the universe protects itself by pitiless publicity." As president, Wilson viewed himself as educator primus inter pares, "the only national voice" in public affairs, as he put it in 1908. If a president "rightly interpret the national thought and boldly insist upon it, he is irresistible."[27]

"Pitiless publicity" became a Wilson mantra. In the highest form of flattery, it was repurposed by reformers fighting for "better wages for working girls" and by his opponent in the 1916 presidential campaign, Charles Evans Hughes. In an advertisement for itself, the *Literary Digest* said, "This is an age of what President Wilson has termed 'pitiless publicity.'"[28]

But as time went on the phrase became a stick with which to beat Wilson. Early in his presidency, a *San Francisco Call* editorial—"'Pitiless Publicity' Again"—observed that he had "learned the art of saying much and telling little." Before the 1916 election, Democrats fretted that Wilson and his administration were doing a poor job of giving out news. Journalists, one stalwart lamented, joked about Wilson's "pitiful publicity."[29]

WOODROW WILSON'S PITILESS PUBLICITY

Wilson's weaknesses warred with—and undermined—his greatness. He expanded the role of the office and enlarged the scope of the federal government, yet he was detached from crucial aspects of governing. Some of this can be attributed to the wide latitude he gave cabinet members. But he paid surprisingly little attention to all-important cabinet appointments, largely leaving them to his factotum House. After Lansing's effort to subvert his peace note, Wilson decided to ignore him rather than fire him. In early 1917, when Wilson's diplomatic efforts were at full throttle, Lansing complained he seldom saw the president. It was a strange way to manage international relations at a time when they were a matter of paramount concern.[30]

In pursuing his ideals, as biographer John Milton Cooper judiciously wrote, Wilson "was bold, extremely sure of himself, and often stubborn." He seized on big ideas, such as peace mediation, and courageously carried them forward. Secretary of the Interior Franklin Lane thought him "less dependent on others than any President in our time." Cabinet secretaries found it counterproductive to urge Wilson to a particular decision by referring to public opinion: "The idea of being induced to act under the pressure of popular demand," Lansing wrote, "was always distasteful to the President and aroused in him a spirit of resistance." At the same time, Wilson was thin skinned. He had no intimates who challenged him forcefully. His smarmy confidant, House, presented himself to Wilson as entirely "self-forgetful" while at the same time filling his self-aggrandizing diary with harsh judgments he planned to leave to posterity.[31]

Wilson's stubbornness was a function of his method of analysis. Leading political scientist though he was, Wilson had little interest in delving into empirical research. He wrote *Congressional Government*, his most important book, without observing Congress at work. He preferred to reason in terms of philosophical principles, and he was intuitive in his application of them. "The greatest forces in the world and the only permanent forces," he said in 1916, "are moral forces." There is little room for constructive argument or compromise with moral decisions arrived at intuitively.[32]

Wilson's strength of character made him an exceptionally effective speaker. Ray Stannard Baker described one of his momentous political speeches: "His face became suddenly alive, his eyes glowed, and as he spoke his entire body, even his restrained gestures, seemed to register the intensity of his emotion. His speech, wholly devoid of flamboyance, instead of rising to oratorical flights, seemed to deepen into a penetrating seriousness."[33]

Wilson believed presidents should no longer be primarily executives. They could delegate that function and assume the political leadership that by tradition resided on Capitol Hill. Knowing his oratory was a potent weapon, he broke with a century-long tradition that presidents did not address Congress in person. Legislators, including Democrats, saw this as a near-imperial intrusion on the separation of powers. Speaking to (and through) Congress was his ace in the hole when he wanted to coalesce opinion, as happened in the wake of his December peace note.[34]

In response to Wilson's overture, the Germans had agreed to a direct, unmediated exchange of views only with the Allies. This would not involve the United States, whom they suspected of favoring their foes, and would not include consideration of a grand scheme to prevent future wars. That would have to wait. The German response left the Allies free to blow their own hole into the hull of Wilson's plan. They said they would not meet unless Germany gave its conditions for ending the war and outlined harsh terms along the lines Lansing suggested privately.[35]

Wilson's response was one of his greatest addresses. In the Senate chamber on January 22, he called for "peace without victory," a brilliant stroke of propaganda that sought to reach over the heads of foreign leaders to animate their citizens. Wilson, who thought of the presidency as a voice of the American people, now cast himself as the voice "for the silent masses everywhere." Although his remarks failed in their immediate purpose, Wilson had boldly projected American leadership abroad. "Never before, it seemed," Arthur Link wrote, "had a single speaker succeeded so well in enunciating the political ideas and principles by which the American people in their better moments had tried to live."[36]

Carl Ackerman was back in the United States in early 1917. He argued in the book he was finishing, *Germany: The Next Republic?,* that Wilson had introduced a new era in which all governments, including that of postwar Germany, would pursue diplomacy in accord with democratic principles: "Instead of a nation's foreign policies being secret, instead of unpublished alliances and ironbound treaties, there may be the proclaiming of a nation's international intentions, exactly as a political party in the United States pledges its intentions in a political campaign." In such an era, Ackerman concluded, "Publicity will be the new driving force in diplomacy to give opinion world power."[37]

For all Wilson's mastery of the wholesale shaping of public opinion, he had little aptitude or inclination for publicity at the retail level. "I have a sense of power in dealing with men collectively," Wilson admitted, "which I do not feel always in dealing with them singly." Progressive Frederic C. Howe, who was a student at Johns Hopkins with Edward Ross, considered Wilson "our greatest lecturer." Outside the classroom he found Wilson "austere, never inviting intimacies." Wilson's preferred method of interacting with Tumulty, whose office was next to his, was by written note. Wilson did not much value Woolley's publicity work. He never thanked him and does not seem to have given much thought to helping him secure a well-deserved government job in the second term. House thought Wilson did Woolley "an injustice."[38]

Wilson's attitudes toward the press contrasted sharply with Roosevelt's. Early in his administration Wilson walked to the new Press Club, over a drugstore kitty-corner from the White House. His off-the-cuff comment, that he enjoyed the visit, made a positive impression, but a more telling remark followed right behind that one. He was not going to come back, as he was president and not free to mingle. At the 1902 Gridiron Dinner, organized by journalists each year with satirical skits, Roosevelt laughed so hard "tears ran down his cheeks." When Wilson attended, he managed forced mirth and spoke of his "immortal office, which may be lifted higher and higher for the guidance of a people and the guidance of free men throughout the world." Roosevelt relished making allies among the press corps, which was becoming larger, more professional, and a greater factor in shaping public attitudes. He voraciously read newspapers, gave reporters long, frank answers, and fraternized with them. He allowed Lincoln

Steffens, a member of his "newspaper cabinet," to interview him while he was being shaved.[39]

Roosevelt banished individual reporters *pour encourager les autres*. At times Wilson seemed inclined to dismiss the whole lot. A telling instance occurred during his first presidential race. Wilson told a reporter he was having so much trouble answering mail he felt like a frog that fell further back every time it tried to jump from a well. The resulting article appeared under the headline "Wilson Feels Like a Frog." In Wilson's mind, the story proved that the press failed to understand the gravity of a president's duties. From then on, Ray Stannard Baker said, Wilson gave reporters as "little as he could." Wilson's views of the press were, Arthur Link noted, "intuitive rather than reasonable." He glanced at newspapers in the morning and concentrated on those that gave him favorable treatment.[40]

Wilson's secretary Joseph Tumulty did his best to improve press relations. The gregarious Irishman cultivated journalists. He encouraged Wilson to write friendly letters to reporters and editors and occasionally convinced him to do one-on-one interviews with sympathetic journalists. At Tumulty's suggestion, Wilson instituted semiweekly press conferences. At his first, eleven days after his inauguration, Wilson asked the reporters to "go in partnership" with him. He wanted them to "help me and everybody else by just swathing my mind and other people's minds in the atmosphere of the thought of the United States." This was one of those grand-but-vague statements for which Wilson became known. "A splendid doctrine, we were all agreed," said Richard Oulahan of the *New York Times*. "But how to translate it into practice was beyond us." The job of the two hundred reporters gathered in a crescent around Wilson was to report his thoughts and actions—and the reactions to them in Washington—to the rest of the country. Wilson told them it was not helpful to play up differences of opinion."[41]

Wilson made quips to lighten the mood in press conferences. He told amusing anecdotes to illustrate his points. Mostly, though, his attitude was that of a "stern, pedagogic" professor lecturing wayward students. "Please, do your best not to let that happen again," he rebuked reporters after the appearance of a story, based on anonymous sources, that speculated on his thinking when war broke out in 1914. Wilson does not seem to have recognized that his lack of candor encouraged such press behavior. His answers were often terse, uninformative, and misleading even though the conferences were off the record. Lying to the press was justified, he told House, when it involved the honor of a woman or "when newspaper men asked questions that involved his foreign policy." It was a remarkable statement from a man who considered himself highly moral, and he meant it. It conveyed his view on how to use the communication powers he held. He took pride in his ability to mislead by "grazing the truth," as he put it, a practice that infuriated Republicans who considered his slippery language unprincipled. The president, said James Kerney, the editor of the *Trenton Evening News* and a Wilson supporter, "was seen less by newspaper people and confided less in them than any President since Cleveland and Harrison. . . . He was saving mankind, and he would let the world know about it in his own good time."[42]

From time to time Wilson toyed with the idea of creating a formal mechanism that would give him greater control over news. He expressed the kernel of the idea in a 1914 letter to Charles W. Eliot, Harvard's progressive former president: "We have several times considered the possibility of having a publicity bureau which would handle the real facts, so far as the government was aware of them, for all the departments. . . . Since I came here I have wondered how it ever happened that the public got a right impression regarding public affairs, particularly foreign affairs."[43]

VERGE OF WAR

Shortly after Wilson's "peace without victory" speech in January, Germany announced it would resume submarine warfare against belligerent and neutral ships sailing in the Allies' zone starting February 1. Two days later, Wilson went to Capitol Hill to announce he was severing relations with Germany. Trying to give the Germans room to back off, he told Congress, "I refuse to believe that it is the intention of the German authorities to do in fact what they have warned us they will feel at liberty to do." The evening before the address, Sweetser encountered Lansing at the foot of the elevator downstairs from the secretary's office. Leaning against a large packing box, Lansing said this was "the most serious crisis the country had ever faced." Lansing added, "America's course was decided on but . . . public opinion would be waited as an encouragement."[44]

A new jolt to American public opinion came a month later. It was a spectacular culmination of habitual German blundering and adroit British exploitation of its communication advantages. The blunder was a proposal by German state secretary for foreign affairs Arthur Zimmermann. Zimmermann, an affable, blond giant of a man, considered himself an expert on the United States based on a single train ride across the country. He had close ties to the German military and extensive involvement with covert intelligence. Susceptible to wild plans proposed by the likes of Captain Boy-Ed, who had been expelled from the United States because of them, he bought into a scheme to propose an alliance with Mexico in the event the United States entered the war. The Zimmermann Telegram, as the proposal came to be known, called on Mexico to "conduct war together. Conclude peace jointly. Substantial financial support and consent on our part for Mexico to reconquer the lost territory in Texas, New Mexico, Arizona." The proposal suggested that Mexico invite Japan, which was then on the side of the Allies, to join the alliance. There is no evidence Zimmermann consulted with the German chancellor before sending the message.[45]

Because Germany had no direct communication link to Mexico, Zimmermann used a roundabout method to instruct his envoy there to present the proposal. He sent the directive to Bernstorff via the State Department line to which Wilson had given Germany access; Bernstorff forwarded the message to Mexico City. The British intercepted the coded message from Zimmermann to Bernstorff and deciphered it. Not wishing to acknowledge that they could read the German code or that they eavesdropped on American diplomatic cable traffic, the British directed an agent to secure a copy of the message from the Mexico City telegraph office. This version of the telegram was passed to US ambassador Page in London, who sent it to Washington. Lansing leaked the telegram to Edwin Hood, a walrus-mustached AP correspondent considered the dean of the Washington press corps. Hood was highly regarded by officials for his knowledge, judgment, and discretion. (In December, he had helped Lansing write his statement softening the "verge of war" comments that undermined Wilson's peace initiative.) Lansing gave him a paraphrase of the telegram on the condition that he not reveal the source. To avoid any hint of Lansing's involvement, the document was passed from Hood to another AP colleague, who wrote the story. The news appeared on March 1. When questioned the next day, Lansing did not deny the telegram's authenticity but declined to give details on the grounds they "would endanger the lives of those concerned."[46]

Germany had a way out. Given the telegram's uncertain pedigree and its outlandish plot, Zimmermann could credibly deny the whole thing. George Sylvester Viereck thought the plan was a "preposterous" fake worthy of British propagandists. "The entire story reads like a dime novel concocted by our guest Sir Gilbert Parker," Viereck wired Postmaster General Albert Burleson. German apologist and Hearst correspondent William Bayard Hale tried to help Zimmermann with a prompt at a Berlin press conference: "Of course your excellency will deny this story." But Zimmermann said the story was true. Lansing was amazed. "If I had been caught that way," he told Sweetser, "I would have denied it from beginning to end." The British were delighted. "No more perfect propaganda could have been conceived," wrote an official in a report that survives in the British National Archives.[47]

A war mood seeped into every Washington cubby hole. The State, War, and Navy Building, noted Sweetser, was "under military rule." No one was admitted without a pass. Inside, the military toiled on war plans. Wilson stopped by to discuss them with Baker and Daniels. The generally rollicking annual dinner held by the Gridiron Club, in which the capital's leading journalists satirized politicians, ended with "a volley of cheers in a great outburst of patriotism." Thirty-two Secret Service agents surrounded Wilson's open, horse-drawn coach as he made his way to his second inauguration on March 5.[48]

Notwithstanding reporters' patriotic outbursts, their frustrations with the administration mounted. Wilson did not apologize for dissembling about his December peace note. In a fifteen-minute scolding, he upbraided reporters afterward for their perfectly reasonable speculation that he was "looking around to see what should be his next move." "Even the newspaper men who represent administration organs," the *New Republic* correspondent told his editors, "are convinced that Wilson does not tell the whole truth." Over at the State Department, Lansing was so furious about an AP story on Wilson's interest in promoting peace he shattered the decorum of his ornate office by cursing and nearly breaking his pipe as he pounded the desk. Sweetser, who did not write the offending story, defended it in heated arguments with Lansing and Polk that began in one office and resumed in another during the course of the afternoon. Sweetser pointed out their lies and contradictory statements. No one understood what the president was trying to achieve, he said, and correspondents were "foundering around in amazement." Lansing said it was none of the public's business.[49]

Lansing directed staff not to talk to reporters. Polk advised embassies in Washington to clam up as well. "Pitiless publicity has admittedly been cast aside," a disgruntled United Press correspondent reported. He contended that "a secret service system to keep tabs on the press is in effect" to ferret out leaks. Lansing tried but failed to reduce the number of reporters admitted to the building and limited their time there to half an hour in the morning and afternoon.[50]

Although Daniels and Newton Baker opposed Lansing's restrictions, the military was eager to manage the press. On June 29, 1916, Baker created a Bureau of Information and appointed an esteemed young officer to head it, Douglas MacArthur. Creel thought the young major oozed "energy, ability and ambition at every pore." MacArthur, who donned a suit and straw boater for the assignment, worked such long hours turning out press releases, arranging interviews, and managing legislation that he had to seek permission to postpone his annual horseback-riding test. He was the army's first public affairs officer.[51]

IF A CENSOR IS APPOINTED, I WANT TO BE IT

Censorship legislation was introduced in Congress in February 1917. It was based on a 1911 act that proscribed information gathering near military installations, but it went much further. The House bill prohibited wartime publication "likely or intended to cause disaffection in, or interference with the success of, the military or naval forces of the United States." The measure died when Congress adjourned on the eve of Wilson's inauguration.[52]

Sweetser sounded an alarm on censorship in one of his unsigned articles for the *New Republic* during this period. Censorship of wireless news to Germany, he reported, had deprived Berlin of information about American attitudes that would have contributed to a more constructive relationship. He argued this should serve as a warning for the United States, which faced "an iron-bound censorship the moment war comes; let it only be hoped that the State Department officials now working on such plans will show more judgment than heretofore and entrust at least a part of the work to trained newspaper men with a practical knowledge of what can and cannot be accomplished by publicists."[53]

While censorship was a matter of concern, measures for the provision of information had enjoyed considerable support for some time. In a 1914 meeting with Wilson, E. W. Scripps proposed a cabinet-level Secretary of the People, a skilled journalist who could "stand between the administration and the press." Scripps offered the good offices of his company "for the purpose of publicity." Wilson showed interest, and Scripps kept pushing. But the idea dropped off the priority list around the time of the *Lusitania* sinking, when Wilson ended regular press conferences. Woolley's Inter-Departmental Committee had some of these publicity functions when it swung into action in 1916 to advertise the good things that the administration did prior to the election. Around the same time an Interior Department appointee proposed "a *permanent* Bureau of Information" representing all parts of the government. The proposal, which ended up in Woolley's hands, called for publications to educate both the public and "those tremendous business forces, and aggregations of capital, commonly called 'Trusts,' teaching them in no uncertain manner of the immense power and resources of the government." The Interior official suggested locating the bureau on Lafayette Square, where it would be close to the White House. As it happened, that is where the CPI would be housed.[54]

As the entry into the war became likely, proposals like these were made with greater frequency. Magazine publisher Cyrus Curtis, who had recently acquired the *Philadelphia Public Ledger,* floated the idea of a nonprofit news service employing reporters who were respected by the public or "certified by men in whose judgment the nation has confidence." House had the impression he and Wilson would be the certifiers. William Bullitt, a correspondent with the *Public Ledger,* suggested the State Department establish a bureau to obtain information from Germany and Austria. The department referred Bullitt to House, who was a clearinghouse for suggestions like these. February 4, the day after Wilson severed relations with the German government, William Willcox, Hughes's campaign manager, visited House to offer the services of the GOP to the president. The publisher of the *San Francisco Call* suggested a "Board of Censorship and Publicity" staffed by Woolley and Creel.[55]

The most eloquent and high-minded proposal came from Arthur Bullard. Bullard had been a settlement worker in New York, editor of the socialist weekly the *Call,* and a foreign correspondent. For him, too, public opinion was a new factor in diplomacy. "All this [government] 'campaign literature'—even the official falsehoods—is added proof of the immense interest with which the public of Europe is taking in the causes, the progress and the outcome of this War," he wrote in *The Diplomacy of the Great War.* In correspondence with House beginning in August 1915, he lamented subversion of the salutary forces of public opinion abroad and was distressed equally by what he saw in the United States. Regarding an army general staff statement that criticism of generals and campaigns should be censored during war, he commented, "A Prussian Staff officer could not have gone further in asserting the supremacy of the uniform." He disliked Wilson's nebulous allusions to sinister domestic enemies; he thought the State Department ran publicity the way monarchies did. In March 1917, he took the next step of proposing a press bureau, writing to House, "I have been talking busily ever since my return with newspaper men, magazine writers and editors. They are all anxious to support the Government in a crisis but are awaiting a *mot d'ordre*." House encouraged Bullard to draw up "a plan on press censorship."[56]

House, who stuck his finger in every publicity pie that came across his desk, encouraged Walter Lippmann to formulate a campaign of his own. Lippmann was a veritable bureau of opinion molding unto himself. His emergence as a public intellectual since his graduation from Harvard in 1910 was phenomenal. House considered him "the ablest American of his age." He was a founding staff member of the *New Republic,* which sought to "brighten the coinage of American opinion." In keeping with Lippmann's predilections, their interest was in elite opinion. Its offices on West Twenty-First Street were staffed by a cook and a waiter who served lunch and cigars to luminaries who stopped by to exchange ideas. "The real preparation of a creative statesmanship lies deeper than parties and legislatures," Lippmann wrote in the first of the three books he had already published. "It is the work of publicists and educators, scientists, preachers and artists."[57]

After the election House submitted to "weekly quizzes" by *New Republic* editor Herbert Croly and Lippmann, who were "interested in doing what little we can to back the President up in his work." Soon Lippmann was sending ideas directly to the president, one of which, in early February, suggested that wartime censorship should be done by civilians with democratic sympathies. "The protections of a healthy public opinion in this country," he wrote, "will be of the first importance." Lippmann volunteered that Wilson would have a good head censor in Franklin Lane, his secretary of interior and a former newspaper reporter, editor, and owner. Although Lippmann made no mention of wanting to participate in this work, his self-interest in finding a position was hard to miss. Lane, however, was an unrealistic suggestion. A man of garrulous geniality, he was regarded as a profligate leaker to the press. A better avenue for securing a government publicity job was through House, whom Lippmann cultivated as House cultivated him.[58]

In mid-March the Germans made good on their threat to sink US merchant ships without warning. Wilson called a special session of Congress for April 2 and cloaked himself in such great secrecy that he insisted on opening his own important mail. Journalists roaming the halls of the executive offices were frantic to know if he was going to call for war, angry that he refused their request to meet with them, and muttered about "pitiless publicity." The War, Navy, and State Departments drew up voluntary censorship rules pending formal legislation. These were unveiled at a Saturday, March 24, conference at the Navy Department. Most of the rules protected information relating to military movements and plans. These provoked some criticism but nothing like agitation over a rule supplied by the State Department. It asked "that no information, reports, or rumors attributing a policy to the Government in any international situation, not authorized by the President or a member of the Cabinet, be published without first consulting the Department of State."[59]

At this point, a new face entered the discussion about creating a formal body to manage news. On March 19, George Creel wrote to Josephus Daniels, "I am in the field for a job. If a censor is to be appointed, I want to be *it*." Daniels was an ideal advocate. The president trusted him. As editor and owner of the *Raleigh News & Observer,* he had good credentials for judging this matter. He had experience with propaganda as a result of heading the Democratic National Committee publicity bureau in the 1908 and 1912 campaigns. Ridicule of Daniels as a rumpled country bumpkin missed the more important aspect of the man. He was a shrewd political operator. Unlike House, who dabbled in press relations, Daniels had an immediate need to find someone to manage news. His department would have responsibility for censorship of wireless communications, given its experience with the technology. The navy was an early adopter of wireless for ship-to-shore communication. With the outbreak of war, it was charged with monitoring the two German wireless stations on the East Coast. Finally, Daniels's experience with Creel had been nothing but happy.[60]

In early 1916, without having met Daniels, Creel defended him in a long article in the *New York World.* Creel, the "journalistic knight errant" as the *World* called him, argued that Daniels earned his enemies with good progressive deeds. He stopped conniving steel manufacturers from inflating navy contracts. He resisted the navy brass's guarding of its royal status and provided education for enlisted sailors. "To wade through the lies that have been told about him, to discover the truths that have been hidden or distorted," Creel wrote, "is to come to a new loathing of the greed that poisons when thwarted and to an added contempt for the public that takes no larger interest in a public servant than to swallow every slander." Creel carried on during the election, claiming Daniels was one of "the greatest secretaries of history." Daniels widely distributed Creel's defense of him.[61]

Creel could expect Wilson to have an open mind about appointing him. Creel's loyalty was vivid during the 1916 campaign. Wilson invited him to the White House for an Inauguration Day luncheon and granted him a rare in-

Secretary of the Navy Josephus Daniels, editor and owner of the *Raleigh News & Observer*, had an urgent need to institute censorship of sensitive war information and championed the appointment of George Creel for that job. During the 1916 presidential campaign, Creel had defended Daniels as one of "the greatest secretaries of history." (Naval History and Heritage Command)

terview, which Creel repaid adoringly in *Everybody's Magazine*. He extolled Wilson's idealism and warmth. Wilson was above politics, Creel wrote. Overlooking the campaign slogans in 1916, he said Wilson's election was not "influenced in any degree by the drama or emotionalism that clever politicians are in the habit of introducing into campaigns in order that the electorate may be beguiled into *feeling* rather than *thinking*."[62]

Pushing his candidacy for the censorship job, Creel's letters and notes to Daniels sounded like commands. "A Bureau of Publicity should be created at once, an independent body with a responsible head," he wrote on March 28. "I think that you should take this up with the President at once. Show him this letter."[63]

THE THREE-SENTENCE ORDER

Addressing a joint session of Congress late on the evening of April 2, President Wilson called for war. "The world," he said, "must be made safe for democracy." On April 6, Congress passed the war declaration by votes of 82–6 in the Senate and 373–50 in the House. Wilson signed it upon receipt at the White House usher's desk. By prearranged signal, a navy officer rushed outside and waved toward the Navy Department, which sent the news to ships at sea. Tumulty informed reporters.[64]

The next day, typing two-finger style on his old Hammond typewriter, Wilson made a short list of what was needed to prosecute the war. One category was measures "safeguarding the nation." These included restrictions on speech. "We are mobilizing the nation as well as creating an army," Wilson told a friendly congressman, "and that means we must keep every instrumentality at its highest pitch of efficiency and guided by thoughtful intelligence." Wilson had not yet determined exactly what instrumentality was needed to mobilize intelligence. He left it to others to come up with a plan.[65]

In March the Council of National Defense had weighed in with suggestions through Newton Baker, its chairman. Created by Congress in late 1916 to coordinate industry and resources for national security, the council viewed itself performing "a well-nigh priceless function in acting as a sort of official incubator for new ideas necessary to win a war under modern conditions." It solicited and passed on suggestions for censorship from, among others, *Collier's* editor Mark Sullivan; Frederick Palmer, who had been the only American correspondent accredited to the British Expeditionary Forces; and Roy Howard, head of the United Press. Baker and Daniels met with representatives on April 3. "Council suggests a board of censors," Daniels wrote in his diary. He and Baker thought, "No." Daniels also heard from Gibson Gardner, Washington Bureau of the Newspaper Enterprise Association, a news service affiliated with E. W. Scripps's empire. Gardner proposed a "Bureau of Publicity focused on censorship." Wilson's cabinet was a similar swirl of competing ideas. In a meeting the day Wilson signed the declaration of war, Postmaster General Burleson wanted to exclude critical newspapers from the mail. "Lansing," Daniels wrote in his diary, "thought no papers should be printed in German."[66]

While these suggestions were made behind the scenes, Bullard's were public. His *Mobilizing America* and a related article in the April *Atlantic Monthly* were progressive manifestos on the imperative of enlightened public opinion in foreign affairs. "Just as the growth of democracy in business tends to fight the sinister profits of secrecy with increasing publicity, and just as we are gradually opening the books of insurance companies, railroads, and other great corporations," Bullard wrote, "so the growth of democracy in government will surely abolish 'le secret du roi.'" The war offered a choice between undemocratic censorship as practiced by the British and French and "wholesome" publicity to unify "the National Mind." Bullard criticized Wilson and the State Department for their secrecy.[67]

On April 4, Creel sent Daniels a plan for a "Department of Publicity" that was more detailed than Bullard's, if still idealistic. It emphasized the provision of positive news. "The *suppressive* features of the work must be so overlaid by the publicity policy," Creel argued, "that they will go unregarded and unresented." He shared Bullard's zeal for bringing the country together: "Administration activities must be dramatized and staged, and every energy exerted to arouse ardor and enthusiasm." Like Lippmann, Creel called for a single civilian head. He envisioned a span of influence to "cover every governmental department." The head of the publicity department would join with the secretaries of the War, Navy, and State Departments to form a censorship board. The department would involve journalists and writers, whose low pay would be in keeping with patriotic ideals. They would work with the press in "frankness, friendship and openness."[68]

Creel's upper hand in the competition for the propaganda job was apparent the evening of April 4 when a group of journalists and writers met at the Players Club in New York's Gramercy Park "to discuss," as Ray Stannard Baker wrote in his diary, "what we could do to help with this crisis—to do our 'bit.'" Bullard was an organizer. Lippmann attended. Neither one said anything that made it into Baker's diary, whereas Creel did. Creel had been in Washington working on censorship plans, Baker noted, and thought "as little as possible should be forbidden: that the duty of the board should be strictly in the line of constructive publicity, not merely censorship." In a letter to Daniels the next day, Creel reported that one hundred writers had been in the meeting; that he had taken no credit for his censorship plan, giving the honors to Daniels; that he did not indicate he was under consideration for a post; that the group was nevertheless unanimous in wanting him to lead the effort, but that he headed off a formal vote. Baker, a vivid diarist, made no mention of such acclaim for his appointment.[69]

Although Bullard knew Creel only slightly, he considered him a good choice for running government publicity. Lippmann did not. Lippmann and Creel had been on a friendly first-name basis when working to support women's suffrage. But their relationship fell apart in 1915, when Creel learned Lippmann was the author of a scathing editorial about him in the *New Republic*. Creel's offense was an article criticizing Paul Kellogg, editor of *Survey*, for praising a Rockefeller Foundation study on labor-industry relations. The study came at a time when the Rockefellers' Colorado Fuel and Iron Company was under assault for its role in the infamous Ludlow Massacre of striking miners. Creel called out *Survey*'s links to philanthropic organizations without taking note of balancing statements Kellogg had made. Creel claimed the widely respected editor's "*intellectual integrity* . . . has been tainted by contact with tainted money." Lippmann called Creel's article "one of the worst cases of brutal stupidity that muckraking has produced." Creel, he wrote, was "a reckless and incompetent person who has at last revealed the quality of his mind." Sharp exchanges between the two men followed.[70]

Now the two men were battling over who would do publicity for Wilson. A few days after the Players Club meeting, House asked Lippmann to prepare a publicity plan and said he would "put it through." Lippmann's plan called for a council that would guide journalists to Washington news and issue "publicity of its own." He recommended that Vance McCormick head the council, assisted by Robert Woolley. It was not a far-fetched idea. McCormick and Woolley were at that very moment discussing how "we might assist the War and Navy Departments by organizing for them a publicity bureau."[71]

House and Lippmann did not prevail. Daniels and Creel did. Daniels was eager to get a censorship operation in play. Creel shared his views on giving out "news instead of suppressing it," except in the case of sensitive military information. Daniels secured support for Creel's appointment from Newton Baker, who also agreed "there should be no censorship of opinion or comment." Daniels made his case with President Wilson in a five o'clock meeting on Monday, April 9. "Talked about censorship," he wrote in his diary. "He will appoint Creel." Two days later Daniels sent Creel's plan to the president. Wilson liked it "very much."[72]

Creel's appointment took several more days of jockeying. In an April 12 letter, Daniels and Baker recommended the president establish a "Committee of Publicity." It was to be made up of themselves and a civilian chairman. It did not mention Lansing, which was fine with him. He did not like Creel's "chairman" title as it implied Creel would be his boss. In a meeting with the president, however, Creel was directed to redraft the letter to include Lansing. The next day, a letter signed by all three secretaries went to the president recommending the establishment of a Committee on Public Information "without waiting further legislation, and because of the importance of the task and its pressing necessity." The letter endorsed the broad authority Creel had envisioned in his plan to Daniels: "It is our opinion that the two functions—censorship and publicity—can be joined in honesty and with profit."[73]

Lansing and Creel were as different as their signatures. Lansing, the conservative son-in-law of former Republican secretary of state John Foster, signed his name with neat, self-conscious flourishes worthy of royalty. Creel had a rapid, slanting scrawl that streaked across the page like a lightning bolt. Lansing considered Creel a wild socialist who should be nowhere near diplomatic news. When Creel brought Lansing the recommendation letter to sign, it was on Navy Department stationery, and Lansing's name was under Daniels's and Baker's. Insisting on protocol, according to which the secretary of state took precedence over other cabinet officers, Lansing ordered the letter to be retyped on his letterhead, and he signed first. Creel was annoyed over Lansing's "petty sensitiveness." Daniels and Baker laughed when Creel told them they had to sign again.[74]

The climax of all this maneuvering came on Friday, April 13, when Wilson signed Executive Order 2594. (From Wilson's point of view, the date of signing was auspicious, as he considered thirteen his lucky number, although the order was dated April 14.) The order created "A Committee on Public Information, to be composed of the Secretary of State, the Secretary of War, the Secretary of the Navy, and a civilian who shall be charged with the executive direction of the committee. As civilian chairman of the committee I appoint Mr. George Creel. The Secretary of State, the Secretary of War, and the Secretary of the Navy are authorized each to detail an officer or officers to the work of the committee." The three-sentence order and the letter from the three secretaries were released to the public. Creel took his oath that day. On Monday he was at work. In his autobiography, written years later, Creel feigned disinterest in becoming chairman. He said his acceptance of the post "was compulsory" since he had proposed the CPI.[75]

A SOLUTION IDEAL FOR WILSON

A remarkable feature of the chain of events that led to the CPI's creation was how little planning went into it. It was not the product of an orderly process. Although the establishment of an agency having the express mission of controlling information represented a sharp break in American tradition, no forethought was given to its implications for democratic government. Nobody appears to have consulted legal counsel to determine the procedure for establishing such an agency or if it were even constitutional, although that would have been difficult to determine inasmuch as it was unclear precisely what the CPI would do or what powers it would have.

In the form the CPI eventually took, however, its creation was a significant encroachment on the prerogatives of Congress. "The offices to which the President is authorized under the Constitution to appoint," as Attorney General Augustus Hill Garland wrote in 1885, "are only those established or recognized by the Constitution or by act of Congress." Similarly, Creel's appointment required Senate confirmation, because he had decision-making power over policy and budget.[76]

Notwithstanding these irregularities in the CPI's creation, some form of executive branch propaganda was inevitable. The Wilson administration was acutely aware that all warring countries engaged in censorship and publicity. The 1916 election showed how well-managed publicity could shape public attitudes. In equal measure, progressives' preoccupation with public opinion pointed to the utility of propaganda. This explains why a large number of individuals, many of them muckrakers, flooded the administration with proposals for censorship and publicity. The progressives placed great faith in centralized authority, especially in government, to bring reason and order to American life. In the same way that government inspectors assured food quality, the CPI would "mature opinion."[77]

The arrangement was ideal for Wilson. The CPI shielded him from the publicity work he did not like. He held no press conferences for the duration of the war. At the same time, the CPI gave him a grand podium from which to speak as leader that he envisioned decades before. Wilson would make "public opinion willing to listen and then see to it that it listens to the right things."

II
OPERATIONS

4

A New Definition of News

There has been, indeed, a change in the whole newspaper game since
the outbreak of the war. The press is expected to suppress valuable
military information and at the same time is expected to give space to the
Government's many statements and explanations of policy and action
intended to enlist the wholehearted support of the people. The Government
has taken upon itself the task of regulating the pulse of the nation so that
enthusiasm will be uniformly maintained at all times.

—David Lawrence, *Saturday Evening Post*

At the time of his appointment in April 1917, George Creel met with President
Wilson for two hours. The purpose, Creel recalled a quarter of a century later,
was "to specify my powers and duties and define the objectives he hoped to have
attained." Creel claimed to have written down phrases that could be recycled
later. Creel should base propaganda on the original Catholic Church meaning
of that word, "propaganda of faith."* Wilson wanted to preach "the religion of
democracy." The president took a copy of his War Message to Congress from
his desk and read the portion that spoke of "the universal domination of right
by such a concert of free people as shall bring peace and safety to all nations." In
Wilson's opinion, Creel said, "a 'war to end war' was a battle cry that should go
straight to the hearts of our own people and all other peoples."[1]

Wilson told Creel that he was to have "absolute control of everything that
related to public information." His mandate was broad. He was to "mobilize
the *mind* of America." As Creel was leaving, the president laid a hand on his
shoulder and "gave several parting admonitions. I was to emphasize the committee as an *information service,* for the Germans had grimed propaganda until

* In 1622 Pope Gregory XV founded the Sacra Congregatio de Propaganda Fide to spread
Catholicism.

the word stood for corruption and deceit. I was to spend no dollar on a secret errand or try to camouflage a single activity. Above all, I must guard against appeals to hate."

The CPI became a megaphone for Wilson's idealistic phrases. Its first major publication, *How the War Came to America,* was the equivalent of the German "White Book" and the British "Blue Book" in its intention to justify the American entrance into the war. Largely the work of Arthur Bullard, whom Creel immediately recruited, it reprinted three of Wilson's speeches, including his War Message. Six million copies were printed. It was translated into more than half a dozen languages.

But Creel's account of the meeting is as much fairy tale as fact. Wilson almost certainly did not refer to a "war to end war." That phrase, which is generally attributed to H. G. Wells, was used by Lloyd George. Nor was it true that the CPI's "information service" was wholly different from German propaganda or that of the Allies, with whom the CPI closely cooperated. Creel's characterization of his "absolute control" over information was an exaggeration. In an honest reckoning of the meeting, Creel would have acknowledged his frustration over the proliferation of government propagandists outside his control.[2]

As a matter of fact, almost nothing about the CPI's work had been settled the first day Creel entered his temporary offices in the State, War, and Navy Building. The president's executive order creating the CPI was as imprecise as the recommendation letter from Lansing, Baker, and Daniels, which called for censorship and publicity to be "joined in honesty and profit." Creel's account of his meeting with Wilson dwelled on the need to inform the public. "We do not need less criticism in times of war," Wilson supposedly said, "but more." The omission of any discussion of censorship is glaring. Censorship was the impetus for creating the CPI. At the time of the meeting Wilson was bent on winning passage for a law that would give him sweeping, unchecked power to rein in speech. That highly controversial provision collided with Creel's original CPI proposal, which the president had endorsed: "The *suppressive* features of the work must be so overlaid by the publicity policy that they will go unregarded and unresented."

The uncertainties and the clashing statements about what the CPI did caused considerable confusion during the first weeks of its existence and clouded its work for the rest of the war. Creel's volatile personality aggravated the problems. By the end of the summer, however, Wilson and Creel achieved something that was not mentioned in Creel's account of their meeting—a re-orientation of government-press relations.

GEORGE CREEL

The story of the CPI cannot be understood without always keeping an image of its volcanic architect in mind. Although only thirty-nine years old when Wilson appointed him, Creel was a firmly established firebrand. He unabashedly described himself as "a newspaper man and magazine writer by profession and an agitator by trade."[3]

Creel was raised in Kansas City, Missouri. His father was an alcoholic ne'er-do-well. The fount of family strength was his mother, who struggled to provide for her children. Creel attributed his belief in women's suffrage to her. His formal education was spotty. He dropped out of high school for a time and had a single year at a small local college. Shortly after finishing high school, he was arrested for distributing a publication of his creation called *Revelations,* in which he and other boys roasted the school board. "The normal condition of Creel," according to a story that dwelled on his youth, "has been one of chronic insurgency."[4]

Creel's turbulent journalism career began in 1896. The *Kansas City World* fired him for quarreling with an editor. In New York, he sold jokes to comic supplements. Back in Kansas City in 1899, he started the weekly *Independent.* Poems and news from women's clubs ran alongside attacks on politicians who displeased Creel. His goal for the paper was "social advancement" and the "the crystallization of a public sentiment." Enflamed by a local clergyman, he replaced the *Independent* in the spring of 1908 with the *Newsbook,* a newspaper animated by the progressive ideal of helping readers "pick the truth from the mass of reports that were not true." Similar news experiments were springing up around the country. Sociologist Edward Ross extolled these as essential to "acquaint the citizens with municipal happenings and affairs." Creel made the case for his in nearly identical words. "The control of [the press]," he wrote, "is manifested not only in the suppression of news, and its distortion where it cannot be suppressed, but in the manufacture of news." Creel envisioned the *Newsbook* as a prototype for a string of weeklies around the country. But it quickly folded, and the *Independent* reappeared.[5]

Creel was a perpetual topic of the news as well as a chronicler of it. He boxed and played amateur baseball, was "the king of wit" at banquets, and wrote a short book of verse titled *Quatrains of Christ*. He made news when he pummeled a rude cable car conductor. He helped elect reform governor Joseph Folk, who appointed him the Kansas City inspector of coal oil, which was used for illumination. While doing this job, Creel did not relinquish the *Independent*. A *Kansas City Post* exposé alleged he collected his pay without doing the work. A quack doctor whom Creel had muckraked may have subsidized the attack.[6]

In 1909 Creel gave up the *Independent* and joined the *Denver Post,* whose two owners probably became acquainted with him when they purchased the *Kansas City Post.* Harry Tammen, a one-time bartender and curio shop owner, and Frederick Bonfils, who became rich through real estate and lotteries, ran a boisterous newspaper that enjoyed the largest circulation between San Francisco and Chicago. Creel called it "the Coney Island of journalism." His relationship with the paper deteriorated when he traveled to Africa with Bonfils to find Theodore Roosevelt, who was on a hunting expedition. The oddball trip was a riff on journalist Henry Stanley's search for Dr. David Livingston the previous century. Creel lost his $1,000 advance. He and the parsimonious Bonfils squabbled over money throughout the trip.[7]

Creel's editorials sizzled. Once he suggested hanging eleven antireform senators. During the libel trial that followed, Creel was invited to repudiate his lynching suggestion. "No!" he said, thumping the witness chair. "I meant it. The hemp—the hemp—the hemp!" This response, which was often noted in profiles of Creel, seems too outlandish to be true, but given his history it could be fact. Creel won the case. He left the paper when it did not endorse the municipal candidates he favored and joined the rival *Rocky Mountain News,* which splashed red ink in headlines and allowed Creel to sign editorials. He began supplying *Everybody's, Collier's,* and other muckraking magazines with such articles as the "The Carnival of Corruption in Mississippi." With Edwin Markham, famous for the poem "Man with the Hoe," and Ben Lindsey, a Denver judge renowned for reforming the juvenile court system, Creel wrote *Children in Bondage* on child labor.[8]

Creel, whom Lindsey called "reformer-in-chief," took another turn at government service in May 1912. He convinced the new mayor, Henry Arnold, whom he had backed, to appoint him police commissioner. Creel took billy clubs from police officers, who were beating drunks, and cleaned up the red-light district. All the while he continued at the *Rocky Mountain News,* a strange arrangement in which he covered himself, initially reporting on his progressive crusades and, in February 1913, on his sensational dismissal from city government. Tension had been building for some time. Arnold, who fell off the reform wagon, rescinded Creel's billy club order. Behind Creel's back, fellow commissioners allowed brothels to resume selling liquor and playing pianos. Creel retaliated by offering a resolution prohibiting police and firemen from going into bars unless "in the line of duty." The rule would apply to his fellow commissioners, one of whom he charged with showing up to work drunk. The mayor asked for Creel's resignation. Creel insisted on a public hearing, at which he challenged all the charges against him except that of "creating dissension." The epithets he used against other commissioners, he said, were justified. On the basis of that admission, Arnold terminated him. Creel expressed pleasure that the issues had been "presented clearly."[9]

Creel spoiled for fights when keeping quiet better served him. After Walter Lippmann attacked him in the *New Republic* in 1915, Creel shot off a letter to the editor: "I have devoted myself to a task of agitation in politics and industry, trying always to stay close to what may be termed the 'under-dog.' . . . You, on the other hand, are academic products, who have come to be commentators by virtue of self-election, based upon self-valuation, aided, I believe, by an endowment fund that spares you the fear of existence. The antagonism between us, therefore, is instinctive and inevitable as that of the house cat for the street dog."[10]

Creel was liable to get in trouble any time he sat down at his typewriter. The odds increased when he spoke. His passions reached tidal wave proportions and swept him away. In an interview with a sympathetic journalist bent on portraying him as an "uncensorious censor," Creel wandered into the subject of young people taking their country for granted. Growing agitated, he stood up and declared, "A boy gets to be twenty-one years of age and becomes a voter automatically, as a matter of course!" Creel slammed down his fist. "We ought to make him work for it, *make him work for it!*" Creel was attracted to the idea of compulsory military training for youngsters to bolster national security and promote "clean living and clean thinking." But on no other occasion did he tie the constitutional right to vote to public service.[11]

Creel frequently claimed he was misquoted. In 1916 he objected to a "viciously unfair" *New York World* article about a Labor Forum meeting. "Everybody in the hall," the story reported, "was shouting, hissing, hooting, applauding, or denouncing Creel." In his complaint to the *World,* Creel insisted he did not impugn "the Stars and Stripes" or incite the crowd. He admitted, "I stated that if my remarks gave offense, I would be outside at the close of the meeting."[12]

Creel was trim, five feet, seven inches tall. His mother admitted he was homely. An admiring 1913 profile in *Collier's* called attention to his mop of black hair "carried straight back as if by the headlong speed with which the man dives into whatever enterprise commands his allegiance." The frequency of profiles increased after Creel was named head of the CPI. His looks rarely went unmentioned. He had deep-set eyes and a "lower jaw with teeth that are set considerably in advance of the upper teeth and that make you think of a bulldog who is very amiable so long as he is let alone." Creel spoke quickly, with racy slang and frequent "damns."[13]

Creel's wife, actress Blanche Bates, star of *The Darling of the Gods* and other plays, added to his celebrity. She was three years older than he and better known when they married in 1912. She owned a colonial-era home on the Hudson River and another well-staffed dwelling in New York City. Bates had her own line into the Wilson White House through friendship with the president's daughter, Margaret, who was in the audience with her at the riotous Labor Forum meeting in 1916. Creel grew irritated at being called "Blanche Bates's husband." He complained that actors were acclaimed "out of all proportion to achievement," especially the achievement of writers. In time the marriage be-

George Creel unabashedly described himself as "a newspaper man and magazine writer by profession and an agitator by trade." (New York Public Library)

came one of convenience. As their son remembered, arguments, shouted from one bedroom to another, were never painful to hear because they were so witty. Bates made "emotion effective without violence" when she was performing, said her close friend, famed singer and actress Lillian Russell; offstage, "she unbottles her immense vitality and energy." [14]

"Neutrality" about Creel, said *Everybody's*, "has been the one impossible attitude." Even his bulldog jaw was seen from different angles. One man thought it "the jaw of a boy who has a chip on his shoulder," while a friend liked the "boyish way" Creel thrust it out when he was about to say something amusing. Despite Woolley's disappointment at not being put in charge of the CPI, he told House, "It is a great thing to have a man of Creel's vision and energy, enjoying the access to the President." *Editor & Publisher* acclaimed his selection. But Melville Stone, general manager of the Associated Press, said Creel "was not recognized as a leading journalist." The *New York Times,* a newspaper that persistently derided Creel, editorialized the first Monday he was on the job: "We are unable to discover in his turbulent career as a municipal officer, or in his qualities as a writer, or in his services to the Woman Suffrage Party in New York, any evidence of the ability, the experience, or the judicial temperament required 'to gain' the understanding and co-operation 'of the press.'" Harry Tammen, still bearing a grudge against Creel from his time on the *Denver Post,* wrote McAdoo to warn him of the troubles that lay ahead with Creel's appointment. "If he doesn't put everybody in the hole and get everything upset, it will be because his whole brain has been revolutionized." [15]

WE MUST SHAKE THAT APATHY

While the need to safeguard sensitive information lent urgency to the creation of the CPI, the administration was also worried about public support for the war. "I accepted the position because I felt that this work was going to be a great deal wider than mere censorship," Creel said. He wanted the CPI to be "a great publicity bureau . . . to bring home the truths of this great war to every man, woman, and child in the United States, so that they might understand that it was a just war, a holy war, and a war in self-defense." [16]

Many segments of American opinion fell in line with the decision to go to war. "At last we are on the right path!" exulted James Garfield, who had long been in the pro-war Roosevelt camp. Peace-minded William Jennings Bryan declared, "The discussion has ended, and the people of the entire country will stand undivided behind the President." German-American propagandist George Sylvester Viereck changed the name of his magazine from the *Fatherland* to *Viereck's American Weekly* and proclaimed "America First and America Only." He advised German-Americans sympathetic to the Central Powers to speak out, but not to the degree British sympathizers did for their side, and offered his pages to the CPI. Bryan and Viereck joined Roosevelt in support of Liberty Loan campaigns.[17]

A great many progressives fell in line too. In 1914 the war seemed to them barbaric and undemocratic, a conflict between German and Austro-Hungarian monarchies on one side, and British and French imperialists on the other. They questioned diverting attention from domestic reform. In 1914, Creel wrote, "Let the fight go on! As in typhoid, it is the last terrible throe that is to clean the system of poison and herald restoration to a finer health than ever before." But Wilson's eloquent rationale for entering the war lifted it into a progressive cause. Ernest Poole, home from covering the war in Europe, was at the Players Club when Creel made his pitch for a publicity plan on the eve of the war declaration. He was swayed by Wilson's call to make the world "safe for democracy." "More and more strongly," he said, "those words beat into my confused thinking at the time. As I read them, how clear and plain they seemed!" Within a few days of its creation, Poole was at the CPI editing Bullard's *How the War Came to America*.[18]

Still, pockets of resistance to Wilson's War Message were apparent. Staying out of war had been a potent campaign message. Six senators and fifty representatives voted "no" on the war declaration. Progressive writer Randolph Bourne chided reformers for focusing on "the war-technique" at the expense of democratic values. Eugene Debs counseled, "There must be no fear, no evasion, and no compromise" in propagandizing against conscription and the sale of war bonds. The Wilson administration feared German-American disloyalty, if not treachery, which British propaganda had amplified and which had been an issue in the 1916 presidential election. Immediately after the war declaration, Attorney General Thomas Gregory ordered the arrest of sixty "alleged ringleaders in German plots, conspiracies and machinations."[19]

Beyond this loomed the question, Why should Americans sacrifice when they were not directly threatened? The conflict in Europe was remote. The United States had not been attacked. Wilson's idealism was abstract. The White House, Tumulty told Wilson, received regular reports of "a spirit of indifference" among Americans. The CPI office had piles of letters "from people in the middlewest and elsewhere wondering why their boys were being sent to war."[20]

The Allies worried that American enthusiasm for the war would prove inadequate. The British owed millions of dollars to the United States. Would the United States lend as much money as was needed? Would it throw troops into the fighting quickly? "Travelling through the country one discovers an extraordinary ignorance and confusion of thought about the war," wrote a British journalist who sounded out American public opinion for the Department of Information. "We must shake that apathy," Arthur Willert warned.[21]

Britain and France sent high-level missions to the United States. Lansing thought they "aroused throughout the Republic a greater zeal for the cause." Gilbert Parker admitted in *Harper's Magazine* that he had been responsible for British propaganda in the United States and then used the confession as an opportunity to promote hatred of the enemy, whose actions were "worthy of Attila the Hun." The British established a War Mission in New York City headed by Lord Northcliffe, whose certainty of the ubiquity of German spies led him to fear he would be assassinated. Like the Democratic National Committee in 1916, it had branch offices in Chicago and San Francisco. The mission's Bureau of Information office looked "like a show room for Daimler's motors," an occupant quipped. The mission was guided by the Department of Information in London and mirrored the breadth of its activities. Although the War Mission said it merely supplied "news and views to the American press when asked for," it kept in touch with the CPI and cultivated influential journalists. "He is a very good fellow," the bureau head said of Carl Ackerman, "and is now working in a friendly fashion with W. and myself." "W" was Willert. Next door to Willert's *Times* of London office in Washington was a Bureau of Information office where he also worked. One of his jobs was to liaise with Creel.[22]

Many journalists were eager to work "in a friendly fashion." Editors, according to a study of sixty-eight newspapers, gave Wilson's War Message "virtually a blanket endorsement, and in scores of instances the document furnished a text for editorial sermons on the war and America's aims." At its annual meeting that month, amid cheers for French and British banners, the Associated Press issued its own declaration of war. Previously, AP president Frank Noyes said, his news service observed "strict neutrality on all controversial points due to the varied and manifold opinions of its membership. To-day, thank God, this is not only not necessary, but the contrary is true, for no trace of neutrality is coursing in our veins." E. W. Scripps told the president he regretted having flogged "He Kept Us Out of War." He had done that to get him elected. As soon as war was declared, Scripps wanted to "instill by every device patriotism in the newspaper offices which are the fountainhead certainly of patriotism."[23]

Many journalists sought government jobs. Four days after Congress voted for war, Willard Straight, a former Reuters correspondent in Asia whose wealth bankrolled the *New Republic,* was upset he had not yet been given work. Soon he had an army commission. Lippmann became Newton Baker's "confidential" special assistant. Frederick Palmer, America's premier war correspondent, gave up an astronomically lucrative *New York Herald* contract of $40,000 a year—more than $800,000 in 2020 dollars—to become an army major and "the pioneer press censor and general utility public relations man" for the American Expeditionary Forces (AEF) under General John Pershing. He knew Pershing from covering the Russo-Japanese War, when he was attached to the Japanese forces. When Charles Edward Russell was asked to survey opinion in Russia, he said he could leave in forty-eight hours. He subsequently joined the CPI staff.[24]

The CPI roster read like "a roll call of the muckrakers." Federal agencies and nongovernment organizations concerned with the government populated their publicity staffs with veteran journalists. "We are losing men," an AP executive lamented, "to the military services or the civil branches of the Governmental or to more lucrative private employment faster than we can replace them." Editors had to hire women, "not because we desire it particularly, but because we are forced to do something."[25]

TO GIVE ALL PROPER INFORMATION

April 16, the first Monday Creel was on the job, he emphasized the CPI's benign approach to news. The *New York Morning Telegraph* wrote, "The primary purpose of the bureau, it was stated, is to profit immediately by the mistakes made abroad in imposing military censorship on the press at the beginning of the war and to give the public all proper information about what the government is doing or intends to do." The *Chicago Daily News* reported, "There will be no effort to withhold any information except such as in the judgment of the press itself it would be unwise to print."[26]

The first meeting of the Committee on Public Information was held the following day at ten o'clock. The committee gathered in the secretary of state's elegant office looking out on the Potomac River. Lansing argued someone from Britain should show them how to carry out censorship. Lansing envisioned a "great censor chief," Daniels wrote in his diary, adding that the operation would cost millions. Later in the day Daniels and Baker conferred with Wilson. He did not approve Lansing's recommendation to import British help.[27]

Nevertheless, the British War Office sent staff to teach their procedures to the navy's cable and wireless censors in New York, and the CPI studied Allied propaganda and worked closely with the Allies. In devising a plan for developing photographs of the war, the CPI contacted Canadian, French, and British officials as to the best approach. Perhaps it is consultation like this that led Lansing to make the following comment after a meeting with Creel and Daniels on censorship: "Creel has come over to my point of view." American censorship, said Edward Cook of the Official Press Bureau, was "largely modelled on our own."[28]

It quickly became clear the Committee on Public Information was a misnomer insofar as the word *committee* was concerned. Its principals met as a whole three times in April to discuss censorship and once in July, judging from Daniels's diary. After that, the gatherings seemed to have ceased altogether. Some of this was due to the crowded schedules of Baker, Daniels, and Lansing, some to Baker's deference to Daniels, who was a newspaperman, and some to Lansing's disdain for Creel, whom he described as having "little conception of vast amount of work to be done." In early May, Lansing reorganized his Division of Information into the Division of Foreign Intelligence. Its duties included press relations. Lansing tried to recruit Arthur Sweetser to head the press operation. When he declined, the job went to Philip H. Patchin, head of the AP's London bureau and well liked by the British. (In late summer Sweetser turned in his press passes for dog tags and was commissioned a captain in the Signal Reserve Corps, where he worked on publicity.) Creel's name appeared on Lansing's calendar with declining frequency.[29]

Creel worked briefly out of a six-by-six-foot room near Daniels's second-floor office and then moved two floors up to the Navy Library. The library's reception room was a compact two-story marble, onyx, and brass jewel box studded with cherubs in each corner. Creel transformed the church-like placidness into a campaign headquarters frenzy. It brimmed with job seekers and idea peddlers while he charged ahead on establishing Wilson's "information service."[30]

The structure of the information service resembled the Democratic National Committee's publicity bureau. It was designed to reach targeted and mass audiences with material journalists could readily use. Like Woolley's operation, it had a number of subdivisions, some of which had few staff but sharp focus. The Cartoon Bureau, when it was formed much later, had only a manager.[31]

The CPI's Division of News was a hub with spokes to government agencies as well as the White House. Its primary concern was managing news out of the war-making departments. The CPI had personnel placed in the War, Navy, Labor, and Justice Departments and the War Industries and Shipping Boards. The operation in the War Department was especially large. Marlin Pew, the CPI representative there, had an office close to Baker's and deputies in the Ordinance Department, the Quartermaster Corps, and the Aircraft Board. Although the State Department wanted to distance itself from the CPI and the Treasury had a strong Liberty Loan publicity bureau, both relied on the CPI for help, as did the Food and Fuel Administrations and independent organizations such as the Red Cross. Every agency benefited in some way.[32]

The News Division attracted experienced journalists. J. M. McConaughy, one of its directors, had been an editorial writer with *Munsey's Magazine* and the *New York Evening Mail*. Leigh Reilly had been managing editor of the *Chicago Herald,* and Pew editor of *Editor & Publisher.* The CPI representative in the Navy Department had worked at Daniels's *Raleigh News & Observer.* Kenneth Durant, who handled general press inquiries, came on a different path, a recommendation of Sir Gilbert Parker, for whom he had worked on British propaganda. In addition to press releases meant "for the telegraph," the division mailed a *War News Digest* to weekly newspapers. The mailing list eventually numbered twelve thousand. Initially the CPI worked with the Council of National Defense to direct news to women. In November it created a Division on Women's War Work. Other units catered to the religious, labor, and the foreign-born.[33]

To enlist writers, as had been done in the 1916 presidential campaign, Creel shot off a telegram to the Authors' League of America. He encouraged members to write helpful articles and offered to assist with information. In August he created a formal Division of Syndicated Features intended for Sunday newspapers. Its head was L. Ames Brown, once the *New York Sun*'s White House correspondent and an active supporter of Wilson in the 1916 campaign. Creel wrote articles, including a weekly column for the *Independent* called "A Message from the United States Government to the American People."[34]

Wellington House attracted more literary giants than the CPI did. H. G.

Wells, Hugh Walpole, and Rudyard Kipling headed propaganda directed at Germany, Russia, and British colonies respectively, all the while turning out books with war themes.* Still, if many of the writers attached to the CPI are less well remembered than their British counterparts, they were popular at the time or became so after the war. Ernest Poole won the Pulitzer Prize for fiction and Charles Edward Russell won one for biography. British-born William MacLeod Raine, who succeeded Brown in Syndicated Features, was famous for western novels, which were adapted for movies. John Balderson, a former foreign correspondent who was a CPI press agent in London, went on to a successful career writing scripts for *Frankenstein, Dracula,* and other movies. The CPI drew on three-time Pulitzer Prize winner Booth Tarkington and Rex Beach, Wallace Irwin, and Mary Roberts Rinehart, who was known as the American Agatha Christie for her mystery novels. In the case of Rinehart, the CPI secured permission for her to visit cantonments. Her war articles appeared in the *Saturday Evening Post* and were syndicated to newspapers.[35]

Wilson had one specific request related to the provision of news. He had long thought that public opinion suffered because "we have no national newspaper, no national organ of opinion." He wanted the CPI to create a government gazette. Creel feared journalists would view such a publication as government competition, but Wilson insisted. The CPI justified the *Official U.S. Bulletin* on two grounds. First, foreign governments—Great Britain since 1665—published gazettes to record government actions. Second, the cost of publication was "absurdly small" compared to congressional expenditures for printing. The first issue appeared on May 10, less than a month after the United States entered the war.[36]

The *Bulletin,* which was published by the News Division, billed itself the "daily government newspaper." It ran between eight and forty-eight pages, Monday through Saturday. The *Bulletin* assisted all government agencies but focused on the war. It published executive orders, proclamations, statutes and regulations, official speeches, and "proceedings of Congress briefly told." It was rich in detail: listings of War Department personnel assignments, casualty lists, and notices of contracts awarded (e.g., the army's purchase of $13,095 worth of canned beans from a company in Freemont, Michigan). The *Bulletin* was free

---

* John Buchan, director of the Department of Information, wrote three famous propagandistic thrillers. The antagonist in one of them, named after German propagandist Baron Gustav Braun von Stumm, was in the words of the novel's hero "an incarnation of all that makes Germany detested." The hero's sidekick was "instrumental in getting the portfolio of Dr. Albert." John Buchan, *Greenmantle,* in *The Best of John Buchan* (London: Prion, 2010), 130, 167.

to government agencies and, until October 1918, to the press, which could re-publish anything in it. Individuals paid a five-dollar annual subscription. Pages were tacked on bulletin boards in fifty-six thousand post offices. Its daily circulation reached 118,000 in August 1918. Edward Rochester, its editor, had been managing editor of the *Washington Post.*[37]

Read the
Official Bulletin

PUBLISHED DAILY UNDER
ORDER OF THE PRESIDENT
OF THE UNITED STATES

BY COMMITTEE ON
PUBLIC INFORMATION
GEORGE CREEL *CHAIRMAN*

WAR
Information

Save writing to Washington for what you
want to know about

The Army and Navy   The Fuel Administration
The Red Cross   Trading with the enemy
The Selective Draft Laws   The War Labor Board
The Food Administration   The War Industries Board
          The Railroad Administration

and all the other permanent or emergency governmental
departments, boards, commissions, committees
and administrations at the Capital and elsewhere.

ASK FOR IT HERE

Ray Greenleaf

President Wilson thought public opinion suffered because "we have no national newspaper, no national organ of opinion." He wanted the CPI to fill that void with a government gazette, which was called the *Official Bulletin.* One of the CPI's most positive contributions, it was the forerunner of the *Federal Register* and other government publications that added to government transparency.

The *Bulletin* and the Division of News, new features of government, drew criticism. But this paled in comparison to condemnation of the administration's censorship proposal.

THE CENSORSHIP CLAUSE

On the day Wilson signed the declaration of war, he issued a proclamation barring enemy aliens from publishing criticism of the government. A proclamation ten days later warned that it was treason to publish information that would "in any way aid and comfort the enemies of the United States." An executive order placed telephone and telegraph lines to Mexico under the War Department and broadened the navy's authority over communication to include submarine cables as well as wireless. Cable censorship was instantly in effect for Asia and Latin America. Transatlantic censorship was delayed until late July so the navy could work with the French and British to synchronize their operations. The goal was to thwart Boy-Ed's agents, as the *Public Ledger* put it, but the Navy and War Departments also could stop reports they deemed prejudicial to the war effort.[38]

At the same time, the administration revived censorship legislation that had died in the previous Congress. The proposed Espionage Act addressed what Gregory called the "new conditions of warfare by propaganda." One provision made it unlawful to communicate "false reports or false statements with intent to interfere with the success of the military or promote the success of its enemies" or to "cause disaffection in the military." A second excluded from the mails any writing or publication "of a treasonable or anarchistic character." The third provision, called the "censorship clause," was the most controversial. It prohibited the publication of any information the president declared to be "of such character that it is or might be useful to the enemy." Almost anything could be barred under such a provision. The wording was similar to Britain's sweeping Defence of the Realm Act, which forbade publication of "information of such a nature as is calculated to be or might be directly or indirectly useful to the enemy." Although this similarity was not advertised by the administration, Jane Addams called attention to it in congressional testimony. She worried about the "spirit of intimidation in the United States at the present moment" and that the bill would stymie discussion of bringing a quick peace.[39]

In the weeks before the war, journalists accepted voluntary restrictions on sensitive military information as "a very excellent and a very necessary provision," as the editor of the *Charleston Evening Post* told Daniels. "Strict adherence to the Government's wishes is a policy which is laid down as absolute law in this office," the editor of the *Philadelphia Evening Ledger* informed Daniels. Although greatly preferring continued voluntary censorship once the country went to war, many editors and publishers were willing to support a formal censorship law. A sign of how far journalists were willing to go came from four diverse and influential New York newspapers. The *Times,* the *Herald,* the *World,* and the *American* drafted a substitute bill, which the *Times* editor forwarded to Daniels in mid-April. It allowed the president to "prohibit the publication or dissemination within the United States, continental and insular, of any and all information, facts, rumors or speculations referring to the armed forces of the government, materials or implements of war, or the military means and measures that may be contemplated for the defense of the country." The proposed substitute was narrower than Wilson's censorship clause, but it gave the president extraordinarily broad authority to silence speech of all kinds, if he chose to use it. The substitute also called for a central censorship board that included a press representative. The American Newspaper Publishers Association endorsed similar language. Nothing came of these suggestions.[40]

The administration swept aside journalists' concerns. When the espionage bill was first proposed, Attorney General Gregory scheduled a perfunctory press briefing on short notice. Confronted with strenuous objections from the handful of journalists who were able to attend, he pledged to give serious consideration to changes. But an hour later the bill was introduced in the House. The *New York Tribune* called the censorship clause "the instrument of the Czar and the Kaiser." The *St. Louis Post* called it "shockingly despotic." Publishers petitioned Congress to delete it from the bill. Journalists, the *New York Evening Post*'s David Lawrence wrote, considered the bill "more far-reaching than any law of England or France."[41]

Edwin Webb, chairman of the Judiciary Committee, led the fight for the bill in the House. "In time of war, while men are giving up their sons and while people are giving up their money," he argued "[newspapers] should at least be willing to give up their right, if they call it a right, to publicly broadcast those things which the President of the United States thinks would be hurtful to the United States and helpful to the enemy." The Republicans naturally seized the opportunity to challenge the president, but many Democrats, including the Senate majority leader and whip and House Speaker Champ Clark, also opposed the legislation. Senator William Borah spoke for many when he described it as "nebulous, drastic and omnipotent, the consequences of which no man can foresee."[42]

With Wilson's approval, a statement was added to the censorship clause that "nothing in this section shall be construed to limit or restrict any discussion, comment, or criticism of the acts or policies of the Government." Arthur Brisbane, editor of the *New York Evening Journal,* urged Wilson to back further away. "Well informed newspaper workers," he wrote diplomatically to the president, "are firm in their belief that desire to nullify the [First] Constitutional Amendment does not at all reflect your state of mind." Wilson did not agree to further changes and replied that he would "not permit any part of this law to apply to me or any of my official acts, or in any way to be used as a shield against criticism."[43]

Instead of allaying fears, Wilson's letter became the "best argument that has been made against the espionage bill," said newly sworn-in Senator Hiram Johnson. The *Milwaukee News* asked, "If the law is not to be enforced, then why enact it? And what guarantee have the American people that no other official will wield it?" It was inconceivable, said a legislator, that "the President, who has frequently advocated 'pitiless publicity,' . . . should have any sympathy with a legislative undertaking designed to accomplish results diametrically opposite." "I know how strongly you feel on the matter of a strict censorship," Tumulty warned Wilson, "but I would not be doing my full duty to you and the Administration if I did not say to you that there is gradually growing bitter resentment on the whole business, which is daily spreading." Wilson, he said, risked going down in history as John Adams did for the Alien and Sedition Acts. Daniels took pains to distance himself from the legislation's censorship provisions, which he considered dangerous.[44]

It was understood that the CPI would be in charge of the censorship. That was what Daniels had in mind when the CPI was proposed, and that is what was reported in the press the day after the CPI was created. The bill, the *New York Times* reported, would give the CPI "statutory authority to carry out its rulings." Creel sought to tamp down concern by insisting he was not bent on heavy-handed censorship. But two stories appearing on the same day in the *Times* illustrate the confusion that existed. "Instead of figuring on means of suppressing news," one story reported, "Mr. Creel is putting in eighteen hours a day devising means of promoting it." In the other story, on the same page, Senator

Henry Cabot Lodge decried the censorship measure under which "newspapers couldn't print anything that the Administration didn't want them to print." He called the CPI a board "appointed to act as censors of the press."[45]

In early May Lansing reinforced these fears by "perfecting" his press operations. He barred all officials except himself from talking to reporters "even on insignificant matters of fact or detail." His twice daily meetings with the press were increasingly perfunctory. "There is much bitterness," Lansing jotted in his desk calendar, about his treatment of the press. The department's handling of the French mission's US tour further alienated journalists. It put so many obstacles in journalists' path that many asked their editors to be recalled. In another one of his unsigned *New Republic* articles, which Sweetser wrote before joining the army, "The nation which has entered this war against autocracy, which has claimed to stand for a democratic open diplomacy, asks its citizens to make enormous sacrifices, to accept universal service in a cause which apparently cannot bear the light of publicity." Lansing's actions, the *New York Tribune* editorialized, was a "foretaste of what will happen if the press gag provision of the espionage bill becomes law."[46]

While Congress debated the espionage bill, Creel drafted censorship guidelines based on the voluntary rules in place before the war. The president read, edited, and approved these. On Monday evening, May 21, Creel briefed Washington correspondents in the Senate gallery. The initially hostile journalists warmed to the idea. "If the voluntary regulations for the press were accepted by them," journalists were led to believe, "there would be no further effort to have a censorship statute enacted." The next day, however, Wilson wrote to Representative Webb to say passage of the censorship clause remained "absolutely necessary to the public safety." Learning of this, the correspondents refused to endorse Creel's proposal when they met again on Wednesday. That day Wilson told senators visiting the White House of the "imperative necessity that a censorship be established." It was not enough, he said, to impose "a moral obligation" on the press. He wrote to Frank Cobb, editor of the *New York World* and a strong supporter of the president, that some papers could not be trusted and it was "absolutely essential for the safety of the country that I should have some power" to control them. Wilson made no effort to reconcile these statements with Creel's voluntary guidelines. Many journalists thought the president was acting in bad faith.[47]

On Thursday David Lawrence tried to straighten out the confusion. Lawrence, a 1910 Princeton graduate, had a personal relationship with Wilson and followed censorship and publicity closely. Correspondents, he told the president, would have endorsed Creel's regulations if the administration had not renewed its call for the censorship clause. "Only you can bring harmony out of the confusion," Lawrence advised the president. He suggested Wilson invite journalists to the White House to hear their point of view and clarify his own. "Instead of an irritated press, ready to pounce on every slight thing and hammer men who are trying only to do their best with a machinery and a people unused to war, we will have a press that will be charitable in its criticism and will inspire the people with confidence in their government." Wilson, he added, should use the occasion to endorse Creel. The next day, Wilson replied. He stood by Creel, but such a meeting was not necessary. "It might look," he wrote cryptically, "as if I were trying to straighten it out when there is really nothing to straighten out."[48]

That same day Creel pressed ahead with what he later called "another act in the serio-tragic drama of misunderstanding." In a speech to journalists, he said he had drawn up advice for the press. There would be no compulsion to eliminate abuse. Instead, the CPI would "crowd it out" with wholesome government news. These, he said, were the terms on which he accepted Wilson's offer to head the CPI. On Sunday, Creel issued his guidelines in the form of a "Preliminary Statement to the Press of the United States." "Hard-and-fast" rules were impossible, the statement said; there would be no interference with "criticism of policies or persons." In line with previous guidelines, the goal was to withhold such militarily sensitive information as troop movements or the testing of aircraft. His guidelines created a category called "questionable matter," such as stories on life in training camps that might inadvertently include information of value to the enemy. Journalists were encouraged to submit all such material "for censorship." In the case of news "plainly of a dangerous character, whether specifically prohibited by these regulations or not, editors are expected to stop it themselves." If in doubt, reporters could submit the material for review. A Division of Visé would mark the story "passed by the Committee on Public Information," which meant there was no objection to it, or "authorized by the Committee on Public Information," meaning the CPI endorsed the news.[49]

This system matched Britain's in several respects. First, it rested on faith that a patriotic press would self-censor. The CPI asked editors to police themselves and each other. When another paper violated the guidelines or when they received matter "dangerous to the public interests," the editors were to notify the CPI. Second, the guidelines held open the possibility of prosecution for "those who published without submission to the committee." DORA made this a powerful threat in Britain, although the government was loath to initiate prosecution, as it would draw attention to information it wanted to suppress. Because Wilson's censorship provision was still under consideration, the CPI said editors were subject to whatever "penalties that may be provided by law." Third, although the Preliminary Statement opposed "private and confidential" censorship directives along the lines of those issued by Britain's Official Press Bureau, the CPI said it would issue "confidential bulletins . . . to the press to acquaint them with subjects to which public reference is considered especially dangerous at the moment."

The Preliminary Statement was a compromise document hastily created. Its proposal to distinguish between news of which it approved and news that it merely allowed to pass proved to be a nightmare to administer. The guidelines stressed reliance on journalists' self-restraint, but the word "censorship" appeared in them. An "Explanation" section added to the confusion. In it, the War and Navy Departments simply reinforced the importance of protecting sensitive military information. But the State Department, in a reprise of its provocative addition to the voluntary guidelines in March, declared it "dangerous and of service to the enemy" to speculate about peace initiatives, precisely the sort of restriction Jane Addams feared, as well as to reveal differences of opinion with Allies and neutrals, or to offend them in some way. These instructions echoed the British Press Bureau's, which enjoined reporters to "refrain from publishing anything which would be prejudicial to His Majesty's relations with Foreign Powers or to the public interest." Lansing's warnings ran counter to Creel's guidelines, which said the fuller "the inter-Ally discussion of their mutual problems the better."[50]

Why Creel issued the rules when the administration was pursuing censorship legislation was puzzling. Congressional leaders and administrative officials, the *New York Globe* said, "should get together on a solution before they publish their individual ideas." The *New Republic* was appalled at Lansing's effort to rule out discussion of peace. "No democracy can remain a democracy and behave itself in this way." Lansing was causing enormous difficulty in other ways as well, Bullard complained to House. He limited press access to State Department officials without informing Creel, and he held up the press guidelines. "Instead of having the control of press matters centralized, as I had hoped," Bullard complained, "the situation is worse than it was in Paris." He thought Lansing hoped to get Creel fired. As the final votes on the censorship clause approached in Congress, Gregory circulated newspaper clippings, many from German-language newspapers, that he believed to show the need for censorship. Having patriotically reined itself in, the establishment press resented being lumped with foreign-language and left-leaning publications that opposed the war.[51]

On May 31, the House killed the censorship clause, 184 to 144, 37 Democrats voting against it. The Senate did not vote on the measure again. The censorship clause was dead. Wilson would have achieved passage of the censorship clause if he had amended it to focus on military security, as the *Times* and other papers suggested, or on the foreign-language press, which he said gave him "a great deal of deep concern." "If the President and his Cabinet had taken the newspapers and correspondents into their confidence and worked out with them the phraseology of a law for those cases where presumably a law is needed," Lawrence reported, "there would have been a censorship law to-day."[52]

Even so, Wilson received considerable power from the other two sections of the Espionage Act that Congress passed without serious press opposition. It was now unlawful to "make false statements with intent to interfere" with military success; to "attempt to cause insubordination, disloyalty, mutiny, or refusal of duty" in the military; or to obstruct recruiting. Postmaster General Burleson, who conspicuously lobbied his former colleagues on behalf of the bill, acquired the power to exclude from the mail "any matter advocating or urging treason, insurrection or forcible resistance to any law of the United States." A dispassionate legal scholar noted that a citizen now ran "considerable risk" by saying the nation "went into the war from unworthy motives."[53]

A TROUBLING QUESTION MARK

The Committee on Public Information remained a troubling question mark in the minds of journalists and others. The confusion during the debate over the censorship clause reinforced the impression that it was to be a censoring body, first and foremost. "I have read in the press and have heard from various sources that there already is a censor board in existence," said a congressman during debate on the Espionage Act, "and that a Mr. Creel is at the head of this board." Lansing's and Gregory's draconian approaches to censorship undercut Creel's efforts to allay concerns. The two men, said the *New York World,* did more to defeat the censorship clause "than all its avowed opponents."[54]

The greatest blame for the stain on the CPI fell on Wilson. He made no effort to clarify what he wanted or to work constructively with the press. Amazingly, there is no evidence he brought Creel in to discuss the conflict that existed between his censorship clause and Creel's voluntary guidelines, which he read and edited. Many years later, Creel admitted to Ray Stannard Baker that Wilson's support of the censorship clause made his job more difficult.[55]

The censorship clause, said *Times* correspondent Richard Oulahan, was a "grave error." Suggestions immediately arose for a new publicity agency to replace the CPI. *North American Review* editor George Harvey, one of those who blasted the administration for its confusing signals on censorship, proposed "a real Department of Public Information" headed by a distinguished journalist who held cabinet rank. *New York World* editor Frank Cobb advised Wilson to consider the idea. Others called for dividing censorship and publicity. It was at this time that McCormick, Willcox, and other leaders of their political parties, with encouragement from House, suggested joining forces to undertake a "campaign of publicity" to unite the country. Creel's name was not included on their short list of people who could lead the nation to unity.[56]

At a minimum, Wilson should have clarified what the CPI was to do. By not doing any of this, the CPI remained a murky organization with no boundaries. This aggravated Congress, which held a deep-seated antipathy to presidential publicity. The 1895 General Printing Act limited expenditures for individual publications and the number of pages that could be produced by the executive branch. In 1908 a senator called news summaries put out almost daily by Gifford Pinchot's Forest Service "a dangerous innovation." The CPI was a giant leap beyond any previous provision of government information. Creel, Lodge said, was a personal agent of Wilson "without definite office. He employs men, he spends large amounts of the public money, and it is considered an impertinence if we ask where the public money is spent." Theodore Roosevelt derided the CPI as a "gigantic news propaganda with the public's money . . . primarily on behalf of the administration."[57]

The CPI's existence also was a source of friction inside the military as well as the State Department. Creel blamed the "admirals and generals, reared in a school of iron secrecy" for forcing the censorship clause on Wilson. The old guard in the Navy and War Departments had little enthusiasm for the CPI. "I don't know anything about publicity," one said, "except that I am against it." This squabbling led to more confusion about the CPI in late June with the arrival in France of the first ships carrying American forces.[58]

News of their arrival was to be held up until the last of the ships docked to avoid alerting the enemy that troops were in transit. Due to a snafu, the AP

New York headquarters received a dispatch about the landings and ran it. Out of fairness, Creel allowed others to report it as well. Military officers were indignant. Baker, it was reported, took authority for War Department news from Creel and gave it to a general. That decision lasted until the evening. An order by Baker a few days later ended the policy of not delaying dispatches if they had been censored by the French, British, or AEF. The new rule required that incoming dispatches go to both the CPI and the War Department for censorship when they reached US shores. This aroused an outcry from the press. After Baker, Daniels, Lansing, and Creel conferred the following day, the CPI announced in a "confidential" note to the press that "the emergency [had] passed" and the old system was restored. But more damage had been done. Senator Hiram Johnson said the War Department and the CPI were seeking to institute censorship that flouted "the expressed will of Congress" when it refused to pass the censorship clause.[59]

WHAT THE GOVERNMENT ASKS OF THE PRESS

Creel's supporters considered him a victim of petty jealousies. "There is a struggle going on in Washington," commented Gus Karger, a respected correspondent with the *Cincinnati Times-Star;* it was a "struggle between bureaucratic and democratic forces." David Lawrence, who was always fair in his reporting on the CPI, described Creel as a "man of bold enthusiasm, a progressive—a liberal—and one who thoroughly understands the newspaper point of view as it relates to the public interest." But many of the misunderstandings and fears about the CPI were due to Creel, for he did much to confirm the impression that he was a partisan bullhorn for the president and a willing censor.[60]

While the Espionage Act was under debate, Creel telephoned the editor of the *Washington Herald,* which was not a Wilson paper, to complain about an editorial criticizing the navy for negligence. During firing practice on the troopship *Mongolia,* bound for France, a faulty shell caused a gun to explode, killing two people. Angry over Creel's telephone call, which it considered intemperate, the *Herald* published a second editorial, this one in the center of the front page, to lodge its own complaint: "If this is not an attempt to control editorial opinion, what is it?" When Creel issued a statement insisting, "No reprimand was hinted or even dreamed of," the *Herald* thundered back again: "Mr. Creel, we feel constrained to say, is putting the most generous and general construction on his conversation with The Herald. This paper regarded it differently and still does, because Mr. Creel is the government censor-to-be if a censorship law is passed." Newspapers across the country reported the exchange. The *Indianapolis News* said the incident indicated the government's intention to use the censorship law "to smother criticism of public officials."[61]

Another firestorm of criticism followed the premature release of news of the first troop landings in France. Two cables from an American admiral reported troopship encounters with enemy submarines. "Submarine opened fire," said one of them, "with one torpedo which crossed bow of USS SEATTLE. Two torpedoes passed close to the HAVANA one crossed bow and one under stern of DEKALB." The second reported, "A submarine approached the group on which the Cummings fired a grenade[;] there was noticed on the surface oil and debris." On July 3, after the ships reached France, Creel prepared a press statement based on the cables. With the flair of a rewrite man on a yellow journal, he wrote a story of "peril and courage": "One [submarine] certainly was sunk, and there is reason to believe that the accurate fire of our gunners sent others to the bottom. . . . The [enemy's] first attack was made in force, although the night made impossible any exact count of the U-boats gathered for what they deemed a slaughter." Creel concluded, "No more thrilling Fourth of July celebration could have been arranged."[62]

Creel's story was designed to play well, and it did, until the AP reported that no attacks had occurred. Creel dismissed this as a "nasty," "unpatriotic" report. As it turned out, the AP story was also inaccurate and based on unsubstantiated background material not meant for publication.* But the report prompted an admission by Creel that he had taken liberties in his story. Because the original navy reports from France had been "rather cryptic," he confessed, "I sat down and elaborated."[63]

Senator Boies Penrose, a belligerently conservative Republican whose size and bushy moustache earned him the nickname "Big Grizzly," called Creel's account a "colossal fraud." He dubbed the CPI the "committee on misinformation." Newspapers flayed Creel for inspiring them to proclaim America's "first notable victory in the war against Germany." "Mr. Creel knows what this process is called in newspaper offices," the *New York Evening Post* wrote. "It is plain 'faking.'" The usually loyal *New York World* said Creel was guilty of "press-agent

---

* The AP story originated with a cable from a reporter in the Irish port of Queenstown, who had picked up the inaccurate tip on the absence of attacks in casual conversation. He prudently marked his cable "confidential," signaling it was not for publication; a British censor stamped the cable "passed for publication U.S.A. only." The AP bureau in London included those words in the cable sent onward to New York, where they were interpreted as suggesting the story was solid.

exaggerations." Weeks later the navy confirmed the attacks but not the sinking of a submarine. By the time of this partial exoneration, the event had seeped into the public consciousness as Creel's "July 4th hoax."[64]

Missteps continued. On a single day in late July the CPI advised journalists not to report three stories—a planned visit by a Belgian mission, details of an official Russian visit to Chicago, and the Commerce Department's decision to transfer ships to the navy—that the State and Commerce Departments and the Russian embassy had made public. In late July, when military authorities wanted the AP to kill a story about another troop landing, Creel made the request. The AP refused. The story contained no sensitive information (no port or country was identified), and censors overseas had cleared the dispatch, which by the rules meant it could go forward.[65]

Creel revised the Preliminary Statement at the end of July. "What the Government Asks of the Press" consisted of twenty-one rules relating only to War and Navy Department information. One typical rule stated that warship arrivals at European ports should not be reported until specifically authorized by the Navy or War Department. The "questionable matter" section was gone; the injunction to submit material to the CPI was softened. The Division of Visé was eliminated. Among other things it had been criticized for inconsistency in deciding which stories should carry official CPI approval and which should be passed without comment. Creel let it be known that the CPI would provide informal advice when asked by the press. He argued that the new guidelines were adequate since transatlantic cable censorship by the navy was now in place to block the transmission of sensitive information that might reach the enemy.[66]

Several days later a confidential memo was leaked in which Baker ordered an end to War Department resistance to the CPI. "These representatives of the committee will be treated with confidence," Baker wrote; the CPI was "the sole medium for issuing war news." The measure, it was reported, strengthened the CPI's control over military information. The decision did not entirely quell guerrilla warfare by army officers. One disgruntled officer told a *New York Sun* reporter, "The Creel bureau frankly asked him day after day whether he did not have some news favorable to the army and the Administration."[67]

A STORM CENTER OF CRITICISM

Propaganda carried out by the Allies and Central Powers was a subject of the news from the first days of the war. Because the CPI was more visible than Wellington House, it received heightened attention. Because it was embroiled in one controversy after another, much of the news was negative. Creel, said David Lawrence, was "a storm center of criticism, some of it deserved and some of it underserved." For partisan journalists, the CPI was an attractive target. *Boston Transcript* editor James Williams, who had been on the Republican payroll during the election, kept his Washington correspondent busy following the CPI. The *Transcript* excoriated Creel's "machine for elaboration and decoration."[68]

As the summer wore on, questions persisted about whether the CPI should—or even could—carry on. "There are certain signs of the disintegration of the Committee on Public Information," the *New York Times* reported almost gleefully. "It is acknowledged by some of its most sincere friends and well wishers that the policy under which it has been conducted has been a failure."[69]

"Creel is hopelessly discredited. Personally, I like him very much but that does not change the situation," Frank Cobb told House. Cobb favored separating censorship and publicity. House, who considered Cobb a good candidate for an official role in publicity, forwarded his letter to Wilson with a note asking, "Why would this not be a good solution?" Meanwhile House, McCormick, and Woolley stewed about what could be done to elevate the publicity effort. Woolley, who was running the Bureau of Publicity for Liberty Loans during its first drive, thought the president should send fifty speakers, organized like a Lyceum Bureau, across the country to counter public apathy. "The Creel matter grows worse," he told House. "It is admirable in the President to stand by him and George's desire to fight it out is fine, but the cause is bigger than the interests of any man."[70]

Anti-CPI darts came from other directions. The dean of the University of Missouri journalism school, Walter Williams, told Daniels a better "publicity service" was needed. The Chamber of Commerce recommended to Wilson the creation of "a definite branch of the government (entirely distinct from the Committee on Public Information) under the direction of the President to conduct a campaign of constructive education of the people as to the war and the important operations of the government regarding the war."[71]

Public disparagement and backroom intrigue did not unhorse Creel. "I am the worst resigner in the world," he told a reporter. "I have not resigned and I do not intend to." Wilson's view was the only one that mattered as far as Creel's continued service was concerned, and he did not like to be pushed. More important, the president had reason to be happy with his appointee's performance.[72]

Wilson's administration revolutionized press relations like the steam engine revolutionized manufacturing. Theodore Roosevelt had made effective use of press releases, to the point of annoying Congress, but these handouts were largely the product of a few bureaus and amounted to a trickle compared to what gushed from the CPI. Creel mass-produced news and established impersonal routines to reach the press day in and day out. The CPI was not limited to handling the flow of news from government agencies. Because Wilson did not hold press conferences and Tumulty ceased giving daily press briefings, the CPI was the principal source of White House news.[73]

Reporters grumbled about occasional inaccuracies and the *Bulletin*'s overall positive tone. Newspaper proprietors were annoyed that each day it consumed nearly three tons of newsprint, which was in short supply. But this was a sign of success. Circulation reached 60,000 the first month and climbed to 115,000 the following year. Despite his initial reservations, Creel became a believer in the publication, and so did journalists who were otherwise critical of the CPI. *Evening Transcript* editor James Williams considered it "very useful." When the CPI decided to charge for the *Bulletin,* a thousand editors asked for the policy to be reversed.[74]

The greatest problem from Creel's point of view was his lack of control over publicity produced by others. Forty-five or fifty agencies had their own propaganda machines. Although it relied on the CPI to distribute its news, the War Trade Board had a journal. The Bureau of Education published weekly bulletins. The Commission for Relief in Belgium, an international organization under US leadership, sent out releases. Legislators boosted the flow of this material by using the postal frank to send it to editors with whom they wished to be friendly. California journalists, Creel was informed, complained they received six pounds of government news every day. In addition, localities had their own news operations. In one state the Council of National Defense had five hundred "war information chairmen."[75]

Editors complained of drowning in news. Much of it, Lawrence told the president, "was badly written and a lot of it ought not to be written at all." This flood, Creel lamented, swamped the information he wanted to emphasize. Lawrence recommended Wilson give the CPI the "power of squelching out the drool." *Editor & Publisher* argued the CPI should have regulatory power over government news, and Creel lobbied Wilson for such authority—all to no avail. "I have protested against it time and again, and have guaranteed, if given control, to cut this enormous mass of matter down to one-tenth of the present volume without loss of effect," Creel complained. "However, the various Departments are insistent upon their authorities."[76]

Nevertheless, the CPI exerted enormous control over the news. The Correspondents' Room at 8 Jackson Place was open twenty-four hours a day, all week long. Its eight telephones answered queries from Washington correspondents. Mimeographed news releases were sent to the press bureaus at the National Press Club. Out-of-town newspapers received CPI news by mail. Journalists professed to find joy in tossing government press releases into the wastebasket, but they needed the CPI's help to keep track of the nearly three thousand agencies engaged in the war. Reporters complained the temperature in the Correspondents' Room "would make even an Eskimo shiver in his sealskins," but they gathered there lest they miss news their competitors would publish. This left less time to pursue stories with alternative points of view. "All initiative and independent investigation stopped," Sweetser complained, "and we became messenger boys for handouts, which naturally became much more frequent than before." It was not possible to use all the government news that came in, the *Boston Post* noted, but "we would regret to be without the information that much of this material contains."[77]

In addition to his soft power over the news, Wilson acquired the hard power of the law. The Espionage Act was the first legislation since the Sedition Act of 1798 to punish expression. Even without the censorship clause, it had teeth. Burleson took an expansive view of its prohibition on "matter advocating or urging treason, insurrection or forcible resistance to any law of the United States." He secretly directed local postmasters to watch for anything that could "embarrass or hamper the Government in conducting the war." Within a month fifteen major publications, most of them socialist in orientation, were barred from the mail. "The effect," the *New Republic* wrote, "is to terrorize all criticism."[78]

More legislation intruding on First Amendment rights passed in later months. These laws also did not give the CPI statutory authority to censor. But it acquired delegated powers to suppress, which added muscle to the protests Creel lodged over stories he deemed wayward. The defeat of the censorship clause, David Lawrence observed, had not settled the matter once and for all. "The newspapers of the country will be virtually on probation."[79]

THE THINGS WE COMPLAIN ABOUT

One of the most significant aspects of censorship during the war was the willingness of editors and reporters to cooperate with the government. Daniels's mailbox overflowed with contrite letters from editors who let an unauthorized photograph slip into the paper or inadvertently mentioned the arrival of two South American ships in New York harbor. The AP made Creel's guidelines "a mandatory general order throughout the service." In June 1917, the War College produced a report intended to show that the press compromised national security, but it substantiated the opposite. It identified only nine transgressions. Ninety-nine percent of all newspapers honored press guidelines, Creel said. Newspapers, Richard Oulahan would later recall with pride, "mobilized themselves, a powerful volunteer army actuated by a patriotic spirit whose operations have no parallel in all history."[80]

Nevertheless, Creel was disappointed. Government news did not always crowd out stories that put the administration in a bad light or that contradicted views the administration wished to impress on the public. Although utter crowding out would not have been possible in a democratic system, no matter how supportive journalists were of the war, Creel persisted in wanting more. When unveiling his voluntary guidelines, he told the press it "often abused" its freedom. He called on journalists to be "associates," in effect asking them to give up their independence. The comment was reminiscent of Wilson's first press conference, when he asked reporters to "go in partnership" with him. Creel did not favor the censorship clause, but he wanted the same outcome Wilson did, a press that did not muddy the picture the CPI presented. "The things we complain about," Creel wrote to Wilson in November 1917, "are not concerned with suggestive changes, but go to the heart of the newspaper business, involving changes in training, aims, ideals and ambitions. News itself must be given a new definition." This statement was far more revealing of Creel's attitudes than his sunny recollection of the two-hour meeting he had with Wilson when the CPI began.[81]

Wilson and Creel were unable to fully realize their progressive dream of reengineering the way journalists thought about their calling. But the CPI's mass production of information changed the way reporters worked. It institutionalized government handouts and journalists' dependency on them. In that sense Wilson and Creel did give news a new definition. The first block of the Information State was cemented in place.

Others would be laid down soon. If the CPI could not completely crowd out undesirable news, Creel could take advantage of the broad mandate the president gave him and bypass the press to "mobilize the *mind* of America." In the next months he enlisted artists, educators, filmmakers, advertising executives, labor and immigrant leaders, and—as the next chapter shows—speakers across the country. The number of CPI orators dwarfed by tens of thousands the fifty Robert Woolley had in mind.

5

All Men Must Harken to My Message

By using speakers instead of writers and platforms instead of type,
Creel not only flanked the newspaper opposition and escaped from the
congestion of the mails; he also evaded the suspicion which the American
people always show towards official propaganda. The speakers whom he sent
out were not recognized mouthpieces for the government, and the
advertising agent who ballyhooed them was a native son and not
an employee from Washington.

—Harvey J. O'Higgins

The common denominator on the Committee on Public Information was progressivism. Whether it was educator Guy Stanton Ford or editor Edgar Sisson, both Republicans, or Charles Edward Russell, a contender for the Socialist Party's presidential nomination in 1915—all were bent to the uplifting purpose of unifying wartime America. Some, like novelist and Denver journalist William MacLeod Raine, had become acquainted with Creel during earlier crusades. Others were familiar faces at the Democratic National Committee during the 1916 election. Maurice F. Lyons, a young attorney who was Woolley's secretary, became Creel's. Of the thirty-six writers who signed the ten-question letter putting Hughes on the spot at the beginning of the election, at least eleven worked for the CPI directly or in some collateral fashion. Muckraker Ida Tarbell, who had recommended Creel for the campaign staff, headed the news department of the Woman's Committee at the Council of National Defense, which furnished stories to the CPI. Harvey O'Higgins, who signed the Hughes letter, knew Creel from his Denver days. A few months after the CPI started, he contacted Creel to offer "to do my patriotic duty for you."[1]

By the time O'Higgins arrived in the fall of 1917, the CPI was packed into buildings that still exist at Jackson Place, on the west side of Lafayette Square. The tree-studded park, with its equestrian statue of Andrew Jackson, had been the focal point of one of Washington's most prestigious neighborhoods. Here had lived literary lights Henry Adams and George Bancroft, secretary of state and Abraham Lincoln confidant John Hay, ministers from Britain and France, Commodore Stephen Decatur, and James and Dolly Madison. The character of the neighborhood changed as federal agencies moved in, but it still offered a pleasant green respite in the war-bustling capital. Wilson could be seen from CPI windows strolling there from time to time.[2]

The CPI initially occupied a three-story red brick townhouse, 10 Jackson Place, and in the coming months spread into numbers 6, 8, and 16. Major Douglas MacArthur, whose trailblazing stint as army press officer was about to end with his assignment to the AEF, helped Creel find the space, whose most famous previous resident was Major Henry Rathbone. Rathbone accompanied President Lincoln to Ford's Theatre on the fateful night Lincoln was assassinated. Rathbone received a serious knife wound from John Wilkes Booth. Given to bouts of depression, Rathbone made news again in 1883, when he was the US consul to Hanover. On Christmas Eve, he murdered his wife. He died in a German insane asylum thirty years later.[3]

With the proliferation of wartime agencies, the CPI was fortunate to find quarters close to the White House. The State, War, and Navy Building, adjacent to the White House, was cramped. A CPI representative in the War Department spent all summer trying to locate a room for developing photographs. Walter Lippmann shared a small office with another aide, future Supreme Court Justice Felix Frankfurter. The CPI buildings, previously used by the Justice Department, were poorly ventilated, dimly lit, and shabby despite a fresh coat of paint. The marble and carved-wood fireplace mantels, the high ceilings and chandeliers, and the wooden handrails lacing from one floor to the next were grand, but the configuration of the rooms was ill-suited to a government bureau. When O'Higgins first climbed the sandstone stoop to the headquarters, the staff was crammed in "vacated parlors and dining rooms, boudoirs, libraries, bedrooms and bathrooms, sculleries and kitchens."[4]

O'Higgins found Creel in his office on the second floor, a former living room that faced Lafayette Square, signing letters without reading them and blotting his hurried scrawl. His large mahogany desk was cluttered with letters, reports, books, articles, and photographs of his two children. "Two batteries of desk 'phones were ranged at either elbow—department wires, private wires, long distance wires and connections with cable offices." While talking to O'Higgins, Creel stripped down to his shorts and changed into a freshly pressed blue summer surge suit brought in by an office boy. "This is one of the disad-vantages," Creel commented, "of trying to live with only two suits of clothes."

O'Higgins, almost exactly the same age as Creel, was a newspaperman, mag-azine writer, fiction author, playwright, and propagandist. In Denver he worked closely with Creel's friend, child advocate Judge Ben Lindsey. When Creel asked what kind of work he wanted, O'Higgins volunteered to patch up relations with the press. Creel dismissed the idea. Press criticism was a given; journalists would never be as wholly pliant as Creel wanted. "As far as the Committee was concerned," O'Higgins concluded, "the newspaper presses had broken down."[5]

Two days later Associate Chairman O'Higgins sat in an office the size of "a horse stall, with an official desk, swivel chair, a yawning wastepaper basket, and a sort of roving commission to do what he was told to whenever Creel had time to tell him." His portfolio grew as the CPI launched one program after another to reach Americans in other ways than newspapers. One of them O'Higgins described as having been brought in by "some genius." It was a "scheme for en-listing volunteer orators to address audiences in theaters and moving picture houses between the acts. Creel jumped at the idea."[6]

THE INGENIOUS SCHEME

The genius was Donald M. Ryerson, a young Chicagoan. His scheme was hatched in a March 1917 dinner at the exclusive Saddle & Cycle Club on Foster Avenue, near Lake Michigan. The dozen or so diners came from the same strata of society as did Ryerson, scion of a steel manufacturing family. Among them were Republican Representative Medill McCormick, whose family owned the *Chicago Tribune,* and a relative of McCormick's, investment banker William McCormick Blair, who was also the grandson of the inventor of the mechan-ical reaper. The men supported universal military training legislation pending in Congress and hit on the idea of making speeches in favor of the law at local movie theaters.[7]

Ryerson gave a trial speech at the Strand Theatre one evening near the end of March. His remarks during the intermission lasted four minutes. On April 2 he and colleagues formed a plan for the Four Minute Men and set up an of-fice at the University Club, where they met that day. Ryerson was voted presi-dent. When the United States declared war on April 6, the group's orientation shifted. The issue was no longer preparing for war but the more urgent one of waging it. The group sent Ryerson to Washington to propose a national program along the lines they had conceived for Chicago. As the story was later told, he was on the next train.[8]

The idea of a local group running a national speaking campaign was audacious, even for self-assured blueblood Chicagoans. The heady mix of youth and surging patriotism emboldened them. On April 16, the first Monday the CPI was in operation, Ryerson found Creel in the Navy Library. Creel agreed on the spot to a national organization of Four Minute Men and made Ryerson the director. Ryerson telegraphed his colleagues in Chicago to confirm that their dinner idea a month before was now an undertaking of the federal government: "Have written arrangements with Creel for organization on national basis on lines of our talk subject censorship from his office first subject universal military service."[9]

Ryerson's proposal had immediate appeal. Grassroots speaking was a staple of political campaigning. In the nineteenth century, local political groups organized themselves as "Jackson Guards," "Batteries," and "Minute Men" to boost their parties' presidential tickets. In the 1916 campaign, it will be remembered, the Democratic National Committee perfected this with orchestrated speakers' programs through regional speakers' bureaus in San Francisco as well as Chicago. Homer Cummings, who oversaw speakers, pointed out to Wilson "the wisdom of making this feature a permanent part of our work in future campaigns." By Cummings's count, the national committee headquarters had been responsible for more than ten thousand speeches. Movie theaters gave Creel a vehicle for similarly reaching the masses across the country. "Every night," one of Creel's associates noted, "eight to ten million people of all classes, all degrees of intelligence, black and white, young and old, rich and poor, meet in the moving picture houses of this country."[10]

Political parties had an advantage in organizing speaking campaigns that the Four Minute Men did not: a national organization built up over many decades. Seasoned party operatives, many working in government, were on the ground in states, counties, and communities. In their desk drawers were lists of loyal party followers ready to swing into action and accustomed to taking guidance from the party's national committee. They also had established methods, such as the party bulletin, to keep members informed.

If Ryerson's scheme was to work, the CPI would have to create its own national backbone. "Had I had the time to weigh the proposition from every angle," Creel said afterward, "it may be that I would have decided against it, for it was delicate and dangerous business to turn loose on the country an army of speakers impossible of exact control and yet vested in large degree with the authority of the government."[11]

Creel initially based the operation in Chicago. By May, he thought it better to place the headquarters in the basement of 10 Jackson Place in a space barely large enough for a desk. On June 16 Creel made the Four Minute Men a division of the CPI. Ryerson's idea of working through Federal Reserve districts was also discarded in favor of a state-based structure. States had social and government networks that did not exist on a regional basis, and state organization was more easily managed than a larger regional one.[12]

After assisting with the transfer to Washington, Ryerson went into the navy, and cofounder William McCormick Blair became the director. If Ryerson's genius planted the seed for the Four Minute Men, Blair's managerial abilities made the idea bloom. Blair, who was barely thirty years old and looked much younger, was a golden boy raised in a house with servants and educated at Yale. Handsome, soft-spoken, and an indefatigable executive, he was on his way to prominence in Chicago investment banking. His division retained a Chicago accent. Bertram Nelson, a University of Chicago speech professor, was associate director. To handle publications, Blair brought with him Ernest T. Gundlach, an exacting editor who had an advertising company on Michigan Avenue. Another Chicagoan, Keith Evans, was business manager.[13]

To build this national-local organization, the division needed Washington allies with ties to states and communities. The most valuable of these was the Council of National Defense, which was one of Ryerson's first stops when he brought his plan to Washington. The CND viewed its local affiliates, which eventually totaled 184,000, as "guardians of civilian morale." The affiliates, which had the task of developing "as fully as possible the facilities for giving broad publicity," were directed to give the Four Minute Men "full support." The relationship was all the more harmonious because Blair was well acquainted with Frederick Lewis Allen, a brilliant young magazine editor who handled publicity for the council. Both were graduates of the elite boys' school Groton.[14]

Cooperation from movie theaters was secured from the National Association of the Motion Picture Industry. The association was created before the war to regulate movie content, a measure taken to prevent outside forces from imposing restrictions on them. The association's executive committee agreed to designate the Four Minute Men the sole government agency authorized to speak in theaters, provided that government agencies agreed the CPI should have this task. Creel achieved this by simply declaring it himself in a letter to

Blair on June 16, the day Blair assumed the directorship. The Four Minute Men were "the only officially recognized organization of speakers to operate in moving picture theaters on behalf of the Government." Blair was authorized to use the letter as "direct authority" with the motion picture industry. Appended to this were letters of endorsement from Robert Woolley, who had become director of publicity for the first Liberty Loan drive, and Herbert Hoover, chief of the Food Administration. Two days later the American Red Cross issued a similar statement. In early July, Blair attended a movie convention in Chicago where a resolution was passed that "in effect threw open to the Four Minute Men every motion picture theater in the country."[15]

A National Advisory Council was established in November 1917. Real estate investor Samuel F. B. Morse, who was on the council, contributed little apart from the illustrious name he inherited. Others were engaged in administration, speaking, and writing. The chairman, William H. Ingersoll, had promoted the country's first low-cost "dollar watches," which were mass produced by his family-owned company. When Blair followed Ryerson into the military in August 1918, Ingersoll replaced him as director. Other members were Mac Martin, whose Minneapolis advertising agency was one of the most prosperous in the country; Samuel Hopkins Adams, a muckraking journalist and novelist; and Solomon H. Clark, head of the University of Chicago's Department of Public Speaking. Likened to Hiram Johnson for his forcefulness on the platform, Clark had advised the Democratic National Committee on ways to improve speaking during the 1916 campaign and did the same for the Four Minute Men. He made over a hundred speeches. He told one Four Minute Men audience that they had more influence than journalists because they reached the masses and because "our work is carefully laid out for us by experts in our main office at Washington."[16]

"It is our idea," Creel told Josephus Daniels, "to build up a great organization of speakers, subject to Government direction and suggestion with references to specific drives." The Four Minute Men undertook thirty-six different campaigns. Following their first, which advocated for the military draft law, they promoted the first Liberty Loan. They devoted six days to "Eyes for the Navy," an appeal for citizens to contribute binoculars, telescopes, and sextants. These were in short supply because the Germans had been the chief manufacturers. A month was given to "Unmasking German Propaganda" and two weeks to "Food Conservation." Keeping speakers energized required the provision of fresh topics. In June 1918, Blair asked O'Higgins to suggest "one or two subjects." The topic the week before the war ended was "Fire Prevention," which had become a social problem. The last theme, confined to a single day, Christmas Eve, was "Tribute to the Allies."[17]

A LOCAL MILITIA WITH A WASHINGTON MESSAGE

Four Minute Men imagined themselves as rekindled Revolutionary War Minutemen—citizen volunteers organizing themselves to meet a national emergency. They were largely financed by their states and communities. They spoke in the local twang. "I am here to-night for President Wilson and our country to ask every one of you to become a modern Paul Revere," one speaker said, "to go to your neighbors with the message of the hour and get them all gloriously awake." A CPI poster depicted a colonial bell ringer standing in front of Independence Hall.[18]

The Four Minute Men, however, were not a bottom-up, organic expression of local patriotism. In the same manner that the Democratic leadership directed midwestern speakers to hammer on the peace issue during the 1916 campaign, the CPI focused Four Minute Men on messages that advanced Washington's agenda. CPI control began with the appointments of state chairmen; it confirmed the appointments of local chairmen, who received an official certificate from Washington. Chairmen took an oath of office; speakers pledged to adhere to "a set of instructions." Blair wanted a force that wore suits and ties but saluted like those in uniform. "We repeat, over and over again, in our letters," he said, "that this is a military organization (President Wilson has himself referred to it as 'part of the reserve officer corps') and that all missions assigned to members must be accomplished with military promptness." A picture of how discipline was imposed emerges from Four Minute Men files in the Tennessee State Archives.[19]

Porter Dunlap was state chairman of the Tennessee Four Minute Men. The thirty-nine-year-old Tennessean had a thin, avuncular face later idealized in Norman Rockwell's illustrations. He hailed from Dover, a village of five hundred people on the Cumberland River, a region pioneered by his forebears. Trained as a lawyer and founder of the People's Bank and Trust, he began dabbling in politics as a clerk in the state General Assembly. In 1914 he directed Thomas C. Rye's successful campaign for governor, earning credit for uniting Democrats who warred over prohibition. (Rye supported enforcement of state laws against the sale of liquor.) That fall the legislature unanimously elected

The Four Minute Men imagined themselves rekindled Revolutionary War Minutemen—citizen volunteers organized in local units to meet a national emergency. But they were not a bottom-up, organic expression of patriotism. The CPI carefully managed Four Minute Men so they rang out messages precisely as the Wilson administration wanted them rung.

Porter Dunlap of Tennessee was one of the first men to be appointed a state chairman of the Four Minute Men. The CPI told him that he was "part of the reserve officer corps in a nation thrice armed because through your efforts it knows better the justice of its cause and the value of what it defends." (Tennessee Department of Treasury, http://www.treasury.state.tn.us/TreasHist/history.html)

Dunlap state treasurer. A progressive who supported Wilson's business and social reforms, Dunlap promised transparency in managing the state's troubled budget. His tenure as state treasurer was remembered as "the first time in history, the state knew what it owed, where it was, and how much it was worth." He was reelected unanimously on the eve of the war. With his political skills, credibility, and identification as a true son of Tennessee, Dunlap was the ideal Four Minute Man state chairman. His appointment on July 27, 1917, was one of the first. It was made at the suggestion of the chairman of the State Council of National Defense, Rutledge Smith, whose program was considered one of the best in the South.[20]

The Four Minute Men Division was in constant touch with Dunlap. He received personal letters, as in August 1917, when he was told, "We are sure that you will be able to organize the state rapidly and with very little effort." A form letter from Blair that same month told state chairmen to "bend every energy, first, to perfecting your branches already established, and second, to appointing competent Chairmen in the cities not already covered." A few months later Blair cautioned Dunlap that it was not enough to simply announce that a community chairman had been appointed. Unless continuously supervised, "they do not carry on their work with the enthusiasm and energy that we require."[21]

Chairmen were supplied with speakers' schedule sheets and expected to keep careful tabs on their activities. Speakers had a glass slide that was projected on the theater curtain to announce their talk. To facilitate message control, the division emulated political parties by sending speakers the *Four Minute Men Bulletin* and the *Four Minute Men News* as well as general CPI publications. The Four Minute Men could subscribe to the CPI's *Official Bulletin* for $2.50 a year, half the regular price. Most of the forty-six *Four Minute Men Bulletins*—one of them ran thirty-three pages—dwelled on a specific campaign theme. They reprised key messages and provided sample speeches, some of which had blanks a speaker could fill in with local references. The *News,* which appeared at three-month intervals, contained lessons learned, speech excerpts, poems, and photographs of Four Minute Men units.

Good suggestions from the field were turned into national suggestions. "Would like to suggest to my fellow Four Minute Men, especially those who are serving big cities," the *News* quoted one chairman, "that they arrive at the theater long enough in advance of the time of speaking to study the make-up of the audience." An Ohio chairman said he gave a dinner at his home for his speakers and "enthused the squad." Picking up on Blair's martial allusions, the Memphis chairman said his unit understood "at the outset they were enlisting for duty and would be expected to respond to every order of the chairman as if it were in fact a military organization."[22]

Guidance was so detailed that Washington told Dunlap how to run meetings with his local chairmen. Blair suggested discussion topics such as "How to Treat 'Hecklers'" and "Is a Question Box at the Entrance Worth While?" Dunlap should invite "prominent motion picture exhibitors" in order to cement good relations with the theaters. He should call the meeting to order at 10:30 and consider greeting attendees this way: "Standing before you today, I feel like a soldier who after battle assembles with his company mates. We Four Minute Men are drafted to fight an enemy at home, our most insidious enemy, the unseen, the masked foe. To oppose a lie with *the truth,* that is our mission. To arouse the enthusiasm of the apathetic, to instruct those who do not understand, and to throw the lime light on anti-Americanism, be the form of that anti-Americanism what it may."[23]

Dunlap and fellow state chairmen were encouraged to court press coverage. Some of this was routine, such as ensuring local newspapers listed the names of speakers at theaters that day. Some was more enterprising. Articles containing "the pith" of each *Four Minute Men Bulletin* were sent to chairmen, who passed them to local newspapers. Blair told chairmen to ensure "photographs of your best speakers are given at once to local newspapers and that you supply

Table 1. The Local Image of the Four Minute Men in the *Tennessean*

Month of Publication	Articles and Images with Washington Orientation	Articles and Images with Local Orientation*	Total Number of Articles and Images
1917			
April	0	0 (0)	0
May	0	0 (0)	0
June	1	0 (0)	1
July	1	0 (0)	1
August	0	0 (0)	0
September	0	2 (0)	2
October	2	2 (0)	4
November	1	5 (0)	6
December	1	4 (0)	5
Total:	6	13	19
1918			
January	2	0 (0)	2
February	2	0 (0)	2
March	4	5 (0)	9
April	4	23 (12)	27
May	9	27 (7)	36
June	5	16 (11)	21
July	4	11 (9)	15
August	6	15 (13)	21
September	10	6 (2)	16
October	5	11 (4)	16
November	3	4 (3)	7
December	2	11 (5)	13
Total:	56	129	185
1919			
January	1	2 (0)	3
February	0	2 (0)	2
March	0	0 (0)	0
April	1	0 (0)	1
May	1	0 (0)	1
June	0	0 (0)	0
Total:	3	4	7

Source: Lauren West

Method: A search of the Nashville *Tennessean*—the dominant morning newspaper—was conducted on newspapers.com. The dates ranged from April 1917 to June 1919. The search date extended into 1919 because the Four Minute Men continued briefly after the war and their war work continued to be a subject of interest. The search terms were "four-minute men," "four minute men," and "4-minute men." The "Washington" orientation identifies those articles and images that suggest Four Minute Men activity was directed by Washington, DC, either from President Wilson, George Creel, the Committee on Public Information, or any other government agency. The remaining articles and images were coded as possessing a "local" orientation (i.e., no suggestion of Washington control).

* A subcategory—shown in parentheses—of "local" denoted articles that listed the names, places, and times of local Four Minute Men speaking that day. They were typically titled "Four-Minute Men to Make Talks Today," "Four-Minute Men Assigned for Today," or "Four-Minute Men Assigned for Tonight."

the press each day or two with an interesting item of real *news* about the Four Minute Men." The chairman in Leominster, Massachusetts, had his speakers write five-hundred-word editorials for the local paper. This, he said, "made the speakers known in the community and gave them some standing." At the end of the war, the state chairman in Kansas had amassed 2,160 column inches of press clippings.[24]

It was a point of pride in Memphis that a local paper ran one Four Minute Man speech in full. When the CPI informed state chairmen it was using farm journals to solicit readers' opinions about organizing rural Four Minute Men groups, Dunlap wrote a similar letter to every paper in the state. By the spring of 1918, the largest morning newspaper in Nashville, the *Tennessean,* mentioned the Four Minute Men more than every other day some months and, one month, more than once a day. While it was no secret the CPI directed the Four Minute Men, table 1 shows that by a two-to-one margin, the stories dwelled exclusively on local activities with no hint of Washington control.[25]

Dunlap's Four Minute Men started out slowly. A final report cryptically attributed this to "illness and unusual handicaps." In November 1917 he had five local chairmen, whereas neighboring Kentucky had twenty-three. Dunlap, however, more than caught up. He had 48 local chairmen by March 31 and 105 by the end of the war. Kentucky topped out at seventy-eight. The Tennessee Four Minute Men organization was above average in size. Its growth was attributable to Dunlap's management skills.[26]

In keeping with the pedigree of their Chicago founders, Four Minute Men were not, with few exceptions, shop clerks and mechanics. They were community leaders to whom others looked when forming opinions. The forty-person unit in Memphis consisted of eleven lawyers, five bankers, two manufacturers, two brokers, two insurance agents, a wholesale grocer, a druggist, an editor and a reporter, an auditor, a physician, a dentist, a college professor, seven Protestant clergy, an Episcopal bishop, a rabbi, and a Catholic priest. The Chicago Four

Minute Men held social gatherings at the toney Edgewater Gold Club. Like Ryerson and Blair, many Four Minute Men voted for Hughes in 1916. A study of Four Minute Men in Los Angeles County found that more than 75 percent were Republicans. One of the CPI's near-miracle achievements was to get local Republican leaders to speak on behalf of Wilson's policies.[27]

Four Minute Men tended to have better-than-average educations and healthy self-esteem. As was often said about Tennessee Four Minute Men, they were good "talkers." The CPI recognized the leadership qualities of its speakers but believed that talent and self-confidence had to be managed. "Let it be borne in mind," Creel said later, "that these were no haphazard talks by nondescripts, but the careful, studied, and rehearsed efforts of the *best* men in each community, each speech aimed as a rifle is aimed, and driving to its mark with the precision of a bullet." Chairmen were told to select speakers "who are certain to abide by the standard instructions of the department."[28]

The CPI admonished Four Minute Men to adhere to strict rules, the first and foremost being the four-minute speaking limit, from which "there must be no deviation." The most important rule after that was to stay on message with whatever drive was under way, a point the *Bulletin* drummed into members. In addition to precooked speeches, bulletins suggested various approaches for a given topic. Speakers could choose the one with which they were the most comfortable. "Extraneous comments" were not acceptable, nor were "personal viewpoints . . . supplementary to those given" by the CPI. "The character of the original message formulated in Washington," the *Bulletin* said, "may not be lost in transmission through the speakers." A scholar of rhetoric observed, "The speaker's *inventio*—his discovery of suitable arguments with which to convince his audience—did not have to be 'invented' but came to him ready-made."[29]

Instructions to speakers became minicourses on propaganda. Speakers were told to use simple language. "Before an audience," the *Bulletin* said, "the speaker will gain by elucidating facts by means of almost childlike picturesque illustrations." Speakers were warned against using derogatory terms, such as "slacker," which might alienate people who had not bought a bond rather than motivate them to open their wallets. Speakers were to ignore questions from the audience or decline to answer them on the grounds it would extend their time on the platform. This last rule foreclosed debate that might undercut the message. The CPI wanted speeches to appear spontaneous but admonished Four Minute Men to be disciplined in sticking to messages. Those who preferred to speak their own words, instead of using a canned speech, were told to write their remarks ahead of time and rehearse extensively.[30]

As with so much else in the CPI, high-minded instructions that purported to enlighten the public were contradicted by guidance that emphasized manipulation. *Bulletin* after *Bulletin* stressed the importance of "facts, and facts only." Four Minute Men were told to be well informed and accurate. When it came to Liberty Loans, they needed to know payment plans and interest rates. "Sound and fury never can understudy sincerity and knowledge. Not for long may noise masquerade as force, nor fine phrases serve instead of facts." But the *Bulletin* was highly selective in the facts it recommended to speakers. Sample speeches made bald statements open to debate: for instance, "On the whole, in this national crisis, despite defects, we may say frankly and without boasting that the outstanding fact after six months is America's stupendous progress." Occasionally bulletins counseled avoiding the pretense of fact, as in this suggested opening for a speech to allay concerns about war profiteering: "I know nothing of 'Labor and Capital.' I know only honest Americans who all want to help in this great fight of the people against Kaiserism."[31]

The desire to make a sale, rather than educate, led to the advertisers' trick of stirring emotions. "We all like to think of ourselves as reasonable beings," William Ingersoll wrote when he was director of the Four Minute Men, "but nature has ordained that men are moved more by feeling than reason." A third of the campaigns had no tangible purpose other than arousing sentiment in favor of the war. When asking listeners to do something concrete, such as contribute binoculars, Four Minute Men appealed to local pride, national honor, hatred of the enemy, and self-interest. "When feeling is aroused," said a *Bulletin,* "it must be directed into the kind of action we want, buying a bond, and buying it at once." Fear needed to "be bred in the civilian populations. It is difficult to unite a people by talking only on the highest ethical plane." A sample Four Minute Man speech asked the audience to fill out a pledge form. "In the evening when the house is quiet, put down your name and the best figure you dare on the white paper. Then go upstairs and look in the crib. Then look at your blank when you come down once more."[32]

The CPI played on group dynamics to motivate and conform Four Minute Men. Those who spoke in three campaign drives received a bronze "4MM4" coat pin. Blair told Dunlap he was "part of the reserve officer corps in a nation thrice armed because through your efforts it knows better the justice of its cause and the value of what it defends." Meetings were held in which Four Minute Men critiqued each other's speeches. Chairmen monitored speakers. The Detroit unit had a seventy-five-person "checking committee." The Nashville Four Minute Men had a "secret advisory committee to visit the theaters and note the effect of speakings" as well as check that speakers did not run over the allotted time.[33]

Without surcease the point was made: "The State Chairman, Local Chairman, and Speakers are governed by standardized instructions issued by the Director in Washington."[34]

FIVE HUNDRED LOGGING CAMPS AND A POOL HALL

The Four Minute Men were well suited to conditions in the South. Tennessee was a poor state in a poor region, with a literacy rate below the national average. All Dunlap's audiences had to do was listen, provided Dunlap could reach them. The state had large cities like Memphis, whose Four Minute Men unit had vice chairmen and its own advisory committee, but also significant rural areas with spread-out populations and little infrastructure. "There are some counties in this State that have no picture show houses," Dunlap wrote Blair in March 1918, "and there are many others having picture show houses, possibly one in a county that reach such a small portion of the population that if the work should be confined to picture shows a very large and well-to-do part of our citizens would be overlooked entirely." To overcome this problem, Dunlap encouraged his chairmen to use "flying squadrons of Four Minute Men" to reach people at gatherings in agricultural sections of the state.[35]

The CPI headquarters at Jackson Place applauded this kind of initiative. Local chairmen, one of Blair's associates wrote Dunlap, did not have to confine themselves to theaters. They could send speakers to "church gatherings, school house meetings, fairs, public sales, in fact any place where a group of people congregate."[36]

Before the war was over, Four Minute Men could be found in grange halls, at picnics, under Chautauqua tents, at five hundred logging camps, and in a village pool hall in North Dakota when the lone church was "unavailable." Tennessee Four Minute Men spoke to an advertising society and workers at a plant and manned an informational booth at the state fair. American Indian Four Minute Men spoke on reservations. Four Minute Men in the Southwest spoke in Spanish. In big cities they spoke in German, Polish, Lithuanian, Magyar-Hungarian, Russian, Ukrainian, Armenian, Yiddish, and Italian.[37]

The CPI did not overlook groups whose political enfranchisement was tenuous. Curtis Nicholson, who oversaw work in the South, urged his chairmen to reach out to black communities. Dunlap did this with an African-American unit of Four Minute Men. No theaters admitted blacks in Brunswick, Georgia, so "Colored Four Minute Men" spoke at churches and lodges. Four Minute Men were almost entirely men insofar as leadership was concerned. Of the 159 local chairmen in Maine only one was identified as "Miss." But a Birmingham, Alabama, ladies' auxiliary had forty members who spoke at theater matinees and to garden clubs. Dunlap augmented his force with ladies who in addition to speaking created "War Savings societies" in stores, factories, and other women's organizations. Boys and girls gave four-minute talks in Nashville schools, as well as at a meeting of the Anti-Cigarette League Federation.[38]

"From all parts of the country," Blair said, "we would receive wires begging us to give up our national campaign for a few nights in order that our organization might be used to further some local campaign, but we were obliged, of course, to adhere to the plan of national campaigns only." Perhaps Blair was unaware of some local efforts with local aims, such as the St. Louis Health Department's use of Four Minute Men to advise citizens on ways to avoid influenza. When it came to carrying out the national plan, however, Blair combined regulation with flexibility. Daniel Roper, who was appointed commissioner of the Internal Revenue Service after helping elect Wilson, wanted to discourage tax dodging every way he could. The Four Minute Men agreed to speak on this theme at forums he arranged through Chambers of Commerce and other organizations.[39]

Blair transformed promising local initiatives into national ones with the same enthusiasm Creel embraced Ryerson's initial proposal. In early 1918, the Four Minute Men of Minnesota sponsored a contest in which students prepared speeches on "War Savings Stamps." This led to the creation of the Junior Four Minute Men. Special bulletins designed for them recommended that the junior orators advise younger children to earn extra money in order to buy war bonds and to urge their parents to "lend to the limit to their Government." When states ran competitions, instructions said, the judges should be the mayor, the school board superintendent, and other prominent local figures. Boys and girls were eligible to compete. "It practically meant doubling the organization," Blair said, "and at a time when it was almost impossible to get clerks at any price."[40]

Colleges were not left out. Like sociology, speech was becoming a discipline with its own departments, journals, and professional associations—and its own progressive aspirations. The war offered an occasion for public speaking to "serve the collective ideal," University of Iowa professor Glenn N. Merry told a convention of fellow speech teachers. While professors like Merry and Solomon Clark were active off campus helping the CPI, others started Four Minute Men programs on campuses in forty-four states. "The war has given us both the impulse and the opportunity to break through traditional limitations," Vassar professor Mary Yost said. Her students spoke for the fourth Liberty Loan in dining halls and on soapboxes during noon recess. Later they left campus to speak to public school students, the Red Cross, and the Duchess County Health Association.[41]

There were other spin-offs. Theodore Roosevelt and baseball star Honus Wagner were Four Minute Men, if only for a speech or two. Actors Mary Pickford and William S. Hart took four-minute turns. At the request of the War Department, army Four Minute Men instructed troops on the causes of the war. Wounded veterans made up a special Men from the Front Division in New York. New Mexico had fifteen hundred Motor Four Minute Men who drove speakers and musicians to far-flung corners of the state. In the fall of 1918, Four Minute Singing began because, Creel said, "People seemed to want to exercise their voices in moments of patriotism." The Four Minute Men Division filled special bulletins with advice for these groups. Songs had to be secular and easy to follow, such as "Dixie" and "When Johnny Comes Marching Home." "It will be well to warn the musician *not to use too slow time.*" Slides with the songs' words helped the audience sing along.[42]

The Four Minute Men gave the CPI a nationwide network of its own. Local offices became distribution centers for CPI and other government pamphlets. Speakers were encouraged to pressure retailers to incorporate a pitch for Liberty Loans in their advertisements. When the military found itself short of walnut needed for gun stocks and airplane propellers, Four Minute Men identified trees of the right size and convinced owners to part with them. Four Minute Men were coordinated for greater impact. Some thirty-five thousand Four Minute Men delivered, verbatim, Wilson's 1918 Fourth of July "message." They could be mobilized quickly, as when Blair got the word on July 9 to honor the French five days later on Bastille Day 1918. By the next evening, a *Bulletin* outlining the special program was in the mail. It provided a speech and a resolution of support for France that was to be adopted by each audience.[43]

Blair jealously guarded the Four Minute Men brand. The name was copyrighted as was its logo, 4 FOUR MINUTE 4. But as the the Four Minute Men grew into a wartime fad, he could not prevent unauthorized imitation. One

Sunday the New Orleans Four Minute Men were given a rest, and "half minute" Boy Scouts spoke in their place. Three women's groups associated with the state Councils of National Defense appropriated the Four Minute Men concept—the Four Minute Speakers in Boston, the Three Minute Women in New Jersey, the Fourteen Minute Women in Indiana. Blair stopped the Boston group and convinced the New Jersey one to confine itself to nontheater venues. The statewide Indiana initiative was 850 strong by mid-1918. Meanwhile, Canada deployed Five Minute Men, and Prime Minister Lloyd George wrote a four-minute message that was read simultaneously in British concert halls, cinemas, and theaters.[44]

Among the seemingly endless variations on the Four Minute Men theme was a contest in Illinois for the best speech on "The Part of the Four-Minute Men in the War." The winner, among the 128 submissions, was Fred A. Wirth of Chicago. It read in part: "I wield the most potent power of Human Endeavor—THE SPOKEN WORD. The Blind do not read—the Ignorant cannot read—the Dullard will not read—but ALL MEN must harken to my message."[45]

ARTHUR BESTOR'S SPEAKING DIVISION

The CPI was not alone in taking the spoken word to Americans. Shortly after America entered the war, more than a dozen federal departments vied with scores of independent organizations in Washington and the states for speaking venues. These bodies were as small as the Army Ordnance Department, which put half a dozen people in the field, and as large as the League to Enforce Peace, six hundred speakers strong. The question naturally arose, How could this cacophony be brought to useful harmony?[46]

An attempt to gain some control followed a meeting of representatives from the Council of National Defense, the Treasury Department, the Food Administration, and the CPI. The group, no doubt with orchestration from Creel, wrote to him on September 6. It recommended that he ask President Wilson to create "A Coordinating Committee on Speakers Bureaus" to be headed by Arthur E. Bestor, president of the Chautauqua Institution. On September 25 Wilson endorsed the concept of a Speaking Division under Bestor in the CPI.[47]

The Chautauqua was the nation's foremost speaking institution. Created in 1874 for out-of-school learning and spiritual renewal, it gathered people at its headquarters on Chautauqua Lake and dispatched speakers across the country. When war came, it threw its patriotic voice into the fray. A balding, slightly pudgy man, Bestor headed the Lecturers and Speakers Division of the US Food Administration. He thought of public opinion as Edward Alsworth Ross did. Paternalistic tutoring was needed to mature the public's crude understanding. "America entered the war chiefly on account of the belief of its intelligent classes," Bestor told an audience at the elite City Club of Chicago. "In a war for which the intellectual group was so largely responsible, the educated people of the country must see to it that America keeps steadfast to its job."[48]

Bestor's CPI division operated with and through a large number of groups. Its Advisory Committee alone represented two dozen organizations whose missions were as varied as the Department of Agriculture, the Commission on Training Camp Activities, the League to Enforce Peace, the Knights of Columbus, and the Association of College Alumnae. The division quickly became more than a clearinghouse. It paired speakers with communities that wanted them and arranged itineraries to move them from one city to another. Bestor had a list of ten thousand people for this purpose.[49]

The variety of speaking tours was wide. Long trips were arranged for Charles Edward Russell, Wesley Frost (an American consular officer who helped survivors of the *Lusitania*), Jane Addams (who promoted food conservation, not the war per se), cabinet secretaries, and other high-value speakers. On an even larger scale, the division organized tours for entire groups that could ignite patriotic sentiments, such as the fifty soldier-speakers General Pershing sent to the United States in spring 1918. It supported war conferences organized by the CPI and the CND. In addition, the Speaking Division did its best to coordinate speaking programs conducted by federal and government-affiliated agencies, by the British War Mission, French High Commission, Belgium Legation, and Italian Embassy, and by a conglomeration of others typified by the National Cash Register Company's speaking teams, which went into communities to give an illustrated lecture, "Wake Up America!"[50]

Coordination required patience, flexibility, and hard work. Schedule changes were constant. Individual speaking opportunities had to be found for Pershing's fifty soldiers, who appeared in forty-three states. An army private gave thirty speeches in factories, schools, shipyards, and meeting halls in Connecticut during a two-week period in May. Three enlisted men spoke in thirty-two of Iowa's ninety-nine counties over a two-month period. Parades and crowds greeted them. They traveled by train and auto. The schedule had to be changed when heavy rains washed out roads. Because the War Department refused to make any arrangements, the CPI organized the tour of 105 heavily decorated French chasseurs alpins. They visited ten military camps and twenty cities. The "Blue Devils" arrived in Nashville on the 6:35 a.m. "sleeper" and left that night at ten o'clock. Porter Dunlap coordinated meetings, meals, and a parade, which seemed to bring out the entire city. Marching with the French soldiers was a long line of military and civic organizations, including sixty-four Four Minute Men, who sang "We'll Hang Kaiser Bill on a Sour Apple Tree."[51]

Bestor piggybacked on the Council of National Defense. Its director, Walter S. Gifford, had been the American Bell Telephone Company's chief statistician, had a spartan office with bare walls, and believed "that everything should proceed in an orderly fashion rather than in a confused, chaotic fashion." By early October 1917, the CND had sixteen state speakers' bureaus and seven more in gestation. Very much like Blair, Bestor operated with a carefully thought-out strategy. The council's bureaus were to assess speaking needs in the state, after which they organized a two-day war conference. The purpose of the state conferences was to energize local citizens "to carry the message to every schoolhouse and crossroads community." With great promotional fanfare, in order to attract a large crowd, a public meeting was held the first evening. The Speaking Division supplied inspirational speakers with national standing and experience in the war. Other sessions informed potential speakers about food conservation, Liberty Loans, and other war programs.[52]

These conferences were often the largest regional public meetings held during the war and were successful in sending the intended ripples across the state. After a war conference in Tennessee, Dunlap's Four Minute Men "developed with remarkable strength and efficiency." Tomlinson Hall overflowed with people on the first night of the Indianapolis war conference. Among the attractions was a 250-piece band directed by John Philip Sousa. A Missouri war conference was held in January 1918 in Columbia, home of the state's major university. It attracted three thousand people. The Food Administration and the CPI provided speakers for eighty subsequent meetings across the state. "We are daily arranging to send speakers to other mass meetings," Bestor was informed in early April. A German Speakers' Bureau was set up to reach the state's large immigrant population.[53]

The Speaking Division did not regulate what speakers said as assiduously as the Four Minute Men did. George Porter, who oversaw CND state programs, thought that "would be getting too far into the Prussian methods we are fighting against." This was practical as well as high-minded. Distinguished speakers expected to speak as they saw fit. But the division brought discipline to bear where it could. Porter wanted to provide a steady supply of materials that resembled "speakers' handbooks of the political campaigns." An organization created by Bestor sought to "collect, catalog and grade patriot citizens of the state" willing to be speakers. He sent out a checklist, "Helpful Hints in Arranging a Patriotic Rally": select an influential chairman, arrange music, decorate with American flags, and so forth down to "Open the meeting with a prayer by some prominent Protestant minister or Catholic priest." Concerned some groups might promote peace without victory, the Advisory Committee conditioned its cooperation with them on each organization pledging that "the winning of this war is its primary concern."[54]

Detailed instructions accompanied Pershing's soldier-speakers. The CPI told hosts to send an accomplished civilian speaker to accompany each soldier, as he was "not an orator." Mistakes, whether in a soldier's behavior or in his speeches, were to be corrected. "He has been informed that you are his Commanding Officer when he is in your state." Bestor complained that whoever selected soldiers on the basis of their speaking ability "needed some coaching himself." In a few instances soldier-speakers blotted the group's record. A Corporal Plant became drunk in Harrisburg and used "such bad language the meeting was adjourned." Still, the overall result was impressive considering Pershing's men addressed an estimated twenty-five hundred audiences numbering between two and three million people.[55]

In September 1918, Creel consolidated the Four Minute Men and the Speaking Division, under William Ingersoll, who took over for Blair. The merger coincided with CPI budget cuts, a development addressed in a later chapter, but the Council of National Defense saw a nefarious hidden agenda. It believed Creel did not value the Speaking Division or Bestor, who had returned to Chautauqua for the summer. "It is an open secret that Mr. Bestor will not come back to head the Division unless he can have some freedom in developing it," said Frederick Lewis Allen, who believed their work "would just die" unless the council took over the division.[56]

Allen had to reconcile himself to Creel's reorganization. When Bestor did not return, his deputy, Indiana University professor John J. Pettijohn, assumed his duties as associate director in the new merged division. He worked well with the CND. The merger brought useful economies. The Speaking Division, which had issued its own bulletins, used Four Minute Men materials. In ten states, Allen acknowledged, "the Four Minute Men and the State Speakers' Bureau are virtually the same. . . . In over thirty states they are separate although associated." State and local consolidation increased after the Washington merger, although Dunlap's operation seems to have remained separate.[57]

The Speaking Division had plenty to boast about in the end. The war conferences were a joint undertaking conceived by the division and the CND. Shortly before the war ended, Allen reckoned fifty-one war conferences had been held in forty-seven states. This was a rare occasion in which Creel offered lower, albeit still significant, figures—forty-five conferences in thirty-seven states. The conferences sparked state councils to carry out county conferences. The division cost little, as expenses were mostly borne by the states. It sought to impose discipline without sacrificing opportunities that went beyond its original mandate. On one occasion it organized a tour in which American and British pilots flew warplanes and made speeches in fourteen midwestern cities. This entailed arranging events and engineering advance publicity to ensure a good turnout.[58]

O'Higgins considered the Speaking Division "a whooping success" because of the effective advertising of events and the oratorical prowess of many speakers. When Russell spoke in Manitowoc, Wisconsin, the audience was so uplifted that the local Council of Defense sent a stenographer with him to his next stop, Fond du Lac, to take down his words, which they had printed for wide distribution. One of the biggest draws was French Catholic priest Lieutenant Paul Périgord. The Speaking Division had him on the road for nearly eight grueling months. Highly opinionated Harold Ickes, who was handling propaganda for the Illinois Council of Defense, considered him "one of the most effective speakers that has appeared on the American platform on any subject connected with the war." If the inspirational "warrior-priest" was in a class by himself, as Creel claimed, hundreds of other American, British, and French speakers left indelible impressions in communities they visited. The appearance of the Blue Devils, parading in dark blue uniforms, black berets, and black spiral puttees, was considered a historic event in Nashville.[59]

SOCIAL MEDIA BEFORE SOCIAL MEDIA EXISTED

Porter Dunlap's highly regarded geniality was constantly tested. When he asked an attorney in Lafayette, Tennessee, to become a local chairman, the lawyer said he was too busy heading the Liberty Loan Committee. "Really I doubt if there is a man here who would be sufficiently interested in this phase of war work to take the lead."[60]

Apart from federal postal franking privileges, which only a third of the state and local chairmen enjoyed, direct federal financial support did not exist. When Dunlap complained about the lack of money, Curtis Nicholson advised him to go to the state Council of National Defense, as Four Minute Men in a few other states had done. Nicholson, who oversaw the southern region, felt certain Dunlap would receive "a liberal allowance for use in sending travelling representatives through the State for organization purposes, defraying the expense of telegrams, letter-heads, stenographic service, clerical service, or keeping records and punching up local chairmen &c." The state council, which did not have state government support, turned him down. Dunlap relied on state treasury staff for clerical support, personally contributed $250 toward expenses, and asked each local chairman for one dollar. One unit assessed its speakers five dollars. Tennessee's money woes were not unique. In its first year of operation, the Colorado Four Minute Men received nothing more than a filing cabinet, some stationery with letterheads, and sixty two-cent stamps.[61]

Despite the insistence on limiting talks to four minutes, a member of the Iowa Council of Defense complained that many speakers considered "themselves Forty-minute-men." A speaker in Kentucky went on for twenty-one minutes. When the lights were finally turned out to shut him up, he claimed the owner was pro-German and did not want him to speak. The audience, Creel was informed, "proceeded to tear up chairs and destroy the furniture in the entire theater."[62]

Nor did everything go according to plan. One speaker felt "unwelcome until that sweet little gal [in the movie] got her lover back." S. C. Purvis, a resident of New Verda, Louisiana, did nothing on one campaign because "farmers [were] busy with cotton." J. A. Farrow in Anson, Texas, did not speak because he "rec'd no literature." With a holdup in the mail to Candle, Alaska, bulletins did not arrive until the campaign for which they were intended was completed. The biggest disruption was the flu epidemic, which sickened a quarter of the population. In the last months of the war, churches, schools, and movies theaters, all places Four Minute Men held forth, were closed. Many of the records kept on speakers had as their last entry the stamp "STOPPED BY INFLUENZA."[63]

Yet Dunlap had tangible success. In 1918 the *Tennessean,* the leading morning newspaper in Dunlap's home state, routinely announced that a dozen or more speakers would appear that day at the Bijou, Dixie, Peafowl, and other theaters. As of that May, Four Minute Men groups existed in all but ten of Tennessee's ninety-six counties. Those ten were in the sparsely populated mountains, and he expected to have them organized in a week to ten days. For the third Liberty Loan drive, just completed, more than seven hundred Four Minute Men in forty-six counties gave 1,389 speeches in ninety-nine theaters, reaching 556,807 people. In addition, 999 speeches were made in other venues, reaching another 210,052 people. By that reckoning, Four Minute Men had reached more than one-third of the state's population, and not all speakers' reports had yet come in.[64]

Consistent with its determination to maintain control, the Four Minute Men Division kept detailed statistics. Some of this data survives on five-by-eight-inch cards filed in long, rectangular boxes in the National Archives. Individual cards recorded the number of talks a Four Minute Man delivered and estimated audience sizes. Audience size, no doubt, was often inflated by zealous speakers. Washington had to make best guesses for gaps in field reports. Even discounting totals by 10 or 20 percent, however, they are striking. At the end of the war 74,500 Four Minute Men were supervised by 7,499 chairmen. A third had been through three or more campaigns. They delivered 755,190 speeches to audiences totaling 314,454,514. This statistic is best understood in the context of the total population in 1918, 103 million people, of whom about two-thirds were twenty-one years or older. The average adult heard about half a dozen Four Minute Men.[65]

If Four Minute Men were not in every hamlet, they were in many towns the size of Dupree, South Dakota, population 213, as well as Guam, Hawaii, the Canal Zone, and Puerto Rico. If some Four Minute Men spoke once or twice, there were others like C. F. Sugg in Tennessee. Although he did not begin until April 1918, he delivered 115 speeches in theaters and 196 in other settings. A Montana woman rode ten miles by horse to give a single talk; an Oregon unit made a five-day trip into the mountains. Junior Minute Men were in 200,000 schools and College Four Minute Men in 217 institutions, despite the program having begun in September 1918. From its early days in a basement, the Four Minute Men Division grew to a staff of forty spread over the entire third floor of both 8 and 10 Jackson Place, as well as in first floor rooms. Thanks to the use of volunteers and to states picking up many of the costs, the total CPI expenditures for the Four Minute Men totaled only $101,555.10.[66]

The patriotism aroused by CPI speakers cannot be measured precisely. But we learn a lot from a New Mexico report that eight in an audience of twelve in a poor Mexican precinct bought bonds. "We are getting similar results over a considerable part of the State," the chairman said. Vassar speakers raised $182,000 and sent more than twenty-five thousand items, such as clothes they knitted,

overseas. Early in its existence, Four Minute Men in Chicago responded to a
request from the Seventh Federal Reserve District for help to promote the first
Liberty Loan and spoke at least once in every one of the 478 local theaters. Four
Minute Men accounted for three-quarters of the 110,000 people who orated
in support of the fourth Liberty Loan campaign. In their campaign soliciting
binoculars, telescopes, and sextants, Four Minute Men supplied 23,852 out of
36,695 donations, according to Franklin Roosevelt, assistant secretary of the
navy. Nashville's Four Minute Men accounted for five hundred of the contributions.[67]

Ryerson's inspiration, Blair's flair for administration, and Creel's frustration
with the press revolutionized political communication. It was not novel to use
scripted speakers to propagandize a cause. The Anti-Saloon League did this to
promote prohibition. But the Four Minute Men, a much larger undertaking,
marked the first time the government employed the top-down structure used
by political parties to reach citizens directly with disciplined propaganda messages.[68]

After the war, radio provided a new communication tool to achieve the
same end. In the 1928 presidential campaign, the Republicans created "National
Hoover Minute Men" to deliver coordinated messages on local stations. When
Franklin Roosevelt became president, he went a step further by reaching citizens with his fireside chats, although audiences had to "find" him on their radio
sets. No one had to seek out the Four Minute Men. Like modern social media
notices that pop up on cellphones and Facebook without a prompt, the Four
Minute Men delivered sound bites to captive audiences.[69]

In his first days at the CPI, Creel devised a system to hand-feed journalists. With equal effectiveness he went over their heads to reach the public directly with speakers. "The Four Minute Men," the *Tennessean* proclaimed, "have
proved one of the best means of reaching the public with information about the
national defense."[70]

Creel, however, was not finished. With equal energy, the CPI opened spig-
ots of information that had recently become available and flooded America
with messages the administration wanted to send.

6

You've Got to Change Their Environment

It was a fight for the *minds* of men, for the "conquest of their convictions,"
and the battle-line ran through every home in every country.

—George Creel

One evening, in the fall of 1917, at a dinner party given by the French High
Commission, the Marquis Crequi Montfort de Courtivron told Creel a heart-
warming story. The Marquis's wife was the daughter of a French general who
fought for the Confederacy. On his deathbed, he asked her "to return his sword
to Virginia." Creel saw an opportunity for a media event and told Arthur Bestor
to orchestrate it.

The sword presentation in the Virginia House of Delegates anchored luncheons, receptions, and a mass meeting in the Richmond Auditorium. Building
further on the splendid opportunity, Bestor organized a French tour of the
South. As an explorer and member of the French Olympic shooting team, the
marquis was a celebrity. Adding luster to the entourage was high commissioner
Marquis de Polignac and his wife, an American socialite he had married days before. The CPI sent along one of its most compelling speakers, Charles Edward
Russell. Russell spoke twelve times in New Orleans, the last stop on the tour.[1]

Ernest Poole wryly observed that only one news-making opportunity "escaped the searchlights that we threw." It involved a more famous sword. A group
of ladies in Mount Vernon arranged to pull George Washington's from its scab-
bard, an act the first president had said should occur only in defense of the
country. "And Creel never knew!" Poole recounted. "With hordes of reporters
and cameramen giving that picture to the world, ye Gods, what couldn't we
have made of that simple little ceremony?"[2]

Creel and his staff routinely turned simple ceremonies into media events.
When a theater publicist suggested holding a July Fourth Loyalty Day in which
the foreign-born could show their patriotism, the CPI staged a grand celebra-

tion at Mount Vernon designed to reach millions. "We who promoted this piece of 'made' news had our eyes not so much on the main performance as on innumerable side shows," said Will Irwin, a distinguished war correspondent who had joined the CPI. When President Wilson spoke at Washington's tomb, a perceptive observer noted, he "did not trouble to raise his voice: He was speaking for the foreign diplomats, for publication, for cable transmission." Parades were held in towns and cities across the country, many of which were filmed for replay later.[3]

The CPI marinated citizens in government messages. It latched on to every propaganda vehicle available. In May 1918, Carl Byoir, one of Creel's associate chairmen, boasted the CPI had "some thirty branches, numbering over 250 men and women, efficiently organized to inform the American public of any war activity." In support of the YMCA's war efforts, Byoir offered "the organized services of ten divisions." At the New York premiere of the CPI movie *America's Answer to the Hun* in the George M. Cohan Theatre, he said the CPI used "every process of stimulation."[4]

Creel thought about the "process of stimulation" the way he thought about cleaning up Denver's red-light district. He moved prostitutes to a tax-supported rehabilitation farm devoid of liquor, mirrors, and player pianos. It was a matter of social engineering. "You can't make people good by law," he told an interviewer. "You've got to get down to causes. You've got to change their environment." Three processes of stimulation offered especially enticing possibilities for changing the environment in wartime America: advertising, motion pictures, and schools.[5]

SPIELING

In July 1918, Carl Byoir wrote to the editor of *Printers' Ink,* the first national trade organ of the advertising profession. "In a sense," he said, "the whole work of the Committee is in the last analysis simply a tremendous world advertising job."[6]

CPI staff often talked in these terms. Creel's history of the CPI carried the title *How We Advertised the War.* He called the committee "a vast enterprise in salesmanship, the world's greatest adventure in advertising." Bestor's instructions for organizing war rallies emphasized, "Plenty of advertising and publicity are absolutely essential." William Ingersoll, who headed the Four Minute Men after Blair left, considered their speeches ads, not oratorical discourse.[7]

Ingersoll was one of many advertising executives Creel employed in some fashion. The CPI also drew from a sister profession that fell into the loose category of press agent and publicist. Bestor borrowed the services of the publicity director of the Redpath Lyceum Bureau in Chicago, Frank McClure. William Wolff Smith, possibly the first government-oriented publicist, was a Four Minute Man in Washington. Smith, a newspaperman, opened his doors in 1902 and roamed the halls of the Capitol and the Willard Hotel lobby, all while reporting on the side. During the war, he was an assistant to the third assistant secretary of war. The idea for the July Fourth Loyalty Day came from Harry Reichenbach, a suave press agent who smoked small cigars and was renowned for kidnapping actresses and other contrived sensations to promote movies. Reichenbach claimed that during a newspaper stint in Uruguay his editorials led to the paper's editor being elected president. Reichenbach called himself a "spieler." Two recruits to the CPI in particular would be remembered as the Thomas Edisons of public relations, as the profession eventually became known.[8]

One of these was twenty-four-year-old Edward Bernays, who was hired for overseas propaganda after flat feet and poor vision kept him out of the military. Austrian-born Bernays, the nephew of Sigmund Freud, had made a small name for himself as a theater press agent. In a promotional stunt that took advantage of the sexual triggers that intrigued his uncle, Bernays draped a ballerina with a limp harmless snake he described as a cobra tamed by her beauty. Already Bernays had displayed his lifelong penchant for promoting promotion. In a 1917 article, he extolled the social value of musical press agents. At the CPI he came up with the idea of naming a ship the *Piave,* after the Italian river by that name, and launching it ceremoniously as a hands-across-the-sea gesture. Ernest Poole considered Bernays "one of the ablest and most devoted young workers on our staff."[9]

Carl Byoir, twenty-eight when he joined the staff, was the other public relations pioneer. Born in Iowa to Jewish immigrants from Poland, he became managing editor of the *Waterloo Times-Tribune* shortly after graduating from high school. The paper was owned by Wilbur Marsh, a wealthy manufacturer of cream separators and treasurer of the Democratic National Committee during the 1916 presidential race. Byoir afterward earned a Columbia University law degree, made a small fortune with the US sales franchise for the kindergarten program created by Italian Maria Montessori, and promoted *Cosmopolitan* so successfully he became circulation manager of all Hearst's magazines. When the Government Printing Office could not keep up with the CPI's needs, he was brought in to solve the problem. Byoir lined up New York printers who had downtime due to seasonal work on mail order catalogs and were willing to charge less than the GPO. Byoir stayed on as associate chairman, shouldering so many problem-solving duties he was known as the "multiple director." [10]

Initially the CPI's associations with the advertising profession were episodic and reactive rather than systematic and planned. Not until the end of 1917 did it develop a formal relationship. As was the case with the creation of the Speakers Division, the need to bring order to dysfunctional chaos drove the decision.

Before the war, advertising executives promoted preparedness, anticipating even greater possibilities ahead. "Ever since England made such important use of advertising in her war need," wrote *Advertising & Selling* in March 1916, "there has been no doubt in the minds of advertising men in this world-leading country of advertising that if war ever comes to the US advertising men would of necessity be drafted for a national service of even greater extent and importance than in England." By the time war was declared, a National Advertising Advisory Board had formed to work on Liberty Loans and other campaigns. [11]

Patriotism and self-interest motivated advertisers. They could rally the country and simultaneously burnish their image, which in many minds was associated with the wildly extravagant claims made for shady patent medicines. Some bankers refused to loan money to businesses that planned to use the money for advertisements. "Advertising has a thousand principles, one purpose, and no morals," the CPI's Samuel Hopkins Adams wrote in *Collier's* in 1909. Creel referred to Adams's landmark muckraking in his own crusading on patent medicine. Reputable companies realized they could sell more if the advertising profession was credible. At the urging of Samuel C. Dobbs, Coca-Cola's sales manager and president of the Associated Advertising Clubs of America, more than a hundred affiliated clubs endorsed the slogan "Truth in Advertising." The war was an opportunity to go further with a demonstration of highly visible public service. [12]

The war also provided an opportunity to demonstrate the powers of mass persuasion. Print ads, once small and drab, had become colorful, artistic, and large. In James Williams's *Boston Evening Transcript,* the average size of ads ballooned from four column inches in the 1870s to sixteen inches in 1918. Window fronts in department stores glimmered. L. Frank Baum, remembered today as author of *The Wonderful Wizard of Oz,* wrote a manual and published the magazine the *Show Window* to instruct business on bringing "goods out in a blaze of glory." Outdoor advertising was no longer plastered only on walls. Framed,

free-standing billboards, an American invention, increased apace with the number of automobiles and the many miles of newly paved roads.[13]

In its galloping enthusiasm to help the government, the advertising community diluted its efforts. This was not only a matter of individual agencies
competing to assert their patriotism. In a mania of professionalization, a large
number of national advertising associations had emerged, and each sought a
role. More than two hundred trade journals, which hoped to copy the success
of *Printers' Ink,* had their own points of view. The National Advertising Advisory Board was of limited help in bringing order. It had no power to rationalize
the use of ad space donated to the government by business and publishers or to
coordinate the services that advertising agencies volunteered to fill that space
on behalf of one government department or another.[14]

While the government wanted help, it did not want to pay for it. Advertising executives argued against this, sensibly, by noting that the government paid
manufacturers for bullets and uniforms, so why not pay for advertising? Besides being fair, advertisers argued, it was more efficient to purchase space where
and when it was most needed rather than relying on whatever contributions
came in. The French and British governments paid for advertising to sell war
bonds. The advertisers had the support of Woolley, who headed publicity for
the first Liberty Loan drive, but not of his boss, Treasury Secretary McAdoo.
McAdoo contended that if the government paid, it would have to place ads "in
every newspaper and periodical in America without discrimination," lest it be
charged with favoritism, and this would be too costly. Congress stood with him.
In September 1917, the House overwhelmingly voted down a proposal to pay for
ads. Opponents argued the press should pitch in because it enjoyed subsidized
postal rates and said advertising agencies had "simply joined the vultures that
hover over this Capitol."[15]

The catalyst for reducing "the waste and confusion" of uncoordinated campaigns came in a meeting of advertising executives in New York on November
15, 1917. Eula McClary, a young progressive publicist whom Creel considered
the "soul of enthusiasm," proposed advertisers include patriotic messages in
every one of their ads during the month of March. "The advertisers who write
copy or sell space," she told the group, "can sell the war to Americans just as truly
as they can sell soap, chewing gum, phonographs or edibles. The war must be
sold to our people if democracy is to be saved." One executive at the meeting
seized on the idea of doing even more. Learning that McClary knew Creel, he
encouraged her to approach him about creating a bureau with which they could

cooperate. The next day she returned with Creel's problem solver, Carl Byoir.[16]

Byoir met with advertising associations, eight of which thrust their hands in the air to offer help. The message to them, as Creel insisted, was "all of you, meeting together, determine the manner of your association." Byoir reiterated the point at the annual dinner of the Association of National Advertisers on December 5. The event was a spectacular display of support for working with the CPI. Surrounded by Allies' flags, the nearly two hundred attendees sang the Marseillaise in honor of the editor of *Le Matin,* one of the speakers. The ANA endorsed Eula McClary's proposal for patriotic advertising and created an advisory board to help the government. Byoir stepped up to praise McClary and insisted the government "was not inclined to assume any leadership in enlisting the advertising forces of the country in the war's cause."[17]

At a December 20 meeting with Creel, a definite plan took shape. Five directors, as he spelled out in a summary of the meeting, would "constitute the sole and authoritative medium of contact between the government and the Advertising industries of the United States. Your work, for the moment, is to be a clearinghouse of all advertising aid offered to the Government. For the present it will be my own task to secure the cooperation of all other departments of Government." Byoir, he said, would represent him in all decisions.[18]

Rivalries continued. Two associations vied for credit for the creation of the CPI's Division of Advertising—the ANA and the Associated Advertising Clubs of the World (formerly the Associated Advertising Clubs of America). Two influential Chicagoans, "billboard baron" Thomas Cusack and William H. Rankin, head of an advertising agency under his name, complained New Yorkers dominated the division. Disagreement about the direction of planning worried Eula McClary to the point she told Byoir she was "quite all broken up over the whole advertising scheme."[19]

Creel had to assuage McAdoo, who was troubled that CPI ad campaigns would divert attention from Liberty Loans. The treasury secretary had little to fear. The CPI made his Liberty Loan campaigns a priority. The Advertising Division supplied national magazine copy, with high-quality illustrations and "certain" space for ads; the twelve Federal Reserve boards handled local advertising; the Liberty Loan publicity bureau in Washington handled billboard campaigns. CPI artists drew powerful posters. The CPI's Four Minute Men took up the campaigns in movie theaters.[20]

The division was in de facto operation by early January and itching for formal recognition. This came from President Wilson on January 20, 1918, when he established the division as "purely a service organization." Thinking in grand terms, Creel informed McAdoo and other senior administration officials, "It is my idea that every advertisement that appears in newspapers and periodicals should have part of the space devoted to a war object."[21]

The division's board was a who's who of modern advertising. The chairman was William H. Johns, a founder of the George Batten Advertising Agency and president of the American Association of Advertising Agencies (AAAA), which represented 115 firms. William D'Arcy, owner of a St. Louis advertising agency, and Herbert S. Houston of the publishing firm Doubleday, Page and Company were president and past president, respectively, of the Associated Advertising Clubs of the World. Lewis Jones, advertising manager for Eastman Kodak, was president of the ANA. He described himself as a "former conductor of propaganda shows." As a result of intense lobbying, Thomas Cusack, with his access to billboards, was added as was Jesse Neal, executive secretary of the Associated Business Papers, which represented five hundred publications. All board members were dollar-a-year men. With the creation of the division, the National Advertising Advisory Board was disbanded. (Eula McClary, who had led the way, went on to become publicity agent for the New York mayor's Committee of National Defense.)[22]

"The advertising agencies are to be put to the test," the AAAA told its members. "This is the golden opportunity of proving to the Government at Washington and to the people of the United States the value of advertising." With advertising's customary enthusiasm for celebration, the AAAA gave a dinner at the Aldine Club, on Fifth Avenue, to show its "appreciation of the wisdom of the Government in creating the Division of Advertising."[23]

A government restriction barred the division from soliciting donations of advertising space. The way around this was to have the asking done by third parties with whom division staff were affiliated or through hints such as this one to a potential donor: "Several advertising committees, in no way connected with this organization, have suggested to various parties that it would be a patriotic thing to contribute space to the Division of Advertising."[24]

Despite his initial reservations, Creel wanted to receive donations only from businesses. They could insert government advertising inside their own ads or buy space and turn it over to the division (giving themselves a credit line if they wished). He adamantly opposed asking newspapers for contributions "unless we ask the packers and steel manufacturers" to give away their products. "You are mistaken if you assume that we are going to ask the newspapers of the country for any free advertising space," Creel told the editor of a newspaper trade journal. "This is not my idea, nor will it be done. The advertisers of the United States organized themselves of their own volition. . . . Their principal endeavor, as I understand it, will be in the direction of influencing the advertisers, not the newspapers."[25]

Within a few days of the division's creation, however, it was accepting editors' gifts. Donations of space, Johns said, "are being rained in on us. . . . We have already on our books nearly half a million dollars' worth of magazine and trade paper space." While some publications continued to object, others expressed dismay when their offers were not quickly accepted. "Do you not think under these circumstances that The Detroit News should be used for any publicity with which you wish to cover this field?" its ad manager asked. By the time the war ended, more than eight hundred publications had donated space.[26]

The Division of Advertising was located in New York, in offices adjoining those of the AAAA in the Metropolitan Life Insurance Tower. From that vantage point in the capital of American advertising, the division functioned, as Johns explained it, as a "national advertising agency," helping government "departments, just as the modern advertising agent helps the advertising departments of his clients." It met with representatives of various government "clients" to understand their needs, created committees in which ad agencies handled campaigns, and administered donated space. The board met as often as twice a week, and Johns devoted more than half his day to division work.[27]

The division's distance from Washington gave it independence, an image Creel fostered in order to shield the CPI from advertisers' complaints, but he did not want the division to have absolute independence. He required routine reports. Byoir, with the help of a former employee in Rankin's Chicago firm, Carl Walberg, routinely supplied ideas and reviewed work. When a couple of sloppy advertisements went out, Byoir had a quick apology from "Blue Pencil" Lewis Jones, known for his careful editing. "My blue pencil," he wrote, "has now done some work on that copy."[28]

The division collaborated with CPI artists. The enlistment of artists was one of Creel's first initiatives. His second day on the job, he telegraphed artist Charles Dana Gibson, asking him to recruit artists for "important national service." The telegram reached Gibson while he was discussing possible war work at a meeting of the Society of Illustrators. The following Sunday the two men met in New York. Gibson agreed to head a Society of Illustrators subcommittee for "Pictorial Publicity." The loosely organized society proved disappointing. Some of its output, Creel told Gibson late in the summer of 1917, was "hopelessly bad, much of it mediocre."[29]

Gibson remedied this, and that November the CPI established a Division of Pictorial Publicity, in time to work with the new Advertising Division. Its office was also in New York City, at 200 Fifth Avenue. Creel insisted the artists donate their time as advertising executives did theirs. The division, Gibson said, was "the greatest chance the artists of the country have ever had to help win the war." He likened the work to what British artists were doing to sell war bonds.[30]

Gibson was considered the highest paid illustrator up to that time. His "Gibson Girls," elegant beauties with thin waists, ample bosoms, and profuse hair piled high, chignon style, were iconic. Handsome as the square-jawed men that he depicted in his art, Gibson was a commanding personality. He gathered distinguished associate chairmen around him: Herbert Adams, president of the National Academy of Design; Cass Gilbert, former president of the Architectural League; and E. H. Blashfield, former president of the Society of American Artists. He drew on great artists—George Bellows; N. C. Wyeth; James Montgomery Flagg, who created the iconic "I Want You" recruiting poster with a stern Uncle Sam pointing at the viewer (inspired by a British poster showing Lord Kitchener in a similar pose); and Joseph Leyendecker, creator of Arrow Collar Man advertisements.

Gibson, like Johns, treated government agencies as clients. Every Friday he presided over a gathering of artists that was part salon and part workshop. On any given night a guest could be an esteemed admiral, a Russian prince, a returned war correspondent, or a shipping tycoon—who held forth inspiringly on some aspect of the war. An "official emissary" from Washington was on hand to outline the visual propaganda a particular department needed. Afterward, the assemblage adjourned to Keene's Chop House and, when they outgrew that watering hole, the Greenwich Village brownstone that housed the arts-oriented Salmagundi Club. Attendance was usually large. For each request, a "captain" was named to select an artist, review the sketch, and coordinate government approval. To include artists outside New York, a Western Committee was set up in Chicago, and deputies were named in Boston and San Francisco.[31]

Advertising campaigns, assisted by these artists, recruited skilled workers for shipyards and "3,000 Red-Blooded Men" for the YMCA in France; urged workers not to jump from job to job without first consulting with the United

States Employment Service; exhorted farmers to go "over the top" in wheat production and rodent extermination; sold Liberty Loans; promoted food and fuel conservation; and encouraged wives to write "cheerful letters" to their husbands in uniform, to make sure they did not "overstay" their leaves and to remind them to "go strong on the gas [mask] drills." Campaigns for the American Red Cross created the image of "The Greatest Mother in the World," a nurse depicted as the Virgin Mary. The original artist was Alonzo Earl Foringer; the idea for his Red Cross Pietà was advertising man Courtland N. Smith's.[32]

Johns and Gibson inundated America with patriotic messages. Their creations became as much a part of American life as Gibson Girls and Arrow Collar Men. Day after day, advertisements, many arrestingly attractive, appeared in newspapers and magazines as diverse as *Good Housekeeping, Atlantic Monthly, American Boy, Cleveland Topics, Hounds and Hunting, New Republic, Snappy Stories, Breeder's Gazette,* and *Ice Cream Trade Journal.* Six hundred publications carried ads for the War Department, more than fourteen hundred for the fourth Liberty Loan drive. The Advertising Division used direct mail, outdoor signs, book jacket covers, theater curtains, streetcars and commuter trains, and windows in businesses and homes. An *Advertising Service Bulletin* provided ads in ready-to-use form.[33]

The Division of Advertising was as much an organizational feat as the CPI's speaking programs. It worked with more than twenty organizations, ranging from the Association of College Printers to the National Association of Theatre Programme Publishers, as well as scores of advertising clubs, thirty-nine advertising agencies, and thirty printing houses. These figures did not account for the need to coordinate with government entities and parcel ad space. Gibson's committee, which reviewed every piece of art, worked with an estimated fifty-eight departments and committees and 318 artists. Indicative of the enormity of the work, the Selective Service registration drive involved mailings to eighteen thousand newspapers, eleven thousand advertisers and advertising agencies, ten thousand chambers of commerce and their members, thirty thousand manufacturers' associations, twenty-two thousand labor unions, and ten thousand public libraries, as well as banks, general stores, YMCA branches, members of the Council of National Defense, advertising clubs, post offices, 100,000 Red Cross organizations, and fifty-five thousand railroad station agents.[34]

Despite his initial reservations, Creel reveled in the free advertising. He computed it to be worth $5 million—more than $850 million in 2020 dollars. In addition to adding to the CPI's impact on the general public, the advertising

"The Greatest Mother in the World," created by artist Alonzo Earl Foringer, was widely used by the CPI's Division of Advertising on behalf of the Red Cross. Note the words just above the eagle: "The Davey Tree Expert Company." The company purchased the advertisement space on behalf of the CPI.

program gave the CPI a means to reach business. For example, Bruce Bliven, the editor of *Printers' Ink,* used the pages of the magazine to boost the CPI and advance ideas the CPI "wanted the business community to act upon." Whatever doubts muckraker Creel harbored about advertising, propagandist Creel thought the war gave it "the dignity of a profession."[35]

From the point of view of that profession, the war was a testing ground for advertising and an advertisement for what advertising could do. Advertising revenue doubled during the war. "Any surface and every surface, and all approaches through the senses," one executive proclaimed, were now appropriate for an ad. The industry perfected techniques for more than selling soap and cereal. They studied consumers in order to better persuade them. The war, *Printers' Ink* exulted, showed it was "possible to sway the minds of whole populations, change their habits of life, create belief, practically universal, in any policy or idea." Advertisers turned progressive idealism on its head. Social engineering to produce better citizens during the war showed the way to produce better customers after the war.[36]

In a final report, Johns and his fellow board members pointed out the advantages advertising had over "news." All came down to the idea of control: control over the words to make them "exact and authoritative"; control over presentation "to ensure readability"; and control over frequency, making "possible the repetition of the lesson until it is learned."[37]

PICTURE MESSAGES

"You may forget what you read—if you read at all," a marketer advised in 1905. "But what you see, you know instantly!" That same year "nickel madness" began in a converted Pittsburgh storeroom, where for five cents patrons watched a movie projected on a burlap screen. The nickelodeon opened at eight o'clock in the morning, wrote E. W. Lightner in the *Pittsburgh Dispatch,* "and the reels were kept continuously revolving until midnight. A human queue was continuously awaiting the ending of a performance." The nickelodeon was a "theater for the people."[38]

By 1917 movie theaters vastly outnumbered vaudeville houses and stage theaters. While stages went dark during tours or seasonal breaks, mass-produced movies flickered everyday. There were picture palaces with thousands of seats and smaller theaters in working-class neighborhoods and prairie towns. Some were "genuine social centers where neighborhood groups may be found any evening of the week," *Survey* noted. By the end of the war, Toledo, population 250,000, had forty-five theaters, and the average Toledoan paid to see sixty-seven movies a year. The low cost of a ticket made it possible for everyone to buy one. Because the films were silent, a child or an immigrant with little English proficiency could get the point.[39]

Creel naturally wanted to exploit the medium. Although the Four Minute Men monopoly on talks during intermission was effective, he wanted CPI propaganda to be the main attraction.

Here was another case in which European belligerents pointed the way. European acceptance of film for propaganda came with initial reluctance. The medium seemed lowbrow and undignified to elite leaders. The Germans readily used war posters to sell bonds, recruit soldiers, and foster conservation, but film, they thought, debased "our people." The British War Office had the same view, dismissing film in 1914 as merely an "instrument for the amusement of the masses." But this contempt evaporated in the heat of war.[40]

Cinema could arouse civilians who endured hardship and doubted the wisdom of prolonged fighting. "The war has shown the overwhelming power of the image," General Erich von Ludendorff told the German War Ministry in July 1917. "It is therefore essential to ensure, if the war is to be brought to a successful conclusion, that film be used to its maximum effect wherever possible." He asked for reports on film propaganda several times a week. The first epic war documentary, using some faked footage, was produced the year before by Charles Masterman's Wellington House along with a related booklet of photographs.* By some estimates, half of Britain saw the film *The Battle of the Somme*. The Germans responded with *Bei Unseren Helden an der Somme* (With our heroes on the Somme). The French were especially advanced in filmmaking. Pathé originated the newsreel, and the French army produced more than six hundred movies by 1918.[41]

The Germans established a film distribution company in New York in 1915. Ambassador Spring-Rice fretted about the popularity of its films in the United States. But German organizational bungling and difficulties importing film due to British control of the seas gave a large advantage to the Allies. By the end of 1916 British, French, and Italian films overshadowed Germany's motion pic-

---

* Blanche Bates, Creel's wife, starred in a propaganda play, *Getting Together*, produced by the British and Canadians. The play, showing comradery among English-speaking servicemen, promoted the idea of "salvation and happiness" thorough military enlistment. *Pittsburgh Press,* April 25, 1918.

tures in American theaters. Maps in the British War Office showed the deployment of their propaganda films abroad as if they were armies. After the United States entered the war, the CPI distributed British films and adopted European film techniques for production and exhibition.[42]

Creel had firsthand experience with the silver screen. His stage actress wife appeared in silent films. He wrote scenarios for Bronco Bill Anderson films as well as one for *Saved by the Juvenile Court,* which was based on his friend Denver judge Ben Lindsey. He played villainous "Bad Steve" in one of Anderson's movies, the 1909 one-reeler *The Heart of a Cowboy,* shot in Denver. President Wilson watched *The Heart of a Cowboy* at the White House in 1918. The *Washington Times* snidely commented that Creel was never again invited to act because "he 'took the play' away from the star." Creel wrote an exuberant article in the *Denver Post* on his experience of filming the movie. The theater was a place of entertainment and uplift, he wrote. It "lessened crime, bettered conditions of living and brought about a marked decrease in saloon receipts."[43]

The 1916 presidential campaign gave Creel further evidence of the power of cinema. "We are living in a film age," argued a campaign planning document, possibly written by Woolley. "The imagination of the hour is impressed almost more by the 'movies' than by the word persuasive in print." The Democrats produced *The President and His Cabinet in Action,* a film that attacked Hughes comically, and a reel that dwelled on "the horrors of war, peace in this country, etc." The Republicans produced films of Hughes at home and campaigning, and one celebrated the return of Roosevelt Progressives to the Grand Old Party.[44]

Several independent filmmakers offered to promote Wilson's campaign. After initial enthusiasm, the president demurred. Thomas Ince, however, helped the campaign with one of his most famous motion pictures, the epic drama *Civilization.* The film glorified pacifism. (The German hero, a sub commander, refuses to sink a passenger liner and goes to jail, where he dies and is reincarnated as Christ.) The movie was in step with Wilson's he-kept-us-out-of-war campaign theme. The president thanked Ince for "advancing the cause I have the honor to represent at this moment." Ince received permission to film himself receiving the president's congratulations at Shadow Lawn. The footage was attached to the end of the movie and considered a good advertisement by the Democratic National Committee.[45]

After the war broke out in 1914, the film industry flashed Wilson's neutrality statement on the screen and promoted preparedness when that became an administration objective. Once the country was in the war, producers were patriotic, animated as the advertising profession was by public spiritedness and self-interest. Their show of support for the war, they hoped, would prevent the government from deeming theaters nonessential and shutting them down.[46]

The industry's point man was William A. Brady, an actor, producer, one-time boxing promoter, and president of the National Association of the Motion Picture Industry. The association's first effort was the creation in May of a committee to help Robert Woolley publicize the first Liberty Loan drive. Brady arranged for appeals to be added to commercial films released during the "the last two weeks of the campaign." Kendall Banning, who organized the CPI Picture Division before receiving an army commission, proposed that Brady's committee cooperate with the CPI. Brady and Creel established a framework for routine assistance to the entire government. "The motion picture," Brady told both Creel and Tumulty, "can be made the most wonderful system for spreading the national propaganda at little or no cost."[47]

Wilson remained a reluctant movie star, at one point declining to adjust his schedule so he could be filmed signing a bill. "I am the worst possible subject for moving pictures," he told Creel. But he was happy the CPI cooperated with the motion picture industry, and on June 28 endorsed the idea in a letter Creel prepared for him. "The film," Wilson wrote, "has come to rank as a very high medium for the dissemination of public intelligence, and since it speaks a universal language it lends itself importantly to the presentations of America's plans and purposes."[48]

The first step was the creation of the War Cooperating Committee. The chairman was D. W. Griffith. Because the famed director was abroad working on propaganda movies for the British and French, Brady did most of the work. "The masters of the motion-picture industry," as the CPI called them, assisted government agencies as well as the Council of National Defense. Mary Pickford, Ethel Barrymore, Marguerite Clark, and other marquee names established the value of star power for political causes. On September 25, Creel created a Division of Films and a Division of Pictures.[49]

The Film Division's first six months were disappointing. Because of military restrictions on civilian photographers, it relied heavily on the Army Signal Corps, to which Newton Baker assigned responsibility for still and moving pictures that were needed for a historical record of the war. The CPI worked closely with the corps, two of whose officers were on Creel's payroll. But it did not produce as much material as the CPI needed, and the division's plans to promote private-sector film production were not realized. The initial scheme of free film distribution chiefly through state councils of defense and the Red Cross was costly and reached few people. Byoir secured the resignation of the division's head in April 1918 and recruited a replacement from the advertising ranks of his old employer, Hearst. Charles S. Hart, who had no motion picture experience, became a government movie mogul.[50]

Headquartered in New York, the revamped division produced its own films. *Pershing's Crusaders,* its first feature-length picture, ran fifty-six minutes and included navy as well as army footage. Through clever deal making, Hart and Creel secured rights to British, French, and Italian newsreel footage, which was used along with Signal Corps film for the weekly *Official War Review.* Hart published a biweekly on government movies, the *Official Film News.* A Scenario Department wanted to show commercial film producers that "government propaganda could be made so interesting that audiences would cheerfully accept it." The department supplied story lines for one-reel films on such subjects as the feeding of troops and the war contributions of American Indians, secured filming permits, and supervised production. Eighteen films were produced this way. The department eventually produced several of its own films.[51]

Hart hired film editors from Pathé, cameramen with war experience from the *Chicago Tribune,* and Paramount Pictures' advertising and publicity manager. The editor of the *Review* was Charles Urban, a blind-in-one-eye American who was Britain's foremost film impresario and previously helped Guy Gaunt distribute British films in the United States. Hart helped the Signal Corps find talented personnel. Corps film production ballooned from 2,500 feet in December 1917 to 118,000 a month at the end of the war.[52]

Hart put distribution on a business basis. In all but three states, where councils of defense shouldered the work, he partnered with commercial firms that reached theaters. Pathé, the largest film exchange, won the rights to distribute the *Official War Review* on condition that it return 80 percent of the proceeds. Leftover film was sold each week to other newsreel companies at a dollar a foot. Similar arrangements were made with commercial distributors who handled individual films.[53]

Hart hyped three movies with "official" screenings in major cities. One was unveiled this way in thirty-four locales. These lasted about a week and were promoted with every gimmick, from planted stories to signs in department store windows. Each film had its own musical score. Theaters, festooned with bunting and flags, looked like the setting of a war rally. George Bowles, who handled foreign distribution of Griffith's *Birth of a Nation,* promoted the films with eight road companies. They worked with newspapers and went into factories at noontime to drum up interest.[54]

Responsibility for showing films in New York was given to one of the country's greatest movie house impresarios, Samuel I. Rothapfel, owner of the Strand in New York City. He began the showing of *America's Answer* with the national anthem sung by one hundred sailors and a tableau vivant of American soldiers poised to "go over the top." The music that accompanied the film had artillery sound effects. The CPI logo was displayed on the screen.[55]

The Internal Revenue Service decided that no theater tax would be levied on tickets to CPI films because it was a government agency. This enhanced attendance. The division recovered more than 75 percent of its costs. The revenue supported film production and promotion, including distribution abroad, and supported other image-producing activities.[56]

Around the time that Hart joined the CPI in the spring of 1918, the Division of Pictures became the Bureau of War Photographs within his Film Division. The bureau distributed images produced by military photographers. By May 1918, it had fifteen hundred photographs available for sale at ten cents apiece. The bureau sent photos to newspapers and magazines as well as businesses such as AT&T. The bureau's Department of Slides serviced teachers, ministers, and lecturers. The transparencies were sold individually for the low price of fifteen cents each. They also were available as slideshows. Initially the Signal Corps produced these. Later the CPI manufactured them in a laboratory at 1820 Eighteenth Street, NW.[57]

Hart's division had responsibility for war exhibitions, which were organized in twenty-one cities. Although chafed that he did not have a large formal role in the Advertising Division, advertising executive William Rankin helped organize, in his Chicago hometown, the largest of all the expositions and came up with the unit's name, the Bureau of War Exhibitions. He believed the word "war" increased public interest. The Chicago War Exposition, which ran for two weeks on the lakefront, attracted 1.5 million people. A second unit—a Bureau of State Fair Exhibits—operated on the same principle at thirty-five fairs. The best way to reach farmers, a planning document observed, was to let people see "the guns, helmets, the gas masks used on the battlefield, photographs, charts and educational displays on food production and conservation, army production and transportation."[58]

A final element of the visual panoply was cartoons. Gibson and others in his division drew them, as did leading newspaper cartoonists John T. McCutcheon of the *Chicago Tribune;* C. R. Macauley of the *New York World,* who helped Woolley in the 1916 campaign; and Rollin Kirby, who was the first to win a Pulitzer Prize in the category of newspaper cartooning. Although not at first keen to establish a formal cartoon unit, Creel agreed in June 1918 to take over the Bureau of Cartoons established under the National Committee of Patriotic Societies, a clearinghouse for organizations promoting national unity. An enterprising young social worker named George Hecht directed the bureau, which sought to "mobilize and direct the scattered cartoon power of the country for constructive war work." A weekly bulletin sent to 740 cartoonists suggested themes for drawings. The bureau acquired and syndicated cartoons related to advertising campaigns. The "importance of 'picture messages' at this time cannot be overestimated," Byoir wrote in the bulletin.[59]

The Chicago War Exposition featured daily mock battles with three thousand soldiers, sailors, and marines, and fourteen warplanes. Gibson's artists painted ninety-foot-wide canvases, which were all the more attention-grabbing because the public could watch the artists at work. Unlike Gibson's division, which was peopled with accomplished artists, the film enterprise began without a single experienced staff member. Its motion pictures did not go down in history as cinematic jewels. Yet in the six months he headed the Film Division, Hart produced sixty-six motion pictures and thirty-one installments of the *Official War Review.* The executive chiefly responsible for feature film distribution had previously done that same job for Charlie Chaplin comedies, and by war's end he managed to achieve an audience for CPI films of the same size as Chaplin's. The *Official War Review,* Creel claimed, appeared in more than half the nation's theaters. Because towns typically had several, if not many, theaters, this approximated near total saturation of the country. If the war had carried on longer, one historian has noted, the government might have become a major film producer.[60]

More than anyone else, Creel established film as a tool for American government propaganda. "I believe in the motion picture just as I believe in the press," Creel said, "and in my work it plays just as powerful a part in the production and stimulation of an aroused and enlightened war sentiment."[61]

ACADEME GOES ALL-IN

Guy Stanton Ford, the dean of the University of Minnesota's graduate school, was a colorful writer, effective platform speaker, friend to scholars, champion of academic freedom, administrative doer, and a picture-book professor with his shock of gray hair, wire-rimmed glasses, pipe, and a Phi Beta Kappa key dangling from his vest pocket. When America went to war, his colleagues organized a drill group. Ford was drill master. He exerted his influence off campus with a letter, distributed by the state superintendent of schools, suggesting high school spring commencements emphasize war issues. After the letter ended up in the hands of Creel, Ford received a telegram asking him to come to work for the CPI. As soon as the university president saw the telegram, he went into a meeting, waved it in the air, and said, "Dean Ford has got the first summons to the university for National Defense."[62]

Campuses across the country were eager to be summoned. At Columbia

Guy Stanton Ford, dean of the Graduate School at the University of Minnesota, turned professors across the country into propagandists. Here he is standing on a balcony at CPI offices overlooking Lafayette Square. (Author's collection)

University, where Ford earned his doctorate in history with a dissertation on Prussia, President Nicholas Murray Butler wrote Newton Baker to declare it would be an honor, "if by any act of ours or by the service of any one, or all, of our great army of students and teachers we can strengthen the hands of the government." The university established a unit of the new Student Army Training Corps, headquartering it in the journalism building. The next year Columbia identified seventy-two professors engaged in war work. As extensive as it was, the list overlooked faculty who also belonged on it. Dormitories became barracks. Lecture halls and laboratory space were turned over to the Air Service Radio School, the Navy Gas Engine School, and the US Signal Corps School of Photography, the latter an assist to the CPI's film and photograph program. "Life and work has been to all intents and purposes suspended," Butler said.[63]

Columbia almost became the "nucleus" of all government publicity. The word was Walter Lippmann's. When he was drafting his publicity plan for House in early 1917, Lippmann became aware of a "fully trained and ready" program just created by journalism professor Walter Pitkin. The former *New York Evening Post* journalist argued that German propaganda, in contrast to the Allies', was "amazingly successful, in spite of its failure to force the government into following its suggestions." By the time war was declared two dozen journalism students were fulltime war publicists, for which they received full academic credit. "Gone are books, gone are classes, gone are all signs of school work," *Editor & Publisher* reported. Pitkin's Division of Intelligence and Publicity provided news of Columbia's war contributions and produced papers on such war issues as "Food Preparedness," for which they received full academic credit. Within a single week, Pitkin informed President Butler, his division received "nearly one hundred proposals from the faculty to write pamphlets and newspaper articles on various topics bearing on aspects of the national emergency."[64]

Pitkin's Division of Intelligence and Publicity on the fourth floor of the Journalism Building became a pillar of Lippmann's publicity plan. He envisioned Pitkin as chief of staff under McCormick and Woolley. After Lippmann's scheme lost out to Creel's, Pitkin carried on until the end of May. Worn out by Pitkin's costly, ambitious proposals, Butler eventually curtailed his endeavors, and Pitkin joined a Columbia exodus to Washington. He affiliated himself with a news service run by the *New Republic* and the Council of National Defense. Among others to leave Columbia University was Dean Frederick Keppel, who joined Lippmann and Frankfurter in Newton Baker's office.[65]

Despite all its war activity, some at Columbia worried they might not be seen as doing enough. When Ford came from the CPI to speak at the university, history professor James Shotwell urged good attendance to counter the "impression growing in Washington that eastern universities are not as active as middle west."[66]

This patriotism came on the heels of progressive education reforms that lent themselves to the CPI's purposes. The percentage of children in school and the number of days they spent each year in the classroom soared. The number of students receiving a high school diploma doubled from 1900 to 1910 and would jump another 150 percent by 1924. While college was still out of the question for many, it was less exclusive. Colleges and universities doubled in number and increased in size, in Columbia's case from about 250 faculty members in 1902 to 700 by 1915. Public universities benefited from federal land grants and generous appropriations from state legislatures that took pride in their institutions of higher learning.[67]

At the same time, higher education simultaneously became more scholarly and more applied. Stronger doctoral programs and emphasis on research were inspired by German universities, where Ford and other budding scholars studied. Ford's discipline, history, was not a recognized academic field until 1884; under German influence American historians pursued "scientific history" through objective study of original sources. Ford's recruitment as dean of Minnesota's graduate school underlined that university's gathering maturity. Simultaneously, campuses added professional schools, such as schools of journalism. On the eve of the war, Bliven identified thirty-seven colleges with advertising courses. Edward Ross criticized the formal lecture system and called for more active engagement with real problems through fieldwork. One of Wilson's most memorable speeches as university president was "Princeton for the Nation's Service." Columbia's Butler was active in Republican politics and not bashful about offering advice to Sir Gilbert Parker, the British propagandist responsible for cultivating elites in the United States.[68]

Academics were eager to follow the path of British university dons who wrote eighty-seven propaganda publications, the so-called *Oxford Pamphlets.** Before Ford was offered a place at the CPI, J. Franklin Jameson, editor of the *American Historical Review* and director of historical research at the Carnegie

---

* American professors scorned a 1914 "Manifesto" in which ninety-three leading German scholars decried "lies and calumnies" against their country.

Institution of Washington, organized a weekend meeting of eminent scholars to consider how to help the government, a problem that had "presented itself to the mind of every history man in the country." The recently created CPI, Jameson wrote in his invitation letter, "gives ground for hope of access in this direction." Jameson, a courtly scholar who taught constitutional law to Wilson at Johns Hopkins University, commanded respect. Arthur Bullard, who was also respected by historians, represented the CPI at the gathering. Out of the meeting came the National Board for Historical Service. First on its list of activities, as NBHS chairman James Shotwell put it, was to serve as "the research end" of the CPI. Staff described the relationship as "intimate" and "official."[69]

Ford had attended the meeting. Once he was ensconced in Washington with the CPI, he built a strong relationship with the NBHS. In the beginning, he lived in a shared house on Connecticut Avenue that included, in addition to a Filipino cook-housekeeper, Charles Merz of the *New Republic* and Columbia professors Keppel, Pitkin, and Shotwell. Shotwell had supported Pitkin's scheme at Columbia, and Pitkin, in place at the New Republic News Service, helped Shotwell with NBHS publicity. They had offices in the same building. Shotwell, who apparently brought Ford to Creel's attention, was a consultant to the CPI and considered himself a member of the staff. Ford sat on the NBHS executive committee. Ford's office was a five-minute walk from the NBHS, and from his window he could see the Cosmos Club, on the other side of Lafayette Square, where they gathered regularly.[70]

The CPI partnered with the NBHS's Enemy-Press Intelligence Service, which it established in July 1917 and considered its "most important single undertaking." The service acquired enemy newspapers and periodicals by the sackful from the British, French, and Belgium missions in the United States, as well as a few other sources. This material was supposed to offer intelligence on "internal conditions and public opinion" in the Central Powers. The service summarized its findings and passed them to various federal agencies and government-related groups. The CPI placed a typist and translator in the NBHS service, used its material for pamphlets, and distributed "extracts suitable for use by the American press." Ford thought this was "one of the best things" the NBHS did in its early days.[71]

When Ford arrived at the CPI, Creel was busy creating the basic CPI structure and distracted by the contretemps over the proposed Espionage Act. It was two weeks before the two sat down to seriously discuss Ford's duties. During the interregnum, Ford took the initiative to publish a document that had just arrived from colleagues at the University of Minnesota. *The War Message and Facts Behind It* consisted of Wilson's call for a congressional war declaration on April 2 along with forty annotations that increased the twelve-page speech to twenty-eight. In Ford's telling, he was shocked to arrive at the office the day after publication to find reporters were upset at having no advance notice. Who was this Ford, they wanted to know, and what did the document say about policy? This reaction revealed how quickly journalists became tethered to the CPI and how newsworthy such publications could be. By the end of the war the GPO printed nearly 2.5 million copies of the pamphlet in eight languages.[72]

Ford believed Creel recruited him to write minor items along the lines of his letter calling for high school graduations to emphasize war themes. Shortly after arriving at CPI headquarters, Ford prepared a national circular that did this. But the *War Message* experience prompted more ambitious undertaking through the Division of Civic and Educational Cooperation that he headed. The new division was to "put into convincing print America's reasons for entering the war, the meaning of America, the nature of our free institutions, and our war aims, together with a thorough analysis of the Prussian system, as well as an exposure of the enemy's misrepresentations, aggression, and barbarities." Ford started with a borrowed secretary and a small office facing Lafayette Square. Later came an assistant, Indiana history professor Samuel B. Harding, and an editorial aide, James W. Searson, an English professor at Kansas State. Searson had handled publicity for the National Education Association and was studying for his doctorate at Columbia.[73]

While Ford often drew from the University of Minnesota and often turned to historians, virtually all the great universities and all the disciplines were involved—government, law, diplomacy and international relations, and English. He also reached outside the university. His housemate, Charles Merz, prepared a synopsis of the war legislation, titled *First Session of the War Congress.* German-born F. W. Lehmann, a former solicitor general and two-time president of the American Bar Association, wrote on the duties of hyphenated Americans.[74]

These publications appeared under three major headings. The first publication in the Red, White and Blue Series, *How the War Came to America,* was made up largely of documents that made the case for US entry into the conflict. Another number in the series was *German War Practices,* a compilation of damning German quotes. The War Information Series included *The Nation in Arms,* with speeches by Newton Baker and Interior Secretary Lane, and *Why America Fights Germany* by John S. P. Tatlock, a literary scholar and medievalist at Stanford. In a series of Loyalty Leaflets were *Plain Issues of the War* by Elihu Root, who had been secretary of state and secretary of war under two Republican presidents, and *Friendly Words to the Foreign Born.*

Other publications were produced apart from these series. *The National Service Handbook* identified "the most useful avenues of service" and described war work being done by various groups. It was inspired by the *Directory of Service,* published the first month of American involvement in the war by Pitkin's publicity bureau at Columbia. Many of Ford's publications were the product of academic teamwork. The *War Cyclopedia: A Handbook for Ready Reference on the Great War* was spectacular in this regard. Through a mass mailing, Ford asked opinion leaders to send in "questions which you know the people in your neighborhood are asking." The 321-page book was edited by Harding, Frederic Paxson of Wisconsin, and famed constitutional scholar Edward S. Corwin of Princeton. It drew on forty-nine contributors, among them such eminent scholars as Charles Beard and Carl Becker. Its entries were extensive, often arcane, and thoroughly propagandistic. An entry for "Corfu" noted the island was a base for Allied forces. The entry for "Education in War Time" read, "No educational institution ought to slacken its work."[75]

The education entry was a de facto slogan for Ford. He wrote to every state superintendent of education and more than eight hundred college presidents encouraging the use of CPI materials and providing postcards to request them. Universities with Student Army Training Corps were required to offer war aims courses that lent themselves to CPI publications. The booklets worked in many other courses as well. *The Battle Line of Democracy,* a compilation of stirring poetry and prose, found its way into English classes. Harding prepared a teacher's guide, *The Study of the Great War: A Topical Outline.* Promoted by the NBHS, it reached a circulation of 700,000, not counting republication in *History Teacher's Magazine.*[76]

In the last weeks of the war, the division launched the publication *National School Service* with the encouragement of the commissioner of education, who worried teachers were inundated with war materials of uneven quality. Ford heavily recruited helpers from Columbia Teacher's College—three people to advise on rural education and William Bagley as editor. The sixteen-page bi-weekly was designed for the schoolhouse, not the college lecture hall. Bagley believed in using education to shape "the socially efficient individual," and the publication promoted hygiene and other progressive goals. But at least half the content carried a war theme—war-related stories to read to students, ideas for class projects such as making propaganda posters, and math problems in which students calculated tonnages of war supplies. The publication was mailed to 600,000 schools. "No one else in the community," Ford told teachers in the maiden issue, "is so singled out as a leader and center of information."[77]

Ford's division produced more than ninety publications. The total print run was estimated at more than seventy-five million. Even then publications had to be rationed. The chairman of the CND's Department of Educational Propaganda lamented he could not send material to the supervisor of Minnesota's rural schools, who was eager to help distribute CPI propaganda. "There is such an enormous demand for the pamphlets by every organization in the country," she wrote, "and the demand is daily increasing."[78]

Because the division employed the nation's foremost academics, its work had authority. Eager to build on this, Ford did not repeat his mistake with *The War Message,* when he failed to put out a press release. Without a trace of ivory tower effeteness, he asked for promotional help from Rotary clubs and the Boy Scouts, whose young members handed out the booklet in their neighborhoods. *The Kaiserite in America* was directed at traveling salesmen, who were in daily contact "with all kinds of people." "Here is an opportunity for the Commercial Travelers of America to do a great work toward winning the war," the booklet began. "You are summoned as specifically as if you were enlisted in the army or navy to aid the national cause."[79]

University involvement permeated the CPI. As we have seen, professors assisted the speakers' program; others monitored the immigrant press. One of the first recruited for this latter task was German-language specialist W. A. Braun at Columbia. Nicholas Murray Butler released him from other obligations to perform this "very desirable" service. A history professor headed a war film scenario department at Harvard, assisted by two faculty colleagues. Scholars prepared lectures to go with slideshows, such as *The Ruined Churches of France,* prepared by a Stanford University faculty member.[80]

As was the case with the advertising and film industries, universities viewed the war as "the opportunity of a lifetime," as a Minnesota professor told Ford. In Ford's papers is a typewritten list, twenty-five pages long, naming all the scholars who worked for the government in one capacity or another. The list, Ford jotted in a note, was "probably not complete." War work allowed history and other disciplines to display, in the words of Franklin Jameson, their relevance "to the fateful exigencies of the present day." Professors were paid at most travel expenses, but patriotism had its rewards. Never before had academics reached so many people. In a far from unique experience, the CPI printed 1.8 million copies of Columbia professor Charles Hazen's *The Government of Germany*. Another 20,500 copies appeared in German. CPI publications could be found in settlement houses and Sunday schools. Little wonder professors were eager to do "popular pamphleteering," as Creel called it.[81]

CUMULATIVE PSYCHOLOGICAL INFLUENCE

Harvey O'Higgins thought the mobilization of advertising agents was Creel's "master stroke," greater even than the Four Minute Men. Advertising amplified everything the CPI did. When the committee sent out a speaker, ad agents arranged billboards, contrived "front-page stories to prepare for his coming, and made his reception as exciting as a political rally, and packed his house." But advertising was only a part of it. Every gear in the CPI machine propelled the others along.[82]

The Advertising Division promoted Ford's publications and Hart's films. D'Arcy, a board member, used his connections with the Associated Advertising Clubs of the World to create more than 140 local war committees "as a point of contact for any and all services" the CPI needed. CPI units reciprocated by helping advance the ad campaigns. In conjunction with the ad campaign to boost shipyard employment, the Four Minute Men devoted two weeks to the topic and an entire issue of its bulletin to a model speech. Gibson's division drew posters to advertise the Four Minute Men. Ford edited Four Minute Men publications and helped create Bestor's speaking division. His *War Cyclopedia* was printed in a slender shape that fit easily in a Four Minute Man's pocket.[83]

In his indictment of fraudulent advertising, Samuel Hopkins Adams said, "We live surrounded by the advertisement. . . . All this persistence can not fail of some psychological influence." The cumulative effect of CPI advertising was powerful in just this way. Woolley wished more citizens purchased Liberty Loan bonds, but all the loan drives were oversubscribed. Lower income Americans stretched to buy government bonds, savings certificates, and savings stamps. Those who kept their money in their pockets nevertheless heard the patriotic messages in these drives. "It cost little to stir up patriotism," two economists noted in a study of Liberty Loans, "and every little bit of extra savings it brought in was a plus."[84]

Americans saw CPI ads while thumbing through magazines or as they drove down the street. When they attended state fairs, often organized by the CPI, they watched CPI-made films. In public libraries they were greeted by war posters, war exhibits, war notices on bulletin boards, and war books displayed on open shelves—at the suggestion of the CPI—"to help make the war a personal challenge and a definite and familiar task to the general public." Children learned CPI lessons at their school desks and repeated them at the family dinner table. The *National School Service* wanted to make "every school pupil a messenger for Uncle Sam." The CPI did not need specific street addresses to reach Americans by mail; Postmaster General Burleson gave it franking privileges to ship bulk mailings "throughout the country."[85]

CPI staff spoke of their work with pride. Byoir called advertising campaigns a "miracle of mechanics." Ford conferred gravitas on the CPI by calling it "a war emergency national university." Nevertheless, the successes in which these men basked entailed costs to the democracy they sought to preserve, a theme taken up in detail in the next chapters.[86]

7

A Test of Loyalty

> Deutschtum, that world-wide, subterranean propaganda of German
> influence, German culture, German hopes and ambitions and future
> domination which had for a quarter of a century established itself
> reproductively as the ichneumon parasite affixes its eggs to the body of
> a helpless host which, later, their brood will prey upon and destroy.
>
> —Samuel Hopkins Adams, *Common Cause*

Samuel Hopkins Adams's novel *Common Cause* is the tale of Jeremy Robson
and his patriotic newspaper in the midwestern town of Fenchester. Robson's
muckraking has led special interests to withhold advertising in order to drive
him out of business. When war comes in 1917, his equally passionate exposé of
local German-American fealty to Deutschtum inspires Fenchester's plutocrats
to put aside differences with Robson to save the *Guardian*. At the end of the
book "a supremely ordinary appearing person" arrives from Washington. One
of the local German-Americans he quietly calls on is a Mrs. Wanser. There have
been reports, he says, that she objected to Four Minute Men speaking at the
movie theater. When Wanser complains she is being spied upon, her accuser
replies, "Certainly. You're a suspicious person. Take my advice. Stop talking, or
if you must talk, talk like an American."[1]

As in Fenchester, in America generally the war triggered an outpouring of
collective patriotism. In New York the Elks, Masons, college students, the city
hotel association, Billy Sunday's Tabernacle, and a group of prominent writers and artists called the Vigilantes joined in boosting Liberty Loans. When
churches in one community purchased advertising space for Liberty Loans,
spirits were so high that church attendance "the following Sunday was very
much increased." Wilson made the Boy Scouts "government dispatch bearers in
carrying to the homes of their community the pamphlets on the war prepared
by the Committee on Public Information."[2]

The Vigilantes was one of many superpatriotic groups. The American Protective League (APL), the National Security League (NSL), and the American Defense Society (ADS) formed to encourage war preparedness. The Vigilantes considered anyone who opposed this "un-American." After April 1917, these groups whipped up enthusiasm for the war and sought out disloyalty. Albert Briggs, a Chicago outdoor advertising executive and founder of the APL, offered its services to the Department of Justice. The department authorized APL members to carry badges embossed with the words "Secret Service." The head of military intelligence, Colonel Ralph Van Deman, asked the APL to serve as his civilian investigative arm.[3]

Those who did not buy bonds were listed on "rolls of dishonor." Those deemed unpatriotic were forced to kiss the flag, tarred and feathered, and in a few instances murdered. Their houses were painted yellow. The APL made unlawful arrests of alleged draft dodgers. Beloved socialist activist Jane Addams, who spoke out against suppression, was cast out of the Daughters of the American Revolution. Although George Sylvester Viereck supported the war and by Creel's admission published a great deal of CPI matter, he had to flee his home to escape a patriotic lynch mob. The Poetry Society revoked his membership.[4]

Perceived threats to national security included socialists and members of the labor movement who believed the war was designed by Wall Street; Amish, Dunkards, and other pacifists who refused to fight on principle; and the foreign-born. German-Americans were believed to foment discontent among all of these groups. In the run-up to his reelection Wilson spoke of citizens "born under other flags . . . who have poured the poison of disloyalty into the very arteries of our national life." He carried the theme forward on June 15, 1917, Flag Day. Informed this was to be a momentous speech, three thousand people gathered to hear him at the Washington Monument despite a violent rainstorm. Germany's "sinister intrigue," Wilson said, still threatened public opinion. "Woe to the man or group of men who seeks to stand in our way in this day of high resolution." At times, the *Washington Herald* reported, the crowd's applause "drowned out the whistling of the gale."[5]

"We are not the enemies of the German people," Wilson said, but his distinction between German leaders and German citizens also was drowned out. When the CPI reprinted his remarks on the front page of the *Official Bulletin,* German perfidy was highlighted in subheads, as was Wilson's "woe to" threat—twice. A pamphlet version of the speech, with similar treatment, was distributed by the millions. Urged on by Wilson, Creel tasked Harvey O'Higgins with preparing materials on "German Intrigue."[6]

"This fight for public opinion is the business of the Committee on Public Information," Creel said. "We do not call it propaganda, for that work, in the German hands, has come to be associated with lies, secrecies and shameful corruptions. Our work is educational and informative, for we have such confidence in our case that we feel no more than the fair presentation of the facts is needed to win the verdict." Creel reiterated this over and over. His colleagues made similar assertions. Guy Stanton Ford told fellow historians, "I have been able to maintain the same standards that I have set for myself both as a member of the history department of the University of Minnesota and as a member of this society."[7]

But while it provided a large amount of factual information, the CPI jumped the tracks it claimed to have laid for itself. It distorted information, played on the public's fears, and fomented hate. It did not go as far as the APL and the ADS, whose "savage intolerances" Creel later decried as "a thing of screams, violence, and extremes." Yet the CPI cooperated with these groups, and its staff endorsed their undemocratic practices.[8]

Samuel Hopkins Adams entered CPI ranks in the fall of 1917. "From now on," he informed his publisher, "it looks as if I should be putting in most of my time still-hunting pro-German and peace propaganda." The CPI did stalk enemy propaganda in the manner of the still-hunter by working noiselessly and unseen in league with government and para-government surveillance agencies. But stealth was not Adams's method. He made his name writing sensational stories splashed on the front pages of newspapers.[9]

This, too, was a favored CPI method. To forge a common attitude about the war, it drummed into the American mind that German spies and propagandists—often in the form of German-Americans—posed an imminent threat. If these bogeymen could not be seen, the CPI argued, their influence was visible each time an American suggested negotiating a peace or uttered another word of dissent. "Germany knows that before we entered the war there was variety of opinion in our midst," the *Four Minute Men Bulletin* primed speakers in advance of a Liberty Loan push, "and she is hopeful that even now when we are in the war, we *Americans* may show divided sentiments.... America faces a *test* of loyalty."[10]

THE HOUSE OF TRUTH

In November of 1917, the CPI created a Division of Reference to gather in one place an information center on government activity. The following March, at the urging of other government agencies, an executive order expanded this into an office "where complete information records may be available as to the function, location, and personnel of all government agencies." The unit's anodyne name, the Service Bureau, belied its value. With the expansion and proliferation of government organizations, whose composition changed daily, citizens found it difficult to know who was doing what and where they might be located. By the summer the bureau was making five hundred changes a day in its personnel directory. Its main office was across the street from the Treasury Department, and it manned information desks originally run by the Navy and War Departments in Union Station. During one week in June, the bureau had 1,630 visitors seeking information, and 150 letters of inquiry arrived daily.[11]

The Service Bureau was not alone in genuine public service. The *National Service Handbook* was a useful directory to war work. The *Official Bulletin* printed news on a wide variety of subjects of public interest. And who could object to the CPI's publication of a "war plum pudding" recipe designed to conserve food or its press release on disease in military camps or a lighthearted feature on an army shortage of lemon drops?[12]

But the CPI was not the "house of truth" Creel claimed it was. It did not limit itself to reaching "the people through their minds." The CPI mind-set was that of a political campaign machine attempting to put across its candidate. Carl Byoir turned down a suggestion for a factual chart with the comment, "Informative material is not part of our task." The CPI, he pointed out, existed "to interpret, as far as we are able, to the people of America the high ideals for which America fights, the justice of our cause, and the autocratic aims of our enemies." Harvey O'Higgins put it more or less the same way: "It is, after all, a question in publicity whether a brief scare-head item on the frontpage—which everybody reads—isn't worth a whole inside page of detailed matter that very few arrive at."[13]

The overwhelming desire to convince drove every CPI bureau to pluck at emotions and use information tendentiously. While this was second nature to the Division of Advertising, it was at odds with what Ford's Division of Civic and Educational Cooperation was supposed to represent. University professors, with whom it worked, were supposedly engaged in dispassionate inquiry. This added legitimacy to the CPI. Columbia University journalism professor Walter Pitkin explained the reasoning this way: "The only group of prominent men who might proceed boldly without incurring such suspicions are university professors." In his 1917 book on war and the rise of public opinion, Carl

Ackerman singled out the influence of professors: "College professors headed by a President who had himself been a college professor contributed more effectively to the decision in favor of war than did the farmer, the business men or the politicians."[14]

Judged by academic standards, Ford's publications flunked. The rush to get publications to press led to unintentional factual errors. The zeal to convince led to purposeful distortion. Notwithstanding the names of the distinguished authors on their covers, and the impressive footnotes and bibliographies, authors of the division's pamphlets routinely selected facts that supported their theses and omitted those that did not. Their reasoning was deductive, linking conclusions to accepted premises. The result was sales pitches disguised as scholarship.[15]

The source material in a school study guide prepared by Samuel Harding, Ford's deputy, was the equivalent of putting a fist on the judgment scales, not just a finger. More than one-third of its references were to other CPI propaganda. A third more drew from the books Allies produced to justify the war from their point of view. "The remainder," noted historian Carol Gruber, "were references to safe and standard sources. The document's picture of the war was so one-sided . . . as to be indefensible as history."[16]

The *War Cyclopedia,* to which first-rate scholars contributed, was a prime example of tendentiousness. It had multiple listings for the Germans: "German Government, Moral Bankruptcy of," "German Intrigue in the United States," "German Government, Bad Faith of," "German Intrigue, Tools" (which had two entries), "German Autocracy," and so forth over many pages. There was nothing comparable on British propaganda or British conflicts with the United States. The entry for "Embargo, British" did not mention the anger that Whitehall policy provoked in the Wilson administration.[17]

Ford's division was responsible for turning Wilson's Flag Day address into a pamphlet, *The President's Flag Day Address with Evidence of German Plans.* The thirty-page publication was so heavily annotated that no room was left on some pages for Wilson's words and on others only two or three lines could fit. Some notes were arcane or irrelevant, but most reprised the CPI's standard talking points on Germany: Germany was responsible for starting the war, it was undemocratic and brutal, and a German victory would require Americans to defend their own shores. Long strings of patriotic German quotations were served up, such as the conclusion of a poem, "Now, people of Germany, ye shall be master of Europe."[18]

As was common in CPI publications, the notes recapped the maladroit plots and propaganda of Heinrich Albert, Karl Boy-Ed, and Franz von Papen. Those incidents occurred before April 1917. None led to prosecution by the Justice Department. With these hapless individuals gone, the CPI strained to wring treachery from unsubstantiated snippets of news. "The extraordinary number of explosions in munition factories so far," the pamphlet noted, "exceeds the normal number even in this dangerous industry as to justify suspicion and investigation." The print run of *The President's Flag Day Address* was 6.8 million, the largest of any CPI publication. The CPI arranged for 500,000 Boy Scouts to distribute a special printing in January 1918.[19]

Conquest and Kultur: Aims of the Germans in Their Own Words consisted of 160 pages of selected German quotations. The principal editor, a young University of Minnesota professor named Wallace Notestein, included statements from Germans who opposed the policies of the kaiser and his military leaders. The CPI editors removed all but one of these, arguing they detracted from the overall effect and would reflect poorly on Notestein, whose name was German. When Notestein proposed the publication go out without his name attached to it, Ford and J. Franklin Jameson of the National Board for Historical Service disagreed. Bylines conferred authority. "There are a few things I do not like," an uneasy Notestein wrote to George Burton Adams, a mentor on the Yale faculty, "but in them I had to yield to others." Adams, a respected historian, told him not to worry. He had done "a very useful piece of work." In his introduction to the publication, Ford wrote, "The pied pipers of Prussianism who have led the German people to conquest and ignominy and to infamy are here given their unending day before the court of public opinion." Ford considered the booklet "the most far-reaching in its effect" of any government wartime publication.[20]

Ford was squeamish about a project to pillory the Germans with words from its military manuals. "War codes," he told the university professor responsible for the publication, "even in humane nations, are likely to contain things which taken out of their texts and apart from the sprit in which they are executed, sound quite as barbaric as similar passages in the Prussian War Code." The CPI nevertheless published *The German War Code,* which invited readers to consider how the German military was programmed to commit "fiendish outrages."[21]

Conversely, the CPI built up the image of the Allies. Working closely with the NBHS, which received a prodigious amount of material from Allied propagandists, it papered over historic Anglo-American animosity—the Revolutionary War, the War of 1812, and subsequent border disputes—as well as disagreements arising after the world war broke out in 1914. One way to do this was to sidestep disagreements, as the *War Cyclopedia* did. The other was to emphasize positive aspects of Anglo-American history. "It should never be forgotten," Ford said, that men like Edmund Burke in England "were the intellectual comrades of Washington, Franklin, and Jefferson." In a letter to a member of the British War Mission, a senior NBHS member expressed delight over "what we are trying to do in the way of breaking down traditional prejudices."[22]

Patriotism was as zealous inside ivy-covered walls as outside. In loyalty interrogations of professors, the University of Minnesota board of trustees reduced a female professor to tears for not helping with Red Cross war work and fired another who wanted the United States to win the war without wiping out the Hohenzollerns "root and branch," a position that Wilson had expressed privately to House. Ford was justifiably proud of helping professors who became the victims of university witch hunts. But one of his suggestions for rehabilitation unconsciously borrowed from the approach totalitarian regimes use to break dissidents. He suggested they redeem themselves by writing a patriotic entry for the *War Cyclopedia*.[23]

Ford's loyalty burst out in a fit of emotion in a speech delivered while traveling for the Council of National Defense in 1918. Straying from his prepared remarks, he told an audience at the Mormon Tabernacle in Salt Lake City that Germany was a nation "without a soul." Afterward he confessed to Creel that he had gone too far. He would let "the Kaiser monopolize God in his war, at least so far as governmental propaganda is concerned." But this was scarcely the only time the CPI evoked God to inspire audiences.[24]

THE BEASTS WE ARE FIGHTING

A few weeks after the United States entered the war, Lansing wrote to President Wilson. "Every agency," he said, "should be employed to arouse patriotic fervor and that whole-hearted devotion to the cause which spring from the emotions even more than from the intellect." Wilson returned the note to him at a cabinet meeting. On it he had written "with approval."[25]

It is nearly impossible to overstate how widely held such views were in the upper echelons of government. Baker thought the best way to implement the Selective Service Act was with brass bands and stirring Four Minute Men speeches. McAdoo hoped to correct the problems that Lincoln's treasury secretary Salmon P. Chase encountered selling bonds to finance the Civil War. "Chase," he said, "did not attempt to capitalize on the emotion of the people, yet it was there and he might have put it to use." McAdoo gave the bonds the uplifting name Liberty Loans. Concerned about public apathy, Tumulty advised Wilson that speakers needed to arouse "righteous wrath" by revealing the "character of the beasts we are fighting." Woolley told House that "a campaign of hate must be resorted to."[26]

The CPI found the use of emotion irresistible. The *Four Minute Men News* admonished speakers to "inspire, not inflame." Yet instructions advocated appeals to fear, "an important element to be bred in the civilian population." A sample speech read: "President Wilson says it is a struggle for democracy against autocracy; it is also a struggle of Christianity against Prussian kultur." Informed that a CPI soldier-speaker told a Knoxville movie audience he "would sooner grasp a snake than shake the hands of a German," Byoir wired the speaker's handler to "eliminate anything from his talk which might excite the violently inclined." Yet Charles Edward Russell, one of the CPI's favored orators, spoke in the House of Representatives of "wolfish Huns whose fangs drip with blood and gore!" Advertisements for CPI films promised scenes of Hun brutality "that would shame a tribe of headhunters." In Creel's most thorough statement on the "the purity of our motives," he drew attention to these warring opposites: "We want a public opinion that springs from the heart and soul—that has its root in the rich soil of truth." Creel never acknowledged the contradiction in himself or the CPI.[27]

High emotion was second nature to Creel. British political scientist Harold J. Laski dismissed his campaign book *Wilson and the Issues* as "reckless pamphleteering." The year before the election Creel made the case for touching emotions. The "average man," he wrote, is "anything on earth but a shrewd, keen analyst of men and affairs. He does not think or read to any great extent.... Out of it all the average American has evolved a certain very passionate idealism that is almost pitifully dependent upon signs and symbols." "America," Creel often said, "must be thrilled into unity and projectile force."[28]

The time had never been better to employ signs and symbols. Modern propaganda would not have been possible without mass literacy and mass circulation publications. It reached full force with the mass reproduction of images. Few people read editorials, said George Hecht, who headed the Bureau of Cartoons. "Cartoons require little time or thought for their complete digest and are therefore editorials at a glance." The whole point of posters was to trigger emotion. "One cannot create enthusiasm for war on the basis of practical appeal," Charles Dana Gibson said, "To light the fires of patriotism, laid ready for the match in every American heart, requires an appeal to the heart."[29]

Charles Hart, director of the Film Division, took advantage of the persuasive powers in moving pictures by hiring talented Bruce Barton to write title cards in CPI films. Barton was a publicist for the War Work Council of the YMCA. "A big problem," Hart told Barton, "is to incorporate in these pictures some telling propaganda which at the same time would not be obvious propaganda but will have the effect we desire to create. We have been informed that you are the master of the short phrase and one of the best caption writers in the U.S." When the CPI's second film, *America's Answer,* premiered in New York, the *New York Times* noted, "Not a man and not a woman in the crowd that filled the seats failed to feel the pull of the war, the urging of its influence, the sense of participation in it."[30]

Barton would become a lion of the advertising profession, an advisor to Republican presidential candidates, a congressman, and author of *The Man Nobody Knows,* which portrayed Jesus as a modern business executive adept at advertising—a field that grappled with the same contradictions as the CPI did. The crusade for "truth in advertising" sought to eliminate false claims, as the CPI claimed to do; at the same time advertisers, like the CPI, were finding it more effective to use nonrational persuasion to shape behavior. Advertising executives turned to science-based measurement of attitudes and psychology. "People," one practitioner said, "can be made to believe almost anything with proper salesmanship."[31]

In the beginning, Creel wanted to stimulate "very passionate idealism." Advertisements asked women to become nurses because "Your Country Needs You" and implored the public to buy Liberty bonds to help American boys in the trenches. Ads used Christmas scenes and the one-word headline "Mother." In one cartoon, a comely Red Cross Gibson girl comforted a wounded soldier. Over a sea of marching troops, John T. McCutcheon of the *Chicago Tribune* drew a large American flag with the caption "The Hope of Civilization." But over time dark appeals of fear and hatred crept into CPI propaganda. Much of it centered on German-Americans.[32]

Germans could be made into a nearly perfect archenemy with which to arouse the public. As we have seen, Germany's intemperate propaganda and ill-conceived, zany sabotage in the United States after 1914 were case studies in how to lose the battle for public opinion. The British took advantage of this in their propaganda, and others reinforced the image of the treacherous German and, by inference, of the treacherous German-American. Anti-German rhetoric was useful to organizations that sought public support for military preparedness before April 1917. German-American disloyalty was a theme in the 1916 presidential election. Wilson—in the words of historian David Kennedy—made "'Americanism' the controlling motif of his re-election campaign." The overthrow of the tsar in Russia in early 1917 gave the Allies a new anti-German propaganda theme. They could buck up their public's enthusiasm for the war by pointing out that all the Allies were now democracies in contrast to imperial Germany and Austria-Hungary. Thanks to the Russian Revolution, James Garfield wrote in his diary, "The Kaiser ought to be shaking on his throne."[33]

German-Americans, the largest group of foreign-born in the country, were perceived positively before the war. They were praised for their industry, thrift, education, and good citizenship. German immigrants, sociologist Edward Ross wrote, "have proved, on the whole, easy to Americanize." Respect for Germany was so pronounced in the nineteenth century that it was referred to positively as the "German epidemic." Senator Henry Cabot Lodge's doctoral dissertation at Harvard celebrated the "Teutonic origins" of American democratic institutions. Ross, Ford, and many other budding scholars studied in Germany.[34]

The never-ending anti-German propaganda changed this image by the time the United States entered the war. German-Americans' reverence for their culture, which underpinned their civic virtues, now made them seem a dangerous people apart. They learned German in school and spoke it in beer halls, a pastime the temperance movement used to argue drinking was un-American. The total effect, historian John Higham wrote, "called forth the most strenuous nationalism *and* the most pervasive nativism that the United States had ever known."[35]

In an article promoting Liberty Loans, Ross confidently asserted a German victory would bring an end to "great poems, dramas, works of art and discoveries of science." Such thinking brought on paroxysms of hate that bordered on the deranged. The headline in a CPI Liberty Loan advertisement aimed at college students read: "In the vicious guttural language of Kultur, the degree A.B. means Bachelor of Atrocities. Are you going to let the Prussian python strike at your Alma Mater?" It went on in a frenzy of mixed metaphors: "The Hollenzollern fang strikes at every element of decency and culture and taste that our colleges stand for. It leaves a track so terrible that only whispered fragments may be recounted. It has ripped all the world-old romance out of war, and reduced it to the dead, black depths of muck, and hate, and bitterness."[36]

Ford claimed that he forbade use of the word *Hun,* a pejorative reference to Central Asian barbarians who invaded Europe in the fourth and fifth centuries. The lone slip, he said, was in the *Cyclopedia.* He instructed an academic team compiling a pamphlet on atrocities to draw only that material from the Bryce report that would "stand up in court." The resulting pamphlet, *German War Practices,* fell far short of the gruesome material the British had pushed out. O'Higgins may have been referring to this publication when he insisted that only one CPI report "was even faintly concerned with atrocities."[37]

But Ford's division did not consistently apply his guidelines. The *Cyclopedia* entry for "Atrocities" referred uncritically to the Bryce report as convincing "those hitherto incredulous that the stories of German cruelty were correct." Other entries referred to atrocities like those in Bryce's report. Next to the relatively tame text in *German War Practices* were sensational marginal subheads on "massacre," "slaughter of innocents," "brutality," and "barbarism."[38]

Creel employed "Hun" in statements and articles, as in "This fight for public opinion, both here and over all the world, will not be won until every man, woman and child enlists as a soldier, standing squarely behind the war, believing passionately in its justice, combatting lies, prejudices, and misrepresentations just as our men in France combat the Hun. Let us fix it so that we will not have to wear gas masks here at home." Arthur Bestor spoke of Germany as "outside the pale of civilized nations," guilty of the "ravishing of women and mutilation of children." A CPI film was titled *America's Answer to the Hun.* CPI posters and advertisements depicted the Hun as a rogue ape in a pickelhaube, the German spiked helmet that became a sinister symbol. The beast whipped children and murdered women, whose rumpled clothing suggested they had been violated. One Liberty Loan ad depicted limp dead bodies hanging Christlike. The headline read, "Must Children Die and Mothers Plead in Vain?"[39]

The German beast directly threatened Americans in their beds. An ad showed a map of the United States overwritten with the words "New Prussia." In a famous drawing for the fourth Liberty Loan drive, which is on the jacket of this book, Joseph Pennell depicted the Statue of Liberty, its head and torch destroyed; in the background New York City was engulfed in flames. An ad promoting Ford's publications showed a German soldier crushing New York with his boot. The text warned, "The next war will come *right* on to our own shores unless—we crush the War idea—unless we crush Germany."[40]

Hecht's Bureau of Cartoons turned to C. R. Macauley for the sort of propaganda he had drawn for the Wilson presidential campaigns in 1912 and 1916. His drawings depicted Germans as blood-drenched apes and vultures and ridiculed naysayers at home. In one cartoon, a scrawny opponent of the war has hidden a pickelhaube under his soapbox. To maximize distribution the Butterfield Syndicate offered Macauley's drawings as "a patriotic cartoon service at your own price." The cartoons had the endorsement of President Wilson, House, and Herbert Houston of the Advertising Division.[41]

CPI staff endorsed Dutch artist Louis Raemaekers, who was considered "the single most influential figure in projecting the Allied vision of the German enemy." Raemaekers achieved in pictures what the Bryce report achieved in words. His work juxtaposed descriptions of German inhumanity with drawings of babies with slit throats and of soap being made out of corpses. Masterman objected to sending the overwrought drawings to the United States, but he was overruled. Willert helped get them published. The British were turning to more strident propaganda, and Raemaekers, being Dutch, gave them cover. The Raemaekers propaganda campaign began in 1916 with secret support from the Foreign Office and the approval of Prime Minister Asquith. Initially only a few publications, such as the preparedness-minded *Boston Transcript,* used Raemaekers's cartoons for fear of warmongering. With the United States' entry into the war, more than twenty-two hundred papers printed Raemaekers's drawings, which also appeared in traveling exhibitions and on postcards.[42]

The Century Company, which published Raemaekers in book form, ran a promotional article by Creel in its magazine. "It is no more possible," the CPI chairman wrote, "to consider this Dutch genius as a mere artist, a worker with paper, ink, and lines than it is to view the Apostle Paul an itinerant orator, Jean of Arc as a military figure, or Rouget de Lisle as a casual song-writer. . . . It is one of the great works of the world which he has done."* Grosvenor Clarkson at the Council of National Defense patted Creel on the back. "If we are going to quicken the spiritual fibre of this country so that it shall become the mighty power of the states that it should and can become, we must do it by utilizing

* De Lisle, a nineteenth-century French army officer, wrote "La Marseillaise," the French national anthem.

Dutch artist Louis Raemaekers was considered "the single most influential figure in projecting the Allied vision of the German enemy." Raemaekers achieved in pictures what Bryce's overblown report on German atrocities achieved in words. This drawing, published in Raemaekers's book *America in the War*, was accompanied by a quotation from Samuel Hopkins Adams on the Germans' "coldly reckoned murder" of innocents.

the human appeal in the most intelligent, candid, and tireless way in every nook and cranny of the nation."[43]

A subsequent volume, *America in the War,* paired Raemaekers's cartoons with statements from President Wilson (a quotation about "vicious spies" from his Flag Day speech), Creel, and CPI colleagues Harvey O'Higgins, Charles Edward Russell, John Spargo, and Samuel Hopkins Adams. Alongside a drawing of the kaiser strung up by his wrists, Adams declared: "To me the deliberate, coldly reckoned murder of the invaded countries' trees and vines so that the children of the slain and enslaved and their children's children may draw no sustenance from the kindly earth—that seems the most perverse, the most detestable, the most typical of all the crimes of Kaiserism. The sterilization of Mother Earth. It took the mind of a Wilhelm to conceive it."[44]

COERCION

The Byoir files in the National Archives CPI records contain a letter from Hans Rieg, the man Robert Woolley called his "bureau of intelligence" during the 1916 presidential campaign. In that race, it will be recalled, Rieg acquired internal documents from the American Independence Conference. Woolley used them to expose the allegedly "secret" foreign-born association supporting Charles Evans Hughes. After the election, Woolley brought Rieg with him to the Treasury Department to organize Liberty Loan publicity. Rieg headed a subdivision to promote bonds among foreign-born Americans.[45]

Rieg's letter in the Byoir file was to Louis Hammerling, the president of the American Association of Foreign Language Newspapers. Disregarding Treasury rules and alluding to proposals from Lodge and other solons to outlaw German-language press, Rieg pressured Hammerling to arrange free space for Liberty Loan advertisements in his clients' newspapers.[46]

> For the reason that neither the Treasury Department nor this bureau desires to solicit nor can solicit, advertising space to be used for the purpose of displaying matter pertaining to the Liberty Loan, to be placed at the disposal of the Government free of charge, I want you to consider this letter absolutely personal. In other words, to not look upon it as an official communication. . . .
>
> It would be too bad to let anything occur which might have a tendency to spoil or in any way distract from the so highly appreciated an[d] so very good showing which papers belonging to your association have made during the last campaign for Liberty Loan bonds.[47]

This was the sort of ham-fisted maneuver British propagandists took great advantage of when it was done by the Germans. The files do not show that Byoir objected to Rieg's letter, and it is unlikely he did. The CPI was not above naked coercion and condoned the use of it by others.

Hammerling was a useful tool for Byoir as well. In addition to controlling ads in seven-hundred-odd foreign language newspapers, Hammerling owned an influential magazine for the foreign-born, *The American Leader*. Byoir, who directly supervised Hammerling's work, had no compunction about leveraging his fear to force the American Association of Foreign Language Newspapers to cut ties with publications deemed disloyal.[48]

Behind this approach lay a shift in thinking about public opinion. The progressive faith was built on the noble idea of giving the public the right facts, which it would accept as a natural course. But in the heat of war, their conviction about the justice of the cause overrode faith in facts. The desire to quickly correct deficiencies in public opinion led to measures that forced compliance.

When promoting the use of its materials, the CPI left no doubt what it wanted done. It pushed photographs and lantern slides on teachers with a letter that read, "Every teacher in every school in the United States should regard it as a solemn duty to secure these Photographs and Slides for class room work as well as for exhibition purposes." The teachers were told they could purchase on the installment plan if necessary. A recommended Four Minute Man speech on Liberty Loans resorted to the strong-arm tactic of peer pressure. The canned talk called for a show of hands as to who would commit to buying a bond. "Look around—count them—all the hands up—Yes, when the hour of danger strikes, the Stars and Stripes unite us all! Now then, don't let our friends remind *you* [to buy that bond]. *You* remind them."[49]

A widely distributed advertisement for Liberty bonds threatened ostracism in the name of decent public opinion.

> I Am Public Opinion
>   All men fear me!
>   I declare that Uncle Sam shall not go to his knees to beg you to buy his bonds. That is no position for a fighting man. But if you have the money to buy, and do not buy, I will make this No Man's Land for you!
>   I will judge you not by an allegiance expressed in mere words.
>   I will judge you not by your mad cheers as our boys march away to whatever Fate may have in store for them.

I will judge you not by the warmth of the tears you shed over the lists of the dead and the injured that come to us from time to time.

I will judge you not by your uncovered head and solemn mien as our maimed in battle return to our shores for loving care.

But, as wise as I am just, I will judge you by the material aid you give to the fighting men who are facing death that you may live and move and have your being in a world made safe.

I warn you—don't talk patriotism over here, unless your money is talking victory Over There.

I am Public Opinion!

As I judge, all men stand or fall!

How Many Bonds Have YOU Bought?

The Treasury Department's promotional efforts, to which the CPI contributed, relied on the same blatant coercion. Liberty Loan workers were instructed to insist that "buying Liberty Bonds is not to be considered optional, but obligatory." The guiding idea of the third Liberty Loan drive was "to compel as many people as possible to subscribe as much as they could afford; at the same time to wage an enthusiastic propaganda campaign to persuade them that they were subscribing voluntarily."[50]

In the pages of *Everybody's Magazine,* where he placed articles while helping the CPI, Adams celebrated the strong-arm sales technique of "blue carding" as part of a series he wrote called "Invaded America." Liberty Loan salesmen pulled out a blue card when they were unable to make headway with a potential customer. On one side, in large type, were the words "Executive Committee, Liberty Loan, Federal Reserve Bank." On the back, the salesman wrote down the target's name, citizenship, family size, and so forth looking for opportunities to press his case. If the target was a farmer who had a homestead, the salesman asked how he could refuse to buy a bond from the government that had given him land. This question-and-answer process often forced a purchase. When it didn't, the blue card became the basis for a subsequent call or a letter—and gave the farmer restless nights.

Adams was unconcerned about the coerciveness of blue carding. People who could afford to buy bonds were obliged to do so. He considered blue-carding especially effective with immigrants. The blue card, he believed, was "an energizing and regenerating force for nationalism."[51]

198

OPERATIONS

SPIES AND LIES

Early on the morning of April 4, 1918, the body of a night watchman was found at the CPI offices on Lafayette Square. He had been shot dead by a single bullet that passed through his lungs and heart. Reports swirled about that "an alien enemy had gone into the building to obtain valuable secret information in the committee's archives." This was not the first instance the CPI's headquarters was the supposed object of German intrigue. A few months earlier, when a staff member fractured his skull in a fall resulting from vertigo, the CPI withheld details. This set off widespread rumors that a German spy had attacked him. The watchman's death also had nothing to do with the German spies. At the end of the day on April 4, an African-American furnace tender named William Clements turned himself in to police. The volatile watchman had violently complained that "negro help" came to work too early. When he saw Clements that morning, he drew a pistol, waved it at him, and pulled the trigger four times. No rounds fired. The watchman had the wrong type of ammunition. Clements, who was carrying a gun because he feared trouble, fired in self-defense.[52]

The specter of German intrigue haunted officials' imaginations. During the 1916 race, Woolley thought German propaganda was behind the railway strike that threatened Wilson's reelection. Attorney General Gregory suspected the Germans of financing the Industrial Workers of the World (IWW), one of the few groups that allowed class loyalty to trump national loyalty. At a meeting of the advisory committee to Bestor's division, a representative of the Bureau of Naturalization declared, "There are practically 10,000,000 people in the country who owe allegiance to some government other than the United States." This was to say, every tenth American was not an American at all.[53]

Officials imbued the press with these fears. Newspapers and magazines carried scare headlines daily: "American Invested with German Spies" (*Literary Digest*); "German Spies in United States" (*Nashville Banner*). The latter story suggested Karl Boy-Ed was recruiting people for an "information mission to the United States." Carrying on his prewar German baiting, *Providence Journal* editor John Rathom printed a daily warning, "Every German and Austrian in the United States unless known by years of association should be treated as a spy." The *Milwaukee Journal,* whose readership was one of the most German in the country, won a Pulitzer Prize for attacking the German culture. One of its prizewinning editorials read like a paragraph straight out of *Common Cause:* "Here, in this trusting, peace-loving land of ours, Deutschtum has in truth been a hydra-headed monster. Evil, cunning, sinuous, it has worked and plotted." Florence Finch Kelly, who helped organize Kansas for Wilson in 1916, took another leave of absence from the *New York Times* to "uphold the morale of people at home." "An immense, secretly operating [German] force of between 200,000 to 300,000" was at large in the country, she wrote in the resulting book.[54]

The logical extension of this obsession was to root out German influence wherever possible. The day after declaring war, Wilson secretly authorized the removal of government employees considered "inimical to the public welfare by reason of his conduct, sympathies, or utterances, or because of other reasons growing out of the war." The man in charge of carrying this out in the State Department was the new third assistant secretary, Breckenridge Long, who had lavishly donated to Wilson's 1916 campaign and vigorously argued that Hughes was ineligible to be president on account of his father's British birth. The handsome, impeccably dressed, and wealthy young diplomat was a xenophobe. "I have caused about 15 officers to go—Consuls, Consular Agents and clerks—because of German nationality or sympathy," he wrote in his diary shortly before American entrance into the war. "Our service will be in much better condition if I can carry out my ideas in 'Americanizing' it from top to bottom."[55]

Government departments with intelligence bureaus in place expanded their operations, and others began similar work. "Virtually the entire executive branch of the Government," the *New York Morning Telegraph* reported, "is now engaged in the new and more active spy hunt that has been inaugurated. They are the State, War, Navy, Justice and Post Office departments, the Treasury, Agriculture, Commerce and Labor departments." McAdoo, who oversaw the Treasury's Secret Service, urged the creation of a coordinating organization under Woolley, who "was well equipped for this work." Nothing came of this proposal, and each department continued to expand its investigative endeavors. "I have today," Gregory commented in August 1917, "several hundred thousand citizens—some as individuals, most of them as members of patriotic bodies[—] engaged in upholding the Government and assisting the heavily overworked Federal authorities in keeping an eye on disloyal individuals and making reports of disloyal utterances."[56]

The CPI was integrated into the burgeoning surveillance system. Surveillance—a word the CPI was unashamed of using—was a valuable accessory to propaganda. "Reports of disloyal utterances" were a barometer of public attitudes that needed to be combatted. In response to a letter from Wisconsin on Senator Robert La Follette's "insidious" antiwar statements, James Shotwell told a State Department official, "We are anxious to keep track of all such propaganda, in order to be able to check on the condition of public opinion in different parts of the country." In addition to receiving reports from intelligence agencies, the CPI produced a "survey of the sentiment of the country as expressed in the foreign language newspapers." Beginning in May 1917, the CPI enlisted "volunteer readers" and by June had "secured the cooperation of college faculties in twenty different places." Nearly seventy professors monitored publications. In some cases, the CPI asked for daily reports. Although the CPI cut back on this work, as others had "taken up the problem," Creel noted in mid-1918, "Reports are made on virtually every paper in the United States that is not printed in English and we try to fight ignorance and untruth with a steady stream of articles selected with particular reference to the race or the problem of bitterness."[57]

CPI surveillance took other forms. The Four Minute Men Critic Committee in Galveston, Texas, " did double duty, checking on speaker performance and reporting "anything they hear in the theaters emanating from possibly disloyal citizens." On behalf of the Department of Justice the CPI urged cartoonists "to ask every loyal American to aid in the task of rooting German interests out of America, by reporting any knowledge concerning German ownership of property in this country." CPI advertisements and publications encouraged citizens to report disloyalty. In his preliminary press guidelines Creel explicitly requested journalists report suspicious activity. People inundated the CPI with "every equivocal word or suspicious action that they could see or hear of, anywhere in their daily lives," O'Higgins said.[58]

Unfounded rumors vexed the government. Many were wildly inaccurate. Soldiers were given alcohol to help them endure trench life. Red Cross sweaters were unraveled when they reached Europe. Germans crucified Allied soldiers. Joseph Tumulty had been shot as a German spy. Military camps abetted prostitution. After *Pearson's Magazine* said the French were charging Allies rent for the use of trenches, Lippmann wrote a colleague at the War Department, "This is one of those mean little tales that do immense damage." The CPI provided a useful service in combating these errant reports. But it also sought to stomp out legitimate criticism of government policy. A *Four Minute Men Bulletin* said that "any line of attack that tries to build up American prejudice against England" or criticize conscription furthered the ends of the "Potsdam gang."[59]

The CPI staff held an exaggerated belief in what Ford called "an extremely active and efficient German propaganda, which had thousands of dollars to our one and which had been in the field for some three years." The German spy system had penetrated every Allied country, the *German War Code* claimed. "Our own country is not yet rid of this menace. We are at war with a country that openly stands for the employment of hired assassins if necessary to overcome its enemy." These views fed off each other. After hearing Will Irwin talk about the "diabolical plots and plans of the Germans," a member of the Advertising Division wrote to him, "I hope you will agree with the Division of Advertising that the enclosed copy is not too strong."[60]

In his unpublished postwar recollections, O'Higgins acknowledged that others besides German agents were responsible for rumors. Some were "imaginative liars who wished to make themselves appear important." Many of the rumors came from people who did not like the Wilson administration. He did not acknowledge that suppression of news was a Petri dish for rumors, as was the CPI's relentless propaganda about spies.[61]

When it came to his attention that a "loyal war worker" of British birth had said that seven thousand soldiers had perished in a recent battle, O'Higgins concluded, "She had apparently been imposed upon by a German rumor monger." Falsehoods about the War Department and Food Administration, O'Higgins wrote in another CPI publication, "could have been invented for partisan purposes by men who were less eager to win the war than to win election. It is much more probable that . . . they are pro-German falsehoods invented for the purpose of weakening the confidence of the American people in the Government's war work." In any case, he said, the falsehoods were "hailed with joy by the enemy." Most criticism of the CPI, O'Higgins said, was lies "from the Kaiserites in America who saw in the Committee their official opponent."[62]

Making Americans fear they were imperiled on their own soil was an effective selling tool. A sample Four Minute Men speech urged audiences to buy "the billions" of Liberty bonds needed to finance the war with this image of the lurking German: "I have just received the information there is a German spy among us—a Germany spy watching *us*. . . . Well, I hope these spies are getting their messages straight, letting Potsdam know that America is *hurling* back to the autocrats these answers: For treachery here, attempted treachery in Mexico and treachery everywhere—*one billion*. For murder of American women and children—*one billion more*. For broken faith and promise to murder more Americans—*billions and billions more*."[63]

The spy mania also offered a way to counter unwelcome views. Challenges to government policy, objectives, or prosecution of the war could be attributed to German influence. As a member of the APL put it, any story or rumor that "makes a people nervous, uneasy or discontented" met the definition of German propaganda. CPI advertisements put Americans on high alert for treacherous dissent. Its "Spies and Lies" ad campaign urged citizens to "report the man who spreads pessimistic stories, divulges—or seeks—confidential military information, cries for peace, or belittles our efforts to win the war." A slogan read, "The German Army has already occupied America. The invisible host of spies is everywhere."[64]

Lewis Jones on the Advertising Division's board wanted the campaign to be as pervasive as possible. "There is a very serious hole in the 'Spies & Lies' campaign," he told Byoir. "Our magazine publicity will reach the educated, though thoughtless man. It does not, however, provide for reaching the uneducated, who are likely to read only yellow journals, and who do a tremendous amount of gossiping." "The subject," Johns suggested, "adapts itself to billboard illustration."[65]

Other divisions reinforced the message. Ford published *German Plots and Intrigues in the United States during the War Period of Our Neutrality.* One of the most widely quoted *Four Minute Men Bulletins* was "Where Did You Get

The CPI emblem was reminiscent of the Great Seal of the United States with its majestic eagle and American flag shield, which bespoke its authority; and it had the added touch of the torch of truth. A CPI advertisement was less subtle. It told the public to "Get the Facts from Washington!"

Your Facts?" Under the rubric of "Types of German Propaganda," it listed socialist propaganda that said this was a capitalists' war; propaganda directed at
blacks who were easy targets due their "illiteracy and credulity"; pacifist propaganda that argued "Christianity and war are not compatible"; and propaganda
on "The Irish question," which referred to Irish claims that this could not be a
war for democracy so long as Britain ruled Ireland. In the two weeks mandated
for lectures on the subject, Porter Dunlap's Four Minute Men gave 356 speeches
to more than one hundred thousand people.[66]

Fear and coercion were seductive shortcuts around the arduous, uncertain
route of rational persuasion. It was similarly expedient to classify dissent as
"enemy talk" and instruct the public, as one CPI ad did, to "Get the Facts from
Washington!" One of O'Higgins's features was called "The Official Facts," a
headline that newspapers often used for his articles.

HIGH-CLASS WRITERS OF FICTION

The CPI occasionally passed information from the State and Justice Departments on German spies to fiction writers. They did not use this to turn out
"trashy or stupid stuff," Creel assured legislators in June 1918. The writers were
too "high class" for that.[67]

The two most prominent writers of fiction and nonfiction on the staff were
Samuel Hopkins Adams and Harvey O'Higgins. Urbane, witty O'Higgins was
a prolific playwright. The courtly, athletic Adams, who knew how to spin a good
tale, was a literary jack of all trades whose output included children's stories and
game books. Both men were literary crusaders. [68]

Adams wrote *Common Cause* in parallel with his CPI duties. The two tasks
informed each other. "I'm frightfully busy trying to make a living and at the
same time do such war work as is handed to me—and it is being handed at an
increasing rate, I assure you," he told his publisher. The gist of the book, he went
on in the letter, was "loyalty vs. German propaganda." The setting for the novel
was Wisconsin (he called it Centralia), where he did research for his "Invaded
America" articles in *Everybody's*. By the time the book appeared in 1919, the
war was over. But a version of it appeared the previous summer in the *Saturday
Evening Post.*[69]

This was not all Adams did to forge a spirit of common cause during his association with the CPI. In short fiction stories he wrote about another small-
town newspaperman who teamed with a government agent to foil a German

plot; about a young man who bribed his draft board so he could enlist in the army; and about a Four Minute Man who, finding that words failed him, punched a Wisconsin Swede who did not show adequate enthusiasm for the war. In the *New York Tribune* Adams attacked the editor of the Yiddish daily *Forward* and Victor L. Berger, editor of the *Milwaukee Leader.* Both socialists were not wholeheartedly behind the war. Adams castigated La Follette, asking the question, "Is Wisconsin against America?" This was apparently fine with Creel, who thought the Justice Department did not act energetically enough in that state.[70]

Adams's "Invaded America" series revealed Germany's poisoning of "the American mind." He repeated the canard about German use of cadavers for soap and fertilizer. He employed the pernicious propaganda technique of arguing that the absence of incriminating evidence showed how insidious the enemy was. Regarding German propaganda, he said, "Of the precise method employed I can not speak with knowledge. It may be that there is a central and secret bureau, a German official press agency, which plans each separate campaign and issues instructions or even syndicated matter." He wondered "whether perhaps my country is too tolerant of the alien within its gates."[71]

Anyone who questioned Adams's line of thinking was, to his way of thinking, disloyal. "The fact is," Adams wrote privately at the end of the war, "that I am in a rather cynical mood as to those untrammeled spirits who tremble lest war methods fix upon us shackles that we never can throw off. Wherever I had talked with men of this mind I have found them to be either pro-German or pacifist at bottom."[72]

Adams called himself a "National Security and Defense Executive." O'Higgins considered himself a "literary conscript for the Committee on Public Information." His writing could be as amped as Adams's was. Shortly before the United States entered the war, he wrote, "The Germans gave us our choice. 'Be German,' they said, 'Or be killed.' . . . We are like the passengers on a larger *Lusitania.*"[73]

O'Higgins specialized in "German lies." His method of operation was to troll through rumors sent to him in search of ones that should be scotched. He wrote *The Kaiserite in America: One Hundred and One German Lies,* the booklet designed for use by traveling salesmen. His pamphlet *The German Whisper* warned Americans that they were under an attack designed by the German General Staff. "As in Russia and in Italy," O'Higgins wrote, "so here also a campaign of German propaganda—a gas attack of poisonous lies and rumors and false reports—has been launched successfully and is now underway."[74]

In mid-1918 O'Higgins started a syndicated feature called "The Daily German Lie." Newspapers across the country ran the column. No publication seemed too insignificant to be on the mailing list, not even the house organ of Niagara Paper Mills in Lockport, New Jersey. The feature resembled Wile's "Germany Day by Day" on German propaganda for the *London Daily Mail*. One especially convoluted column blamed the Germans for the false atrocity stories that were leveled against them. The Germans, O'Higgins argued, put out the false stories in order to inflame American troops, who would then commit similar crimes, thereby making the German soldier fight all the harder. False stories of atrocities, O'Higgins warned his readers, discredited "the well-authenticated cases committed on Belgium girls during the early days of the war."[75]

"It would be practically impossible," O'Higgins wrote in response to an inquiry about German atrocities, "to exaggerate the truth of the German atrocities committed in this war."[76]

DANGEROUS ORGANIZATIONS

At the end of 1917, a Boston minister asked Newton Baker if the American Defense Society had "the endorsement and approval of the US Government in its propaganda." Baker turned to George Creel for advice. "It is one of these 'worthy' organizations," Creel replied, "that persists in doing stupid and even dangerous things. It is not possible for me to attack it, but I refuse to recognize it in any way, and whenever the opportunity presents itself, I am kicking out some of its supporters."[77]

Creel had uneasy relations with the ADS and organizations like it. They criticized him for lack of patriotic enthusiasm; in his memoirs, Creel called the ADS and the National Security League "obnoxious." But at the same time the CPI was interwoven with them.[78]

Arthur Bestor headed the National Security League's Committee on Patriotism through Education, which published a speakers' handbook of its own. In July 1917, his Chautauqua Institution hosted an NSL-sponsored Speakers Training Camp that included CPI participation. When Bestor created the CPI's Speaking Division, he sought help from Robert M. McElroy, a Princeton professor who was educational director of the NSL. A committee under McElroy produced "a detailed plan for a national campaign to be conducted by the allied societies under the direction of the Bureau [sic] of Public Information." McElroy, a handsome, muscular presence wearing a silver NSL lapel pin, was to be remembered for an intemperate speech at the University of Wisconsin. The state, he said, had to choose between German and American. When the attention of rain-drenched students flagged, McElroy shouted out, "By God, I believe you are traitors!"[79]

The Vigilantes was the brainchild of Hermann Hagedorn, a pro-Roosevelt German-American author and poet. The idea was hatched "one dour Sunday afternoon" in November 1916 in the home of playwright Porter Emerson Browne. "Germany," Browne said of the inspiration for the group, "has unsheathed and brought into play one weapon that the Allies and ourselves didn't even know existed. . . . It is propaganda." The Vigilantes developed "intelligent public opinion" through syndicated articles, poetry, posters, and speeches to "quicken the people of America into a sense of the country's peril." By May 1917, the group was sending typeset stories every Friday to newspapers in towns with populations over five thousand inhabitants, divvying up stories among those in each town to avoid duplication. It reached ten thousand weeklies through the American Press Association.[80]

Pro-Roosevelt critics of Wilson were members of the Vigilantes. But so were Wilson disciples Charles Hopkins Adams, Charles Dana Gibson, Ernest Poole, Bruce Barton, and Ida Tarbell. In one of his first planning meetings, Hagedorn met at the Players Club with the president of the NSL and a director of the ADS. In addition to supporting those organizations, the Vigilantes boosted Liberty Loans (Woolley was a member of the Vigilantes), the Red Cross, and the American Alliance for Labor and Democracy, a group the CPI quietly sustained. Ernest Poole asked Hagedorn to write articles for the CPI's Foreign Press Bureau.[81]

In late 1917 Creel encouraged the American Defense Society to move its publicity bureau to Washington in order to work closely with the CPI. The ADS, which had Roosevelt as its honorary president, was in the vanguard of the "one hundred percent Americanism" movement. Its American Vigilance Patrol was on the lookout for "seditious street oratory" and urged police to arrest the orators for disorderly conduct. Writers working with the CPI served on the ADS publicity committee. Creel wanted the ADS to expand its work by adding journalists "of the type of Samuel Hopkins Adams and Harvey O'Higgins."

The strong funding the ADS received from wealthy Republicans made it attractive to Creel, who was always looking for additional revenue to do his work. An affiliation with the CPI appealed to the ADS because it would give the organization access to "secret telegrams and messages constituting revelations which the American people are entitled to know but which the Bureau of Information [the CPI] has hitherto been unable to issue for lack of competent help." Articles produced by the ADS-funded staff would be issued under auspices of government agencies "after being vised by Mr. Creel." An ADS internal memorandum noted, "The Publicity Bureau could handle many topics (such as an attack on Senator La Follette) which a government agency could not handle."[82]

Although the idea did not come to fruition, it indicated Creel's flexibility in partnering with patriotic organizations of which he disapproved. A few months later, the CPI asked the ADS for its publications, saying many of them "can be used to great advantage in our work in Mexico and Spanish America." About this time Creel congratulated the founder of the ADS on drumming George Sylvester Viereck out of the Authors' League of America.[83]

FROM A THOUSAND SOURCES I AM TOLD

The Great War was half a world away. It was never a fight for American security. Wilson based involvement on the idealistic end of helping bring a just peace. Stories on spying and disloyalty made the war seem more proximate and threatening. During the debate over the Espionage Act, the administration emphasized that German propaganda was a continuing menace. "The germ is still alive," the *Indianapolis Star* dutifully reported, "and it would be a fatal blunder for the authorities not to take notice of this fact, the department of justice officials say."[84]

The government continued to plant scare news. The Vigilantes reveled in their access to "much valuable" government information on enemy propaganda, which they passed on without any hint they were being used by government authorities to shape public opinion. News stories carried unsubstantiated assertions of the most general sort. Enemy propaganda was a continuing threat, wrote Isaac Marcosson, who sought the CPI's help for a *Saturday Evening Post* article. Government agents, he reported, had evidence "of a fresh campaign to distort and shape public opinion" in favor of ending the war. He did not say what that evidence was.[85]

In early 1918 the British slipped cables to the French and the Americans that it intercepted relating to Joseph Caillaux. Caillaux was in jail on charges of treason in order to keep him out of the way. Like the French, the British feared Caillaux would use his influence to bring about a negotiated peace that precluded all-out victory. A French newspaper coined the word "defeatism" for him. The British director of naval intelligence, said an American diplomat in London, "thinks of nothing but hanging Caillaux." One cable contained comments that Caillaux made during a visit to Argentina in 1915. According to a "confidential agent," he was contemptuous of the French leaders attacking him, believed that the Germans did commit atrocities, and cautioned that German praise for him and his peace message "injures his position in France."[86]

None of this proved Caillaux was a traitor, but it was made to seem so by the CPI, which was given the cables. The *Official Bulletin* splashed the Caillaux revelations across its front page. To heighten the impression of sinister collusion with the Germans, the CPI included a German government press notice that ordered journalists to keep Caillaux's name out of the news, as Caillaux had asked. No mention was made of the fact that the French forbade its press to mention the former minister because it would encourage peace talk. The *New York Times,* which along with other newspapers dutifully reported these putative revelations, did not say in its story that Caillaux believed the Germans were guilty of atrocities. It emphasized instead that Bernstorff used cable lines for "unneutral" purposes.[87]

The CPI was a two-way conveyer belt for spy information. O'Higgins sifted through the reports of disloyalty that were sent to him by journalists, community leaders, and citizens. He passed those that might warrant action to the Justice Department. He also received tips from army intelligence. Ford drew on Justice Department, War College, and State Department records in the preparation of *German Plots and Intrigues.*[88]

Before coming to the CPI, Adams wrote a *New York Tribune* column called "Ad-Visor" to expose dishonest advertising. The *Tribune* created a Bureau of Investigations to ferret out information he could use. In September 1917, Adams used the same muckraking style to expose German treachery, this time with the help of Justice Department investigators who seized papers the year before from the New York office of Wolf von Igel, secretary to Captain von Papen. The papers belonged in the same category as the contents of Dr. Albert's briefcase. They documented subsidies to journalists, connections to Irish revolutionaries working against the British, and possible sabotage of a canal in Canada. With Lansing's blessing, Adams prepared, as Creel put it, "a skillful analysis . . . that showed German intrigue down to the last sordid detail." The *Official Bulletin* carried the "revelations," and newspapers across the country did their part to play up the "official expose." The managing editor of the *Brooklyn Eagle,* who complained about the flood of CPI news, had no objection to this handout. He wanted more CPI stories of the "Igel type." Von Igel's papers belonged to a period before the war (he had gone home before he could be tried for conspiring to destroy a canal in Canada), but the clear implication of this "news" was that German subversion was alive and ubiquitous.[89]

In keeping with Wilson's Flag Day speech, Creel claimed the CPI did not vilify Germans, only their leaders responsible for the war. But this was not so. The bestial figures in CPI posters, cartoons, and advertisements occasionally resembled the kaiser, but often they were quotidian Germans in uniform. The "suspicious" Mrs. Wanser in Adams's *Common Cause,* who objected to Four Minute Men interrupting movies, was a housewife. Ford's booklet *Conquest and Kultur* was not limited to statements from the kaiser, his ministers, and his generals. It quoted German professors, stage directors, writers, clergy, journalists, a physician, a letter-writer to a German-American newspaper, and a second lieutenant on the German general staff. "It is well enough to attempt to differentiate between the German and his government," Arthur Bestor wrote in a National Security League publication, "but most Germans make no such differentiation."[90]

After the war, Creel complained the CPI did not deserve criticism for "bloody" Liberty Loan advertisements, but it did. Many of the posters produced by Gibson's artists did not identify themselves as associated with his division or the Committee on Public Information, an omission that Creel complained about to Gibson. One omission was Joseph Pennell's famous, evocative poster of a flame-engulfed Statue of Liberty, with merciless Hun planes swooping overhead. He conceived it while attending a CPI meeting in which the request was made for drawings for the fourth Liberty Loan drive. The CPI helped produce it. The CPI's name appears nowhere on it. Similarly, a poster with a bloody handprint—"The Hun—his Mark"—showed no CPI affiliation even though the division used it as a representative example of the work it did. "Nine out of every ten posters which you see on the boards for any department of government," Byoir told a Chicago audience, "were created by the organization that Mr. Creel has built."[91]

In 1915, Joseph Tumulty told Wilson it was imperative to show action in combatting German intrigue, lest he lose public support. "The country every day," he said, "reads of the efforts of these hyphenated Americans to destroy manufacturing plants, to poison and control public opinion in every way." Officials' fear of opposition to the war—and their desire to squelch it—led to wild exaggerations of the threat from the one element of the population that could be easily labeled un-American, those of German extraction. The CPI energized this continuous propaganda feedback loop. It encouraged Americans to imagine spies and treachery everywhere, which led to "sightings" that reinforced the impression and led to calls for more diligent searches for hidden treachery. "From a thousand sources," Creel told a group of journalists, "I am told of the wonder of German propaganda." But American propagandists had propagandized themselves.[92]

"Not infrequently as many as 1500 complaints reach the Department of Justice in a single day," Gregory said. "It is safe to say that there is nothing whatever in 95 per cent of these cases, and yet all are thoroughly investigated in order that we may cull out the small number which justify prosecution." Having a German name, reading a German-language paper, attending a church with a German name were grounds for harassment. After McAdoo strenuously objected to the American Protective League's use of the term "secret service," which made them sound as though their members were Treasury Secret Service agents, the Justice Department ordered APL agents to put away their badges. APL directors complied half-heartedly by telling their members not to use their badges "except when approaching one who cannot read English."[93]

Despite the widespread fear of spies, the Germans did not leave a spy-sabotage network behind when the United States entered the war. Only one agent was convicted. Lothar Witzke, a handsome young German, was apprehended when he crossed from Mexico into Arizona to start an uprising through the IWW. The plot was as bizarrely unrealistic as Zimmermann's plot to induce Mexico to reconquer lost territory in the United States. Witzke carried a crude Russian passport and a piece of paper—easily decoded by the British—that identified him as a "German secret agent." Nine days before the war ended, a US Army military court sentenced him to death. Wilson commuted the sentence to life imprisonment. Witzke was released in 1923.[94]

8

Working from the Inside

> When the campaign is tremendous don't think it just happens; something has
> to be done to get millions of people to think the thought you want them to
> think and then to get them to act on that thought.
>
> —Carl Byoir

In 1935, Carl Byoir told military officers at the Army War College how to mobilize "all the living forces of a nation to secure a given course of conduct or action." They must become behind-the-scenes "stagehands." The first step was to
create front organizations "with names that establish in themselves the soundness of the movement and the integrity of its purpose." He uttered the word
integrity without any sense of irony.[1]

The CPI routinely partnered with other organizations. The Council of National Defense supported the Four Minute Men. Ford's education division relied on the National Board for Historical Service. Bestor's Speaking Division
coordinated oratory among government and extragovernmental organizations.
The Wisconsin Loyalty Legion, "the right-arm distributing agency of the CPI,"
promoted Adams's *Common Cause* among state newspaper editors. The CPI
cooperated with extremist patriotic organizations that it did not fully endorse.[2]

These connections were obvious to see. But others were not, especially when
it came to targeting two groups whose loyalty the CPI was especially keen to
secure, immigrants and labor. Some of this deserves to be remembered as wholesome. The Division of Work with the Foreign Born enlisted immigrants to
work with immigrants. This effort, Creel said, "steered clear of the accepted
forms of 'Americanization.' We worked from the *inside,* not from the outside,
aiding each group to develop its own loyalty league, and utilizing the natural
and existing leaders, institutions, and machinery." As positive as this sounded,
however, it was at odds with the democratic idea inherent in Wilson's admoni-

tion that Creel was to "spend no dollar on a secret errand or try to camouflage a single activity." The CPI worked from the inside *and,* to the degree it could, out of sight. It designed the organizations to appear organic and veiled its affiliation with them. Despite Creel's claim that "we gave counsel, not commands," the CPI stage-managed the organizations' activities, with Byoir playing a leading role in the deception.[3]

Creel was no stranger to sleight of hand. He was caught in the act in 1914, when Frank Walsh, chairman of the US Commission on Industrial Relations, led an inquiry into the treatment of workers by the Rockefellers and other owners of Colorado mining companies. Creel praised the commission's work in two *Harper's Weekly* articles that muckraked the coal companies for "poisoning public opinion" to cover up their guilt in the Ludlow Massacre. It was in this reporting that Creel launched the attack on *Survey* editor Paul Kellogg that drew Walter Lippmann's scathing rebuke. It will be recalled that Creel's criticism of Kellogg focused on his conflict of interest in praising the Rockefeller Foundation's inquiry into mining practices while his magazine was receiving foundation support. Creel did not acknowledge that he was doing something similar. He was a close friend of Walsh since his Kansas City days and on the payroll of Walsh's commission. There is no evidence Creel felt chastened when Kellogg called attention to his conflict of interest.[4]

Creel condoned similar behavior by his CPI colleagues. Samuel Hopkins Adams sold propaganda articles without noting his CPI affiliation. In one instance where he was more forthcoming, the admission was too coy to be illuminating. "Nowadays," when he picked up his pen, Adams said in an author's sketch accompanying a short story, "it is mainly in the conscientious endeavor to earn the dollar a year which a recklessly extravagant Government pays me, or to write articles or fiction dealing with the one all-engrossing subject, the war."[5]

The impulses that led CPI staff to lean on emotions also led it to operate in a way progressives found loathsome in trusts, the surreptitiousness with which they operated. When Ray Stannard Baker muckraked the railroads, he showed how they planted news, withheld advertising from unfriendly publications, and bought newspapers outright. "Now it is a good thing for the people to have all the arguments," he concluded, "provided, *they know the source from which the arguments come.*" One of the many ironies of the CPI was its relentless insistence that German propagandists subverted American public opinion through insidious subterfuge while at the very same time concealing its own activities.[6]

JULY FOURTH LOYALTY DAY

The July Fourth Loyalty Day inspired by theater publicist Harry Reichenbach in 1918 produced a spectacular national display of patriotism with Wilson at its center. At two o'clock the president and representatives of foreign-language groups boarded the presidential yacht *Mayflower* at the Navy Yard for a trip up the Potomac River. "The hills of Mt. Vernon were black with thousands of people," recalled Attorney General Gregory, who was among the perspiring throng of officials and diplomats. Frederick Lewis Allen, who came with two friends in a rented Ford, noticed Creel was "hustling about apparently telling people where to go and making arrangements in general." Irish tenor John McCormack started the ceremonies with "The Star-Spangled Banner." When he repeated the refrain "then conquer we must," Wilson extended his hand. As a light southerly breeze took the edge off the late afternoon heat, the foreign-born laid wreaths on George Washington's tomb. "We, who make this pilgrimage," their spokesman said, "are the offspring of thirty-three different nations—and Americans all." Wilson responded with a speech envisioning a new world organization for peace. Straining on tiptoe to see the president over the crowd, Allen again noticed Creel, standing between the orating president and his wife.[7]

This would have been a grand Independence Day no matter what. The war spirit was high in the country. New navy vessels were launched in San Francisco that day. But the dominant motif was the unfurling of foreign-born patriotism in unison with the Mt. Vernon event. Parades, folk singing, and tableaux sponsored by Allied nations took place all over the nation's capital. The New York City parade, which the *New York Times* called a "demonstration of the loyalty of Americans of foreign birth," lasted more than ten hours and had more than seventy thousand marchers. Harrisburg, Pennsylvania, had a "glorious Fourth," proclaimed a local paper, "a riot of color, bands, flags, and nationalities." "If ever the Melting Pot of the Nations showed the strength and glory and knitting powers of freedom, it was at yesterday morning's Fourth of July parade," proclaimed the *San Francisco Chronicle*'s front page. "From the Embarcadero to the City Hall, Market Street was lined with patriotic multitudes."[8]

Loyalty Day was the largest public event the CPI organized. It was the sort of thing Creel liked to boast about, and he did so well after the fact, when he tallied the committee's accomplishments. At the time Loyalty Day took place, however, the CPI adopted Byoir's stagehand role. While expressing exuberance for the celebration, Creel credited the "foreign element" with taking "advantage of the day to express their devotion to America." The United Press Washington bureau chief knew Creel was behind the "peach of a stunt." But the *Times,* the *Harrisburg Telegraph,* and the *San Francisco Chronicle* ran many columns without a single mention of the CPI. Frederick Lewis Allen, who was on the Council of National Defense and worked closely with the CPI, noticed Creel bustling, but was apparently unaware of the CPI's role in orchestrating the event.[9]

The first illusion in this Loyalty Day theater was the impression that patriotic immigrants inspired it. This, argued Will Irwin, prevented "the enemy from saying that the government had bludgeoned the foreigners into taking this action." Irwin described the procedure this way: "The head man of all our thirty-three foreign-born groups, charmed with the idea," petitioned President Wilson to endorse their desire to "manifest, by special celebrations, our loyalty to this country and to the cause for which we fight." Irwin went on, "Wilson, with the fire having been built under him, fell into line and issued the appropriate proclamation. We wrote the copy in our office; he merely added a few 'may I nots.'" The *Official Bulletin* gave all credit to the foreign-born groups, briefly noting Wilson asked the CPI and the Council of National Defense to cooperate. The suggestion that Wilson make a presidential "pilgrimage" to Mount Vernon to deliver his speech came from Creel. When the president balked at using Washington's tomb as a July Fourth prop, Creel brought "the foreign-born into play" by getting them to request Wilson to do so. It was Wilson's idea to travel on the *Mayflower* rather than by car. The deftly directed occasion stood out "in the life of the Committee," Creel said when he got around to bragging, "as one of the few events that swept from start to finish without attack, obstruction, or untoward happening."[10]

Loyalty Day was the culmination of organizational efforts that began, piecemeal, the previous fall and produced associations with such evocative names as the Jacob A. Riis League of Patriotic Service, which united Danes. Like the July Fourth event, the purpose of these leagues was to promote and demonstrate loyalty. They adhered to Byoir's principle of "a set-up with names that establish in themselves the soundness of the movement and the integrity of its purpose." Pianist, composer, and future prime minister of Poland Ignacy Paderewiski rallied Poles. German-born New York banking partners and philanthropists Jacob Schiff and Otto H. Kahn lent their names and money to the American Friends of German Democracy. Dr. Antonio Stella, an esteemed New York physician dedicated to improving living conditions among his fellow immigrants, was president of the Roman Legion of America.[11]

Whenever possible the CPI played down its involvement. It openly stood behind the American-Hungarian Loyalty League, whose name Creel suggested, when its head, Alexander Konta, insisted on it. Konta felt government recognition would offset claims he was disloyal. Creel had favored the league standing "by itself, just as the other organizations stand." Nevertheless Hans Rieg, who was well-connected with immigrant populations, was for months unaware the Hungarian League was a CPI invention.[12]

The American Friends of the German Republic began without CPI impetus. After taking a new name that hit a more suitable note for propaganda, the American Friends of German Democracy fell under the CPI's aegis but maintained the impression of independence. In February 1918, it staged a mass meeting in New York's Grand Central Palace. News stories reported the "three hours of condemnation of the Kaiser" without any mention of the CPI. "The Friends of German Democracy was formed by me and is financed by me," Creel reassured Attorney General Gregory, who was questioning the organization's patriotism. "Everything it does is under my direction." But Creel did not want the link known. "We are not advertising it," he told a State Department colleague. The organization should be left unhindered without "reference to me."[13]

Byoir traveled across the country to help ethnic leaders establish local clubs. He came with money and strategic advice. In order to get the Sons of Herman to join forces with the Friends of German Democracy, he wrote its president, "It might be advantageous for all concerned if the officers and members of your organization could work out a plan of cooperation." They did. Byoir authorized Julius Koettgen to urge the organization to change its constitution, which required members to do business in the German language.[14]

Management of such an impromptu collection of immigrant organizations was difficult. Alexander Konta of the American-Hungarian Loyalty League presented an especially difficult problem. His league thrived. It had satellite offices in half a dozen cities and twenty-five thousand members, each of whom paid a one-dollar fee. But Konta's budget, like that of sister organizations, was not large, and his spending habits troubled Byoir. When the CPI urged ethnic groups to self-finance the mobilization of their people for the July Fourth Loyalty Day, Konta threatened to resign. A few days later, he told Byoir that he appreciated that the "suspicion of subsidization would spoil" the appearance

Carl Byoir believed propagandists should be behind-the-scenes "stagehands," creating front organizations "with names that establish in themselves the soundness of the movement and the integrity of its purpose." He used the word "integrity" with no sense of irony. (War Department, Army War College, Historical Section, World War I Branch)

of spontaneity, but without CPI money, "You can count me out. . . . If you do wake up, I hope you won't call on me at forty-eight hours' notice." It is unclear how Byoir resolved this or how much Konta's league contributed to the event, although other Hungarian societies participated.[15]

Byoir closely supervised Louis Hammerling, the Austrian-born president of the American Association of Foreign Language Newspapers. Hammerling's value went beyond his near monopoly over advertising in seven-hundred-odd immigrant newspapers. He was influential in ethnic communities and skilled in politics, having worked for the Republicans in recent presidential campaigns. As soon as Hammerling saw the announcement of the July Fourth Loyalty Day, he offered to arrange meetings and distribute releases to the foreign-language press. Hammerling got the impression that he was an assistant director at the CPI.[16]

DIVISION OF WORK WITH THE FOREIGN BORN

By May 1918, CPI activities with immigrant groups expanded to the point that Creel felt he needed a coordinating body. The Division of Work with the Foreign Born had fourteen bureaus, each responsible for a segment of the immigrant population. It absorbed the Foreign Language Newspaper Division, which monitored ethnic and overseas newspapers and translated materials. One of its first tasks was planning the Fourth of July Loyalty Day. The head of the division was social reformer Josephine Roche.

Roche, who worked in New York settlements during graduate studies at Columbia University, was one of the Denver "gang," as Judge Ben Lindsey called Creel, O'Higgins, and others in his progressive circle. During his turbulent tenure as police commissioner, Creel hired her as an inspector of public amusements. In addition to keeping youth away from alcohol and sex, she fought prostitution. Not yet thirty years old, the square-jawed, badge-wearing Roche carried herself with authority, but as Creel put it in an admiring article, she wanted to avoid "all necessity of making arrests." Her solution to prostitution was to shut down brothels, treat venereal disease, and help prostitutes find respectable employment.[17]

After the outbreak of war in 1914, Roche raised funds for Herbert Hoover's Commission for Relief in Belgium but was not keen for America to fight. That stay-out-of-war view led her to support Wilson in his 1916 reelection campaign (a close call for her because he did not support a constitutional amendment giving women the right to vote). When the offer to join the CPI came in the spring of 1918, the entire Denver gang was in a patriotic harness, including Judge Lindsey, who was on a five-month European speaking tour financed by the CPI

As head of the Division of Work with the Foreign Born, Josephine Roche sought not only to mobilize support for the war but also to overcome "years of neglect and even injustice" toward immigrants. (Edward Costigan Papers, University of Colorado–Boulder Library)

and the British Bureau of Information. Roche surrendered to the impulse to overcome "years of neglect and even injustice" toward immigrants. In addition to informing immigrants, she wanted to serve them as an intermediary with the federal government.[18]

Creel shared Roche's point of view. He liked to use variations of the phrase "It has been years since the melting pot has done any melting." A year before America went to war, he lamented that immigrants did not speak English, lived in "sordid colonies," and "failed to transfer their allegiance, a domestic peril that threatens the permanence of American institutions as gravely as any menace of foreign foe." He largely blamed this on American institutions, not on the new-comers who needed education, protection from con men, public employment bureaus, and health clinics.[19]

The Division of Work with the Foreign Born was one of many American-izing organizations. In February 1918, the CPI asked mayors for a list of the organizations doing local Americanization work. The survey identified thirty-two different groups. Given the perceived authority of the CPI, the letters had the unintended effect of suggesting to some mayors that they were now federal agents for Americanization. The Council of National Defense, with CPI ap-proval, had to send out a letter to clear up the confusion. One especially dy-namic leader of Americanization was Frances Kellor, who had helped organize Republican women's cross-country "Billionaire Special" on behalf of Hughes. She recruited Roche in 1913 to head the educational arm of the Progressive Party in Colorado. Kellor's interest in foreign transplants was kindled when then Governor Hughes put her on a commission in 1908 to improve conditions for aliens. She later guided the Committee for Immigrants in America. In 1915, the committee foreshadowed the CPI's Loyalty Day with a national Fourth of July "Americanization Day." The slogan was "Many Peoples, But One Nation." When war came, as John Higham noted, "One Nation" took precedence over "Many Peoples." Kellor's committee along with others advocated surveillance, suppression, and the forced study of English.[20]

Roche's division, Creel boasted, worked from the inside by organizing "the various foreign language groups into loyalty leagues and through the foreign language press, through their societies, through their leaders." Roche conducted a national "Americanization Survey" to identify churches, clubs, and businesses involved with the foreign-born. Instead of devoting its energies to eliminating foreign languages, her division spoke in them in order to connect with those peoples. When she learned that organizations doing similar work did not appoint immigrant staff as executives, she decided to be "the exception" (see table 2). The approach was practical as well as idealistic. "In our schools, our churches, our press, and in our social life, English should be the one accepted language, and this must, of necessity, be our goal," Creel wrote to Wilson. "But the ideal of tomorrow cannot alter the facts of today."[21]

The CPI's approach to the foreign-born was strikingly similar to the 1916

Table 2. The Division of Work with the Foreign Born

Name	Director	Location
American-Hungarian Loyalty League	Alexander Konta	123 East 23rd Street and 20 Exchange Place, NYC
Czechoslovak Bureau	Mrs. Anna Tvrzicka	16 Jackson Place, Washington, DC
Foreign Information Service	Donald Breed	16 Jackson Place, Washington, DC
German Bureau	Julius Koettgen	6 West 48th Street, NYC
Italian Bureau	Antonio Stella Basquale de Blasi	Metropolitan Tower, NYC
Russian Department	Joseph Polonsky	6 West 48th Street, NYC
Jugoslav Bureau	Peter Mladineo	16 Jackson Place, 6 West 48th Street, NYC
Lithuanian Bureau	Julius Kaupas	16 Jackson Place, 6 West 48th Street, NYC
Polish Bureau	John Wedda Miss Wadnda Wojeieszak	Union Trust Building, 6 West 48th Street, NYC
Scandinavian Bureau	Edwin Bjorkman	235 West 23rd Street, NYC
Ukrainian Bureau	Nicolas Ceglinsky	10 Jackson Place, 6 West 48th Street, NYC

Source: CND Report. The Council of National Defense pieced together the division's organization from CPI records as best it could with the following introductory comment: "This service was created in May 1918 and discontinued in May 1919. Miss Josephine Roche was Director. The office was located, successively, at 16 Jackson Place, 1621 H Street N. W. and 16, 10, and 8 Jackson Place, Washington, D.C., and 6 West 48th Street, New York City.

"The function of this division was to distribute to the foreign-speaking people in this country information on America's purpose in the war and the part they were asked to take in that crisis."

The names of the directors reflect Josephine Roche's desire to put the foreign-born in charge of their own organizations. The table reflects something else about the division, that much of its work was murky. The list does not have the names of the front organizations that the CPI used, except for the American-Hungarian Loyalty League.

Democratic National Committee's. At the same time Woolley's publicity bureau linked Hughes with supposedly un-American immigrant groups, it appealed to immigrant voters by distributing materials in their native languages and dispatching speakers who spoke in their tongue. Laurence Larson, an eminent Norwegian-born University of Illinois history professor who assisted the CPI, advised the best way to reach Scandinavians was by bringing a "first class" Swedish-American on the staff. "Occasionally during presidential campaigns," he said, "the national committees have secured Scandinavians for work of this sort."[22]

Roche's bureaus helped immigrants. They translated CPI and other government publications, created their own materials, and sent speakers to foreign-born "colonies." Materials went to immigrant associations, which pushed them onward to their constituents and to foreign-language newspapers. Bureaus sought "to rectify wrong conditions affecting the foreign born." They answered inquiries written by immigrants and visited communities (the Jugoslav Bureau made an extraordinary 124 visits to 53 localities). The Division of Foreign Language Newspapers provided immigrant editors with news from their home countries. News releases contained information on the prevention of venereal disease, war risk insurance, land reclamation, vocational training, and naturalization. Roche's division produced positive stories on immigrant acts of loyalty for use in English-language and ethnic newspapers.[23]

Still, the chief objective of the division was to do well propagandistically while doing good civically. It educated immigrants on the conscription laws and income tax. Stories of immigrant loyalty highlighted acts the CPI wanted to encourage, such as the purchase of Liberty bonds and military service. There was much gained by giving home country news to foreign-language papers. The CPI exercised considerable influence on news read by German-Americans. "For three years the German-American papers have been cut off from their foreign exchanges, always the most important part of the papers," William Churchill, the chief of the Foreign Language Newspaper Division, told Creel. "If we undertook to let them have this look-in they will feed out of hands on all the propaganda we supply." The division played up news of German and Austro-Hungarian military setbacks and brutality to their own citizens. The American Friends of German Democracy, which functioned more openly as the German Bureau in Roche's division, had its own bulletin, employed four field organizers and collected information on German groups and "the methods by which German propaganda made headway and the successful methods of overcoming it." The latter was passed on to intelligence agencies.[24]

Edwin Bjorkman exemplified the sort of "first class" person Larson had in mind to work with Scandinavians. Born in Sweden, he became a naturalized US citizen in 1915. He worked for Swedish-language newspapers in the Midwest before breaking into mainstream journalism with the *Minneapolis Times, New York Times,* and *World's Work.* "Genuinely patriotic" and "positively anti-German," the way Larson hoped, Bjorkman served with the New York militia during the Spanish-American War. In the fall of 1914, while visiting Sweden, he passed intelligence to Wellington House, which subsequently put him in charge of counteracting German propaganda there. With the British not wanting to propagandize openly in Sweden any more than in the United States, Bjorkman was ostensibly a correspondent with Reuters and the *London Daily Telegraph.* In the summer of 1917, he headed to the United States to make the case, as he informed the British Department of Information, for "America's taking her proper place beside you in the propaganda work as in everything else." By the end of the year he and Creel finalized the details of his employment with the CPI.[25]

Creel told Bjorkman to begin in Chicago, which had a vibrant Scandinavian community, and then proceed to Minneapolis and "to any other points that your judgment will suggest as wise." Bjorkman had an aptitude for organization as evidenced by his formation, as a young man in Sweden, of the Swedish Wholesale Clerks' Association. The plan he outlined for Creel called for the organization of Swedes to "appear spontaneous." He established the John Ericsson League of Patriotic Service by early March 1918. A Swedish news service was in place the end of April.* His message was "Furl your Swedish flag and gently lay it aside."[26]

When Roche's division was formed in May, Bjorkman was put in charge of the Scandinavia Bureau, which included Danes, Norwegians, Swedes, Finns, and, by reason of his "knowledge and sympathies," the Dutch. He was adamant on the need for materials in the Swedish language. (When the governor of Iowa proclaimed only English should be spoken in school, conversations in public, and the pulpit, Bjorkman complained to Creel. This may have prompted Creel's note to Wilson on the importance of foreign languages for propaganda.)[27]

Over a twelve-month period ending in 1919, the bureau produced an average of three releases a day, including weekends. The bureau prepared a weekly summary of news from overseas. The bureau admitted to exercising censorship

---

* John Ericsson (1803–89) was a celebrated Swedish-American mechanical engineer and inventor.

by discouraging Swedes from running articles by certain individuals "as their tone was not suitable or American. These suggestions were not only followed, but taken willingly and in the right spirit." As adamantly as Bjorkman opposed outlawing foreign languages, he believed "safeguards" were necessary to know what was said "in the lodges of the Swedish Secret Societies." He asked editors to inform "us of every lie and foolish rumor brought to your attention."[28]

Although exhibiting a "slight tendency towards opposition in the beginning," Swedish papers made use of bureau materials, as table 3 illustrates. This was consistent with other papers served by the Scandinavian bureau. The success of the bureau, the editor of its Dutch news service commented, lay in not "approaching the foreign born as strangers" and writing "in the language which they still understand best." The CPI had no objection to newspapers using its material in editorials without attribution.[29]

Table 3. Swedish-Language Newspapers' Use of the CPI Swedish Service

State	No. of papers	Extensive	Medium	Small use
New York	6	2	2	2
Massachusetts	3	1		2
Connecticut	1	1		
Pennsylvania	1		1	
Illinois	14	2	2	10*
Minnesota	9	1	4	4
Michigan	1	1		
Kansas	1		1	
Iowa	2	2		
Nebraska	1		1	
Utah	1	1		
Colorado	1	1		
Oregon	1	1		
Washington	4	2	1	1
California	3	2	1	
Texas	1			1

Source: Robert E. Lee to Roche, [1919], box 2, EB.
* Includes one fraternal and seven religious papers.

"Organization work is dear to me," Bjorkman told Finns meeting under the auspices of their CPI-created Lincoln Loyalty League, "and details of it I need not mix into."[30]

AFRICAN-AMERICANS AND PACIFISTS

Roche's bureaus were limited to people of European extraction. None touched Hispanics or Asians, although the latter had small roles in the July Fourth fete. African-Americans were treated by the CPI, as they were by America generally, as a group apart. The CPI worried that blacks were "especially susceptible to pro-German propaganda and lies which are continually being circulated." A CPI Negro Division was proposed, but Creel chose to make his "counter drive" against German lies in the black community through existing divisions and in cooperation with Emmett Scott, an associate of Booker T. Washington whom Newton Baker appointed his special assistant on race relations. (A realist, Scott said the source of black susceptibility to German propaganda was to be found in lynchings: "THESE LYNCHINGS BE IT REMEMBERED, WERE NOT 'Made in Germany.'")[31]

Byoir urged black editors to secure business sponsors for CPI advertisements. The Film Division produced *Our Colored Fighters,* which showed in churches and social centers as well as movie theaters, and wrote scenarios that were produced by others. Black Four Minute Men spoke to black audiences (although the associate director of the Four Minute Men for the southern part of the country thought no one "better able to help the negro, educate him, and inspire him to loyalty than the white people with whom he comes in contact"). The CPI's Division of Women's War Work was "particularly active among the colored women" in an attempt to combat "a great deal of rumor and propaganda" among that group.[32]

At the suggestion of military intelligence, which paid special attention to "Negro Subversion," Scott proposed a conference of thirty-one black journalists to get their agreement that "Negro public opinion should be led along helpful lines." Byoir helped arrange the three-day gathering, in June 1918, in the Interior Building. Wilson, whose record on race was abysmal, turned down Creel's suggestion to meet the journalists informally because black delegations always went "away dissatisfied." Creel addressed them instead.

At the journalists' request, Creel arranged press accreditation for a black war correspondent with the American Expeditionary Forces. Ralph Tyler, a rarity, had worked for a white-owned Ohio newspaper and was active in Republican politics. He went to France as a member of the CPI staff. "I am getting good propaganda stuff," he wrote Byoir in September 1918. Tyler recounted "the splendid endurance and valiant fighting of the Colored soldiers." The CPI killed his stories about French women's willingness to socialize with blacks. Privately he told Scott of rampant discrimination: "For the Colored soldier over here, this war is a tragedy."[33]

When it came to combating pacifism, Creel found an institutional ally in the Church Peace Union. The union began as a "peace education" organization funded by Andrew Carnegie. In 1917, the CPU concluded the best avenue for the clergy to exert its influence lay in winning "the war against autocracy" and establishing a League of Nations. The CPU served as the CPI's agent promoting "the moral aims of the war" among churches and especially among African-Americans and women. The CPU highlighted its affiliation with the CPI in red letters on its stationery. This "delighted" Creel and inoculated the CPU against charges its peace agenda was disloyal.[34]

Like the Four Minute Men, Roche's division pursued the progressive goal of rational top-down organization to establish correct thought and action. And like the Four Minute Men, which appeared to be local while taking cues from Washington, the CPI created the impression of autonomy among foreign-born communities. The difference was that the CPI pulled strings that were far less visible in the case of immigrants. Julius Koettgen, secretary of the Friends of German Democracy and its prime mover, believed membership was stunted because German-Americans feared joining a group with the odious word "German" in its title. They did not realize it was a CPI-affiliated group.[35]

The CPI was even stealthier in its work with labor.

THE GREAT PROBLEM OF LABOR

In December 1917, Creel encouraged Cyrus McCormick, the Chicago manufacturing titan of farm implements, to help finance the American Alliance for Labor and Democracy. McCormick was Wilson's classmate at Princeton and one of the president's longtime political supporters. "This is our most important body," Creel said of the AALD, "and I am eager to have it stand on its own feet." Financial contributions, Creel added, would "not only please me, but others who are above me."[36]

Creel's oblique reference to Wilson was indicative of the alliance's cloaked relationship with the administration. After the war, in his "Complete Report" on CPI activities, Creel did not mention the alliance except to list it among the organizations with which "direct relationship was constantly kept up" and to include six alliance publications among those put out by the CPI. The report likewise breezed past the CPI's Division of Industrial Relations and Division of Labor Publications, merely listing their expenditures in a financial summary. Nowhere did it mention Robert Maisel, director of the alliance and for a time director of the CPI Division of Labor Publications.[37]

The attitude of labor was a major concern for the Wilson administration. Strikes spiked when living costs rose despite government cost controls and limits on profits. This threatened industrial output crucial to winning the war. The American Socialist Party had the potential to foment unrest in union ranks. After the country went to war, pro-war members such as Ernest Poole and Upton Sinclair bolted; Charles Edward Russell was expelled. The antiwar party left behind opposed the draft and Liberty Loan drives and was generally viewed as an instrument of the enemy. A cartoon in the *St. Louis Republic* summed up the sentiment. Captioned "Birds of a Feather," it showed a draft dodger, an IWW member with a Bolshevik's beard, and the German spy perched side by side on a tree branch. Uncle Sam, armed with a rifle, hid nearby. Creel regarded propaganda toward labor as an extension of CPI efforts with the foreign-born. He called it an "attempt to Americanize the labor movement."[38]

O'Higgins's first assignment when he moved into his cramped office on Lafayette Square was "the great problem" of selling the war to labor. Other branches took on the same task. Four Minute Men spoke on "The Shipbuilder" and "Mobilizing America's Manpower." The Film Division produced *Labor's Part in Democracy's War*. Ford's division published *Labor and the War,* a speech by Wilson to the American Federation of Labor, among its Loyalty Leaflets. The *Friendly Word,* a weekly Russian-language magazine published in the CPI's office in Vladivostok, devoted space to industry and labor. Bjorkman's Scandinavian bureau used alliance material so extensively that at one point it was "the major part of our releases."[39]

In early 1918, the CPI created the Division of Industrial Relations, headed by Roger W. Babson, a New England business genius with a Kentucky colonel beard and a talent for Dale Carnegie prose. He founded Babson's Statistical Organization, which analyzed business reports. Although a Republican, he was active in Wilson's 1916 campaign because he opposed going into the war. Wilson, he said, was "trying to apply the teaching of Jesus to the running of a government and to international relations." He claimed to have participated in a meeting with Woolley where it was decided to use the "He Kept Us Out of War" slogan. He fell in step with going to war in April 1917 out of the belief that Great Britain had to be defended. He thought the Germans were winning the war because of their propaganda, not their military, and went to Washington to use "my knowledge of publicity methods."[40]

Babson initially referred to his job as director of the Pay Envelope Division. The "pay envelope" conceit—the phrase referred to the target audience of workers—originated with his Statistical Organization, which sold short stories in booklet form that businesses passed out to encourage workers to "Make More." Babson wanted to use the concept to "interest employees in the war." In a pitch to Byoir, he said his stories had a following of 200,000 workers. "My purpose of uniting with Mr. Creel is to increase my 200,000 to one or more million." The booklets, measuring less than three inches on a side, fit comfortably in a worker's pocket.[41]

Brimming with other ideas, Babson distributed Ford's literature to labor audiences, published *Labor Bulletins,* and produced posters directed at workers, the latter including confidential supporting material for employers. Babson did not hold back on emotion. One of his stories, "Human Bait," related a supposedly eyewitness account of the Germans tying a French soldier to barbed wire in no man's land. When his comrades tried to rescue him, they were picked off by snipers.[42]

Babson's division lasted a fleeting four weeks. In a rare instance of giving up turf, Creel handed off Babson to Secretary of Labor William Wilson, who was starting an Information and Education Service. Babson's work, Creel said, was "fundamentally within the province of your department." Babson's desire to tell capital how to view labor and vice versa was a "delicate" subject that might generate controversy the CPI did not want. Babson's service at the Department of Labor possessed features of the CPI with its news releases, posters, motion pictures, and speakers. Babson and the CPI cooperated. In June, for instance, the CPI News Division began to handle news for Labor. This was overseen by William L. Chenery, with whom Creel had worked on the *Rocky Mountain News* editorial page. Creel conceived a Babson-like plan for a CPI employer-employee program to promote national unity headed by the president of Commonwealth Steel Company, but nothing came of it.[43]

LABOR'S OWN CREATION

The American Alliance for Labor and Democracy, which became the focal point for CPI outreach to labor, avoided the problem of adverse publicity by veiling the ties between the two entities. The idea for the AALD originated with Samuel Gompers, president of the American Federation of Labor (AFL). On July 26, 1917, a day after meeting with Gompers, Creel wrote, "As I explained to you, I must insist that the entire movement be governed and directed by organized labor." The AALD appeared to be strictly "labor's own creation." The existence of CPI funding was closely held by Gompers. Initially, it was unknown to Secretary of Labor Wilson. When a similarly disguised arrangement with labor was suggested to Secretary Wilson, he rejected it. The United States was not like European governments, he said. "It is one of the great safeguards of Democracy that no such fund is available."[44]

Gompers was a short, portly man with a bullfrog face, a gift for oratory, and a thirst for convivial drinking. (He called prohibitionists "fanatics, long-haired men and short haired women.") Born in the East End of London, he was indentured to a cigar maker at the age of ten. When he moved with his parents to New York, he became involved in Cigarmakers' Local Union No. 15. Gompers became the AFL's first president in 1886. He built it into the most powerful labor group in the country with nearly thirteen million members. His enthusiasm for improving life for workers never took him into socialism, which he thought of as he did prohibition, a "fad of fanatics." Gompers flew the American flag above that of the AFL pennant at its seven-story headquarters on Massachusetts Avenue in Washington. He supported Wilson in 1912. The AALD grew out of his conviction that something had to be done to fight the "treasonable" acts of "German propagandists and agitators" in the labor movement.[45]

Gompers was president of the alliance. The director, Robert Maisel, was head of the National Labor Publicity Organization, a clearinghouse in New York for labor publications. He had worked on the *New York Call,* the principal organ of the Socialist Party, with whom he split over the war. Gompers used Maisel as an emissary to pro-war socialists.

Two prominent apostate socialists took leadership positions. John Spargo, called an "indefatigable publicist for the cause of evolutionary, democratic socialism," began his working life as a stonecutter in his native Cornwall, England. He was four-square for peace right up to Wilson's call to war, when he wired the president, "From now on, spiritually I am clad in khaki. I am ready for any service which is demanded." When Wilson complained to Spargo about "a very sullen resentment" among labor, Spargo met with Gompers. Together they came up with the idea for the alliance. Spargo became first vice president. J. G. Phelps Stokes, scion of a wealthy New York family, became treasurer. Stokes was enthusiastic about the alliance's openness to pro-war radicals. "From what Maisel tells me," he informed Spargo, "the possibilities are immense."[46]

Frank Walsh saw the alliance "alive with possibilities," as he told Creel. The two men had been "inseparables" in Kansas City, a bond built on their shared zeal for reform. When Creel published his first issue of the *Independent* in 1899, a drawing of Walsh dominated the front page. Walsh's causes ranged from successfully defending the son of Jesse James against charges of train robbery to serving briefly as editor and publisher of Bonfils and Tammen's sensational, crusading *Kansas City Post*. His championing of workers led Gompers to call him "Labor's Tribune." During Wilson's 1912 race for the White House, Walsh organized a Social Center Bureau at the Democratic National Committee dedicated to child welfare, sanitation, and workmen's compensation. Wilson appointed him chair of the Commission on Industrial Relations. Walsh put aside his pacifism in 1917 because he did not want to break with an administration that seemed committed to advancing labor's interests. Wilson appointed him cochair with former president Taft of the National War Labor Board. He also sat on the alliance's executive committee. Walsh dined or lunched with Creel "almost every day" at the Cosmos Club.[47]

Maisel headquartered the alliance on Chambers Street in Manhattan, a short distance from city hall. The CPI Division of Labor Publications was housed there as well, although the connection was murky. Materials sometimes carried alliance identification, with no mention of the CPI. As a collateral duty, Maisel surreptitiously gathered intelligence for Gompers on the activities of socialists that might impede pro-war propaganda. Maisel's inclination to spy may have led to an offer of employment from military intellegence, which he declined.[48]

One closely watched group was the People's Council of America for Democracy and Terms of Peace. The socialist body based its organization on the workingmen's councils in Russia and shared the Bolsheviks' desire for a quick peace by negotiation. The People's Council planned "a national anti-war propaganda campaign condemning the capitalist countries of Western Europe for starting a commercial conflict." The alliance, Maisel believed, was in "a fight to finish" with the council.[49]

Within a few days of being formed, the alliance organized a meeting in Minneapolis to counter a national conference planned for the same time and place by the People's Council. As a result of violent local press criticism, difficulty renting space, and the Minnesota governor's statement that it was not welcome, the People's Council moved to a different venue, Chicago. An alliance statement asserted, "Not even at the bequest of the so-called Peoples Council will the organized workers of America prostitute the labor movement to serve the brutal power responsible for the infamous rape of Belgium." Hostility continued in the coming months. Spargo thought the People's Council sabotaged distribution of AALD materials. The People's Council disrupted alliance rallies directed at foreign-born Jewish garment workers in New York who made uniforms and tents.[50]

The AALD's core message was that the war was good for the worker, if not immediately, then soon. "Out of the war will arise the golden days for the men who toil," proclaimed an alliance publication. It promised "better wages, better hours, better shop conditions, better opportunities, a fuller life, more leisure." John R. Commons, a University of Wisconsin labor economist and a member of Walsh's Commission on Industrial Relations, drove the point home in pamphlets that Ford published under the name of the alliance. "A democracy in which the wage-earner has his share of influence is coming," Commons wrote, "and if it does not come as it should, the reason will be that some wage-earners are misled and don't know democracy when they see it, or don't support when they know it."[51]

The hard sell was a common feature of the alliance. On the AALD's behalf, Gustavus Myers, a muckraker with a scholarly bent and an interest in parapsychology, attacked the People's Council for asserting that German socialism had been progressive. This was a "German myth," he wrote, created by Berlin's propagandists to "weaken the respect and loyalty of other peoples for their own countries." Alliance publicity director Chester M. Wright, like Myers a fallen-away member of the Socialist Party, had been managing editor of the *New York Call.* He distributed typeset stories and editorials that newspapers could easily use. The articles opposed radical labor and Bolshevism, promoted Gompers, and celebrated the war heroism of workers. Creel was impressed with Wright. He told Julius Koettgen to consult him on the Friends of German Democracy bulletin. The alliance, Wright told Creel, was a "club" to beat other organizations in line if they "have not the spirit of doing loyalty work. We can always say to them, if your organization will not do the right thing, the Alliance organization will go over your head and do it. You will understand what I mean to convey. We have done this in a number of cases."[52]

In order to attract followers, Wright argued, the alliance had to be more than "simply a flag waving organization without sympathy for the labor movement." When the labor loyalty program broke down in Detroit, Creel and Walsh sent him to investigate. He concluded that poor working conditions made the workers unreceptive to alliance pro-war propaganda. Walsh brought eleven of the workers to Washington at government expense to meet with his War Labor Board.[53]

Mostly, though, the CPI was careful about wading into disputes. From his initial investigations into labor, O'Higgins concluded the government "had to conduct the war against Germany without taking sides" among groups that used the conflict to advance their own causes. Being neutral was never easy for Creel, and he held the typical muckrakers' attitude toward trusts. But at the CPI, he wanted to concentrate on keeping workers working. When the editor of *McClure's* queried Creel, "Do you want us to build up a sentiment for conscription of labor or do you want to prevent the necessity of conscripting labor?" Creel responded: "This Committee cannot take part in the industrial dispute." The fight should be against all kinds of "slackers," he said, "so that the class line would be wiped out entirely, and suspicion removed that one side or the other was attempting to use a national emergency for its own selfish purpose." While the alliance directed its efforts at labor, Byoir enlisted business executives, including a Ford Motor Company advertising manager, to help him reach manufacturers of war materials. The executives wrote letters, which Byoir monitored, asking them to promote the war with their workforce.[54]

CREEL'S SUPERVISION AND DIRECTION

Gompers's interest in a partnership with Creel stemmed from the CPI's access to Wilson's war chest. The CPI paid the AALD's rent, salaries, and printing, and arranged for it to use the postal frank. Money gave Creel a whip hand. In the first days of the alliance, Gompers told Maisel that it would be under the "supervision and direction" of Creel. Byoir paid attention to details, such as Maisel's decision to hire a Jewish writer for six weeks. He and Creel commissioned publications and reviewed (and sometimes killed) them.[55]

Creel worked closely with Maisel and Spargo in planning the alliance's Minneapolis conference, held September 5–7, 1917, and in blocking the People's Council from securing a venue for its parallel gathering. Creel gave detailed instructions to Walsh, who had been named the "temporary chairman" of the conference. On September 1, Creel told Walsh that he had spent the "day with the 'Alliance' putting the last touches to the Minneapolis meeting!" His letter contained detailed instructions. Walsh was to ensure the main resolution emphasized that the United States was engaged in a *"war of self defense."* Other resolutions called for fair wages, progressive taxation, and the right of free speech. This last point was not heartfelt on Creel's part. A reporter with the Socialist *New York Call* was barred from covering the conference. Creel did not want the alliance to criticize authorities who banned the People's Council from using its First Amendment rights of peaceful assembly. Rather, he wanted "patriotic societies and civic organizations [to] pass resolutions condemning the People's Council as pro-German and disloyal." Creel told Walsh radical resolutions should come at the end of the meeting, when public attention to the conference was likely to flag. "All the luck in the world," Creel told Walsh. "Stick close to Gompers and see that the program moves with zip."[56]

The next day a chartered train, the Red, White and Blue Special, pulled out of Grand Central Station bound for Minnesota. Two bands and a Metropolitan Opera singer were on hand for the sendoff. The CPI paid half the $6,000 cost of the trip and handled conference press releases. After the gathering was over, Walsh reported back to Creel that his ideas had been put into effect: "You probably noticed that they all went into the resolutions."[57]

Gompers shared Byoir's views on the value of piggybacking on other organizations. He helped the National Civic Federation set up a bureau to "keep eyes and ears open for every utterance or suspicious action against the interests of this Government." The information was passed on to the Department of Justice. He urged AFL branches to establish local alliance chapters. "Minutes count," Gompers said in a letter to his locals. "The pro-German cause gains by every moment of American delay." By the summer of 1918, according to Wright, the AALD had branches in ninety-six cities. The alliance pushed Liberty Loans, first on the east side of New York and subsequently across the country. Four British labor leaders were imported for a speaking tour. According to Maisel's February 1918 report to the alliance executive committee, over a million pamphlets had been distributed nationally; its weekly news service reached the "entire labor press" and 150 dailies; and two hundred meetings were held as far

afield as Tucson, Los Angeles, and Laramie. Earlier that month, "Labor's Loyalty Week"—Gompers' idea—led to rallies across the country. The militantly
patriotic American Defense Society and the National Security League threw
their support behind the program.[58]

The alliance was not a perfect picture of labor solidary. Only about half the
170 delegates to the Minneapolis conference were trade unionists; the rest were
socialist intellectuals. Maisel acknowledged the alliance had little support in
"large war industrial centers in the east." Bitter debate erupted when Gompers sought an endorsement of "the patriotic work" undertaken by the AALD
at the AFL's annual convention in November 1917. Delegates questioned what
patriotic work the alliance did. They were outraged it did not stand up for the
free speech rights of the People's Council. "I may endorse a given system of patriotism," a socialist labor member said, "but if it is the system of the American
Alliance for Labor and Democracy I shall not do so." In a long speech on the
AALD's founding and principles, Gompers made no mention of the CPI.[59]

When it came time to vote to endorse the alliance, 21,602 were for and 402
opposed. But it was hardly a ringing vote of confidence. To pass the measure,
supporters framed it as a referendum on loyalty and Gompers. Dissatisfied
members refused to fall in line. The Pennsylvania Federation of Labor president wrote an open letter asking Gompers to identify the source of alliance
funds. The Pennsylvania labor leader suggested the money came from capitalist
"enemies of labor," a misperception revealing how shrouded the CPI's role was.
Gompers indignantly declared "it was not a letter deserving an answer." John
Fitzpatrick, president of the powerful Chicago Federation of Labor, objected
to the lack of democracy in the AFL. The Irish-born Fitzgerald told Maisel he
would not create an alliance branch because no one had satisfactorily answered
his questions about the alliance's covert activities.[60]

Spargo and Stokes offered resistance of a different kind. They viewed the alliance as a platform on which to build a new party in line with their radical, if
pro-war, politics. As Stokes said to Spargo, who became chairman of the short-
lived Social Democratic League of America, "I have no doubt that there are
some people who are trying to use us. I see no reason however why we should
not, in this incident, reciprocate."[61]

Gompers learned of Spargo's plans from his spy, Maisel. When the conservative Gompers complained the new party was "violative of the purpose and
spirit" of the unity-conscious alliance, Spargo responded hotly. If the alliance
were as truly nonpartisan as it claimed to be, "our right to indulge in any politi-

cal activity—even the creation of a party—which is not demonstrably contrary to the avowed principles of the Alliance cannot be denied." A few weeks later he discovered Maisel was working "under cover" (at the urging of Gompers and Creel) to undermine the party's founding meeting in Chicago in October 1917.[62]

Wright argued that the alliance's success was "due to the genius of Mr. Maisel, who, whatever his shortcomings may be, has a faculty for getting people to do things." But Maisel's shortcomings as an executive became a mounting source of frustration. The executive committee complained meetings were a waste of time since his "method of conducting business" never improved. Gompers told Maisel that he agreed with Creel on the "entire failure in your letters to suggest campaigns and plans to the achievement of a specific object." Stokes, the alliance treasurer, and Byoir reprimanded Maisel for sloppy financial procedures. In addition to being frustrated with Maisel's management style, Creel tired of his constant pleas for more money.[63]

Creel hoped financial problems could be solved through fundraising. This was the origin of his letter to Cyrus McCormick. To reach Jewish workers, he suggested that Gompers appeal "to a number of rich Jews and get them to start a daily that will serve our purpose." Others directly picked up costs; for instance, the Council of National Defense paid for telegrams to announce the Minneapolis conference. When Creel urged Maisel to seek donations, Gompers personally contributed one hundred dollars in "hope that it may stimulate others." But few were stirred. A fundraising campaign in Chicago cost $200 and "brought no results."[64]

In July Creel informed Gompers that he was ending funding. When Gompers pled with him and Wilson to continue, Creel agreed to provide limited funds. Babson at the Labor Department covered some costs but turned down many requests. With his budget severely constricted, Maisel had to work out of his home.[65]

New projects were still conceived. Byoir felt the CPI needed an industrial information bureau. The CPI arranged for the idea to be approved in the name of labor at an alliance meeting, but lack of funds stalled the project. Creel tried to create a Jewish Loyalty War Committee aimed at New York's pro-Russian Jews. Creel aborted the plan out of frustration with factional disputes among the people he sought to involve. One camouflaged project, however, did get off the ground.[66]

The AFL's interests reached into Latin America, where it encouraged labor unity, discouraged radicalism, and promoted the Allied cause in the war. In July, Gompers received reports that German agents were agitating in Mexico. To counter this, he conceived a counterpropaganda program throughout Latin America. This found support in a meeting with Byoir, Secretary of Labor William Wilson, and others. Two days later Gompers asked Wilson for a private meeting to relate new information about "the Mexican situation." "I am under word of honor to convey it to no one but you," he said.[67]

Out of these discussions came Wilson's agreement to provide $50,000 to fund a bilingual newspaper based in Texas. Although Gompers initially understood Wilson wanted everything "done openly," the president decided to give the money out of his war fund to the CPI, which laundered it through the alliance. Stokes was told to spend the money without "too close adherence to technicalities." *El Obrero Pan-americano* began publishing on August 28. It lasted until the war ended in November.[68]

THE THIRD-PARTY TECHNIQUE

Gompers hoped the alliance, without Maisel at its head, could effectively carry on as an AFL propaganda arm. The Red Scare hysteria sweeping the country was its undoing. This was ironic. The alliance, like the AFL, vigorously continued to denounce Bolshevism in Russia, so much so that Frank Walsh resigned from the board.* (He believed it was up to the Russians to decide their future.) But when workers went on strike over wages, layoffs, and the length of the work day, rumors spread that the AFL was riddled with Communists. The AFL needed its resources to support the strikers. Unable to turn elsewhere for money in this political environment, the alliance shut its doors in November 1919.[69]

The People's Council disbanded around the same time. As a result of the post office's suppression of the mails, it was nearly impossible to send a letter, complained the organization's director, let alone mail publications. Supporters were asked to distribute materials door to door. Financial contributions fell off. The People's Council's successor was the People's Freedom Union, established to assist colleagues jailed for sedition.[70]

Although the alliance did not survive, the concept did. It was a prototype for the CIA's covert use of labor organizations to promote American foreign

---

* This was not Walsh's only disappointment. He thought the alliance failed to advance industrial democracy. He also resigned from the National War Labor Board out of frustration with Wilson policies he considered too favorable to big business.

policy during the Cold War. The secret funding and direction of the alliance, Ronald Radosh observed, "comprise the first example of how an American administration has used organized labor to serve its own purposes."[71]

Byoir's stage managing is credited with inventing a durable, if derided, public relations tactic, the third-party technique. After the war, he employed it on behalf of a number of businesses, including railroads, whose use of front organizations for manipulating the news Ray Stannard Baker once muckraked.

9

Nail Up the Damn Thing

If you have no doubt of your premises or your powers and want a certain result with all your heart, you naturally express your wishes in law and sweep away all opposition.

—Justice Oliver Wendell Holmes, *Abrams v. United States*

During a visit to England in September 1918, Edward Bok, editor of *Ladies' Home Journal,* was appalled by London women's "uncontrolled solicitation" of American servicemen in streets, hotel lounges, and restaurants. "We should not be asked to send our boys here to be morally crucified," he told a group of American correspondents. Four reporters filed stories with Bok's blistering comments. The dispatches passed through navy censors in New York, who shared space with the CPI's Wireless-Cable Service. When the stories were brought to the attention of Walter Rogers, the director of the news service and Creel's liaison to the censors, he requested that the newspapers suppress them for fear of harming Anglo-American relations. "Not only was the request complied with," Rogers informed Creel, "but each of the papers cabled its correspondent to file no more on the subject."[1]

That was not the end of Rogers's worries. What if Bok continued to make such remarks and used his magazine to criticize CPI censorship of his views? Rogers asked a navy censor in London to take the matter up with the influential editor. The censor reported back that Bok realized "the mess he was stirring up and intends to drop the matter."[2]

Propaganda is always censorious. Publicity omits contradictory facts and opinions, and the logical next step is to suppress dissonant thoughts expressed by others, as when Charles Dana Gibson enthusiastically passed on a suggestion to Creel: too many pictures in the press presented a youthful, vigorous kaiser;

better to show his crippled left arm and "sinister countenance." "Flattering pictures of the Kaiser," he advised, "should be discouraged." Creel agreed. Because no law allowed the CPI to block such pictures, he suggested Gibson's division unofficially "reach the papers individually."[3]

The American Expeditionary Forces lumped censorship, press relations, and propaganda against the enemy in a single unit, G-2-D. G-2-D's bias toward suppression was reinforced by its location on the army's table of organization.* It was a subunit of intelligence operations. A disgruntled correspondent referred to the AEF press office as "a department of the Army's Secret Service." Publicity and censorship, a G-2-D officer observed, "are so closely related that practically all their activities are interlaced and it is impossible to keep them entirely separate."[4]

Frederick Palmer, the AEF's chief press officer, made the point more colorfully: "When the censor and the propagandist meet behind the black curtain, they are as friendly as two lawyers in the anteroom after slanging each other in court, and they go the lawyers one better by plotting together, since, unlike the lawyers, both are employed by the same client."[5]

Although Creel insisted the CPI did "not touch censorship at any point," it more than touched censorship, officially and unofficially, at many points. This was not lost on journalists. The *New York Tribune* referred to "the official censor—in other words George Creel." *Der Deutsche Correspondent* in Baltimore identified him as "Vorsteher [head director] der Zensur-Bureau." After the war, *Le Figaro* said Creel was "the most redoubtable representative of Anastasie in the world." "Madame Anastasie" was a cartoon depiction of a censorious old shrew with giant scissors.[6]

Creel could have mitigated his scissor-wielding image by suppressing his volatile personality. But his intemperate attitude toward stories he did not like during the first weeks of the war continued. "The President did Creel no service when he gave him, of all jobs, this particular job, which includes administrative supervision over the mails, the telegraph and cable services, and ten thousand newspapers," Mark Sullivan wrote. "Wilson might just as appropriately have appointed Billy Sunday."[7]

---

* The link between press work and intelligence was common elsewhere and especially pronounced in Germany. The War Press Office, the lead agency for all government press relations, was in the military general staff's office III B, whose primary job was military intelligence.

OBEY THE LAW. KEEP YOUR MOUTH SHUT.

In March 1917, in an oft-related conversation, President Wilson worried out loud to *New York World* editor Frank Cobb. "To fight you must be brutal and ruthless," he said, "and the spirit of ruthless brutality will enter into the very fibre of our national life, infecting congress, the courts, the policeman on the beat, the man on the street." First Amendment rights "would go." This was not the only time Wilson expressed such concerns. It was unclear if Wilson feared the direction patriotism would take the country or if he foresaw the consequences of his own thinking on the subject. In November 1917, Creel suggested Wilson meet with representatives of the Open Forum, a speakers' organization that promoted both the war and, as its name implied, free speech. Creel argued it was a good opportunity to "share your views as to where free speech leaves off and disloyalty begins." Wilson declined, saying, "It would be extremely difficult to state correctly and wisely my views about free speech just now."[8]

In the summer of 1917, a lawyer who was minister to Spain during the Cleveland administration wrote an article in Hearst's *New York American* challenging the constitutionality of the new conscription law. Creel sent the article to Wilson, who in turn asked Gregory, "Do you think there is anything we could do to this wretched creature, Hannis Taylor, or is he too small game to waste powder on?" After doing an analysis of the article worthy of the British Foreign Office's scrutiny of Hearst's reporting, the Justice Department suggested hunting bigger game.[9]

Lansing encouraged the British to reconcile with Hearst's International News Service. Although unenthusiastic, they agreed to restore its cable privileges if the administration requested it openly. Wilson, who suspected Lansing was behind this, was not interested. He told Polk, "I should be most unwilling to do so, indeed would do so in no circumstances." An exception to the cable ban was made for an INS reporter accredited to the AEF because the British saw value in his work "for advertising purposes."[10]

To Creel's surprise, the British lifted the ban in early 1918. He had the impression the Treasury Department was "the medium of arrangement," which was partly true. Lansing, McAdoo, and House made the British realize that the ban angered newspapers that relied on INS and might prompt a backlash with Congress. When Creel learned of an editorial in Hearst's *New York American* suggesting the United States annex Mexico, he asked the Censorship Board to consider denying the mails to the paper.[11]

Wilson was angry that Hearst's *New York American* printed his Memorial Day proclamation in 1918 without mentioning his calling on Americans to pray for victory. This was a simple editing error, which the editor explained in an affidavit, a precaution he had good reason to take. Wilson asked Gregory if legal means existed to "bring this habitual offender to terms." For months Gregory's Bureau of Investigation and the Military Intelligence Division, with CPI help, investigated Hearst in hopes of making such a case, all in vain. The tidbits it turned up were often along the lines of a note from an agent who learned the Key West Elks Club barred Hearst's *New York American* from its reading room.[12]

If Wilson was not able to squelch speech to the extent he wished, he had strong allies in Gregory and Postmaster General Burleson, a curious pair of Texas friends who had responsibility for enforcing the Espionage Act. Slight and severely hard of hearing, Gregory went through the day puffing on small black cigars and relishing the opportunity to tell jokes. Although soft-spoken, he left no doubt where he stood on dissent. A German alien had nothing to fear, he said, "so long as he observes the following warning: 'Obey the law. Keep your mouth shut.'" Tall and ruddy, with muttonchop sideburns, Burleson wore black suits and carried a black umbrella, which he tapped on the floor as he walked. Burleson's hooked nose and cold eyes gave him a "fighting face," thought Ray Stannard Baker. After Burleson barred the August 1917 issue of the Socialist *Masses* from the mails, Wilson suggested going easy as the journalists were "sincere men." Burleson threatened to resign. "Well," Wilson said with a laugh, "go ahead and do your duty."[13]

Writing to Max Eastman, the editor of the *Masses,* Wilson said that he did not know how to draw the line between permissible and impermissible speech. When the magazine sought a legal remedy, Burleson took another step against it. Because one issue of the magazine had not gone through the mail, thanks to his stopping it, the *Masses* was technically no longer a continuous publication and thus ineligible for second-class privileges. The *Masses* folded.[14]

"I have no propaganda bureau," Burleson said, implying he was disadvantaged against unfair complaints about him. He was thin-skinned and almost as compulsively truculent as Creel. When the *New York World* invited him to respond to criticism of "his administration and of himself," he drafted a heated twenty-five-page response. He answered friendly letters of concern about censorship with long letters that tediously reprised statutes and insisted he tried "to do injustice to no one." He could have built bridges with the press when he was invited to comment on the positive contributions that journalists made during 1919. Burleson wrote a four-page lecture instead on the shortcomings of journalists. "Too many newspapers," he wrote, "are guilty of laxity in respect to their public duties." [15]

Two laws that were passed after the Espionage Act enhanced the power of Burleson and Gregory to control speech. The congressional debate over these was not nearly as contentious as over the Espionage Act. The Trading with the Enemy Act, passed in October 1916, gave Burleson absolute censorship authority over foreign-language journals that used the domestic mails, and it permitted censorship of mail as well as radio and cable communications with foreign countries. The next year, in the spring, Congress again showed itself compliant to administration wishes by voting for the Sedition Act, which gave the government more power to prosecute dissent. Gregory argued that this was required to reassure citizens and lessen mob violence. "Most of the disorder throughout the country," he said, "is caused by the lack of laws relating to disloyal utterances." [16]

In his conversation with Cobb, Wilson had worried that tolerance would wither in the war; in effect, Gregory argued for legalizing "popular demand" for intolerance. Unlawful under the act was the "uttering, printing, writing, or publishing any disloyal, profane, scurrilous, or abusive language intended to cause contempt, scorn, contumely or disrepute as regards the form of government or the United States, or the Constitution . . . ; and words or acts supporting or favoring the cause of any country at war with the United States, or opposing the cause of the United States therein." [17]

The courts, too, were compliant. Having undergone little judicial testing, the First Amendment was unsettled law. It was commonly understood to rule out prior restraint but not prosecution after publication, and legislators could set the boundaries. Freedom of the press in wartime, the CPI's *War Cyclopedia* said, rested "largely with the discretion of Congress." When the first case under the Espionage Act reached the Supreme Court in 1919, the justices unanimously upheld the conviction of two socialists who distributed pamphlets opposing conscription.

The next week the court ruled on *Debs v. United States.* In a June 1918 speech in Canton, Ohio, the lean, balding Eugene Debs had inveighed against government prosecution of dissenters, Samuel Gompers, and plutocrats who benefited from a war that need not have been fought. The court, again unanimously, rejected his First Amendment defense. Later that year, in *Abrams v. United States,* a case involving Russian-Jewish anarchists who opposed the war, Justice Oliver Wendell Holmes changed his point of view. But he was in a minority with Justice Louis Brandeis. "It has been a source of great satisfaction to me," Burleson said in 1919, "that in every instance where my action was challenged, the courts upheld my action, in effect saying: 'The Postmaster General did no more than his duty.'"[18]

As for the public at large, it was generally supportive of the war and the war measures upheld by the courts. To be sure, almost 337,000 men did not register for the draft, but that was a relatively small number compared to the twenty-four million who did. Opinion leaders were strikingly unified in believing the war should be prosecuted aggressively at home as well as abroad. The press was instrumental in maintaining this harmony. The initial enthusiasm journalists displayed for the war continued to a degree that historians have underappreciated. There was no possibility the Dutch-born Edward Bok would speak out of turn for long. He was proud that his magazine was "the semiofficial mouthpiece of all the various government war bureaus and war-work bodies." When he went to London, he frankly viewed himself as a government publicist.[19]

Every day, front pages rang out headlines along the lines of "Hun Airmen Fiendish." While it was true that editorials criticized the administration for slow airplane production and news pages carried Theodore Roosevelt's anti-Wilson vituperation, the press was largely a cheerleader. Hearst declared himself to be an American first. He supported the draft law. In the eyes of Hiram Johnson, he was "slobbering" in his support of the administration. With encouragement from the State Department and the post office, the *New York Tribune* displayed its loyalty by attacking Hearst anyway as "the leading spirit of German propaganda in the United States." Samuel Hopkins Adams wrote a series of pseudo-exposés for the newspaper that focused on "Herr Hearst's" reporting before the war started, decried Hearst's calls for negotiated peace, and claimed Hearst opposed censorship in order to continue his unpatriotic news reporting.[20]

The press published CPI material, sometimes in full. In an editorial accompanying the Four Minute Men's "Where Did You Get Your Facts?," the *Evansville Journal News* said every American had the duty "to hold himself ready to fire ammunition at any person who tells any story or repeats any rumor which smacks of German origin." The editor of the *Des Moines Capital,* who headed the state Council of Defense, admonished citizens on their "patriotic duty to find out what your neighbor thinks." He asked Carl Byoir for all the CPI's literature. "We will make good use of same." In the spring of 1918, with Byoir's encouragement, the publisher of the *New York Globe* started a campaign called "Win the War Newspapers." He enlisted some 125 newspapers to publish an official daily statement of three to four hundred words.[21]

Initiatives like this popped up everywhere. The *New York Evening Telegram* published the phone numbers of the police and the Secret Service and directed readers to "Paste This in Your Hat" in case they heard of a plot. The Pittsburgh Press Club's "intelligence bureau" assisted the Department of Justice by monitoring twenty-seven counties and by publicizing statements government wished to broadcast. The *Pensacola Journal* invited readers to sign a card that pledged, "I will endeavor to silence disloyalty and detect plots or designs inimical to this country." "Replies have already deluged me," the editor wrote to Daniels.[22]

In 1918, the second year Pulitzer Prizes were awarded by Columbia University, two students at the journalism school won one for a slim publication that lauded the press for publicizing government war programs and for its "suppression of ill-timed sentiments." *Editor & Publisher* persistently criticized the government's refusal to pay for advertising to promote Liberty Loans; it insisted in April 1917 that "any censorship of the press in the United States, even in wartime, is illegal." Yet it sponsored an award for the best editorial on behalf of Liberty Loans and a few months into the war argued, "The Government must find some effective means for suppressing seditious publications." "The President," it editorialized, "is entitled to immunity from attack from the rear."[23]

REGULATION AND INTIMIDATION

It was as though Dr. Jekyll and Mr. Hyde wrote Creel's pronouncements on the press. "There is not a newspaper in the United States that is without earnest desire to do the thing that is best for America," said Creel, Dr. Jekyll-like, in his first week on the job. "It is upon this theory that I mean to base my policies and official actions." Mr. Hyde appeared in his Preliminary Statement to the Press in May 1917: "The term traitor is not too harsh in application to the publisher, editor, or writer who wields this power without full and even solemn recognition of responsibilities. It is not alone the people of the United States who are on trial, but the press of the United States as well."[24]

As a journalist Creel had taken full advantage of press freedom. Mark Sullivan called him "the most insistent on 'pitiless publicity,' the most violent of muckrakers." Creel resisted Wilson's proposed censorship clause in the Espionage Act and occasionally spoke against it afterward. Other CPI staff had gold-plated records of fighting for press freedom. After joining the CPI staff, Arthur Bullard publicly said the "Wilson motive" in the espionage bill was to suppress "irritating news." Ernest Poole signed a statement opposing the initial version of the espionage bill.[25]

Nevertheless, Creel and his colleagues believed speech had to be fenced in, although they were not precise as to where to pound in the posts. "What you complain against," he told radical journalist Louise Bryant, "and what many others complain against, I imagine, is the suppression of what is termed 'free speech.' Never at any time has it been the inalienable right of a citizen to say what he pleases. From time immemorial, this right has been limited by law, and today, when the Nation fights for its existence, it is merely the case that another limitation has been added."[26]

Congress, Creel said, had the power to set limits because it was elected by the people. "We have no right to kick against a law after Congress passes it." Harvey O'Higgins linked free speech advocates with sedition. "The cry that is now raised for freedom of speech and freedom of the press," he said in an *Atlantic Monthly* essay, "is raised by persons who have enjoyed these freedoms and been judged guilty of abusing them." Charles Hopkins Adams argued that it was perfectly acceptable to ignore the law in order to stop unpatriotic speech. In one of his *Everybody's* articles, he praised Council of National Defense representatives for secretly monitoring German-American saloons and threatening to revoke liquor licenses if patrons derided government policy. "It is by no means certain that this would stand in law," he conceded, "but the Council is more concerned with getting things done." Even Bullard said, "We cannot permit traitors in the newspaper business any more than in the Army. . . . In times of great national danger we would all gladly consent to temporary limitations of our accustomed liberties."[27]

Creel asserted, in italics, that the CPI did not *"seek or exercise authorities under those war laws that limited the freedom of speech and press."* This was not true. From the first days of the war, the CPI sought and exercised control over cable censorship of news dispatches, which grew from 25,000 words a day to over 200,000 after censorship of Atlantic cables went into effect on midnight July 26. It was the navy's job to monitor cable traffic. Initially Daniels had wanted Creel to have executive control over censorship, but at Creel's urging the responsibility was given to Commander David W. Todd, director of Naval Communications, with the CPI playing a supporting role. Then, in August, Creel recommended that he should have executive control after all on the grounds that he needed the authority to streamline the process. The procedures were not changed, but a strong partnership was developed. As a Navy Department directive noted, "There is close co-operation between the Committee on Public Information and the Chief Cable Censor." The navy had control over military matters, the CPI over political and economic policies. The appearance of "divided authority [was] more apparent than real," the navy noted in its instructions to censors. The *Official Bulletin* was similarly clear: "The rules and regulations of the cable censorship, within the sole and specific relation to press dispatches, are laid down by the chairman of the Committee on Public Information." Creel was involved in the hiring of censors. His staff worked with the British authorities to plug holes in censorship. In July 1918, when Creel revised guidelines for the press, the British issued them as a notice to their own press.[28]

What Creel said and what he did were often out of sync. He insisted, "It is the announced policy of the Navy Department that all news of accidents, disasters, battles, etc., will be made public as promptly as possible. This policy will be rigidly followed." Yet in August Creel advised Commander Todd to stop all incoming communications discussing conspiracies and disasters that seemed based on rumors. The vague mandate gave Todd's novice censors wide discretion.[29]

Creel was similarly contradictory regarding outgoing cables. Creel's Preliminary Statement to the Press assured correspondents from Allied nations they could "cable their papers free from interference by our censors." But he told Todd to watch for cables with opinions "intended to contaminate neutral countries."[30]

> Messages of correspondents arranged with this insidious intent should be deleted of this offensively opinioned matter. A record of the attempts of correspondents from day to day to cable German propaganda in this manner should be kept and referred as evidence to the Committee on Public Information, which will then be in a position to bar the offender from the use of the cables and to take such other steps as may seem necessary.[31]

Drawing from material passed to it by navy censors, the CPI put together a list of pro-German foreign correspondents working in the United States. Edgar Sisson told censors to be especially vigilant with these dispatches. "Any attempt on their part to color news is not possible," he said. "Delete phrases, paragraphs, or if the entire dispatch is colored, suppress it." He suggested the navy assign an individual to focus specifically on the biggest offenders on the watch list.[32]

The CPI reiterated its censorship authority from time to time. "The control of the censorship of all press cablegrams will be vested in The Committee on Public Information," a navy directive said in October 1917. Eight days later came an internal directive to censors that they would be guided "by the regulations issued by the Committee on Public Information." Censorship was to be kept to a minimum, but if a report was thoroughly troublesome, "the censor is not to hesitate in suppressing the entire dispatch." Furthermore, "All references to strikes, riots or activities which are attributed to an anti-war sentiment are to be suppressed. All reports regarding the activities of the 'Industrial Workers of the World,' or similar anarchistic bodies are to be suppressed." [33]

Creel and the president were largely shoulder to shoulder with regard to censoring. In May 1918, Creel forwarded an analysis by British correspondent Arthur Willert of the president's attitudes toward Irish independence. "Acting under my blanket instructions, to the effect that censors should not pass matter purporting to give your views," Creel wrote, "the whole cable was killed with the exception of the opening graph." The first graph was one sentence. The portion killed amounted to more than three pages. Creel asked if Wilson approved. Wilson did. He said the reporter "had no authority'" to speculate on his thinking.[34] This despite Willert's close cooperation with the CPI.

Censorship of domestic news stories remained voluntary. Emendations to the CPI guidelines came from time to time. The rules were relaxed on January 1, 1918, for instance, giving the go-ahead to publish information on "dry docks, repair, and construction work." The CPI issued "confidential" requests to editors, as the British did, although in far smaller numbers. The tone was conciliatory, as in: "It is hoped the reasonableness of these suggestions made in the common interest will appeal to you." This request asked for care in publishing letters from soldiers, even if censors passed them as acceptable to mail home, because soldiers often did not have a full picture of what was happening. "Letters should be treated as the uncensored correspondence of war correspondents." [35]

Creel complained that journalists thought "voluntary censorship was not voluntary, that the uncontrolled thing they were doing was not *really* uncontrolled, and that while they could not speak with definiteness, certainly there was a 'catch' that would some day become apparent." While Creel dismissed these impressions as nonsense, he gave the press definite reasons to worry there was a "catch." "Mr. Creel," said the *New York Sun*, "on several occasions has sought to emphasize that the alternative to refusing to cooperate with him would be a strict enforcement of censorship rules backed by authority to compel newspapers to follow them." Creel could refer renegades to the Justice Department and the post office. The War Industries Board rationed newsprint and forbade the creation of new newspapers. "The Executive Branch," said David Lawrence, "has enough power to intimidate the press and in time of war intimidation can be worse than censorship."[36]

A letter to A. Mitchell Palmer, the fervent alien property custodian, underscores the wide range of methods Creel was willing to consider to suppress unwanted information. Created in October 1917, Palmer's agency took control of German-owned banks, breweries, factories, and newspapers, in the case of the latter "to put an end to an insidious outlet for German propaganda which has been in operation for some time before America entered the war." Creel told Palmer, "If we can put your representatives in editorial control, we will have some powerful weapons for real fighting."[37]

CENSORING AND SELF-CENSORING OF PICTURES

CPI censorship also touched visual images. Its Bureau of War Photographs had responsibility for approving requests by civilians to film or photograph at military facilities. The bureau sometimes asked for input from military and Justice Department intelligence bureaus. In consultation with army and navy intelligence officers, the CPI reviewed the images afterward to determine if they compromised national security. The National Board of Review, a movie industry censor body, assisted the CPI. The board reviewed films to determine if CPI permission was needed and requested content changes that went beyond narrow security concerns, for instance removal of a scene from *Daughter of France* in which ballet girls entertained soldiers in a wine cellar. The CPI received a daily report on each film that the board reviewed.[38]

The CPI sparked a controversy when it suppressed Universal Film Company's *The Yanks Are Coming*. Universal had not acquired the necessary permissions to film in the Dayton-Wright Airplane plant. Military aircraft manufacturing was a sensitive subject because of slow production as well as security. The Signal Corps required that all airplane production information and photos go to the CPI for review. Universal argued that Creel had already favored similar films produced by Hearst. When it appeared Universal might defiantly show the film in a New York theater, Department of Justice agents were on hand. The film was not shown. Someone wrote on a poster for the film in front of the theater that "Creel-Hearst Committee" had stopped it. The charge that Creel favored Hearst was preposterous, but the CPI's display of power was real. The controversy was front-page news in New York.[39]

Additional censorship power was derived from the Trading with the Enemy Act, which prohibited the export of a movie without a license from the War Trade Board. The board, which was chaired by Vance McCormick, delegated responsibility for reviewing movies to the CPI. In July 1918, Byoir worked with the National Association of the Motion Picture Industry to establish content guidelines. Films were to present a positive impression of the United States, for instance, to "avoid mob scenes and riots that might be entirely innocent in themselves, but distorted and used adversely to the interests of the United States." Films set in the Civil War or showing slavery were stopped. Customs and military officials helped review films. Exported film was consigned to an American embassy official abroad who could give it a second round of censorship. By one estimate, some one hundred films, out of a total of eight thousand, were denied permission for export. "I do not think that too much attention can be given to the censorship of motion pictures," Creel told Colonel Ernest J. Chambers, the chief press censor of Canada.[40]

The CPI's control over film exports amounted to de facto censorship of films at home. Foreign sales accounted for 30 percent of profits. Studios could not afford to make films that would not pass muster for an export license. Creel had other leverage over studios. The foreign ties of movie moguls made them vulnerable to charges of disloyalty. The heads of Paramount and Fox were Hungarian Jews; the president of Universal was German born. The studios also feared that the government would classify the movie industry as nonessential. As it was, the Fuel Administration shut down theaters on Tuesdays in order to conserve power, and the War Industries Board banned the construction of new theaters. The board noted that the efficient use of materials laid a requirement on movie producers to make "wholesome pictures." Creel pled the case for keeping projectors spinning in theaters, telling the head of the Fuel Administration that dark theaters would put Four Minute Men out of business. A trade newspaper, the *Dramatic Mirror,* said Creel, in his fight to make movies essential, had "endeared himself to the heart of every movie man and fan."[41]

"This censorship of motion pictures," Creel said, "goes much further than military information, but is wholly persuasive." By "persuasive," he meant voluntary, but his powers to help or hurt moviemakers made him much more convincing. The movie industry submitted films for review that did not fall under authorities officially delegated to the CPI. "There is no law for it," Creel said, "but we have secured a voluntary agreement with the industry that all still photographs, no matter by whom made, and all motion pictures that deal in any manner with the war and with Americans aims, shall be submitted to this committee for censorship."[42]

The CPI had no problem with films that depicted bloodthirsty Huns. In 1918, Major M. L. C. Funkhouser, the movie censor in Chicago, cut scenes of egregious German barbarity from *Four Years in Germany,* a film based on a memoir by James W. Gerard, the former American ambassador to Germany. Funkhouser was an unusual departure from local censors who often exceeded the CPI's eagerness to suppress. Creel believed the film was "powerful and effective . . . in its appeal to the people of America." When Gerard complained to Creel about Funkhouser's action, Creel suggested he contact the Illinois governor to urge the Chicago censor's removal.[43]

Among the films the CPI stepped in to alter was *The Caillaux Case.* In this celluloid drama, Caillaux is portrayed as the "evil genius of France." He and his wife take money to spread German propaganda. She wants a German title and shoots the editor of *Le Figaro* because he has information on the plot. While Joseph Caillaux sits in prison, Madam Caillaux is dragged into the street by a mob and forced to kiss the French flag. The CPI reviewed the film less than a week before it was to be released in early May and requested revisions. The State Department had not liked the scene in which Lansing provided evidence to convict Caillaux, which was uncomfortably close to reality, and the Marquis de Polignac with the French High Commission told Creel it hurt France's image in the United States. Fox altered the film, a costly process that took until August and still did not satisfy the French or Creel, who said more changes had to be made. When the cutting was done in September, Philip Patchin, who handled publicity at the State Department, told Creel, "I find myself wondering what they are going to do with it. The only good stuff was objectionable, and I am afraid there is not much left."[44]

The CPI also objected to a film in which a French village "offered no resistance to the Hun invaders" and a German officer was depicted as honorable. Creel asked for changes in *The Curse of Iku,* the story of a brutal Japanese warlord and a shipwrecked American, because it "gave offense to a nation now America's comrade in arms." The revised film, retitled *An Eye for an Eye,* turned the Japanese into Malaysians.[45]

The CPI self-censored a film it had acquired for its own propaganda. The footage came from a secret agent in Scandinavia who promised a naval film showing atrocities of submarine warfare. "The price was so modest, the description so bloodcurdling, the possibility for working up horror among the neutrals so obvious that we accepted the offer at once," Will Irwin recalled. On the night of its arrival at Jackson Place, the staff watched it in a basement office. The Germans were handsome and happy. Before they sank a ship, they took off its crew. The captives were smiling. The CPI had purchased German propaganda. "Nail up the damn' thing," Creel said.[46]

THE CENSORSHIP BOARD

Pursuant to passage of the Trading with the Enemy Act, President Wilson created the Censorship Board on October 12, 1917. The board was to coordinate the multiple censorship functions that were now carried out by different executive branch agencies. This body had representatives from the State, War, and Navy Departments, the War Trade Board, the Committee on Public In-

The Censorship Board, established in late 1917, had representatives from the State, War, and Navy Departments, the War Trade Board, the Committee on Public Information, and the Post Office. The dominant force was Postmaster General Albert Burleson, who worked through Chief Postal Censor Robert L. Maddox. But Creel, seated at the far right, was an active member. (Harris & Ewing, Library of Congress)

formation, and the post office. Chief Postal Censor Robert L. Maddox was the chairman.

As much as the censorship apparatus burgeoned, it was understaffed for the tasks it set out for itself and suffered from overlapping responsibilities and uncertain authorities. When a history was put together on the duties of the chief military censor in the summer 1918, no written authorization could be found "for direct administration of telegraph and telephone censorship." The chief military censor confessed that no one knew when his position was created.[47]

Adjustments to censorship procedures were unending in an effort to figure out what worked best. In the last months of the war, the Military Intelligence Division (MID), where army censorship was housed, deferred less to the CPI.* It took over responsibility for granting permission for photographers to visit army facilities and for reviewing their pictures, a step that streamlined the process. The chief military censor had felt "hedged about like an oracle who could only be consulted by the Committee's representative." The MID initiated and distributed press advisories and consulted the CPI representative, a reverse of how it had been before. The MID upbraided editors and publishers who did not keep their "columns free from news matter which might in any way be useful to the enemy."[48]

The members of the Censorship Board were not always in a state of easy agreement. Early on, a turf battle took place over foreign mail. The New York headquarters for this censorship—as well as the related censorship stations set up as far afield as Manila—was a collective endeavor of the post office, the two branches of the armed services, and the War Trade Board. The post office argued it should direct this, as other functions of censorship were directed by individual agencies. The post office's case was buttressed by the fact that it was funding this censorship because Congress had not yet appropriated funds. Creel and the rest of the board believed they should collectively control censorship of foreign mail, as this was a military function in other countries.

The dispute was eventually taken to Wilson, who sided with Burleson. But tensions persisted. "The name 'Executive Postal Censorship Committee' is a misnomer," the navy representative in New Orleans complained of the operations at his station, "since the members, other than the [post office] chairman, are shorn of all effective voice and all executive power, and consequently the

* Military intelligence was organized as a Military Intelligence Section in May 1917. It became the Military Intelligence Branch in February 1918 and the Military Intelligence Division in August of that year.

other members find their usefulness restricted, their activities curtailed, their energies dissipated and their patriotism impugned."[49]

Creel ran into difficulty convincing the post office to give blanket mailing permits to some foreign-language newspapers that the CPI relied on. These permits alleviated a newspaper from the time-consuming chore of translating war-related articles into English for review by postal authorities. In one of the more vexing instances of hampering the CPI, W. H. Lamar, the post office solicitor, turned down a permit for a weekly backed by the CPI's American-Hungarian Loyalty League. After "a most exhaustive examination," Lamar said, the post office concluded the paper's loyalty "is a very forced one." If it were really loyal, he added, "it will have no objection to printing matter which does not require the paper to bear the expense of translation."[50]

Creel was an active member of the board. He took part in most meetings, which were usually held near Maddox's office. He made reports on censorship activities. He helped set censorship rules, at one point winning adoption of a resolution that barred individuals from mailing single copies of a publication to someone living abroad, a measure that aimed to stop spies from secretly transmitting sensitive information in this way. His Foreign Language Newspaper Division translated articles for the post office. "I feel very strongly that the Censorship should not become a secret service organization for the detection of crimes," he wrote to Maddox. "I do feel, however, that when offenses against the law are obvious, with proof of crime standing plain before the Censor, that it is our duty to refer it to the proper authorities."[51]

On April 3 the Censorship Board, after some discussion, affirmed that Creel had the "full authority of the Board to deal with the matter of newspaper censorship." That same day, Creel reiterated that Walter Rogers would continue to be in charge of censoring the communications sent abroad by correspondents for foreign newspapers. Censorship of English-language newspapers remained voluntary. The CPI meanwhile stepped up its efforts to control magazines and books.[52]

Previously, at the behest of the War and Navy Departments, the CPI asked magazine publishers to voluntarily submit articles and books containing "any information relating to military or naval affairs" prior to publication. The CPI would return the material "with such recommendations as the Government may desire to make for the preservation of proper military secrecy." At the April 3 meeting, the board discussed going a step further and requiring "all magazines in the country . . . to submit articles to the Censorship Board several weeks before publication for proper censoring." This came to nothing. Prior censorship of an English-language publication had no support in law. But another means of achieving the same end was possible under the Trading with the Enemy Act. Magazine publishers, like movie producers, wanted access to foreign markets. They were willing to pledge themselves to patriotism in order to be on the Censor Board list, with which Creel was also involved, that gave them a blanket right to export. The military censor took the additional step of contacting publishers any time British censors objected to an article. The publishers were asked to discontinue such articles or "prepare to lose a large part of their foreign circulation through censorship." The military censors thought this exerted a "wholesome disciplinary influence" over the press and compensated for any "laxness of the existing postal censorship."[53]

The Trading with the Enemy Act gave the board similar leverage over book publishers, who were troubled by declining book exports. They approached the board with the voluntary offer to self-censor. A representative guaranteed that publishers would export only books that were "pro-American in sentiment," that they would submit books for review, and in general "would go to any lengths provided the flow of books abroad could be restored." Creel was directed to establish procedures. A copy of each book was submitted to military intelligence. A list of approved publishers was given to censorship stations, which were to pass their publications without review. Another list, drawn up with CPI assistance, identified publishers ineligible for export. Although these measures applied only to exported books, publishers did not want to produce books for domestic consumption that could not be sold abroad.[54]

Burleson maintained a high-handed secrecy about censorship. When Congress asked for information about his instructions to postmasters, he said disclosure was "incompatible with the public interest." He brushed off Champ Clark, the Speaker of the House, who passed him a letter from a constituent questioning the withholding of a publication from the mail. Burleson said it contained "abusive language about the Y.M.C.A.," which was recognized by the government as part of military forces. The New York postmaster, he stated, could not send copies demonstrating this to Clark "since they are nonmailable under the law."[55]

Burleson's attitude was in keeping with the suppression of information on censorship in other warring countries. He could not go so far in suppression as other countries, given American traditions of open government. But the Espionage Act had an effect. The search for subversion was institutionalized in both government and vigilante intelligence bureaus that worked behind the scenes to ferret out enemy activity. "You must work under cover," the American Protective League advised members in its newsletter, *Spy Glass.* "You can't go to the man you are investigating and invite him to give up the facts you require." The withholding of information detailing these activities was justified as necessary to protect national security.[56]

"The Censorship Board operated silently and effectively. Individuals were not notified when their foreign mail, outbound or incoming, was confiscated or destroyed: it was, in a word, *"spurlos versenkt,"* said two scholars, using a term that was applied to the German sinking of ships that disappeared without a trace. Postal censors were directed to withhold from the public "any information relating to the time or place of censorship of mail; the process of censorship, or the jurisdiction of the several Committees over mail matter, or any other information about the Censorship."[57]

Creel held a view similar to Burleson's (and censors in every belligerent nation). He told a reporter he "did not want anything whatever published in regard to cable or mail censorship. . . . No one should know just where the censorship is working." He was thus unhappy about a June 1918 story that censors in San Antonio burned seven railway cars full of "Hun propaganda"—newspapers, magazines, and books in Spanish and German destined for Mexico. Obviously based on information provided by a censor eager to brag about his bureau's good work, the story reported that the bureau had a list of more than thirty-eight thousand names of disloyal persons and firms. Creel asked the United Press to "lay off" such news. "Not only is secrecy essential to an effective operation of this border censorship," he said, "but our relations with Mexico, as you know, are very delicate."[58]

CREEL GIVETH AND TAKETH AWAY

No accounting of the CPI is complete without reference to the many instances when Creel used his power to improve news coverage. He pushed to allow correspondents to accompany the first troop ships to France, which Newton Baker suggested to Pershing. The general "earnestly urged" that this not be done and with equal vehemence opposed the proposition that "any reputable American newspaper be allowed to send one correspondent" to the AEF. Only sixteen

correspondents were accredited as of July 1917. This was more than the twelve
the French accredited to their forces and the five the British accredited to theirs
but a pitifully small number nonetheless.[59]

"I felt that the Pershing expedition was largely to be regarded as a fife and
drum corps," Creel told Mark Sullivan, "and that every man should be permitted to go with it, who could raise the money and present proper credentials."
Many reporters without AEF accreditation arrived in Europe with "letters from
the Creel bureau" asking that they receive "every possible courtesy" from the
army. The CPI facilitated passports, organized short trips to the field for visiting correspondents, and helped reporters visit navy installations and ships. By
the end of the war, according to one authoritative military account, 36 American correspondents were accredited to the AEF, and 411 were allowed to visit
the AEF.[60]

Creel battled the War Department over its decision to issue casualty lists
with only the names of wounded or deceased soldiers. Without home addresses,
the lists were worthless to newspapers. President Wilson took Creel's side. Creel
was similarly successful in overturning Pershing's decision to forbid mention of
the cause of death. To help ease constraints on correspondents in Britain and
France, Creel enlisted his friend George Barr Baker. Baker was executive officer
of US Naval Cable Censorship in New York and a former reporter in Britain.
Creel provided Baker with a letter from Wilson endorsing his mission to Britain and France. Baker streamlined censorship, which was bogged down by censors in Paris who reviewed dispatches after they had been approved by the AEF
censors in the field. Baker also upgraded the communication lines used to send
dispatches from the AEF front.[61]

Creel was more liberal than his Censorship Board colleagues. When a complaint came in about Sullivan's supposedly unpatriotic speeches, Creel stood
up for him. He intervened on behalf of publications he believed were unfairly
harassed by postal censors and complained to Maddox that censors tore out
pages from magazines when they had no authority to do so. He was outraged
that the Military Intelligence Branch, in its search for "literary infection," put
authors Ambrose Bierce and G. K. Chesterton on the list of books banned
from military installations. He refused to release the list through the CPI, telling Tumulty that "to give these lists to the public is to work grave injustices to
loyal people." Amos Pinchot, one of the most outspoken liberal critics of suppression, was willing to give Creel the benefit of the doubt on his stewardship
of the CPI.[62]

Creel acquitted himself well with regard to the lynching of Robert Prager, a German-American, in Collinsville, Illinois, on April 3, 1918. The mob, whose leaders were found not guilty, said he was a spy. The lynching highlighted the wave of injustices across the country. Creel "went to the president at once" to suggest he speak out. After an inordinately long lapse, the president finally decried mob violence on July 26. Creel sought maximum attention for his pronouncement.[63]

Creel was one of many Wilson advisors who favored dismissing the charges against IWW members rounded up in mass arrests in September 1917. After the war, he added his name to the list of people who believed the defendants in the Abrams case should be given amnesty. Although "utterly out of sympathy" with the defendants, he said, "From the first I have held the views so ably presented by Sir Frederick Pollock." Pollock, an eminent British jurist, argued "spy mania" tainted the trial, the penalty was excessive, and the application of the Espionage Act unconstitutional. By the standard of the trial, Pollock wrote, "every strike of workmen employed in producing anything of warlike use would be an act of resistance to the United States, though the strike might be caused merely by a dispute about wages or hours of work."[64]

But what Creel could give he could take away. The ability to facilitate passports was also a means of holding them up, which Creel did. The CPI's defense of speech was often based on desirable ends rather than democratic principle. When military intelligence barred *Current History* and *Mid-Week Pictorial* from export, Creel argued for sending them because they were good propaganda. Bestor recommended working with the controversial socialist-leaning Nonpartisan League in the Northwest because "it has audiences which otherwise cannot be reached." Creel agreed. "Our one task," he said when objections were raised, "is to carry the message of America to every part of the United States in order that all people may understand the justice of this war." All the CPI asked "of any man or body of men, any organization, sect or class of citizens," Harvey O'Higgins said, "was 'Are you for the war?' If they were, the Committee was ready to work with them and to defend them from every enemy who sought to charge them with pro-Germanism."[65]

Guided by this philosophy, Creel's response to criticism was the same as Wilson's, a reflexive desire to silence it, even if the subject matter was far afield from sensitive military information. This broader scope was apparent in the division of labor worked out with the chief naval censor in which he and his staff "acted on all strictly naval and military matters" and the CPI "accepted responsibility for decisions in matters of a political character." While admitting no hard-and-fast rules that covered every element of censorship, one of the "general principles" for cable censorship was "All matters that might indicate serious dissensions among the American people or the people of the Allies shall be suppressed."[66]

Creel deserved credit for arranging the accreditation of Ralph Tyler, a black correspondent, to the AEF. But Tyler's dispatches and personal letters were subject to "special care" by censors and vetted again by Emmett Scott at the War Department. The army worried "that under the existing conditions in France, as affecting the colored soldiers, he may fail to exercise, at all times, the best judgment." Tyler was supposed to devote his attention to the positive activities of his own race. He did not report the discrimination he witnessed. The CPI killed his stories about French women's willingness to fraternize with blacks. Scott warned Tyler that "press authorities of the War Department have regarded it as expedient that some of your letters be 'expurgated' in a measure, to conform to strictly military policies."[67]

Creel remembered Attorney General Gregory as "a vicious old reactionary." He denied having "intimate relations with the Department of Justice, the Post Office Department, Military Intelligence, or Naval Intelligence. On the contrary, my relations with all of these agencies were bitter to the breaking point." The CPI files refute this. The CPI was routinely in contact with those entities. Creel raised no objection when the chief naval censor informed him that censors cut large portions of a news cable to London carrying Roosevelt's criticism of the Wilson administration. It was not exceptional for military intelligence to ask Creel to follow up on a troubling story in a Hearst newspaper. Roche's division sent the MID copies of reports on foreign-language newspapers, and the MID believed the CPI would "look with favor upon any plan this Division might propose for the handling of the censorship of film for shipment abroad."[68]

Creel wrote to Bruce Bielaski, head of the Justice Department Bureau of Investigation, to suggest books that should be suppressed and passed along a circular mailed by the People's Council of America, the group that was at odds with the CPI front American Alliance for Labor and Democracy. "It seems to me," Creel told Lamar in one of many such notes, "that not only should the Post Office proceed against this paper, but that the whole matter should be turned over to the Attorney General." He suggested that Gregory prosecute a journal that said nurses overseas engaged in prostitution.[69]

PATROLLING FOR ENEMY UTTERANCES

The Justice Department operated "upon the theory that, where propaganda cannot be met with criminal proceedings[,] it must be met by country-propaganda or publicity or control of publicity, the matter falls within the scope of your [CPI] activities." When Assistant Attorney General John Lord O'Brian complained the CPI did not follow up as it should, Creel said such material should be sent "to me personally. I am very anxious to get it." After the war was over, he wanted "to smash the lie" that the Justice Department had been negligent in monitoring loyalty. "I want to prove that the Department was vigilant from first to last, and effective throughout," he told O'Brian, "and that almost all those who deserved to be punished, were punished."[70]

CPI staff constantly patrolled for "enemy" utterances. They pored over a story in the *New York World*—a thoroughly pro-Wilson newspaper—on the lack of military preparedness, doing a line-by-line analysis to show errors (and show the reporter's perfidy), which was sent to the president. After the collector of customs in Los Angeles forwarded a socialist proclamation, Creel urged him to "pay as much attention as possible to the press in your vicinity." Herbert Putnam, the librarian of Congress, gave office space to the CPI, where it screened books, alerted Creel to books that others deemed questionable, and informed Creel of individuals who checked out such volumes. Robert Murray, the CPI's representative in Mexico and a longtime reporter for the *New York World,* forwarded a clipping from a newspaper, *El Democrata.* It reported that a certain "Jose Bracamontes of Youngstown, Ohio," had written to a man in Aguascalientes that his son had been "impressed against his will into our army" and was "compelled" to buy Liberty bonds. "Is it worth while," he asked Creel, "to have some of our people hunt up Mr. Jose Bracamontes . . . and ask the gentleman what he means by writing such fibs to Mexico?"[71]

Whether or not this was followed up is not clear from CPI files, but trivial matters were often pursued. When a reader of the *Washington Evening Star* suggested a photograph of wooden barrels of rosin bound for munition factories might "suggest to some pro-German that so much rosin would make a fine fire," Creel chided the company responsible for the photo for not submitting it for review. When a patriotic individual alerted Creel to Dr. Sigmund Freud's *Reflections on War and Death*—which had a section devoted to "disappointments of the war"—Creel called the book "to the attention of the proper authorities." Learning that a Boston University professor was talking about class struggle,

Creel asked a member of the CND to get the professor to "change his tone in the interest of unity." O'Higgins alerted the editor of the *Argus* in Caledonia, Minnesota, of a report "that a prohibition lecturer in your community has been making untrue statements about the government in its relations to liquor." "Pro-German" agents, he warned, were claiming the government allowed sugar to be shipped abroad to be used for spirits while Americans were supposed to conserve. He asked the editor to publish a notice that corrected the record.[72]

Indicative of the CPI's opportunistic, and erratic, censorship was *Two Thousand Questions and Answers about the War.* The idea for the book occurred to one of the proprietors of the Review of Reviews Company, which published a magazine by that name, when he read a patriotic question-and-answer feature in an Australian journal. The *Review of Reviews* acquired rights for that material and added its own. The principal author was Julius Muller, the author of *The Invasion of America,* an imaginary account of the German conquest of the United States. In his typical state of haste, Creel wrote an introduction proclaiming the book "a vital part of the national defense." Ford read *Two Thousand Questions* after it was published and arrived at a different verdict. He told Creel that it was "a pacifist pro-German affair" containing nothing that condemned the Germans. Ford was dismayed that the book contended that British and French imperialism resembled German imperialism and that it praised German education. Creel complained to the *Review of Reviews,* and Ford followed with a seven-page critique and an implied threat: "I can hardly regard with equanimity the extensive distribution of this book." The book was revised. Among the changes was a new section on German atrocities and an explicit endorsement of the Bryce Committee findings as based on evidence "exhaustively considered."[73]

Creel had a strong working relationship with his Canadian counterpart, Colonel Chambers, a slight, balding man with a walrus mustache. Chambers, who once was a newspaperman, told Creel censorship was "one of the most powerful engines of war at the disposal of the Government." He went about his work with gusto, removing from Canadian soldiers' letters such statements as war "was worse" than hell. He detested Hearst and was slow to follow the British lead in reinstating INS cable privileges. When Chambers said he had prohibited the book *War—What For?,* Creel asked the librarian of Congress to remove the volume from its shelves and supply the names of people who had asked for it. Creel was helpful when Chambers complained about New England news stories that portrayed French Canadians as military slackers. Creel wrote to editors, including of the *Harvard Lampoon,* suggesting they "quietly pass word around among journalists in that part of your Country to desist from publishing statements which cannot conceivably do any good and which are calculated to cause harm by producing a feeling of resentment."[74]

In the first weeks of the CPI's existence, Arthur Bullard headed a Division of Foreign Correspondents and Foreign Language Publications, a unit soon reorganized out of existence. He thought the stories netted by cable news censors were a "waste of time" to monitor. He had a similarly benign view of the foreign-language press in the United States. "I have not seen any of the foreign-language papers which seem to me to make any immediate strong action imperative." The major problem, he said, was that they were poor and corruptible. Instead of repression, it would be better "to stimulate them to a higher ideal of journalism."[75]

This was not the prevailing view on the staff. With Bullard's help, Ford put together the network of university professors who monitored foreign-language newspapers under CPI supervision. "I distinctly feel that your people are running as close to the line as any group," he told Norwegian-born Laurence Larson at the University of Illinois. Ford wanted verbatim transcripts and sent Larson a copy of the Espionage Act. With regard to an Illinois newspaper he particularly wanted watched, Ford commented that with the Trading with the Enemy Act "the government will be in a position to deal promptly with such cases." This jibed with Larson's views, who believed "something ought to be done to quiet" certain German-language papers. The Swedish press, he said, was "loyal, but the loyalty is negative." It did not oppose the war, but neither did it "promote Americanization." Edwin Bjorkman's censoring was not limited to leaning on editors to stay away from certain writers; he recommended revoking the mailing permit of a paper that discredited his work.[76]

Foreign-language newspapers that aggressively supported the Central Powers at the start of the war shifted gears once America entered it. They demonstrated loyalty by printing nothing that could antagonize the government, adorning front pages with American flags, promoting Liberty Loans, changing their names into English, and using CPI material. If they wanted to be critical, they quoted from English-language papers. Justice Department raids of foreign-language newspapers were a reminder of their vulnerability. Also, by cutting war news, they did not have to pay for the translations necessary for use of the mail. Dissent diminished. Few were denied the mails, and most were given blanket mailing permits. "By the end of the war," historian Carl Wittke noted, "German papers were publishing 'open confessions' of conversion from their earlier pro-German position."[77]

This did not guarantee their survival. German-American newspapers suffered unofficial censorship at the hands of readers and advertisers who deserted them for fear of being identified as disloyal. By the end of the war, half of all German-language publications had disappeared. The number of French- and Italian-language newspapers was unchanged, and the number in Spanish increased substantially.[78]

"The owners and editors of these [German-language] publications," Julius Koettgen told Creel, "feel that the full success of our movement means the death of their enterprises. Some of their sheets will probably end by becoming American newspapers printed in the English language." Koettgen attacked individual publications. The *Evansville Demokrat,* he said, "was put out of business in the course of conflict it engaged in with the Friends of German Democracy." At the same time, he fretted that the loss of some papers was not in the CPI's interest. In many cases, he noted, it was the "weaker papers for which our mat [print-ready] service is intended that pass away."[79]

NO RIGHT TO DESTROY PUBLIC CONFIDENCE

"We have the right to demand to be told everywhere and always the truth," Georges Clemenceau wrote early in the war. "The Tiger," as Clemenceau was nicknamed, championed press freedom and crusaded for Jewish officer Alfred Dreyfus, who was falsely accused of selling military secrets. By one count he toppled eighteen governments over a sixteen-year period. When Clemenceau was a senator, the minister of the interior suspended his newspaper *L'Homme Libre* for exposing miserable medical care for wounded soldiers. Clemenceau started a new paper, *L'Homme Enchaîné.*[80]

In 1917 politicians who had suffered at Le Tigre's editorializing hand ruefully acknowledged they needed Clemenceau's leadership. With French morale wilting and French troops mutinying, the renegade became the premier. It was he who jailed Caillaux on charges of treason and left him languishing in prison without a trial.* Favorable newspaper comments on Caillaux were censored. "Why should you think I want to make my task harder?" Clemenceau asked a *Christian Science Monitor* correspondent. "The French press is irresponsible. Do you suppose I'm going to have it filled with defeatist articles? No, the newspapers must walk warily, or I shall close them down without mercy."[81]

* Caillaux made no secret of his interest in seeing the war come to an end and kept company with controversial figures with similar views. One of these was French financier Paul Bolo-Pasha, who was suspected of using German money to buy *Le Journal.* Bolo-Pasha was executed for treason along with the spy Mata Hari.

American newspaper readers did not encounter, as French readers did, swaths of blank space where censors killed stories. Official government censoring of domestic news was limited to the mails and fell almost entirely on radical and foreign-language press. The size of that enterprise was considerable, nonetheless. Nearly sixteen hundred people, opening 125,000 pieces of mail daily, handled post office censorship, according to Burleson's 1918 annual report. In his annual report for that year, Gregory said, the cases brought under the speech section of the Espionage Act exceeded "the number of those brought under any other of the war laws, except the selective-service act." The Department of Justice prosecuted more than two thousand dissenters. "Because there were essentially no instances in which the government could prove that dissident speech had *actually* caused insubordination, mutiny, refusal of duty, or obstruction of the recruiting or enlistment service," legal scholar Geoffrey R. Stone commented. "Almost every prosecution was framed as an 'attempt.'"[82]

Sentences were extreme: fifteen years to a Vermont preacher who refused to preach on behalf of Liberty Loan Sunday, twenty years to an Iowan who said American boys would return from Europe mad. In the Abrams case an informer received a three-year sentence and the others as much as twenty years. "For a similar offense in England," said Sir Frederick Pollock, "the usual sentences would be imprisonment for six months, or twelve at the outside." After the war, the president accepted Gregory's recommendation to release or reduce the sentences of two hundred individuals convicted by overly patriotic juries. He would not, however, relent on Eugene Debs, America's Joseph Caillaux.[83]

The worry over unwanted speech was out of balance with the amount that actually occurred. "Most of the Press and Magazines, as you know," Merrill Rogers of the *Masses* correctly noted, "have gone over on the side of War and the Masses is in a very slim minority." No evidence showed the enemy subsidized these left-leaning publications. In a couple of instances, frustrated war reporters violated censorship rules established by the AEF in France, but these were rare, as were violations of the CPI's voluntary censorship guidelines. "We guarded [sensitive military] facts as jealously as if they had been family skeletons," said Fred Essary, the *Baltimore Sun* reporter who had helped Woolley during the 1916 campaign, "and even debated the propriety of confiding so much as a line of what we knew to our own editors."[84]

In an exuberant moment, Creel proclaimed there had not been a single violation of the guidelines. But this was not far off. At the end of the war, army censors concluded, "there were practically no violations of the voluntary censorship and very little information was published, either through accident or design, which might in any way be construed as damaging to the interests of the United States." In Ford's estimation mistakes were inadvertent and often the fault of social editors "who announced that a wedding of a certain captain was being solemnized because his regiment (name and number given) was sailing at such a time." Time and again, the press stood behind repression. The *Washington Post,* one of the more frequent violators of the guidelines, nevertheless said, "Enemy propaganda must be stopped, even if a few lynchings may occur. The people know what they want."[85]

Creel's voluntary guidelines were a wise strategy. Besides patriotically restraining their reporting, editors howled when a competitor gained a news advantage by violating the rules. But Creel could not restrain himself. His adamant claims that the CPI did not touch censorship were blatantly at odds with reality. The CPI had plain-to-see censorship power, a seat on the Censorship Board, and hypersensitivity to facts and comments not covered by the guidelines or the law. Implied consequences for angering the CPI and Creel's pugnaciousness buttressed the CPI's informal, ad hoc power.[86]

Creel was a man of emotions. Sometimes they carried him to liberal ends. Sometimes, in the words of Justice Holmes, Creel would "sweep away all opposition." In the summer of 1918, an editorial in the *Danville (IL) Commercial-News* called out the CPI for "flooding the country with a lot of 'news' that is not news" and for wanting publishers to submit for review all books and magazine articles "dealing with any phase of the war." The first assertion was arguably true. As to the second, Creel had wanted to review all magazines and books on the war but could not devise a practical plan to do that and concentrated instead on publications touching on "military and naval affairs." Confusion was inevitable, and many editors had the same impression as the *Commercial News.* Guy Stanton Ford, who passed the editorial to Creel, noted publishers were sending him books in accordance with a supposed "policy of supervising all war literature." Nevertheless, Creel admonished the editor, "I do not think you have the right, as an American, to attempt to destroy public confidence."[87]

10

Officials of Doubtful Status

We know our rank and status which is more than can be said for you.
You are a strange fish and we don't know where to place you. We
will have to look up precedents or perhaps create one.
—Third Assistant Secretary, US Legation, Beijing, to
CPI Commissioner Carl Crow

In the first months of the war the large frosted globe in George Creel's office was for little more than decoration. The CPI's first job was domestic, to "hold fast the inner lines." But by January 1918 he was eager to take on the world. Creel informed Wilson in a report that month that, with the inner lines secure, the "greatest need" was abroad. "We are now able to commence 100 per cent operation in all confidence. It is for this that I ask sanction. There is no detail in connection with these activities that we shall be ashamed to reveal. No paper will be subsidized, no official bought, no corruption employed." Wilson agreed that the time had come to look abroad in view of what had been accomplished inside the United States. "The country," he told the British ambassador, "had not been so thoroughly united for years."[1]

The CPI sought to reassure the Allies of "L'Effort Américain" on the battlefield, to encourage neutral countries to stay neutral, if not turned in the Allies' favor, and to cause enemy citizens to lose faith in their government and enemy soldiers to throw down their arms. Beyond this Wilson and Creel saw the loftier possibility of selling the United States. CPI emissaries, the president said in a letter to one of them, were privileged to "acquaint those countries with the life of America, our aims and our ideals." One ideal in particular stood out, that this was a war for a stable democratic order with the United States in the lead.[2]

Propaganda on the outer lines presented problems that did not exist domestically. Conditions varied from country to country. The work had to be done at great distances from Lafayette Square. The overall objective ran against a diplomatic tradition that considered propaganda bad form. Envoys led rarified lives. The hoi polloi were irrelevant except to fetch coffee for them in meetings with frock-coated counterparts at the foreign ministry. Allied propagandists were an additional source of frustration. French military censors delayed American dispatches about the AEF to give their troops better press. A CPI representative complained, "The British won't work with anybody unless they can boss the whole job."[3]

The United States had never done anything like what Creel proposed abroad. This terra incognita magnified the worst tendencies of his management style. Inefficiency, erratic planning, and bureaucratic wrangling marred the CPI's performance. As will be taken up in the next chapter, this was also the case with CPI propaganda against enemy military forces, but with an important difference. The CPI had little to show with regard to field propaganda against the enemy. Its work in friendly and neutral nations established a new approach to foreign affairs.

The CPI moved beyond the concept of hard power based on economic leverage and military might. It thought in terms of the soft power derived from shaping public attitudes and opinions that promoted American foreign policy interests. If Creel's execution left much to be desired, the concept of public diplomacy was one of the CPI's most significant accomplishments.

OVERCOMING WILSON'S RELUCTANCE

Creel's proposal in January 1918 was not the first to call for overseas propaganda. Two days after the United States declared war, David Lawrence of the *New York Evening Post* proposed that Wilson organize "a staff of newspapermen *to undertake in secret* the whole question of a pro-American propaganda in Latin America." Frederic Wile, a persistent roman candle of publicity proposals, argued for a bureau in London that would use "every form of modern publicity." Ambassador Page endorsed Wile's idea. Macneile Dixon, who took over Gilbert Parker's propaganda portfolio in London, thought it "quite as necessary" for Americans to carry out propaganda in his country as it was for his office to do so in the United States. He complained, "We have never been able to get into touch with [the CPI]. It would be of greatest advantage if we could."[4]

Declining Allied morale in the coming months ratcheted up the sense of urgency. Felix Frankfurter, a special assistant to Newton Baker, returned from Europe in August with warnings that Joseph Caillaux might secure a place in government and open peace negotiations. He recommended "continuous publicity" in Paris under someone who kept "in discreet and effective contact with French public men and opinion."[5]

Such admonitions—and there were many more—did not move Wilson. His initial thoughts about publicity were strictly domestic. His three-sentence executive order creating the CPI said nothing about its working abroad. Arthur Bullard, who thought the United States should do to the British what the British propagandists had done to them, gained the impression in his time at CPI headquarters that it "would have nothing to do with Publicity work abroad." While Wilson had an eye on foreign audiences when he delivered speeches on the war, he wanted to keep a certain distance from the Allies. He made a point of saying the United States was "associated" with them rather than "allied." He told Creel it was not "advantageous" to belong to the inter-Allied propaganda committee. In October 1917, he flatly rejected a unanimous recommendation from Bestor's advisory committee to send speakers abroad. When he turned down a subsequent proposal to send a speaker to England, Wilson commented that the English should never have sent speakers to the United States. Creel circumvented Wilson's prohibition by arranging speakers through other executive branch departments as well as the British War Mission. (He also encouraged the War Mission to send speakers to the United States.)[6]

The first crack in Wilson's wall of resistance grew out of the overthrow of Tsar Nicholas in March 1917. The future of the Provisional Government was in doubt, as was its willingness to fight. After receiving suggestions "from a number of quarters" that a commission be sent to Russia, he dispatched one under Republican statesman Elihu Root to assess what should be done to keep the country in the war. Shortly after his arrival in June, Root urgently cabled Washington that German propaganda was demoralizing Russian soldiers. He called for "immediate counter attacks by the same weapons." Root and other delegates personally advanced $30,000 to start the work. Approval of the modest expenditure did not come until Root was back home. Wilson would not commit to do more when he met with Root in August.[7]

This foot-dragging angered Root, as did Wilson's decision to turn the matter over to Creel, who convinced the president to give the CPI responsibility for publicity in Russia. Root refused Tumulty's suggestion that he meet with Creel to discuss what was being planned. In November Creel dispatched Edgar Sisson to Petrograd with a budget far smaller than Root had recommended. Wilson did not let Creel send Russian-born men to explain America's war aims.

"We must wait," he said, "to see our way before pushing forward any faster than we are."[8]

Shortly before Sisson set off for Russia, Creel set up a fledgling Foreign Section. In addition to Sisson, it was made up of a CPI representative sent to launch a motion picture campaign in Italy and Spain and of an overseas news service. Wilson may have given way on the service because it had a similar mission to the *Official Bulletin,* whose creation he had insisted upon at the start of the war.[9]

The Wireless-Cable Service aimed to correct an American disadvantage in explaining itself to the world. In the nineteenth century, Reuters in Britain, Havas in France, and Wolff in Germany had formed a cartel in which each had the exclusive right to sell news in specific regions defined by their country's colonies and special relations. Each had close ties with its government, including financial support, which they repaid by distributing propaganda and filtering foreign news reaching their readers. The Associated Press, a junior partner, could sell cartel news in the United States but not directly distribute its own abroad. For some time Walter Rogers, a former *Chicago Daily News* reporter, had been proselytizing on the need to reach foreign readers. When the United States entered the war, Charles Crane, a wealthy, politically active Chicagoan who financed progressive news ventures, sent him to study Asian news practices, which confirmed Rogers's belief that something had to be done. At the suggestion of House, he approached Lansing, who had no interest in his findings, which he said did not bear on the work of his department. Creel thought it essential to "become articulate throughout the world" and put Rogers to work creating the CPI service.[10]

The Wireless-Cable Service was launched at 20 Broad Street in New York. News left via navy communications lines and was transmitted onward with the help of Allied facilities. By January 1, 1918, according to the Office of Naval Intelligence, Rogers "had established cable and radio communication around the world for the distribution of news beneficial to this country and the Allies." "Compub"—the service's cable address and cognomen—emphasized war news: the Supreme Court's upholding of the draft law; statistics on the production of war-making commodities; the establishment of thirty-two America First clubs in Colorado by Czechs, Slavs, Italians, Germans, and Italians; and Caillaux's treachery. It reported that Germany distorted CPI statements to conceal from its people "the unselfishness of the Americans in entering the war." Proximity to navy censors, with whom the CPI shared office space, allowed Rogers to monitor, as well as suppress, the dispatches that European correspondents in the United States sent to their home countries. To compensate for shortcomings in these reports, the CPI news service emphasized "points which the foreign correspondents failed to mention."[11]

On October 31, Creel added the Foreign Press Bureau under progressive journalist Ernest Poole. By mid-November Poole was sending out more than fifty articles a week. Initially, Poole prioritized giving "a true picture of this country" to Russia, from which he had just returned. The "Poole Service," which sent its articles by mail, went beyond stories about American war work. The hope, Poole told Creel, was to highlight the "innumerable experiments and efforts made in this country toward more and more democracy and general social welfare." The CPI drew from government reports and speeches, republished articles that had appeared domestically, and commissioned contributions from Booth Tarkington, Edward Ross, William Allen White, and other well-known authors. Country specialists wrote and translated material. "Before I knew it," said Hamilton Owens, editor in chief of the Poole service, "I had a staff of about seventy-five people working in a building on Madison Avenue." Poole had the unpleasant task of knocking on doors in their building to commandeer offices.[12]

As the news service got under way, reports of declining morale among the Allies grew dire. In November, respected former minister and viceroy of India Lord Lansdowne argued for a negotiated peace. "Lansdownism" in Britain, like Caillauxism in France, became a byword in agents' intelligence reports for unpatriotic quitters. It was at this time that Lloyd George, worried about public opinion, elevated the status of propaganda by creating the Ministry of Information. In Italy, the executions of recalcitrant soldiers soared (reaching 750 by war's end). In early 1918, the chief of Italian propaganda told an American diplomat he expected "machine guns in the streets to repress disorders." French troops trudged to the front mimicking the bleating noises of sheep going to slaughter; mutinies occurred in sixty-eight divisions. Wilson could no longer ignore the outer lines.[13]

The Foreign Section would eventually consist of Rogers's and Poole's units, a Foreign Film Division (that included a pictorial service that provided photographs and posters), and a large corps of CPI representatives posted in individual countries as Sisson was in Russia. Creel's vision for these representatives was ambitious, but the plans amounted to little more than vague statements redolent with platitudes.

THE GREAT DIFFERENCE BETWEEN
TRENTON AND PARIS

Creel envisioned CPI commissioners working "in a dignified, modest and thorough manner in keeping with the character of the New America as opposed to the America with which Europeans associate boasting, flamboyancy and commercialism." The common denominator in his plan was commissioners who "knew the country" to which they were posted.[14]

Carl Crow, the CPI's representative in China, fit the bill. He was better versed in the country than most diplomats there. In 1911 he helped start the first American newspaper in the country, the *China Press,* which aimed to counter the colonial mentality of British papers with American attitudes about self-determination. Crow enjoyed access to Sun Yat-sen, who led the overthrow of the Qing Dynasty in 1911, and wrote the popular *Handbook for China.* In 1915 he left the Far East and bought a fruit farm in the Santa Clara Valley. When war came, he sought a commission in army intelligence. Army investigators scotched this when they learned he once had as a house guest "a very pretty Canadian girl" who was allegedly a German spy. Crow sold the farm and headed across the Pacific to work for the CPI in China instead.[15]

Other representatives were accomplished but not for knowing "the country." Many were progressives with a progressive's taste for publicity to advance a good cause. Charles Merriam, sent to Rome on the advice of his Chicago friend Walter Rogers, was to political science what Edward Ross was to sociology. He was the first member of the University of Chicago faculty hired under the designation "political science" and founded the behavioralist movement. Instead of humanistic study of political institutions, behaviorists used statistical field research to understand the election process and governing. He ran successfully for the Chicago city council. This was useful experience for propaganda, but his knowledge of Italy was derived from what he read aboard ship on the way over.[16]

Frank Marion was president of the Kalem movie studio, where he excelled in sales. It was he who was sent to promote American films in Italy and Spain at the end of 1917. In the topsy-turvy way things were done, he ended up as the commissioner in Spain. Creel envisioned putting "a man of broad European experience" in Paris, which was supposed to anchor CPI overseas operations. Instead, he sent James Kerney, editor of the *Trenton Times.* Kerney spoke no French and had no foreign experience. His ticket to Paris was Wilson, whose political career the affable New Jersey editor had supported. Wilson wanted

Kerney to send him confidential reports, a ploy he often used to circumvent diplomats, whom he distrusted. "There is a great difference between Paris and Trenton," Kerney said, "and you notice it more in Paris than in Trenton." When diplomats criticized Kerney's lack of sophistication, Creel reversed himself on the importance of foreign expertise, saying the critics wanted someone in Paris "who speaks French, acts French and is as little like an American as is possible."[17]

In June 1918, Creel told Kerney to employ the American wife of the Marquis de Polignac and an American actress, who was a friend of Creel's wife and married to a Frenchman. He left it to Kerney to figure out how they could be helpful. Often appointments were a matter of expediency. The commissioner selected for Peru, Bolivia, and Ecuador was the American editor of the Lima-based English-language *West Coast Leader.* His reporters spread CPI propaganda, and his business staff drove advertisers away from the pro-German *La Crónica,* which supposedly changed its slant as a result. The CPI drew heavily on military intelligence attachés, who already were on the ground and following public opinion. A navy lieutenant with press experience spent more than six months in South America setting up CPI offices as well as establishing censorship functions in the region. Others were amateurs, if earnest. A military intelligence officer in Costa Rica, who recommended wide diffusion of CPI materials, opined that the country was "the egg nearest decomposition in a basket where the explosion of one would set off our other bad eggs. Any stench raised in Central America would divert slightly our military resources but might seriously cloud the political horizon."[18]

By Creel's count, the CPI had seventeen commissioners, twenty-two diplomatic and consular representatives, and ten American citizens acting as CPI agents. In preparing its postwar report on the CPI, the Council of National Defense could not identify the full staff Creel cobbled together. "As far as could be ascertained," it said, "special commissioners were employed for work in Denmark, England, France, Holland, Italy, Mexico, Romania, Russia, South America, Spain, Switzerland." (See table 4 in chapter 12.) Insofar as the CND was able to discern, South America included Argentina, Brazil, Chile, and Peru. One difficulty in making a tally was identifying the intelligence officers who assisted the CPI. "President and Secretary Daniels are absolutely opposed to use of Army or Navy or Diplomatic representatives as directors of open propaganda work," Creel cabled a commissioner. "Our idea [is to] employ them fully under cover of our Committee with its own director in charge." Not mentioned in the CND report were Sweden, Panama, El Salvador, Uruguay, Australia, Japan, and

China, all of which are referenced in the CPI files and one of which (China) definitely had a commissioner. Crow's omission may explain why he never received notice to close his office at the end of the war.[19]

The turnover in personnel was dizzying. The Foreign Section was headed successively by Creel, Arthur Woods, Will Irwin, Sisson, and Harry Rickey, who had been chief of Scripps's Newspaper Enterprise Association. When the war ended, Poole took over. Woods, a former New York City police commissioner with no foreign or journalism experience, quit after a week. "Just then I showed up," Irwin said. Creel thought he "dropped from heaven." Irwin had a laureled career as a muckraker and war reporter and experience handling publicity for Herbert Hoover's Europe-based Commission for Relief in Belgium. Irwin considered his specialty to be "the theory and psychology of journalism and of the kindred profession of advertising." The CPI London office was headed successively by Rickey, Henry Suydam, Charles Edward Russell, Russell's son John, Perry Arnold, and Paul Perry. When Russell became fed up, his son was appointed on the spur of the moment. "Who is running Compub London?" a CPI representative asked in frustration in October 1918.[20]

Communication was vexing. To some extent this was a function of the long distances involved. But the CPI aggravated the problem. "Although it may seem incomprehensible to you, as it is to me," Marion informed Creel in April 1918, "I have not received a letter nor a piece of printed matters of any character from our Committee since arriving in Spain, December 1st. None of the Official Bulletins of the Committee are sent to me, and I know nothing whatever about the Committee's policies as except what I may pick up in an occasional American paper arriving here six weeks late." A friend of Creel's in the Madrid embassy chided him for not being more responsive. "Madrid is four to eight weeks from Washington *by post* and hence *very* far off—but by cable is farther if cables are unanswered." "Please answer this question," a commissioner once wrote to Sisson, underscoring the words in pencil to reduce the chance they would be overlooked or forgotten.[21]

On top of this, communications often were uselessly vague. Commissioners were merely told to be "independent in so far as every fundamental decision is concerned, but you are, of course, to advise with the American Legation and maintain at all times a close and understanding contact." This gave them unlimited room for personal interpretation of their jobs and elevated the hostility American diplomats harbored for the enterprise.[22]

CRASHING A PRETTY GOOD CLUB

Carl Crow, "a smallish man with glasses and a ready laugh," got on well with people. The third secretary whom he called upon when he arrived in Beijing had been a poker-playing pal when Crow was a journalist in the Far East. But his comradery was on hold as far as Crow's CPI job was concerned. The diplomat called Crow "an American official of doubtful status." After waiting several days in vain for word on what rank he would hold, Crow printed calling cards with a title that put him on a par with the third secretary. "There were no official or political traditions behind us," he said.[23]

State Department antipathy was in full bloom with Hugh Gibson. In the spring of 1918, Creel recruited Gibson from Lansing's Division of Information to help coordinate CPI propaganda. A talented diplomat remembered for his wit and possible invention of the Gibson martini (with a pickled onion instead of an olive), Gibson was nevertheless a dubious choice if one wished to bring greater harmony to the CPI's work in Europe. After Gibson served in the American legation in Belgium, Brand Whitlock, Wilson's appointee as minster, commented, "It is hard to work with snakes and cads like Gibson. . . . While I was recommending him for promotion to the Department, he was conspiring against me."[24]

The lack of clarity as to what Gibson was supposed to do would have led to problems no matter what. Gibson was described to American and foreign officials as having oversight of "the general plan of propaganda strategy" and working in "close cooperation" with the CPI, the AEF, and "various other Government officials." In introducing Gibson to Kerney, Creel skipped even these generalities and told him to use Gibson as he thought best. In late April, Irwin told Gibson he was in charge of all propaganda in enemy countries and everyone had been so informed. The easily exasperated Gibson wrote in his diary that he received nothing official from Washington on this. In a letter to Irwin in May, Creel spoke breezily of Gibson's "roving commission."[25]

This spawned conspiracy theories. Kerney in Paris and the CPI commissioner in Bern thought Gibson wanted their jobs or to be their boss. When Gibson traveled to Rome, he found Merriam "touchy." "Gibson's functions here are very uncertain, and this has caused some confusion," Merriam complained to Creel. "It would greatly improve the situation if his relation to the Committee work here were more clearly defined, otherwise there is room for a good deal of friction."[26]

Gibson recognized the need for propaganda, especially propaganda directed at the Central Powers. He offered concrete suggestions. He correctly objected to statements overpromising what the United States would deliver militarily, calling it "press agentry." But he had a disdain for the CPI's innovation of directing propaganda at people. He dismissed as "piffle" a campaign to distribute leaflets to school children. The idea had merit. The youngsters would take the literature home to their parents.[27]

Gibson got on well with Will Irwin, whose international experience was deep. He considered most other CPI staff "utterly unfitted" for their work and maligned them. Kerney was "my little playmate." Merriam "was inclined to spin a web of psychological theories about things that did not lead anywhere." Creel had energy without follow-through: "He shares the belief of the Greek Sophists that a thought is a thing." Gibson made good points, but it was not helpful to make them so insistently. An adroit bureaucratic fighter who knew how to protect himself, Gibson worked ventriloquist style by attributing negative observations about CPI shortcomings to others. But eventually his badmouthing came to Creel's attention. In late July Creel separated him from the CPI.[28]

Gibson's subversion, however, did not end. He worked on the fringes of the CPI and was joined by others, none more wholeheartedly than his friend Hugh Wilson, the chargé d'affaires of the American legation in Switzerland. Wilson came from a wealthy Chicago family, graduated from Yale, and studied at the École Libre des Sciences Politiques in Paris. Diplomats, he thought, "belonged to a pretty good club" that he wanted to keep exclusive. When the consular service was merged with the diplomatic service, he objected because the latter possessed "higher thought." He was thus openly hostile to the commissioner Creel sent to crash his club in Bern. Although many rungs down his ladder of thought, in Wilson's mind anyway, the socialite-suffragist proved to be more than his match.[29]

Forty-two-year-old Vira Boarman Whitehouse epitomized the *Social Register.* The *New York Times* acclaimed her "one of the most beautiful and girlish of the young matrons in society." The *San Francisco Examiner* said she was the "prettiest woman in New York." In photos, she struck a high society pose as the wife of Norman De Rapelye Whitehouse, the senior partner in a wealthy New York brokerage house that his family established a century before. But there was another side to Whitehouse. She grew up in New Orleans, where she had received an education at Newcomb, one of the first women's colleges in the South. In New York, she was a leader of the suffrage movement, whose "primary job," a historian noted, "was to manufacture public opinion."[30]

Whitehouse was the publicity director for the unsuccessful drive to secure the vote for women in New York in 1915. When a new campaign was launched in 1917, she was elevated to chair of the New York State Woman Suffrage Party. Of the five states voting on enfranchising women, New York was considered "hopeless." Whitehouse ran the campaign with the focus and intensity Woolley brought to Wilson's reelection. She declared women could no longer work "like amateurs," taking holidays and succumbing to other distractions. They canvassed public sentiment, organized rallies, distributed pamphlets and press releases, and rallied workers, immigrants, and others. The measure passed with nearly 54 percent of the vote. Woman suffragists proclaimed, "No such campaign was ever conducted in the United States for any cause as that in New York." They presented Whitehouse with a gold leaf wreath inscribed, "From the women of New York State, whom she led to victory Nov. 6, 1917."[31]

While in Washington to receive the honor in early December, Whitehouse asked Creel if he had war work for her. They knew each other from the 1915 suffrage campaign, when he was executive head of the Men's League for Woman Suffrage in New York. Creel was laying plans ahead of securing Wilson's formal approval for overseas propaganda and offered Whitehouse several places abroad. She chose Switzerland, about which she knew little beyond what she had picked up as a tourist. She spoke some French and bad German. Unfazed by her lack of experience, she set conditions for accepting the assignment: she would "have an acknowledged position as representative or director of the Committee on Public Information in Switzerland, and should be expected to do only legitimate work." Her appointment letter arrived on New Year's Eve with an ominous footnote: her appointment would not be announced.[32]

This violated a major tenant of public relations: don't suppress controversial information that is going to come out anyway; when it leaks, it will be bigger news than otherwise. When the story appeared that Whitehouse was about to begin "an elaborate educational campaign" overseas, a source told the *World* that "she was not an appointee of the Administration, but was selected for the post and appointed by George Creel." A follow-up story added that neither Lansing nor Wilson was consulted and that Lansing opposed publicity abroad. Lansing tried to sweep up the mess with a denial, but Whitehouse did not have the diplomatic passport she had been promised when she left New York Harbor on a cold, windy January 10.[33]

When she reached Paris, Whitehouse was handed two items, a Swiss press report that her husband was on his way to Switzerland to do propaganda and a State Department telegram informing her that the legation was authorized to say she was traveling to Bern to study children's and women's issues. "It is not now and never has been the policy of the United States to conduct persuasive activities in any foreign country," the telegram said. "It relies entirely upon frank and open presentation of its aims and objects and the secret and corrupt methods of its enemies have never been attempted and will not be." Whitehouse mistakenly assumed this was the State Department's doing. Actually, the author was Creel, who had ill-prepared the ground for her arrival and sought a convenient way to get her into Switzerland.[34]

Not that the legation objected to this message. It had requested repudiation of Whitehouse's mission. When Whitehouse arrived in Bern, the minister, Pleasant Stovall, was in the United States. Hugh Wilson, Stovall's deputy, gave her a reception as chilly as the Swiss Alps. No women were then diplomats, and he thought, in general, "the political activity of women, especially of beautiful ones was highly irregular." He told her propaganda was a waste of time, as the Germans had discredited it among the Swiss. He refused to accept Whitehouse's letter of appointment as a CPI publicist. Until he had orders from Washington to the contrary, he would only honor the directive saying she was studying women's and children's issues. He had publicly denied she would be doing such work, he pointed out to her, and a reversal would force the legation to say that it had lied. He asked her to lunch so she could meet his wife. Wilson, Whitehouse told Creel, "has put every sort of subtle obstruction in my path.... I am developing a fine case of nervous indigestion."[35]

Several days later a young foreign service officer, Allen Dulles, made her stomach churn more. Dulles's qualifications for membership in Wilson's club were impeccable. His grandfather John Foster had been secretary of state. Robert Lansing was his Uncle Bert. Dulles spent weekends at his uncle's estate raptly listening to Captain Guy Gaunt, the British spy and surreptitious propagandist, recount his exploits. Bern marked the beginning of his lifelong love affair doing what Gaunt had done. The sleight of hand he suggested for Whitehouse was that she pass herself off as an AP reporter. "The fact that it was as much a lie as the woman and children fiction," she told Creel, "recommended it strongly to him." After reading the initial news stories about Whitehouse's mission, Dulles congratulated Uncle Bert for recognizing the futility of her mission. She did not realize how "necessary it is to disguise [propaganda] before shoving it down people's throats."[36]

Another source of resistance was Carl Ackerman. He was now a correspondent for the hugely popular *Saturday Evening Post,* a confidant of House, and as interested in propaganda as when he covered Washington embassies at the start of the war. In May 1917 he showed House a draft article on Germany's manipulation of its citizens' opinions in its "war of conquest." House drew from it in making suggestions to Wilson for his Flag Day speech that year. That summer Ackerman reported in the *Post,* "We don't know how to fight with news!" House convinced Ackerman to go to Switzerland for the magazine and to act as his "undercover personal agent" to monitor enemy public opinion and make recommendations. He could send reports in code via diplomatic channels. The *Post* endorsed Ackerman's split employment. In late 1917, he wrote in the *Post* that the Germans intended "to conquer the world after the war with news and business." At Hugh Wilson's request, he began drafting a plan to fight back.[37]

Whitehouse arrived as Ackerman was finishing his plan. His booming voice belied his five-foot-nine height, and he was full throated on the inadvisability of bringing in a woman who would wreck his plans and his involvement implementing them. "Only an experienced and well-known journalist [should] be entrusted to this work," he wrote to House. He did not favor her open approach as it was best not to "advertise what we are doing" to shape opinion. "No paper in Switzerland will dare publish her news," he said.[38]

Copious communications winged their way between Bern and Washington. Hugh Wilson said Whitehouse should go home. Whitehouse blasted Wilson for refusing to say how many copies of a presidential speech had been distributed. That information, he said, was "deeply confidential." Creel wrote Whitehouse that the president had informed the State Department "of his approval of our plans." A vice consul reported to the State Department that Swiss detectives overheard Whitehouse say she was starting her work. Swiss authorities, he said, planned to arrest or expel her if she did. This sniping was too much for Lansing's deputy, Frank Polk. He commanded Hugh Wilson to let Whitehouse move ahead.[39]

Then Minister Stovall returned to his post. Stovall, founder of the *Savannah Press* and childhood playmate of the president, was "in no way qualified" to be minister in the view of Dulles and his colleagues. They liked him best when he did what they said, which normally happened. He told Whitehouse that neither open publicity nor a woman suffragist belonged in Switzerland. She responded that she refused to operate secretly. On the suffragist issue, she called his bluff. She would offer her resignation if Stovall put his objection in writing. He declined.[40]

Expecting the State Department would command Stovall to give her full support, Whitehouse went to Paris in mid-March to consult with Kerney on setting up her office. There she received a cable from Creel saying she could inaugurate work "without connection with the legation or endorsement by it." Whitehouse submitted her resignation.[41]

To salvage the situation, Creel offered Whitehouse an undefined position in Paris. She suspected he did not want her back in the United States airing her grievances. She was still the chair of the New York State Woman Suffrage Party, and her voice would carry far. As it was, the *New York World* ran a front-page story on her resignation. Related stories appeared around the country reporting her disagreements with Stovall. When she declined the Paris assignment, Creel cabled that he would force the legation to take her on, if that was what she wished. "I mean to do the thing you want done." If she preferred, he said, she could have special missions in Europe. She asked for particulars on the missions, but neither those nor the promised State Department endorsement arrived.[42]

Whitehouse announced she was going home to see Creel. Twice, when she was about to board a ship in Bordeaux, she was told to return to Paris to receive a new directive. The first, from Creel, again asked her to work in Paris. She cabled asking for specifics and again received none. The second message, from Irwin, told her to go to Bern and start working. He said nothing of State Department authorization. Whitehouse was on the *Niagara* when it sailed on April 12.[43]

That same day Ackerman informed House that cooperation was impossible between the legation and Whitehouse, who "was in a belligerent frame of mind." Stovall informed the president that Whitehouse was obstinate and should not return; he told Lansing she was "personally hostile to me." At Stovall's urging, Ackerman cabled Polk to ask for her job and offered himself to Creel as a substitute if he needed one. Gibson, who was at the time still working with the CPI, considered Whitehouse beautiful and charming but "not particularly intelligent" and too exuberant in her plans for large public displays.[44]

After Ackerman lobbied him over lunch in Lausanne, Gibson pressed Irwin to "take Ackerman on." "Ackerman's idea," Gibson said, was "to work solely as a representative of the New York Times [in Bern], with no official label" and no public acknowledgment given to his appointment. A senior representative of the *Times* in Europe had endorsed the scheme. Also on April 12, Creel wrote Norman Whitehouse that his wife wanted to get things settled quickly, "but my own feeling is that [the legation envoys] have prejudiced her work so thoroughly in Switzerland, that a return would be useless." He did not mention that

President Wilson considered the legation's intransigence "one of those mistakes which apparently cannot be corrected without making matters worse."[45]

Friends and foes underestimated Whitehouse. Whitehouse generously credited Creel with turning events in her favor. But she was the chief architect of her victory. She rebutted the spurious accusations against her, had a clear strategy

Vira Whitehouse, a New York socialite with an iron will, successfully battled hidebound, antagonistic American diplomats in Switzerland to establish publicity as a tool of diplomacy. She bought Sonny so she would have friend in Bern. (Frontispiece in *My Year as a Government Agent*)

for what she wanted to do in Bern, and pressed her case. After a meeting with Tumulty, she wrote him, "I should like to cry from the housetops of the necessity and economy of a liberal policy of education publicity (which we must no longer call propaganda) in both allied and neutral countries." Tumulty passed the letter to Wilson. Whitehouse, Philip Patchin told Gibson, came to Washington "with murder in her heart as you said she had, and proceeded to raise the devil around here. She dominated George and had things her own way." The State Department was going to give her "every bit of cooperation possible." He added, "You should do the same over there. Incidentally, I hear that she rather has this in for you."[46]

Whitehouse returned to Europe with a diplomatic passport and two letters from Wilson. One endorsed open publicity; the other told Stovall she came "with my entire approval." In London she bought a dog to ensure she had a friend in Bern, where she opened an office on July 1.[47]

I WILL ARRIVE IN PARIS WITH BLOOD IN MY EYES

Whitehouse's relationship with the legation was one of civil enmity. She had no time for the envoys' leisurely lunches. She barely spoke to Stovall. The military attaché found her an office in a three-story house outside of the town center. To reach the grand neighborhood, she had to take a bridge over the Aare River and ascend a steep hill. Whitehouse could not move into the quarters for two days because the attaché lost the keys. Competent staff, as well as typewriters, were as scarce as office space. "We have one stenographer, who works from 9 in the morning until the day is well done," she reported in mid-July. "We have an old lady to translate and people who drift in each day looking for a position we put to work and get what we can out of them."[48]

Surrounded by France, Germany, Austria, and Italy, and made up of cultural groups speaking those languages, Switzerland was highly contested. "Every means should be exerted," Pershing wrote to Newton Baker, "to bring her in on the side of the allies, or keep her out altogether." The harboring of spies, correspondent Herbert Corey commented, was the principal occupation "outside of the cheese business." German intelligence took note of Whitehouse's arrival. She believed she was "constantly shadowed." In order to acquire a stenographer with translation skills, she hired a known German spy who worked hard, though sullenly. "It wears on our nerves to keep everything under lock and key and away from her," she told Kerney, "but perhaps she will fall in love with Mr. Fife and change her sympathies." George Fife oversaw Whitehouse's Swiss news service.[49]

Switzerland functioned as an international clearinghouse for the clandestine gathering and disseminating of information. After coming to power in November 1917, the Bolsheviks set up four diplomatic posts, one of them in Bern. Their envoy's sole purpose was propaganda, pursued "in such a way that you can never be accused of propaganda." The Allied nations were so secretive about their propaganda that Whitehouse had difficulty sizing up its effectiveness.[50]

In contrast to Whitehouse, the German propaganda chief was one of the most important people in his embassy. The chief's office, said Count Harry Kessler, who combined cultural propaganda with espionage, "resembles a large ministry." The Germans, Whitehouse informed the Bern legation's military attaché, bought and subsidized newspapers and displayed photographs "on billboards in every corner of Switzer[land]." Kessler's cultural propaganda included music, theater, art, cinema, and "even varieté"—this last word describing theater with a range of performances from acrobatics to magic. The consul general in Lucerne had the triple mission of spying, propagandizing, and smuggling.[51]

Whitehouse concentrated at first on CPI news. Stories were translated into French and German (Italian was not attempted), typed on a stencil, and run off on a smudgy mimeograph. A weekly bulletin summarizing current news went to newspapers. Whitehouse scored a major victory in persuading the official Swiss news agency, Agence Télégraphique Suisse, to distribute CPI articles. An agency for smaller papers also took articles. In September, she reported that Swiss papers were running two thousand paragraphs of her American news service a week, which was now "on a par with Havas, Reuter, etc., and many times leads them in the day's news."[52]

Whitehouse traveled around the country to meet editors. Her staff monitored the Swiss press to gauge sentiment and refute falsehoods. They distributed Wilson's speeches in pamphlet form, editorials from American papers, and CPI stories to journals devoted to medicine and farming. Labor stories went to socialist publications. Businesspeople and consuls received special bulletins. In October nearly two thousand enlarged war photographs were exhibited in thirty-three towns.[53]

Cinema was a German priority. Before Kessler left for Bern, General Ludendorff summoned him for a briefing on his plans for film. The Germans seemed to have unlimited funds for this purpose. Under pressure to counter with film propaganda of her own, she planned to form a company to control cinema houses in the principal towns with heavy German influence. During a stop in London on her way to Bern, she thought she secured agreement for a joint venture from Lord Beaverbrook, who presided over the new Ministry of Information. But the British representative in Bern was not supportive. Instead, she had to work through a newly formed Inter-Allied Commission on film that met Mondays at 2:30 and accomplished little, apart from annoying her.[54]

Creel devised an ingenious plan to maximize film propaganda overseas. To qualify for a CPI export certificate from the War Trade Board, the exporter had to agree that 20 percent of every shipment included CPI films and that no American commercial films would go to movie theaters that showed enemy films or refused to show CPI films. Whitehouse's Inter-Allied Commission colleagues, however, did not accept Creel's dictum on withholding films from theaters that showed enemy movies. In addition, the British argued that American commercial films, which were superior, had to be considered theirs because the film reached Europe though arrangements with British firms; the French made similar self-interested assertions. Under this thinking, both the British and French claimed American commercial movies had to be paired with their propaganda films.[55]

As these disputes dragged on, Whitehouse endeavored to acquire American films directly through the diplomatic mail. This arrangement was thwarted by the American representative of the War Trade Board in Switzerland, whom she considered old, slow, and adverse to publicity. Taking the same passive-aggressive stance as Hugh Wilson, he said that he was not authorized to cooperate and threw up procedural obstacles. In the end his opposition and interallied noncooperation were mooted by the influenza epidemic that closed Swiss theaters for long stretches.[56]

The embattled Whitehouse was relentless. She encouraged Swiss editors to write friendly editorials by pointing out how dependent their country was on American food. In a sly form of subsidization, she bought all the "surplus numbers" of editions with such editorials and sent them to the United States for distribution among leading American newspapers. She pressed CPI staff to follow up. "YOU MUST HAVE THESE DISTRIBUTED AND COMMENTED UPON IN OUR PRESS!" she told one of Poole's deputies. A few weeks later he reported back, "Your scheme is bearing splendid fruit." Perturbed over a glitch in Rogers's news service, Whitehouse shot off a letter to Kerney: "Do what you can about this, and if it still goes on I will arrive in Paris with blood in my eyes." She convinced AEF intelligence to supplement her staff.[57]

Whitehouse's tenaciousness came into play again when the Hapsburg monarchy began to disintegrate. Concerned that unruly successor states were jockeying for power, Wilson called on the peoples of the region to exercise restraint. Whitehouse was told to publicize the message throughout the defunct empire. This was a monumental task in any case but all the more difficult at that particular moment. Influenza had decimated her translation staff; a printers' strike impeded reproduction, and inoperable telegraphs and stalled mail service rendered distribution nearly impossible.

Whitehouse turned to Rosika Schwimmer, an "envoy especial" of the new Hungarian republic. The two women knew each other from a 1914 suffrage convention, where they had clashed over condemning the war, which Schwimmer advocated, or focusing on securing the vote, which Whitehouse wanted. Respecting Schwimmer's grit, Whitehouse asked her to distribute Wilson's message. Fearful that a lone Hungarian woman would be suspicious to Allied troops, Whitehouse requested that military attachés provide a written endorsement of her mission. When they refused, she asked Stovall. He objected to Schwimmer as a woman and a Jew. The best he would do was a nebulous, illegible note. Taking matters into her own hands, Whitehouse accompanied Schwimmer across the border, a nine-hour ride over dimly lit roads. Several days later, Schwimmer informed Whitehouse, "The appeal has been taken up everywhere with great sympathy and much understanding."[58]

"Somehow or another we have gotten together a very efficient and busy little organization," Whitehouse told Creel in late October. The disguised propaganda that belligerent nations heaped on the Swiss fueled cynicism. But Whitehouse's open approach worked. The Swiss were interested in the United States, about which they were not well informed. A consensus developed among the likes of Kerney, Colonel Ralph Van Deman with AEF intelligence, and even Gibson that Whitehouse's methods "made a real hit." Allen Dulles wrote to Uncle Bert, "Mrs. Whitehouse—I am frank to admit—is doing good work, much better than I had thought possible. She is having a real influence in placing American news in the Swiss press and is in touch with a great many influential Swiss. . . . The influence of America in Switzerland is tremendous now."[59]

By the time of the armistice, Whitehouse was sick of her unheated hotel room and lack of hot water except on Saturdays. Creel begged her to stay a little longer. "She is," he told her husband, "by far *the best* of our foreign representatives."[60]

CHARLES MERRIAM'S ODE TO UNCIVIL SERVICE

Whitehouse devoted the first third of her memoir of her time in Bern, plus twenty-seven appendixes, to her travails with the legation. In a memoir spanning his entire career, Hugh Wilson was sufficiently irked with CPI propaganda in Bern to devote a full chapter to it. Memories formed in other foreign capitals were equally bitter.[61]

The ambassador in Madrid refused to recognize the legitimacy of Frank Marion's mission. When Marion said he intended to carry on anyway, the ambassador produced a cable from Washington that said Marion could do nothing without his approval. Creel took the matter to Wilson, who ruled in the CPI's favor. Fights with military intelligence officers were a problem in many posts but acute in Spain, where the officers were especially truculent. One punched the first secretary, and the two commenced to bite each other. The Mexican government, sensitive to the Wilson administration's meddling, ordered the deportation of CPI representative Robert Murray for "pernicious propaganda." The order was rescinded, but Creel had other concerns. While serving as the *New York World*'s Mexico correspondent, Murray did double duty as a political advisor to Wilson's campaign and as an agent of the State Department. He kept his *World* affiliation while he was a CPI representative. Creel was troubled by his using his position for journalistic advantage and his "tendency to irregularity in his accounts." Theater agent and self-styled "spieler" Harry Reichenbach, whom the CPI sent to Europe, was rude to foreign officials, misrepresented himself as the agent for the National Film Corporation, and said, according to a military intelligence officer, "The present staff of the Bureau of Public Information were a bunch of 'boobs.'" Reichenbach was "a genius in some ways," Creel said after firing him.[62]

Charles Merriam left a particularly bitter trail of memories. He was warmly received by Ambassador Thomas Nelson Page, a Virginia novelist who served Smithfield ham and spoon bread at embassy functions. Page feared Italy might leave the war. He wanted to counter anti-American German propaganda and opened a small office in the embassy attic for that purpose. "It is a matter of great importance," he told Lansing, "that we should set ourselves seriously to this work. I have on a number of occasions sent telegrams about this matter, more or less urgent, but so far I have apparently had little success in impressing my views on whoever the matter has been referred to at home." "The Ambassador is very much interested in the work," Merriam told Creel when he arrived in April, "and is very cordial in his attitude."[63]

At some point in his career Merriam penned a poem, "Ode to Uncivil Service and Administrative Management," and stuck it in his papers. It read, "I long to be / Where men are free / Without a rule to follow / Or a law to be obeyed /

As the CPI commissioner in Rome, University of Chicago political scientist Charles Merriam infuriated the American ambassador by posing as "a kind of secret special plenipotentiary." Such liberties were not uncommon among CPI commissioners abroad. Merriam later founded the behavioralist movement, which used statistical field research to understand public opinion as it played out in elections and governing. (University of Chicago Library)

Without a Sovereign / Or a sanction." This could have been his credo in Rome. With financial resources and independence, he headquartered himself in a suite of eleven offices on the top floor of a building six minutes from the embassy, far enough so it would not encroach on him. He assembled a staff of fifty, some of outstanding talent, and took on grandiose airs. He arrived in Rome as Captain Merriam, an army commission derived from being president of the Aviation Examining Board in Chicago. In addition to retaining the title, he elevated himself from CPI commissioner to high commissioner. Walter Wanger, a twenty-three-year-old Signal Corps officer who handled film, addressed him as "Your Excellency."[64]

Merriam acquired an Italian noblewoman as a mistress, told Irwin he needed his own code so he could "speak quite frankly about the whole situation here," and held forth in the bar of the Grand Hotel. "His power truly seems to be considerable," an Italian official commented. "He has often asked that messages that would be useful to President Wilson be communicated to him directly." After visiting Rome, Charles Edward Russell reported that Merriam was "about the most popular foreigner in Rome." It was a heady experience for Merriam. He recommended sacking the entire American military mission to Italy for incompetently propagandizing Austro-Hungarian forces and suggested military strategy that had been planted in his mind by the Italians. Much of this went over State Department cable lines.[65]

The once hospitable Page called Merriam "a reformer, crank, a politician." He informed Washington that Merriam "usurped functions pertaining solely to Military and Naval Attaches offices" and posed as "a kind of secret special plenipotentiary." Wanger, too, had "lost his head." When asked what he did for Merriam, Wanger refused to say anything except that he was a "confidential agent" for him. The conservative Page had limitations, among them failure to realize the importance of socialist opinion in Italy. His staff, which egged him on, was not above self-interest and vindictively hampered Merriam. The military attachés called him the Black Pope. But the ambassador's anger was justified. Merriam had done "a remarkable job," Creel told the head of military intelligence in Washington, but he had to be recalled. Page ordered Wanger out of Italy. When he learned the young officer had gone to Paris, the ambassador pettily asked the military to send him home as a "dangerous" person. Page laid the blame for the Merriam fiasco on "the lack of specific instructions to people [Creel] has sent here."[66]

Merriam was not the only one to aggrandize himself. Air Service Sergeant

Kingsley Moses, a budding writer who had been published in the *Smart Set,* referred to himself as executive director of the Speakers Department in Italy. Edgar Sisson, as we shall soon see, presented himself as a personal representative of Wilson in Russia. Kerney made the same claim in Paris. In both places, the ambassadors, the duly appointed representatives of the president, objected. The ambassador in Paris asked Gibson to find examples of "foolish propaganda" that he could use to discredit Kerney. As much as Whitehouse liked the gregarious Irishman, she thought he was more interested in the trappings of the job than the job itself. "He talked when he could have been working."[67]

CREATIVITY AND SYNERGY

CPI outposts operated like miniature CPIs. They combined under one small roof the CPI's diverse domestic functions. This was a formidable task but one that lent itself to the creativity the CPI always seemed to exhibit.

Foreign operations benefited from synergies with domestic activities. As noted, materials used for home audiences were repurposed for distribution abroad. Charles Dana Gibson worked with the Foreign Press Bureau, which sent out art captioned in local-language captions. Joseph Pennell's war drawings were widely circulated in Spain. For a time Edwin Bjorkman was housed with the Poole service. Two people in Scandinavia reported to him.[68]

The CPI's immigrant-centered July Fourth Loyalty Day emerged from and was handled by the Foreign Press Division under Will Irwin, who projected it overseas. Allied capitals showed solidarity with their own demonstrations, news of which jammed AP wires. Merriam reported 100,000 "assembled" in Rome, 50,000 in Milan, and 30,000 in Florence. Public schools were closed in Italy. El Salvador declared a national holiday. The CPI followed up by exporting motion pictures of parades showing German-Americans marching under unfurled flags.[69]

In the same manner that the CPI partnered with the organizations at home, overseas commissioners collaborated with the American Red Cross, the YMCA, and other do-good American groups working abroad. George Fife, Whitehouse's news editor, initially came to Switzerland to help the Red Cross with propaganda. Wilson approved Creel passing $4 million to the YMCA. The YMCA, which considered itself the "war auxiliary of modern democracy," bucked up Italian, French, and Russian troops.[70]

The degree of improvisation was impressive. Exporters were asked to insert propaganda in their catalogs. In Buenos Aires, packinghouses, banks, shippers, and various American merchants enclosed CPI literature in their correspondence. Edward Bernays, whose work was directed at Latin America, arranged for American businesses to give window space to propaganda displays. An enterprising member of Murray's staff in Mexico created a newsletter for distribution inside the United States in the belief that relations would improve if United States citizens understood the country better.[71]

The CPI fashioned a creative, if coercive, scheme to propagandize Italians. Many Italian-Americans enlisted in the Italian army. They remitted their pay to their families in the United States via Italian consulates. The CPI arranged for the pay envelopes to contain a letter suggesting the families write positively to relatives in Italy about the US war effort. "Probably most of the recipients thought that continuance of their pay depended on writing the suggested letters," Will Irwin recalled, "and we, I confess, did nothing to correct this impression.... American mails into Italy swelled to such a point that the Italian postal censors groaned."[72]

When Whitehouse arranged a US tour for journalists from the six largest Swiss newspapers, she called on her husband to help. He met them at the pier in New York, wined and dined them, and accompanied them around the country. The trip lasted more than a month and was aggravating, as the journalists did not always cooperate. "I did this," he told his wife, "because I knew that you desired that I should."[73]

Wilson continued to frown on speakers' programs. In September 1918, he told Daniels he wanted the names of anyone going abroad. He did not like people "assuming to speak" for the government. Commissioners circumvented this, as Creel had done early in the war. Edward Riis, the commissioner in Denmark and son of the famous Danish-American muckraker Jacob Riis, took to the stump himself. With good results, Marion imported a Spanish-language professor to speak. Whitehouse arranged for Swiss intellectuals to speak on American war aims. Kerney put two hundred French university lecturers on the road armed with CPI materials.[74]

The speaking program in Italy was unsurpassed among CPI outposts. Rudolph Altrocchi, who preceded Moses as head of "oral propaganda," was an Italian-born professor of languages at the University of Chicago. The Red Cross helped identify speaking venues by putting together a list of fifteen hundred names and addresses of leading citizens in towns and cities. Merriam sent these individuals a weekly newsletter. From July through September 1918, speeches were made in 139 cities and more than 200 smaller communities, reaching an estimated five million Italians. Altrocchi built hoopla around engagements, on one occasion instructing a consul to proclaim "American day," arrange bands and posters, and show CPI war films. When he spoke in Prato, "the most defeatist hole in Italy," a procession took him back to the hotel. Merriam had the inspiration to import wounded American soldiers of Italian extraction while they convalesced. "They turned out to be our best propagandists," Creel said, "preaching the gospel of democracy with a fervor and understanding that would have shamed many an heir of Plymouth Rock."[75]

DECEPTION

The CPI abroad was a miniature of the CPI at home in another manner. When sending a commissioner into a country, the CPI announced to the host government it would be "open and aboveboard." It explicitly told commissioners to avoid bribery and subsidies to newspapers. It was more transparent than propagandists in other countries. But the secretly funded prolabor *El Obrero Panamericano* was not an exception. It was part of a pattern of deception that characterized CPI work everywhere. As was the case at home, expediency was too tempting to avoid.[76]

As much as Vira Whitehouse argued for working in the clear, she was open to alternatives. "I note Mr. Sisson's telegram of July twenty-first that we are not to buy or subsidize newspapers," she wrote to Washington. "I think this is a good plan or policy to adopt but I think there may be conditions under which an exception should be made. If such a condition arises I shall take the liberty of cabling you." When Northcliffe told Whitehouse he wanted to use his newspapers "to stir up" officials about subversive German activities in Switzerland, she provided a mass of "more or less confirmed rumors to one of his writers." One of her first stops on reaching Bern was the offices of *Freie Zietung,* a biweekly newspaper run by German exiles that circulated in Germany and Austria. On Creel's instructions, she provided an initial subsidy of $50,000 and more later.[77]

The CPI slipped money to writers and editors in Spain. It worked through agents who reported to navy and military intelligence. At a meeting of agents, one of them reported that a bribed reporter in Cadiz "had done good work by a little faking: he has pretended to learn from incoming passengers a lot of admirable news about the United States." Marion praised his "excellent scheme" and recommended other agents try the same thing. The consul in La Coruña was asked to have local reporters on hand when ships arrived so they could hear "cheerful talking" by American passengers. The CPI offered to pay the reporters.[78]

Creel told Gibson that a *New York Herald* reporter heading to Russia was really going "to serve our publicity division in Petrograd." Robert Murray was to avoid subsidizing newspapers, but Creel said he could pressure American firms to advertise in favored papers. The CPI condemned this practice when done by the Germans. In Italy, Merriam contemplated a similar scheme with one of the pro-war newspapers, *Popolo d'Italia.* To test the waters, he sent a *Chicago Daily News* correspondent, who served as an unpaid advisor to him, to see the editor, Benito Mussolini. The future Italian leader said, yes, he would be happy to have the money. The *Daily News* reporter never learned if Merriam followed through.[79]

The CPI drew on its ties with pro-war American labor in familiar ways. With the urging of Wilson, who suspended his concern about individuals speaking abroad for America in this case, Creel encouraged Gompers and others to travel to bolster their brother workers overseas. These emissaries were seen as a counterweight to Bolshevik propagandists. Chester Wright, the publicity director of the CPI's American Alliance for Labor and Democracy, accompanied the Gompers mission and wrote articles for home consumption. The CPI secretly funded the American Socialist and Labor Mission to Europe to win support for the war and Wilson's peace terms. The mission included Charles Edward Russell and AALD founder John Spargo, who stayed in Italy for two months.[80]

Friends of German Democracy operated in Switzerland and in France in the same manner it did in the United States by hiding its links to the CPI. Frank Bohn, a former labor organizer, was told by Creel to "appear as a newspaper man." He was to promote the overthrow of the German government, secure insight on German public opinion, and speak and write on anything that would demoralize the enemy. He passed funds to German exile groups. While he admitted he was representing the CPI, Bohn told the chief of AEF intelligence, "This fact is never to be publicly stated. I am the representative of the Friends of German Democracy." Creel provided funds to Bohn, as Whitehouse advised, so they would not be identified as coming from the CPI. Bohn, Gibson thought, was "a most attractive fellow, full of enthusiasm"; his cloaked propagandizing was "the right sort." Eventually, however, reports came in from military intelligence that he was "indiscreet." When the Germans associated him with the government, Creel took him "out of there at once." "Because Bohn's work could not be kept a secret, and because the committee entered into an agreement with the Swiss government that its work would be open," Creel privately told a military intelligence officer, "I ordered Bohn to return." In other words, the CPI stopped when it would be found out to have lied.[81]

The CPI was involved with a sub-rosa scheme in Sweden to reorient news, which in that country had a pro-German slant. Allied reports were delayed and downplayed. Planning by the British, French, and Americans to combat this began early in 1918. At the center of this initiative was a young naval intelligence officer named Edward Robinette, a Philadelphia banker who was previously a member of the Commission for Relief in Belgium. Robinette, who helped the CPI with propaganda in Sweden, envisioned inducing "men of brains and with large sums of money" to create a rival news operation that appeared independent. They would crush the pro-German Svenska News Bureau by denying it the services of Reuters, Havas, and AP, setting up a new agency underwritten by friendly Swedes, and arranging the purchase by a friendly Swede of two newspapers.[82]

Olaf Gylden, a retired admiral and diplomat, directed the news service. He insisted it was "in no sense a foreign concern." He said the funding came from Swedes, without noting that they were supporting a plan concocted by "the three Entente Governments as represented by their Ministers in Stockholm." The Allies committed to providing 280 tons of copper wire and other materials to a holding company that could sell them for a profit to cover expenses. The service became operational in May.[83]

The AP bureau chief in Stockholm, Miles Bouton, regarded the scheme as a "grave blunder," no better than what the Germans were doing and sure to be recognized for what it was. "Sympathy cannot be gained by strong arm methods," he wrote to AP general manger Melville Stone. Bouton's AP boss in London, Robert Collins, concurred. The Swedish newspapers, Collins told Stone, considered this "an attempt to force upon them a foreign news service." He and Bouton blamed Robinette, who was tactless and had "no experience of newspaper work." British intelligence intercepted Bouton's letter to Stone and passed it to the State Department. In the eyes of American officials, Bouton did not evidence "sturdy Americanism." He had a German-born wife, wrote evenhandedly about Germany when he was posted there, and commented to a German-American acquaintance, "Doesn't it make you tired to hear people at home calling Germans Huns and barbarians?" When he learned that Robinette maligned him, Bouton threatened the young officer "with a sound thrashing." Following an investigation by military intelligence, the State Department took away Bouton's passport. The AP discharged him. "Mr. Stone regards the scheme as you do," Collins told Bouton when he first voiced his concerns, "but the war has changed a good many things."[84]

Robinette "has done wonders," said Will Irwin. The young naval officer was awarded the Navy Cross, the highest decoration short of the Congressional Medal of Honor, for establishing "a news service in Sweden for the benefit of the Allies, which all the representatives from other allied powers had been absolutely unable to accomplish." Northcliffe, who helped Robinette secure the support of Reuters and Havas, thought he "would have had full reward" if he were British, that is to say, presumably, a knighthood. "He has been two years there, and practically got control of the Swedish Press."[85]

Carl Crow objected to the Germans' use of front organizations in China even as he employed his own version of Byoir's third-party technique. He did not want to give away CPI news for free, as that would mark it for what it was, propaganda. He created a dummy company instead, the Chinese American (Chun Mei) News Agency. "We didn't charge much for the service," he said, "and we were not too insistent on collecting the fees." He used the revenue to cover other expenses. This was so successful that Crow hired a well-known Chinese scholar to translate Wilson's speeches and convinced a Chinese publisher to issue a book of them. Crow guaranteed the purchase of a large number of copies. His dummy news agency used the royalties to buy full-page ads for the book. A north China warlord bought five hundred copies and made the book required reading for his officers. When it came time to officially summarize his work for the CPI, Crow said nothing of these activities.[86]

Crow adopted Gilbert Parker's strategy of reaching American opinion leaders through surrogates. He sent postcards to American missionaries and representatives of American oil and tobacco companies, asking for names and addresses of local officials, scholars, and gentry. The resulting list of twenty-five thousand people received copies of the book of Wilson's speeches compliments of the missionaries or businessmen who supplied their names. Addressees were invited to write to Wilson in care of Crow, who promised to translate the letters. He received thousands of responses, far too many to translate into English and forward to the White House. Crow's postcard scheme led to the identification of several Americans who were pacifists or German sympathizers. The American minister, Paul Reinsch, had the malcontents expelled. According to an American Chamber of Commerce report, more than four hundred Americans acted as volunteer CPI agents, monitoring Chinese opinion as well as distributing literature.[87]

This was not the only instance of the CPI engaging in surveillance overseas. In February 1918, Van Deman invited Creel to swap information on "the latest changes of popular feeling within Germany as regards the United States." The CPI responded positively on the value of learning how "public opinion anywhere in the world is being misinformed." Kingsley Moses, who considered intelligence gathering an essential aspect of his speakers' program, told Merriam that one of his people "had a man arrested for openly preaching opposition and sedition." Merriam thought of himself as an undercover agent among radical and discontented elements and seems to have gained better political intelligence than the embassy. In this, Merriam compensated for Ambassador Page's distaste for engaging the left.[88]

Propagandists quite rightly did not want the enemy to know what they were doing. "Permit *absolutely nothing to pass* in regard to American efforts to spread propaganda in enemy countries," read a note in a handwritten log for censors. But the CPI used its suppressive powers in less defensible ways. "As you know, we have no censorship of the press, but permit the freest discussion of all domestic differences," Creel told a British military attaché. "We deem it very unwise, however, to let much of this matter go out of the country, as it is bound to give a false idea of our war preparedness, our unity, and our resolution. For this reason, we have suppressed dispatches to England and to France that dealt with the recent coal order, with the Congressional charges that our war preparations have broken down, and with domestic dissention." (The "coal order" referred to the Fuel Administration's directive that factories east of the Mississippi River shut down for four days.) Kerney cabled Irwin, "Extremely important to prevent publication in France news which seeks to indicate American workingmen antagonistic to socialism stop recommend earnestly censorship of all news to Europe of such character." "The whole matter [of overseas propaganda] is one of infinite detail," Creel told a member of Congress, "and much of it highly confidential. The fact that we are not able to say much about it has kept people from realizing the vast amount of work that we are doing."[89]

When Vira Whitehouse returned to the United States, she was chagrined when people presumed that she had done anything clandestine. Whitehouse personified the best of the CPI. Her intentions were noble. But her indignation was delusional.[90]

MIXED RESULTS

"I am not going to end by drawing any conclusions from this record of my year as a government agent," Whitehouse closed her memoir. "They seem to me either too obvious or too confused. I shall simply leave the record as it is."[91]

That record in allied and neutral countries is as difficult to characterize as the office space its commissioners inhabited. Whitehouse was impressed with James Kerney's enormous office in the Élysée Palace Hotel, where the AEF had headquarters. He had other rooms in the French Bureau de la Presse and the embassy. In a visit to the American embassy in London, she had trouble locating Charles Edward Russell's office until an elevator operator directed her to "one little back room on the top floor."[92]

Cable delays and slow mail delivery hampered the use of CPI news. Due to interrupted communications, Marion had to "fake a service" in Spain in March 1918. Features about American life had less appeal than war news, for which commissioners clamored. As open as the Swiss were to learn about America, bituminous coal production statistics held little interest. Henry Suydam, who worked in the Netherlands as well as London, described the Poole service as "local, blatant, flamboyant, trite, flippant, parochial, smug, and sentimental, whereas it should be none of these things. It smacks too much of press-agents and advertisements." The CPI, he said, needed to take the British approach of "oblique propaganda." The British suggested to Russell that the Poole service be abolished. Russell agreed on its limitations but was all too aware that the British had little interest in privileging American news. He was furious that they would not let him photograph American troops passing in review before the king.[93]

The trouble with the Poole service, Irwin told Russell, was "that it resembled a ready-made suit of clothes that fits every one a little, but no one in particular. We determined, therefore, to specialize and expand it." A British unit was created to oversee news for that country. Edwin Bjorkman was given responsibility for Scandinavia. The Swedes, he noted, did not want "patriotic appeal" or stories about a Swedish-American clergyman who became an army chaplain unless "he comes from the city of Calmar." Irwin thought each commissioner needed a "person whose job it is to travel through the country and gather information for our use [on] what the people are saying about us with a view to ascertaining what our needs are in the way of propaganda."[94]

All this said, the amount of news sent abroad was impressive. A May 1918 summary of daily cable transmission showed 1,400 words to the French Maison de la Presse in Paris, which forwarded them on to Portugal, Spain, Italy, and Switzerland; 500 words to London, which forwarded the news to Scandinavia and Holland; 500 words to Asian countries; 250 words to Mexico, Russia, and the West Indies and Venezuela. In some weeks, Poole's weekly mail service ran as much as eighty thousand words in English and thirty thousand in Spanish. Another service, "Homestuff," consisted of brief reports of sports scores, patriotic events, and measures to help returning soldiers culled from American newspapers. The primary audience was the homesick serviceman. Despite the uneven quality of news for foreign audiences, it was not without redeeming value, as Whitehouse's successes makes clear. No longer were American events and points of view filtered through the typewriters of foreign journalists. Over time improvements were made. "In general I might add that this stuff has greatly improved," reported John Russell, who took over his father's London post. An estimated 70 percent of Poole's service was used by the British in September. The British brought out in pamphlet form Booth Tarkington's "American Facts and German Propaganda" in a print run of 850,000 copies.[95]

This was only one part of the propaganda distributed abroad. Notwithstanding Merriam's controversies, the final report from Italy showed the fruits of his entrepreneurship: 4.5 million postcards; 154,854 Italo-American ribbons and buttons; 68,574 Wilson posters; 66,640 war posters; 200,000 American paper flags; 30 cloth flags; 33,000 copies of "Star-Spangled Banner" sheet music; 326,650 booklets of Wilson's speeches; 364,650 American war information pamphlets; 200 United States maps; 300 photographs of Wilson; 35 engravings of Wilson. Photographic displays were organized in three thousand Italian communities.[96]

The CPI left flops and successes around the world. The man appointed to head the work in Brazil failed to arrive. The ambassador assumed the job. "The uncertainty as to who should have a permanent direction of the propaganda work," the final Brazil report stated, "embarrassed the whole matter and made it less effective than it otherwise might have been." In Lima, a Liberty Loan drive brought in $700,000, an astonishing amount by an impromptu commissioner in a poor foreign capital of fewer than 200,000 inhabitations.[97]

Whitehouse did not make much progress on film. Marion did. Guy Croswell Smith, director of films in Scandinavia, believed Creel's approach of linking commercial films with propaganda "practically drove German propaganda and drama films from the Scandinavian market." An advantage on the American side, he noted, was that its commercial films were superior. One of the CPI's

postwar legacies was the opportunity it gave American commercial film companies to learn international markets, which they later dominated.[98]

CPI propaganda had consequences less easy to measure. Wilson's calls for
self-determination energized independence movements in the colonized world.
It contributed to unrest in Spain by giving succor to Catalonian and Basque agitation for autonomy. Some argue that the American projection of *Wilsonismo*
to the great masses of Italians headed off a Bolshevik-inspired revolution in that
country, which next to Russia was the most susceptible of all European countries to a leftist uprising. Sisson's damage to Russian-American relations takes
up an entire chapter of its own in his book.[99]

PUBLIC DIPLOMACY

The CPI's signal achievement was not individual accomplishments in one country or another. It was the implementation of Wilson's New Diplomacy, a progressive idea of international relations. The CPI went over the heads of governments to shape the attitudes of their citizens about the United States, about
their own domestic politics, and about creating better ordered world comity.

CPI commissioners had barely begun their work when the war ended. Although he had started work earlier, Carl Crow's appointment was not official
until September 1, 1918. Commissioners would have compiled a more impressive record if they had more time. But they field-tested ideas that became staples
of public diplomacy. Murray arranged the first CPI press tour to the United
States, an idea replicated by Whitehouse and others, and set up reading rooms
in seven Mexican cities. In the Mexico City room, adorned with red, white,
and blue bunting, Mexicans took classes in English and bookkeeping. CPI staff
understood the value of reaching average citizens in the "real Italy" of villages.
"It is impossible to exaggerate the importance of propaganda work among the
contadini [peasants]," wrote Arthur Bennington, a *New York World* authority
on Italy who helped Merriam. Crow's mailing list scheme in China, said the
American Chamber of Commerce there, enabled "the American Government
to speak directly to the Chinese people." Rogers and Poole projected America
abroad as never before. As Rogers foresaw, "The international publicity expert
may henceforth be largely responsible for international relations."[100]

The idea of government-to-people diplomacy slowly took hold in the postwar years. In a 1939 handbook for envoys, British diplomat Harold Nicolson
ruefully noted it was no longer "considered unfitting and unwise for a states-

man to make public pronouncements to his own people which public opinion in other countries would know to be totally untrue." But he had come to believe the press attaché was of "great usefulness and considerable importance, and the system should be extended to every important mission."[101]

World War II brought into being the Voice of America (VOA), the broadcast equivalent of Rogers's Wireless-Cable Service. Other US broadcast organizations followed. The United States Information Agency was created in 1953 against the background of the Cold War. USIA projected American ideas overseas, as the CPI did with a press service, speakers, and exhibitions. At USIA headquarters, Creel's photograph hung first in a row of images of agency heads. The term *public diplomacy* came into use in the mid-1960s. *Soft power* was conceptualized nearly thirty years after that. "Conventional wisdom holds that the state with the largest army prevails," wrote Joseph Nye, a scholar and former State Department official who coined the term, "but in the information age, the state (or the non-state actor) with the best story may sometimes win."[102]

Walter Rogers suggested that every embassy and legation should have an official responsible for propaganda. Patchin dismissed this as a "quite pious idea but a futile one." It was futile at the time given Lansing's pinched views on publicity and the deadweight of diplomatic tradition. In time, however, Rogers's idea came to be seen as the best means of managing propaganda as well as the overseas activities of other government agencies, whose proliferation also had caused confusion during the war. Under the "country team" concept, ambassadors oversee most government agencies operating in a given country.[103]

Disagreement about the mission of public diplomacy and its place in the bureaucracy has nevertheless persisted. By 1977, overseas propaganda had undergone thirty-one major studies over three decades. USIA began as an independent executive agency. In 1999, it was abolished. Its broadcasting arms were placed under the United States Agency for Global Media; other activities were integrated into the State Department, a decision that became a subject of intense debate. With regard to mission, the VOA served as an instrument of the Central Intelligence Agency during the Cold War. In 1967 it was given a new charter that required it to provide balanced news. VOA reporters are outside the country team. Many considered their independence essential to their credibility as well as an example of democratic values. Many, however, persisted in arguing for "weaponizing" the VOA so that it provides "news that supports our national security objectives."[104]

The use of journalists for veiled propaganda reached a high point in the

Cold War. Allen Dulles, who was named director of the Central Intelligence Agency in 1953, built on his idea that Vira Whitehouse should disguise herself as a journalist. Dulles's agents posed as journalists, and the CIA subsidized stories in foreign publications. With the acquiescence of print and television executives, American reporters gathered intelligence and acted as intermediaries with foreigners. A Senate inquiry in the 1970s found the CIA used at least fifty American journalists from 1952 to 1976. Other estimates run to four hundred. Frank Bohn and Robert Murray were forerunners of these practices.[105]

Laws now restrict the clandestine use of American journalists. But the Pentagon secretly funded foreign journalists in Iraq after the 2003 invasion and developed a network of putatively independent military experts to promote the government line on television. These commentators were former senior military officers and contractors with financial ties to the military. They were given special briefings that they were not to disclose prior to appearing on the air. Internally the Pentagon called them "message force multipliers."[106]

Wilson's New Diplomacy was inspiring. "Instead of a nation's foreign policies being secret, instead of unpublished alliances and iron-bound treaties, there may be the proclaiming of a nation's international intentions, exactly as a political party in the United Sates pledges its intentions in a political campaign," Carl Ackerman wrote in 1917. "If there was this candidness between the governments and their citizens there would be more frankness between the nations and their neighbors. Public opinion would then be the decisive force."[107]

As the CPI (and Ackerman) showed, however, the New Diplomacy left plenty of room for undemocratic practices. Creel is the father of public diplomacy in all its aspects.

11

A Hazy Affair

[Creel] asked me to try to get something started on propaganda in enemy
countries. We can get things started whenever they answer my telegrams
and tell me what we can have in the way of money, staff and
participation in the various inter-allied boards.

—Hugh S. Gibson, diary, May 5, 1918

George Creel was a master at putting a bright gloss on CPI initiatives that
turned out badly. But he took a different approach when it came to propaganda against enemy troops. When he wrote his postwar *Complete Report of
the Chairman of the Committee on Public Information,* he sped past the subject
with scarcely a side glance.

The report's table of contents promised a section titled "Enemy Propaganda." The reader who opened the book to this potentially potent topic found
two short paragraphs under a renamed section "Enemy Propaganda Studied."
Elsewhere in the report was a cryptic and inaccurate reference to a July 1918
meeting in Paris when a "special group of experts" was put in charge of AEF
field propaganda. The truth was that Creel, at that moment, was fighting a
pitched battle in Washington to keep control of over-the-trenches propaganda.
Creel's report did not say that he prevailed or that the CPI afterward did nothing to carry out the work. Creel did not mention James Keeley, the CPI man
who was in charge, or Heber Blankenhorn, the young army captain who, more
than anyone else, brought field propaganda into being.[1]

Creel's mismanagement of field propaganda exceeded the bungling of CPI
propaganda in allied and neutral countries. Nothing redeemed the CPI apart
from its belief that field propaganda was a good idea. The spare account in
Creel's *Complete Report* swept the embarrassing episode under the historical
carpet. Little has been written about it. The story is worth telling not only because it fills out the history of the CPI. Field propaganda against enemy com-

batants, which the AEF eventually oversaw, marked the advent of a species of psychological warfare deemed essential today but was then, in many military minds, considered a waste of time.

EXPERIMENTATION AND RIVALRY

Propaganda against the enemy—whether against military forces behind barbed wire or civilians in their homes—required ingenuity. It had to be projected over perilous trenches or great distances. This led to experiments worthy of Rube Goldberg.

One French brainstorm was to stuff fake German sausages with messages urging surrender. Airplane pilots dropped this ersatz food on civilians in the hope they would forward it to loved ones at the front. Leaflets were floated into Germany from Switzerland in leather sacks buoyed up by cork. Hugh Gibson watched a French trial in which propaganda was shot over enemy lines in artillery shells. The first four rounds were duds. When shells did fire, the contents were blown to bits. Harry Reichenbach, the fabulous stunt-making theater agent who worked for the CPI, boasted of entrenching motion picture projectors on the Italian front and aiming them at the snow-covered Alps, which served as a movie screen visible to the Austrian troops. He said it worked. "We would start our program with a comedy two-reeler," he said, "interspersed with a few stereopticon flashes in German." One read: "Italy has just invented the deadliest of all gases. The doom of the foe is at hand!"[2]

The best way to reach enemy civilians was through neutral nations. Literature was smuggled through countries near Germany and Austria. George Sylvester Viereck praised Whitehouse, the "propagandist extraordinary of the Administration," for making use of disaffected Germans and "German officials susceptible to Allied allurements." Another technique was to give propaganda to captured soldiers who took it home with them when they were exchanged. Swiss, Danish, and Dutch newspapers were a valuable propaganda vehicle against the enemy because, in an amazing deviation from its heavy censorship practices, the Germans allowed foreign-language newspapers to circulate inside the country. The Germans considered it a sign of their confidence in their cause. (At the same time, of course, they subsidized newspapers in neutral countries to get their point of view across to those populations and the Allies.) The CPI commissioner in the Netherlands, Henry Suydam, said all the news given to the Dutch press was "chosen with regard to the ultimate effect on the German masses." Suydam described this as "counter-espionage."[3]

The news coming out of Poole's service did not directly call on the enemy to capitulate. The stories would not have qualified as news if they had. Instead, they conveyed an image of the United States as a robust nation pursuing the war vigorously. On the other hand, leaflets dropped over enemy lines were direct: American military forces were growing menacingly large, prisoners were treated well, defeat was inevitable. Wilson's widely distributed speeches promised a fair treaty. The Allies used these themes, too. There was an element of cynicism to this, since they did not fully embrace Wilson's words. But the messages were too effective to forgo. The United States' entry into the war, said an Italian propagandist, "was a certificate of the moral purity of the Allied cause."[4]

Influencing enemy opinion did not become an Allied priority until late in the war. In November 1917, the Central Powers routed the Italian army at the Battle of Caporetto, an overwhelming defeat attributed to demoralizing enemy propaganda. The idea took hold that the Allies had to counterpunch all along the battle line. This view grew stronger with Allied successes on the battlefield and harsh conditions behind German and Austrian lines. "We can't hope to administer our gloom tablets with any hope of effect until the patient is feeling worse," said Hugh Gibson, who took a strong interest in this endeavor when he came to Europe to assist the CPI. In February 1918, Lord Northcliffe, who had left the British mission in New York, became director of the newly created Propaganda in Enemy Countries, which reported directly to the prime minister. The French created a similar organization. Northcliffe did not convene an Allied conference on enemy propaganda until August 1918.[5]

When steps were taken for concerted action, they foundered on poor organization and disagreement. The French wanted to concentrate on German soldiers, who threatened their borders; the British wanted to focus on Austria-Hungary, where morale was especially poor. Anglo-Italian cooperation against the dual monarchy was hindered by the different postwar political objectives they wished to promote. The Italians' objectives hinged on territorial claims they did not want to give up.[6]

James Keeley, whom Creel appointed to head the United States effort at shaping enemy opinion, came away from Northcliffe's conference unimpressed. "We expected to find three organized and working Inter-Allied Propaganda Boards, one in Paris, one in London and one in Padua, which would be landmarks in the field, with which we could have to deal and to which we would immediately designate liaison officers," Keeley reported four days after the meeting. "Those boards are ghosts." The French, he said, were intent on smuggling materials through Switzerland, the Belgians on emphasizing newspapers, and the British on using balloons. "There is considerable stirring of the ground but no clear and scientific ploughing and not an American machine on the whole farm." The CPI was represented in Padua by a young Harvard lecturer whose expertise was Italian painting. Squabbling among the Allied representatives limited success against Austria-Hungary.[7]

Another obstacle to American propaganda against enemy forces was domestic, only in this case the War Department, not the State Department, was the problem. The United States entered the war ill-prepared to fight on the scale required. American troops went into limited combat under Allied commands at the end of 1917, but the AEF did not undertake an independent combat operation until the following September. The War Department had to institute a system of conscription, build training camps, and equip soldiers. (It did not have adequate rifles for training until early 1918.) This was an enormous undertaking for an egregiously undermanned general staff.[8]

Given the urgency of getting all this done and the constant criticism that fell on the military for not proceeding fast enough, the idea of penetrating the minds of the enemy with untested techniques was met with yawns and resistance. The War Department did not have a distinct military intelligence section in Washington until May 1917, several weeks after the CPI was created. Such intelligence work as was done had consisted mostly of mapping and investigations. "Incredible as it may seem," wrote E. Alexander Powell, a journalist turned army major, "when General Pershing set sail for France in the spring of 1917, the entire personnel of the Military Intelligence Section, as it was then called, consisted of four officers (of which one was myself) and three clerks." The army chief of staff did not want Newton Baker to be bothered with plans to do more. It was the same in Britain. Propaganda against the enemy, a British general sniffed, "was a minor matter—the thing was to kill Germans."[9]

A few days before the declaration of war in 1917, Stanley Washburn, an American journalist who had been in Russia for Lord Northcliffe's *Times,* sent a memorandum to the State Department warning that the slow pace of getting American troops to the fighting front would cast doubts about the earnestness of the United States' commitment. He argued for field propaganda against German troops "as we can instantly affect the morale situation, long before we can contribute troops." His plea had no effect.[10]

In his constant quest for government war work, Frederic Wile proposed in June that Pershing's staff set up a system to undertake his specialty for Northcliffe's *Daily Mail,* "searching the German Press for news and views of military importance," as well as interrogating prisoners and translating documents taken from German soldiers, all of which were useful in framing propaganda. In the coming months Wile solicited numerous letters recommending that he be given a job, including one from Creel to the army general staff's intelligence chief, Ralph Van Deman. In 1918, he was finally invited to send reports to AEF intelligence. Wile referred to this as a "special type of duty . . . on a major's basis." He also had a desk at Crewe House, a Georgian mansion that was North-cliffe's headquarters.[11]

The man who finally broke through the army generals' disinterest in field propaganda was an unlikely candidate for such an accomplishment, a balding, chain-smoking former journalist of German-American extraction who wore horn-rimmed glasses and had an obsession for chess.[12]

HEBER BLANKENHORN

When war came to America, Heber Blankenhorn was a labor reporter and edi-tor at the *New York Evening Sun.* Like many of the socialists with whom he was in contact, Blankenhorn was not keen on the war. He changed his mind when he was persuaded a victorious Germany would become a threat to the United States. Rejected for military service on account of poor eyesight, he cast about for other war work. Samuel Gompers, who regarded Blankenhorn a dangerous socialist, threw him out of his office. He had a warmer welcome at the CPI from

Against great military resistance, Heber Blankenhorn became the father of military psychological operations. Information oper-ations are today "a core military competency on par with air, ground, maritime, and spe-cial operations." (US Army Special Opera-tions Command History Office)

his friend Ernest Poole, who put him to work at the end of 1917 writing features for use by Sisson in Russia. Like the progressive journalist he was, he had "faith that if you can find the facts and tell them, they will be persuasive."[13]

In January, Blankenhorn sought to take advantage of his toehold in the CPI and approached "that thunderous steam engine Creel" with a scheme to propagandize enemy troops with Wilsonian idealism. Creel was discouraging. The CPI had arranged for leaflets to be dropped on the Russian front. On the western front the CPI used French "printing plants and airplanes and publicity machinery until we can create our own." But creating more, he said, was problematic. The CPI did not have the infrastructure to undertake the work, and the army "won't listen to me when I suggest anything that has to do with operations." Will Irwin, heading the Foreign Section, confirmed Creel had gotten nowhere with the army general staff. In his January request to Wilson for approval to engage in propaganda abroad, he said nothing about propaganda directed at the Germans, civilian or military.[14]

Blankenhorn found a more sympathetic ear in Major Charles Mason. Mason headed military intelligence's information section. He, as well as Colonel Dennis Nolan, the AEF intelligence chief, thought it was time to propagandize enemy troops. Impressed with Blankenhorn, Mason arranged a captain's commission and put him in charge of a new Propaganda Subsection, shortly afterward renamed the Psychologic Subsection, in the Foreign Intelligence Section. One of his jobs was to liaise with the CPI.[15]

On January 31, barely a week after the habitually rumpled reporter donned his army uniform, Creel submitted a plan to Wilson for implementing the overseas campaign the president had approved earlier that month. Again, he said nothing specifically about field propaganda. But Creel had the War Department in mind when he wrote, "Pressure from various quarters has been brought to bear on the Army Authorities to undertake Propaganda along the lines of the different European organizations." Creel's proposal assigned responsibility for all propaganda abroad to the CPI. He gave no leadership role to the War Department, although he suggested it help pay for the work.[16]

By March, Creel had Kerney and Gibson in Paris investigating methods of delivering propaganda against the enemy. Frederick Palmer, who was assisting the CPI, encouraged Creel to move forward. "Strongly suggest concentration educational facts on enemy country immediately," he cabled. "German soldiers and people begin to feel effect of heavy casualties and failure of offensive." Irwin considered it a priority to get "propaganda across the lines to Germany and Austria."[17]

Irwin told Gibson in early April that he had found someone to do the "mechanical work" of enemy propaganda, but the army was dragging its feet on giving him a commission. Three days later he told Gibson he had lined up men to liaise "between us and the armies," but Kerney resisted. Kerney said he could find his own help and rejected Irwin's contention that he was too busy to adequately oversee propaganda toward the enemy. An inventor came to Irwin with an idea for balloon delivery of propaganda that relied on an automatic feed regulated by a timer. This seemed promising, but it was "the devil and all to get experiments through the army routine." Kerney, in the meantime, had trouble coordinating with the French. Clemenceau told him to do nothing pending a reorganization to create the Centre d'Action de Propagande contre l'Ennemie. "We don't seem to be getting things done," Irwin complained to Gibson. "Creel and I greatly dissatisfied."[18]

An inter-Allied conference in Paris in March on unifying propaganda showcased American disunity. The US delegation was haphazardly thrown together, some members having been invited independently by Allied officials. Creel asked Frederick Palmer to head the delegation. When he begged off, the delegation arrived without a chief. Kerney, who assumed leadership, brought no harmony. Each country was asked to outline what it was doing. "No member of the American delegation being qualified to make such a general report, each one explained something of the work in his particular field," the AEF representative reported. Kerney and Marion, who had come up from Spain, openly squabbled. Gibson was annoyed that no one bothered to write a report to the embassy on what had transpired.[19]

"Virtually everybody in France took it upon himself to select the American representatives," Creel complained. The embarrassing outcome was not his fault, he insisted, since he had no involvement after Palmer declined. He did not address the fact that he should have ensured that someone oversaw the organization of the delegation. As he had said a few weeks before, "no other department of Government has the right to take part in this work, except upon the express invitation of the Committee."[20]

BLANKENHORN PERSISTS

Kerney related his travails to Colonel Nolan, the AEF intelligence chief. Kerney said that he received cables asking for "information which he had already cabled in response to previous requests." Nolan heard from a State Department official—Gibson one imagines—that CPI policy "seems to be a changeable one."

The CPI, Nolan reported to Washington, had "little system" in its work. But like Creel, he failed to acknowledge the army's own failures, which were admitted in an AEF memorandum around this time. The AEF had joined the French in shooting propaganda over the trenches with rifle grenades, the memo noted. But the overall AEF effort was unsatisfactory, leaving leadership to the CPI. The biggest defects were lack of a plan and "much duplication."[21]

This dual foot dragging frustrated Stanley Washburn, now an army major with the AEF. Washburn's interest in public opinion was nurtured by his father, a Republican elected to both the House and the Senate. In 1912 Washburn fils handled publicity for Hiram Johnson, Roosevelt's Bull Moose running mate for president. Northcliffe sent him as a correspondent to Russia in 1914 with instructions to shape positive attitudes toward the Allies. Washburn expanded his brief by urging Tsar Nicholas to pay more attention to Russian opinion as well. Now with the AEF, he interviewed German prisoners and concluded enemy morale was sinking. "We are approaching a point of balance in military operations," he wrote to Creel, "and it is worth millions now to attack the morale of the Germans on a broad scale." His plan called for propaganda that followed the principles of commercial advertising by being continuous, interesting, and widely distributed. He proposed dropping as many as ten million leaflets a day in a joint venture between the AEF and the CPI. "Over here it seems difficult to do anything on a broad scale in regard to propaganda except through you," he told Creel. "It is perfectly immaterial to me who does the work as long as it is done."[22]

An army interloper with Washburn's relatively low rank commanded no attention among West Point–trained officers. Hugh Gibson found him "ready to blow up with rage because the A.E.F. do not act at once on his ideas." Perhaps because he did not like pressure by someone in an army uniform or because of Washburn's anti-Wilson Republican views and his ties to Hiram Johnson, Creel was uncooperative. At the mention of his name, Washburn learned, Creel "went into the air." Washburn had a warmer reception from his old boss Lord Northcliffe, who read his propaganda plan to the British cabinet. As satisfying as that may have been to Washburn, it had no effect on the AEF or Creel.[23]

Back in Washington, Blankenhorn pressed on with the small staff he assembled. He had a bent for research, one of his strengths working on labor issues, and produced systematic "estimates" of various countries' susceptibility to propaganda. *The Psychologic Factor: Its Present Application,* a study he prepared, argued that the psychological aspects of war were equal to military, eco-

nomic, and political factors. Relations with the CPI were cordial in many respects. Creel and Colonel Ralph Van Deman, who headed military intelligence
in Washington, cooperated in swapping domestic and foreign information
gleaned from censorship. In April 1918, Van Deman offered to put in a good
word with the White House on increasing Creel's foreign propaganda budget.
In addition to being the conduit for much of the military intelligence gathered
abroad, Blankenhorn passed along requests from military attachés for print and
visual propaganda and collaborated with Irwin on the testing of balloons for
delivering propaganda. This aside, Blankenhorn considered the CPI too slow to
move field propaganda from theory to practice and, in any event, thought this
should be army work, despite the indifference with which his ideas were met.[24]

One of his few early successes on the army side was with Colonel Van
Deman, who was building military intelligence with impressive enterprise and
broad vision but did not quickly appreciate the value of Blankenhorn's concept.
Blankenhorn turned this around when he pointed out that propaganda leaflets
had been used in the Battle of Bunker Hill. But few on the general staff were
even aware the Psychologic Subsection existed. Interest in field propaganda was
episodic and perceptions of it confused. In April, Pershing informed Washington that the AEF had "close liaison" with Kerney and was ready to undertake
enemy propaganda. Several weeks later Chief of Staff Peyton March queried
Nolan, "Does American expeditionary forces propaganda cooperate with Creel
Commission Representatives?"[25]

Blankenhorn sought to rectify this by conducting briefings for the general
staff and sending memoranda up the chain of command. In another ploy, he
sought out Tomáš Masaryk, who visited Washington to develop support for an
independent Czech republic after the war. Masaryk favored hastening the collapse of the Austro-Hungarian Empire by means of propaganda over their lines
and agreed to Blankenhorn's suggestion to give a talk on the matter to the War
College. Blankenhorn also tried to reach Newton Baker through his assistant
Frederick Keppel, the Columbia University dean who joined the secretary of
war's staff. Keppel assured him of Baker's sympathy, but nothing concrete came
out of his office.[26]

In late May or early June, Blankenhorn arranged to attend a dinner party
that included Ralph Hayes, Secretary Baker's personal assistant. Blankenhorn
cornered Hayes and complained about the lack of response from Baker's office. When Hayes denied that responses had not been forthcoming, Blankenhorn bolted from the party and went to his office to retrieve unanswered

memoranda. Because the material was classified and a watchful officer was on duty, he wrapped the secret documents around his waist under his jacket. Hayes took the documents home. When he returned them to Blankenhorn that night, Hayes handed him a green card on which was written "Appointment with the Secretary of War," the meeting to take place the very next day at eleven o'clock.

The meeting included General March and Colonel (soon general) Marlborough Churchill, whose lineage traced to the famous British family. Churchill had become director of military intelligence in place of Van Deman, who was transferred to France. With his feet propped on an open desk drawer, Baker asked questions. Neither of the two senior officers exhibited knowledge of Blankenhorn's plans and looked to him for answers. Baker ended the meeting by blessing the idea and said he would consult with the president. What Wilson said to Baker, if the issue was raised, is unknown. But the go-head in principle remained in place.[27]

Blankenhorn knew his plans could still fall through. Charles Merz, who had written pamphlets for the CPI and wanted to go to France with him, suggested enlisting the help of Walter Lippmann, his former colleague at the *New Republic*. By this time Lippmann had left Baker's office to join the Inquiry, a semisecret study group of over one hundred experts organized by House to plan for the postwar world. The idea for the Inquiry had been planted by Felix Frankfurter following his trip to France in the fall of 1917. In addition to pointing out the urgent need to shore up support for America's war aims, he recommended the preparation of materials for the eventual peace conference. Wilson referred to Frankfurter's letter when he directed House to create the Inquiry. Lippmann could give Blankenhorn two things he needed. First, he had a good command of the political-economic issues that would inform "America's war of ideas" abroad. Second, Lippmann had personal connections with Baker and House. Lippmann, Blankenhorn said, "may be able to hasten the organization of this greater agency by getting the matter directly before the president."[28]

"Do you not think that the time has come for cooperation between us?" Blankenhorn wrote to Lippmann on June 14. Striking what was no doubt a welcome tone, Blankenhorn criticized Creel. "When Mr. Creel reports that a million copies of a presidential speech were dropped into Germany he cannot tell where they were dropped, or when or by whom. He trusts, perforce, to the French, and has no 'check-up.' Our Allies offensive propaganda has been sporadic and skeptical of itself." The two men met the next day, a Saturday, in New York.[29]

Blankenhorn's offer strongly appealed to Lippmann. It gave him a convenient exit from the Inquiry, where his golden boy image, ambition, and arrogance made him unpopular. At the same time it satisfied his desire to engage directly in propaganda. That desire had been thwarted when he lost out to Creel in the spring of 1917 to establish a publicity program. He made other suggestions along the same line afterward. When he went to work for Baker, he proposed as one of his jobs following "public opinion in this country and elsewhere." Lippmann gave Herbert Hoover, director of the Food Administration, a plan for a propaganda bureau to arouse support for conservation. (As with the publicity scheme he proposed when the war began, he suggested Vance McCormick as executive head.) Now, at long last, he could do propaganda in a big way.[30]

Lippmann sought House's approval for accepting the offer. The appeal of Blankenhorn's propaganda plan, he said, was its emphasis on projecting Wilsonian idealism. Lippmann asked House to sound out Wilson on the wisdom of taking the position. As was the case with Baker's assertion that he would consult with Wilson, there is no record House consulted the president. But House was enthusiastic about the job. He wanted Lippmann to retain his connection to the Inquiry. He was to examine postwar problems that "in your judgment may seem appropriate." This nebulous bifurcated loyalty to the AEF and the Inquiry gave Lippmann considerable independence.[31]

Walter Lippmann realized his dream of being a war publicist when he joined Heber Blankenhorn's "Propaganda Shock Troops" in Europe. His wartime experience subsequently led him to "attempt a restatement of the problem of freedom of thought as it presents itself in modern society." It was "no longer possible," he concluded, "to believe in the original dogma of democracy." (Walter Lippmann Papers, Manuscripts and Archives, Yale University Library)

In securing Baker's approval, Lippmann did what Blankenhorn wanted him to do by reiterating the need for money and men. He again struck an idealistic note. "The thing should have a distinctly American flavor," he wrote, "and should of course take as its text the utterances of the President." Lippmann was commissioned as a captain. Merz was made a lieutenant. Blankenhorn considered Lippmann his "chief tangible asset."[32]

Resistance seemed to evaporate. CPI acquiescence fell into place almost effortlessly when Blankenhorn and Churchill met with Creel and Irwin on June 20. At least Blankenhorn thought so. "This afternoon," he ebulliently wrote in a note for his files, "Mr. Creel formally relinquished to the army the distribution of American propaganda into enemy countries" as well as "executive responsibility" for all field propaganda. The CPI would cooperate. Blankenhorn's memorandum carried no hint of astonishment that Creel suddenly ceded leadership to the army for all enemy propaganda, including through neutral countries. "Plan approved can you come here at once the iron is hot," Blankenhorn asked Lippmann by telegram.[33]

The day after the CPI meeting, Blankenhorn, Churchill, and March met again with Baker. Blankenhorn presented his plan for sending a unit of propaganda officers to the AEF. They would prepare materials, with "C.P.I. in cooperation," and would have sole responsibility for its distribution. The plan was silent on the mechanics of working with the CPI.[34]

Baker agreed. "The education, over the lines," he said, "must be absolutely honest." Blankenhorn would head the AEF Propaganda Subsection, located in G-2-D, which also handled press relations, censorship, and other informational activities. He was to develop plans to be implemented during the winter lull in fighting. The section would defer neither to the Inter-Allied Propaganda Board, as Creel favored, nor to Creel. "It is the Secretary's idea that the Army shall be the judge as to what propaganda is distributed," Churchill noted. "In other words, he is not willing to have the Army made a messenger boy for the C.P.I." Baker said he would visé propaganda material himself.[35]

Blankenhorn assembled an eclectic staff. Besides Lippmann and Merz, he recruited Yale English professor and future actor Edgar Montillion "Monty" Woolley; a newly minted Princeton graduate, George N. Ifft, who came from an Idaho newspaper family and was fluent in German as a result of his father's service as a consular officer in Germany; Ludlow Griscom, whose diplomat-uncle was a liaison between Pershing and the British War Office and who became a distinguished Harvard ornithologist; and Arthur W. Page, the son of Ambassador Page and an editor at the family publication *World's Work*. Page joined the team after it reached France.[36]

Blankenhorn and his men boarded ship on July 14 and pulled out of Hoboken, New Jersey, the next day. "Already my world is completely one of khaki," Blankenhorn wrote to his wife when he had been at sea for two days; "throngs, orders, movements, bigness—a great task."[37]

A GREAT TASK DERAILED

Blankenhorn's "Propaganda Shock Troops," as one war correspondent called them, arrived in Brest inauspiciously on July 22. No arrangements had been made for them. They were marched through fog, rain, and mud to barracks built in the time of Napoleon, where they were given candles and three blankets. Blankenhorn described Lippmann's anger the next morning: "Behold Walter, the pundit, the calm Olympian, the collar of his uniform crushed with being slept in, startling passersby and himself as he shook a fist in the direction of the barracks and shouted 'J-C-, that place is a prison.'"[38]

Blankenhorn and his men found their way to AEF headquarters in Chaumont, where they made a favorable impression, Pershing told Baker. Pershing, however, understood most of the materials would be prepared in Washington and, in any event, was reluctant to go too far too fast with such a delicate matter as propaganda. Because field propaganda was not to take place for some months, Blankenhorn, Lippmann, and Merz went to London to learn the methods used by the British and others that could be incorporated into their own efforts when the time came. Lippmann, who used part of his time to collect intelligence for the inquiry on British peace conference plans, was in his element, dining with H. G. Wells in the palatial Reform Club and conferring with Guy Gaunt. "I begin for the first time," Gibson wrote in his diary, "to have some hope that we can accomplish something."[39]

Then, without warning, unwelcome news intruded into meetings "with the great ones." The bearer of the bad tidings, indeed a personification of them, was James Keeley, an individual none of Blankenhorn's team considered worthy to direct them, as he was sent to do. Keeley, a Chicago newspaper editor, was another one of Creel's impromptu appointments. Creel needed someone to head enemy propaganda, and Keeley happened to be in London advising Wellington

House about its publicity in America. His enthusiasm for propaganda included its suppressive aspects. "A war is on," he wrote to his family, "and every day impresses on me the necessity and value of censorship."[40]

Conceptually, Keeley was Northcliffe's counterpart. They knew each other well from their journalism days, and Northcliffe urged him to take the job. But the differences were stark. Northcliffe had been thinking about enemy propaganda since the beginning of the war; hence his employment of Wile to monitor German opinion and Washburn to shape Russian views. Although English-born, Keeley specialized in sensational Chicago stories he called "bell-ringers." His sole overseas reporting trip, which he assigned to himself when he was editor of the *Chicago Tribune,* was to track down a local banker who absconded to Morocco with depositors' funds. Gibson dismissed Keeley as "a rounder of the sort that sheds little credit upon us."[41]

Keeley's instructions drastically altered Blankenhorn's previous understanding. Keeley was to be in charge of over-the-lines propaganda directed at enemy soldiers. The AEF would only handle distribution. Beyond this, however, Keeley was on weak footing. Northcliffe had staff and considerable power derived from reporting directly to Lloyd George. Keeley, Lippmann told Gibson, had "no instructions from home, cannot get answers to his cables, has no plan, no ideas, no staff, in fact nothing but a room at the Ritz and a cigar."[42]

Keeley's surprising appointment was the culmination of misunderstandings in the June 20 meeting with Creel and Irwin. The supposed agreement had been verbal. No one did the sensible thing of producing a memorandum of understanding until July 10, when Churchill sent one to the CPI. Irwin immediately rejected it. The CPI "had final judgment" in all field propaganda, he replied on July 12. At the time of the meeting, Creel was frazzled by heavy criticism and worried about the safety of CPI staff in Russia, which was then under the control of the Bolsheviks. It was unimaginable that he would have agreed to the terms Churchill and Blankenhorn thought they secured, if he had been paying attention. It is also possible that Blankenhorn and Churchill were guilty of selective listening and wishful thinking.[43]

Creel's unwillingness to relinquish control was reinforced by the appointments of Lippmann and Merz, which he learned about subsequently. He was also unhappy to learn that Baker told Pershing he intended to "personally scrutinize" propaganda material prepared by the AEF. Churchill had recommended this "as reserve ammunition" if differences arose with the CPI. In addition to annoying Creel, the assertion perplexed AEF staff, since it was unrealistic for Baker to engage in such detail.[44]

This drama unfolded out of earshot of Blankenhorn, who was on his way to Europe. Not until September did he receive an act-by-act description of what happened from Colonel John Dunn on the MID staff. Upon hearing Irwin's objections, the MID's first thought was to locate written instructions that should have been given to Blankenhorn "from higher authority." MID had found nothing when Churchill met with the CPI to sort things out. By this time Edgar Sisson, who was back from Russia, had replaced Irwin as head of the Foreign Section. Sisson came to the MID offices on the evening of July 22. His natural chilliness was a few degrees lower than normal, leaving the impression that the MID-CPI relationship was on the rocks. Churchill gave in. Under the so-called Creel-Churchill Agreement, drafted by Sisson and sent on July 23, the CPI would produce field propaganda; the army would distribute it over enemy lines and have nothing to do with propaganda against enemy civilians. Keeley would be the US representative to the Inter-Allied Board, which would direct policy.[45]

Churchill had good reasons to make peace. Why imperil relations with the CPI over ownership of an untested, low-priority initiative? Issues of more importance to the army needed to be resolved with the CPI. "I must say," Dunn told Blankenhorn, "that the most perfect coordination and cooperation of effort has resulted from that night's session." Shortly afterward, Creel agreed to cede more authority to the MID to handle press relations as they saw it. Beyond this, the practical reality of Creel's power must have contributed to Churchill's willingness to be accommodating. Wilson was likely to side with his CPI chairman in a dispute over propaganda. Creel met with the president the day after Churchill sent his initial memorandum with his flawed understanding of the MID-CPI agreement; Creel likely discussed it with Wilson.[46]

Blankenhorn admitted the verbal agreement of the June 20 meeting had been "a hazy affair." But he was not resigned to the latest agreement. When he learned of it via Keeley's cables, Blankenhorn fired off messages in hopes of restoring his original understanding. He told Keeley he was not at liberty to enter into a permanent agreement until he heard from the War Department. In the interim, he and Lippmann worked out a temporary division of responsibilities with Keeley, whose uncertainty about what to do made him pliable. The CPI was "responsible for editorial preparation, translation, printing, etc., with the advisory aid of M.I.B." The AEF would control distribution. They would have joint offices "whenever necessary, so that they shall be in the most complete personal constant and exchange of information and views." With regard to inter-Allied meetings, Keeley would have an AEF propaganda officer as an assistant.[47]

Keeley's limitations were apparent at Northcliffe's conference, which convened on August 14 and ran for several days. He was frankly unclear what he was supposed to convey as the head of the US delegation. Blankenhorn and Lippmann attended as observers. Northcliffe's condescending deputy, who had shown only "polite interest" in the CPI when Russell stopped by at an earlier date, described the US delegation "as pupils, having a most earnest desire to learn."[48]

BUREAUCRATIC TUSSLING CONTINUES

The beginnings of American field propaganda were a bureaucratic roller-coaster ride. One minute Blankenhorn was stymied. The next he was free to do his work largely unimpeded, as happened following Keeley's dismal performance at Northcliffe's conference. With the winter lull still some time off and his belief that "possible conflict with Lippmann and his group smoothed over," he returned to the United States for consultations. Under the circumstances, complained Keeley's deputy, G. H. Edgell, it was "difficult to begin any operation" in Italy. The circumstances, however, had the opposite effect for Blankenhorn. They left the field open to the AEF at a critical moment.[49]

The moment materialized on the afternoon of August 28, the day Keeley reached the United States. Major Joseph Stilwell burst into Blankenhorn's third-floor office in Building B at Chaumont. Stilwell, head of Fourth Corps intelligence, wanted "some propaganda—quick" to counter rumors among German troops that Americans shot prisoners.[50]

Because Blankenhorn's status remained uncertain pending clarification from the War Department, AEF intelligence chief Dennis Nolan was reluctant to give him wide latitude. But he let Blankenhorn's men pounce on Stilwell's request. "Leaflet Number 1," edited by Lippmann and ready for distribution in one day, carried General Order 106 on the treatment of German deserters and a description of rations they were guaranteed. Ground patrols and airplanes threw the leaflets over enemy lines on August 29. Reports came in of German soldiers stuffing them in their pockets. "You're a hell of an outfit," Stilwell told Blankenhorn.[51]

Blankenhorn rejoiced at the success, only to be set back again. This time the cause was Lippmann. In letters and cables to House in late August and early September, in which he provided reports useful to the Inquiry, he derided the CPI and Keeley. He suggested "a new expert organization" independent of Creel and along the lines of Northcliffe's. It should be housed in military intelligence and headed by a true diplomat, namely Hugh Gibson. The goal of this new venture, he argued, should not be limited to winning the war. It should also prepare European thinking for the just, progressive peace called for in Wilson's speeches.[52]

Gibson, who had been dismissed from the CPI by this time, had plenty of opportunity to egg on the young journalist. They dined with each other in Paris, sometimes twice a day, and were often joined by Arthur Frazier, with whom they formed a devil's triangle of CPI haters. Frazier, a seasoned diplomat who was a liaison with the Allies' Supreme War Council, saw the value of propaganda but not the CPI's execution of it, as he too spelled out in letters to House. He liked Lippmann and not Whitehouse, the latter view probably fueled by Hugh Wilson, who lodged with Gibson when he visited from Bern. Lippmann thought the diplomats in Bern were "the very best young men in the diplomatic service."[53]

Toward the end of August, Creel briefed Wilson on the cooperative agreement he had reached with military intelligence. This satisfactory resolution came into question a couple of days later when Wilson learned of Lippmann's discordant commentary and suggestions, much of which passed through State Department channels. Neither Baker nor House had told him of Lippmann's AEF assignment. The angry president wanted to know why he had been sent. Not incorrectly, he conflated Lippmann's views with those of the *New Republic,* which criticized the administration for the suppression of speech and the CPI for promoting the war instead of arousing "public opinion in the constructive problems of settlement." "I consider his judgment most unsound," Wilson told House, who had forwarded some of Lippmann's correspondence. Creel wanted Lippmann recalled.[54]

With Baker traveling, Wilson summoned the War Secretary's deputy, Benedict Crowell, for a "little war conference." Wilson told Crowell that he wanted "propaganda entirely in my own hands. . . . If any agency of the Army is attempting to organize propaganda of any sort or to take a hand in controlling it, I would be very much obliged if you would 'call them off.'" Churchill cabled Blankenhorn to cease his work until given further instructions.[55]

Wilson authorized Creel to write a directive giving the CPI control over army propaganda. Sisson drafted this with the new wrinkle that military intelligence was to give the CPI the "editorial service" of its officers upon request. The draft may never have been signed, perhaps because it was unnecessary. When Crowell provided a reasoned explanation why field propaganda required military involvement, Wilson allowed Blankenhorn to proceed upon assurances the CPI was not being "supplanted." In accordance with Sisson's memorandum, Crowell told Wilson that military attachés in Madrid, Bern, Rome, and elsewhere would be ordered to "to place themselves at the disposal" of the CPI. The directive, sent by Churchill, was unambiguous. Attachés had "no authority whatever to initiate propaganda or to interfere with or criticize the work, methods or personnel of the representatives of the Committee in this field." House, in the meantime, told Lippmann and Frazier to stop the criticism.[56]

Around the same time Pershing proposed that the State Department lend Gibson to the AEF to oversee policy aspects of field propaganda, for which Gibson had already begun planning. The proposal emanated from Nolan, Blankenhorn, and Lippmann. Baker liked the idea and forwarded it to Lansing. The answer came back a firm "no." "The president," Baker informed Pershing, "has definitely placed the responsibility for propaganda work on the Committee on Public Information, represented in Paris by Mr. James Keeley, and has disassociated the State Department from it."[57]

"It will be an extremely difficult matter to carry out the policy which will be directed by the Committee on Public Information," Nolan told General Marsh. But they never had to. Blankenhorn's fortunes again took a positive turn. Keeley lingered in the United States, and no one with the CPI in Europe stepped in to guide field propaganda in the last weeks of the war. "Curious that at the wind-up Creel apparently cleared himself out of the field," Blankenhorn said.[58]

CAPTAIN PAPERS

On September 12, the AEF launched its first major independent combat operation, at Saint-Mihiel in northwest France. Five days later Blankenhorn lofted a British ninety-foot balloon—they never received American-made balloons—with four pounds of leaflets suspended from a slow-burning fuse whose length was roughly calculated by meteorologists. Blankenhorn plowed ahead in the next weeks despite shortages of gas for balloons. Colonel Billy Mitchell, chief of the First Army Air Service and considered the creator of the US Air Force, flatly told Blankenhorn his leaflets had "no place in combat operations." "Captain Papers," as Blankenhorn came to be known, convinced pilots to do the work quietly until Mitchell finally got on board.[59]

AEF intelligence, historian George Bruntz concluded, kept "a closer watch" on German morale than its counterparts. Blankenhorn told Churchill they were going about their work "more scientifically" than the British. Lippmann and Ifft, both German speakers, grilled prisoners about what newspapers they read, which Reichstag spokesmen they believed, whether they had been well fed, and whether they knew "what Bernstorff did in America." Another unit in G-2-D combined the surveillance and suppression aspects of propaganda by going through prisoner mail and censoring it. Once the leaflets were dropped, the AEF questioned German defectors to assess how effective their propaganda was in getting them to surrender. In effect, Blankenhorn used the prisoners as focus groups to evaluate various messages. This evidence-based measurement of what the enemy found persuasive was a progressive enterprise, if ever there was one. And only the AEF could do it, Blankenhorn rightly told Churchill.[60]

Notwithstanding the lack of formal sanction from Washington, Gibson continued to work "very closely" with Blankenhorn. The AEF also had its way on not coordinating their work with the interallied boards on enemy propaganda in London, Paris, and Padua. The boards' ineffectiveness, Pershing said, leaves "us entire liberty of action for conducting our own propaganda."[61]

During a visit to France in September, Baker received an extensive, carefully reasoned memorandum, probably written by Lippmann, laying out the practical reasons the military should control field propaganda. Baker preferred to let the informal arrangement stand. His aide Ralph Hayes, who helped Blankenhorn get a hearing with him months before, stayed behind and was assigned to Blankenhorn's propaganda unit in G-2-D. There was no "sign of help from Creel's men," Blankenhorn noted several weeks later, "despite our inquiries."[62]

On October 17, Van Deman advised Baker that "the whole propaganda matter is a mess and that it is necessary to give us definite instructions as to our powers and duties, that is to say the powers and duties of the army." Two days later, Pershing asked Baker for full responsibility for field propaganda. This time the answer was the long-awaited one. On November 1, the AEF was informed the CPI "did not desire to participate in either preparation or distribution." James

Keeley, who had returned from the United States, wrote to his family, "Some army officers had been doing some enemy propaganda work and doing it very well." At that late date, he decided not to waste the $50,000 he had on hand for propaganda. "As a propagandist I am either the most wonderful success or a stupendous failure," he wrote his family. "The moment I arrived the enemies against whom I was to campaign all and severally laid down their arms, and so my targets vanished."[63]

"It was a fine little organization going at the end," Blankenhorn told Churchill in December. The grand plans he had drawn up for the lull were put aside in favor of finishing off the demoralized enemy as quickly as possible. AEF dropped three million leaflets in the last eight weeks of the war. The chief objective was "to fetch people over the line," as Blankenhorn put it. This did not preclude using Wilson's words promising the enemy a just peace and, in effect, inciting the overthrow of their government. Wilson encouraged the latter by his statement "There can be no peace obtained by any kind of bargain or compromise with the governments of the Central Empires." Toward the end of the war, an AEF report noted, "almost all the propaganda was written in Washington, by President Wilson, in the Armistice notes addressed to Germany." Blankenhorn deviated from Baker's command to keep propaganda "absolutely honest." The rations promised in Leaflet Number 1—the most heavily used leaflet—were not always provided immediately. Leaflet Number 3 encouraged surrender by providing imprisoned deserters with a postcard they could fill in to tell their family they were well. The army had no intention of taking the time to forward these to loved ones.[64]

"Although its chief weapons were only brains, ink and paper," United Press correspondent Webb Miller wrote, "the Field Propaganda Section undoubtedly saved many lives, brought in many prisoners and weakened the German morale and shortened the war thereby." A precise estimate of the Propaganda Subsection's impact was not possible, said Nolan, who was now a general. "Enough facts are at hand, however, to make us feel sure that the effects were considerable."[65]

The Germans, who had been the first to use psychological operations, conducted "propaganda raids" in the final days of the war. But their morale collapsed despite Field Marshal Paul von Hindenburg's warning that the Allies were assaulting "the German spirit . . . [with] poisoned arrows dipped in printers' ink." German authorities claimed that leaflets insulting the kaiser and their government violated international law; they threatened to hang pilots who dropped them and were captured. Despite German general staff orders that troops should not read propaganda, Ackerman reported that enemy prisoners frequently carried leaflets.[66]

In early November, German sailors mutinied, German soldiers deserted in large numbers, and German workers went on strike. When the kaiser abdicated on the ninth, he threaded his way through pockets of revolutionaries to reach exile in Holland. The last days were a shock to Germans. Their government's propaganda led them to believe that the shortages of food and other hardships they endured were leading to certain victory.[67]

THE BRIGHT SPOT OF AEF-CPI PRESS RELATIONS

Despite wasting a lot of time in senseless fights over field propaganda, Creel found ways to cooperate with the AEF in improving news coverage of the war. In this, he had assistance from his good friend Martin Egan, an executive at J. P. Morgan and a prototype of the all-purpose corporate public relations counselor, although he disliked the term when it came into use after the war. The blond, affable Irishman described himself as "assisting the firm's public relationships."[68]

J. P. Morgan, which had financed the Allies from the start of the war, encouraged its staff to do their personal part to help. When the United States was still neutral, Egan helped Captain Guy Gaunt run down secret bank accounts used by the Germans. Henry Davison, a Morgan partner, took Egan with him when he became chairman of the War Council of the Red Cross in Washington.[69]

Pershing and Egan had a warm relationship dating from the Boxer Rebellion, when the former was an army captain and the latter an AP reporter. In the spring of 1918, the general called him to France "to act as a kind of special agent." Pershing was concerned about the state of "press information and press propaganda," as well as field propaganda, which needed "the right man to take hold of it." Before leaving, Egan rushed to Washington to confer with Creel, who also wanted to improve AEF press relations. Egan convinced Pershing of the insufficient "contact and communication between the American people and their troops in France."[70]

Working with Kerney, Egan arranged a central office in Paris to facilitate trips to the front by journalists and distinguished visitors. He also helped realize Creel's idea of a daily news service from the front, which CPI commissioners were pleading for and AEF intelligence officers regarded as "unthinkable." The

CPI placed journalist Maximillian Foster, who had been helping the YMCA, at AEF headquarters beginning in September. "Each day," Creel said, "[Foster] writes a very remarkable story that we put on the wires for use in all countries of the world other than the United States."[71]

Foster's stories were sanitized to stress success, although this was not far from the way independent journalists reported. CPI representatives in Allied and neutral countries were enthusiastic about Foster's reports. All the newspapers in Spain used them, the CPI commissioner in Madrid enthusiastically reported.[72]

Gibson spread the word Egan was dismayed and wanted to give up. Egan may have been frustrated, given all the difficulties surrounding CPI-AEF relations. But he had a far better attitude than Gibson did. He was "quite favorably impressed" with Kerney when they first met in France. Given Egan's expertise in war reporting and publicity as well as his close relationships with both Creel and Pershing, it is a pity that he did not have a large role in field propaganda from the beginning.[73]

A NEW THING IN ARMY HISTORY

"The use of propaganda as a military weapon against the enemy in the field . . . was a new thing in American army history," Blankenhorn wrote after the war, and it was not widely appreciated. "No *communiqués* were issued about its operations."[74]

The postwar fate of Blankenhorn's Psychologic Subsection in Washington illustrates what a triumph it had been to create it in the first place. The unit languished in MID until 1925, when it was abolished. Between 1925 and 1935, no officers were assigned to study psychological warfare. In World War II Blankenhorn was brought back into military service by the same man who took him on in 1918, Charles Mason, by that time a colonel. Mason could not find Blankenhorn's final report from World War I and wanted him to prepare a new one. In a reprise of his earlier experience, Blankenhorn found "not merely indifference to the idea of combat propaganda leaflets but . . . marked hostility from skeptical G-2 officers." He eventually left the general staff for the Office of Strategic Services under William J. Donovan. After the war, the military continued to struggle with the concept. "They spent millions of man-hours without any accepted definition of psychological warfare," said one of its foremost practitioners, Edward Lilly. By the time of the Vietnam War, psychological operations was not yet a career field.[75]

The importance of psychological propaganda, which Blankenhorn argued for in *The Psychologic Factor,* is now undisputed. In 2003, the year of the US invasion of Iraq, the Pentagon issued a secret internal report, *Information Operations Roadmap.* It called for "transforming IO into a core military competency on par with air, ground, maritime and special operations." Whereas the grand nineteenth-century military theorist General Carl von Clausewitz limited the value of information in war to knowledge "of the enemy and his country," information operations ranged from disrupting the enemy's cyber systems to creating "information intended for foreign audiences, including public diplomacy and Psyops." Psychological operations had become so extensive, the Pentagon report acknowledged, that it touched American domestic audiences.[76]

Blankenhorn is remembered as the father of military psychological operations. No glory accrued to the CPI. Had Creel stepped aside when it was clear he did not have the capacity to lead the effort, Blankenhorn's team would have functioned more efficiently and effectively. Even if Creel had the resources, chief responsibility for field propaganda should have fallen to the army from the beginning. "I am of the opinion," Nolan observed, "that the propaganda to be used on enemy troops should be prepared in France by people who understand the psychology of the German soldier."[77]

The problems that Blankenhorn encountered in getting acceptance of this view were endemic to the overworked War Department. Van Deman, who is considered the father of American military intelligence, had to use the same subterranean ploys Blankenhorn did to get Newton Baker's attention. Thanks to Van Deman, the tiny Military Intelligence Section that existed when E. Alexander Powell joined grew to 282 officers and 1,159 civilians by the time the conflict was over. Little wonder that Van Deman, to whom Blankenhorn's ideas should have been especially attractive, was not quick to grasp them. He was overwhelmingly busy.[78]

Churchill's delay in preparing his memorandum on the June 20 meeting with Creel was symptomatic of another larger problem. The army did not have an effective central coordinating authority. Paperwork was routinely backlogged. Orders, written in haste, were often sketchy and misplaced.[79]

After the war, Lieutenant Colonel Walter Sweeney, who had been with G-2-D, wrote in *Military Intelligence: A New Weapon in War*: "Perhaps it was natural that the Intelligence Service should have been misunderstood and used wrongly or not at all, as was sometimes the case, because, as has been stated, it was a new thing to the American Army and its growth, like that of a mushroom, was almost over night. . . . It did not give anywhere near the return it would have given had its powers and limitations, its true purposes and sphere of usefulness, been clearly understood by the army at large." [80]

Blankenhorn and his "chief tangible asset," Lippmann, made matters worse. Their back-channel communication annoyed Pershing as well as Wilson. Churchill laid the blame on their "youth and enthusiasm." But in Lippmann's case, youth was matched by arrogance. Lippmann described himself as Baker's and House's "personal representative," just as Merriam and Kerney had enlarged themselves. He seems not to have done Blankenhorn the courtesy of informing him of the pot-stirring letters he wrote to House. He annoyed Blankenhorn by exceeding the authority given to him. Lippmann told Gibson that Blankenhorn "was not capable of running anything," a statement that was as untrue as it was self-serving. [81]

Shortly before the armistice, Lippmann went to Paris to work full-time on Inquiry matters. In a farewell letter, Major A. L. James, who commanded G-2-D, said Lippmann should be gratified. At long last the CPI had "no jurisdiction in the matter of the preparation or distribution of [field] propaganda." Lippmann sought an additional measure of gratification when he returned to the United States. "One of the genuine calamities of our part in the war was the character of American propaganda in Europe," he wrote in the *New Republic*. "It was run as if an imp had devised it to thwart every purpose Mr. Wilson was supposed to entertain. . . . One would never have dreamed from these 'personal representatives of the President' who were all over the place that America had purposes and interests and ideas and reservations together with its whole-hearted determination to win the war." [82]

The CPI was never guilty of underselling. Unlike Blankenhorn's team, which made a close assessment of enemy thought, the CPI had a looser approach. It did not prepare public opinion for the final settlement, a tragic mistake for which Wilson was responsible. Vague promises of a just, nonvindictive peace built up hopes that collapsed at the peace table. But Lippmann's critique was itself excessive. It was much easier to focus field propaganda, which had specific military objectives, than it was to focus propaganda reaching a wide range of countries in the form of news. Rogers and Poole deserved the credit that many journalists gave them. As for Wilson's overpromising rhetoric, Lippmann had argued for using it in field propaganda.[83]

In the past Creel almost gleefully attacked Lippmann as an elitist, a charge that fit Lippmann's subversive machinations at the AEF in league with Gibson. This time Creel did not. His final report omitted Lippmann's name as it did Blankenhorn's and Keeley's. There was too much blame on all sides to get into this argument.[84]

Creel, however, could not breeze past all of his mistakes so easily. The repercussions of one of these, committed glaringly on the home front, epitomized his spontaneous truculence and became an enormous distraction at the time he should have been answering cables from his foreign commissioners. "A foolish, tactless remark made about Congress in a small meeting in New York provoked a Congressional investigation in Washington," Vira Whitehouse observed. "It was time stolen from the great and serious work of winning the war."[85]

12

Acrimonious Contention

From the very moment of its creation, the Committee on Public
Information has been the object of harsh criticism—from both the press
and the public, Congress and various Government officials.
— *The Fourth Estate,* February 9, 1918

In the spring of 1918, with criticism raining down on George Creel and the
Committee on Public Information, Guy Stanton Ford and a few colleagues approached their volatile director with advice: "George, you must make no more
speeches."

"Sure, sure," Creel replied. "I'm not going to make any more. I've got just
one engagement."[1]

On Sunday evening, May 12, Creel gave the speech in New York City. A
thousand people crowded into the Church of the Ascension on Fifth Avenue
and West Tenth Street. The overflow crowd drifted up on the altar steps.[2]

Creel became a man possessed when he took the podium. As much as he
wanted to blur the CPI's association with its foreign-born organizations, he
blurted out in a speech that the CPI "has organized, and now directs, a round
dozen of societies and leagues." He tended toward philippics. He habitually
spoke through clenched teeth. Instead of protecting himself by working off a
script, he relished being freewheeling. The question-and-answer session at the
Church of the Ascension lasted well over an hour. Creel was at turns witty, com-
bative, and disingenuous.[3]

What did he think of Roosevelt's criticism of the administration? "I would
regret if we were robbed of Roosevelt's criticisms," as they made friends for Wilson. What about Creel's recent remark, "I shall always be proud to my dying
day that there was no rush of preparation in this country prior to the day the
President went before Congress" for a declaration of war? Instead of distanc-

ing himself from the comment, he stood by it, calling it evidence of how earnest Wilson had been about keeping the country out of war. Creel insisted that Burleson did not crush publications and that "there should be no Government control of public opinion." Referring to Creel, someone cheekily asked, "Has the censor any authority over the Postmaster?" Creel replied, "The censor—the censor—who is the censor? Certainly not I." To the complaint he "hadn't said anything at all about public opinion," the subject of his speech, Creel said anything the audience took away from his talk was public opinion.

One of Creel's answers reverberated far outside the church. Republican statesman Elihu Root had called for electing that fall only those legislators who had "loyal hearts" in maintaining the war against Germany. Creel was asked if current members of Congress had loyal hearts. He could have dodged this. Questions were submitted on scraps of paper that he was free to toss aside. Instead, he answered flippantly, "I don't like slumming, so I won't explore into the heart of Congress."

Creel was trying to be funny, and some people laughed. But Louis Wiley, business manager of the *New York Times,* saw trouble ahead. Wiley was the newspaper's "social lion," always out and about and attuned to the consequences of the news. He walked over to Lieutenant Commander George Barr Baker, who was in the audience, and offered a suggestion. Baker, who worked in the navy censorship bureau in New York, should ask newspapers to keep the comment out of the news. At 10:45 that night he dispatched two ensigns to see what could be done in the newsrooms of the *Sun, Tribune,* and *World.* The young officers viewed their task as a fool's errand. The *Tribune,* one of them noted in an after-action report, was "probably willing to pay large sums to obtain matter that could be printed to the detriment of Mr. Creel." It would be especially damning for someone from the censorship office, "under the directorship of Mr. Creel, asking that one of his hasty remarks be suppressed. I saw no one in the newsroom that I dare approach."[4]

The New York newspapers reported the slumming comment. Stories and editorials appeared across the nation carrying the comments of infuriated legislators. "Revolution in Congress," Josephus Daniels wrote in his diary. Illinois congressman Joe Cannon wanted to "take Creel by the seat of the breeches and the back of his neck and throw him into space." Majority leader Democrat Claude Kitchin said Creel was "unworthy of the respect of any decent citizen." Congress had just passed the Sedition Act, which authorized "the prosecution of persons who utter words intended to bring the Government of the United States into contempt." Creel, the *New York Sun* said, was guilty of doing just that. The *Tribune* suggested, "Congress should abolish him."[5]

"I feel it best to drop out of sight as far as possible," Creel said several days later in response to a speaking invitation. The refractory CPI chairman considered himself a victim of the news media. He was making "no more speeches," he replied to another invitation, because "it seems absolutely impossible to prevent distortion and misrepresentation."[6]

Dropping out of sight was impossible. Creel, in Harvey O'Higgins's words, was "as accessible as a municipal drinking fountain." His perceived power and combustible personality and the CPI's unprecedented mission made him an object of scorn, resentment, and fear—inside the administration, with Lansing especially hating him; among quasi-official bodies, which viewed him as a rival and perversely found him a useful target in their loyalty campaigns; on Newspaper Row, one block east of the White House, where journalists chafed at his heavy-handedness; and at the other end of Pennsylvania Avenue, where outraged legislators finally brought his budget to heel following his Church of the Ascension speech.[7]

Creel was, in the words of the *New York Tribune,* the "Terrible Infant" of Washington. "Whatever may have been the rights or wrongs of his controversies, his career had been one of turbulence and mud-splattering; he had denounced and been denounced," the *New York Times* commented after his slumming remarks. "His name stood for acrimonious contention."[8]

A TONG IN THE WILSON TRIDENT

When Washington journalists held their annual Gridiron Club dinner on December 7, 1917, the newsmen did not check their patriotism at the door of the New Willard Hotel or their tradition of roasting the news makers who attended. The walls and tables were adorned with American flags. Food conservation czar Herbert Hoover scribbled "ok" on a printed menu with oysters on wheatless crackers and a spiritless punch because hard liquor had been "interned" in Washington by order of Congress a few days before. When it came time to light a fire under the dignitaries, no one was singed more than George Creel, who sat next to Hoover at the long head table.[9]

The burlesquing journalists recalled the "July Hoax" in which Creel embroidered the navy's encounter with enemy submarines. They joked that the "censor" had "deleted" the contents of his hipflask. Most poignant of all was a skit in which foreign "High Commissioners" were briefed on the American government. Didn't it have three branches, one of the commissioners asked?

"Four," the American interlocutor replied, "the Executive; the Congress, the Judiciary, and the Committee of [*sic*] Public Information."

What did the CPI do? "Inculcate a proper popular respect for the Administration. Right now it's the whole cheese. . . . I mean it's all to the good—the main squeeze—the grand gazebo—the lallapolooza—understand?"

Political power is magnified if an individual leads an influential agency in which the president takes a personal interest, if the official enjoys the president's confidence, and if these two conditions are well known. Wilson's interest in the CPI was palpable. He told Lansing in a moment of pique over Lippmann's renegade activities with army intelligence, "I am very jealous in the matter of propaganda." Wilson's interest in the CPI lapped over Creel to an unusual degree. Everyone understood the CPI was the Creel Committee and called it such in conversation and news stories. "There was no doubt," Ray Stannard Baker said, "that he completely dominated that organization."[10]

"The Three Tines of Wilson's Fighting Trident"

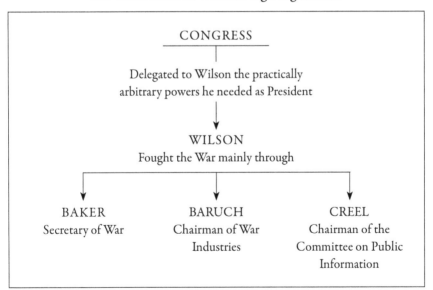

CONGRESS

Delegated to Wilson the practically
arbitrary powers he needed as President

WILSON
Fought the War mainly through

| BAKER | BARUCH | CREEL |
| Secretary of War | Chairman of War Industries | Chairman of the Committee on Public Information |

Source: Mark Sullivan, *Our Times: Over Here, 1914–1918,* vol. 5 (New York: Charles Scribner's Sons, 1936), 370.

"The three tines of Wilson's fighting trident," Mark Sullivan said, were Newton Baker, overseeing the fighting in Europe; Bernard M. Baruch, directing war
industries; and Creel, mobilizing emotion. Sullivan produced a diagram to illustrate his point. Herbert Bayard Swope of the *New York World* said the president called only three officials by their first names: Dudley Field Malone, a liberal attorney who was appointed collector of the Port of New York; a second
person whose name he could not remember; and Creel. It was a flip remark by
a man who liked to be an insider and not bankable as fact. Its significance lay in
Swope's perception, held by many, of Creel's influence.[11]

Boris A. Bakhmeteff, the Russian ambassador to Washington, acted on the
perception when the Bolsheviks seized power in St. Petersburg in November
1917. He desperately wanted to make the case for nonrecognition of the new
regime. In that chaotic moment, when it was unclear if the Bolsheviks would
hold sway more than a few days, he asked for an appointment with Lansing and
was put off. This did not trouble Bakhmeteff greatly, as he believed that Lansing
would have little influence with Wilson, and he telephoned Creel to ask for a
meeting as soon as possible. Creel came to his home at midnight. The next afternoon Creel telephoned Bakhmeteff. He had seen the president and "everything
was all right." Creel had little or no impact on the nonrecognition policy that
the administration adopted, but the ambassador thought that he played "a very
important role." Each time Bakhmeteff repeated the story at cocktail parties, he
reinforced Creel's image as a man of power.[12]

"The President had an affection for Creel, who had won his heart, while his
brilliancy compelled his admiration," said Josephus Daniels, himself a favorite
of the president. Frederick Palmer considered Creel "closer to the President
than many Cabinet members." Publicist Ivy Lee, who tangled with Creel during
the labor unrest in Colorado, reported, "They say Creel enjoys the confidence
of President Wilson as few men in Washington do." Creel saw Wilson almost
daily, said James Kerney, with a touch of exaggeration.[13]

The Wilson-Creel bond had social sinews as well as professional ones.
Creel's wife, Blanche Bates, was friendly with the president's daughter, Margaret, who visited Bates's country home. Wilson took his wife to see Bates in the
feature film *Daughter of the Gods* on their first wedding anniversary. Creel gave
Wilson openings to be warm and intimate. When submitting an initial budget
in May 1917, Creel made no provision for his salary. Wilson no doubt enjoyed
directing him to include his $8,000 annual salary.[14]

The distance from the CPI stoop at 10 Jackson Place to the White House
portico was 220 yards. Creel often made the quick walk at five o'clock in the

afternoon, when Wilson liked to see him. Creel, one of Washington's best sto-
rytellers, made him laugh at the end of a trying day. Creel was abundantly loyal.
Wilson's enemies were Creel's, said Frederic C. Howe. Creel "was brilliantly
profane in excoriating them, particularly Senator Lodge. Mr. Wilson appreciated his devotion."[15]

Wilson liked to communicate via concise notes. Some days Creel sent more
than one. Many were in the vein of suggesting a presidential thank you to the
Four Minute Men or a meeting with the Lithuanian National Council. Other
times Creel's missives were weighty. When the Root mission first recommended
immediate initiation of propaganda in Russia, in June 1917, Creel offered to digest it for the president. This gave Creel the opportunity to make a pitch for
the CPI handling the task. "I do not think the State Department should have
anything to do with it at all," he told the president. He wanted the CPI to be
in charge.[16]

Wilson was not a rubber stamp for Creel's propaganda proposals, but he was
perceived as such. From Vira Whitehouse, Hugh Gibson heard that Creel gave
Wilson an ultimatum after learning that Lippmann was trying "to steal his job
in Paris." If Wilson did not back Creel, he would quit. In Whitehouse's telling
of the episode, Creel was bragging. Wilson's support of Creel was apparent in a
comment he made to Polk on the incident: "The jealousies and misjudgments
on the other side of the water [to wit, Lippmann's] happily greatly exceed those
on this side." In January 1918, Wilson gave Creel more than a polite pat on the
back, writing "I want to say how much it has gratified me and how entirely the
work being done by the Committee meets with my approval."[17]

Wilson edited letters and statements Creel drafted for him, taking out hyperbole and correcting spelling and grammatical errors that Creel made as he
wrote in his usual white heat. From time to time Wilson corrected speeches that
Creel was himself about to deliver. Once Wilson said teasingly, "I'm afraid, dear
boy, that I was born without your passion for adjectives."[18]

"Creel has made a couple of bad gaffs lately and the national sport seems to
be bating him," Gibson wrote in his diary following his Church of Ascension
speech. "However he will probably weather the storm as he stands high with
the Great White Chief who does not desert his friends."[19]

CREATIVE ENERGY AND FRUSTRATING FRENZY

Probably in the summer of 1918 someone took a photo of the "Official Family of the Committee on Public Information at their Home in Washington."

Women and men spill out of the red brick buildings at Jackson Place. They are packed together, many heads barely visible. In the center, a man is standing at an awning-draped window. By all appearances it is Creel. At the moment the camera shutter is pressed, he has turned. Perhaps something just occurred to the kinetic chairman and he is giving a directive. Perhaps someone is taking advantage of Creel's moment of stasis to get a long-awaited answer to a question.

These staff members were only part of the official family, which grew to some four hundred scattered in seven buildings in Washington, ten in New York City, and outposts overseas. The Division of Films had a New York office, which was in touch with the movie industry, and a Washington office, where it was in touch with government agencies, as well as a laboratory for processing film in Washington. Charles Dana Gibson's artists had a small office in Chicago, and Rogers had one in San Francisco.[20]

The creation of an organization of these proportions in a few months was remarkable. Similarly remarkable were the attainments of the people Creel hired. On any given day one could have coffee with an acclaimed playwright (Harvey O'Higgins), take lunch with a renowned war correspondent (Will Irwin), and say hello to the nation's best illustrator (Charles Dana Gibson). The lower ranks held individuals with extraordinary accomplishments and pedigrees. By the end of his career William Churchill, head of the Foreign Language Newspaper Di-

In this grainy photo of the CPI staff in front of their Jackson Place offices, a man can be seen at the window, just turning around. (See arrow.) It is no doubt George Creel, who was "always off [on] some other possibility or [to] see some other man etc." (Photo found in Arthur Bestor's papers at the University of Illinois)

vision, had been librarian of the San Francisco Academy of Sciences and consul general to Samoa, whose language he mastered. A dozen of his ancestors came to America on the *Mayflower*.[21]

Rapid growth, a brilliant staff, an idealistic mission, and Creel in the lead engendered an esprit de corps. He worked so hard that his friend Martin Egan urged him to come to his country place for a "week-end rest cure" with breakfast in bed. Although an unrepentant militant to the public, he privately told jokes on himself. His commitment to progressive causes was as vivid as a neon sign. He defied convention in hiring Josephine Roche and Vira Whitehouse. When the play *Watch Your Neighbor* cast a woman in a role similar to Whitehouse's, it was considered a joke. The setting of the play was a conference in spy-infested Switzerland. "The necessary love interest is none too plausibly brought in by making the American delegate a girl," the *New York Times* said. "But, then, the piece cannot be spoken of in the same breath with plausibility." Despite the frustrations Whitehouse experienced at Creel's hands, she dedicated her Swiss memoir to him.[22]

The CPI staff, Edward Bernays recalled, "went ahead with enthusiasm on a widespread front. When anyone of us got a bright idea, it was very likely to be accepted." They thought of "themselves as crusaders" and worked long hours. Creel had "the gift of inspiring loyalty, of winning trust," O'Higgins said. He "had his faults, but if I were picking a friend, I should prefer Creel's faults to the lickspittle virtues of most men."[23]

Creel was equal parts exhilarating creative energy and frustrating frenzy. Virtually everyone agreed Creel was "not much of an executive." He created, re-created, and abolished units so often in the brief life of the committee that it was impossible at the end of the war to determine what exactly had existed or the correct dates of operation. (See table 4.) Creel sent incessant notes with ideas and direction. He wrote and edited materials and "consistently interfered to endorse or to veto" projects. Guy Stanton Ford wrote to his wife of his difficulty extracting a decision during a long meeting. Creel was "always off [on] some other possibility or [to] see some other man etc." Rogers felt compelled to write on the top of a letter to him, "This is important! Read it!" Poole similarly wrote to his boss. "I want to help you the most I possibly can—and I cannot do this unless you will either give me a *little* more of your time or a *little* more power to decide things myself."[24]

People, Bernays said, were hired based on "their enthusiasm for the cause, not their training and experience." Poole, for instance, was a "nervous fellow"

Table 4. Organization of the Committee on Public Information

Section, Division, or Bureau	Organized	Discontinued
DOMESTIC SECTION		
Advertising Division	December 1917	December 1918
Business Management Division:	October 1917	June 30, 1919
Distribution Division:	June 1917	December 1918
New York Bureau of Circulation	October 1917	December 1918
Mailing and Printing Department	May 1917	February 1919
Stenograph and Mimeograph Department	October 1917	December 1918
Civic and Educational Cooperation Division:	May 1917	December 1918
National School Service	August 1918	December 1918
Executive Division:	April 1917	June 30, 1918
Bureau of Cartoons	May 1918	July 1918
Bureau of State Fair Exhibits	June 1918	December 1918
Film Division:	September 1917	June 1918
Allied War Expositions	July 1918	June 30, 1919
Bureau of War Photographs	March 1918	December 1918
Slide Laboratory	June 1918	December 1918
Foreign Language Newspaper Division	April 1917	March 1918
Four Minute Men Division:	June 16, 1917	December 31, 1918
Speakers Bureau[1]	August 1918	December 31, 1918
Industrial Relations Division	February 1918	March 1918
Labor Publications Division	August 1917	December 31, 1918
News Division	April 1917	December 1918
Official Bulletin Division	April 1917	March 31, 1919
Pictorial Publicity Division	November 1917	December 1918
Picture Division[2]	May 1917	March 1918
Reference Division[3]	November 1917	March 1918
Service Bureau	March 19, 1918	April 1, 1919
Speaking Division[4]	October 1917	August 1918

Syndicate Picture Division	August 1917	July 1, 1918
Women's War Work Division	November 1917	July 1, 1918
FOREIGN SECTION		
Executive Division:		
Special Commissioners[5]	July 1, 1918	March 31, 1919
Film Division:[6]	July 1918	July 1919
Foreign Picture Service[7]	October 1917	November 15, 1918
Foreign Press Bureau:	November 1917	June 30, 1919
Foreign Press-Cable Service	November 1917	June 30, 1919
Foreign Press-Mail Service	November 1917	December 1918
Work with the Foreign Born Division:[8]	May 1918	May 1918
American-Hungarian Loyalty League		
Czechoslovak Bureau		
Foreign Information Service		
German Bureau		
Italian Bureau		
Jugoslav Bureau		
Lithuanian Bureau		
Polish Bureau		
Russian Department		
Scandinavian Bureau		
Ukrainian Bureau		

Source: CND Report. The Council on National Defense created this table after the end of the war, when it was charged with closing out the CPI's activities. It is re-created here verbatim, except for typographic corrections and minor adjustments in formatting. In addition to tracing the evolution of the CPI's organizational structure, it reflects the chaos that attended that growth. The CND could not find beginning or ending dates for some units and acknowledged that it was unable to fully identify every unit. Some dates, such as those for the foreign commissioners, are wrong. The Four Minute Men, as another example, were abolished on Christmas Eve. Elsewhere in the CND Report, the Labor Publications Division is described murkily as "the outgrowth of the American Alliance for Democracy." In any event, the CND Report is the best that we have to work with.

1 The Speakers Bureau was the Speaking Division until taken over by the Four Minute Men Division in August 1918.

2 The Picture Division was made a part of the Film Division in March 1918.

3 The Reference Division was absorbed by the Service Bureau in March 1918.

4 The Speaking Division was made a Speakers Bureau of the Four Minute Men Division in August 1918.

Table 4 (*continued*)

5 As far as could be ascertained, special commissioners were employed for work in Denmark, England, France, Holland, Italy, Mexico, Romania, Russia, South America, Spain, and Switzerland.

6 The Film Division had nine branch officers in foreign countries.

7 The Foreign Picture Service was taken over by the Film Division, Foreign Section, November 15, 1918.

8 The branches of the Work with the Foreign Born Division were organized at various times and the dates of organization and discontinuance cannot be given. [A more detailed but still incomplete summary of this division is in table 3.]

and not considered much of a manager himself. Some hiring decisions were obvious mismatches. William Bullitt, a journalist who would make a name for himself in diplomacy, was brought on to turn State Department reports into articles on foreign affairs. It was not much of an idea even if the ambitious reporter had been suited to such a routine job, and he quickly gave it up.[25]

Will Irwin arrived at the CPI with high hopes. He believed the CPI "should take the lead in this job [of advertising abroad], just as the French, in the ideal organization of the Alliance, ought to take the lead in military affairs and the British on the seas. It is our special trade." But he was soon complaining of the lack of teamwork and money and, as he told Martin Egan, "the general incompetence of several people now in the field." From the start Irwin expected to return to Europe as a journalist, but that decision was hurried up. He wrangled with Creel over a labor mission to Europe, secretly funded by the CPI, because he felt it needed more liberal members if it was to be effective. In a "stormy" July meeting, Creel called him a Bolshevik sympathizer based on an army report that Creel had confused with someone else, as Irwin learned when he angrily went to see the head of military intelligence. Shortly afterward Edgar Sisson, a Creel favorite, took his place. "My leaving this place—and it was not a case of resignation but of being forced out—was just a piece of office politics," Irwin told a friend. When he wrote about the CPI later, Irwin did not reveal his animus toward Creel, but did not hold back privately. "He cannot find words adequate to damn Creel on every count," Gibson recounted after seeing Irwin in Paris. Irwin told Gibson that Creel was Wilson's "Court Jester & loved as such."[26]

Ford gave as balanced an assessment of Creel as anyone: "Creel was not a logical administrator. In fact, from any other standpoint than the job he was doing, he was no administrator at all. We did not have staff conferences." Yet he "had an instinctive flair for hitting the high spots, seeing where the job was, and with it all a certain humility that was always amazing to me." He deferred to others, but did not always consult. "You had to catch him by the coat tails before he hit the ceiling and exploded about something. Then we were in hot water with Congress."[27]

The siege mentality created by Creel's travails strengthened staff loyalty. "Creel was wonderful when the Committee was small," Maurice F. Lyons, his secretary, said shortly after his slumming speech, "but with his added duties and trials has proven himself to be almost superhuman." "I have seen him day after day stand up under trials that would break a dozen ordinary men," Byoir told a critic, "and the thing is that he has made so few mistakes in a field that was all pioneer work."[28]

"The more I see of this perfectly tremendous business," Ford told his wife, "the more I am amazed that things can go so well. It is because everyone is in it & for it and making it go."[29]

ADMINISTRATION JEALOUSIES

No one called the CPI offices at Jackson Place placid. But they were the calm eye of a hurricane compared to the turbulence Creel generated around it.

Organizations that partnered with the CPI found Creel trying. J. Franklin Jameson of the National Board for Historical Service told a congressional critic of the CPI that Creel's "temperamental peculiarities" so annoyed Republicans that they did not notice "the real merits of the work which he and his associates have been doing." James Shotwell, the first chairman of the NBHS, found Creel "impulsive and outspoken" with the annoying habit of throwing around American slang. Even so, Shotwell recognized Creel was not self-seeking. "He was a roughneck through and through but an honest man." One of the young professors from whom Ford sought assistance took persuading before he agreed. Working with Creel, he had been told, was "playing with fire."[30]

The Wilson administration had its petty jealousies. Joseph Tumulty, relishing his proximity to the president, resented Creel's close relationship with him. Among Wilson's senior wartime administrators, however, Creel got on well with Josephus Daniels, with whom he worked more closely than any other cabinet head. Baker was supportive, despite his endorsement of Blankenhorn's plan to supersede the CPI with field propaganda. Bernard Baruch became one of Creel's "dear friends."[31]

If never perfect, CPI coordination with Baker's and Daniels's departments improved. Creel and Lansing coexisted in a permanent state of dysfunctional antipathy punctuated from time to time by contests for authority. Irwin recalled being in Creel's office when some aide in the State Department called to say Lansing disagreed on some matter. "Tell that hypocritical, double-dealing boss of yours that I will slap his face publicly if he tries any more such tricks upon me." The comment seems impossibly extreme until one remembers Creel's slumming comment.[32]

A proposal from *Everybody's* to serialize a book by Brand Whitlock led to a contest of wills between Creel and Lansing. Whitlock, a journalist and four-term mayor of Toledo, was minister to Belgium. When the Germans displaced the Belgian government to Le Havre, he moved with it. Creel had a double purpose in wanting Whitlock's articles on Belgium published. They made inspiring publicity, and Whitlock, Creel's friend, could replenish his bank account. (He was paid $35,000 for the serial rights.) Lansing objected to serialization as bad precedent. Creel turned to Wilson, who overruled Lansing. "Belgium: The Atrocities" and other articles, illustrated with Raemaekers's drawings, appeared in *Everybody's* throughout 1918.[33]

Secretary of State Robert Lansing quarreled with Creel from their first encounter, and he often lost. Lansing considered Creel, a Wilson favorite, a radical who should be nowhere near diplomatic news. Creel said Lansing was so dim "his ideas were annual." (Library of Congress)

Breckenridge Long, who occasionally became involved in publicity, operated as Lansing's factotum when, toward the end of 1917, he proposed measures for improving press relations. Among insiders, Arthur Sweetser told Lippmann, Long was considered "absolutely unqualified" to be third assistant secretary. Long's hefty campaign contributions, and possibly his zealous attacks on Hughes, earned him the job. He did not mention Creel by name in the two letters he wrote to Wilson. But Long's suggestion to create a board of journalists invested with "great" power to censor news was an obvious slap at the CPI and reflected Lansing's preference for heavy-handed treatment of the press. The proposal was pretentiously written, unrealistic in wanting to bar journalists from reporting American losses on the battlefield, and short of specifics on implementation, other than to say board members must be "absolutely loyal to the administration." Wilson told Long the CPI was doing the best it could.[34]

Lansing's decision to keep the CPI at arm's length was mutually detrimental. "We are taking very little part in what they are doing and are informed of what is going on through the telegrams which are sent through the Department." Patchin complained to Gibson, "We are never consulted." In this atmosphere, the recriminations mounted. "The whole legation is *poisoned* by antagonism to your department—Do you know that?" Whitehouse informed Creel. "It seems that it must come from instructions or lack of instructions from Washington."[35]

House was an altogether different kind of rival. He had no official title and no bureaucracy at his command. He engaged in issues Wilson bid him to undertake and weighed in on matters that interested him. Publicity was one of those matters. Because he was close to Wilson, he was sought out by journalists, whom he advised on how to "handle the news from Washington correctly." As befit an éminence grise, he had to be paid attention. "I do not know how far House speaks for the President in this matter of propaganda," Lord Northcliffe told Lloyd George in late 1917, when he headed the British Mission in New York, "but in the course of our interviews he referred to it again and again." House's relentless effort to draw British spies, political actors like Robert Woolley, and journalists like Carl Ackerman into his orbit had an operational side. In addition to gleaning their ideas, which he sometimes passed to Wilson, he used these individuals to achieve objectives he considered worthwhile.[36]

House floated numerous propaganda schemes, some quite inventive and inspired by William Wiseman, who had taken rooms in the New York City building where the colonel lived. A joint and complicated publicity-cum-intelligence operation in Russia won Wilson's approval in mid-1917. It employed British novelist Somerset Maugham and a Czech-American named Emanuel Voska, who reappears later in this book. The secret mission to bolster Russian enthusiasm for carrying on the war ended around the time Sisson went to Russia. House also concocted the idea of a debate on war issues to be published simultaneously in the pages of the *New York World* and *Berliner Tageblatt.* He thought this could bring about peace. House broached the idea to Wiseman and Lord Northcliffe, who approved, as did *World* editor Frank Cobb. When Wilson vetoed the plan, House persisted without success. It would "bring out disagreements" with the Allies, Wilson wrote with emphasis; they "*have not the same views with regard to peace that we have* by any means."[37]

House's overlap with the CPI brief manifested itself in one of the most powerful pieces of American propaganda during the war, Wilson's Fourteen Points speech spelling out American "War Aims and Peace Terms." The address aimed to dissuade the Bolsheviks from negotiating peace with Germany, to encourage liberal Europeans to maintain support for the war, to spell out what Wilson meant by a reasonable peace without victory, and to reiterate his case for the

Colonel Edward M. House in his New York apartment, where he cultivated journalists, politicians, and British spies. With a strong interest in propaganda, he was Creel's most formidable rival. The CPI chairman called him "a high-class sponge, with the added beauty of being easy to squeeze." (Edward Mandell House Papers, Manuscript and Archives, Yale University Library)

creation of an association of nations to guarantee "political independence and territorial integrity."[38]

Creel claimed CPI patrimony for the speech. Because his assertion has been accepted by many historians, it is worthwhile to describe in detail what really happened. Creel's claim begins with a January 3 cable from Russia in which Sisson asked, "If President Wilson will re-state anti-imperialistic war aims and democratic peace requests of America thousand words or less, almost placard paragraphs, short sentences, I can get it fed into Germany . . . and can utilize Russian version potentially in army and everywhere." As Creel described his next steps, he immediately took the cable to Wilson, who needed urging. Wilson supposedly said he "had never tried his hand at slogans and advertising copy." Two or three days later, Wilson called Creel to the White House to "let me read the address." Wilson gave him a copy of the speech with editorial marks as a souvenir. Sisson argued that his cable "very likely had an effect in shaping and simplifying the external form of the 'Fourteen Points,' decided the movement of their expression, and led the President to address to the Russian people the general introduction to the concrete Peace terms."[39]

The problems with these assertions begin with timing. Wilson set the speech in motion before Christmas, when he asked House to have the Inquiry prepare background on war aims. Lippmann was one of the authors. On Friday evening, January 4, House arrived at the White House with a memorandum and toiled with Wilson over the weekend on the speech. The detailed description of that process in House's diary makes no mention of Creel, Sisson, or placard paragraphs. It may be that Creel saw Wilson on January 3 or 4, but neither Wilson's nor Creel's papers indicate this. What they do show is a request from Creel, dated January 4, for a meeting on Monday, January 6, and a note the next day in which Creel vaguely said he had "a memorandum of suggestions" and "much cheering news to give you from Petrograd." The Monday meeting was set for 4:30. It was too late in the process for serious rewriting. That would have been the likely occasion for Wilson to let Creel read his completed speech. Wilson delivered the speech the next day at noon.[40]

Sisson and Creel were not the only ones to claim credit for the speech. The US ambassador to Russia, David Francis, did as well, citing two telegrams he sent to Wilson. Arthur Bullard, working for the CPI in Russia, said "everyone is claiming the exclusive honor for having influenced the President" to deliver the speech. What is true is that Wilson's speech served the propaganda purposes

Sisson envisioned. It derived power from the succinctness of its points, as in "A free, open-minded, and absolutely impartial *adjustment of all colonial claims.*" The CPI papered the world with the speech. In Petrograd alone Sisson put up two million related posters and handbills.[41]

House and Creel did not interact with each on the same level of intimacy that House did with Woolley or Ackerman. Creel's name appears in House's diary on two occasions prior to his Church of the Ascension speech—and eight days in all (compared to twenty for Ackerman, whose correspondence with the colonel was vastly greater). Prior to the 1916 campaign, Creel asked House what he should write to help the president, perhaps because he was angling to be part of Woolley's publicity bureau. Creel sent publications and reports to House. House suggested names of people who might be appointed to the CPI. These communications paled in comparison to House's more meaningful contact with Arthur Bullard and others on the CPI.[42]

Creel could not fail to see that House's agenda intruded on his. He must have known the colonel championed Lippmann's propaganda proposal on the eve of the war in 1917; he may have been aware that House was a conduit for Lippmann's complaints from Europe in the summer of 1918. Creel had to suspect that the feline colonel was not his champion with Wilson and that he would usurp his authority if he could.

Be that as it may, little evidence exists of open hostility between the two men until after the war. In 1926, Creel used House's self-serving published diaries to show his treachery to the president. He told Ray Stannard Baker that House exaggerated his influence with Wilson and that House "asserted that he had presented matters to Mr. Wilson when he had never spoken of them at all." House also kept his reservations about Creel for a later time. In his diary in late 1917, House noted that Creel was "prejudicing the President against Lansing," but he does not seem to have taken that up with Wilson. After the war, he told George Sylvester Viereck, with whom he developed a surprising friendship, that Creel "was responsible for the excesses [in selling the war]. Wilson was at all times ready to weigh things."[43]

The two men had good reason to avoid open enmity. Each enjoyed a privileged relationship with Wilson. As Irwin put it, "No man except Colonel E. M. House stood on more familiar relations with Wilson than George Creel." Confrontation was in neither one's interest. When the Lippmann-inspired imbroglio over field propaganda angered Wilson, House distanced himself from it. He told Hugh Frazier, "Cables with reference to propaganda are causing friction here and I should prefer not to have reports of this character made to me." When Cobb and another journalist brought House a plan to mobilize writers to explain the war, House made a point of telling Wilson that he "steered them away from any conflict with Creel, and they understand that it is necessary to in no way encroach upon his field."[44]

House had no compunction about urging the removal of Ambassador Stovall, who was a boyhood friend of the president, or Tumulty. "Wilson ought to get rid of Daniels," he told McCormick, whose help he tried to enlist, "and you should be appointed in his place." House was probably happy to see Creel stumble over his "slumming" remark. At the end of the fractious week following his comment, House dined with Wilson, who worried that Congress would withhold money if Creel was not fired. "I suggested he might send him abroad in some capacity, and to this he agreed if it could be done," House recorded in his diary. "He wondered if Frank Cobb would undertake the work. I believed he would." But House does not seem to have pushed beyond that, perhaps because he knew Wilson's loyalty to Creel foreclosed drastic action.[45]

Shortly after his "slumming" comment, Creel wrote to House, "I am eager to see you for a long talk." Whether or not they met is unclear. But by the end of 1918, House was addressing Creel as "George" in letters.[46]

THE SUPER PATRIOTS ATTACK CPI PURITY

A culture of surveillance and incrimination gripped the nation. The CPI, which had energized campaigns to sniff out disloyalty, became a victim of them.

The American Defense Society worked with the CPI when it was in their mutual interest and criticized Creel for not wanting to forbid the use of the German language, which he resisted because it would preclude getting his propaganda to those groups. The ADS wrote to him in March 1918, "We protest that the attitude of the Committee is so pacific that now some of its work amounts to giving comfort to the enemy."[47]

Such critiques were tinged with self-interest. The Vigilantes, which had ties to the CPI, was led by Hermann Hagedorn. He and other members were aligned with Theodore Roosevelt, whose hatred of Wilson was pathological. Hagedorn tried to set up a German-American organization with a mission similar to the CPI's Friends of German Democracy. Creel "vigorously opposed it," and the idea died. Hagedorn also blamed Creel for blocking his appointment as a racial advisor to the Interior Department.[48]

The CPI had the same hot-cold partnership with the National Security League as it did with the ADS. The NSL mounted a disingenuous publicity campaign against Creel based on his hastily written introduction to *Two Thousand Questions and Answers about the War.* "The National Security League," the *New York Sun* reported, "took pleasure last night in announcing that at its request the George H. Doran Publishing Company had withdrawn from circulation a book which it had published."* The NSL failed to mention that the CPI had taken action weeks before to suppress the book and replace it with one that corrected supposed errors. Whatever satisfaction Creel might have taken in proclaiming the NSL guilty of "singular dishonesty and indecency," the episode was one more instance in which he was seen in a negative public light.[49]

Creel's willingness to work with the populist Nonpartisan League embroiled him in a controversy with business interests. The league was formed in the Midwest to address farmers' complaints about high fees at grain elevators and lofty interest rates on mortgages. It attacked state political leaders who backed business. When some league members argued the war benefited the rich, conservatives said they purveyed "damnable Hun propaganda." Creel stepped in to reorient the league by arranging for its president to meet with Wilson and Hoover. As a result, Creel told Wilson in February 1918, "The League is one of your foremost supporters, is backing the war, and is backing Hoover." Creel told the president he did not give the league "approval of any kind," but it appeared that he did when CPI speakers were linked to the league in places like Minnesota. By April Wilson felt compelled to tell Creel to back off, as "we are getting into deep water in that part of the country." In an attempt to patch things up, Creel stated publicly that he had not given approval for the league. In fact, however, he had inferred approval in a letter to an Oklahoma farm leader. Creel said the government did not consider "it an act of disloyalty to be a member of the League." When the letter was used in a handbill, anti-league forces painted him a socialist.[50]

In a perverse twist, the shrouded nature of the CPI's ties to its foreign-born organizations made them more vulnerable to attack. When the Department of Justice investigated the Friends of German Democracy, Creel had to step in. "Quite confidentially," he told A. Bruce Bielaski, chief of Justice's Bureau of Investigation, "the organization was formed by me and supported by this Com-

---

* The capacity of patriotic groups to devour their own is evident in the fact that the president of Doran had just been named to the NSL advisory board.

mittee." Creel also had to explain to Bielaski that the American-Hungarian Loyalty League was a CPI organization.[51]

Defending the league's chairman, Budapest-born Alexander Konta, was more difficult. Well regarded in Hungarian intellectual groups and married to the daughter of a St. Louis brewer, Konta was a power broker among his people. Early in 1918, military intelligence chief Ralph Van Deman pronounced Konta "thoroughly loyal." But reports to the contrary continued to surface along with concerns over his financial practices with the league. Konta resigned. He later acknowledged to a Senate committee he was in touch with Bernhard Dernburg and Heinrich Albert before the United States entered the war but insisted on his loyalty. After the war was over, Creel defended Konta against "brokenarched" representatives of the Justice Department.[52]

Despite his indiscretions, Creel was wary of associations that might call CPI loyalty into question. He "kicked out" Louis Hammerling, president of the American Association of Foreign Language Newspapers, when he learned Hammerling considered himself a member of the CPI staff. "I have no charges to make against him myself," he confided to Bjorkman, "but the various investigating branches of government worried me no little." A similar fate seems to have befallen Walter Niebuhr, associate director of the Division of Films. The case against Niebuhr, a German-American who had edited an Illinois newspaper, became a tangle of allegations about disloyalty, some of which were suggested in a story by Carl Ackerman. Evidence of disloyalty was flimsy. Before the United States went into the war, Niebuhr had worked on films to promote preparedness, but Creel dismissed him after a briefing by military intelligence. Niebuhr's name, like Konta's, appeared without prejudice in Creel's postwar chronicle of the CPI.[53]

No one was safe from suspicion and accusations. Before joining the CPI, Vienna-born Edward Bernays was investigated by MID, met personally with Van Deman, and arranged letters of recommendation from executives at *Vanity Fair*, *Harper's Bazar*, and the New York Hippodrome. On the eve of her departure to Europe, Creel told Whitehouse that a "great many people have written to me, stating that you are now, and always have been, a very strong proGerman." Rumors had it she was a German spy.[54]

By early April, his exasperation soaring, Creel requested that Ralph Van Deman conduct an "instant investigation" of every person on his staff. The substantive findings were not particularly damning. Only fourteen people fell under some kind of suspicion. Their transgressions mostly amounted to pro-

German statements before the war, a few radical comments, and charges of disloyalty from which they had already been absolved. But the sixty-odd-page report was full of gratuitous comments based on hearsay and supposition provided by anonymous informants. Sisson, a Republican, was a socialist, a charge apparently based on his having gone to Russia for the CPI. A Dutchman who worked for Irwin had made negative but unspecified comments about the government and seemed "utterly unfit to be associated with a bureau of the Government." A translator working for Ford "was accused of mistranslating a speech of Paderewski's into Polish." Irwin, it was pointed out, believed "the Bolsheviki to be men of high ideals and correct ideals who sprang them at the wrong time." E. S. Rochester, editor of the *Official Bulletin,* "was a frequenter of the Occidental hotel, the proprietor of which, one Bucholtz, was under suspicion of being disloyal." The News Division employed socialists and "is evidently in need of a thorough house-cleaning." An unnamed informant, who visited the CPI, told the investigators it was full "of Labor people and I.W.W.'s."[55]

In July, Creel refuted the charges in a letter to Marlborough Churchill, who replaced Van Deman. But there was no end to the attacks. The day after Creel wrote to Churchill, he answered charges made by Ralph Easley. Easley, a Gompers man who considered the IWW an "auxiliary of the German espionage system," told Creel about intelligence he picked up at the City Club in New York, an elite gentlemen's club with a civic do-good agenda. Some members said the CPI employed wild radicals of the IWW type. "Greenwich Village is moving to Washington," one member told Easley, an allusion to the socialists who frequented that part of New York. A "Greenwich Village restaurant," the informant said, had reportedly set up shop around the corner from the CPI offices on Jackson Place.[56]

NOT AN EASY MAN TO GET ON WITH

Toward the end of the war, correspondent Reginald Wright Kauffman wrote a novel "to typify the evils of censorship." The antagonist in *Victorious* is a censor with "a cadaverous face" and dull eyes. Lieutenant Garcia's foreign name is starkly out of sync with the hero, a young freckle-faced journalist named Andy Brown. When he is not whoring, Garcia takes bribes to cover up inadequate airplane production. Brown and his fellow journalists are furious over being barred from reporting that American troops have finally gone into battle. If they make trouble, the correspondents are told, "We'll get the Committee on Public

Information, back home, to blow you up for fakers." Brown bucks the censors to reveal how poorly troops are equipped. Losing his accreditation, he joins the army and dies saving Garcia's life.[57]

In no respect was Kauffman a pacifist. The correspondent for the *Philadelphia North American* belonged to the American Defense Society and the Vigilantes. Andy Brown's dying words are, "The Cause is bigger than its mistakes!" But Kauffman matched Creel in pugnacious, skewering prose. His flagrant resistance to censorship led to the revocation of his AEF press credentials. His complaints about censorship echoed Andy Brown's. The novel gave him an opportunity to take a swipe at the CPI, which he disliked as much as his friend Herman Hagedorn did.[58]

In the years to come, many of presidential media advisors would be roasted at Gridiron dinners. But Creel was a bigger target than most due to the jarring new relationship he forged between the White House and the press. "From one man and with a pencil [the CPI] has grown into a department of such magnitude it almost staggers the imagination," the trade journal *American Press* editorialized. It had become "a gigantic news and publicity machine the likes of which never entered the thought of any living American before. The great news gathering organizations fade into pigmy proportions alongside the activities of the Committee on Public Information, which uses every known medium of publicity to reach the people."[59]

As previously noted, but worth repeating given its significance, journalists came to rely upon and resent the CPI. On two occasions, Harry Tammen and Frederick Bonfils, Creel's antagonistic former employers at the *Denver Post,* angrily protested to McAdoo and their Colorado senators, as well as to Creel, that they had not been given some CPI material. In one case the CPI had split its syndicated features among Sunday papers in each community so each would have exclusives. The *Denver Post* wanted it all. The nation's press, a western newspaper complained, "must resort to the only source left, the pitiless publicity of the paid piper."[60]

Even more irksome than the surfeit of handouts was censorship, the evils of which were often put at Creel's doorstep. This was not always deserved, but Creel's outsized personality and personal attacks on people made it seem so. As vehemently as he denied being a censor, even his friends referred to 10 Jackson Place as the "office of the censor."[61]

"Censorship has caused much confusion," the AP noted. The press was unaccustomed to it and censors had to "feel their way experimentally." Not everyone expressed frustration so charitably. Furious over cable delays, *New York Times* managing editor Carl Van Anda stormed into Rogers's New York office in March 1918 to demand that the censoring of incoming *Times* cables cease, that two or three hours be set aside each day for handling press cables exclusively, and that rates be lowered. All this was refused. Van Anda was back again in May when the aurora borealis delayed the transmission of *New York Times* cables.[62]

AEF correspondents were unhappy with censorship of the trivial issues (such as Frederick Palmer telling Kauffman to stop coloring the French in terms of "wine and women") and of the monumental (such as equipment shortages, the reporting of which led to Kauffman's fictional Andy Brown losing his credentials). The appointment of highly regarded Palmer as chief press officer was supposed to bring about comity. But he was seen as rigid, and as an army major with a reserve commission, he could not push stories through the system. "Palmer has *no* power and all the correspondents know it," Wythe Williams complained to his bosses at the *Times*. When Palmer was relieved of his censorship duties, he was glad to move into a less thankless job.[63]

Journalists wanted responsibility for regulating themselves. David Lawrence, Carl Ackerman, and others called for a censorship advisory board made up of journalists. The *Baltimore Sun* argued for a war publicity bureau organized by the newspapers under "a leading journalist of their own selection." Consulting with government departments, this individual would "determine what should be suppressed and what should be published." Kauffman and Williams independently made the fatuous argument that Congress should be responsible for censorship.[64]

The American War Publicity League in France, conceived in Paris in late 1917, indirectly criticized both the CPI and AEF press relations. The league "was no association of irresponsibles," wrote Kauffman, who was a member. It wanted to counter two misimpressions. The first was that over optimistic expectations had been built up on the speed with which the AEF would get into the fighting; the second that American reporters treated the war as they would "a murder trial or a baseball game," making it difficult for the public to render "intelligence" support. The league recommended that American newspaper owners organize themselves in Washington to achieve better results. Norman Hapgood was elected president of the league. He tapped the old-boy network of the 1916 Wilson campaign by enlisting help from Vance McCormick. The league came to nothing. Pershing refused to meet with it. Clemenceau told Hapgood he preferred censorship over accurate reporting.[65]

Although Creel deserved credit for facilitating news from the front, he insinuated himself into the suppressive side of AEF press relations. He kept tabs on Kauffman, whom he considered "guilty of misrepresentation." When mail censors intercepted two articles by Wythe Williams attacking censorship and even suggesting graft in connection with it, Creel alerted the AEF. In a memo to Williams, Colonel Nolan cited Creel's view of his reporting as evidence why he should lose his accreditation. Williams thought the AEF should adopt CPI voluntary censorship, except "Creel has proved himself a mis-fit."[66]

The *New York Tribune*'s Heywood Hale Broun worked for the CPI, a mismatch that did not last long. As a war correspondent he was notorious for the flippant salutes he gave to Palmer. Broun lost his credentials over stories he wrote upon returning to the United States. Creel blocked accreditation for other *Tribune* reporters until he had assurances Broun's violation was not part of a *Tribune* policy to discredit the war effort. He attacked Broun in the *Independent* over a minor story he wrote on censorship. "That Mr. Creel has done a gross injustice to me hurts nobody but me and Mr. Creel," Broun responded in the *Tribune*. "Probably it hurts me most. Creel is harmed only in his immortal soul. I find it hard to wait until judgment day for satisfaction."[67]

Creel constantly made news. Journalists considered him "the most picturesque figure in the public life of Washington today." In early April 1918, he flew from Washington to Baltimore with a message for a Liberty Loan meeting. The publicity stunt did double duty as a demonstration of the capabilities of army pilots and airplanes. After putting the plane through rolls and dives that forced Creel to put his head between his legs, the pilot made a violent landing at Pimlico racetrack. The plane's nose stuck in the earth, splintering the rudder and propeller. Pilot and passenger could not get out of the cockpit until a ladder was found. Apart from nausea, Creel was unscathed. Newspapers had yet another colorful story about him.[68]

Creel had his cheering section. Some pointed out the CPI "was new and experimental," as the *Cherokee (OK) Republican* allowed; Creel was "doing a big and creditable service to the country." Arthur Brisbane, who purchased the *Washington Times*, told Creel no newspaper in town was "really friendly to him." He offered to take whatever the CPI put out, "from a paragraph to a page, exactly as you want it." This had to be heartening, but the fact that friendly journalists had to defend Creel illustrated the drumbeat of negative headlines he generated: "Why Pay for Comedy When We Have a Creel Committee" (*Washington Post*); "The Censor Needs Censoring" (*Norfolk Virginian Pilot*); "A One-Creel Drama" (*Muskogee Phoenix*). As table 5 shows, when Creel was the subject of a story, it was typically negative. His blunders made him ideal for a type of feature commonly run in those days: short quips or jokes commenting on the current scene. When Creel's name was mentioned in passing in a news story, the results were relatively favorable. The CPI was held in higher esteem than he was.[69]

Creel admonished his staff not to defend the CPI against criticism. If they could not stand the heat, they should leave. He insisted he did not care about being criticized. Yet he compulsively responded to criticism, often by starting out with a disclaimer that he was not prone to answering criticism and followed by heated refutation. "As you know, I have never made a single reply to any newspaper criticism, no matter how unjust or untrue," he wrote to fair-minded David Lawrence, and then proceeded to denounce an *Evening Post* editorial as

Table 5. George Creel in the News

George Creel's name appeared in 326 articles in the *Hartford Courant,* the *Nashville Tennessean,* and the *Los Angeles Times* from April 1917 to December 1918. These stories were identified by searching "newspapers.com" with the terms "George Creel" and "Creel." This tabulation shows the attitudes of the stories toward the chairman of the Committee on Public Information.

Stories	Positive	Neutral	Negative
Creel as the focus:			
Articles	9	6	66
Fillers/Jokes/Quips*	0	0	87
Editorials	1	0	45
	10	6	198
Creel mentioned:			
Articles	4	99	2
Fillers/Jokes/Quips*	0	1	1
Editorials	1	4	0
	5	104	3

Source: Lauren West

* These are items only a few sentences long. They were a common entertainment feature at the time. They typically commented on the contemporary political scene and personal life of public figures.

having no "word of truth in it from beginning to end." "If these sort of lies were paid for by German money," Creel told another critic, "they could not serve the German purpose more absolutely."[70]

Creel's counterattacks could backfire egregiously. He said he was misquoted on the benefits of Wilson not adequately preparing the country for war and regretted that no stenographer was there to record the milder statement he actually made. Then a stenographer came forward to verify that Creel had said what he was reported to have said. He resuscitated controversies best left to die. In a speech to journalists in Columbus, Ohio, months after the July Hoax, Creel said the AP reporter who questioned his embellished submarine attack story had been branded a liar by a British court of inquiry and expelled from the base where he was located. As "a matter of record," he added, the AP's premature reporting of the first troops in France around the same time was made possible by bribing a telegraph operator. Neither charge was a matter of record or remotely accurate. The AP board, made up of esteemed newspaper executives, was incensed. "Creel was a public scandal," said normally cool-headed Victor Lawson, owner of the *Chicago Daily News*. Creel needed to be fired. The board thought Congress should investigate him.[71]

A set-to with Kauffman was a parody of Creel's needless quarrels. In September 1918, Kauffman damned the CPI film *America's Answer* as misleading. In a letter to the editor of the *New York Tribune,* which was published under the headline "Creeling Again," he pointed out that the footage did not match the events it purported to depict. The time of year was wrong, the location was wrong, and the caption "the Huns, retreating before our men" appeared under men in Canadian uniforms. Although the letter was buried in the paper and easy to ignore, Creel wrote to the editor, "Only a fool or a Kauffman could have read into the pictures any intent to make people believe that the words 'our men' referred to American soldiers." Kauffman, a Republican, and Creel continued the argument in personal letters full of name-calling and shouts as to which of them was more politically partisan.[72]

Creel asked Walter Rogers, with the help of navy censor George Baker, to look into the *Chronicle* because it was "spending a great deal of money, circulating attacks upon me, and I have the curiosity to know who pays for the magazine, and the names of those actually in charge." The report came back that the *Chronicle* was a society journal circulated to a private list of subscribers. Its angel was a stout matron residing at New York's Ritz Carlton.[73]

Jason Rogers, publisher of the *New York Globe* and a CPI supporter, was more diplomatic than Creel could ever be after Creel called a *Globe* editorial "another example of sheer stupidity and utter recklessness." Creel's attitude, Rogers replied, explained "better than words why you are so grossly misunderstood. You put things too d— bluntly instead of saying them so the other fellow can come back pleasantly with some degree of dignity and kindliness."[74]

Criticism of Creel by his former brethren in the press reached a crescendo around the time of his comments on preparedness and "slumming." The *New York Times* liberally ran CPI material in its pages but from Creel's first days in office had little good to say about him. Louis Wiley privately suggested that he be replaced by Frank Noyes, the president of the *Washington Star* and the Associated Press. The *Times* editorialized, "Actual or inferential responsibility for the doings and utterances of Mr. George Creel cannot any longer, consistent with the public welfare and comfort, be borne by the Administration."[75]

When the American Newspaper Publishers Association met in April, Hopewell Rogers, the ANPA president and business manager of the *Chicago Daily News,* called for the creation of "a newspaper body in Washington with both the ability and the judgment to gather information as to the business methods of the Government." Newspapers would use its findings to "properly criticize or condone those responsible for the conduct of our affairs." This, Rogers argued, would allow "us to rid ourselves of the incompetent and disloyal head of that department, who glories in our unpreparedness."[76]

Creel demanded the ANPA investigate the CPI. Its newly elected president Frank Glass of the *Birmingham News* was willing to do so. When he encountered difficulty recruiting prominent publishers, Glass asked Wilson to bless the undertaking, which he proposed to broaden into an inquiry into "*the entire publicity question.*" The members "would be experts in publicity and in the psychology of reaching public opinion in strategic ways. They could clarify the present confusion, and would suggest means of coordination between all sources of news and the agencies for its diffusion." Wilson refused. Journalists "would wish to see the thing changed *de novo,* and my expectation would be that they would make recommendations which I would not accept and that the new situation created by my failure to accept them would be more unpleasant than the present situation."[77]

"Dumb," Creel blurted out during a walk one day with war correspondent Herbert Corey. "Thick-headed, saps." He was talking about journalists. Creel, Corey thought, "had been called on to transform the Washington correspondents almost overnight from a body of reporters to a body of propagandists and he found the going slow. He spoke of them only in words of one syllable. They used the same formula in speaking of Creel. The advantage was on their side, naturally, because there were more of them and they could say what they had to say in more different places."[78]

By the time the war was over, Creel was shorthand for everything wrong with government-press relations. When AP general manager Melville Stone conferred with George Barr Baker in Paris on improving news transmission, the subject turned to French restrictions. Stone's bureau chief Elmer Roberts offhandedly observed that the chief French censor was "a sort of George Creel of the Clemenceau administration. He is not a very easy man to get on with."[79]

CONGRESS AND CREEL

From the first, the Committee on Public Information had contentious relations with Capitol Hill. Wilson created the CPI without congressional hearings or approval. Its funding came from Wilson's National Security and Defense Fund. Congress had no opportunity to set its budget or review its work. Legislators criticized Wilson's creation of other wartime agencies for similar reasons. The CPI's lack of accountability was especially grating, however, because of long-standing legislative hostility to a chief executive shaping public opinion with which they would have to contend.[80]

By tradition legislators believed they—the voice of the people—set policy, and the president implemented it. They had regarded President Roosevelt's publicity efforts as executive overreach. The CPI dwarfed anything Roosevelt dared to attempt. In February 1918, senators went straight to that underlying issue in complaining the CPI's use of paper limited the print run of the *Congressional Record*, "the only uncensored publication in the United States." One agitated senator claimed, incorrectly, the CPI used $5,000 worth of paper a day. Time and again legislators said, in these or similar words, the CPI was "founded upon somewhat doubtful authority."[81]

Legislators became intensely aware of the CPI during the debate over Wilson's proposed censorship clause, which Creel was expected to implement. To many in Congress he remained chiefly a censor without legitimacy. Lodge called Creel "an unknown somebody plucked from the bushes the day before yesterday." As the CPI grew into a large propaganda ministry, legislators complained they did not know what it was doing. After the *Official Bulletin* appeared, Senator Frank Brandegee asked, "Under what authority it is published, and how the expense of it is paid?" When the CPI announced it was working overseas, an Indiana legislator introduced a resolution to ask why. "It seems to me that this committee is assuming more authority than has been delegated to it by Congress."[82]

Partisanship was not absent. When the administration stumbled in war making, Republicans used it as an opportunity to attack it. "The Republicans hate President Wilson as the Devil hates holy water," Congressman Edward Pou told Creel. Wilson reciprocated. His relationship with Lodge was a microcosm of this enmity. Lodge, a Senate leader and close friend of Roosevelt, was the first senator with an earned doctorate and possessed intellectual and moral self-assurance; Wilson, a bitter enemy of Roosevelt, was the first president with a doctorate and equally certain. The two men did not stop at questioning each other's policies; they questioned each other's character.[83]

Republicans viewed the CPI as a publicity agent for Wilson. Senator Boies Penrose called Creel the "editor of the Court Chronicle." His penchant for getting in trouble made him a useful "whipping boy," as Ford put it. Wilson loyalists winced at his mistakes. Each new one added to the litany recited routinely on the House and Senate floors.[84]

In March 1918, captions on four army photographs of training airplanes at a factory created a firestorm of criticism. A CPI writer incorrectly wrote that hundreds of planes had been shipped and "thousands upon thousands will follow." It was an innocent slip, but did not seem so under the circumstances. Airplane production was far behind schedule, which brought forth charges of incompetence (which was true) and corruption (which Kauffman reprised in his novel *Victorious,* but which was not true, as an inquiry led by Charles Evans Hughes later concluded). A Republican senator brought the errant airplane captions to the attention of Lawrence Rubel, the head of the Picture Division. Rubel withdrew the photos but neglected to keep them out of the *Official Bulletin.* A senator called it "a crisis of extraordinary magnitude." The Senate Committee on Military Affairs summoned Rubel for an explanation.[85]

The National Security League called for legislation to create a five-person committee, three of whom did not hold public office, to supervise the CPI. Although nothing came of that, the controversy did not die. In July, the *Paris Herald* ran a story in which it said that Newton Baker, who was in Europe, had seen "1,000 American monoplanes and biplanes in flight." A few weeks later the CPI issued photos of Baker inspecting planes. The two events were conflated by Missouri senator James Reed, who called Creel "a licensed liar." As unfair as this was (Baker was inspecting French planes), Creel was guilty of exaggerating air readiness. For instance, he told Judge Lindsey, whom he sent on a speaking tour, to mention news reports of high production levels.[86]

Reed, a Democrat, had a special reason to hate Creel. As a young journalist in Kansas City, Creel excoriated him for his association with city boss Tom Pendergast. Other legislators joined Reed in long-simmering grudges. In 1914, Creel portrayed then-governor Hiram Johnson as a naked opportunist. "Like the one speck of rot," he wrote in *Everybody's*, "his lack of faith and vision, his incapacity for disinterested effort, are being absorbed by the rank and file and petty greeds are crowding out all warmth and breadth and brotherhood." To legislators' charges he had gone too far, Creel later claimed he gave "a fair and dispassionate study of Johnson as a presidential candidate." The article provoked a "beehive of protest"—the phrase was Lincoln Steffens's, who visited *Everybody's* offices at the time—and the editors had to cut two pages from a war article by Frederick Palmer to publish all the refutations.[87]

In search of evidence of Creel's recklessness, legislators excavated the piles of writing he produced as a journalist. During the debate over the Sedition Act in April 1918, Senator James Watson read into the record editorials that Creel wrote in Denver. One impugned the founding fathers as a bunch of "rich men" who wanted to protect their property. Watson was not above quoting out of context, but several articles were truly incendiary, among them Creel's claim of "crimes in high places" and the statement the Senate was "a body that sits in despotism." Watson called Creel a "slivering sneerer" who could go to jail under the Espionage Act.[88]

In the summer of 1917, Robert Woolley told Creel he should resign if he was required to undergo a congressional investigation, as his usefulness would be over. Creel stood his ground as various punishments were proposed. Penrose called for an investigation of the July Hoax. During an investigation of War Department delays, Representative Frederick Gillett, a dogged opponent of Roosevelt's fledgling publicity machine, complained of the lack of information about CPI salaries. "The longer the publicity [on the CPI's budget] is delayed in these matters," Gillett said, "the more pitiless it will be when it comes." Creel provided a sketchy report.[89]

Matters probably would have gone on inconclusively were it not for missteps in the spring of 1918. It was shortly after Rubel's overblown picture caption that Creel rejoiced in the nation's lack of military preparedness in a speech to the National Conference of American Lecturers. Legislators were outraged at such a comment when Americans were dying in battle. People who agreed with Creel, Gillett said, "are in jail and others are in lunatic asylums." Gillett used the occasion to reiterate that Congress did not know how the CPI spent its money. "George Creel, expensive luxury!" exclaimed David Lawrence in the wake of these attacks. "The efforts of the committee are constantly being discredited in congress and elsewhere." The CPI's work was valuable, he observed, but should confine itself to being a medium for the statements of others.[90]

Creel's next gaff came in response to an inquiry from Representative Allen Treadway. At home in Massachusetts, Treadway was appreciated as the affable owner of the famed Red Lion Inn in the Berkshires. In the House of Representatives, the tall, athletic Republican was known for combativeness against "hapless political opponents." In this case he charged that mail to AEF soldiers was held up in favor of copious CPI materials. A House resolution asked the postmaster general for information about mail practices. This was a simple request, without Treadway's charges included. Creel, however, prepared a response for Burleson that accused Treadway of "an assertion the absolute baselessness of which could have been ascertained by a telephone inquiry." This was mild by Creel's standards of insult, but the recipient was no ordinary citizen. At Treadway's instigation, a special bipartisan committee was formed to review the letter, which it found "impertinent." The committee recommended returning it to Burleson. The House agreed without a single dissenting vote. By the *New York Times*'s reckoning, this was only the fourth time in history the House had taken such action.[91]

Creel's slumming remark was worse. He maligned all of Congress, not a lone member. Legislators called for withholding CPI funds if Creel were not sacked. As Wilson indicated to House, replenishment of his National Security and Defense Fund was in jeopardy. Creel offered his resignation. Perhaps, as House wrote in his diary, the president toyed with giving Creel a new assignment. Daniels, with whom the president also conferred, acknowledged that "Creel came very near losing his job." But Wilson conveyed a different message to Daniels than to House. "Our friend Creel is in trouble and we must save him," Daniels recalled. Wilson called Creel on the phone: "If necessary, I will go up there myself as your counsel."[92]

In the event, Daniels went to Capitol Hill to see Edward Pou, who represented his North Carolina district and was a longtime friend. Pou chaired the Rules Committee, which had under consideration a resolution from Treadway calling for an investigation of Creel's remarks. Pou said he had never seen legislators "so incensed." The only way out was for Creel to apologize. Pou would stall on Treadway's resolution until tempers calmed. At first Creel refused to express remorse. "It was all the President and I could do to persuade him to accept Pou's advice," Daniels said. Creel's apology was far from abject; he confessed to giving "a quick and thoughtless answer that lent itself to exaggeration and distortion." Treadway noted it took Creel five days to express contrition.[93]

Unsatisfied, the committee demanded that Creel address five charges, summarized by one newspaper as "that Creel is a Socialist; that Creel does not believe in the American form of government; that in his so-called 'muck-raking' days he had attacked the constitution and the judiciary; that I.W.W. members are employed by the committee; and that its news releases have proved inaccurate."[94]

The Democrat majority in the House might have headed off any inquiry, but Democrats also had concerns. In a meeting with the president on May 23, a week after Creel's apology, Swager Sherley, chairman of the House Appropriations Committee, said hearings about the replenishment of Wilson's war fund should include discussion of the CPI, given its potential to abuse its power. Wilson told Creel to provide Sherley's committee with details on CPI spending quickly, as it was late in the budget process and a subcommittee needed time to "do the very thing that we want them to do, namely go into the matter until they comprehend it." Meanwhile, Gillett, a member of the subcommittee, succeeded in removing the CPI's domestic budget from the president's war fund and making it subject to congressional approval based on hearings. Financial support for foreign activities would continue from Wilson's war fund.[95]

THE HEARINGS

At 10:30 on Tuesday morning, June 11, an appropriations subcommittee held the first of three hearings that week on the CPI. The grilling lasted for hours, producing 169 pages of testimony that went into detail on each CPI unit, including the jobs of clerks. After the first day of questioning, Creel told several colleagues to meet him that evening to strategize, then failed to show up at 10 Jackson Place. William McCormick Blair, Guy Stanton Ford, and Carl Byoir, however, were essential in making the case for the CPI. They responded in detail to many questions. Individuals of the stature of Ford and Blair, and Byoir's deep knowledge of CPI operations, lent credibility to the organization.[96]

Every complaint lodged against the CPI was rehashed. On the last day,

Creel was subjected to intense questioning on his personal conduct. When excerpts of editorials from his Denver days were read, Creel nervously chain-smoked cigarettes, "throwing one down after the other." During a break, Creel conferred with his lieutenants in the hallway. "God," he said, "what am I going to do if they keep this up?" Creel sought to minimize his transgressions. He said that he wrote his Denver editorials "in the heat" of seeking reforms. "They were untrue in the sense of being campaign exaggerations." The mistake in his slumming speech was not what he said but that he spoke extemporaneously, which left him "at the mercy of misconstruction."[97]

Gillett thought Creel's writing was inexcusable. Another legislator said German propagandists "could make very effective use now of these utterances." By the final day, Creel's habitual stiff-necked confidence gave way. He turned to William Blair at the witness table with him. The chief of the Four Minute Men was a skilled executive. Creel asked him to tell the committee if "I am a good business man and good executive." "Yes," Blair said. "I think you have shown it in the last year by building up out of nothing an organization which to-day covers our country."[98]

The proceedings provided a primer on the CPI's domestic work. Sherley confessed that he had thought the CPI was devoted almost entirely to suppressing information. Congress had, at last, a sense of the range of CPI activities. Creel acknowledged on the last day that Congress should have oversight. Joe Cannon, a former Speaker of the House, had dropped in on the hearings, which he seemed to enjoy. He occasionally told the stenographer to stop so he could tell an off-color story. Cannon said Creel left a "good impression" of his organization.[99]

Wilson's war fund request of $2,098,000 for CPI domestic work reached the House floor the next week. In a letter to Sherley on the eve of the vote, Wilson put in a special word for it. "I should feel personally crippled if any obstacle of any kind were put in the way of that work." Congress renewed the president's war fund. On the unanimous recommendation of the subcommittee that reviewed the CPI, the House cut its domestic budget request by 40 percent to $1,250,000. This passed both houses.[100]

Creel tried to shrug this off. "From all I can gather, my maiden appearance before a Congressional Committee was a success," he told Wilson. "I did not, however, as some papers said, recant a single belief. I did say that I would have phrased things differently if I were writing the same articles today." Wilson's assessment was more measured. He was glad CPI relations with Congress improved, but the size of the budget cut "puzzled" him.[101]

Congress got what it wanted, some control over the CPI. Such vindication as the agency received did not extend to Creel. Despite his leeriness of government publicity, Gillett endorsed the CPI appropriation "apart from any question of personality." Legislators gave Creel "a merry scoring on the House floor" during the debate over the CPI appropriation. A Republican representative, uttering a common refrain, said the CPI's good work came "in spite of rather than by the support of the gentleman who is the head of it. Mr. Creel is not only temperamentally but he is socially and politically unfit for the position that he holds." Creel remained in his job for one reason, Pou told him. "You had the great good fortune to have the man in the White House back of you."[102]

THE CPI ADJUSTS

Every belligerent nation struggled with how best to organize propaganda. Although the German high command was regnant on propaganda issues, the number of military and civilian propaganda offices in Berlin totaled twenty-two in early 1918. This led to bureaucratic tensions and conflicting messages to the public. That March, a new agency, Reichszentrale für Heimatdienst, was given the task of coordinating domestic propaganda. In the last days of the war, when all was lost, the Reichstag gave the civil chancellor coauthority over censorship.[103]

In Britain, propaganda officials complained of "constant enquiries without ostensible cause." In 1917 Robert Donald, a newspaper editor and one-time publicity manager for Gordon Hotels, wrote reports at the request of Lloyd George, his friend. He noted the "absence of harmony between one branch and another and the existence of inter-departmental jealousies," and then became a party to them. When Buchan's Department of Information superseded Masterman's Wellington House that year, an unwieldy advisory committee was created with Donald as "a sort of generalissimo over Buchan." In 1918, Buchan's department was superseded by the Ministry of Information under Lord Beaverbrook. Beaverbrook was surprised afterward to learn that the separate department on enemy propaganda was to be created under Lord Northcliffe. Beaverbrook resigned in October 1918 over a turf issue with the Foreign Office and was never replaced.[104]

Vira Whitehouse thought the British investigations were "almost as bitter as the congressional investigation of Mr. Creel's department, and probably as hampering to its work." But the experience in the United States was not the same. In Britain, as well as France and Germany, laws and regulations to suppress speech did not meet the political resistance that stymied Wilson's censorship clause in 1917. Another difference was that the Creel committee survived the entire war.[105]

Creel did, however, have to make adjustments. A provision in the congressional appropriation forbade the use of the funds for anyone between the ages of twenty-one and thirty-one years of age who qualified for military service. This forced Creel to move Byoir to the foreign payroll, which was covered by Wilson's funds. The reduced budget forced Creel to trim activities. He attributed his decision to end support for the American Alliance for Labor and Democracy on the appropriation. He scrapped a program to reach factories with the help of industrialists. The work of the Division of Syndicated Features was slimmed down. The CPI discontinued free subscriptions of the *Official Bulletin* for newspapers. In October, Ford complained that he did not have sufficient money for reprinting publications.[106]

Creel also eliminated the Division of Women's War Work. The hearing on CPI finances had questioned its need in light of similar units at the Council of National Defense and the Labor Department. The division had started in November 1917, after Clara Sears Taylor, a Denver journalist and suffragist, came to Washington in search of war news about women, found little, and approached Creel. She began in a vestibule at Jackson Place. The division grew to twenty women working on an entire floor. After being cut loose from the CPI, Taylor and many staff went to the Labor Department, where they sold the war "to every workingman and every working woman in the country."[107]

Creel felt pain in other ways too as a result of the congressional inquiry. His reputation suffered abroad as well as domestically. The congressional hearings made for good counterpropaganda in Germany. Criticism of Creel was reported in the Berlin press, which argued the CPI had "shaken the *morale* of the American people." He heard that in Britain, "I myself am discredited."[108]

CARRYING ON

Unlike Creel's treatment of field propaganda, which he could brush past in his accounts on the CPI, he felt obliged to write lengthy, inaccurate self-justifications on his highly visible troubles with Congress. Creel's friends and colleagues noted that he was worn down from hard work and criticism. Creel, said Lincoln Steffens, "has got little but abuse and is often deeply depressed." Eula McClary, who pressed for the creation of the Division of Advertising, wrote to Daniels, "Have you noticed how awfully tired George Creel has become? You also appreciate that the newspapers are laying in wait to give him more and severe drubbings." She suggested the administration give him an overseas assignment to get him "away from the continuous criticism." That "would be good for his health, as well as a good thing for the Committee."[109]

Withal, the Committee on Public Information and George Creel carried on along the same lines it had before. Creel's leadership remained chaotic, as he forecast it would be when he responded to Sherley's concern that the proliferation of divisions was costly and inefficient. "During the coming year there are some divisions that I am going to throw out entirely, while there may be some new ones I will create," he said without an apparent twinge of doubt about his unorthodox approach to management. "But I have them scattered in this way so that I can see what each one is doing and judge as to the value of their activities."[110]

Journalists continued to complain about pitiless publicity. Creel's name became a synonym for fake news. When concerns arose over stronger censorship, the New York Times editorialized on the "rash, intruding, Creelish hand." "In this dearth of topics to comment on," the Evansville Courier editorialized during a slow news day, perhaps facetiously, "we remind our brother editors that George Creel is still at the head of the bureau of public information. Now is the appointed time for an offensive against Creel. Let everybody throw a brick."[111]

After the hearings on Capitol Hill, Creel told Whitehouse, "A new atmosphere obtained and on every hand there is a disposition to help. It was a very unhappy and trying time, of course, but it is over thank heaven, and I do not think there will be any repetition." Republicans, nevertheless, continued attacking the CPI. Treadway called for an inquiry into whether the CPI gave preference in war film footage to Hearst's film company. Creel appeared before the Military Committee to address the concerns. In July Illinois Senator Lawrence Sherman, who was Lincolnesque in appearance and homespun wit, said the effort to convert Creel "into an essential pillar of stable government makes the resurrection of Lazarus seem commonplace."[112]

During the appropriations hearings, Creel repeated his vow to give up public speaking. Immediately afterward he bounded onto podiums. But his next big mistake—his greatest blunder of all—came about by working behind the scenes to persuade Wilson to let him release what became known as the "Sisson documents." The documents, faked by White Russian dissidents and given to Edgar Sisson, portrayed Lenin and his comrades as German agents. The sensational report, which the CPI spread through the nation's newspapers, added to rampant fears of a German-Bolshevik conspiracy at home as well as abroad.[113]

"History will dismiss [the Sisson documents] in a line without serious comment, except by special students of war morals," said Norman Hapgood, who closely followed Russian affairs. "In a treatise by some future investigator on fictions of the world-war, they might hold a distinguished place."[114]

13

The Sisson Documents

I have in my possession documents proving completely and conclusively that
the German government not only created the Government of Bolshevik
Commissars, but that during the whole farcical negotiations for peace
this government was operated by the German General Staff.
—Edgar Sisson to George Creel, April 8, 1918

On the afternoon of Friday, January 11, Edgar Sisson, the CPI's chief representative in Petrograd, hurried to the Smolny Institute. In his hands was a copy
of Wilson's Fourteen Points speech, ready for release. "I have not pounded
the typewriter so fast since old newspaper days," he excitedly informed Creel.
Smolny, once a school for maidens belonging to the nobility, headquartered the
Bolsheviks, who pasted crudely written signs ("Bureau of Foreign Affairs") over
the nameplates on the classrooms. Walking through the long, vaulted corridors,
Sisson found his way to "the deepest back room" where Vladimir Lenin worked.
Since arriving in November, Sisson had frequented Smolny "camouflaged as a
newspaper man" to avoid giving the impression the American government recognized the regime. Sisson presented himself to Lenin as the head of the American Press Bureau.[1]

Lenin the man—short, dumpy, bald—was not the Lenin that his propagandists projected in towering statues and inspirational murals. Arthur Bullard met
Lenin in Switzerland in 1905 and found him to be one of the least impressive
political exiles. "He has always seemed to me the very opposite of magnetic—
dreary." But Lenin could be warm when need be. Speaking in English, smiling,
he welcomed Wilson's message as "a great step ahead toward the peace of the
world."[2]

Wilson's speech reached out to the Russians, who were negotiating a separate peace with the Germans in the town of Brest-Litovsk. The Bolsheviks,
he said, acted "in the true spirit of modern democracy" by insisting that the

negotiations be conducted in the open. In Point 6, he said that Russia should not have to give territory to the Germans. Sisson hoped Wilson's words would encourage dissension at the peace talks and encourage the Bolsheviks to stay in the war. If not that, they might at least insist on terms that kept the armies of both countries in place. This would prevent the Germans from shifting some forty divisions to the western front.[3]

Propaganda, not bullets, was the weapon that counted most in the Bolshevik rise to power. During Marxist wrangling in 1903 Lenin took for his side the name "Bolsheviks"—"men of the majority"—despite the fact that they were outnumbered by what came to be called the "Mensheviks"—"men of minority." Recognizing propaganda value in Wilson's speech, Lenin dashed to the telegraph office to send it to Leon Trotsky, chief of the Russian negotiating party in Brest-Litovsk and no less a propagandist than Lenin. Trotsky was called "the Pen."[4]

Sisson adopted the Bolshevik technique of papering the city with posters. "President's speech placarded on walls of Petrograd this morning," he cabled Creel. More were distributed outside the city. Altogether the CPI printed 3.5 million posters and handbills. A million printed in the German language appeared to have some success demoralizing the enemy on the German-Russia front.[5]

Distribution of Wilson's Fourteen Points speech was a high point, if not *the* high point, of Sisson's propagandizing in Russia. His report to Creel was giddy. Lenin, he said, "was as joyous as a boy" over Wilson's recognition that the Bolsheviks were "sincere." But a comment about the conversation that Friday afternoon hinted at the low point that lay ahead for the CPI. After basking in Wilson's acknowledgment of Bolshevik honesty in the negotiations, Lenin threw up the palms of his hands and lamented, "Yet I have been called a German spy." The remark referred to rampant rumors and acerbic political jokes that Lenin was a German pawn in taking Russia out of the war.[6]

Sisson did not dwell on this in his report to Creel. Instead he said, "The Bolsheviks are not acting like the German agents they were supposed at the beginning to be." They had the will to fight. But in his 1931 memoir *One Hundred Red Days,* he told the story a different way. He believed Lenin's comment was calculated to mislead. The words "German spy," he said of his reaction, "enshrined themselves in the brain of this maker of catch phrases." Sisson, the propagandist, had been propagandized! In this retelling, he portrayed himself as too crafty to be thrown off the scent by Lenin's guile.[7]

Sisson's subsequent acceptance of forged documents purporting to reveal Lenin as a German agent illustrates yet another technique in the Great War: disinformation. As Inspector Javert to Lenin's Jean Valjean, Sisson eagerly assisted in his own seduction by anti-Bolshevik propagandists. Utterly certain of the veracity of documents that confirmed his bias and Creel's, the pair threw the full weight of the government behind them.

THE ADDITION OF INTERNAL INTELLIGENCE

When he left the United States on October 27, Sisson was bent on realizing "our plans for the enlightenment of Russia," as Wilson had put it. He expected the Provisional Government under Alexander Kerensky to welcome Americans' stay-in-the-war message. On November 7 the Bolsheviks seized power. Because the frontier was closed, Sisson's unheated train did not reach Petrograd's Finland Station until Sunday, November 25. He and a military courier who happened to be traveling to Russia as well were the first Americans to enter the city since the revolution. In the early morning light they could see bullet-made pockmarks on buildings along the wide streets. Bolsheviks had replaced all of the officials to whom Sisson had letters of introduction. Nevertheless, Creel directed him to "drive ahead full speed regardless expense."[8]

But in what direction? Russia, Robert Lansing quipped, was an "unanswered and unanswerable riddle." Civil war wracked the country. Foes ranged from White Russian armies to former civil servants bent on sabotage. No one knew if the Bolshevik regime would survive. "Bolshevism has reached the end of its powers," said a German envoy. Accurate information was scarce. "What surprised me most during the first months of Soviet rule in Russia," Bullard said, "was the breakdown of the ordinary service of information. The lack of 'news' was more devastating, more de-civilizing, than the food shortage."[9]

Although Sisson may have been the "organizational genius" that Creel told Wilson he was, he was poorly prepared to put that talent to use in a confusing country he was seeing for the first time. In Chicago he had been drama editor and city editor for sensational newspapers. *Collier's,* when he was managing editor, dedicated itself mostly to domestic muckraking. When he edited Hearst's *Cosmopolitan* during the early war years, the focus was fiction that one historian characterized as "sex in society, sex in adventure, sex in mystery."[10]

Sisson was a slight man. He admitted he could not handle the weight of a typical Russian fur coat. Wire-rimmed glasses and pinched features accented his distant, dyspeptic demeanor and his noticeable penchant for secretiveness. He relished camouflaging himself as a newspaperman at Smolny and disguised the writing in his journal with innocuous phrases and symbols. His interest in ferreting out German-Bolshevik plots may be traced to his experience with muckraking. Here was a chance to expose something big. But the intrigue that abounded in Petrograd was nothing like that of beef trusts and ward bosses, which for all their deceit coexisted with stable government and rule of law.[11]

The best of Sisson's outstanding staff was Arthur Bullard, his polar opposite in temperament and experience. A wispy man with a red Vandyke beard, Bullard had the look of a shy scholar. Largely forgotten today, he was one of the most thoughtful, knowledgeable foreign correspondents of his generation. Although only thirty-eight years old when he arrived in Moscow that summer, he had reported from Panama, the Caribbean, North Africa, the Balkans, and Russia, where he covered the 1905 revolution. In addition to books on current affairs, he wrote two novels dealing with social issues. Bullard exemplified progressive faith in informed opinion. "I would rather be engaged in moulding public opinion at home," he said, "than in registering its decisions as a diplomat." The personal papers of diplomats and fellow CPI workers are filled with admiration. Guy Stanton Ford thought he "was the finest man" in the CPI.[12]

Largely forgotten today, Arthur Bullard was one of the most thoughtful, knowledgeable foreign correspondents of his generation. He was widely admired as "the finest man" in the CPI. (From George Creel, *How We Advertised America*)

Bullard returned to Russia in the summer of 1917. He was restive at CPI headquarters, where he was helping Creel jump-start his organization. Ernest Poole, another astute observer of Russia working at the CPI, added impetus. A little after midnight, after a pensive June evening on a Lafayette Square bench, Poole crossed the street to Bullard's office to say the revolution was too important to miss. Poole secured credentials from the *Saturday Evening Post* and Bullard from *Harper's*. Poole returned home at the end of 1917 to head the Foreign Press Bureau. Bullard worked informally on propaganda, without pay, for the American consulate in Moscow until Sisson arrived and put him in charge of the Russia News Division.[13]

Bullard disagreed with the administration's focus on keeping Russia in the war. Russian forces had suffered more than two million casualties. Soldiers were throwing down their arms. They wanted to be home for Bolshevik land redistribution. Bullard thought the better approach was to build good long-term relations. One of his most farsighted ideas, which he repeatedly pressed on Sisson, was to send Russians to American universities in the manner of Rhodes scholars. "As soon as the peace is signed," he argued, "there will be a rush to the foreign universities. We ought to get a large share of those students for America." Nothing came of that proposal, whose value was eventually recognized, after World War II, in the government-funded Fulbright Program.[14]

Another one of Bullard's superior ideas was a series of "Letters from an American Friend." The letters were a primer on American history, institutions, and ideals. They succeeded because they were democratic in their open-mindedness and honesty. "We are keenly conscious of our own shortcomings," he wrote. "We hope that you will learn the lessons of freedom more quickly than we have done." The letters showed the potential for propaganda to rise to the level of dignity.[15]

Bullard quickly outgrew his first office in Petrograd and took another overlooking Nevsky Prospect, the main avenue. But his work was not easy to carry out. As one member of his staff noted, "The most powerful weapon of all those used by the Bolsheviki, absolute control of the printed word, was perfected only gradually but with extraordinary skill." Bullard found it difficult to maintain a mailing list of newspapers because the "liveliest papers sooner or later get suppressed and come out under a new name." The Bolsheviks' voracious appetite for propaganda contributed to a "paper famine." By dangling money in front of him, Sisson convinced the commissar of printing to let him use the shop that printed the Bolshevik broadsheet *Isvestia,* but in February the government confiscated a poster as it rolled off the press. Dissemination of a speech by Wilson was thwarted when soldiers returning from the front commandeered a train and threw off its freight. The CPI had high hopes for reaching the illiterate masses with film propaganda. But the YMCA, which received financing from Wilson to bolster morale of Russian soldiers and help the CPI, was only able to bring in two documentaries.[16]

The Bolsheviks' grip on information turned the gathering of ordinary news into a clandestine activity. A high degree of creativity was called for. The American consulate in Moscow used a Greek-born American export merchant with the colorful name Zenophon Blumenthal Kalamantiano. Kalamantiano turned his extensive connections into an information-gathering network that used the espionage technique of cut-outs so that "only two or three men were to know and have any contact with Kalamantiano. Each of those men had two or three men in contact with them, and so on." CPI staff viewed their work as "a mixture of Public Information and efforts at Intelligence Service." Sisson took this to an extreme. "The fact simply is," he told Creel, "that to outward publicity I have added internal intelligence." He told his wife he had "channels running to every seat of power."[17]

Conditions lent themselves to freelancing. Communications with Washington were difficult. It took two days for a cable to arrive. Sisson first learned of Wilson's Fourteen Points speech from the newspapers; the embassy had neglected to forward the message to his office. American ambassador David Francis, a businessman and former governor of Missouri who relished his cigars, whiskey, and poker, was not much better equipped for his task than Sisson was for his, and he was on a shorter leash. The United States along with France and Britain did not extend diplomatic recognition to the Soviet government. Lansing and Wilson believed the Bolsheviks were not, in the former's words, "the real agents of the sovereignty of the Russian people" and were unlikely to last. Francis was told to "take no steps with Lenin or Trotsky."[18]

Sisson was not the only one to step into this vacuum. There were two others: Burly, self-confident Raymond Robins, who made millions prospecting gold in Alaska and headed the American Red Cross Commission, and General William Judson, who in addition to being the army attaché had an independent brief as head of the American Military Mission. None of the trio felt an obligation to keep the ambassador informed of their interactions with Bolsheviks. Francis was told that Sisson was Creel's representative and "personally charged" by Wilson to do direct propaganda. When the ambassador asked if he had credentials, Sisson impertinently replied, "You have instructions; adhere [there] to." Francis said he knew his instructions; he wanted to know Sisson's relationship to the embassy. Sisson changed the subject to ask about possible mutual friends in St. Louis. Francis cabled Lansing, "The impression prevails here that Sisson is personal representative of President Wilson and it is reported that Sisson originated such an impression." This "twilight zone of divided authority," as Sisson put it, existed in other CPI posts, but the consequences were more momentous in Petrograd.[19]

Before Sisson left Washington, Wilson warned him to "guard particularly against any effect of officious intrusion and meddling, and try to express that disinterested friendship that is our sole impulse." Sisson had scarcely unpacked his bags when he joined Robins and Judson in conspiring against the ambassador, whom they believed lax in developing informal lines of communication to influence Bolshevik negotiations with the Germans. Judson and Robins considered Sisson a useful messenger to Wilson, and he obliged. "No fruitful work can be done here by any division of our Government," Sisson cabled Creel at the beginning of December, "so long as Francis remains in charge of Embassy."[20]

Sisson sent the cable in a code of his own devising that State Department cryptographers easily deciphered. Wilson was angry when Lansing showed him the message. Creel shot off a cable to Sisson: "President insists that you avoid political entanglements and personal matters." Creel assured Wilson that Sisson understood, but Creel was as much the problem as Sisson was. In a letter in January, Creel told Sisson his previous message was merely "to satisfy opposition and not at all as a rebuke. Have communicated irregularly because I wanted you to have a free hand, using your own judgement. God bless you."[21]

FOMENTING HOLY WARS

Carl Ackerman's eagerness to be useful to officials made him a victim of one of the most notorious fakes of the twentieth century, the *Protocols of the Elders of Zion.** The *Protocols* described a plan for Jewish world domination. Tsarist secret police concocted these putative secret minutes to make it seem that liber-

* A British journalist exposed the *Protocols* in 1921. The fabricated document lived on as a "warrant for genocide." Adolf Hitler incorporated it into his anti-Semitic rants. The Nazis published a party edition of the *Protocols,* and the Nazi Ministry of Education put it on its lists of basic school textbooks. Norman Cohn, *Warrant for Genocide: The Myth of the Jewish World Conspiracy and the Protocols of the Elders of Zion* (New York: Harper, 1969), 201.

alizing movements in Russia were inspired by Jews. After the 1917 revolution, anti-Red Russians repurposed the *Protocols* to discredit Lenin, Trotsky, and others of Jewish lineage as leaders of a Judeo-Bolshevik plot to take over the world. Ackerman, at the time working for the *Philadelphia Public Ledger,* wrote two front-page stories on the *Protocols.* The headline of one of the articles captured their overall tone: "Red Plot to Smash World and Then Rule with Universal Czar." The stories were forgeries of a forgery. "Jews" were replaced with "Bolsheviks," and "people" with "goyim." Ackerman called the *Protocols* the "Red Bible" and claimed the Bolsheviks used "diabolical methods" to topple governments. Ackerman described his sources as a "prominent American diplomat," who received the documents from an intelligence officer. He told his editor he saw photographs of the original Russian edition.[22]

Ackerman's articles, which appeared in 1919, were a fitting coda to the multitudinous attempts during the Great War to sow political dissent abroad, sunder alliances, and bring about regime change. As we have seen, Germany tried to turn Mexico against the United States with the Zimmermann telegram. They supported antiwar leader Caillaux in France. The plot line in the war novel *Greenmantle* by British propagandist John Buchan was a German scheme to foment a holy war among the Allies' colonies in the Middle East. In one of many real German plots in that region, a rabble-rousing propagandist and spy named Wilhelm Wassmuss organized a revolt in southern Persia. He was captured by pro-British Persian tribesmen and, like Dr. Albert and his briefcase, left behind a codebook when he escaped. It fell into the hands of British code breakers.[23]

Propaganda was useful for promoting destabilization. The Germans plied Russian prisoners with peace propaganda before sending them home. The Bolsheviks returned the favor by radicalizing German prisoners. The CPI sought to drive a wedge in other countries' domestic politics and was willing to strike up strange alliances to do so. It joined with the Bolsheviks to foment revolution in Germany, although they had different kinds in mind. Wilson's Fourteen Points speech was aimed at the Russian people. As if conducting a political campaign from afar, Wilson hoped to override the Bolshevik government and persuade Russians to reenter the war.[24]

Whatever twinges of remorse propagandists felt when lying to their own people, they had less compunction about doing so abroad, for instance, creating fake German newspapers, as the French did, and spreading blatantly false rumors that the Bolsheviks "nationalized" their women, which the *New York Times* picked up from the British press. Russia was especially vulnerable to such propaganda, given the Bolsheviks' tenuous grip on power. The shortage of accurate information left an open field for oppositional parties to plant lies that, under the tumultuous circumstances, seemed plausible. In 1917 the Root mission reported that "thousands of German agents . . . swarmed across the border immediately after the revolution" brought down the tsar.[25]

"German agent" propaganda was an old canard. Anti-tsarist revolutionaries alleged that mad monk Rasputin insinuated German agents in the court and was part of an imagined German plot to spread cholera with poisoned apples from Canada. The tsar's ministers, it was said, were secretly negotiating peace with Berlin. In the strange house-of-mirrors world of disinformation, the Germans promoted the "German agent" lie to undermine the image of the tsarist regime. By turning similar charges against the Bolsheviks, opponents delegitimized the regime and legitimized their revolution to bring about its demise. To make their case, Lenin's adversaries pointed to his return to Russia from Switzerland in the spring of 1917. Routes through Britain and France were closed to him because those countries did not want him back home spouting his end-the-war rhetoric. The Germans, to whom those slogans were mellifluous, made special arrangements for a three-day train ride across their country. Lenin downplayed the trip, but a journey with thirty-odd revolutionaries could not be kept secret. Another charge leveled at the Bolsheviks was that the Germans subsidized their activities. How else, it was argued, could they publish forty-one newspapers in 1917?[26]

In July of that year, the Provisional Government investigated these whisperings. Trotsky was arrested. Lenin shaved his beard, donned disguise, and fled to Finland. The government amassed more than twenty volumes of evidence. In the end it could not prove the German-agent charges, but the Bolsheviks could not convincingly lay the gossip to rest after Lenin returned to Petrograd. When Russian forces experienced military defeats that summer, the *Paris Herald* blamed the Bolsheviks in a story with the headline "Traitors Bring Fresh Reverses to Russians."[27]

A MAN POSSESSED

Sisson's descent into this disinformation labyrinth of half facts and bald lies began the following year, on February 2, when Robins gave him a sheaf of German circulars and letters, many translated into English. These indicated that before the war and up to October 1917, the Germans financed the Bolsheviks.

Two days later Ambassador Francis was called upon by a large, shadowy journalist who went under the name Evgenii Petrovich Semenov and was alternatively known as Solomon Moiseevich Kogan and Kohn. Semenov, whose pallid features were accentuated by a long black beard, had been an anti-German propagandist in the Provisional Government's military secret service. He handed Francis a photostat of a document that purported to show that Trotsky was only pretending to negotiate with the Germans at Brest-Litovsk, when he was secretly cooperating with them. Semenov said he lifted the document from Bolshevik files at Smolny. Francis turned this over to Sisson, who made direct contact with Semenov. Semenov later said of Sisson that "his soul of a newspaper man and an agent was all astir."[28]

Semenov added to Sisson's pile of incriminating papers. The documents showed that the Bolsheviks approved the assignment of German personnel in Russia; that Trotsky authorized the provision of passports to German spies going to England, France, and the United States; and that the Germans directed Russia's economy. Particularly astonishing was an order by the German general staff insisting that Lenin, Trotsky, and others be elected to the Bolshevik's Central Executive Committee.[29]

Sisson was not the only one to receive these documents. Copies floated around the city like confetti. Some appeared in an anti-Bolshevik newspaper in the Don Cossack region. A British envoy saw a stack of them on Trotsky's desk. Robins, who refused to tell Sisson where he acquired the documents that he had passed along, believed they were fake and feared their publication would estrange Bolsheviks and Americans when it might be possible to keep Russia in the war. Robin's hopefulness stemmed from an announcement Trotsky just made at the stalled Brest-Litovsk negotiations: the Bolsheviks would not fight *and* would not agree to the peace terms. The Germans responded to this diplomatic sit-down strike by announcing a resumption of hostilities.[30]

Sisson regarded Robins's ideas as half-cocked or worse. One morning, he told Robins to decide if he was a Bolshevik or an American. Robins told Sisson that he "must not be well and should go back to bed." The rupture soon was complete. They had dined together every day; now they did not speak. Francis was torn between their opposing views, but instructions from Lansing on February 18 tipped the embassy in Sisson's favor. The State Department had reviewed the first documents and directed Francis to find more evidence of German-Bolshevik intrigue. Wilson approved a request for $25,000 to purchase more documents.[31]

Like a man possessed, Sisson threw himself into building his case against the

Bolsheviks. With the German army back in the field and threatening Petrograd, the American embassy evacuated the city. Before departing on February 27, Francis told Sisson that Trotsky wanted him to stop his sleuthing. Sisson dismissed the warning as "designed to frighten me." When the Germans dropped bombs on the city to signal they were serious about going back to war, Sisson remained in place. He kept his work secret from Robins for fear he might inform Trotsky, although Trotsky's warning indicated his activities were known.[32]

The British Secret Service in Petrograd, whose head was persuaded of the authenticity of Sisson's documents, put him in touch with a group that had tapped the Bolshevik telegraph lines to Brest-Litovsk. The eavesdroppers said they were willing to raid the Bolshevik files in the Smolny, which was vulnerable as a result of the government's relocation to Moscow. Sisson wanted originals of the photostats Semenov had supplied. The raid supposedly took place on the night of March 2 and yielded fourteen items Sisson deemed original.

In total, Sisson collected sixty-eight documents, the majority from Smolny, plus the German circulars and letters provided by Robins and a single intercepted telegram from the Soviet negotiators in Brest-Litovsk to their leaders in Petrograd. George Kennan, who undertook a thorough analysis of the documents in 1956, pronounced them "unquestionably forgeries" with a few insignificant exceptions. Faking was evident for technical reasons—the use of identical typewriters for Russian and German documents, documents from organizations that had ceased to exist, and so forth—and for reasons of implausibility. "No experienced intelligence organization, particularly in wartime, would list the names of its agents even in its internal correspondence, much less in official communications to a foreign government," Kennan noted. Also, Semenov and the anti-Bolsheviks that Sisson enlisted were, to say the least, suspect.[33]

This did not mean the documents were utterly unhinged from truth. As with all effective disinformation, the documents' power to persuade lay in their plausibility. Their authors had inside knowledge of goings-on in Smolny and enhanced their forgeries with facts. The persistence of rumors of German support for the Bolsheviks strongly suggested there was something to them. And, indeed, there was. The Germans did help the Bolsheviks. German documents captured during World War II and documents found in Soviet archives after the collapse of communism show the Germans funneled millions of marks to the Bolsheviks. The German state secretary told his ambassador in Moscow in May 1918 to lavish money on the Bolsheviks, "as it is greatly in our interests that the Bolsheviks should survive."[34]

The specifics are difficult to pin down even today. German subsidies flowed through intermediaries. The Bolsheviks sanitized government files once they came to power. How much Lenin knew about these subsidies is unclear. The cautious revolutionary left a paltry paper trail. As astute as he was, Kennan incorrectly concluded that German support for the Bolsheviks ended with the November Revolution. Among the authentic documents to surface is an August 1918 letter in which Lenin instructed his political agent in Bern to be unstinting in spending on propaganda. "The Berliners will send some more money: if the scum delay, complain to me formally."[35]

But even if one were sure Bolsheviks benefited from German gold, were they German agents? The forged documents left plenty of room to imagine treacherous connivance if one desired to believe it was true. But that facile conclusion left out factors pointing to another conclusion, which Kennan and other historians agree is the correct one. German gold did not buy Lenin.[36]

The Bolsheviks and the German "scum" who helped them had parallel interests in ending war on the Eastern Front. German state secretary Zimmermann for once hit on a viable plot when he supported Lenin's transit by train. It would well serve Germany, he said, if "the radical wing of the Russian revolutionaries should prevail." In August 1918, Lenin made more or less the same comment on the "coincidence of interests" with regard to the train trip. "We would have been idiots not to have taken advantage of it." "Each side," historian Robert Service concluded, "was confident that it had tricked the other." The Bolsheviks' mistake was to think their propaganda would bring swift revolution to Germany and thereby negate the peace terms the Germans imposed on them.[37]

Bullard believed the documents, which he had not studied himself, might be authentic but was not taken in by the German agent canards. Shortly after the November 1917 revolution, he had warned Creel and House it was "a dangerous mistake" to believe them. "The situation is much more complicated than German intrigue." The Bolsheviks independently wanted to leave the capitalist war. Their strength lay in promising peace. Lenin was a deceitful revolutionary opportunist, not a German stooge. The Bolsheviks took German gold with every intention of "betraying their benefactors at the first—and every—opportunity." This point of view led to a violent argument with Sisson, who damned Bullard for "seeing both sides" of everything.[38]

Manipulation and countermanipulation, Bullard argued, were rampant. He himself had slipped funds from the American Friends of Russian Freedom to revolutionaries in 1905. Around the same time a colorful Japanese colonel named Askashi Motojirō created a spy and propaganda network to weaken

Russia internally. He financed Lenin and other anti-tsarist revolutionaries. Not unlike the Germans, who gave Lenin safe passage through their country, the French and the British allowed supporters of the pro-war Provisional Government to return through theirs. After the war was over, Bullard commented, "such tactics were universal."[39]

Neither Sisson nor Creel heeded Bullard's warnings. They pushed all their Russia chips into the center of the table on a bet Sisson's revelations would discredit the Bolsheviks. On Sunday evening, March 3, the day after the raid on Smolny and coincidentally the day the Bolsheviks agreed to Germany's onerous peace terms, Sisson boarded a train at Finland Station, impatient to leave Petrograd with his big story.

AN ANTICLIMACTIC RECEPTION

Sisson's desire for a speedy return home was thwarted by Finland's Red-White civil war, which disrupted travel, and the precautions he took to protect his papers. Fearful that the documents might be discovered by Bolshevik guards, he entrusted a portion to an American military officer whom he subsequently met up with in Sweden and arranged for a Norwegian courier to carry the rest to the American minister in Christiania (Oslo). While in Christiania, he arranged for translation and wrote a report during two nearly sleepless nights of work. Sisson's ship did not pull into New York harbor until May 6. Creel's welcoming telegram sounded as if he had survived a daring mission behind enemy lines. "God Bless you. Such a relief to have you back."[40]

During Sisson's journey, the State Department warned him not to share his documents with anyone, including the British Secret Service in London, when he passed through. He was permitted to leave copies with the embassy, which was also directed to keep them strictly confidential. These instructions were issued at the direction of Wilson.

Fearing that publication would lead to reprisals against the CPI staff in Russia, Sisson sent a message on April 24 from London to Washington asking that Bullard and his team be "ordered out of Russia" in two weeks' time. The same day Will Irwin directed Bullard and his staff "immediately and with all possible secrecy to leave for the present all territory controlled by Bolsheviki." Russian assistants were to carry on in Moscow. Sisson also suggested recalling the Red Cross, which was done, and the embassy staff, which was not.[41]

Forced to wait in Archangel until late June for passage on a British ship, Bullard fumed. The CPI's work was smashed in Russia, he wrote to Creel. He told Sisson, "I am trying to reserve judgment until all the facts are in. You used to damn me for being too judicial, but if I were not I would certainly be damning you." He considered Sisson's attitude insulting: "Don't take yourselves seriously, my children, I used you as camouflage for my work, about which I do not care to trust you. Your job is over." Bullard suspected the order to leave related to Sisson's documents and cabled Creel, "For us here in Russia, our work seems more important than the probable results of any publication of evidence against the B—stop. They have weathered similar attacks before—stop." Bullard spoke "for all the men in our employ in requesting authorization to return to the job."[42]

Sisson was unabashed. "You were offered up deliberately," he cabled Bullard, "and I make no apologies stop drastic action was needed to attract Washington attention." Creel's enthusiasm for the documents equaled Sisson's. "Sisson returned from Russia last night," he crowed to Ernest Chambers, the chief Canadian censor, "and has a big story." Creel spent much of the night going over Sisson's papers and the next day told Wilson that they were "absolutely conclusive and contribute the most amazing record of double-dealing and corruption. I am having a clean copy prepared, and I can bring Mr. Sisson over at any time you indicate."[43]

Sisson did not get a hero's welcome from Lansing when he and Creel met with him on May 9. Exactly what Lansing said is unrecorded, but Sisson was in a sulky mood when he was handed off to Leland Harrison, who handled secret intelligence coming into the department. When Harrison asked his opinion of the documents, Sisson said brusquely they spoke for themselves. Sisson's attitude, Harrison said, was that of a "newspaper man who had secured what he thought was the greatest scoop in history and which was not being made use of by his superiors." Copies of the papers were turned over to the Division of Russian Affairs. "I have been told that the President has stopped the publication of Sisson's material for the present," Philip Patchin told a colleague.[44]

Following that anticlimactic reception, Sisson took over Irwin's duties as head of the Foreign Section. Three weeks after Sisson's return, Creel sent a note to the president asking if he had read the documents or wished to see Sisson. If Wilson responded, it is not in the files. Creel was in no position to push. On May 12 Creel uttered the infamous "slumming" comments that put his job into jeopardy and forced him to focus on Capitol Hill.[45]

Wilson's failure to pay attention to Sisson fit a pattern. Russia was a Wilson administration obsession. Not only did it want Russia to stay in the war, but the Bolsheviks were a rival in the quest to win hearts and minds of the world. Both Wilson and Lenin spoke in idealistic terms, and both used propaganda that went over the heads of governments to their people. Yet Wilson was perversely reticent to consult people who returned from Russia with information he could use to better understand conditions there. He perfunctorily met with Root, whom he sent to Russia on his behalf, and would not see Ambassador Francis or William Boyce Thompson, Robins's Red Cross predecessor in Russia.[46]

Despite his initial orders to acquire damning documents on the Bolsheviks, Lansing, as well as others in his department, acquired some doubts about their validity. Bullard may have had an impact on this, as he persisted in warnings about them that can be found today in State Department files. Shortly after Sisson left Petrograd, Bullard wrote a cautionary letter to House arguing that the administration should adopt a "wait-and-see policy." The documents would not discredit the Bolsheviks inside Russia and could distort thinking abroad. "It is a queer quality of this evidence that, while it is not very impressive to the Russian, it looks to the stranger like the most damning evidence."[47]

These doubts about the documents do not fully explain why the administration failed to act on them immediately. Not everyone doubted their authenticity. After welcoming Sisson to London in April with, literally, a warm embrace, Ambassador Page read the documents and—ignoring Lansing's admonition to talk to no one about them—informed the Foreign Office he was "completely convinced." Although put off by Sisson's manner, Leland Harrison saw "no reason to doubt their authenticity." His record of the meeting with Sisson indicates the documents were withheld not because of doubtful authenticity but because officials did not want to use them "until the psychological moment had arrived," that is, when the Germans were stumbling. When that time came in late summer, however, the documents stayed in the files. A later memo speaks of "an unfortunate misunderstanding." Perhaps officials promised to review the documents and failed to do so. Such a study may have been held up while the department awaited a similar batch of documents purchased in Russia after Sisson left. Those papers did not arrive until after the war was over.[48]

Over the course of the summer, Creel said later, in his memoir, the materials were "submitted to every known test by various agencies of government, experts on ink, paper, and typewriter faces being called in." The administration held back "when their authenticity had been proved to the satisfaction of all" out of hope the Bolsheviks would "break away from their treacherous alliance." No evidence exists for either statement. Sisson said nothing in his memoir about the holdup.[49]

During the unusually hot Washington summer, Sisson argued to anyone who would listen that "a world told the truth about Germanic-Russia conspiracy would be a world immune from their poison." In June the CPI foreign news service, now under his direction, distributed a story on intercepted messages that seemed to support the German agent thesis. One of the messages referred to a German bank account opened "at Comrade Trotsky's request." Post office censors found similar documents in the luggage of a one Mme. L. Nikiferoff. (Her husband worked in the foreign department of General Electric.) Some of the documents duplicated Sisson's, and three added to them, giving the government "a most valuable weapon against Teutonic duplicity," according to the post office analysis. Sisson agreed.[50]

PUBLICATION

What, then, brought about the change of fortune for Sisson's "valuable weapon"? We have no record of a formal decision by Wilson or even of Creel's interaction with him on the subject. What we do know is that Creel was better able to lean on the president now that his battle with Congress was over. His strongest argument related to a decision Wilson had recently made with considerable reluctance. That decision was to join an Allied military intervention in Siberia that violated Wilson's Fourteen Points declarations for self-determination and against aggression.[51]

The president's decision was based on a complex rationale. Part of this was to protect Allied stockpiles of war matériel in Archangel and Murmansk that had been intended for use against the Germans by the previous Russian government. Part was to enable anti-German forces—including Czech soldiers who had fought with Russia—to reach the Eastern Front from Siberia. A third justification was that an invasion had the potential to weaken, if not topple, the Red government. This third reason was never explicitly stated, but it was obvious to many. The introduction of foreign troops, the *Nation* editorialized, "will encourage every revolutionary group" opposing the Bolsheviks. Czech and White Russian forces clashed with Red forces seeking to control their eastern territory. In an *aide memoir* the administration stated that Allied military support was permissible "to steady any efforts at self-government or self-defense in which the Russians themselves may be willing to accept assistance." This view, a respected US diplomat said, rested on the "feeling, even the conviction, that the Bolsheviks were German agents." Wilson showed he was open to that argument in a December 1917 speech to Congress. The Russians, he said, had been hoodwinked by "masters of German intrigue."[52]

Sisson made the case for intervention in late May. The Bolsheviks were not a legitimate government. The American embassy should be closed so as to avoid any appearance of condoning their regime. Intervention should be in concert with Allies, and the Russians should be called upon "to rise and stand with us against their German masters." The memo was widely distributed. A copy ended up on the desk of Postmaster General Burleson. If a copy did not reach Wilson, Creel could have made the points personally.[53]

American troops arrived in Vladivostok on August 16 and in Archangel in the north on September 4. Wilson's permission to publish shortly afterward showed, once again, that the CPI enjoyed greater credibility with him than the State Department did. Wilson did not bother to inform Lansing of his decision. The CPI sent out the documents with Sisson's commentary on Friday, September 13, for publication on Sunday. A stunned State Department learned of this on Saturday morning. The immediate concern was the safety of US diplomats in Russia. The Bolsheviks had jailed British and French envoys for political activities. With Creel in Chicago giving a speech, Lansing immediately sent a letter to Sisson asking the CPI to recall the release.[54]

Only two weeks before Lansing had met with Creel about "better liaison with this Dept.," Sisson's condescending and intellectually dishonest reply to Lansing's request to hold back the documents erased whatever détente had been formed. Sisson conveniently forgot all about his urgent request months before, when he believed publication was imminent, to recall CPI, Red Cross, and embassy staff for fear of retribution. Now he told Lansing the "peril is difficult to conceive." If the American envoys were really worried, they should seek sanctuary with the Swedish consul. Lansing sent Wilson a copy of his letter to Sisson, and Breckenridge Long called the White House to ask that it urgently be brought to the president's attention. After follow-up calls, Long learned the CPI release was not recalled.[55]

By sending out advance copies of the documents, the CPI gave newspapers time to prepare their stories for their Sunday edition, a day when readers had plenty of time to read their newspapers. The CPI ensured still greater play by organizing the materials into installments that could appear over five days. The news swept over the country to a degree that rivaled coverage of Wilson's major speeches. Most stories appeared on the front page. Newspapers reprinted many or all of the documents, which "proved," "substantiated," "revealed," "showed," "bared," and left "no room for doubt" that Lenin and his associates were German agents. The head of the United Press Washington bureau complained to Creel that the Associated Press seemed to get more of the documents than they did. "I think the Lenin-Trotsky story is one of the biggest you've ever put out."[56]

Editorial writers drew the conclusions Creel and Sisson wanted drawn. The documents ranked with the "notorious Zimmermann note," the *Evansville Journal News* wrote. The *Boston Evening Transcript* made no criticism of the CPI this time: "The data supplied by Mr. Sisson are conclusive." A *Philadelphia Inquiry* headline blared, "Secret Papers Tell Lenine and Trotzky Betrayed Russia." *Current History* called them "complete proof of what the world had long suspected, namely that Lenine and Trotzky and other members of the Bolshevist Government of Russia were paid German agents." Nowhere, the *New York Times* wrote, did the documents show that "a German officer ever commanded Lenine or Trotzky to press his trousers for him; but the correspondence, as a whole, proves that if any such order had been given they would have regarded it as comprehended within the terms on which they entered the German service."[57]

Upon receipt of the documents from Compub, the CPI commissioner in Denmark, George Edward Riis, called a nighttime meeting. He told his staff to get out the entire text in the morning. "The next day all the Danish newspapers gave it all the space that was possible," he reported, and carried on for three days. The commissioner in Holland was similarly upbeat. "Bolshevik disclosure printed practically in full in all important Dutch newspapers. Dutch press has accepted disclosure as authentic with editorial comment to German disadvantage." "Congratulations on Bolshevik exposures," Whitehouse told Sisson. "Making big impression here."[58]

THE GOOD WORD AND FULL FAITH
OF THE GOVERNMENT

The Sisson documents presented a problem inherent in national security reporting. Few newspapers had the skills to evaluate them. For that, an editor needed an expert on Russia who was supported by experts in the forensics of faking. Even then, the analysis could not be done over a weekend, and no newspaper could afford to undertake a lengthy review while its competitors rushed to print. As a result, journalists had to accept the documents as valid based on the word of the government. In the few cases when they did not, Creel called it an act of treason.

On the left, the *New York Call* denounced the documents as forgeries. Louise Bryant, the wife of radical journalist John Reed, advised Creel they were fakes: "I would stake my life on it." She had a cordial relationship with Creel and may have thought her words would carry more weight than her husband's. He was an avowed enemy of Sisson, whom he called "the weasel." Any hope Bryant would make an impression was dashed in a same-day response. "These documents," Creel said, "were issued by the full approval of the Government after a very careful investigation by the Government, and the Government stands squarely behind their authenticity."[59]

Reed's history with the CPI could make up a small chapter all by itself. Creel tried to hire the socialist firebrand shortly after the CPI was created. It was a mismatch if ever there was one, and Reed declined. In Russia, he helped Sisson send propaganda into Germany. But Sisson alienated Reed by lecturing him on being a Bolshevik tool. Sisson was enraged when Trotsky named Reed the soviet consul to New York. A Russian-American Jew on the CPI payroll, Alexander Gumberg, had ties to the Red leadership, and Sisson sent him to talk Lenin out of it. Gumberg provided documents showing Reed had cooperated with Sisson on propaganda. The appointment was a silly idea to start with, and Lenin reversed it. When Reed left for the United States, Sisson struck again, suggesting that authorities confiscate his notes for a planned book. Port officials did this when Reed arrived in New York on April 28. Sisson recommended the authorities take their time studying Reed's papers, which they also did. For a time Reed's papers sat on Sisson's desk. They were not returned until September, apparently through House's intervention. Reed's history became a seminal volume on the Russian revolution, *Ten Days That Shook the World*.[60]

Writing in the November issue of the left-wing *Liberator*, Reed charged Sisson with intending "to give color or excuse to an uninvited intervention" in Russia by American forces. He subsequently produced a detailed analysis debunking Sisson's revelations, published in pamphlet form. Reed, Creel told Polk, was "a very dangerous person to have loose." Creel sent a newspaper clipping on Reed to Thomas Gregory and said Reed was the "center of the Bolsheviki movement in this country." In making the case for his documents, Sisson insisted that Reed was the one who "indulged in real forgery."[61]

Damning by radical association was one tactic. Another was intimidation. When the German-language *New Yorker Volkszeitung* observed that "it is clear from the very outset to anybody who knows Lenine or Trotsky and their meaning to the International, that these cannot be treated as facts," Creel wrote to the editor. "Please inform me at once," he commanded, "with regard to your reasons for asserting the honesty of Lenine and Trotsky and the dishonesty of the Government of the United States."[62]

The State Department was publicly silent. Inside the building the documents remained a matter of concern and wonderment. "Even the most anti-Bolshevik men in the Russian Bureau of the State Department doubt their authenticity," William Bullitt, now working in the State Department, told House. "Does the publication of the documents by Creel mean that the President has been convinced of their authenticity?" Bullitt considered Creel a "mountebank" for convincing Wilson to allow the documents to become public. Attempts to reel in Creel failed. On September 20, Philip Patchin informed him British intelligence considered the documents fakes. Creel said British reservations were based on misguided ideas as to "what constitutes effective propaganda."[63]

Sisson's sworn enemy, Raymond Robins, shared the views of John Reed, with whom he had regularly dined in Russia, and did what he could to counter the German agent arguments. When sociologist Edward Ross was gathering information for a series of articles on Russia, he fell under Robins's sway and asked for "a list of indications (utterances and actions) of Lenin and Trotsky which do not jibe with the theory that they are German agents." He debunked the theory and in a 1923 book explicitly said Sisson's documents were forgeries. By the time Robins returned to the United States in June 1919 his opinions on cooperating with Russia were viewed with alarm. Military intelligence advised the State Department to warn him against publicly discussing Russia policy. Robins continued his criticism privately. This had an impact on the *New York Evening Post,* the lone establishment newspaper with the temerity to question the documents when they first appeared.[64]

The *Evening Post's* integrity as an organ of responsible liberalism gave it greater influence than its twenty-five thousand circulation suggested. Oswald Garrison Villard, the newspaper's president and grandson of abolitionist William Lloyd Garrison, inherited the newspaper and its sister weekly magazine, the *Nation,* from his German-born railroad tycoon father. Wilson's progressive policies earned Villard's support. But the pacifist owner became disenchanted during the 1916 presidential campaign when Wilson pushed for military preparedness while supporters chanted "He Kept Us Out of War." "There has never been any doubt in my mind that it was the slogan which re-elected Mr. Wilson," said Villard. Wilsonian propaganda disturbed him. "All the press, it seems to me, is suffering from inspired statements given out in Washington and the obvious controlling of opinion," he admonished his Washington correspondent David Lawrence. "Don't let us forget this and let too much of the sham and hypocrisy of the carrying on of this war in Washington get into our writings."[65]

The *Evening Post*'s independence was costly. It never fully recovered from an 1897 boycott imposed by New York merchants who were angry over the paper's exposure of their improper customs practices. All papers suffered during the war from high inflation and soaring costs for newsprint, but the *Evening Post*'s policies added more red ink to its ledger. The newspaper was not as antiwar as its owner, but Villard's unwillingness to give in to violent anti-German sentiment drove away advertisers and readers. The newsroom heard stories of subway commuters reading an antidraft editorial and dashing the paper to the ground. By August 1918, Villard was obliged to sell the newspaper to Thomas Lamont, a former journalist who was a partner at the house of Morgan. The financier gave editor Rollo Ogden freedom to carry on as he saw fit and had no direct hand in the decision to attack the Sisson documents. But he was sympathetic. Before buying the paper, he became convinced the Russians were not German agents and considered the Allied invasion of Russia "misguided." Lamont's tutor was Robins's predecessor William Boyce Thompson, who shared Robins's opinions on Russia. When the Sisson documents were released, the paper consulted Robins.[66]

The *Evening Post,* which did not publish on Sundays, attacked the documents on Monday as "a strain upon credibility." They needed to be subjected to expert evaluation. "Mr. Creel owes it to the country to do his best to find out whether we are really face to face with the most extraordinary cabal in history or whether Mr. Sisson is the victim of a gigantic hoax." The newspaper's criticism continued throughout the week, and on Saturday it published a story in which a propagandist with the Red regime in Finland called the documents "brazen forgeries." The Finn based his opinion on investigation done by Robins. Two days later, an AP correspondent located Robins, who was with Thompson in Arizona. Robins said he was "under instructions from the State Department and could not make any statement." The story was widely reprinted along with Creel's countercharge that the Finn was a liar.[67]

The *Evening Post,* Creel wrote to Rollo Ogden, "cannot escape the charge of having given aid and comfort to the enemies of the United States in an hour of national crises." In one of several letters attempting to force the paper in line through browbeating, he complained to Lamont that Ogden not only "refused to accept the evidence put forward by the Government, but acting as if he were the avowed advocate of Lenin and Trotsky, he demanded that the Government should take the witness stand." These were extraordinary charges to level against a one-time Presbyterian minister who came to work in a frock coat and wing collar. He was regarded as one of the country's finest editorial writers. Creel's anger was boundless. He told Lamont that the *Post* behaved as though it had taken German money. The *Evening Post's* response to these charges was to ask, "Who is the 'Government' whose good faith and judgment the *Evening Post* has impugned? Is it Mr. Creel?"[68]

Magazine criticism was sparse. The *Nation,* where Villard now devoted his full efforts as editor, decried Wilson's murky rationale for invading Russia, adding, "It does not help to give out documents of doubtful authenticity alleging that Trotzky and Lenine are in German pay" inasmuch as the Bolsheviks, despite their excesses, were likely to stay in power. The *New Republic,* whose editor also consulted Robins, said some of the documents had been discredited in Europe. It reserved final judgment until they had been tested for accuracy.[69]

Creel did not respond to the *Nation,* which was embroiled in a highly visible contretemps with the administration. Burleson had revoked its mailing rights over the September 14 issue in which the magazine derided Gompers's mission to assess European labor attitudes and said Wilson's suppression of civil liberties made "democracy unsafe in America." In one of only two such instances, Wilson countermanded his postmaster general.* Creel could easily have ignored the short *New Republic* article as well. The magazine was more supportive of Wilson than the *Nation.* But Creel administered his standard scolding to Croly about government authority. When Croly replied that the CPI "is not infallible," Creel doubled down: "The Committee on Public Information, the direct creation of the President and acting at all times under his orders, gave to the press of the United States a series of documents tending to prove that Lenine and Trotsky and their immediate associates are, and have been, paid and directed agents of the German Government."[70]

Despite their initially promising reception, the Sisson documents met re-

---

* The magazine said Gompers did not go as a fact finder but as a propagandist like Creel, "a salesman, bearing the burden and heat of the day as he 'sells the war' to his fellow countrymen."

sistance abroad. Naturally the Germans and the Russians denounced them. A trusted authority in Switzerland told Whitehouse that he was "absolutely convinced" the documents were forgeries, and she stopped distribution. The French were loath to waste precious newsprint on the lengthy documents. A CPI staff member informed Washington that "most of the reliable Russians still in Paris agree with those Frenchmen who know Russia and the Russian language that a number of Bolshevik documents 'bear the stamp of the man-ufactured article.'" In Russia, the pushback came from within the CPI. The Bolsheviks had closed down the CPI's office in Moscow the week American troops landed in Vladivostok. But a rump operation in Siberia, established that summer, carried on under Bullard, who returned to the country. He arranged a translation that gave the documents an "entirely different interpretation."[71]

Creel's biggest disappointment overseas came from America's chief ally, Great Britain. British authorities issued a secret press advisory calling for sup-pression of the dubious documents. Claiming to act on instructions from his government, Paul Perry, then in charge of the CPI London office, protested to Foreign Secretary Alfred Balfour. In a subsequent meeting with five offi-cials from various parts of the government, he demanded they identify which documents were fake and publish the rest immediately. Perry said Lansing was "seriously interested in the matter" and considered failure to publish a "slight on America." Balfour subsequently learned that Perry had not told the truth; Lansing concurred in the British decision. But a higher authority, Wilson, sided with Creel. Against the advice of Lansing and Polk, he ordered the State De-partment to inform Balfour of his strong feeling.[72]

Creel "was almost in tears" when he protested to Arthur Willert that they were losing the opportunity to disillusion "extremist friends of Bolshevism at home." Creel and Sisson assured Willert that the attorney general and Wilson had reviewed the documents. Willert decided to "take a chance, go whole hog." He wrote a story summarizing the documents. It slipped past the British censor and appeared in the *Times*. Willert explained his reason for appeasing Creel: he was influential and "very decent in giving us a free hand over here." Besides, Willert said, even if the documents were doubtful, who would question them "save discredited Bolshevisks [*sic*]" and Germans.[73]

Balfour could not understand why the president insisted on publicizing doubtful materials but relented after British envoys were safely out of Russia. Perry's dishonest characterization of Lansing's interest in publication of the documents, a British official noted, was "most discreditable" to the CPI. The

Foreign Office and the Ministry of Information "will have to look very sharply after [CPI] publicity activities in England."[74]

AN EXPERT REVIEW:
IMPORTANT SERVICE, NOT LABORIOUS

The *Evening Post*'s criticism concerned Creel enough that on October 18 he asked for an expert review by the National Board for Historical Service. The review committee consisted of Samuel N. Harper, a Russian expert at the University of Chicago, and John Franklin Jameson, the eminent historian who founded the NBHS. Jameson was not an expert in Russian affairs. Harper was closely allied with the administration's Russia policy and already had opined favorably on the documents' authenticity in the *Christian Science Monitor*. Jameson failed to recruit a third member to the hastily assembled committee despite the inducement: "important service, not laborious." Harper said he could devote three days to the work once he arrived from Chicago, which suited Creel, who urged them to finish quickly.[75]

Their report was made public on October 26, a mere eight days after Creel asked for a committee to be formed. Neither Robins nor State Department skeptics testified. Creel and Sisson did. Sisson hovered over the two men while they worked. Jameson and Harper saw "no reason to doubt the genuineness or authenticity of the fifty-three documents" from the Smolny. They felt unable to judge the rest with complete confidence but considered only two of them truly problematic. Translations of the documents, they acknowledged, were sloppy.[76]

The other question to be addressed was the validity of Sisson's interpretations. Harper believed "nothing in the documents" proved Lenin was a German agent. He and Jameson offered to say Lenin was aiding the Germans. They were told "that such a statement would not help to promote the emotional upsurge necessary for the mobilization of all our resources to be thrown in the struggle." The compromise was to avoid the subject altogether, which they did by stating that they had been asked to pronounce only on the genuineness of the documents. Creel and Sisson, Jameson told Harper, were "well pleased with our report." The CPI rushed the pamphlet version of the documents into print with the Harper-Jameson report included as a seal of approval.[77]

"My experience with the Sisson documents showed clearly the pressure to which University men are subjected in time of war," Harper later wrote in a draft of his autobiography. "My position was particularly difficult because my area of study was under the control of a new group which was talking peace, and I felt it was my academic duty to explain why the Bolsheviks were working against a continuation of the war." When the memoir was published after Harper's death, the passage was omitted.[78]

The NBHS report did not alter the *Evening Post*'s opinion. The *Nation* ridiculed it and singled out Harper for blame. The report, the magazine said, called "for stern rebuke from every American historical scholar who values the good name of his profession, but fairly justifies a Congressional investigation of Mr. Creel and his Committee in the whole affair."[79]

The CPI's view dominated. Villard had been forced out as president of the Philharmonic Society and shunned by his Harvard classmates as a result of his antiwar views. His critiques of the documents were similarly dismissed as those of a crank. "I find the members of the academic tribe holding the *Nation* in very little esteem," Jameson told Harper, "ever since it was turned over to the uncovenanted mercies of Oswald Villard."[80]

The Sisson documents strengthened the narrative Wilson's propagandists were establishing of German-Bolshevik subversion. In its refutation of the *Evening Post*'s critique, the *World* noted the documents "are in line with what is known by all intelligent Americans as to the methods used by Germany before we entered the war." The *Literary Digest* said newspaper editors found "great satisfaction in adding legal proof to their moral certainty, and when the Government guarantees the authenticity of the documents proving that Lenine and Trotzky are German agents, it gives them an opportunity to speak their minds without hesitation and without reserve."[81]

Evening Post Washington correspondent David Lawrence spoke to the underlying dynamic when responding to Villard's complaints that he was too accepting of the government line. "For my part, I am willing to trust the Government and if necessary to trust my life to it. It seems to me that a true American can make no other choice at this time. We are either for the Government or against it. And in dealing with spies and propagandists the Government cannot afford to err on the side of leniency."[82]

A CORNERSTONE OF THE RED SCARE

Shortly after the Sisson documents appeared, House asked Wilson why he permitted Creel to go ahead with publication. The president replied he was "thoroughly satisfied" with their authenticity. "I told him I had my doubts," House wrote in his diary in September, "and I thought their publication meant a virtual declaration of war upon the Bolsheviki Government. He admitted this."[83]

Following the incursion into Russia, Lenin declared a state of war existed with the Allies. On a drizzly September day, the week the Sisson documents became public, the lone American diplomat remaining in Red-controlled Russia crossed into Finland. Diplomatic relations did not resume until 1933, when Bullitt became ambassador.

The Sisson documents, bricks in the wall that separated the two countries, had a continuing significance. In assessing that impact, the place to start is Bullard's premature departure from Petrograd as a result of Sisson's directive. The Wilson administration lost on-the-ground observation from one of America's most astute Russia watchers as well as someone who could promote understanding. He would have accounted for the most effective Allied propaganda in Russia even if the British and French propaganda had not been greatly curtailed there. "We can and ought to be their best friend during these trying times," he told Creel. "And the fruit of the friendship we can now plant will be of incalculable value later on. It is the only way I can see to make this old world of ours really safe for democracy."[84]

The rump CPI operation in Siberia reached a small portion of the country and did not have clearly defined goals. "We are rather in the position of advertising something and not knowing what it is," Bullard complained. "Buy it! Buy it! What is it? We don't know, but we are sure it will do you good." In one respect, however, the CPI did have a clear message. Its foreign news service relentlessly sold the wisdom of the Allied invasion. A story by Harvey O'Higgins ludicrously reported that Czech soldiers stranded in Russia were "saving Siberia from the Germans." The invasion's real achievement, if it can be called that, was to further damage Russo-American relations.[85]

The administration badly miscalculated. It assumed the great mass of Russians could be induced to throw off the Bolsheviks for a democratic government and enthusiastically fight the Germans. "It was perfectly possible to make them have heart in the war," Charles Edward Russell told Wilson when the Root mission, of which he was part, returned to the United States. An education campaign was needed. "If it is addressed to Russian's passion for democracy, and if it shows him that his beloved Revolution is in peril, he will be ready to fight with all his strength." Wilson replied that Russell's thinking "runs along the lines of my own thought." If one believed the Russians really wanted to fight, it was an easy next step to believe the Bolsheviks, who took the country out of the war, were an alien political element acting on behalf of the Germans.[86]

The Sisson documents reflected and reinforced this foreign policy. They also reflected and reinforced the mounting Red Scare domestically. By seeing what it wished to see in Russia, the administration followed the same line of thinking that led to the German spy mania at home. Any opponent of the administration's policy was, by definition, a German agent or influenced by one. The CPI helped hammer irrational fears of Bolshevik subversion into the minds of the public.

To be sure, radicals threw crude bombs in the United States. One of Lenin's many calls for a Bolshevik-led world revolution was addressed explicitly to American workers. Maps on the wall of Blankenhorn's Psychologic Subsection at AEF headquarters were filled with red marks to denote Bolshevik strikes and uprisings in Europe. But the grievances of striking American workers were not manufactured in the Kremlin. They were rooted in domestic conditions. Inflation had cut the buying power of the dollar in half since 1913. Special interests dialed up public anxiety. Manufacturers discredited strikers by calling them Red. The hunt for Bolsheviks gave the leaders of the National Security League and its sister organizations new opportunities to carry on. The press perpetuated the national hysteria. The same day the *Philadelphia Public Ledger* published Carl Ackerman's second *Protocols* story on the Bolshevik plan for world domination, the newspaper reported in separate stories that Reds infiltrated Sunday schools and that the rallying cry of American farmers was "Shoot Reds or Ship Them." Ackerman explicitly linked the *Protocols* to labor strikes in the United States.[87]

Government officials, the source of Ackerman's scoop, pressed their case for Red menace with greater intensity. Wilson's new, politically ambitious attorney general A. Mitchell Palmer added an antiradical unit to the Bureau of Investigation under young anti-Red zealot J. Edgar Hoover. "Palmer Raids" rounded up forty-five hundred suspected Communist aliens across the country without warrants. William Adams Brown, who worked for Bullard in Siberia, was shocked upon returning home to find "a wave of hysteria against every form of radicalism. It seemed for the moment as if America also were losing confidence in the strength of her own institutions, and veering toward the Bolshevik and Tsarist view that all men must be made to conform to the dominant point of view."[88]

The Sisson documents made the leap from German treachery to Bolshevik treachery by portraying them as one and the same. Newspapers reported that the documents uncovered "Bolshevik-German Plots against the United States," as one headline thundered. The plots were carried out by "agents, agitators and agent destructors" who had been sent to America. The CPI titled its pamphlet containing the Sisson documents *The German-Bolshevik Conspiracy.* The documents, historian William Appleman Williams argued, "provided the cornerstone in the foundation of symbol meanings upon which rested the great Red scare."[89]

The notorious Abrams trial discussed in chapter 9 hinged in part on the symbolic nature of the documents. The seven Russian-Jewish defendants had circulated leaflets calling for a general strike to protest intervention in Russia. The government argued that Russia, against which the United States had not declared war, was an extension of Germany, on which war had been declared. By this tortured logic, the defendants' puny interference with intervention fell under the Sedition Act, which outlawed speech that would hinder American prosecution of the war. The defense intended to parry this by showing the Sisson documents "were forgeries and that the Bolshevik government was not and is not pro-German." The judge would hear none of this. He cut off the first defense witness, Raymond Robins, ruling that his testimony on the Sisson documents had as much to do with the case "as the flowers that bloom in spring." What the judge meant was the German-Bolshevik conspiracy was beyond debate. As he said at another point, "We are not going to help carry out the plans mapped out by the Imperial German Government, and which are being carried out by Lenine and Trotsky." In light of this, the defense abandoned its plan to call Sisson as a witness.[90]

Contrary to Villard's suggestion that Congress investigate the Jameson-Harper report, a special Senate subcommittee confirmed its thesis. The subcommittee was set up in late 1918 at the suggestion of Palmer to investigate the attempts of German brewers in the United States to shape public opinion. It quickly broadened its scope to rehash the plots of Dr. Albert and Captain Boy-Ed and at the very end shifted to Bolshevik propaganda with the testimony of Archibald E. Stevenson. Stevenson, a New York lawyer who became a special agent with the Justice Department's Bureau of Intelligence, was a prototype of Cold War Red baiters who spun extravagant theories of ubiquitous Communist treachery. He portrayed William Jennings Bryan, Oswald Garrison Villard, and Villard's mother as part of this web as a result of their pacifist beliefs. In the

Cold War such people would be labeled fellow travelers. In Stevenson's grand scheme, enemy propaganda was a constantly morphing virus that insinuated itself in America. In the first phase, before the war, "the German element" organized itself into clubs and associations; in the second it sought to keep America out of the war; in the third it hampered the war effort; and now in the fourth it promoted domestic revolution. When asked if Bolshevik propaganda could properly be added to the subcommittee's original German-focused mandate, he did not hesitate: "Yes. The Bolsheviki movement is a branch of the revolutionary socialism of Germany."[91]

This question was not posed to Stevenson by chance. The administration was troubled by mounting criticism over the Russian incursion. Under the influence of Robins, Senator Hiram Johnson sponsored a resolution calling for withdrawal of American troops. He was critical of the CPI's "regular and consistent propaganda of misrepresentation" that painted the Russians as German agents to justify the invasion, which ran counter to Wilson's pledge to honor self-determination. His measure lost by a single vote, cast by Wilson's vice president to break a tie. By broadening the hearings, the Democratic majority had an opportunity to blunt criticism for sending American forces into Russia.[92]

Ambassador Francis's testimony justified American support for regime change. He insisted that no more than 10 percent of the Russian people backed the Bolsheviks. Although he admitted the Bolsheviks would have taken financial support from anyone, he emphasized that Lenin "was a German agent from the beginning." John Reed and a few others who testified opposed intervention, but virtually no criticism was made of the Sisson documents. Concerned he was a target of military intelligence and Hoover in the Justice Department, Robins refused to say anything about the documents. They did not come up at all when Samuel Harper testified. The dominant impression of the documents was articulated by an anonymous witness, in executive session, who considered their acquisition "one of the most remarkable pieces of work done in our Secret Service." The statement must have pleased the intrigue-minded Sisson, who did not testify because he was in Europe. *The German-Bolshevik Conspiracy* was an appendix to the hearings.[93]

A WORLDWIDE CONSPIRACY

In late 1918, Sisson sent House two copies of his CPI pamphlet. There was no difference, he wrote, between "Russian Bolshevik or German Bolshevik. There is no need. They are one by their own definition of the international 'Dicta-torship of the Proletariat.'" Advisors on Russian policy should never "forget the cynical, sardonic, manner of thought of the so-called International Bol-shevik. Often he is a laughing, always a jibing devil." Sisson believed the Bol-sheviks marked him for assassination, as happened to a Russian admiral found with similar papers, but publication of the documents protected him. "To have harmed me afterward would have been a silly form of confession."[94]

After returning to journalism as a vice president at *McClure's,* Sisson did not stop promoting the documents. "It seems to me," he wrote in June 1919, "that it is now the duty of the State Department to meet the attacks upon the docu-ments." The next year the department agreed. "Nothing has yet come up in our study here to throw any serious doubt on the validity of either the Sisson papers or the Department's [subsequent] series," said Allen Carter, head of the Russia Division. Bullard, who had joined the Russia division staff, attributed this en-thusiasm for establishing the genuineness of the documents to the failure "to destroy Bolshevism by force of arms." The government needed to "burnish up our arguments" in order to attack the Communists with words. Harper, a part-time advisor, devoted time to the documents in hopes of doing some burnishing of his reputation. Sisson plied the division with letters containing "important new" pieces of information. One letter was twenty-eight pages long. Bullard thought the documents were "a serious tragedy."[95]

After the ordeal of pressing Balfour to allow publication of the Sisson doc-uments, an exasperated American diplomat in London exclaimed, "I sincerely hope I may never hear of Sisson or his papers again as long as I live." But he did. In May 1920, the department ordered fifteen outposts to find out what they could about people mentioned in Sisson's documents and those acquired later. "It is hoped that evidence will thus be secured which will definitely determine once and for all the authenticity of these documents." Six months later a simi-lar request went via the War Department to "40 or 50 of the more important points abroad."[96]

Military intelligence rendered a favorable analysis of handwriting on the documents. When a military attaché in Bern combed through trial records of the terrorist section of the German general staff, he thought he found evidence that tended to prove the genuineness of one of Sisson's documents. J. Edgar Hoover assisted the State Department, which reciprocated with information on suspected Bolshevik sympathizers. Harper gave Hoover evidence of Bolshevik plans for world revolution. Harper looked into the possibility of an international German-Jewish-Bolshevik cabal.[97]

Hugh Wilson, now in Berlin, complained of the constant requests for information on the Sisson documents. "I am curious to know who in the Department has such an acutely developed historic sense that they are willing to spend months of labor on what is after all past history."[98]

Eventually the campaign to substantiate the documents fizzled. A conclusive answer required examination of the originals, which Creel had given to Wilson. Twice Creel asked for the papers to be returned to him and was denied. Bullard failed as well. Wilson would not let anyone look in his files, Creel complained. After Wilson's term ended no one was sure where the documents were. So it stood until 1952, when President Harry Truman cleared out his office. For more than thirty years they were in an envelope in the back of a White House safe.[99]

In the meantime, the documents lived on the way modern-day fake news does when it confirms fanatics' fantasies. Father Charles Coughlin, who spread anti-Red fear and anti-Semitic hate to millions over the radio in the 1930s, used the documents and the *Protocols of the Elders of the Zion* to make his case. Both remain ammunition for white supremacy conspiracy groups today.[100]

In a vivid illustration of the difficulty of erasing misinformation, the Sisson papers were treated as a new discovery after the fall of the Soviet Union. Dimitri Volkogonov, a historian and former head of the Russian army's psychological warfare branch, found copies when he plowed through the recently opened archives of the secret police. The documents with their secret classification, he said, proved Bolshevik treachery. Lenin had "debts to repay, and this could only be done by national defeat." Volkogonov was unaware George Kennan had decades before shown them to be fakes and that the Bolsheviks had classified them years before, not to hide that they were German agents but to keep the misleading documents from circulating.[101]

THE POWER OF BLACK PROPAGANDA

Publication of the Sisson documents, Creel said during the Red Scare years after World War II, revealed "the first direct interference in our domestic affairs by Communist agents. The technique used then is much the same as that employed ever since; bold attack on whatever is said or done against them and then unceasing repetition of lies until they take on the look of truth."[102]

Creel's indictment could have been made against the Committee on Public Information.

The Sisson documents were not a simple matter of being duped. Creel and Sisson recklessly ignored warnings the documents were false. Against the advice of people far more knowledgeable than himself, Sisson gave the fake papers an interpretation spawned by his febrile imagination. Today we have a term for what Sisson brought on himself, *black propaganda*—that is, false information unwittingly distributed by the very people who are being deceived. Such propaganda has great force when it comes with the imprimatur of a trusted authority. Russian agents could not have found a better conduit than the CPI. Not only did it publish the bogus documents. Evoking government authority in support of them became a mania for Creel. When Philip Patchin informed him that British intelligence found anomalies in the documents, he responded, "I submit this is hardly a ground on which to question documents officially issued by a division of the government of the United States under authority of the President." In other words, the British had no right to make up their own mind. Such was Creel's state of mind by the end of the war.[103]

The Sisson-Creel combination played to both men's weaknesses, the one being inclined to sensationalism and the other to impetuousness. Wilson's reliance on two men with no credentials for pronouncing judgment on a German-Bolshevik conspiracy and his failure to tell the State Department that he approved publication constituted administrative malpractice. Wilson had warned Sisson to stay away from "political entanglements" and then followed him into an adventure that haunted policy toward the Soviet Union for years to come. "Sisson's belief in the authenticity of the documents later communicated itself quite extensively to State Department officialdom," Kennan argued, "and added an unnecessary burden of suspicion to the formation of their judgment about the Bolsheviki."[104]

The lesson taught by the Sisson documents is not easily learned. Disinformation has become an ever-higher art form. The internet and social media, for instance, have exponentially increased the ability of adversarial nations to undermine each other's elections. In the 2016 US presidential election, a fifty-thousand-strong army of Russian bots—web robots—sent out fake messages that were retweeted by Republican candidate Donald Trump's campaign. The base power of disinformation, however, lies not in technology but in human nature, the desire of people to seek confirmation of their beliefs.

The United States' path to war with Iraq in 2003 eerily recalled that element of the Sisson documents. To make the case for an invasion, the George W. Bush administration relied heavily on Ahmadi Chalabi and fellow Iraqi dissidents who wanted Saddam Hussein ousted. Chalabi lined up a parade of Iraqi defectors to provide compelling and inaccurate stories of Hussein's terrorist connections and his stockpile of weapons of mass destruction. In addition to selling the invasion to the public, the campaign solidified the administration's conviction that it was right to do what it wanted to do. "It's dangerous," Chalabi was known to quip from time to time, "if you believe your own propaganda."[105]

14

Getting Ready to Get Out of Business

So far as direct service to newspapers is concerned, the Committee on Public
Information last night said good-by to Chairman George Creel and Night
Watchman Barcages locked the front door of the historic old residence on
Jackson Place and threw the key away. The seed planted in various government
departments is taking root, but the moth plant, cut off by the whirlwind
of peace, has closed a valiant though storm-tossed career.
— *Washington Herald,* December 1, 1918

During his three-day congressional grilling in June 1918, Creel was categorical
as to what would happen to the Committee on Public Information when peace
arrived. "We have always gone on the assumption that this organization was
purely an emergency organization," he testified, "and would disappear as soon
as the war was over."[1]

As that day approached and newspaper headlines chronicled the crumbling
of the Central Powers, staff began to think about life after the CPI. Harvey
O'Higgins told his old friend Judge Ben Lindsey in late October that he expected to return to theater work in New York soon. "I have a hunch that the
Committee on Public Information will cease the moment that peace is declared." On November 9, Creel declared he was "getting ready to get out of
business."[2]

Two days later, Armistice Day, President Wilson told a joint session of Congress, "The war thus comes to an end." Within twenty-four hours, Creel announced that "demobilization" of the CPI would begin. The domestic bureaus
would cease operations at the end of the month. The foreign operations would
continue for a short time. A representative of the Advertising Division told
Printers' Ink it was winding up a fund drive for the Red Cross and a conservation campaign for the Fuel Administration. "If it is deemed advisable by those
in authority, we shall 'shut up shop' with good grace."[3]

Censors immediately gave news dispatches "wider latitude." On November 14, the CPI called a halt to voluntary press censorship. Two days later Carl Ackerman and other correspondents received notice that the Censorship Board was following the CPI's lead on news. Because other communications were still subject to suppression, censors remained at their desks for a week "so that there might be no error in the sorting and expedition of press matter at the cable company stations in New York."[4]

The CPI's demise brought forth gushers of stories and editorials. The overall sentiment was relief. Some gleefully administered another kick in the CPI's shins; some let bygones be bygones. Creel, the *Herald* said, was zealous, but sincere. "He made mistakes because all good men make mistakes rather than 'play it safe.'" Despite their frustrations, reporters learned "the value of a central distribution agent and reference room." Censorship had been "more irritating than painful," the *New York Times* said backhandedly. "Perhaps it was just as well that [Creel] was not a very good—that is, a very effective—censor."[5]

But another sentiment crept into newspaper commentary as it became apparent the CPI's obituary was premature. Creel had once again spoken hastily. The dates for closing some bureaus slipped; a few activities seemed destined to carry on indefinitely. Delighted as it was with the prospective demise of "Creeled" news, the *Indianapolis News* worried that the *Official Bulletin* would survive to "guide and to amuse us." Worse news lay in the announcement Creel would accompany Wilson to treaty negotiations in Paris.[6]

Thus, the CPI began the final fraught episode in its short history.

The CPI was cobbled together piece by piece. It was taken apart the same way, but with less enthusiasm. Many staff felt they should carry on, and some did. O'Higgins stayed for months to supervise closure of headquarters. To its bitter end the CPI remained entangled in controversy, only now it was more vulnerable. In the midterm elections just before the armistice, the Republicans reclaimed control of both houses of Congress and could more easily exact punishment on the CPI. "Creel is still Creel," Illinois Republican senator Sherman declaimed, "and the chairman of public information will be the same journalistic drunkard in the journalistic wine cellar, as he was in Denver and that he has been in Washington."[7]

When Congress ended the CPI's funding on June 30, 1919, a controversial financial autopsy continued. Several years passed before the last shovel of dirt was thrown on the CPI grave.

RELUCTANT DISMEMBERMENT

The CPI was hitting its stride as the war ended. In September it attracted 1.5 million people to its grand Chicago War Exposition and staged its large labor conference in Minneapolis. The foreign operation was gelling. Although they were resigned to the CPI going out of business eventually, staff continued to plan more activities. At the end of October, they considered producing films for the Federal Board for Vocational Education to help disabled servicemen. Six days before the armistice, Sisson told Bullard, "Keep your news-distributing organization at high pitch of efficient." He notified CPI representatives overseas, "If Germany accepts terms, Committee work of news distribution in foreign countries will continue throughout period of session of peace conference." Even James Keeley, who had done virtually nothing with battlefield propaganda, was told to "hold yourself in readiness to shift your organization to meet any changing conditions."[8]

The government was not ready to give up its wartime habits of combating subversion. The State Department released a batch of intercepted telegrams from Bernstorff relating to German propaganda activities in the United States. The *Official Bulletin* ran a long story on them. Attorney General Gregory said the American Protective League was still needed. General Churchill with MID told a former CPI news liaison, who was now on the army payroll, that he wanted "careful scrutiny of the press" for anything that warranted prosecution under the Espionage Act.[9]

The CPI unsuccessfully tried to suppress a movie that depicted a German officer as kind and honorable. Fearing "deliberate propaganda" by the Germans in the United States, Ernest Poole argued for "prompt and vigorous effort to meet such hostile efforts now." In a late November dinner speech at the American Slavic Conference, Creel warned of a new wave of German propaganda perpetrated by German women who had written letters to Wilson's wife. "These women, who never grieved for a single moment when the Lusitania with her innocent men, women, and children was torpedoed, who never lifted their voice in protest when the babies of Belgium were slaughtered at the breasts of their mothers, . . . are now flashing their cry to America for sympathy and for help, while the male propagandists are holding out their hands dripping blood and begging for mercy." This was a harsh statement in light of starvation on the central European home front.[10]

Lamenting demobilization, Poole's managing editor Hamilton Owens said, "I had an enormous staff of able people gathered from all over the country, speaking all kinds of languages, at the end of the war, and they were all dumped. . . . It seemed a shame that all that talent should just be disbanded like that." Charles Dana Gibson's Division of Pictorial Publicity passed a resolution that it should continue its work. George Hecht pled for a temporary stay of execution for the Cartoon Bureau, which had been a link between government departments and cartoonists around the country. "The bombing of the bridge ought to be delayed at least three or four months," he told Creel. Nevertheless, Creel decreed the Cartoon Bureau would end on December 1, along with the speaking program, the Division of Civil and Educational Cooperation, and the News Division. Gibson's was to go two weeks later, at the same time as the Advertising Division and the Division of Publication and Distribution.[11]

While these units met or came close to meeting Creel's end-of-November date for closure, exceptions were made for practical reasons. Hart's Film Division shut on December 1, but sales continued into the next year. War Expositions continued through the postwar Liberty Loan campaign. Although his division was eliminated in December, Guy Stanton Ford and another employee were temporarily put on the rolls of the Foreign Press Bureau. Creel told Wilson it would be "a serious loss" to kill the *Official Bulletin,* and the decision was made for it to carry on at least through the peace negotiations. The *Bulletin* staff, which formerly occupied ten offices on the second and third floors at 10 Jackson Place, squeezed into three rooms at 16 Jackson Place. Its editor, Edward Rochester, grumbled to Creel, "You can't get a quart of milk into a pint bottle."[12]

The Service Bureau, the CPI's center for guiding people through the federal bureaucracy, did not close until April 1, 1919. Its directory was transferred to the Bureau of Efficiency and later to the Bureau of the Budget, where it was discontinued. The CPI's journal for children, the *National School Service,* was moved to the Bureau of Education in 1919 and edited by J. J. Pettijohn from the CPI's former Speakers' Bureau. The journal folded after nine issues when the Republican-led Congress cut its funding.[13]

The Division of Work with the Foreign Born had a longer afterlife. Determined and enterprising as ever, Josephine Roche transformed it into a nonprofit organization under a different name, the Foreign Language Information Service. The FLIS retained its goal of transmitting useful government information to immigrants. Arabic, Chinese, and Spanish were added. Roche stepped aside after four years. The FLIS lived from grant to grant. For a time, it was integrated into the Red Cross. In 1939, it succumbed to persistent financial problems.[14]

When Wilson offered farewell praise for the Four Minute Men, he was clear the division should shut and stay shut: "The name of the Four Minute Men (which I venture to hope will not be used henceforth by any similar organization) has become part of the history of the great war." William Ingersoll, who had replaced William Blair as its chief, nevertheless urged the Open Forum, which promoted debates and speeches, to invite the Four Minute Men to affiliate with them. The Open Forum responded with "a plan for the serious discussion of public matters to make democracy safe for America," but no affiliation came about.[15]

The speed with which the CPI was dismembered made careful planning and orderly execution difficult, besides which, as one critic observed at the CPI's end, "God did not make [Creel] an executive." Just before Christmas, when he was with Wilson in Paris, Creel abruptly closed the seventeen departments of Poole's Foreign Press Bureau, which expected to carry on during the peace negotiations. The announcement was all the more jarring because it came with less than a week's notice and took effect on New Year's Day. Creel made the draconian decision out of frustration with criticism that the CPI's overseas work was too long on its deathbed.[16]

Creel's impulsive "Christmas message," as it was derisively called, angered the bureau's ninety-odd journalists, lecturers, college professors, and linguists. A *New York World* reporter stopped by the bureau's eleventh floor offices on Madison Avenue. The disgruntled staff vented their unhappiness with Creel and his style of management, which was duly recounted in the *World* story. "It was the wish of Chairman Creel, the members explained, that as much as possible of the work of the bureau should remain unknown in America." It rankled the staff that while they spent Christmas worried about finding new jobs, Sisson, Byoir, and other lucky CPI colleagues were with Creel in Paris and still drawing salaries.[17]

CREEL'S UNFAVORABLE EFFECT

While putting his "emergency organization" out of business, Creel agitated for a personal continuing role with Wilson at the Paris treaty talks. Wilson gave him a berth on the USS *George Washington* with his small personal party, which included his physician Admiral Cary Grayson, his secretary, and Secret Service men. But when the liner slipped out of Hoboken, sirens and whistles blasting, Wilson had made no decision as to what Creel would do when they reached France.

The announcement that Creel and others from the CPI were going to Paris set off alarm bells. When Hugh Gibson informed Lippmann and Merz that the Sisson party was on its way, he noted in his diary, "I took all the joy out of their young lives. . . . The C.P.I. is evidently up to its old tricks of trying to run the whole show & G.C. is probably coming with the President to grab off some of the glory." William Wiseman, who continued as an interlocutor with Wilson and House, told Wilson's legal advisor, David Hunter Miller, he "feared that Creel's coming with the president may have a very unfavorable effect." Noting the potential trouble that lay ahead, David Lawrence reported that Creel "had lost the confidence of the press." Joseph Tumulty advised Wilson that Creel should have no part of press relations due to his unpopularity at home.[18]

Reminders of Creel's turbulent effect appeared almost daily in newspapers.

CPI staff arriving in France at the end of the war. Their mission generated a new round of criticism for the CPI. Edgar Sisson is third from the left; fourth from the left, in back row, is Kenneth Durant. William Chenery is seventh in line, also in the back row. Edward Bernays and Carl Byoir stand, in that order, on the far right. (Bain News Service photograph collection, Library of Congress)

One of the first episodes to roil public opinion was a presidential proclamation, published in the *Official Bulletin* on November 16, that Burleson would take temporary control of marine cables. This was justified. Lack of cooperation among cable companies in handling the heavy load of postwar messages delayed crucial diplomatic communications. But critics saw the proclamation, which the *Bulletin* did not announce until two weeks after it was signed, as part of a nefarious plot to "creelize" news from Paris. "Is the partisan Burleson to hold the wire," the *Chicago Tribune* editorialized, "and is the rhapsodic quack doc of journalism, Creel, to fill it?"[19]

Immediately after this came an announcement that seemed to confirm that the answer to this rhetorical question was "Yes, Creel would fill it." At the direction of Ernest Poole, Edward Bernays gave out a news release stating a United States Official Press Mission to the Peace Conference under Sisson was heading to Paris. Its declared mission was to "interpret the work of the Peace Conference by keeping up a world-wide propaganda to disseminate American accomplishments and ideals." Journalists' worst fears were coming true. The CPI was not to disappear. Capitol Hill glowed with the white heat of condemnation.[20]

Creel was vehement in his denials, each of which further minimized the role the CPI would play. The Sisson mission "did not in any manner constitute 'an official peace press mission.'" It went to Europe to close up the CPI's foreign activities. He was going to Europe to help. The CPI would facilitate the transmission of correspondents' stories from the peace conference without tampering with them in any way. Creel promised the "fullest and freest flow of news" from Paris. Rumors that he would have a role with publicity were "absolutely without foundation."[21]

Sisson and his party were on the high seas when news stories based on Bernays's press release appeared. Creel cabled ahead, "Tell Sisson on arrival publicity to be avoided absolutely." But as soon as the party landed, Sisson called Creel's disclaimers into question. Speaking with reporters in Paris, he said the CPI would neither censor nor serve as "press agents" for the president or the peace commission, but it would issue statements on behalf of negotiators to prevent misunderstandings. Sisson or someone else—perhaps Bernays—told reporters, "Every American official communication to the press must pass Mr. Creel." A new burst of condemnation followed. Journalists considered these comments "a direct controversion" of Creel's assurances censorship was abandoned. Throughout the war Creel had inspired editorial cartoonists; they now achieved their high-water mark in Creel ridicule.[22]

The allegations of Creel-Burleson collusion to thwart news were figments of agitated imaginations. Similarly, journalists and Wilson's opponents over-reacted to a misleading report the CPI would ration cable space for news. The congestion of cable lines, not Creel, made news rationing necessary. Creel helped correspondents by securing guaranteed cable space for them and letting them allot it among themselves. He also convinced the War Department to provide correspondents with transport to Europe.[23]

Privately, Creel blamed Bernays for "stupid and misleading publicity." But Creel's public claim that he harbored no ambitions for managing the press in Paris was not credible. His staff believed that he had an expansive publicity agenda in mind. They left New York, Bernays recalled, "mentally prepared to handle the releases of the American delegates, maintain liaison with the American and foreign press, and assume for the delegation and the President the generally accepted functions of a press mission." When Sisson boarded the ship for Europe he carried a letter of introduction from Creel to "THE CIVIL, MILITARY, AND NAVAL REPRESENTATIVES OF THE UNITED STATES AND OF THE ALLIED COUNTRIES." It stated Sisson was in charge of "the Committee's cable, wireless, and operative organization in the different countries." Byoir may have had an even stronger mandate for action. When Creel sent instructions that Sisson should "absolutely" avoid all publicity, he added, "Tell Byoir not to use his letter under any circumstances and to destroy all photographic copies."[24]

In anticipation of taking on such a mission, Bernays had been directed to purchase 3,360 stencils, 144 pounds of ink, 100 bottles of varnish, other materials used for mimeographing and reproduction, and, inexplicably, a maternity kit. Sisson's party, later enlarged, included an accountant, three secretaries, and a treasury official—who could help close offices but do other jobs as well. Among those with Sisson were Carl Walberg, who worked with the Advertising Division; Kenneth Durant and William Chenery, who had handled press relations; and experts in German affairs. Sisson established a press center in a six-story mansion a few steps off the Champs-Élysées that was formerly owned by James Gordon Bennett, the deceased proprietor of the *New York Herald* and its sister newspaper in Paris.[25]

The press center, Creel insisted, was an act of unrequited kindness that he abandoned when journalists abused him for it. The CPI could easily have done more with the building and with Sisson's staff if the opportunity presented itself. The most generous assessment of Creel's ambiguous, shifting statements before reaching Paris was that his plans were inchoate and flexible. To journal-

ists, who assessed the situation from the outside, a position involving press relations seemed a distinct possibility, given Creel's CPI experience and his status
as a Wilson favorite. If Wilson asked him to work with the press, who could
deny the president? And, indeed, a press position was under consideration, although the prospects dimmed with each new negative story that followed Creel
to Europe.[26]

A MAN IN SEARCH OF A MISSION

On the morning of December 4, the day the *George Washington* set sail for
France, Creel arrived late. With Wilson aboard, the ship was sealed off. Reporters delighted in watching the agitated CPI chairman "exert official pressure"
to be allowed to board. "Without him in the party, without his illuminating
literary touch," a reporter noted archly, "one shudders to think of the consequences."[27]

Two days out, when nasty weather hit, Creel was sidelined by seasickness.
His frustrations over being a man without a portfolio were as obvious as the
turbulent ocean through which the ship streamed. More than one person commented that Creel complained he "did not know a god-damn thing about
what the president is thinking." Grayson, who served as Joseph Tumulty's eyes
and ears on the presidential party, noted Creel's discomfort in a letter written
shortly before reaching France on December 13. Creel, he said unsympatheti-
cally, was "very much disturbed as to what his duties with the President are to
be when he arrives. He has tackled the President several times to let him handle
and digest his paper work, or serve him in any other way that he possibly can,
but the President is standing pat."[28]

In Paris, Creel had Room 75 at the Crillon Hotel, in the center of the action.
He bustled about, dashing off on Christmas Day with Sisson and Byoir for a
visit of battlefields and rushing back to the Crillon for dinner with a French dig-
nitary. He used these opportunities to hold forth on the CPI's outstanding accomplishments. Will Irwin, who dined with him and H. G. Wells one evening
in London, complained to his wife of Creel's relentless self-promotion, "There's
only one talent worth anything in this world—window dressing. Because I lack
it utterly, I have failed with the goods right on me. George has it. He has been
leaping from court to court as the great American propagandist."[29]

As Wilson continued to stand pat, Creel remained a minor figure in the
great peace drama. He did odd jobs for the president and picked fights. House

warned Wilson that a "head-on collision" was in the offing with Lansing. "Lansing's dislike for Creel," he said, "was only equaled by Creel's dislike for Lansing." "That Mr. Creel has been peeved since he reached Europe is an open secret," wrote a reporter with the *Kansas City Post,* which had never been overly fond of its hometown boy. "Following his usual custom, he crowded next to the president when his corps of movie operators were filming the landing—but that was the last time Creel was able to shove himself into the limelight."[30]

While a press job was under consideration for Creel, other ideas were floated, including the paper-digesting job Grayson referred to in his letter to Tumulty. In this he would be Wilson's "foreign secretary," the Paris equivalent of Tumulty's job at 1600 Pennsylvania Avenue. But on the way over by boat that role was effectively assumed by Gilbert Close, Wilson's stenographer and his secretary at Princeton. When Wilson became angry about the men who Lansing put together for a secretariat, House suggested a team, working under himself. On the team would be Creel as well as House's son-in-law Gordon Auchincloss and diplomat Hugh Frazier, who was a member of Gibson's anti-CPI cabal. Apart from expanding House's power, this scheme had nothing to commend it. As discussed in more detail in the next chapter, no job in Paris worked out for Creel. The main press position, directing the Press Bureau of the American Commission to Negotiate Peace, was given to Ray Stannard Baker.[31]

By Christmas Day, Creel reached the limit of his easily frayed patience. He announced he was severing his relations with the government. He had finished his close-down of the CPI and was returning home. Press accounts said he was leaving "in a huff." Then, amid extensive press coverage of this latest Creel commotion, the story changed. He would not return home right away. He was to accompany Wilson on his triumphal visit to Italy, where he could buck up CPI staff suffering from their estrangement from Ambassador Page. From Rome he would undertake a special mission to central Europe.[32]

This mission, which has received scant attention from historians, was a continuation of Creel's intemperate behavior, albeit so extreme it could have been written as a farcical caricature of what had come before.

CREEL'S MISSION TO CENTRAL EUROPE

Creel proposed his central Europe mission to "save my face." The purpose he envisioned was to extend CPI wireless service into those enemy countries and to distribute CPI materials. The mission also could gather intelligence on the region, which House felt was badly lacking. Creel argued that he could "discharge two tasks on the one errand."[33]

The proposed dual mission sparked the interest of the four American commissioners: House, Lansing, veteran diplomat Henry White, and former army chief of staff General Tasker Bliss. After some deliberation, however, they decided it was more prudent to have a separate mission for intelligence gathering. Creel could go to central Europe strictly for propaganda purposes. Joseph Grew, the commission's secretary, told Creel the commission did not want to "run the risk of possible criticism and embarrassment at the peace table of having any of its representatives identified with propaganda work in territory the future status of which is to be discussed at the conference. This issue is clear and unquestionable."[34]

Creel's mission conveniently solved some problems. Wilson had a handy opportunity to give his loyal aide something to do. Lansing and House got Creel out of the way. But "the risk of possible criticism and embarrassment" that Grew feared was palpable. Creel had no experience abroad apart from his faux Stanley-finds-Livingston search for Roosevelt in Africa for the *Denver Post.* He was notorious for taking an expansive view of his duties, and two of the men he brought with him were no less independent—Sisson and Czech-born Emanuel Voska, whose exploits constitute a fantastic chapter of the war.

Voska, commissioned a US Army captain, was highly regarded. Wilson heard "very favorable" reports about him. When Hugh Gibson met Voska in Paris, he thought him "bent on creating all sorts of trouble where trouble ought to be created." Voska was a born political troublemaker. He began life in Bohemia as a stonecutter specializing in cherubs on tombs. When he irritated authorities with criticism of Hapsburg rule of Czechoslovakia, a government official suggested he emigrate to America. By the time the war began in 1914, Voska had a prosperous marble business and was active in the Czech community. He used these ties to create an organization dedicated to promoting US entry into the war. An Allied victory, he correctly reasoned, would lead to an independent Czechoslovakia.[35]

Voska worked with British spies Guy Gaunt and William Wiseman to plant anti-German stories in that most willing British propaganda outlet the *Providence Journal.* To gather intelligence and steal documents, German-speaking Czech-Americans in Voska's network found jobs in Austro-Hungarian and German consulates as well as the German embassy itself. After the United States entered the war, he helped Josephine Roche's foreign-born division organize

Liberty Loan drives among Czech- and Slovak-Americans, assisted Will Irwin direct CPI propaganda at Czech revolutionaries in Europe, and in 1917 set up espionage networks in central Europe and Russia. This last exploit is the one, mentioned in a previous chapter, that was dreamed up by House and Wiseman. Breaking into the Petrograd apartment of a female spy, his men acquired documents that showed payments to Bolshevik leaders. The money, he believed, originated with the Germans. This, no doubt, endeared him to Sisson.[36]

Voska was resourceful and daring, absolutely the wrong person to discourage the freelancing inclinations of Creel and Sisson. Because House, Lansing, and the other commissioners wanted to disassociate themselves from the Creel mission, they effectively handed the three men license to do as they saw fit in Poland, Czechoslovakia, and Hungary, fragile countries struggling to find their way in the postwar world.

Continuing the practice of other CPI staff overseas, Creel conferred titles on himself. He was sometimes Wilson's assistant, sometimes his personal secretary. He remembered none of the lessons he should have learned from his ill-fated Church of the Ascension debacle the previous May. Publicly and privately, he held forth on any subject that came to mind.

Creel arrived in Prague with his fourteen-person party on January 13. The trip on a Czechoslovak troop train was uncomfortable and prolonged by violent snowstorms. The welcome was warm thanks to Voska's connections. At a reception, Creel assured everyone the United States was thoroughly behind the new government and its president, philosopher Tomáš Masaryk. He ended with "Glory to the Czechs!" He was more wound up in an interview with a Czech newspaper. He declared the United States would provide agricultural supplies. "America is ready to give you everything." Creel declared. "America, England, and France have but one favorite, and that is you—you are the dam against Germanism and Bolshevism." At a farewell dinner, he said that he would emigrate to the Czechoslovak Republic if he were ever forced to leave the United States. In an interview with the London *Times*, he criticized the Allies for not taking over the German wireless station at Nauen. "Disquieting" reports of these statements reached the commissioners, who struggled to recall the purpose of Creel's mission.[37]

Officially Voska translated and arranged printing of CPI materials. Unofficially he was a political actor. Sisson and Byoir—as Sisson told the story—conceived a plan for Voska to get radicalized Bohemian coal miners to go back to work. Voska told the miners that Bohemian workmen in the United States helped finance their campaign to become an independent nation. This was the CPI's "last big job," Sisson told House. "Voska was the mace that smashed the Bolsheviks."[38]

Around the same time Creel's mission became tangentially involved in the Czech invasion of the Duchy of Teschen. The coal-rich enclave had been divided between Czechoslovakia and Poland in late 1918. Poland kept the three districts in which its people made up the largest share of the population. Czechoslovakia received the fourth. Neither side was happy with the division, and an escalation of tension resulted in a Czech force marching into the Polish-held districts on January 23. The Czechs gave their action the appearance of having international sanction by creating an "Inter-Allied Military Commission" made up of four Allied officers attached to Czech forces. One of them was Voska's son, Arthur.

When the invasion began, the four officers demanded the local Polish commander immediately evacuate the duchy. Their names were affixed to a similar, widely posted proclamation. In the investigation that followed, all the officers except Lieutenant Arthur Voska said they acted on orders of the Czech minister of defense. He said he took orders from his father but later changed his story to conform to his brother officers. Voska senior was summoned to Paris, where General Bliss questioned him. Voska insisted he had known nothing of the impending invasion. The American Commission terminated his involvement with the CPI and reassigned his son.[39]

In his autobiography, Creel described the episode as a Polish invasion that the Czechs had to repel. He claimed to have traveled to Poland with the approval of Masaryk to mediate and "out of the conversations came a true and eventual agreement." The historical record does not support this. In any event, when the Teschen dispute was settled in 1920, Czechoslovakia received more territory than in the original agreement. In American diplomatic circles it was believed that Creel's overblown comments about America's unswerving support emboldened the Czechs to attack Teschen.[40]

When Bliss questioned Voska, he asked about another CPI escapade. The lone historian to delve into Creel's central European mission, Gregg Wolper, calls it the "affair of the Czernin letters." The phrase is aptly reminiscent of the Sisson documents. In this instance, Sisson arrived at the belief that the Germans, not the Serbs, started the Great War by engineering the assassination of Archduke Franz Ferdinand. Voska probably planted this idea. He claimed evidence could be found in letters and documents associated with former Austrian foreign minister Count Ottokar Czernin and housed in archives in Vienna and Konopiště, the archduke's summer residence outside Prague. Voska stole the papers and translated them. When questioned by Bliss, he said he worked under Sisson's direction but made no mention of its breaking-and-entering aspects.[41]

The report Voska prepared on the letters was full of equivocation. The documents and letters, he told Sisson, "proved there was a German-Magyar conspiracy against Franz Ferdinand." Further on, however, he admitted to having "no positive proof," although it was "evident" the Serbs did not hatch a conspiracy to kill the archduke. "If we do not prove absolute conspiracy by the German government in connection with the Sarajevo tragedy, we shall at least expose the intrigues of the Hapsburgs against the German imperial family as well as the intrigues of Kaiser Wilhelm against the Hapsburgs." The supposed German's motive for the assassination was fear that Franz Ferdinand, heir apparent to the emperor, would block Germany's planned expansion to the Far East. This was nonsense.[42]

In late March, when he was in the United States, Creel released the "Czernin letters" as the latest example of diabolical German scheming. The CPI disguised Voska's involvement. In a bald lie, it said the letters were "turned over to Edgar Sisson at Prague by the custodian official of the Bohemian government, on January 24, 1919." Sisson "accepted the privilege of using them in behalf of the United States Government." Press attention was nothing like that for the Sisson documents.[43]

On Creel's final stop in Budapest, the local press described him as "very talkative." He criticized the French for being difficult to work with in Paris and called for the creation of a confederation in central Europe modeled after the United States, with Hungarian president Mihály Károlyi as president. He privately dispensed military and political advice to Károlyi, who was struggling to survive threats from the right and the left while holding on to his territory. Among Creel's suggestions was a plan to reclaim Transylvania from Romania by joining with Serbia, which had its own border disputes with the Romanians. Károlyi pointed out that his defeated nation was not in a position to pit one Allied nation, Serbia, against another, Romania. Creel promised to intervene on their behalf with Wilson. The commissioners dismissed his various suggestions "as typical and ridiculous." Creel's admonition to Wilson that the Károlyi regime was worth saving became moot when a Bolshevik revolution toppled the Hungarian government in late March. In a *New York Times* interview, Creel blamed the Allies for letting this happen.[44]

The Creel mission distributed 2.5 million CPI pamphlets in central Europe. It connected Prague, Cracow, and Budapest to the CPI information service in Paris. This was an accomplishment. But the reckless mission caused unnecessary diplomatic disruption and spread bogus information in the form of *The German-Bolshevik Conspiracy,* which Voska had translated into Bohemian and Polish and which Sisson talked up wherever he went. When Bliss informed his fellow commissioners that Sisson was digging up evidence of the kaiser's plan to kill the archduke, Lansing related the fiasco of the Sisson documents and proposed that Bliss investigate him. Sisson, Lansing said, was a "dangerous person." [45]

CREEL STILL DISGRUNTLED

Despite Creel's claim he would supervise the closing of CPI foreign operations, he left this to Sisson in Paris and Harry Rickey, who was in charge of the remnants of the Foreign Section in New York. In early February they ordered closure of all overseas offices the next month except for London and Paris. Representatives were to "dispose of office furniture and fixtures at best prices possible" and send their files to Washington. The CPI in Siberia was to arrange for "distribution of all pamphlets etcetca [*sic*] which are left or which arrive after you leave stop this includes Russian translation of Sisson's Bolshevik pamphlet."[46]

As was the case at home, foreign representatives were disappointed. "The interest of Italy in all things American is very keen," Kingsley Moses complained, "and the demand for American news keeps increasing weekly." In a sign that some diplomats had come to see propaganda as a complement to their work, consuls in Siberian cities lamented the decision to withdraw the CPI. "Compub was helping more than any other one American organization to explain away other mistakes in our Siberian policy," the consul in Irkutsk wrote. Due to illness, Bullard had come home the previous December. His replacement warned that shuttering the CPI sent a bad message to Russians in Siberia: "America quits." The Siberian office was closed in mid-March. Not until late June did all the staff leave.[47]

The lone reprieve went to Carl Crow in China, or so he thought. Crow worked largely under the minister, to whom the CPI deferred. Although Sisson's final report listed Peking as demobilized, Crow claimed he "never received any official notification, no discharge, either honorable or dishonorable or non-

committal." As far as he was concerned, he remained perpetually "in the employ of the Committee and helping to carry on the Great War on the Shanghai
front." While that was jocular, written some years later, Crow paid himself from
the profits of his dummy company for months. He occasionally sent comments
on Chinese press coverage to the American treaty delegation in Paris, although
he doubted anyone read them.[48]

Creel was not eager to return to the United States. His disappointment at
not having another assignment came out on a visit to his old friend Ambassador Brand Whitlock in Belgium in mid-February. One morning Whitlock
found him eating breakfast in front of the fire and mentioned Wilson had just
appointed journalist William Allen White as one of two men to represent the
United States in a conference with Russians at Prinkipo, a conference that was
later called off. Creel "suddenly got up, and went hurriedly over to the window,
turning his back and looking down into the street, struggling with some emotion." It was, Whitlock wrote in his diary, "a touching little tragedy." Creel told
Whitlock he felt "some lack of appreciation on the President's part, a certain
high, frigid, and impassive impersonality."[49]

Many of those who worked for Wilson had similar experiences. But when
Creel returned to Paris, the president gave him a new mission, this time to assess
Irish attitudes about home rule. The issue had serious political implications for
Wilson. Irish-Americans wanted him to press the case for Irish independence
at the treaty talks. As much as anything, though, the motive was once again,
as Wilson told Creel, to counter rumors that "you are no longer in my good
graces, and I do not mean to let the impression gain ground." Creel's performance on this short assignment was not as fraught as the central Europe mission had been.[50]

Afterwards, Creel wanted still more to do. In an afternoon meeting with
House in Paris the last day of February, the colonel found Creel "disgruntled
with the President and pretty much everyone else. He says he will resign tomorrow as Chairman of the Bureau [*sic*] of Public Information." In a letter to Wilson that day, Creel provided a report on his trip to Ireland and said he expected
to leave in three days. "All the domestic work has been closed up. All foreign
work has been discontinued save the news distribution machinery with offices
in New York, Paris and London." He had removed himself from the payroll and
would work without pay on the remaining liquidation issues. His resignation
took effect on April 1. "How deeply I have appreciated the work you have done

as Chairman of the Committee on Public Information," Wilson wrote to Creel. "The work has been well done, admirably well done, and your inspiration and guidance have been the chief motive power of it all."[51]

In reality much remained to be done at home. Harvey O'Higgins, who was acting while Creel was away, told a congressional committee many decisions had been put off. "We are all in a state of complete uncertainty," Josephine Roche fretted, "which I trust will be cleared up upon George's return. We are expecting him within a week or ten days now." Despite Roche's hope he would quickly set things right, he was soon embroiled in two new controversies, the disposition of the *Official Bulletin* and the final financial reckoning of the CPI. Creel's days as the enfant terrible of the Wilson administration were not over.[52]

THE OFFICIAL BULLETIN

The flow of press releases did not cease when the News Division closed. Executive branch departments that the CPI had serviced took over those tasks, often transferring CPI staff to their payrolls. These news releases had value, but they did not give a systematic, full picture of government activities. Nor could editors, however earnest they were about showing the workings of government, begin to publish all of them. The space in newspapers was too limited and, even if it were not, many handouts held little interest to the average reader.

This is where the *Official Bulletin* came in. By broadening its scope beyond war-making agencies and by limiting itself to unadorned notice of contracts, regulations, and official pronouncements, the *Bulletin* could make the government more transparent to the people whose money it was spending. The climate in Congress, however, was not conducive to this in 1919.

The Government Printing Office, which produced the *Bulletin* and other executive branch publications, answered to legislators through the Joint Committee on Printing (JCP). A four-person Republican majority dominated the committee as a result of the politically upending congressional elections in November 1918. The two Democrats on the JCP were docile, at best, when it came to defending the CPI or government publishing generally. One of the Democrats sneeringly referred to the rise of government publicity during the war as "this mimeograph evil."[53]

In a yearlong review of government publications, the JCP eliminated 111 of them. It subsequently axed another 255. The committee claimed to have "nipped in the bud the greatest propaganda scheme the country has ever escaped." It singled out the CPI as the root of all mimeograph evil. "Cravings of the limelight," it said, "undoubtedly were inspired by the bombastic activities of the Committee on Public Information, headed by that master publicist, George Creel." The *Official Bulletin* especially irked the JCP.[54]

The Sundry Civil Appropriations Bill, passed in the House in February 1919, included a unanimously approved provision ordering the *Bulletin* to cease on April 1. The measure did not become law before the session ran out. But something similar was sure to spell the demise of the *Bulletin,* and Creel issued an order to end publication on the date specified in the bill.[55]

This would have put the matter to rest if Rochester, the *Bulletin's* editor, had not been determined to keep the publication going. In the last months of war, he lined up endorsements from cabinet secretaries and floated plans to refashion it as a joint venture of several agencies. After the JCP scotched these ideas, he turned to Roger Babson, whom Creel had handed off to the Department of Labor. The provision of basic information such as the *Bulletin* provided was along the lines of *Babson's Reports,* which the consummate entrepreneur had created earlier to track and forecast markets. On the advice of the attorney general, he and Rochester renamed their publication *United States Bulletin,* sans the "official" in the original title. Babson's acquisition was announced in the *Bulletin* on March 31, the day before it was to go out of business. The notice said the Labor Department authorized Babson to continue the *Bulletin.* It identified Babson as a department employee, a position he would hold until the end of June.[56]

The obvious irregularity of this arrangement, in which the Labor Department authorized the continuation of a publication it did not control but which was overseen by a person who worked for the department, drew the attention of the JCP. The JCP's inquiries led the secretary of labor to deny that his department had any connection to the *Bulletin.* More irregularities came out when the JCP held hearings on the journal in August 1918. The *Bulletin's* business manager also had been a department employee, on a part-time basis, during the first weeks Babson owned it. An anonymous informant claimed Babson hauled off equipment and files from the CPI offices in the dead of night. This could not be proved. Babson and Rochester acknowledged copying the mailing list with Creel's written permission. The list was technically available to anyone who wanted it, but Babson and Rochester's affiliation with the CPI made the copying seem shady.[57]

Babson testified that he had not known Congress wanted to discontinue the *Bulletin*. This drew a barbed comment from one committee member. How could the owner of a publication that followed official happenings fail "to know anything about legislation affecting itself"? In its final report, the JCP said Babson had "lost no opportunity to advertise himself at Government expense" through Labor Department publications. He had come "into possession of the Bulletin, its name, good will, prestige and value as a going concern . . . without paying the Government for any of those valuable assets." Another party had expressed an interest in acquiring the publication but never received a response from the CPI when it inquired about the possibility. No bids were solicited.[58]

The JCP charged Creel and his colleagues with a "deliberate effort to loot" the *Bulletin*. It recommended that the Justice Department consider proceeding against them. No charges were pressed, but Creel ensured the topic did not fade from the news by writing a letter, which he made public, denouncing the JCP and its chairman Senator Reed Smoot. "The war is over," he wrote, "and I am no longer compelled to sit silent under your malice." Creel asked Attorney General Palmer what protection he had "against the deliberate slander of a member of Congress." Babson and Rochester chimed in. They called Smoot an "an obnoxious cancer in the side of American public life" and accused the JCP of doing what it said the CPI did, taking "invisible control over a large portion of the Washington news." Babson vowed to use the *Bulletin* to protect government departments from being silenced by the JCP. He said Smoot, a Mormon, was acting vengefully because Babson had attacked the church.[59]

Babson's *Bulletin,* which focused on commercial information emanating from the government, struggled financially. It appeared twice a week initially, then weekly, and finally was sold to Babson's cousin, who made it into a commodity and investment publication. Babson's *Bulletin* was a prototype for the Washington newsletters that proliferated afterward.[60]

The JCP critique of the *Bulletin* and other government publications took the principled view that the executive branch was acquiring an enormous advantage in making its case to the public. But principle alone did not animate legislators. The chief motivation was partisanship. In 1920, the JCP asked for the power "to pass on the publication or discontinuance of all Government journals, magazines, and periodicals." As soon as Warren Harding was elected president, the JCP lost its zeal for trimming publications. In 1922, it pushed through legislation shifting the responsibility for supervising publications to the president's Bureau of the Budget. Republican representative Albert Johnson, one of the most outspoken opponents of Wilson's publications, championed the new law. "Why should I be obliged to say that one journal published by the Federal Government is a bad thing? How do I know?"[61]

This pattern was to be followed in coming years. Legislators objected to executive branch publications when a member of the opposite party was president and shifted their point of view when one of their own sat in the White House. With Congress writing virtually no meaningful legislation curbing government publications, the number soared to between fifteen and twenty thousand by 1938. This broadly estimated range illustrated how difficult it became to know how much information the government put out.[62]

When federal activity exploded during the New Deal, something had to be done to ensure an accessible public record of the myriad decisions being made. The result was an improved iteration of the *Official Bulletin* under a new name. The daily *Federal Register* first appeared in 1936. It published rules and regulations, executive orders, and presidential proclamations without editorial comment. The archivist of the United States oversaw the *Register* via an administrative committee. An annual compilation of the rules in the *Register* was later created, the *Code of Federal Regulations.* In due course other topics covered by the old *Official Bulletin* were picked up by the *Weekly Compilation of Presidential Documents,* made up of press materials released by the White House, and the *Commerce Business Daily,* which lists proposed procurement, contracts, and sales of government property.[63]

The JCP uncovered true excesses. One army camp journal ran 104 pages with layout and design rivaling *Ladies' Home Journal,* and another in the same camp was akin to *Vanity Fair.* But the *Bulletin* was not extravagant and should have carried on in a form more in line with postwar circumstances, as the *Federal Register* did. Wilson and the CPI deserve credit for originating the idea.[64]

LOST RECORDS AND A FINAL ACCOUNTING

The CPI's financing lapsed the last day of June 1919, the end of the federal government's fiscal year. On July 20, the day after the budget for the next fiscal year was approved, army trucks rolled up in front of the lone building now occupied by the CPI on Jackson Place and carted off the files that had not been lost, thrown out, taken home by staff, or transferred to other agencies. Not that officialdom cared much about the records that were left behind. Congress made no provision for their disposition. The files were dumped in a large room in a building used by the federal Fuel Administration, which was demobilized at the same time.

Almost exactly a month later, Wilson signed an executive order requiring that "the chairman of the Committee on Public Information relinquish and transfer to the Council of National Defense all papers, files, records, public property, assets, and liabilities, and all effects of whatsoever kind, and that upon such relinquishment and transfer the Committee on Public Information shall cease and be at an end." The 640 file cabinet drawers in the Fuel Administration building were transferred the next day to the CND. The files arrived in a disorganized fashion and, according to the CND director at the time, Grosvenor Clarkson, cried out for "a complete investigation." The next week, Clarkson appointed Emmons K. Ellsworth on his staff to make sense of the papers and provide a final accounting. The CND carried over three people from the CPI to help.[65]

The CND was a logical choice for this task. It was custodian of the records of the shuttered War Industries Board and the Fuel Administration. But it was a bitter decision for Creel. The CND had been a competitor and critic as well as a collaborator. Its largely conservative leadership, Creel told Wilson shortly before the war ended, helped tilt the midterm election toward the Republicans and silenced the liberal voices Wilson needed to establish the peace he envisioned. Creel urged Wilson to quickly "demobilize the Council of National Defense so that the Chauvinistic, reactionary state organizations may be put out of business."[66]

The haphazard dissolution of the CPI records was not unique to the United States. The British Ministry of Information was the first of that nation's war-related ministries to be obliterated after the war ended. As recounted in an internally written history, which deviated from bureaucratic blandness to wax eloquently about the ministry's demise, "The telephone ceased to ring, the furniture set off joyously on new Odysseys, the files and card-indexes vanished none knows whither; and by the end of the year, after all the struggles and achievements of the Ministry, there remained only a few faithful charwomen, singing the great deeds that had been done, and the kindheartedness of the gentlemen that had done them." The British government was eager to discard this aspect of its victory. Five tons of records disappeared, the majority destroyed by order of Parliament. The government rewarded many officials with knighthoods and other honors for their war work, but neither Buchan nor Masterman was on those lists.[67]

To make sense of CPI records, Ellsworth had to re-create its organizational structure. This was like putting Humpty Dumpty back together. He acquired some lost records, increasing the number of file drawers from 640 to 789. But many were not recovered. The files of the Division of Pictorial Publicity remained in the hands of Charles Dana Gibson. None were found from Babson's short-lived Division of Industrial Relations. It was difficult to say how much was missing. There was no telling, for instance, how many records were kept by the semi-independent Division of Advertising in New York or front organizations under the Division of Work with the Foreign Born.[68]

Many files from overseas offices probably did not make it home. In 1925 two boxes presumed to contain household goods and labeled "Arthur Bullard" were found in the San Francisco General Intermediate Depot at Fort Mason, California. These were sent to a Lieutenant A. L. Bullard in Fayetteville, Arkansas, who returned them to the government. They were CPI records from Siberia. In 1930, when Bullard's widow was collecting her husband's papers, Creel found a few by rummaging through the CPI papers he had taken home with him.[69]

"As far as can be ascertained," Ellsworth's final report said, "there were 22 main divisions of the Committee created at various times." The organizational detail Ellsworth put together—used for table 3, in chapter 8, and table 4, in chapter 12—had shortcomings. Some errors were inconsequential, for instance, that the end date for the Four Minute Men was the last day of 1918, when it actually ceased to exist on Christmas Eve. Others were more significant. Ellsworth could not identify start-stop dates for foreign-born front organizations or compile an accurate list of foreign commissioners. Nevertheless, it is the best summary that exists.[70]

The more immediate issue was the troubled state of CPI finances. Rumors of these problems circulated before the war ended. Major A. L. James with the AEF told Gibson he worried a congressional investigation of the CPI would produce "a scandal over expenditures." In Russia, Bullard lamented, "I certainly will go to jail when I get home over these damned accounts." After the CND began its work, Rochester wrote fretfully to Creel, "If the council makes a report showing the finances of the committee to be in a tangled condition and otherwise illustrate confused and conflicting records, I fear that the Congress will jubilantly exclaim, 'We told you so.'"[71]

Ellsworth discovered unpaid bills, uncollected receipts from films and exhibits, and uncashed checks. When Creel complained about the slow pace of the audit, Ellsworth explained that the absence of records made it "necessary to start the auditing from the very bottom and work up to a point where we could ascertain what had been done before we could do any further work."[72]

The messy finances were rooted in the circumstances under which the CPI grew. It had started quickly in sui generis fashion, rather than fitting into the orderly structure of an existing organization, and it ended abruptly when Congress zeroed out its budget. Front organizations had been difficult to manage, as shown by the troubled spending habits of Alexander Konta with the American-Hungarian Loyalty League and Robert Maisel with the American Alliance for Labor and Democracy. Overseas, commissioners' offices often lacked adequate accounting staff. Their funds came from Wilson's wartime account, which had fewer controls than regularly appropriated funds. Also, the CPI was a conduit for funds that were not entered on its books. It was unclear to Ellsworth what responsibility the CPI had for money it passed from Wilson's wartime fund to the Red Cross and the YMCA. "I do not believe," Sisson told Ellsworth of money he passed along in Russia, "it was the intention of the Committee on Public Information to ask the Red Cross officials for an accounting of these funds." In any case, no one could realistically expect the books in Russia to be well taken care of. The banking system was taken over by the Bolsheviks, and Bullard and his staff were ordered to leave quickly in 1918. In early 1920, "after many hours of exhaustive research and effort on my part," Ellsworth admitted defeat on Russia accounts.[73]

Still, some accounting failures were not easily excused. Robert Murray's books in Mexico were marred by lost financial statements, unaccounted expenditures for "petty cash" amounting to several hundred dollars a month, and the absence of justification for reimbursement on travel. Byoir, who was supposed to be a good manager, did not have receipts for expenses from the central European trip, which took weeks to clear up.[74]

Ellsworth's hair-pulling frustrations burst out in his response to a query from Senator Francis E. Warren, chair of the Senate Appropriations Committee. In light of a CND request for $32,000 to pay for the audit, the senator asked for a rundown of work done to date. In his October 23 letter, Ellsworth poured out a tale of financial horrors. CPI staff "threw up their jobs" after the armistice, leaving disorder behind. Thousands of dollars' worth of checks had accumulated in a safe, in file trays on a desk, and on the floor "without any effort whatever for collection." An auctioneer who sold CPI property did not turn over the proceeds. "An army officer in Roumania" had been left with several thousand dollars. Advances were not to exceed $1,000, but some were much more than that, in one case amounting to $500,000. And so forth.[75]

Ellsworth might have written with more restraint if he had known the letter was going to be leaked. His letter, the *Washington Post* reported, revealed "a lack of financial and business responsibility in that body that has amazed Members of Congress. It would seem that the committee on information [*sic*] had information on pretty much everything under the sun, or professed to have, save its own financial status and what was done with the millions placed at the disposal of George Creel."[76]

Newton Baker reassured Creel that Clarkson was sorry about the bad publicity, but Clarkson's tepid public explanation did nothing to offset the impression left by Ellsworth. Creel's rejoinder showed that Ellsworth had overstated many of his complaints. Staff abruptly left the CPI for the obvious reason that it was abolished, and no continuing funding was provided to finish in any orderly way. Wilson's fund was not subject to congressional restrictions on advances. But headlines like "Creel Denies Work Was Left in Chaos" reinforced the impression that something must be wrong. Creel complained to Daniels about the "cruel and unjust attack. . . . It is virtually the case that we live under the fear of another."[77]

Those fears were realized a few months later when Senator Smoot, still on the anti-CPI warpath, won approval for a resolution calling on the CND to provide a full report on CPI finances. Creel viewed the resolution as nakedly partisan and engineered by the CND. Clarkson, he told Daniels, was "my enemy at all times" and close to Republicans.[78]

While all of this was going on, Creel had to make a living. He pounded out magazine articles and delivered incendiary speeches warning of the spread of Bolshevism, lauding the CPI's contributions to the war, and ridiculing the State Department and Congress. With advertising help from William Rankin, who had worked with the CPI's Advertising Division, he founded an American branch of the British-based Pelman Institute, whose correspondence courses offered questionable instruction for improving mind and memory. Creel's advertisement for the self-help course—"Pelmanism is able to guarantee advancement and increase incomes"—had the whiff of the patent medicine ads Creel had once decried. Pelmanism's "science of success," as Creel described it to Wilson, went bankrupt in 1921.[79]

But the CPI remained constantly on Creel's mind. He wrote two book-length defenses of it that appeared in 1920: *Complete Report of the Chairman of the Committee on Public Information*, published by the Government Printing Office, and *How We Advertised the War*, published by Harper. A reviewer referred to the latter as "a sort of *apologia pro vita sua*."[80]

Creel complained about the time he lost coming to Washington at his own expense to answer questions about CPI finances. "No war organization has such a record of economy and carefulness in expenditures," he told Daniels. "Please help me to end this nightmare." "Not only are my former associates shamed," he told Newton Baker, "but I myself am vitally injured." Daniels and Baker provided Creel with a letter exonerating him. Knowing his proclivities for attack, they insisted that he not release it publicly, as that would "provoke controversy and give an opportunity for critics of the Administration and of you to indulge in newspaper comment."[81]

The CND report was submitted to the Senate on June 9, 1920. Even then Ellsworth's work was not done. Late that year he told a congressional committee it would take three or four more months to recover all the funds that had been advanced to staff. He complained to Creel in March 1921 that Murray's accounts were still unresolved.[82]

When it came time to issue the final report, Herbert N. Shenton, who replaced Clarkson as head of the CND, cautioned Ellsworth that any error or misinterpretation would inevitably draw counterattack from Creel. The report was far more measured than Ellsworth's negative letter to Warren, but much less celebratory than the story Creel told in his books and elsewhere. The CND reported total CPI expenses of $8.2 million. Creel's report put the total at $7.2 million. He proudly and loudly pointed out that receipts from films, publications, and photographs reduced the cost to taxpayers. In a speech to the Associated Advertising Clubs of the World, he went so far as to claim the CPI was "virtually self-sustaining." On paper, he was somewhat more careful. Ellsworth put the total amount spent, minus receipts, at $4.9 million. Creel's report said expenditures were almost half a million less. In *How We Advertised the War* he adjusted the amount upward to slightly below Ellsworth's totals.[83]

After the CND finished its work, the files that Ellsworth had laboriously assembled went to the War Department, where they were as forgotten as the Sisson documents in Wilson's safe. They resurfaced in the mid-1930s when a member of the Library of Congress staff, Cedric Larson, located them on a tip from a lieutenant colonel with the Army War College library. A card in the library indicated the files were in the custody of the Army Industrial College, housed in the old Munitions Building three blocks from the White House.[84]

Larson found nearly twenty-five cabinets in the basement "bulging" with CPI records. Bulging though they were, however, tens of thousands were missing. Some were destroyed under a mandate to eliminate "Useless Executive Papers." Others disappeared for unknown reasons. The remaining papers—172 of the 789 drawers collected by Ellsworth—were sent to the National Archives, which recently had been created for such a purpose. The archives' summary of them laconically noted the organization of the records was complicated by their fragmentary nature, their disordered condition, and the CPI's "nebulous character."[85]

THE CONTINUING NEED FOR PROPAGANDA

Despite the ignominious end of the CPI's files and finances, it celebrated itself in its final days. Whitehouse, who headed home on Christmas Day, enjoyed a grand evening in the palatial Biltmore Hotel in New York. She had, said a woman there, "fought, in her way, just as valiantly and just as tellingly as any soldier." Charles Dana Gibson's division celebrated with a dinner dance of more than six hundred people. Nashville's Four Minute Men gathered in the Commercial Club to give gifts to Porter Dunlap and other leaders; all the speakers received a red, white, and blue pin inscribed "One Hundred Per Cent." When one of them rose to speak, someone yelled, "Go to it, Julius. You make Shakespeare and Longfellow look like pikers."[86]

Creel's dinner was at the new Hotel Washington, which overlooked the White House. The fete was hurriedly organized as he was about to leave for Paris. More than 125 people attended. Daniels and Baker were at the "love fest," but not their fellow member of the Committee on Public Information Robert Lansing. Gus Karger—correspondent with the *Cincinnati Times-Star,* president of the National Press Club, and a Creel stalwart—was toastmaster. "Now George Creel's work is done and he is about to leave us," Karger said. "We shall miss him, sadly miss him; darned if I don't believe that even Congress will miss him. We shall never see his like again, for God made only one George Creel." Creel was presented with a bronze tablet designed by O'Higgins and the Pictorial Division.[87]

Yet mixed in with the applause and farewell gifts was the lingering feeling that the need for publicity had not ended. Ralph Van Deman wrote to Vira

Whitehouse precisely on that "fateful hour—11 o'clock, November 11, 1918—the hour at which the armistice goes into effect." He wondered "how much longer our propaganda work will go on. There is probably much need of it, perhaps now more than ever." Whitehouse agreed: "My own view is that there should be some sort of permanent organization to present the American side of questions which may arise, not only in the peace settlement but afterwards, but I don't want to have anything to do with it!"[88]

Others expressed the same concern. Ernest Poole, who like Whitehouse was eager to leave the CPI, believed the era of open diplomacy demanded the use of "publicity to reach widely the great mass of people in other countries with significant facts about the life and purposes of this nation." Robert Woolley, who initially watched the CPI with trepidation, regretted its demise. Its job, he told Creel, was "of the greatest importance and I for one wish it were possible to continue it."[89]

In an important way the CPI did go on. It was no longer a government entity, to be sure. But it became the foundation for the Information State that emerged during the twentieth century. As is discussed at the end of this book, all modern government propaganda has antecedents in the CPI. It changed the way America was governed on a daily basis.

Yet the comments by Whitehouse and others referenced a short-term challenge that was *not* met. That was the urgency of promoting the peace Wilson envisioned. The history of the CPI, as the next chapter shows, is incomplete without an account of Wilson's failure to mount an effective publicity campaign after the war. The CPI could have compensated for its undemocratic failings by helping Wilson at that crucial moment. But it had so alienated the press and so aroused partisan wrath that its continuation was impractical, and the president did not create an alternative publicity apparatus. This failure to win the battle for public opinion after the shooting stopped greatly hindered Wilson in attaining the lofty peace objectives he and the CPI had proclaimed as the reason for entering the war.

"The Americans came into this war simply for an idea," H. G. Wells wrote on the eve of the peace negotiations. "All human institutions are made of propaganda, are sustained by propaganda and perish when it ceases; they must be continually explained and re-explained to the young and the negligent. And for this new world of democracy and the League of Nations to which all reasonable men are looking, there must needs be the greatest of all propagandas."[90]

III
LEGACIES

15

More Important Now Than Ever

The peace treaty was the supreme salesmanship opportunity of the age.
Its miserable failure, at least as far as the people of the United States are
concerned, is truly a superb fiasco of selling. As a nation we were not
sold. Congress was not sold. The treaty failed—in every popular
sense as well as the purely legal one.

—Edward Hungerford, *New York Herald* correspondent

It was a political moment that Wilson's advisors remembered with bitterness and recriminations.

In late October, while haggling with Germany over terms for ending the fighting in Europe, the president faced another contest, this one at home, the midterm congressional elections. Up to that time the imperative to prosecute the war with "loyal hearts" had produced an "informal political truce," in the words of Homer Cummings, vice chairman of the Democratic National Committee. But the white flag inched lower as voting day approached.[1]

The Democrats, who believed the odds favored them, were flat-footed during the first months of the campaign. Vance McCormick, chair of the Democratic National Committee, was preoccupied with his duties as chairman of the War Trade Board. Cummings was not named acting chairman until early October. The major speaking drive came late in the campaign and was curtailed by the flu epidemic, and the Democratic National Committee did not have adequate funds for a "publicity substitute."[2]

On October 25, at the urging of Democratic candidates who clamored for a strong presidential endorsement, Wilson issued a blanket appeal that tied the election to his ability to prevail at the negotiating table in Paris. He made it seem that a vote for a Republican was an act of national disloyalty: "The Republican leaders desire not so much to support the President as to control him. . . . I am asking your support not for my own sake or for the sake of a political party, but for the sake of the Nation itself, in order that its inward unity of purpose may be evident to all the world."[3]

For some time the Democratic National Committee had been framing the election of its candidates as an act of patriotism. Its campaign manual told party workers to emphasize "Straightout Americanism and loyalty to the Government." But Wilson's self-righteous letter professing to be above politics, when he clearly was not, invited the Republicans to take off the gloves. "Bi-partisanship," Robert Woolley said, "went with the wind."[4]

"This is not the President's personal war," Republican legislators said in rebuke. They used Wilson's letter to show he was the partisan one—more partisan, said Republican National Committee chair Will Hays, than a "reckless stump orator" in ungratefully impugning the patriotism of Republicans who had loyally supported the war. At the same time, but more deftly, Hays did what he criticized Wilson for doing. He argued that a sound peace could only come with the election of Republicans. In a telegram to James Williams of the *Boston Evening Transcript,* he said a Republican Congress was needed "for the problems of peace which means so much for the good of the country stop pass this word in your own way to as many papers as you can suggest." Williams, who was close to Henry Cabot Lodge and still toiling behind the scenes for the Republicans, made the *Transcript* "the most dyed in the wool League-baiter in the United States," and other Republican-leaning organs of news fell in line.[5]

Every election campaign is about the last one in that the losing side seeks to build on what its opponent did well. In 1916 Willcox did not act on the suggestion to place Albert D. Lasker in a role comparable to Woolley's. Hays corrected this mistake. Lasker's appointment was the first ever of a professional advertising executive, and he was not just any ad executive. He was considered the father of modern advertising. His Chicago firm Lord & Thomas was the most successful in the world. He was the first to train copywriters and test advertisements. During the war, he helped Agriculture Secretary David Houston with National Vegetable Canning Week. But he abhorred Wilson's postwar internationalism. One of his campaign triumphs was an extreme anti-league pamphlet, *After the Peace, What?* Lasker used it to focus campaign workers on the issue.[6]

Charles Evans Hughes believed he would have won in 1916 if Hays had run his campaign. He was probably correct. The jug-eared Hays was a towering political genius in a 110-pound body. Creel thought Indiana's State Council of Defense, which Hays chaired, was the best run of all the state organizations. It excelled at organizing speaking conferences across the state, not forgetting to put Republicans on the stage as much as possible. Like Woolley, Hays recognized the need to lay the ground for the next presidential campaign as soon as the last one is decided, and his organizing ability was visible in the midterms. "The Republican organization is working more harmoniously than ever before," the British embassy informed the Foreign Office, which keenly followed the campaign because of the effect the outcome would have on the Paris negotiations. "Public utterances against the partisanship of the President are greater in volume than those of the Democratic Party in defense of his actions." In Colorado, Judge Lindsey told Creel, "Every Republican candidate from constable up to county or state tickets raved about [Wilson's letter] as though he had been personally insulted by the President and his loyalty and his patriotism had been brought into question."[7]

On November 5, American voters reversed the power equation on Capitol Hill. The day before, the Republicans were the minority in both houses. Now they were the majority, with Wilson's enemy Lodge the Senate majority leader and chairman of the Foreign Relations Committee. The election, Creel told Mark Sullivan, "worked vast and fundamental changes in conditions" at the

Will H. Hays did unto the Democrats in 1918 and 1920 what Robert Woolley did to the Republicans in 1916 by taking advantage of publicity blunders to help torpedo the peace pact. (Indiana State Library)

treaty negotiations. The October 25 letter, Ray Stannard Baker observed, "was one of Wilson's greatest political blunders, and it has been amusing, in going about among the various friends, to find how each of them tries to throw the blame for advising the President upon the others."[8]

Woolley was an exception. After helping with the first Liberty Loan drive in 1917, he was rewarded with a place on the Interstate Commerce Commission. He was still called on for political advice, and Tumulty summoned him to the White House to read a draft of Wilson's appeal. It was the end of a tiring day. Woolley hastily read the letter while Tumulty cleared his desk, so the pair could drive home together. He raised no objection. But when he read the letter in the newspapers over breakfast two days later, he realized it was "political dynamite. . . . The truth is I was called and found wanting."[9]

The president, too, was found wanting. "For nearly six years Mr. Wilson had manipulated the Government of the United States with a skill that was almost uncanny," Frank Cobb of the *New York World* said. "Then at the very summit of his career he made his first fatal blunder." Wilson, Gus Karger told his friend William Howard Taft, had grown impatient with public opinion: "He would no longer 'larn' them; he'd just tell 'em,'; and they would not be told."[10]

Not everyone agreed Wilson's letter turned the election. David Lawrence believed war restrictions produced a backlash. If so, the letter was still a colossal public relations blunder. The midterms are problematic for a president's party. When a loss of seats occurs, the president can chalk it up to tradition. But Wilson raised the stakes by making the vote a referendum on his presidency. The loss weakened him at home and abroad.[11]

The letter became emblematic of the missteps Wilson subsequently made as he strove to create the new world order promised in his Fourteen Points. He did not adjust to the reality that he could no longer count on patriotism to carry through his objectives. Wilson needed to reach across the political aisle and refurbish the tools and strategies that helped him previously. In the 1916 election he had Woolley's publicity bureau; in the war he had Creel's CPI. But he appointed no publicity chief and created no publicity machine to sell the treaty. Advice poured in urging less aloofness and more attention to publicity, but Wilson thought he could carry the day largely on his own by speaking from the lofty perch that had served him well in the past. It was a lot to put on the shoulders of a frail man whose political judgment was deteriorating along with his health.

PRESS-AGENTING THE PRESIDENT

The Committee on Public Information was born in the 1916 presidential campaign, where Woolley, Creel, and others perfected publicity techniques to elect Wilson. It died after the 1918 midterm elections brought in a Republican-controlled Congress. Throughout the course of its existence, the CPI's partisan cast set the tone for Wilson's wartime presidency.

Government publicity privileges the voices, images, and ideas of the administration issuing it. Heartfelt as it may have been, when War Secretary Baker praised returning soldiers, he advertised the government's good will, as well as his own. When Treasury Secretary William McAdoo went on the stump to promote Liberty Loan campaigns, he raised his national visibility. This was useful to a man who aspired to be president. Alien Property Custodian A. Mitchell Palmer publicized his way into the job of attorney general and, with his equally well publicized anti-Red raids, hoped to make the next leap to the White House. He so aggressively advertised his uncovering of German plots during the war that President Wilson had to remind him publicity was Creel's job.[12]

So it was with President Wilson. The *Official Bulletin*'s publication of his Fourteen Points speech was a public service. Citizens needed to know what he had in mind for the peace. But the public also needed to know Republican objections to his plans, and the *Bulletin* did not publish those. Every component of the CPI contributed to this advantage. Wilson, Charles Dana Gibson said shortly after his speech, "was the great Moses of America. He points out the promised land, the milk and the honey. The work of the artists will be made easy by putting into pictorial form the last message of the President."[13]

It was a simple matter to push the boundaries of the president's information franchise beyond the easily defensible, and Creel's proclivities in this regard were pronounced. He was as partisan as a campaign button. He judged people based on which side they were on, as Guy Stanton Ford said. He was widely regarded as "a Wilson publicity agent." The Republican-dominated Joint Committee on Printing noted this partisan tendency. One of the many examples that caught its eye was a story in the May 1919 issue of *National School Service*, which had moved to the Bureau of Education but maintained a CPI attitude. It asked teachers to cultivate "the League of Nations attitude" in their students.[14]

Creel tried to offset charges of partisanship by pointing out that Republicans filled half of the CPI's twenty-six top positions. Of the remaining thirteen, Democrats held five and independents eight. This, however, did not signify what Creel said it did. Many of those Republicans and independents voted for Wilson, as Representative Gillett pointed out during the June hearings on the CPI. In anticipation of those hearings, Creel polled his staff on their political affiliations. "Voted for Wilson for President both elections," Walter Rogers telegraphed. "As long as term meant anything definite classified myself as progressive Republican."[15]

Although Blair actively campaigned for Hughes, his Four Minute Men were considered Wilson's "telephone." In 1918, Four Minute Men recited Wilson's full Flag Day speech from the previous year at industrial plants and schools. In 90 percent of the Four Minute Men campaigns, speakers were given prompts with some reference to Wilson. "Think of it!" read one sample speech. "Last winter the country immersed in peace! In the White House a man of peace, a man of patience, whose every effort it was to keep us *honorably* out of war, to keep us away even from *thoughts* of war. Of whom, tell me, can this be said more truly than of America's President, Woodrow Wilson? But peace became impossible."[16]

Virtually every time Creel complained to an editor about a story, the issue was not the publication of "militarily sensitive information," the focus of his voluntary guidelines. His complaint was that the story cast the administration or the handling of the war in a bad light. Creel, O'Higgins said, had a rule against writing "anything personal" about government officials to "escape the charge of being a 'personal press bureau.'" But O'Higgins was assigned to write an article defending Josephus Daniels along the lines of the defense Creel wrote during the 1916 campaign. Censorship had a similar partisan tilt. "Many were arrested or deported for radical propaganda, but none, so far as I know, for reactionary propaganda," said Norman Hapgood, who grew disillusioned with the effect of propaganda on discourse. Arthur Willert, whose patriotism was unassailable, complained to Wiseman about the "strong political censorship" his reports received in the United States.[17]

In March 1918, *Metropolitan* magazine criticized Harry Garfield, chairman of the Fuel Administration, for restricting coal production in one of the coldest winters on record and for good measure argued that Wilson should never have been elected. Creel responded with "The Case for Mr. Garfield," published in the *Independent*. The *Metropolitan*'s editor retorted in an open letter, "Is it right that you should use the time and money of your bureau, which is supported by the American taxpayers, to defend members of the administration from criticism in the public press? Are you not in fact the personal press agent of the President and members of the Administration?" Creel's rejoinder showed the ease with which partisanship can be dressed as patriotism: "We consider it right to spend that money to defend the Government and its war measures from misstatement that weakened the faith in the nation's war work." Creel's "belabored defense," Lawrence wrote in the *Evening Post,* confirmed the public's impression that the CPI was "primarily interested in defending the Administration against attacks."[18]

Wilson did not stop the CPI from defending him or from promoting him, which was one of its strongest impulses. The *Official Bulletin* boasted of publishing "all the utterances by the President since the entry of this Government into the war." Some pamphlets consisted solely of Wilson's speeches. CPI files are filled with communications along the lines of a cable from Frank Marion in Spain: "Kerney and I agree that the most important phase of our work here is to pressagent the president." Creel considered it a sign of Marion's success that the *Christian Science Monitor*'s correspondent in Spain reported, "What may be called the Wilson cult is truly making astonishing progress in Spain." In every Allied country, streets and babies were named for Wilson; his image, distributed by the CPI, was in storefront windows and homes.[19]

At his farewell dinner at the Hotel Washington, Creel spoke of "the undergrowth of irritation and the poison ivy of politics" that bedeviled the CPI. This irritation got worse as the war drew to a close and partisanship surged. The CPI's successes became liabilities. Indiana senator Harry S. New, a former chairman of the Republican National Committee, told Hoosiers at the state party convention that the Democrats were making the midterm elections about loyalty to the country. "Mr. Creel, with his bunch of socialistic, muck-raking misfits, is employing this sort of propaganda in every form at his unlimited command—the bulletin, the movies and the Chautauquas. The money of the tax paying public foots the bills."[20]

The CPI lent itself to political controversy even when it was not guilty of a transgression. A New Jersey candidate for office asked movie theater managers to show pro-Wilson slides supplied by the Democratic National Committee. "At this critical period of our history," he said, "supporters of the President are needed in Congress." When the letter became public, Hays blamed the CPI, which had the power to put theaters out of business. His statement also drew attention to a letter Hans Rieg wrote on Treasury Department stationery urging the foreign-language press to publish Wilson's October letter "as prominently as possible" and send copies of their stories to the Democratic National Committee.[21]

The CPI was an expression of Wilson's partisanship. Had the CPI been more restrained, it would not have been so useful to Republicans in the 1918 election and might have carried on under reduced circumstances. Instead, it hardened partisan behaviors in Wilson that worked against him in time of peace. This became self-defeating. Wilson had more to lose in the League of Nations fight than the Republicans, who could defend their "no" votes as a victory for American sovereignty.

At each turn, it seemed, Wilson invited the Republicans to be partisan.

During the midterm campaign, Charles Evans Hughes parried Wilson's October call to unify the nation by electing Democrats. "Unity should be preserved by taking counsel together and hearing the voice of all parties after the methods of a republic and not by abject submission according to the example of autocracy," he told an audience at the Union League Club. After the armistice was signed, however, Wilson clung to the same attitude that led him to reject the proposal to meld the resources of the Republican and Democratic National Committees to build bipartisan support for the war. (Had he made a minor concession, for instance, giving a joint committee a limited publicity brief, he would have spiked some Republican criticism during the war years.) When Wilson selected his peace commissioners, only one of the four, Henry White, was a Republican, and the elderly diplomat was a nonentity as far as the party leadership was concerned. Taft, Root, and Hughes would have been better choices and in mid-November the betting odds were even on Hughes being named (and 100-to-1 on Lodge). They favored the league; their judgment would have been useful in shaping the league; they had party credibility. Hays considered Wilson's appointments his "second great mistake" after the October letter.[22]

With no meaningful representation on the commission, Republicans had less incentive to pull punches. Wilson, they said repeatedly, lost the vote of confidence he called for. "Our Allies and our enemies, and Mr. Wilson himself," Roosevelt said, "should all understand that Mr. Wilson has no authority whatever to speak for the American people at this time. His leadership has just been emphatically repudiated by them." As evidence that Wilson refused to honorably acknowledge his loss of authority, Roosevelt pointed to the Sisson mission's announcement, prior to its departure to Paris, that the CPI would "interpret the work of the peace conference by keeping up the world-wide propaganda to disseminate American accomplishments and American ideals." Wilson, Roosevelt said, had no standing to do that.[23]

In late 1917, Northcliffe described Wilson to an AP correspondent as a global force, "the dictator of the world." In January 1919, he held a radically different view. "Mr. Wilson has lost his power in the United States," he said privately. "Whatever he does over here is subject to the approval of the Foreign Relations Committee of the Senate and that in reality Mr. Roosevelt is the American to support." Roosevelt died a couple of days later. The Foreign Relations Committee was not going away.[24]

YOU HAVE SPUN A NET FOR ME

CPI propaganda had other postwar liabilities besides accentuating partisanship. CPI images of Hun brutality and CPI stories of German-Bolshevik conspiracies worked against the fair treaty that Wilson had promised—a promise the Germans believed when they signed the armistice. "In the state of mind existing at home and abroad a sane peace was no longer possible," George Sylvester Viereck said. "It may be said that American propaganda was not only successful but too successful. Woodrow Wilson the propagandist defeated Woodrow Wilson the statesman." Despite his having negotiated an end to the fighting, Wilson could not count on the support of immigrant groups whose home countries did not get the results they wanted in Paris. German-Americans organized rallies against the treaty and what Viereck called the "League of Damnations."[25]

The administration's trampling of civil liberties also alienated Americans on the left. If anyone could be said to want a world free of war, it was pacifist Oswald Garrison Villard. After the November election, he told Tumulty that Wilson did not have "the liberal support he needs in this trying hour when the real victory of the war is still to be won." Creel told Wilson the same thing. "When you raised it to the level of a war for democracy, you rallied, to the support of the war, all the progressive and democratic elements," he said. But by the elections, "All the radical, or liberal friends of your anti-imperialist war policy were either silenced or intimidated. . . . No one had been able to tell the public what was really at issue in the elections."[26]

A final liability was the outsized image the CPI built of Wilson. Wilson's speeches, Creel said, were "our most effective weapons." The Allies used them in their domestic propaganda to bolster the morale of their people and demoralize the enemy. While possibly hurrying the end of the war, this propaganda had two adverse by-products. First, the adoring throngs that cheered Wilson in Europe may have contributed to his conviction that he had European public opinion behind him, when, on the contrary, they supported their leaders at the treaty table. Second, CPI propaganda created impossibly high expectations as to what the president could accomplish in Paris.[27]

On board the *George Washington* bound for Paris, Wilson worried to Creel, "It is a great thing you have done, but I am wondering if you have not unconsciously spun a net for me from which I cannot escape." The fault, of course, was also Wilson's. Creel "oversold" his words like so much patent medicine. But Wilson had fallen into the deadly trap propagandists set for themselves by becoming infatuated with their soaring promises, forgetting they will be finally judged by how they implement them. He was, as he once said of himself, "intoxicated by the exuberance of my own verbosity."[28]

KEEPING THE PRESS AT ARM'S LENGTH

"Propaganda more important now than ever," Tumulty cabled Wilson in April 1919, when the president was nearing the end of the peace negotiations in Paris. The same advice had been coming from others for months.[29]

Before the election, Creel told Wilson of "the instant need of some clear and complete statement of America's war aims and peace program." The press and the public were "muddled," Creel said. After the election, Creel insisted, "You will have to give out your program for peace and reconstruction and find friends for it."[30]

McCormick and Frank Cobb, who was on a leave of absence from the *World* to help House in Paris, thought the biggest challenge for Wilson was not in Europe. Wilson should stay in Washington to manage postwar domestic problems and find treaty friends. The commissioners could handle the negotiations and refer questions to him. Such an arrangement would strengthen his position by putting him above the negotiators in Paris. Winning American public opinion would strengthen his hand in Europe.[31]

Wilson shrugged off such advice. He did not want to focus on public opinion to any large degree; nor did he want to articulate clearly what he wished to accomplish. For months, his objective had been to keep peace aims out of the public conversation and concentrate on maintaining a fighting attitude at home and abroad. When David Lawrence wrote positively about the semisecret, postwar planning group the Inquiry in late 1917, Wilson admonished him, "You newspaper men can have no conception of what fire you are playing with when you discuss peace now at all, in any phase or connection." In an address to Congress two days before sailing to Europe, Wilson appealed for public support without offering any specifics as to what the public was to stand behind. Lodge read Wilson's speeches, he told Root, and found "they are all in the clouds and all fine sentiments that lead nowhere."[32]

Wilson arrived in Paris without a strategy for informing the public about what he was doing and pulled together a press operation the same way he created the CPI in 1917, on the fly. A number of names were suggested besides Creel's to do the work. House recommended Cobb, a steady Wilson supporter, to explain "the policies you stand for." Cobb, however, had a falling out with House over the colonel's withholding of information from Wilson and the State Department, and he returned home. Lippmann, also working for House in Paris, suggested George Barr Baker for cable matters, as he would foster openness with the press.[33]

From the various suggestions, Wilson conceived a complex, fuzzy scheme of overlapping responsibilities. Maximillian Foster, the CPI's correspondent at the front, would liaise between Wilson and the reporters. Creel would disseminate information "through the world and the United States." Ray Stannard Baker was to handle publicity for the commission. House let Baker believe the appointment had been his idea. Creel later told Baker it had been his suggestion. Baker considered House's slipperiness "pretty abominable."[34]

Creel tried to be a player, for instance by offering advice to Wilson on his itinerary in Rome. But he clashed with Baker within a few days. He was battered by the negative news stories about his proposed press headquarters in James Gordon Bennett's twenty-room mansion, with its numerous servants. His frustration with press criticism erupted in a message in early January to Rogers. No matter what the CPI did to help, he complained, correspondents were "liable to wax ugly, creating some trouble that would expose me again to the charge of interference with the free flow of news or attempt to control public opinion." He told Rogers to keep Foster away from the press. Foster's presence irritated them and exposed Creel to more criticism. Rogers dropped Foster from the payroll. Soon, Creel was on his way to central Europe, leaving the field entirely to Baker. Rogers carrying on with the transmission of news.[35]

At his peak, Baker "was considered the greatest reporter in America." He was the lone journalist to cover Guglielmo Marconi's first secret transatlantic wireless transmission. He exposed corruption, wrote a pathbreaking book on race relations, and penned homely sketches of country life under the name David Grayson. Baker endorsed individuals, not parties, depending on their ideas. In the 1916 election, he was a leader in the Wilson Independent League. Unlike Creel, he was soft-spoken, judicious in his opinions, and agonizingly self-reflective. He quit the Vigilantes because, he wrote in his diary, they "scream & sing the hymn of hate!"[36]

When Wilson tapped him for the publicity job, Baker was concluding a nearly yearlong mission arranged by House to assess opinion in Britain, Italy, and France. Working under a "plan of camouflage," he was ostensibly a correspondent for the *New Republic* and the *New York World* but confined himself to reports for a small circle of Washington officials. The assignment stemmed

Ray Stannard Baker, head of the American Press Bureau during the Paris treaty negotiations, was disappointed Wilson did not use the conference to fashion a "new diplomacy" that was transparent and attentive to public opinion. Behind Baker is his deputy Arthur Sweetser (theblackenvironment.blogspot).

from Wilson's concern that liberal elements in Europe were drawing inspiration from the Bolsheviks and might push for a negotiated peace—and his distrust of information from his embassies.[37]

Baker was reluctant to take the press assignment in Paris. He wanted to return to his rural home in Amherst, Massachusetts, where he gardened and raised bees. But public service won out. He took up his office at the grand address of No. 4 Place de la Concorde. Reporters trooped to his American Press Bureau in such large numbers they wore its aged red carpet to shreds.[38]

Baker hired Arthur Sweetser, who also was conveniently on hand, as his assistant. During the war, Sweetser moved from the Signal Corps to the Military Intelligence Branch in Washington at Blankenhorn's request. Blankenhorn hoped to take him to France. That did not work out. But in the same way Sweetser had dropped everything to cover the war when it broke out in 1914, he rushed to Europe in 1918 as a freelance reporter when he was mustered out of the army. His experience covering the State Department commended him for the job as Baker's assistant, as did his high hopes for the conference. "My ambition from the onset of the war has of course been to attend the peace meetings," he told Herbert Croly, for whom he wrote a few stories. "The public must be brought into touch with the situation, given the best and most accurate information."[39]

For Baker, the conference was an opportunity to achieve the acme of progressive-minded public opinion molding. Publicity would not be an arm of American diplomacy. It was to be its heartbeat. He believed the American peace commission was "organized upon the initial assumption that it was a great public undertaking, that it would have to keep open the avenues of communication with the people of all the world and provide means of present and future publicity."[40]

The American peace commission's communications system was, indeed, extensive. It included a courier service and telephone system for western Europe, a postal service, a printing plant, a photography department, and a department to make a historical record. The CPI in New York sent a biweekly summary of American news to Paris and arranged for the Paris press corps a special allotment of nine thousand words a day over navy wireless, without charge—a third for official documents of news value, a third for the wire associations, and a third for individual newspapers, the latter divvied up by the reporters themselves. Compub in New York forwarded individuals' stories to the respective newspapers. The correspondents were free to send other dispatches by wireless and cable at their own expense.[41]

When the lengthy, complex treaty was ready for unveiling, Sweetser prepared the fourteen-thousand-word American summary. Baker and Rogers arranged transmission. Baker thought that it was "the longest single continuous cable dispatch ever sent up to that time." One of Baker's innovative ideas was for American experts at the conference to draft briefing papers for the correspondents, many of whom had little experience covering foreign affairs. This met resistance from Lansing. Wilson once again overruled him.[42]

The barrier to reaching Baker's progressive vision of worldwide publicity was the president. The following short note from a nameless correspondent in Paris is among the personal papers Baker donated to Princeton: "Mr. Wilson is a very secretive individual, and we have had a chance at him directly only three or four times. Baker sees him every day and we see Baker for news from the President, and also unload on Baker all the bile collected in our systems. . . . We all like Baker very much, he is distinctly the ablest man we have had in charge of news dispensing since the war began."[43]

Baker's daily meetings with Wilson began in March, after the president returned from a five-week trip to Washington. Baker met with the president each evening and briefed the reporters afterward on what had transpired during the day, to the extent the president allowed. This was the first time a president had a subordinate act as his daily, full-time personal intermediary with the press. The arrangement foreshadowed the formal job of "presidential press secretary."*

Ideally press secretaries serve two masters: the president, whose message they must faithfully convey, and the press, who serve the public. "I honestly endeavored at Paris to do the real work of publicity," Baker told his friend Norman Hapgood, "getting out the *facts* & the background, as well as to report exactly what was being done, so far as I was permitted to do; and when I wasn't permitted to pass on certain information I told the correspondents so."[44]

Baker set a high standard. His view was in tune with democratic principles. But this was not Wilson's preferred method of dealing with the press. His daily debriefing with Baker was not a vehicle to engage the press so much as a means of keeping it at arm's length, as the CPI had previously done for him. Usually, Baker said, his daily briefing of the press "was disappointing."[45]

---

* The first full-time de facto press secretary at the White House was George Ackerson, appointed by Herbert Hoover. The title was not used until Franklin Roosevelt appointed Stephen Early, a one-time AP reporter who had worked in the CPI. Greenberg, *Republic of Spin,* 192.

A FEELING OF BETRAYAL

"Seventy men from all corners of the earth are seated around the long horse-shoe of a green-baize table in the Clock-Room of the Foreign Office on the Quai d'Orsay," Simeon Strunsky of the *New York Evening Post* wrote. "Newspapermen from all corners of the earth . . . strain eye and ear, through the arches of the adjoining reception room."[46]

Strunsky's report was one of many written about press coverage of the negotiations. The stories were reminiscent of those filed about Centcom's Doha media center in Building 406 during the US invasion of Iraq. They reflected journalists' awareness of the magnitude of the event and their frustration covering it. "The tremendous interest involved in the peace conference and the secrecy with which the negotiations have been conducted," the AP said, "have made the assignment one of the most difficult which American journalism has ever undertaken."[47]

The treaty negotiations were a high historical moment. This had been the most far-reaching, devastating war ever—sixty-five million troops mobilized, twenty million military and civilian deaths, twenty-one million wounded. Now, the first-ever plan for permanent world peace was in the offing. With wartime censorship lifted, reporters could be reporters again. At the high point, some 500 covered the proceedings, 150 of them Americans. Many shared Baker's enthusiasm for a "new diplomacy" that was transparent and reflective of public opinion.

Wilson elevated these expectations in the first of his Fourteen Points, which called for "open covenants of peace, openly arrived at, after which there shall be no private international understandings of any kind, but diplomacy shall proceed always frankly and in the public view." Wilson expressed the same view to William Wiseman, who was advising the president as well as his own government: "Negotiations should be conducted publicly for the whole world." But fruitful negotiations were impossible if conducted in front of a public grandstand, and Wilson's subsequent actions showed the statement was not meant literally. House asked Cobb and Lippmann to come up with a formula that would clear up the confusion. They suggested that open covenants, openly arrived at, meant there would be no secret agreements. Lippmann later confessed, "I was never sure that was what President Wilson meant when he coined the phrase."[48]

The first meeting of Prime Ministers Georges Clemenceau, David Lloyd-George, and Vittorio Orlando, and President Wilson—who came to be known as the Council of Four or Big Four—was behind soundproof doors on a gloomy cold winter day, January 12. The leaders decided to limit publicity to a daily communiqué. American journalists responded with a petition that threw Wilson's "open covenants" in his face. To various degrees journalists from other countries followed the Americans' lead. At the urging of Tumulty, who cabled about the snide editorial comments at home that this was another case of "pitiless publicity," Wilson earnestly pleaded the correspondents' case with his fellow leaders. They relented slightly to allow coverage of plenary sessions. He also beat back a French proposal to censor telegraph and cable transmissions of official communiqués.[49]

"The Peace Conference," one reporter concluded, "is well on its way to the abandonment of the first of the Fourteen Points." Only six heavily scripted plenary sessions were held. Strunsky characterized them as "stage-management" to bless decisions made in secret. The daily communiqué was soporific.[50]

One might expect the reporters to forgive Wilson's "open covenants" as unfortunate hyperbole. But a recurring feature in their reports and in their memoirs was a feeling of betrayal. Such was the power of Wilson's rhetoric that it had been widely believed. And such was the crashing disappointment when he showed that he had no intention of following through when he clearly could. As chairman of the committee working on the League Covenant, he could have admitted reporters but did not. Nor did he issue official communiqués on its work.[51]

Herbert Bayard Swope had taken a leave from the *New York World* to handle publicity for Baruch's War Industries Board during the war. He had a warm sympathy for Wilson on most occasions, but not this one. Swope was a leader of the disgruntled reporters in Paris. He considered the press restrictions "more drastic than any heretofore undertaken" and a "lack of good faith."[52]

WORKING SILENTLY

Hugh Gibson understood the need to negotiate behind closed doors but blamed Wilson for keeping the public so much in the dark. "Few professional diplomats," Gibson said, "have proceeded by means that were so secret." Openness was essential in the sense Baker and other progressives had talked about publicity. Publicity was a vehicle for leading. Had not Wilson written in 1887, "Whoever would effect a change in a modern constitutional government . . .

must make public opinion willing to listen and then see to it that it listens to the right things"?[53]

Wilson's failure to signal early on what "right things" he had in mind for the League Covenant, historian Thomas Bailey observed, was "one of his most costly errors in the handling of public opinion." If he had articulated the plan he drafted before leaving Washington, even without full specifics, he would have invited partnership in the process; critics would have revealed themselves; he could have made adjustments in the draft where called for. This would have allowed him to bring a better draft to the negotiations. By holding his draft close to his chest, Wilson merely delayed the inevitable. When he returned to Washington briefly in February, he was bombarded with valid objections. Back in Paris in March, he had to ask for changes in the draft. This, Bailey argued, "increased the strain on Wilson, added to the general confusion at Paris, and introduced a not inconsiderable amount of genuine delay."[54]

To good effect, Wilson had an impromptu off-the-record meeting with reporters on February 14, the day he presented a draft of the Covenant in a plenary session. But the success did not prompt a greater effort to shape public opinion. He could not control American journalists, as Clemenceau did the French, so he sought reasons to avoid all but the few he personally liked. Reporters respected Wilson's insistence that his comments to them were off the record. But a lone exception from the February 14 meeting, which was probably due to a misunderstanding, gave him reason to say flatly he could not trust correspondents. He refused to see one group of reporters because it included a journalist he did not like.[55]

Alone among the Big Four, Wilson did not meet regularly with correspondents. He did not even bother to tell them, or Baker, how hard he worked to convince his fellow chiefs of state to open plenary sessions. "It probably never occurred to him to tell even Mrs. Wilson," Baker said. When Lawrence suggested to Wilson the lack of openness was politically damaging, he impatiently replied, "I don't give a damn about the politics of it—if this thing is a success we will get the benefit of it, and if it isn't, we will be attacked anyhow."[56]

The best way to handle the correspondents, Wilson informed Lansing, was for the commissioners to brief them each morning. "This I am sure is preferable to any formal plan or to any less definite arrangements." This in-between approach was of minimal value. The commissioners often were not fully informed when they held their fifteen-minute press meeting. "We will all be glad," Lansing complained at the rather late date of January 4, "when the President can settle down and disclose the application of his principles." They did not find out about Wilson's decision to give German concessions in China's Shantung Province to the Japanese until Baker told them. Baker considered these newsless meetings "farcical." Tasker Bliss and House stopped attending.[57]

A danger in this arrangement was that Wilson's stand-ins could offer interpretations that reflected their thinking, not his. This was especially so with House, whose differing views with Wilson led to estrangement during the negotiations. He saw reporters alone every evening at six o'clock at the Crillon. House's son-in-law Gordon Auchincloss, who was a member of the American delegation, also spoke liberally to the press. One morning Wilson's wife overheard Auchincloss ask House jocularly, "What shall we make the president say today?"[58]

Perhaps the anecdote, dredged from Edith Wilson's memory, is inaccurate. But unruly interactions with the press proliferated. Wilson's confidential secretary Gilbert Close, various intelligence officers, and Philip Patchin with Lansing's Division of Foreign Intelligence briefed reporters. Tumulty figured into this mix. With the CPI dissolved, he resumed his press duties at home and managed public relations in Paris through Wilson's physician, Cary Grayson. Tumulty's instructions, often frantic in their concern over the bad press Wilson was receiving, could be quite detailed. "Don't forget the movie men," he cabled Grayson, reminding him to "picture human side of president." "President's smile is wonderful," he said in another cable. "Get this over in some way." "At work on your suggestions," the obedient admiral replied. Grayson became one of the journalists' most reliable sources. The French journalists even sought him out. It was quite a role for a man who was so unimpressive in his navy uniform that a guest at a Paris reception asked him to "Call me a cab."[59]

Special interests outside American circles were all too eager to supplement these helter-skelter streams of information. "Intrigues and propaganda are everywhere," Lansing complained. The one certain thing in journalism, Sweetser said, "is that if the truth is not given out, something else will be printed. . . . The press was beset on from every angle, by interviews, written material, trips, confidential luncheons and dinners, even decorations." French officials, who treated their newspapers as a bureau of the Foreign Ministry, passed them Wilson's October letter and Roosevelt's denunciation of it to weaken the president during the negotiations. They ran a press center at the elegant Hotel Dufayel. It was replete with excellent food and wine, endless receptions for officials, and walls covered with depictions of naked women. The press called it the "House of a Thousand Teats." The French built up sentiment for a vengeful treaty with special trains to see the wreckage left by the Germans. "It was propaganda *de luxe*," said *New York Herald* correspondent Edward Hungerford, a walrus-mustached reporter with experience in these matters as a Wells Fargo advertising manager.[60]

Secrecy was as extreme. The Big Four initially wanted to bar reporters from witnessing the presentation of the treaty terms to the Germans on May 4 on the grounds the Germans would use it as a propaganda opportunity. This attitude encouraged leaking. While the conferees refused to reveal the treaty, purloined copies could be bought on street corners. Reporters relied on the "red-eyed rumors" that washed through the Hotel Crillon's lobby and the Chatham Bar, the latter a "harbor to anchor in and watch the ebb and flow of aviators, detectives, civilians, slackers and soldiers." On one occasion Wilson allowed Baker to whisper in the ear of Swope and a couple of other American reporters about French demands for heavy indemnities on the Germans. But this was not his style. Nevertheless, he could not stop leaks by his own delegation, let alone the strategic leaks by other delegations.[61]

The drip, drip, drip eroded Wilson's position by sowing disharmony and confusion. The *Chicago Tribune* got its hands on an advance copy of the treaty from the Chinese, who were furious that it transferred German concessions in Shantung to the Japanese in contravention of pledges in the Fourteen Points for the fair adjustment of colonial claims. The antitreaty *Tribune* published the document and sent a reporter to Washington to deliver a copy to the equally antitreaty Senator William Borah, who unlike Wilson met with reporters at his office daily and took their calls at home. On June 9, Tumulty told the Senate that Wilson was not ready to transmit the treaty, which by tradition was his prerogative. After heated debate that same day, the Senate voted 42 to 24 to print Borah's copy in the *Congressional Record*. Senator Gilbert Hitchcock, Wilson's point man on the treaty, argued that publication of the document was an act of German propaganda. Antitreaty Senator George Norris said the Senate was expressing the president's idea of open covenants. Publication of the treaty, Karger told Taft, "gained something" by making "clear the indecency of [Wilson] withholding it from the public.[62]

Wilson's reluctance to engage public opinion was a topic of fretful conversations in Paris cafés. Americans filled diaries and letters with woeful comment. "You know as well as I do the resentment which has been aroused by the President's failure to explain what he is doing," Lippmann told House, "but do hope you will consider seriously the importance of having some voice in America capable of speaking for the President at this time. The news which comes out of Paris by way of the correspondents is distrusted and the official communiques which are issued are about as interesting as a railroad time-table."[63]

Referring to news of mounting opposition in Washington, Gilbert Close told his wife, "It becomes more and more evident every day that it is time the President got home and did a little plain talking himself." Close decided against suggesting this to Wilson given his mounting irritability with his staff. "He might think it best to fire me."[64]

Tumulty, Creel, and Baker continued to implore Wilson to meet with reporters and explain what he was doing. But Wilson told Swope the only way to succeed in the face of leaks and intrigue was "by working silently," the opposite of what was called for. "*The greatest failure* of this whole peace conference," Baker wrote in his diary, "is the failure to take the people into our confidence, the abrogation of the first of the Fourteen Points."[65]

INCHOATE PUBLIC SUPPORT

Before the war, Arthur Bullard predicted the peace would not be worked out "solely by the diplomats grouped about their 'green table.'" "The real decision will depend on public opinion at home. No diplomat, returning from this congress, will ride up the avenue of his capital, waving his silk hat to a uniformed, admiring crowd, who shout approbation to such a vague and bombastic phrase as 'peace, with honor.' The coachman will turn about in his seat and say: 'Your Excellency, why did you annex all the African swamp?'"[66]

Wilson returned home convinced he would prevail. He had persuaded his fellow leaders in Paris to wrap the Covenant inside the treaty, so they would be voted as one. Although this senator or that might not like one part or another of the pact, they would not deny a president who toiled to bring home a treaty that promised so much for the world. This false sense of security came out in a conversation with Baker in May. The treaty, Wilson said, enjoyed "good support" among Americans. Yes, Baker replied, "but they do not know what is in it." When Wilson became visibly annoyed with this line of conversation, Baker dropped the subject.[67]

Wilson had support, but it was not overwhelming. In April the *Literary Digest* polled newspaper editors on the league: 718 approved, 181 did not, and 478 approved conditionally. Put another way, nearly half the respondents expressed a degree of doubt. Even if Wilson took the survey as a proxy for positive American opinion, it did not measure the intensity of sentiment. The negotiations had dragged on for months. The Senate did not vote until November 1919, a full year after the armistice was signed. This left opponents ample time to win over the public, which, in any case, was preoccupied with the rising cost of living and the Dempsey-Willard boxing match. Treaty fatigue set in. How many citizens would lean on their senators to pass Wilson's treaty and the League Covenant? Chicago newspaper publisher Herman Kohlsaat told House, "The great majority of our people are still behind the President—I fear they are very far behind him." Traveling through the West in August 1919, Woolley found that 70 percent of voters favored the League, but not "whole-heartedly." "Every day the president delayed in making his case," Woolley told House and McCormick, "he makes his job more difficult."[68]

The peace pact was open to legitimate criticism. The treaty levied heavy reparations on the Germans, hardly the just outcome Wilson had promised them. Wilson had acquiesced in allowing the victors, apart from his own country, to divide Germany's colonies among themselves. The widely reviled Shantung agreement was Wilson's "African swamp."

The chief objection to the Covenant centered on Article X, which pledged mutual defense. The idea of automatically coming to the aid of any nation in trouble ran against the strong American tradition opposing "permanent alliances," which George Washington articulated in his farewell address and which was read each year in the Senate on the anniversary of its delivery. Article X also carried the idea of protecting existing borders rather than allowing for self-determination. Villard's *Nation* derided the president for failing to stick to his principles. Lippmann, who had been an architect of Wilson's Fourteen Points, thought the treaty was "illiberal and in bad faith." He gave Borah inside information acquired while he was with the Inquiry. This helped the senator put Wilson on the spot when he met with the Foreign Relations Committee.[69]

Wilson's strongest support group was the League to Enforce Peace, headed by Taft. With no authority beyond the ability to persuade, the LEP was from its inception in 1915 engaged in educating Americans on the value of a global alliance to preserve peace. At its peak, it had 400,000 members, many of whom were American thought leaders, and a staff of 115 in its New York headquarters. It had state and county chapters and a lobbying arm in Washington under former CPI executive Harry Rickey. A former associate director of the Four

Minute Men was the extension secretary responsible for speakers. Gus Karger, who had press agented Taft, played a large role in publicity. The LEP advertised in the press and held regional conferences. It sent former secretary of commerce Oscar Straus and magazine publisher Hamilton Holt to Paris to show the world that the Americans were behind Wilson. Favorable American opinion toward the Covenant in the spring of 1919, historian John Milton Cooper observed, "owed less to Wilson than to assiduous organizing and publicizing by the LEP."[70]

On the other side was a parallel, opposing organization, the League for the Preservation of American Independence. Although not as powerful as the LEP, it had prominent members and close ties to the Republican Party—and employed the CPI tactics of speaking tours, canned articles, and advertisements. Phonograph records were made of some speeches. One of the league's founders in the spring of 1919 was Senator George H. Moses. Moses, a New Hampshire newspaper publisher, edited the weekly *Bulletin* of the Republican National Committee during the midterm elections, filling its pages with anti-Wilson vitriol. He also was a vocal member of the Joint Committee on Printing.[71]

While Wilson's attention was riveted on the green table in Paris, Will Hays built up resistance at home by keeping "the general public informed as far as possible concerning the daily progress in Paris, especially the factors that might affect the welfare of the United States." Hays recognized that American sentiment, while favoring the treaty, was inchoate. People did not understand the technical details in the 268-page treaty. His goal was to educate them on the value of the reservations that Lodge wanted attached to the treaty and help him unify Republican senators with disparate ideas of how to handle the treaty. Hays, wrote Gus Karger in the *Cincinnati Times-Star,* "is to Moses them out of their difficulties."[72]

To these same ends, Hays orchestrated a letter in which Republican statesman Elihu Root laid out his apprehensions. Root's main objection was to Article X's effect of sacrificing United States sovereignty to guarantee existing national boundaries. "Change and growth are the law of life." He also made the case for aggressive Senate scrutiny. Treaty negotiations were normally handled by delegates who were supervised by the president. Since Wilson was his own delegate, Root said, he needed supervision.[73]

Hays, who hoped Root's letter would encourage LEP members to endorse reservations, thought it had "just the effect we had hoped for." A second letter from Root to Lodge laid out additional objections. Hays printed it in pamphlet form and circulated it with "no stamp of political party headquarters." Digging into the bag of tricks parties used in political campaigns, Hays facilely created doubts about the peace pact: the president violated his "open covenants" statement in order to bamboozle the public; Wilson had Bolshevik advisors; the presence of Creel in Paris proved he wanted to muzzle the press. Lodge and Hays described internationalists as "anti-American." Wilson made vilification easier with statements that were arrogant and disrespectful of the democratic process. In a meeting with the Democratic National Committee during his home visit in February, he called critics of the league contemptible without "even good working imitations of minds. . . . If I did not despise them, I would be sorry for them."[74]

The LEP, with its close ties to the Republican Party, was of no value in parrying personal attacks. Taft joined with Hays in calling for the election of a Republican Congress in 1918. And in the end, the LEP's determination to see the League Covenant passed without alteration eroded. With nudges from the political puppeteer Will Hays, Taft sketched out reservations of his own after Wilson presented the treaty to the Senate in July. Taft asked Hays not to circulate the draft widely, but Hays made it public. Taft's naïve strategy to win over foes of the treaty left the LEP in disarray from which it never recovered.[75]

TOO LITTLE, TOO LATE

Wilson needed an organization dedicated to defending him and his treaty. Whatever was put in place would have had to be smaller and less well-oiled than would have been the case if it were created much earlier. Wilson had two obvious choices. One was to use the Democratic National Committee's publicity machinery, which needed bolstering but at least existed. Alternatively, Wilson could have authorized the creation of a separate body. Private money could have been found for that purpose. Financier Andrew Mellon and steel manufacturer Henry Clay Frick, among others, funded the League for the Preservation of American Independence. Henry Ford was a donor to the LEP and funded a pro-League pamphlet written by Breckenridge Long. Henry Morgenthau, who oversaw financing for Wilson's campaigns in 1912 and 1916, could have done the fundraising. In anticipation of the 1918 election, he pleaded with Wilson to "concentrate the mind" of the public.[76]

The large number of CPI staffers who went to work for the LEP showed how easy it would be to repurpose remnants of the CPI under private auspices, if not governmental ones. In April 1919 Tumulty unsuccessfully tried to convince Wilson to keep Roche's foreign-born division as a vehicle to reach those disillusioned elements. A leaflet prepared for the farewell dinner of Charles Dana Gibson's division showcased the enthusiasm that existed for carrying on. "Let us not forget that our duty is not yet done," the leaflet exclaimed. They felt "fortunate to be alive at this time and be able to take advantage of the greatest opportunity ever presented to artists."[77]

In the last issue of the *Four Minute Men News,* William Ingersoll urged his speakers to remain civically active. His men, and offshoot groups, brimmed with pent-up energy. In the fall of 1918, newly elected state legislators addressed the Nashville Kiwanis Club for four minutes on the theme "How We Can Best Serve Nashville and Davidson County." The *Tennessean* was still announcing Four Minute Men talks in January and February of the following year. Methodist Minute Men spoke out for European reconstruction. In the next three years, according to the 1922 *Methodist Year Book,* sixty-five thousand Five Minute Men raised funds for the church and the Red Cross. Reaching old Four Minute Men with a new mission would not have been difficult. The unit's mailing list still existed in CPI files, and state and local chairmen remained active in their communities. "To permit these elaborately organized pieces of machinery to disintegrate just because we have won the war appears to many to be sinfully wasteful," the head of the Open Forum said of the Four Minute Men in March 1919.[78]

The best candidates to direct such an effort were the ones whose names had come up frequently before, McCormick and Woolley—or both together. McCormick, whom Wilson brought to Paris to assist with the negotiations, was a seasoned political campaign manager, owned newspapers, followed publicity closely, and served on the LEP executive committee. In Paris he was alert to pernicious French propaganda, met often with journalists, and on the whole thought the American delegation was "at a great disadvantage here in regard to publicity." As the Paris experience also showed, he had Wilson's ear. Woolley's credentials were compelling in complementary ways. He was a match for Hays's creativity and craftiness. He was adept at working the press. Recognizing this, Creel earlier had promoted the idea of Woolley heading LEP publicity.[79]

However it was organized, whoever led it, Wilson needed "fighting propaganda," as *Herald* correspondent Edward Hungerford put it. By this, Hungerford meant billboards "spilling out unctuous, and terse and even witty epigrams about the League of Nations"; wide, systematic circulation of speeches; direct

mail; the recruitment of columnists and wits; and, if possible, board games
for kids. This was CPI-style publicity based on the fundamental concept of
attention-grabbing repetition. But Wilson had no appreciation of this. He did
not know what every politician knew, Ray Stannard Baker said: in seeking victory, an idea "had to be repeated a thousand times, published in every newspaper, put in the movies, set to music!"[80]

"To tell the truth," Wilson admitted during the 1916 campaign, "I am not a
fertile suggester of campaign methods." He readily went along with publicity if
it was conceived and executed by others. By not bringing on someone to guide
overall communications during the peace process, he deprived himself of such
advice. Strikingly, neither House nor Creel pushed him to create a new organization. Before the war ended, House assumed Creel would "continue at home
in the same capacity as now for he will never be more needed than then." Although House made suggestions for publicity work in Paris, he did not argue
for a bigger effort at home. By the summer of 1919, House was not in a position
to press the point. Wilson no longer spoke to him. As for Creel, his attitude, it
seemed, was that if his CPI could not do the work—no organization could. He
confined himself to urging Wilson to meet with the press and laid all the publicity problems on journalists' shortcomings and Republican partisanship. Such
publicity as was carried out domestically under Wilson's aegis fell to Tumulty,
who possessed good political instincts and established rapport with journalists
but had other duties and no organization under him.[81]

In effect, Wilson elected to do his own "fighting propaganda." The moment
for this did not come until September 3, 1919, when he began a whistle-stop
train trip to sell his peace pact. The train shot into the heartland, where opposition was strongest, and thundered westward. Wilson traveled eight thousand
miles and delivered thirty-two major addresses and eight lesser ones. It constituted one of the most heroic chapters in American political history. And it was
one of the most heartbreaking.[82]

Tumulty, who had implored Wilson for months to make this campaign by
train, did his best to make it effective. His "maneuver sheets" organized appointments and logistical details. Advance men worked with local bipartisan
committees that were set up. Tumulty helped Wilson improve his speeches as
they went from city to city. Wilson's remarks were quickly transcribed, mimeographed, and handed to the twenty-one reporters on the trip. Karger helped
distribute them to fourteen hundred dailies, the costs of which were covered
largely by Henry Ford. Wilson talked informally to the reporters, which led to

better newspaper copy. Baker helped by writing a series of articles for *McClure's* defending the treaty. These were reprinted as *What Wilson Did in Paris,* which was published in record-breaking time.[83]

The train trip was Wilson's first and only occasion to go to the people with a defense of his treaty. His speeches were powerful. News of the enthusiastic turn-outs along the way made Lodge grimace. But the trip was far from perfect. Some stops, such as in Senator Borah's home state of Idaho, were a waste of time. Wilson ignored valuable opportunities to say nice things about senators when he was in their states. He misstated facts, for instance that the United States had veto rights in all League matters. He lapsed into wartime habits of calling opponents pro-German and pro-Bolshevik. "Hyphens are the knives that are being stuck into this document," the exhausted president proclaimed on September 25 in Colorado. "I want to say—I cannot say too often—any man who carries a hyphen about with him carries a dagger that is ready to plunge into the vitals of this Republic."[84]

The heartbreak came that day with Wilson's physical collapse. His trip was over. The Paris negotiations had taken a physical toll on Wilson, and this trip strained him to the breaking point. Railroads cleared the tracks so Wilson could be whisked back to Washington. A few days later he suffered a severe stroke and paralysis on his left side.

Baker thought the trip came much too late. He should have made it before the congressional elections the previous year, as Wilson had considered doing, in lieu of writing his incendiary October letter. In addition to being too late, it was too little. A single train trip was a long way from a full campaign. There were no billboards, nothing set to music. Instead of risking his fragile health, Wilson should have stayed in Washington to work with those who could be brought to his side by allowing a few mild reservations to be attached to the treaty.[85]

Following his train trip, Wilson could not have fought for public opinion if he had wanted to. He was more out of the public eye than ever. What followed was perhaps the greatest act of censorship in the war. Wilson's wife, Tumulty, and Grayson covered up the severity of his illness, which left him bedridden and too weak to carry out his duties as president. For fear of agitating the sick man, they kept news from him. This impaired his ability to assess public thinking or adjust his own. Wilson's first visitor on official business was not until November 7, when he met with Senator Hitchcock. The feeble president was adamant he would not accept Lodge's reservations. Hitchcock remained on a short leash, effectively leaving the Democrats without a leader who could search out compromise.

While Wilson was confined to his bed, master parliamentarian Lodge dragged out Foreign Relations Committee hearings to unsell the treaty to the public. By refusing to consider reservations, Hays said, the president was "pounding against a stone wall of patriotism which has already become impregnable and is daily increasing in width, strength and height."[86]

When the time came to vote, Wilson's treaty and Covenant fell far short of the necessary two-thirds for ratification. Thirty-eight were in favor of ratification without reservations; fifty-three were opposed. Hays, who had worked so hard for this day, spent it mostly in Lodge's inner office. After the vote, the senator gave him a photograph of himself, autographed and dated "November 19, 1919." The *Boston Transcript* celebrated the defeat of "the evil thing with a holy name."[87]

THE DEATH OF THE LEAGUE

Baker, Creel, and legions of other faithful allies wanted Wilson to bend. "It would be a great mistake to kill the Treaty because of the reservations," Cobb told Taft. A treaty with reservations was better than no treaty at all. The LEP placed ads in newspapers begging Wilson and senators "to set aside partisanship."[88]

Wilson would not budge. When a second round of voting took place in March, the treaty again failed passage. In May Congress passed a resolution offered by Senator Philander Knox to repeal war declarations against Germany and Austria-Hungary. Wilson vetoed it. "'He kept us out of war,'" one Republican legislator quipped; "now he keeps us out of peace."[89]

Wilson made the 1920 presidential election "a great and solemn referendum" on the treaty. Ohio governor James Cox, the Democrats' candidate for president, and his running mate, Franklin Roosevelt, got behind Wilson initially, but eventually backed off. Tumulty and Creel failed to dissuade Wilson from his solemn referendum argument, which smacked of his counterproductive letter of October 1918. Many opinion elites, as well as the public, thought the ailing president was petulantly inflexible. Arthur Willert believed the president's "obstinacy . . . the greatest personal tragedy the world has seen."[90]

Immediately after the electoral losses in November 1918, Woolley told Wilson they would prevail in the 1920 race for the White House with the slogan "He made an end of war." When the time for that campaign arrived, Woolley was not sanguine. He considered George White, chairman of the Democratic National Committee, inept. Woolley was unwilling to give up his job to join the staff because he believed his ideas would never be accepted. "I feel sure you do not appreciate the deplorable conditions at the New York headquarters," he told Creel. Charles Edward Russell considered the absence of Woolley a calamity. "If Mr. Woolley had a double, you would have to search no farther," Russell complained to a campaign staffer. "As he hasn't, the thing to do is to get somebody as near like him as you can." Such a person was not found.[91]

Toward the end the race Woolley and Creel pitched in. They reprised their 1916 gimmick of putting Hughes on the spot with a list of troubling questions. In this case the target was Taft on account of his shifting position and agreeing reservations to the peace pact were acceptable. Creel quickly wrote a protreaty book, *The War, the World and Wilson,* which the Democratic National Committee promoted with a flyer that read as though it were written by him. "Step by step, stab by stab, Mr. Creel follows the Republican majority's conspiracy of hate, showing just how the treaty was killed."[92]

Hays zeroed in on Democrats' weaknesses. When White complained that the Republican textbook unfairly did not include the text of the Covenant, Hays challenged him to publish a joint pamphlet containing all the treaty documents and all the Republican reservations "to help clarify the situation." The ploy drew a contrast with Wilson's lack of openness. Lasker stayed on the campaign staff on the condition that Republican candidate and senator Warren Harding would never support the League. He personally contributed nearly $40,000 to pay for anti-League pamphlets. He had motion pictures constantly whirling and staged media events galore. A coiner of brilliant slogans for soap, cigarettes, and breakfast food, he conjured a winner to sell Harding. Notwithstanding Harding's waffling to avoid irritating Republican factions with different views on the treaty, Lasker's slogan was: "Let's have done with wiggle and wobble." This was directed at Wilson for promising to keep the country out of war, then ending the war without a crushing victory, and now pushing for Article X, which could draw the United States into a new conflict. Billboards with the slogan went up across the country as soon as Harding uttered the phrase in a speech in a seemingly spontaneous (but in fact carefully planned) way.[93]

To win over Americans of Greek, Italian, German, and Hungarian extraction—who felt their homelands were double-crossed in Paris—the Republicans took a page from the CPI playbook. Their Foreign Voters Day had features of Loyalty Day on July 4, 1918. With flags waving, Harding denounced attempts to pick on national groups instead of celebrating them.[94]

On election day Wilson held to his false hope. He told his cabinet that Cox would prevail because of the "great moral issue" at stake. Harding won more than 60 percent of the national vote. It was the best the party had ever achieved. Eugene Debs, still in prison, won more than 3 percent of the votes cast, a tenth of what Cox received. The League, Harding said two days after the election, was "now deceased."[95]

It fell to Wilson's opponent in 1916 to get the United States out of the war. Hughes, whom Harding appointed secretary of state, wanted to secure United States membership in the League. But he knew he could not win the fight. He told Sweetser, who went to work for the League in Geneva, that "a state of mind existed which it was impossible to ignore." He shrewdly combined Senator Knox's resolution to end the war with treaty provisions that benefited the United States. Because it relied on language used by Congress and the Allies, it satisfied both parties.[96]

SACKCLOTH AND ASHES

Wilson did not originate the ideas behind the League of Nations. His contribution, as historian Thomas Knock put it, was "propagation and grand synthesis." The peace process presented a moment to finish the job of selling that he started before the United States went into the war. It was the supreme moment for using propaganda for thoroughly altruistic purposes.[97]

The treaty left a trail of woe. With the absence of the United States, the League was enfeebled at birth. The Germans exited Paris embittered by the treaty. Its harsh terms were "a godsend" for Adolf Hitler's propaganda, historian Margaret MacMillan wrote. The treatment of non-Europeans "stirred up resentments for which the West is still paying today." The disappointment over the Shantung concessions fueled the rise of the anti-West Chinese Communist Party. Carl Crow attributed the intensity of Chinese outrage to the high expectations created by the "official American war propaganda which I circulated so industriously." Crow had made Wilson into a "super-hero" in China.[98]

"What are you going to do now there will be no more wars?" someone asked Frederick Palmer outside the Hotel Crillon one day. "From what I have seen of the Peace Conference," replied the great war correspondent and former AEF censor, "I am convinced that more wars are already in the making." During one of his many hours of having nothing to do in Paris, Lansing scrawled a poem: "For seeds of war are asprouting / On every treaty page / And future peace looks gory / For this peace-loving age." "We failed to give liberty to Europe," lamented Frederic Howe, a civic organizer, journalist, and public official who joined other progressives in abandoning domestic reform for world reform. "We might have saved America."[99]

Wilson pursued a grand vision with conviction and courage. He labored in Paris under great physical strain and against great resistance. "It is certainly discouraging," Gilbert Close told his wife, "the way people try to stab him in the back every time he turns around." Notwithstanding the compromises Wilson made in Paris to achieve the League Covenant, the treaty would have been worse had it not been for him. But his failure to show as much flexibility at home rendered the compromises useless by sinking the Covenant in the Senate.[100]

The immediate source of his failure was illness. It made him more intractable, impaired his judgment, and led to the abrupt end of his one grand attempt at propaganda. After his physical collapse the Democrats were rudderless while Lodge and Hays engineered the demise of the peace pact. Poor health and the amount of work Wilson shouldered in Paris made it more difficult for him to engage in publicity work. His illness, however, does not fully account for his failure. Wilson's stubbornness and sanctimoniousness and his aversion to courting the press and political opponents were not new. Those traits had existed for a long time. Illness only exacerbated them.

Wilson had been self-destructively rigid before with regard to propaganda. In 1917, he could have secured passage of the censorship clause by accepting minor alterations. He fought it out and lost. When it came to selling his policies, he was disinclined to personally engage journalists, who could broadcast his message. Wilson "was relieved when the war brought him the opportunity to abandon the press conference," said James Kerney, his newspaper friend. Wilson's "heart was not in it, and he wanted to be left alone. He never seemed to realize how difficult he made the situation for both the correspondents and himself."[101]

Wilson could delegate to a fault, as evidenced by the censorship power he gave to Burleson. But on issues that mattered most to him, he took too much control and locked people out. Because he did the important foreign policy work himself, he did not feel the need to fire Lansing until illness made him irascible. He pushed Lansing out in early 1920 on the spurious charge that he usurped Wilson's authority by holding cabinet meetings during his illness. Wilson, who did not hold a cabinet meeting until April 13, 1920, could as easily have thanked him. "There is no man in the world who better understands the democratic spirit in its broad manifestations—and few with less of the easy democracy of people friendship and the give and take of intimacy," Baker confided to his diary. "It is apparently a strain upon him to have people argue with him about anything whatsoever."[102]

Wilson profoundly transformed the communication functions of the American government, but he did not grasp how much. He enlarged the executive branch in his first years in office and expanded it more during the war. This growth required a presidency that was more engaged in persuasion—persuasion of members of his administration, of Congress, of key constituencies, and of citizens. In some respects, Wilson epitomized what it would mean to be "educator in chief." He dared to break tradition by going to Capitol Hill to address legislators directly. He created the CPI to keep thinking in line with his goals during the war. Time and time again, he was described in terms similar to George Sylvester Viereck's, "High Priest of Propaganda." All this, and yet, when the need for propaganda was as great, if not greater, than at any other time, he treated it as a secondary matter.[103]

Edward Bernays insisted Creel should have continued with the original plan of having the CPI handle publicity in Paris. He believed it could have altered "the course of history." If the CPI had continued, Harvey O'Higgins thought, "We'd be in the League of Nations today, and we'd be the teeth in it." While this ignores the political realities that made the CPI's continuation impossible, someone in Paris should have had responsibility for thinking about and coordinating efforts to shape public opinion while Baker managed press relations. An organization was needed at home to devise publicity plans and execute them, a lesson that President Franklin Roosevelt learned.[104]

Roosevelt launched a massive publicity campaign to secure US support for the United Nations. The State Department officials who led this were admonished, "It is imperative that we exert ourselves to satisfy the earnest public demand for information." The department held hundreds of briefings inside and outside Washington. The Woodrow Wilson Foundation, created in the early 1920s to perpetuate Wilson's ideas, almost went broke sending out UN literature on behalf of FDR's UN proposal. The State Department created a unit to interact with Congress, and Roosevelt included prominent Republicans in the delegation that negotiated the UN charter for two months in 1945. The presidency, Wilson wrote in 1908, "will be as big and as influential as the man who occupies it." A large president, as he aspired to be, cannot exist apart from the effective communication of ideas and ideals, as he had said.[105]

This imperative goes to the heart of democratic government. As Bullard said of foreign policy, voters had "a right to demand the clearest and most unequivocal definition of general policy." The Senate had the constitutional right of treaty ratification, and this treaty called for vigorous debate. The obligations under the Paris treaty asked a lot of the American people, who wanted to put the war behind them. If Wilson could persuade the country and legislators to accept what he brought home without change, so be it. If not, he had to compromise. But just as Wilson looked for excuses to avoid the press, he erected false barriers to accepting revisions. "I could not accept any amendments," he told Creel, "because it was not within the right of any one of the signatory powers to amend the treaty in any particular, and I was obliged to reject all the amendments suggested to me because they were not made in good faith." The statement was self-servingly blind to reality. Many senators offered reservations in good faith, and the Allies signaled they would accept them.[106]

Compromise would have led to better outcomes. First, Root, Hughes, and Lodge proposed reservations that deserved serious consideration. Significantly, the United Nations Charter did not include the collective security provisions of Article X. Second, once the United States was in the League it could make changes along the lines Wilson envisioned. It was a brand-new idea that would inevitably undergo modification. Third, by making the Republicans partners in the peace pact, Wilson would have deprived Hays of the treaty as an issue in the 1920 race. Finally, compromise over the treaty would have affirmed the values Wilson espoused when he called on the country to go to war so the world could be "made safe for democracy."[107]

This was a tragedy worthy of Shakespeare. Wilson articulated a farsighted, noble vision of an increasingly interdependent world and the leadership his country could bring to maintaining peace. He failed because he would not make reasonable concessions. This denied the United States a place at the head of the League's green baize table. As John Milton Cooper observed, American global leadership was absent for an entire generation, until a new war brought it back.[108]

In 1931, on the anniversary of the armistice, Ray Stannard Baker wrote his friend Louis Brandeis of his feeling that day. "I have been recalling, how vividly, the event of thirteen years ago today in Paris—the crowds, the noise, the delirious joy of it all. The war was ended! In a deeper sense, to some of us who were there, War itself was ended. The wolf was dead in Arcady and the dragon by the sea! A new age was beginning. . . . Since then I have not care[d] to celebrate this day. I do not care to see the flags flying. Most of all, I do not care to hear the windy oratory. What is there to celebrate? Why not a day of sackcloth and ashes?"[109]

16

The Question

A President whom [the public] trusts can not only lead it,
but form it to his own views.

—Woodrow Wilson, 1908

How can we ever again believe anything? Wholesale lying on the part
of trusted Government in the last war will not soon be forgotten.

—*Richmond Times-Dispatch,* 1925

The history of propaganda in the war would scarcely be worthy of
consideration here, but for one fact—it did not stop with the armistice. No
indeed! The methods invented and tried out in the war were too valuable for
the uses of government, factions and special interests.

—Will Irwin, 1919

On November 11, 2018, under a bright blue sky, the leaves golden with autumn
color, dignitaries from many nations and citizens such as myself crowded into
the Washington National Cathedral to commemorate the end of the fighting
exactly one hundred years before. In the presence of Woodrow Wilson's tomb,
on the south side of the nave, celebrants recited prayers and sang hymns, recounted sacrifices made on battlefields, and remembered the dreams of world
peace spun by the bloody conflict. In passing, a speaker called the Great War
"the founding catastrophe of the modern age, ushering in the greatest period of
change in human history. A world forever changed."[1]

Immediately after the war one of those changes reverberated through the
staid editorial rooms of the *Encyclopaedia Britannica.* Censorship, war bias, and
the "perversion of fact"—the editors concluded—had "cut a Grand Canyon
gash in the whole intellectual structure of the world." The 1911 edition, which
was supposed to remain current for years, had no entry for "Propaganda." In the
three-volume supplement the editors felt obliged to publish, "Propaganda" ran
nearly ten pages of small, densely packed type. The author was a former British

military officer who conducted field propaganda and was attached to Northcliffe's British War Mission in New York City. "Those engaged in a propaganda may genuinely believe that success will be an advantage to those whom they address," Peter Chalmers Mitchell wrote candidly, "but the stimulus to their action is their own cause. The differentia of a propaganda is that it is self-seeking, whether the object be worthy or unworthy, intrinsically or in the minds of its promoters."[2]

The warring nations had conducted propaganda of a magnitude previously unimagined. The United States joined them in propagandizing its own citizens, its allies' citizens, and its enemies in their trenches and in their homes. Although it claimed purer motives than even its allies, the Wilson administration used the same tools as the enemy and employed them as perniciously. When the peace came, propaganda was entrenched in governing. The word *propaganda* appeared in the *New York Times* once a month in 1875; in 1919, it averaged three times a day.

By 2018, the one-hundredth anniversary of the war's end, the president of the United States propagandized daily from his Twitter account. His statements triggered emotions of fear and hate; they often were as false as the Sisson documents. The president's opponents decried individual tweets. Almost never did anyone recognize that the practice fit into a continuum that began a century before. Less recognized still were the disturbing parallels for discrediting inconvenient fact and opinion. During the Great War, critics of government policy and action were guilty of "enemy talk"; today they spread "fake news." In both instances, the great majority of those who accepted those judgments were decent Americans who wanted to do the right thing.

A world forever changed. And yet we are only vaguely aware of the Information State that emerged out of the Committee on Public Information's experiment at mass mobilization of opinion or of the threat that it poses to democracy.

Propaganda has become the air government breathes, vital to its operation; like air, it is difficult to discern as a pervasive daily enterprise, let alone control. When the word is mentioned, evasion and euphemism are employed. It is freighted with sinister overtones thanks to the Great War. It has the curious property of being done by every government leader and admitted by none. The CPI's *War Cyclopedia* carried a lone entry for propaganda. It appeared under the heading "Propaganda, German." The first iron law of propaganda is that only the enemy does it.[3]

A PROPAGANDA BEHEMOTH

The Information State began in a six-by-six-foot room near Josephus Daniels's office. Creel had no staff, a vague mandate, and no models to fall back on. Notwithstanding constant reorganization, mistakes, and unrelenting criticism, the CPI became a propaganda behemoth. It reached every crevice of the nation, every day, and extended widely abroad.

The CPI was a publishing conglomerate, with pamphlets, a six-day-a-week government newspaper, and news services at home and overseas. When the News Division closed on December 1, 1918, it had issued six thousand press releases—more than ten a day, including Saturdays and Sundays. By the end of its existence, the Syndicated Features Division achieved a newspaper circulation of more than seven million readers a week. The Division on Women's War Work sent out almost twenty-five hundred stories in the nine months it existed. The Division of Work with the Foreign Born issued more than twenty-three hundred press releases.[4]

Newspapers used CPI news releases and photos. They often published CPI releases as written, the Sisson documents being a conspicuous example. In Porter Dunlap's hometown of Nashville, the *Tennessean*'s pages averaged one item a week clearly marked as coming from the CPI. The CPI believed the readership of its syndicated features, written by some of the nation's best writers and often not printed with CPI identification, reached a total of twelve million monthly. Even if not identified as originating from the CPI, its releases generated independent stories and affected journalists' thinking about the news.[5]

The Division of Pictorial Publicity under Charles Dana Gibson produced 1,438 poster designs, cards, advertisements, cartoons, seals, and buttons for ninety-eight agencies and committees, ranging from the Federation of Neighborhood Associations to the Salvation Army. The CPI distributed tens of thousands of slides taken by the military. Its advertisements were ubiquitous in newspapers and magazines. The Bureau of Cartoons' weekly *Bulletin* reached every cartoonist it could identify. Families watched CPI films in theaters across the country.[6]

The CPI created organizations, repurposed existing ones, and piggybacked on others. The Division of Work with the Foreign Born had eleven branches, as far as we can tell, and reached twice as many immigrant groups. The CPI worked with Gompers's AFL to create the American Alliance for Labor and Democracy, which, according to one estimate, eventually had 150 branches in forty states. It, too, pumped out press releases. The Four Minute Men were an organizational feat: an eye-popping total of seventy-five thousand grassroots speakers harmonized by Washington. The motion picture industry, advertising associations, universities, and other professional bodies gave the CPI other pathways to American homes and minds. The Boy Scouts, traveling salesmen, and corporate titans did the CPI's bidding. The state Councils of National Defense helped the CPI reach into cities across the country.[7]

Publicity was not considered a diplomatic tool in 1914. By 1918, when the CPI had outposts in some fifteen countries and a news service that spanned the globe, diplomats who once sniffed at rubbing shoulders with the hoi polloi thought "it would be well to continue our propaganda activities." Although the CPI failed miserably in field propaganda, its botched effort, taken over by Heber Blankenhorn, foresaw what could be done.[8]

The CPI did not control every information spigot inside the government. But it was a conduit for all of them. It had a coordinating role for speakers and advertisements. Departments benefited from the *Official Bulletin,* the CPI's press distribution system, and the Four Minute Men, who took up their causes. No department could do without the CPI, not even the hostile State Department, which used it to spread rumors of German spies as well as routine matters.

Superpatriotic groups outside the government shaped opinion. But their reach and effectiveness did not come close to the CPI's. The basic law of propaganda, Sisson said, was to "reiterate cumulatively." The CPI had access to the government printer as well as its own taxpayer-supported printing contracts to handle the overflow. The post office distributed its materials. Through various agencies, it had the power—a meaningful threat—to block mail and the export of films, magazines, and books, to curtail ink and paper, to shut down movie theaters. It spoke with unmatched authority. Its emblem, adorned with the American eagle, evoked the Great Seal of the United States of America with its motto "E Pluribus Unum."[9]

USURPING DEMOCRACY

The CPI was commendable in the transparency principle behind the *Official Bulletin;* in Arthur Bullard's thoughtful earnestness; in Josephine Roche's determination to combat the "numerous un-American conditions and injustices" that victimized immigrants; in Vira Whitehouse's tenaciousness in Switzerland;

in the Four Minute Men's constructive urgings for food conservation and donations of binoculars to the navy; in the Service Bureau's responses to the eighty-
six thousand public inquiries it received after the CPI took over in the spring of
1918. When the CPI was fact-based and open, it vivified American democracy.
Yet for all the patriotic sincerity of its staff, for all their good works, the CPI was
out of sync with democratic values.[10]

Democracy privileges process. It presupposes that open, vigorous deliberation ensures better outcomes. The CPI subverted this. It did all the things that
Creel insisted it did not do. It ignored facts and opinions that spoiled its narrative. Its publicity was tendentious. To an extent not seen in future American
wars, it tugged at heartstrings, triggered hate and fear, and used other "crude
methods," as David Lawrence wrote, to "arouse the people's interest in the war."
Its propaganda often carried an implicit threat, and sometimes a direct one, of
ostracism if one did not conform. It secretly subsidized organizations and publications. It censored, and it said it didn't. It cooperated with burgeoning federal
domestic surveillance agencies, whose witch hunts culminated decades later in
congressional hearings on the intelligence community's excesses. If the CPI did
not routinely go as far as some private groups in fearmongering and jingoism—
and was at times an object of their scorn—it validated their messages.[11]

The CPI's propaganda, even when benign, was nonconsensual. It spent the
public's money to tell them things that they did not ask for or necessarily want.
An individual could choose not to pick up a newspaper or walk into a movie
theater. But everyone drove along roads where CPI posters were ubiquitous.
Traveling outside Denver, William Johns, chairman of the Division of Advertising, wrote a July 4 postcard to Carl Byoir on the ubiquity of the CPI's famous
Red Cross poster of the Virgin Mary as a nurse. "It has been interesting to see
the 'Greatest Mother' poster in the windows of towns on the prairies, towns
hardly as big as this postal [card] out in the flat arid lands."[12]

The emotional posters along roadways, the one-dimensional press releases,
and the pro-war lessons taught in classrooms deprived Americans of a full understanding of the war. Creel tried as best he could to get more journalists to the
front. But he squelched anything that contradicted the images of happy marching soldiers or of gleaming tanks bound for the front. Creel successfully fought
for the publication of the names and addresses of the dead. But the black-and-
white lines of type were bloodless. CPI films showed troops valiantly charging
the enemy. They did not show mangled bodies splayed in the mud. The CPI
denied citizens the means of reckoning the true cost of the war. "We never told

the truth—not by any manner of means," Will Irwin confessed in an article a year after the war. "We told that part which served our national purpose."[13]

The CPI limited citizens' choices. No memorandum in the files spelled out its goal of stymieing the discussion of alternatives to the Wilson administration's policies. It simply happened, as it does with all propaganda—another iron law that we can derive from the war. To keep the public buying war bonds to finance the war, the CPI manufactured fear of an imminent threat to the nation. The "German whispers" campaign—its warnings to beware of "spy talk"—made thoughts of negotiating an early peace treason. Direct and implied appeals to patriotism—encouragement to suspend judgment—permeated CPI propaganda. The CPI wanted the public to cheer, not think. Many later echoed Lloyd George's acknowledgment that if the facts had been known about the losses on the battlefield, people's demand for peace could have been difficult to resist.[14]

Propaganda reverses the democratic idea that elected and appointed officials answer to the people. Rather, it aims to make the people answer to the government. This reversal was egregious in the case of the CPI because of the intensity of its propagandizing and its lack of accountability. Congress, whose elected members are as close to the vox populi as federal government gets, had little sway over Creel's operation. When the CPI was created, Congress had no say in its funding. Wilson allocated money from his war chest. When Congress took control of CPI domestic spending shortly before the war ended, Wilson's fund continued to pay for foreign operations.

The CPI's ability to do so much with so little was a miracle of ingenuity that relied on private subsidy. William McCormick Blair, Francis Marion, Samuel Hopkins Adams, and others worked for token amounts. The eight top executives in the Division of Advertising were dollar-a-month men. Its entire payroll came to $179 a week. Professors, artists, and community leaders like Porter Dunlap were out-and-out volunteers. If one accepts Creel's estimates, the free advertising space donated by newspapers and magazines was roughly equal to the CPI's tax-supported budget. Poole created an Auxiliary Committee whose members, himself included, supplemented his Foreign Press Bureau's budget with money out of their own pockets. Ford Motor Company gave "thousands of dollars' worth of material to the Government as a free gift." George Eastman at the Kodak Company said the CPI in France "could use his organization there in any way that will prove beneficial." The National Negro Press Association paid the expenses of Ralph Tyler, who took no salary while he was accredited to the AEF. The Art Institute of Chicago provided a small office for Gibson's artists; its lone staff member was a volunteer stenographer. The list goes on. This was undeniably patriotic. But it further removed the CPI from congressional oversight.[15]

A more significant circumvention of congressional accountability lay in Creel's appointment and the creation of the CPI, both of which were arguably unconstitutional. Creel qualified as the first presidential "czar," a term today used to describe a White House appointee, unconfirmed by the Senate, who heads an agency, administers policy, and issues rules. The case for requiring Senate confirmation lies in Article II of the Constitution: The president may "*nominate, and by and with the Advice and Consent of the Senate,* shall appoint Ambassadors, other public Ministers and Consuls, Judges of the Supreme Court, and all *other Officers of the United States,* whose Appointments are not herein otherwise provided for, *and which shall be established by Law*"* (emphasis added). Creel's position was not, as it should have been, established by law. He was not confirmed in it. Congress never explicitly authorized the CPI's propaganda functions. The closest it came to correcting this constitutional anomaly was through enactment of the sundry appropriation law in June 1918, many months after the CPI was created. Written in a hurry and vague, the appropriation language provided funds to the CPI in connection with "work that may be specially assigned to it by the President."[16]

Given its power over the thoughts of citizens and the lack of legal authority for its work, the CPI marked a significant step toward the imperial presidency that emerged afterward. Spurts of growth have been dramatic in time of war, when national security concerns spurred Congress and the public to cede more power to the chief executive. This has undermined the system of checks and balances essential to American democracy. As partisan as they may have been, the Republicans had good reason to object to the CPI's existence.[17]

WILSON AND DISSENT

Propaganda exhibited the same iron-law characteristics in every nation, but with variations in execution. The British were far more adept than the Germans, the difference lying chiefly in the lines of authority over propaganda. The military dominated in Germany, civilians in Britain. The CPI excelled at adver-

---

* The same case for unconstitutionality applied to two agencies that became part of the executive branch after the CPI was created: the War Industries Board under Baruch, and the National War Labor Board under former president Taft and Frank Walsh.

tising, a field Americans pioneered. It also reflected the ideas and personalities of Woodrow Wilson and George Creel.[18]

Wilson did not have a thought-through plan for the CPI when he signed the executive order establishing it. This can be explained by his many preoccupations in those early days of war. As Daniels, Baker, and Lansing wrote in their proposal for the CPI, they could not wait on legislation. The CPI offered a quick solution to the urgent need for censorship of sensitive military information. In a sense, though, Wilson had been thinking about the CPI for years. Presidential communication was a central theme in his scholarly studies of government.

Wilson's philosophizing had a democratic cast to it: the president was the "spokesman for the real sentiment and purpose of the country." The primacy that he gave communication suited his oratorical abilities. He was the Great Communicator before the term was applied to Ronald Reagan. Yet, pari passu with Wilson's pledges of pitiless publicity was impatience with debate. In Wilson's view, the president should communicate in order to dominate. "A President whom [the public] trusts," Wilson wrote in the same breath as the passage quoted above, "can not only lead it, but form it to his own views." This explained his attitude toward Congress. Legislators could—and should—be marginalized by a president who controlled communication. He was similarly impatient with the press, which should, in his view, wait on his pronouncements. He disliked the messiness of news and, unable to bend it utterly to his will, isolated himself from it as much as he could. "It is an odd thing," Ray Stannard Baker wrote in his Paris diary, "that while the President stands for 'pitiless publicity'& 'open covenants openly arrived at'—a true position if ever there was one—it is so difficult for him to practice it. He is really so fearful of it."[19]

American traditions did not allow for the heavy censorship possible in Germany, France, and Great Britain. Wilson's party would not push through the censorship clause he proposed. That he persisted in seeking its passage, rather than compromise, revealed the limits he wanted to put on speech. Wilson, Creel told Baker after the war, "was against free speech in the height of the war. He said there could be no such—that it was insanity and that men could, by their actions to America, stab our soldiers in the back." But Wilson's dislike of dissent ran deeper than the fear that it would hinder victory. Wilson could have easily pardoned Eugene Debs, whose antiwar statements no longer posed a threat of any sort. The gesture would have won the approval of liberals, whom Wilson needed in his peace-pact fight. But he could not rise to the occasion

out of practicality or compassion.* Although the need to protect military information evaporated with the armistice, Wilson agreed with Attorney General
Palmer that it was necessary to strengthen laws against sedition.[20]

Tumulty had feared Wilson's suppression of civil liberties would put him in
a class with John Adams and his odious Sedition Acts. And it did. Conditions
did not require the president's heavy-handed stifling of dissent, if they ever do.
It is unlikely that Charles Evans Hughes would have allowed Burleson the freedom he had to suppress speech. In January 1920, when the New York Assembly
refused to seat five duly elected socialists, Hughes took it on himself to write
to the Assembly Speaker, "This is not, in my judgment American government."
Hughes chaired a state bar committee seeking a reversal. He failed, but as constitutional scholar Zechariah Chafee noted, the action "made the conservative
press and sober citizens realize the absurdity of the Red Menace."[21]

Creel complemented Wilson. Creel understood the mechanics of publicity
as Wilson did not. His energy and creativity transformed Wilson's ideas into
action. He urged Wilson to meet with the press and wished him to be less severe in suppressing of speech. But in an odd turn for an individual who was one
of the least restrained journalists, he shared Wilson's annoyance with journalism's unruliness. His reflexive censoriousness encouraged Wilson's suppressive
instincts.

There is much to be said for an alliance such as the one struck by Wilson
and Creel. Subordinates should reflect the views of the individual voted into
the White House. But Creel did not have the right temperament to manage
government propaganda. While Congress would never embrace the CPI fully,
he invited its hostility. He created enemies when he did not need to.

Had the publicity job fallen instead to Lippmann, who wanted it, its scope
likely would have been smaller than the CPI's. That may have necessitated the
creation of another agency, as McCormick and Woolley suggested in the summer of 1917, when they did not know what the CPI would eventually become.
In any event, it is difficult to imagine Wilson and Lippmann working well together. Woolley was a better choice. He was aggressive and creative, without
Creel's pyrotechnics. Woolley had executive skills, possessed superior political
judgment, knew how to practice restraint, and was much craftier than Creel.
Perhaps he could not have softened Wilson's partisanship, but he would not
have aggravated it.[22]

* President Warren Harding commuted Debs's sentence to time served, effective Christmas
Day 1921.

Wilson missed other opportunities. He could have accepted the advice, persistently given to him, to separate censorship and publicity. Franklin Roosevelt did that in World War II, when he created an Office of War Information and an Office of Censorship. Creel could have been confined to the provision of information. Wilson could have embraced the suggestion from journalists that they oversee censorship through a board of advisors or even in an executive fashion. This would not have been a matter of letting the journalistic fox inside the Wilson chicken coop. Publishers and editors would have sternly policed each other, taking political heat off the Wilson administration. In this scenario the administration would have been the fox in the journalism chicken coop.

"There are no other such propagandists as the Washington correspondents, if they are properly handled," Frank Cobb said. "They are not only willing but eager to do the Government's publicity work." But Wilson did not grasp easy opportunities to capitalize on this goodwill. His "attitude toward journalism often made ours a ticklish job," Will Irwin said. He "had little sympathy and less understanding" of the way the press worked.[23]

PROPAGANDA BECOMES A PROFESSION

Not everyone reacted the same way to the "Grand Canyon gash" that propaganda cut in the "whole intellectual structure of the world." The power of propaganda instilled fear in some and exhilarated others.

A great soul-searching followed the war. Opinions that had put the radical press out of business became matters of wide discussion. Were the Germans really to blame for the war? What American interests justified going to war? Were bankers behind it? Americans were not directly threatened. Did a false neutrality favoring the Allies drag America into the war? Had Wilson cynically promised to keep the country out of war? Had he, and the public, been seduced by his rhetoric? By going to war, progressives complained, the United States won nothing worthwhile and set back domestic reform. Historian Carl Becker, who was in the CPI fold, rebuked himself for having been "naïve enough to suppose, during the war, that Wilson could ever accomplish those ideal objects which are so well formulated in his state papers." A great many Americans—a full 70 percent in a 1937 survey—believed it had been a mistake to intervene in the war.[24]

Propaganda figured into these discussions. At last, criticism of British propaganda was not the nearly exclusive province of frustrated German-Americans. Out in the open was discussion of British deceit, British deftness at avoiding controversy as it molded public opinion, and British success at cultivating House and Wilson. Opinion journals, which criticized the CPI throughout the war, went deeper to analyze its penetration of American institutions. The *American Mercury* explored "George Creel's herd of 2,000 historians." Despite his poetic liberties, George Sylvester Viereck wrote one of the better studies of propaganda. "Inflaming popular emotion during the War," he wrote, "they had created a Frankenstein monster" that hampered Wilson's ability to forge a just peace.[25]

"In retrospect it hardly seems possible that a large, throbbing land, practi-cally filled with inspired editors and old ladies and professors and a few wage-earners, would bite into such an apple as the Allies offered us, without first determining that there was no worm at the core," said Herbert Corey, one of a handful of reporters who covered the fighting in Europe from the start. "But we did bite in. From August 1914 to April 1917, we had been well and copiously fooled." The war put the press on guard. The realization came that they needed to be a brake on government propaganda, not an accelerator. The first national code of journalism ethics, written in 1923, deemed partisanship "subversive of a fundamental principle of journalism."[26]

"Propaganda" was not the only dirty word. The war exposed the contradic-tion in progressive views on "publicity." Progressives had basked in being publi-cists who provided the facts the public needed to reach sound decisions about what was broken and how to fix it. But during the war, this belief tripped over the other progressive ideal of managing society, exemplified by Wilson's idea of leading people to think along the pathways he traced for them. The CPI, staffed with progressives who prided themselves on exposing trusts, created an information trust. The government, previously the object of exposure and re-form, now sorted the right facts from the wrong ones. After the fighting ended, the techniques perfected in the war were taken up by private special interests to thwart social, economic, and political improvement. Ray Stannard Baker had believed the solution to misleading railroad publicity was "true publicity," the more the better. Now journalists no longer said with pride that they did "pub-licity," and they condemned the proliferation of it by others.[27]

Frederic Wile, who became a commentator in the new medium of radio in the 1920s, complained of the Grand Army of Publicity that descended on Washington to influence legislation. It all started, he said, when the Allies and their enemies came ashore in America in 1914 to shape the country's views.

"When Uncle Sam himself became a belligerent in 1917, one of the first leaves he took from the notebook of war-experienced Europe was that which dealt with publicity as a fine art." In a speech to the Women's Club of New York a few weeks after the armistice was signed, Frank Cobb decried government propaganda that "goose-stepped" public opinion and the "private propaganda" that emerged along with it. Before the war, the number of publicity agents could be counted. "How many there are now, I do not pretend to know," Cobb said, "but what I do know is that many of the direct channels to news have been closed, and the information for the public is first filtered through publicity agents. . . . God forbid that our supreme achievement in the War should be the Prussianizing of ourselves." These were remarkable statements by journalists who had been eager propagandists for the Allies and the Wilson administration. They testified to the way the war took the wind out of progressive sails. "The reformer's occupation is gone," wrote journalist William Allen White.[28]

Walter Lippmann, an enthusiastic would-be propagandist during the war, wrote disturbing critiques afterward. In April 1919, after returning from Paris weighed down with disappointment over the treaty negotiations, he told the editor of the *Atlantic Monthly* of his "discovery that opinion can be manufactured. The idea has come to me gradually as a result of certain experiences with the official propaganda machine, and my hope is to attempt a restatement of the problem of freedom of thought as it presents itself in modern society."[29]

The Wilson administration, Lippmann believed, succeeded "in creating something that might almost be called one public opinion all over America." He produced three books muckraking public opinion. It was "no longer possible," he wrote in the most enduring volume, *Public Opinion,* "to believe in the original dogma of democracy." In small communities, people could form intelligent opinions on issues that fell inside their experience, but they did not have the tools and experience to grapple with national problems. By thinking otherwise, "We expose ourselves to self-deception and to forms of persuasion that we cannot verify."[30]

A few on the CPI staff had misgivings. Roche, Bullard, and others were dismayed by Wilson's failure "to turn Paris into a rostrum from which he could have addressed the world audience." In his 1920 novel, *Blind: The Story of Our Times,* Ernest Poole's hero comes home sightless from a wound suffered fighting in France. "Washington," he says, "has been invaded by an army of ideas—a host of strange new aims and methods born in the clash and din abroad and now entering here to bore and burrow their devious ways deep into our national institutions. We are being driven to drastic powers of control over the whole nation's life."[31]

But for the great majority of those who worked alongside Creel, the bright light of their earnestness removed shadows of doubt. Ford indicated no misgivings when he told a Minnesota audience, "For the first time in the history of America, the voice of the national government was carried directly and regularly into the schools of the whole country." Said Harvey O'Higgins, "Those were great days—the greatest that Washington ever saw or is likely to see.... Couldn't have found anywhere a better cheerleader than Creel." "We challenge anyone to charge Creel and his organization with a single dishonorable objective or method of operation," said Frank Bohn fifty years later at a retrospective conference on the CPI. He did not mention that he had worked in Switzerland under the cover of the Friends of German Democracy.[32]

Many were inspired to wield the arts of persuasion after the war. "Now, being Associate Chairman of the Creel Committee didn't make me the best public relations man in America," Byoir told his staff years later. "It did give me the broadest education that anybody had ever had in the history of the world as to what you could do with this power of publicity or public relations."[33]

Edward Bernays returned from Paris convinced "the activities like those of the Creel Committee with the people of the world could be employed for peacetime purposes." When he hung out his shingle on East Forty-Eighth Street in New York, he cast around for a term for his work, at one point calling it "publicity direction" and eventually choosing "counsel on public relations." He borrowed the term "counsel" from law, "hoping its professional implications would carry over to the new field." "Whether in the problem of getting elected to office or in the problem of interpreting and popularizing new issues or in the problem of making the day-to-day administration of public affairs a vital part of the community life," he wrote in his 1928 book *Propaganda,* "the use of propaganda, carefully adjusted to the mentality of the masses is an essential adjunct of political life."[34]

Universities became a microcosm of the elation and anxiety over the newfound power of propaganda. On one side were new fields of scholarship that studied its deleterious effects on democracy. Journalism schools, which proliferated, inculcated in their students a skepticism of official pronouncements. "It was everywhere assumed that public opinion, clarified by general education, assured the continuation of representative government and free institutions in the United States," said Carl Ackerman of the youthful hopefulness he had. Now, as dean of his alma mater, the journalism school at Columbia University, he acknowledged "these confident assumptions are challenged or denied." With scientific study of the impact of journalism on public opinion, he argued, journalists could fight the power of propagandists. Pushing in the other direction were new university departments of psychology, marketing, advertising, and public relations. In 1923, Bernays announced he was teaching the first public relations courses in the nation, at New York University.[35]

The forces propelling propaganda were self-perpetuating. When one side found a better way to make its case, the other sides were compelled to improve on it. "Propaganda has become part of political warfare—both in domestic and foreign policy," wrote Walter von Hofmann of the German War Press Office at the end of the war. The day after Germany's surrender, a directive went out to the Foreign Office press officers. These "attorneys of politics" were to stay in place. Hofmann thought the Germans needed to emulate the British propagandists.[36]

"Propaganda has become a profession," Harold Lasswell wrote in *Propaganda Technique in the World War,* the first serious study of the topic. "The modern world is busy developing a corp [*sic*] of men who do nothing but study the ways and means of changing minds or binding minds to their convections. ... It is to be expected that governments will rely increasingly upon the professional propagandist for advice and aid."[37]

THE INFORMATION STATE AND DEADLY NIGHTSHADE

In two significant aspects United States propaganda departed from the propaganda practices in the Great War: the organizational structure changed, and the legal powers for chloroforming unwanted speech were weakened.

The Committee on Public Information was the first and last United States ministry of propaganda. Afterward proposals to re-create a central information agency surfaced from time to time. President Harding considered establishing a department of administration publicity under an assistant secretary. But comparisons to Creel and the CPI kept surfacing, and the idea "went to an unmarked grave." During World War II, Creel recommended that Franklin Roosevelt re-create the CPI. The Roosevelt administration found it difficult enough, in light of the CPI's history, to create a fragmented propaganda apparatus.[38]

In any event, a large centralized propaganda bureau was not as efficient as it might seem. Each government department—and often bureaus within a department—wanted to promote itself and was better able to do so than an outside organization was. The CPI recognized this when it put its press officers inside government agencies.

The second departure from the war experience was a reinterpretation of the First Amendment. The Espionage Act, the Trading with the Enemy Act, and the Sedition Act forced the courts to take their first sustained look at free speech. Initially judges upheld the government. But in calmer times after the war, the courts shifted. The minority views of Holmes and Brandeis in the Abrams case became the majority view. Particularly significant advances came in the 1930s, when Charles Evans Hughes was chief justice of the Supreme Court.

These two deviations from the wartime pattern did nothing at all to impede the growth of the Information State. On the contrary, decentralization made it easier for information bureaus to proliferate. When lodged inside individual agencies, they were less visible and did not require congressional authorization the way a propaganda department would. The reinterpretation of the First Amendment made it easier to criticize the government, but it had no effect on the rest of government propaganda. As legal scholar Geoffrey R. Stone noted, "It would have to be a very extreme case to imagine a court holding that the government's own speech violates the First Amendment because it has, in effect, swamped, the marketplace of ideas. As a constitutional matter, we tend to give broad leeway to the government's own propagandizing, and there is no judicial precedent declaring government speech itself unconstitutional under the First Amendment."[39]

The control of propaganda is one of the thorniest problems of democracy. Like the plant deadly nightshade, which can promote sanity or bewitch, depending on how the potion is administered, government information can sustain democracy or undermine it. The Government Accountability Office (GAO), which monitors the executive branch on behalf of Congress, is equally concerned with stopping propaganda and ensuring the executive branch adequately informs the public. In the words of founding father Elbridge Gerry, "In a republic every action ought to be accounted for."[40]

The positive side of government information falls into three categories. First, the government is a public almanac, albeit published daily. It provides information as diverse as weather forecasts; statistics on trade, traffic accidents, K–12 educational attainment; and health alerts. The severity of the coronavirus epidemic, a Grim Reaper that swept its way across the planet while this book was in its final stages of production, epitomized the essentiality of reliable government information. These public services help citizens make better decisions, decisions that can be the difference between life and death. Second, the government informs the public about what it is doing, whether awarding a contract for bridge repair, imposing new safety regulations on mining, or detaining immigrants on the Mexican border—the sort of information that made the *Official Bulletin* useful. Democracy is impossible without transparency. Finally, also as part of the democratic process, officials are obliged to make the case for the policies they wish to pursue and the actions they take. Democracy is a contest of ideas and an exercise in choice. Wilson was not wrong that the chief executive should seek to lead opinion.

But how does one wall off the undemocratic aspects of the Information State? No legislation can require the president and his appointees to provide all facts on all sides of a question. It is impractical to write legislation barring presidents from using rhetoric that scares the public. No law could have conceivably stopped the CPI from warning the public of "German whispers," as overblown as it was. Sometimes the evocation of fear is justified. A president can legitimately speak in favor of raising the minimum wage or enhancing border security, but how does one separate that from using a federal agency's public communication machinery, supposedly designed to inform, to advertise the merits of such legislation? These two functions are as difficult to separate as Siamese twins. Time and again the GAO has noted that the line "is almost impossible to draw."

The few laws governing propaganda are problematic. Congress has not defined "publicity" or "propaganda." One category of offending information is "purely partisan materials." No violation has ever been found because no political message can be "completely devoid of any connection with official functions." The GAO is "reluctant to find a violation where the agency can provide a reasonable justification for its activities." The executive branch has little incentive to enforce antipropaganda laws that restrict its operations. The Department of Justice has never prosecuted a violation of the laws governing propaganda. Congress episodically launches investigations, but legislative intervention follows the pattern of the Republican-dominated Joint Committee on Printing, which lost interest in executive branch publications once Harding walked into the White House. In 2005, Senate Democrats introduced the "Stop Government Propaganda Act" to thwart the Bush administration's video press releases. They were the minority party, and the bill failed.[41]

A significant difficulty in controlling the Information State is that it is amorphous, seen as if looking through frosted glass. We see shapes, but specifics are elusive. "It is unlikely that anyone in the Federal Government knows how many people are engaged in 'opinion-shaping' information activities," Senator William J. Fulbright wrote during the height of the Vietnam War. Since then, government information has become more difficult to measure and evaluate on even the most basic level. With the increase in the number of jobs involving the dissemination of information, the GAO could not do a complete census if it wanted to, said a former GAO official specializing in information.[42]

A 2016 GAO study identified some five thousand employees engaged in executive public relations. Their salaries amounted to half a billion dollars annually. The study did not cover a number of agencies, including the military, and counted only individuals listed under the occupational code "Public Affairs." Many of those concerned with information hold unrelated titles or do the work part time. How should the government classify those on the State Department's Policy Planning staff who, as a part of their work, consider plans for countering Jihadist recruiting videos, or a special assistant who tweets excerpts from the Secretary of Transportation's speeches? The Environmental Protection Agency alone had some two dozen Twitter accounts. Early in its first term, the Obama administration identified twenty-four thousand federal websites. These activities do not include advertising and public relations carried out by government contractors. This totals at least $1 billion a year, although again this cannot be taken as a complete tally. Contractors purchase advertising space in all forms of media and provide marketing research, opinion polling, message-crafting assistance, and more. The Executive Office of the President alone spends an average of $40 million a year on such contracts. This does not include all the techniques presidents have to enlarge their images and voices, as President Trump showed when he insisted his name appear on stimulus checks mailed to pandemic-distressed Americans in 2020. The CPI was masterful in stage-managing Wilson's July Fourth Loyalty Day speech at Mount Vernon in 1918. Today presidents enhance July Fourth speeches by ordering a Blue Angels flyover. Military marching bands generate patriotic feelings and confer authority. The Department of Defense has 136 bands, costing half a billion dollars a year. None of this showed up in the GAO study.[43]

"It is almost impossible to know even within the institution where the important [communications] work is being done," said a State Department consultant on public diplomacy in 2012. The information bureaucracy is adept at thwarting scrutiny. Over the years public affairs officers have been listed as assistant supervisors of employment in the Labor Department (in FDR's administration) and air force chaplains (in the Truman administration). In 2008, Army vice chief of staff General Peter W. Chiarelli set out to determine how many people were involved in strategic communication, which was greatly enlarged under Secretary of Defense Donald Rumsfeld and criticized for spinning more than informing. Chiarelli "couldn't do it," said his principal public affairs officer. Many strategic communications personnel held unrelated job titles. Commanders did not cooperate in identifying them. The commanders feared Chiarelli would eliminate the positions. They relied on these communicators to promote themselves as well as their programs.[44]

THE RECURRING PATTERN OF PROPAGANDA

The Information State would have emerged without the Great War. Recognition of the importance of public opinion took hold before the conflict. But the tools were primitive, and the number of people involved small. In 1911, the *New York Times* complained the government was employing as many as eight press agents. Necessity being the mother of invention, the war accelerated the development of strategies and tactics for managing public opinion in an organized, persistent, and pervasive way. "The work came first," Guy Stanton Ford said of the CPI's operation, "and the methods came afterwards."[45]

"The War," Roger Babson said, "taught us the power of propaganda." Never again would the government undertake propaganda from scratch. Never again would the government leave public opinion unattended. "For the first time in history, we are now confronted nearly everywhere by *mass* opinion as the final determinant of political, and economic, action," said the *Public Opinion Quarterly* in its maiden issue, January 1937.[46]

The CPI established patterns that persist: the use of every available communication tool to fill every space in the public sphere, appeals to patriotism and accusations of "un-Americanism" to discredit unwelcome views, and the conviction that the goals of propaganda are more important than preserving democratic processes. "With the existence of democracy itself at stake," said Creel in a moment of great clarity, when giving a speech in Chicago in 1921, "there was no time to think about the details of democracy." These, too, are iron laws. "It is a quality of propaganda that high-minded persons on both sides commend their cause by identical arguments," said the *Encyclopaedia Britannica* in 1922, "and that high-strung persons soon come to believe what they wish to be true."[47]

Surveillance and propaganda remain interlocking components of the enlarged federal government that emerged from the war and have held sway over citizens since. Not all surveillance falls into the category of the intelligence gathering done by Ralph Van Deman and Herbert Hoover, although technological advances have enhanced intelligence agencies' ability to monitor views of foreigners and American citizens alike. The measurement of public opinion, initially a matter of observation and instinct, became a science with the emergence of polling in the 1930s. The next iteration was internet-driven "surveillance capitalism," which has refined the slicing and dicing of information about consumers and, collaterally, about voters to the point that moods can be measured.[48]

The links between running for president and governing remain as strong as they were when Woolley's Publicity Bureau was an incubator for the CPI. While in Italy, Charles Merriam said he could "do some very effective propaganda at home on the strength of what I have seen here." Back at the University of Chicago, he pioneered the modern data-driven election campaign based on deep statistical analysis of voter behavior. "It is clearly in evidence," he said, "that the science of creating and transmitting public opinion under the influence of collective emotion is about to become the principal science of civilization to the mastery of which all governments and all powerful interests in the future will address themselves with every resource in their command."[49]

The use of these techniques is cumulative. Barack Obama harnessed social media to win the presidency. In office, he created an Office of Digital Strategy to reach the public directly via social media. More than half the staff had worked on an Obama presidential campaign. Donald Trump rode into office on a tsunami of tweets. As president, he kept the Office of Digital Strategy and used tweets to shape the news agenda, call out his critics, and bolster his base for the next election.[50]

The relentless study of the means to better shape opinion is a feature of government. Obama also created a Social and Behavioral Sciences Team, nicknamed the "nudge unit," to encourage citizens to behave responsibly, for instance to stop smoking or start a retirement savings program. At the Defense Advanced Research Projects Agency (DARPA), whose research paved the way for the internet, scientists turn science fiction into science with their studies of the brain. In one study neurologists have traced blood flow to the brain to measure the effectiveness of messages. They are "moving fiendishly fast" in understanding how to make those messages more persuasive, said Read Montague, a Virginia Tech neuroscientist working with DARPA. DARPA's program is aimed at foreign enemies. But nudging and brain study breakthroughs can be repurposed for partisan political propaganda at home.[51]

Propaganda "by its very nature involves concealment," wrote Lucy Salmon, a fellow faculty member with Wilson early in his career and a student of news. This is another iron law. The judiciary strengthened free speech guarantees, but suppression of information remained. Massive surveillance, as the writers-support organization PEN International has pointed out, keeps people from pursuing sensitive subjects and communicating with sources. The government can classify information that would open it to criticism. The classification stamp went down on more than forty-five million government documents in 2017, according to one government report. The number is understated given the difficulty making a tally. The cost of protecting secrets in 2017 was nearly twice the budget of the Environmental Protection Agency.[52]

When possible, presidents follow Wilson's pattern of bypassing journalists. Although FDR interacted with the press as effectively as his presidential cousin Theodore Roosevelt, journalists complained about the control his press officers exerted over information. Despite President Obama's pledges for openness, he held fewer press conferences than his immediate predecessors and, in the view of many journalists, had "the most closed, control-freak administration" in memory. In 2014 national intelligence director James Clapper barred officials in seventeen agencies from speaking with reporters without authorization even on unclassified subjects. The Trump administration took steps to silence officials within a week of his inauguration and barred testimony that used federal scientific data on climate change, a phenomenon the administration disputed.[53]

CYNICISM AND DISENCHANTMENT

"Public Opinion," said Amos Pinchot, a liberal who reluctantly supported the war, "is the ultimate basis of all political power and of all social institutions in a free country and anything which taints or debauches it is an evil far more vital and harder to reach than the mere short-comings of government." The Information State is a threat to democracy not only in its tendencies to pollute public opinion. Propaganda corrodes public confidence in democratic institutions and processes.[54]

The realization of the power that lay in government propaganda during the Great War wrenched the national psyche. "Gradually the whole horrible truth about the war is being revealed," Reinhold Niebuhr, a Detroit minister and budding public intellectual, wrote in his diary in 1923. "Every new book destroys some further illusion." Frederic Howe lamented, "My attitude toward the state was changed. I have never been able to bring it back. I became distrustful of the state." "We seem to be approaching a state of government by hired promoters of opinion called publicity agents," said philosopher-activist John Dewey. Too often elections were determined by "the portrait of a candidate with his firm jaw, lovely wife and children."[55]

For Harold Lasswell, who studied under Charles Merriam, this disillusionment was a sign of systemic failure. "The whole discussion about the ways and means of controlling public opinion testifies to the collapse of the traditional species of democratic romanticism," he wrote. "That credulous utopianism, which fed the mighty words which exploited the hopes of the mass in war, had in many minds given way to cynicism and disenchantment."[56]

Continued revelations of the evils of government propaganda cemented these feelings. The Vietnam War introduced a new word into political discourse, "credibility gap." The origin of the gap, said political philosopher Hannah Arendt, was that the government treated the war like a political campaign in which the goal was to create an image of the war, rather than look at contrary facts. These facts emerged sensationally with the leaking of official documents that came to be known as the Pentagon Papers. The government's failed attempt to suppress their release added to the impression that deception was, in the minds of those who did it, an acceptable tool for governing. "In the Pentagon papers," Arendt wrote, "we are confronted with people who did their utmost to win the minds of the people, that is, to manipulate them."[57]

The short-term expediency of propaganda comes with the long-term cost of ideals. Promoting the German-Bolshevik conspiracy may have helped make the distant war seem a proximate peril. But it fueled repression during and after the war. Demonizing the Germans made it more difficult to prepare public opinion for the peace terms Wilson had in mind. His soaring rhetoric led to crushing disillusionment when it was not realized. Shortly after his Fourteen Points speech, Vira Whitehouse observed, "Mr. Wilson's idea of diplomacy is to tell so little of a topic—leaving out the essential points—that he deceives his hearer."[58]

New propaganda strategies are created all the time to stay ahead of the public's cynicism. They may succeed for a time but ultimately reinforce citizens' perceptions that government is not leveling with them. Less than 17 percent of Americans expressed trust in Washington in 2019. "The moment government begins its direct propaganda," Frank Cobb told CND director Grosvenor Clarkson in 1917, "people begin to wonder if it is not suppressing something for the protection of itself, and the reaction is inevitable."[59]

Cynicism puts the nation at risk. Lack of faith in government delegitimizes leaders and makes it easier for demagogues to gain a following through malicious use of communication tools. External adversaries leverage public distrust of government by planting misinformation that disrupts elections and casts suspicions on those elected to govern. "Cyberattack," a phrase unheard of in intelligence threat assessments before the Obama administration, is now at the top of the list. "If social media's greatest contribution is democratizing communications, their greatest threat is in abetting cynicism and distrust," writes David Cole, legal director of the American Civil Liberties Union. As the Sisson documents show, the public and their leaders eagerly accept grossly inaccurate political information that affirms their convictions.[60]

The press, a bulwark against propaganda, has also been breached. After the war journalists were never entirely successful at keeping officials at arm's length. News media relied on the Bush administration's assurances that Iraq possessed weapons of mass destruction. Still, independent journalism became the default position after 1918—until recently. Technological advances have strengthened propagandists and disrupted fact-based reporting. The low cost of technology makes it much easier for partisans to confuse and distort. With declining revenue from advertisers, who are less dependent on newspapers and magazines, the news media cannot afford to patrol government as they did.[61]

"The question is no longer one of establishing democratic institutions," Chief Justice Charles Evans Hughes said, "but of preserving them." The Information State calls for Information Statesmen and Stateswomen who champion principled government communication. These people must come, to a large degree, from Congress, the strongest institution we have to control executive power. Legislators must impose restraints on propaganda the way arms control negotiators limit nuclear weapons to achieve national security. An independent board could be established by law to report annually to Congress on government information policy and trends. This would make it easier for the press to cover the quotidian aspects of the Information State rather than the occasional sensation, as happens now.[62]

Where outright propaganda is called for, as with public diplomacy, it should be a lesson in the presentation of facts and honest introspection on the American experience, as Arthur Bullard demonstrated in his "Letter from an American Friend." "The fundamental issues surrounding these activities remain essentially the same as those that confronted the Creel Committee fifty years ago," said a scholar during the Vietnam War. The most fundamental of all was, "What is the proper role for propaganda in the foreign policy of a democratic society?"[63]

The public has a role to play. Straining for a happy ending to his pessimistic *Public Opinion,* Lippmann argued that expert-led intelligence bureaus should guide the public's thinking. This progressive nostrum was naïve. The experts have biases and their own agenda. Every source of information must be questioned. In place of the idea that people should be led to the right thoughts, people must learn to think critically for themselves. Of his war experience Ray Stannard Baker said, "I acquired a new regard for the value of informed public opinion & a new distrust for leadership."[64]

Any check on the Information State depends, in the first place, on recognition of the dangers that lurk in it. That is the purpose of this history. The origins of government propaganda reveal the susceptibility of well-intentioned people to subvert the democratic principles in which they believe deeply. Like Hughes, Creel understood, "Democracy is not an automatic device but the struggle everlasting." Yet in his zeal to make the world "safe for democracy," he did not recognize that he chipped away at its foundation. "The great Drama is of the Ages," wrote the editors of the postwar edition of the *Encyclopaedia Britannica,* "and can only be appreciated with all its Acts on record."[65]

Epilogue

Government propaganda was a new undertaking, and the new attracts the young. Many of those involved had long careers ahead of them, often working at the intersection of politics, news, and publicity. Others in the autumn of their lives had poignant final years that illuminate aspects of this new phenomenon of manipulating the masses.

CARL ACKERMAN, who felt like "an agent of public opinion" when he covered Washington at the start of the war, left journalism to become a corporation agent of public opinion. His clients included Eastman Kodak, Union Carbide, General Electric, and General Motors, firms that learned from the war that they could build customer loyalty by selling a pleasing idea of themselves. During the 1924 campaign, Ackerman wrote a biography of Charles Dawes, who was elected vice president on the Calvin Coolidge ticket. In 1931 he became the dean of Columbia University's School of Journalism. "The primary obligation of the press in peace and in war is to serve as an instrumentality of the public, not as an agency of government," he told a gathering of American newspaper editors in 1941. The following year he established a journalism school in China with secret funding from the Office of Strategic Services, the predecessor of the CIA. The OSS used the school to recruit Chinese journalists to its service.[1]

SAMUEL HOPKINS ADAMS's *Common Cause* appeared just as the war ended. "If you are a red-blooded American, you will want to read 'Common Cause,'" said a Wisconsin newspaper. "If you are a pacifist you won't like it." Adams continued to give readers what they wanted. By the time of his death in 1958, he had written more than fifty books, ranging from serious and racy novels to romance and light-hearted fiction, histories, biographies, books for children, science fiction, mysteries, a game book, and a western. A short story for *Cosmopolitan* became director Frank Capra's *It Happened One Night,* with actors Clark

Carl Ackerman began the war as a self-styled "agent of public opinion" and never lost his enthusiasm for shaping events as well as covering them. After leaving journalism, he was a public relations counselor and political consultant. As dean of the Columbia University School of Journalism, he established a journalism school in China with secret funding from the Office of Strategic Services. Its goal was to produce Chinese spies and propagandists. (Columbiana)

Gable and Claudette Colbert. It was the first film to win all five major Academy Awards (Best Picture, Director, Actor, Actress, and Screenplay).[2]

ROGER BABSON, the business wizard who helped the CPI reach labor audiences, founded Babson College. In 1940 he ran for president as the candidate of the Prohibition Party.

After the war, navy censor GEORGE BARR BAKER handled publicity for Herbert Hoover's American Relief Administration, which provided food to eastern and central Europe. In 1924 he was the publicity director for Calvin Coolidge's race for the White House and in 1928 helped Hoover's campaign in a similar fashion.[3]

Ray Stannard Baker remained an energetic writer on numerous subjects, but the chief one was Woodrow Wilson. In addition to his little book *What Wilson Did in Paris,* he wrote a three-volume study of the peace conference and, with William E. Dodd, edited a four-volume collection of documents related to Wilson's presidency. In 1924, in the last letter he ever wrote, Wilson gave Baker exclusive rights to all his papers for a full biography. Creel, who had hoped to coauthor a book with Wilson, told Edith Wilson the decision "was, quite naturally, a bitter blow to me." The last of Baker's eight volumes on Wilson's life appeared in 1939. The biography won the Pulitzer Prize. "Publicity," Baker said at the end of this life, "is indeed the test of democracy."[4]

Edward L. Bernays devoted the rest of his long life (he died in 1995 at the age of 103) to public relations. He promoted vices such as smoking by women (by suggesting they would lose weight) and virtues such as reading (by encouraging interior designers to use bookshelves, which then would be filled with the output of publishers, whom he represented). During the Eisenhower administration, he helped the United Fruit Company, whose control over Guatemala was threatened by land reform. Bernays portrayed the democratically elected president as a Communist and urged American intervention, which occurred through a CIA-staged coup. "Propaganda," he said, "is the executive arm of the invisible government."[5]

"If I still have any political ambition left in my life," Count Johann von Bernstorff wrote to Frank Polk when the United States declared war on Germany, "it is solely directed towards helping to mend what now has been broken." After the war, Bernstorff was cofounder and president of the German Association for the League of Nations. The League, he argued, "will transform itself into the United States of Europe." Singled out by Adolf Hitler as bearing responsibility for the German defeat in World War I, Bernstorff took refuge in Geneva, where he died in 1939. (Bernstorff's military attaché Franz von Papen, who was expelled in 1915, was vice chancellor under Hitler, an arrangement that he hoped would contain the führer. He was acquitted at the Nuremberg War Crimes Trials. Naval attaché Karl Boy-Ed, also expelled, married the daughter of an American Episcopalian bishop in 1921. He wanted to settle in the United States but was denied a visa. In 1930 Boy-Ed was killed when he fell off a horse.)[6]

EDWIN BJORKMAN, who oversaw CPI work with Scandinavian immigrants, became associate director of the League of Nations News Bureau. The short-lived agency was established to build American support for the League in the United States. Later Bjorkman edited the *Asheville Times* and directed the North Carolina Federal Writers Project.[7]

WILLIAM MCCORMICK BLAIR returned to his career in Chicago finance. When the firm for which he worked went under during the Depression, he started his own with financial assistance from the steel manufacturing family of DONALD RYERSON, the first director of the Four Minute Men. William Blair and Company still exists, with offices worldwide. Blair became one of Chicago's most civic-minded citizens.[8]

After the war, HEBER BLANKENHORN returned to the subject he favored in his newspaper days, labor unions, only now as an advocate. "For close to three decades, in every major labor event having to do with public opinion," a historian wrote, "one could find Blankenhorn tugging at someone's elbow—asking questions, supplying the answers to these questions, and pointing out alternative courses of action." In the 1930s he staffed a Senate committee investigating industrial espionage of the labor movement. He learned of the practice while in military intelligence, where he saw secret reports supplied by corporations on so-called Red unions. "I remembered that nefarious undercover system," Blankenhorn wrote in an unpublished memoir, "and knew that it was nationwide and I swore to myself if I ever got a chance I'd hit that as hard as I could." When he returned to intelligence work in World War II, he had to start over again explaining the value of field propaganda. At the end of World War II Blankenhorn left the service as a lieutenant colonel. In 2014, he was posthumously named "a silver knight" on the honor roll of the Army Psychological Operations Regiment.[9]

L. AMES BROWN, who headed the CPI's syndicates feature division, wrote a book pleading for the elimination of wars before becoming president of Lasker's Lord & Thomas.[10]

ARTHUR BULLARD was recruited as chief of the State Department's Russia Division after the war. In 1924 he was an assistant to the Democrats' nominee for president, John W. Davis. Believing that public opinion was "the most important question" facing the fledgling League of Nations, Bullard became the Geneva representative of the League of Nations Non-Partisan Association, an organization that promoted that body. His friend Ernest Poole, among others, attributed his untimely death in 1929, at the age of forty-nine, to the hardships he endured in Russia. "On his last afternoon, his mind went back into the past," his wife told House, "& he was talking of Russia & the Revolution." [11]

ALBERT BURLESON ignored an order from Wilson to end postal censorship. He did not tell his local postmasters to stop withholding mail until the summer of 1919. To the end of the administration he would not give second-class privileges to the successor of the *Masses,* the *Liberator,* as well as others. When the Harding administration restored its mailing privileges, one of Burleson's men said the officials were "violators of their oaths of office." Burleson's wife put up an indirect defense of his wartime anti–free speech position in a short novel published in 1921. In it a congressman's reelection is imperiled by charges, spread in a handbill, that he is a socialist. She saves the day by purloining the handbills before they can be distributed. When her husband asks if she is afraid, she replies, "I didn't believe the law could punish me for stopping such a monstrous *lie!*" [12]

In 1925 CARL BYOIR was described as "undoubtedly the most successful public relations counsel now in business." He was also one of the most controversial. Immediately after the war, he became part owner of a patent medicine company whose exaggerated advertising drew the attention of the Federal Trade Commission. With George Sylvester Viereck on its payroll, Carl Byoir & Associates won a contract to promote tourism in Germany shortly after Adolf Hitler was named German chancellor. (Nazi propaganda minister Joseph Goebbels saw political value in tourist propaganda.) This became the subject of congressional hearings. Later Byoir promoted the Chinese Nationalists. The Chinese canceled the contract when they learned he also helped their enemy, Japan. Byoir's use of front organizations on behalf of railroads—the third-party technique he perfected at the CPI—led to prosecution under the Sherman Anti-Trust Act for conspiracy to put truckers out of business. The case went to the Supreme Court, which sided with Byoir. "Deception, reprehensible as it is, can be of no consequence so far as the Sherman Act is concerned," wrote Justice Hugo Black, a champion of First Amendment rights. Carrying forward another practice from the war, public service messaging, Byoir raised millions to eradicate polio. His firm, the third largest in the country at the time, was acquired by Foote, Cone, & Belding, the advertising giant that was itself an offshoot of Albert Lasker's Lord & Thomas. That new firm was later acquired by Hill and Knowlton.[13]

When the French government put JOSEPH CAILLAUX on trial in 1920, it could not prove treason. He was found guilty, instead, of "having had relations with the subjects of an enemy power." Because he had spent so much time in jail, he was released and banished from major cities. Caillaux made a political comeback, once again becoming finance minister. He remained in the Senate until 1940. During his wife's trial in 1914, it was rumored he would divorce her and that both he and her victim, *Le Figaro* editor Gaston Calmette, were competing for the affection of another woman. Joseph and HENRIETTE CAILLAUX remained married, perhaps because the trial made it impossible not to be. An intimate of Madame Caillaux said they grew to hate each other.[14]

GEORGE CREEL remained a human cyclone, touching down as before in journalism and politics. *Collier's* billed him as "national trouble shooter, stormy petrel of politics, relentless reporter." During the Great Depression, Creel was West Coast chief of Franklin Roosevelt's National Recovery Administration. When he loudly resigned on the grounds his powers were too limited, Roosevelt gave him the additional job of regional head of the National Labor Board. Creel was a candidate for California governor in 1934, losing to Upton Sinclair in the primary. He eventually viewed Roosevelt as a "bleeding heart." Creel headed California Democrats for Nixon in a 1950 Senate race that stands out as one of the dirtiest up to that time. He numbered himself among "the tens of thousands who admire [Senator Joseph] McCarthy's almost single-handed fight against the Communists and 'fellow travelers' who have weaseled their way in the policy-making departments of government."[15]

CARL CROW's CPI staff became the "nucleus" of Carl Crow, Inc., China's first advertising agency. In his memoir *Four Hundred Million Customers,* he boasted of placing the first ads in China for lipstick and vanishing cream as well as the first fashion book and a manual of poker rules, which sold better than his wartime translation of President Wilson's speeches. He worked for the Office of War Information in World War II.[16]

Kenneth Durant, who worked on British and CPI propaganda, became director of the American branch of the Telegraph Agency of the Soviet Union (TASS).[17]

Guy Stanton Ford resumed his deanship of the University of Minnesota Graduate School and was named its president in 1938.

Guy Gaunt and Arthur Willert were knighted for their services. Gaunt used his propaganda skills to win a seat in Parliament. Willert joined the Foreign Office, where he oversaw press relations. William Wiseman became a partner in the New York investment firm Kuhn, Loeb & Company.

Hugh Gibson became minister to Poland and Switzerland and ambassador to Belgium and Brazil. "It is a new thing to try women in the diplomatic service," he wrote of the first woman to receive an appointment in the foreign service—who, as it happened, was posted to Switzerland when he was minister. "I shall be curious to see how it works out." The third secretary, Lucile Atcherson, was an active suffragist. Gibson wrote a satirical letter to the State Department in which he imagined various problems that would arise. Would she have to dress like a man in a formal coat, breeches, and opera hat? In an end-of-career memoir, Gibson admitted foreign service officers needed training in "Public Opinion."[18]

Samuel Harper continued at the University of Chicago until his death in 1943. His involvement with the Sisson papers nagged him. When drafting his memoir, he concluded the sorry saga of the documents with an anecdote. In 1934, he was traveling from Berlin to Moscow with a German scholar. During a stop, the pair went on the platform to stretch. As they talked of this and that, the German asked, "Are you also a little ashamed of some of the things you had to write during the war?" Harper ended the story there, letting the question answer itself.[19]

President Harding named Will Hays to succeed Burleson as postmaster general. In 1922, on the recommendation of Albert Lasker, Hays became the first president of the Motion Picture Producers and Distributors of America (today the Motion Picture Association). In the face of silver screen scandals and calls for policing movie content, he instituted a self-censorship regime known as the Hays Code.

GEORGE HECHT, who headed the CPI Cartoon Bureau, established the highly successful *Parents Magazine* and *Better Times,* the latter devoted to charity and social work.

In 1926 EDWARD HOUSE published the four-volume *Intimate Papers of Colonel House,* which drew on the self-aggrandizing diary that he diligently maintained during his relationship with Woodrow Wilson. His appetite for courting people and being courted was as strong as ever. He struck up a friendship with George Sylvester Viereck, who wrote *The Strangest Friendship in History: Woodrow Wilson and Colonel House.* House, Viereck wrote, was "a genuine philosopher and a gifted statesman." Creel referred to House "as a high-class sponge, with the added beauty of being easy to squeeze."[20]

CHARLES EVANS HUGHES's lone political failure was his loss in the 1916 presidential race. After his death in 1948, a poll of diplomatic historians ranked him as one of the three best secretaries of state, a post he held under Harding and Coolidge. (John Quincy Adams and William H. Seward ranked ahead of him.) At the Department of State, he forged the first-ever international disarmament agreement. In 1930, Hughes became chief justice of the Supreme Court. He was reckoned, with John Marshall, as one of the two best chief justices up to that time. He led the court's strengthening of First Amendment freedoms. While chief justice, he encountered FREDERIC WILE at a Washington garden party. Wile asked him how he felt about being hailed as a blossomed liberal for his free speech decisions. "Wile," Hughes said, "I blossomed out as a liberal a long time ago, but the trouble is, it never bore fruit."[21]

WILL IRWIN did not lose his zest for journalism and activism. He crusaded for the League of Nations, which he said could have headed off the Great War had it existed; produced a campaign biography for Herbert Hoover; argued the Red Scare was overblown; and wrote frequently on propaganda. "The war had brought to attention a new method in politics and diplomacy," Irwin observed in *Propaganda and the News.* "Government had proved that the press could be gagged and the news slanted, biased or juggled to produce almost any temporary effect they wished; and that in time of war at least, people would endure the process. Here was a weapon of statesmanship too useful to abandon in time of peace."[22]

Toward the end of the war, WILLIAM H. JOHNS briefed the executive board of the American Association of Advertising Agencies on the Division of Advertising's accomplishments. Washington, he said, had been educated "very largely to the value and use of advertising and also to the advantage of using organized, skillful direction in advertising." The division reappeared in the next war as the Advertising Council, which collaborated with the Office of War Information. The Ad Council, as the nonprofit is called today, carried on. It produces and distributes public service announcements for the government and do-good organizations, usually with the parallel objective of promoting business interests.[23]

Former *Chicago Tribune* editor JAMES KEELEY, who accepted Creel's offer "to propagand the enemy," became a press agent when he returned to Chicago. He assisted Warren Harding in his campaign for president and helped Chicago meat-packers fight charges of price fixing.[24]

Upon his resignation ROBERT LANSING opened a law office at 8 Jackson Place, neighboring the CPI's old offices on Lafayette Square. In his memoir, Lansing complained that Creel handed out information too freely and did all he could "to discredit me." (In *his* memoir, Creel said Lansing was so dim his ideas were "annual.") One of Lansing's nephews, cold warrior JOHN FOSTER DULLES, was President Dwight Eisenhower's secretary of state. ALLEN DULLES, his other nephew, was director of the Central Intelligence Agency under the same president.[25]

ALBERT LASKER went on to advance other advertising innovations, most notably introducing advertising to radio. In time he shed his midwestern isolationism and was as ardently for the United Nations as he had been against the League of Nations. When he left advertising, he became a philanthropist. He was far ahead of his time in advocating national health insurance. "A liberal," he said, "is one who knows that, if he is to survive, all others must survive."[26]

In 1926 DAVID LAWRENCE, who had devoted much of his time during the war to reporting on the good and the bad of government publicity, launched the *United States Daily*. It looked a lot like the *Official Bulletin*. "Despite the remarkable growth of the government," the newspaper said in its maiden issue, one could not find "in any single publication the facts of what actually is being done day by day in Washington." The *Daily* morphed into the weekly *U.S. News & World Report.*[27]

WALTER LIPPMANN became America's foremost newspaper columnist and public intellectual. Throughout his career, he struggled with the vital question that arose out of the war: How could the public be adequately informed if its views were so easily manipulated? In his writing on the subject, he did not acknowledge his burning desire to be a propagandist during the Great War or the advice he gave officials on propaganda in the next war. In a review of Creel's history of the CPI, *How We Advertised the War,* Lippmann wrote, "There is probably no good way of conducting government propaganda. There is probably no healthy way in which a government based on consent can enter upon the business of manufacturing consent." Lippmann said Creel's book resembled "the class albums which are distributed to graduating seniors as a memento of their bright college years and as an assistance in remembering names and faces at future reunions."[28]

BRECKENRIDGE LONG made large donations to Franklin Roosevelt's 1932 presidential campaign, as he had to Wilson's in 1916. FDR appointed him ambassador to Italy, where he supported Mussolini's invasion of Ethiopia. Later Long was an assistant secretary of state with responsibility for the Visa Division. Still disdainful of foreign elements, as well as deeply anti-Semitic, he squelched official reports of the Holocaust and did what he could to "delay and effectively stop" Jewish refugees seeking a safe haven in the United States. He was relieved of visa supervision after an internal report noted, "If men of the temperament and philosophy of Long continue in control of immigration administration, we may as well take down that plaque from the Statue of Liberty and black out the 'lamp beside the golden door.'"[29]

DOUGLAS MACARTHUR, the first US Army public affairs officer, set sail for Europe in 1917 with press accolades in his wake. Thirty-seven journalists covering the War Department sent a letter of appreciation to his boss, Newton Baker: "The major has helped through us to shape the public mind." By World War II, General MacArthur, with his swagger and corncob pipe, was a master at self-promotion. When he was proconsul of defeated Japan, one of his public affairs

officers told reporters, "We believe that a correspondent has a certain duty towards the Commander of the Forces he represents, and it is the Commander-
in-Chief's desire that nothing of a political nature be released as coming from
his staff of correspondents, and nothing that may be in any way criticizing the
efforts of any Commander of any of the Allied nations."[30]

CHARLES F. G. MASTERMAN was "one of the most brilliant, misunderstood,
and tragically fated men of our time," wrote JOHN BUCHAN, who superseded
him as Britain's chief propagandist. While a member of the Asquith cabinet
before the war, Masterman was compared to Winston Churchill. He briefly
served in Parliament after the war, but "was neither the journalist nor the politician of earlier days," the *Times* of London said in his obituary of 1927. Drink
and drugs wrecked his health. The death notice mentioned "his highly confidential" work during the Great War. Wellington House's existence was not publicly acknowledged until 1935, and Masterman was not awarded any honors for
his propaganda work. When Buchan became governor general of Canada in the
1930s, he was raised to a peerage as 1st Baron Tweedsmuir.[31]

Charles F. G. Masterman, who established
Wellington House in September 1914, was an
accomplished writer and social reformer. He
rose rapidly in politics, attaining cabinet rank
in Prime Minister Herbert Asquith's government. But Masterman received no public
credit for his war work and in 1927 died in
relative obscurity. The British Ministry of Information also disappeared. But as happened
with all governments, propaganda would continue under new institutions that used techniques the war had spawned. (Imperial War
Museums)

"Is propaganda politics or [government] administration?" CHARLES MER-
RIAM ruminated. "I don't know. It's a strange breed of cat." Under his chairman-
ship, the University of Chicago's Political Science Department became the lead-

ing program of its kind in the country. "Merriam's hand can be seen in virtually every facet of modern political science," fellow scholars wrote of his impact. As a member of the Commission on Freedom of the Press in the 1940s, he argued the news media were not the only conduit for constructive information. The government was "carrying on an immense function of information and analysis" and could do even more. But his enthusiasm for this did not preclude the need for civic education so the public understood "the new techniques of political power in the modern world."[32]

Lippmann's *New Republic* colleague and fellow field propagandist CHARLES MERZ became editor of the *New York Times* editorial page.

HARVEY O'HIGGINS returned, as he said he would, to the theater and writing. In 1921, he coauthored a stage version of Sinclair Lewis's *Main Street*. With a medical doctor, he wrote *The American Mind in Action,* a volume that sought to isolate those personal qualities that were "characteristically American." He died in 1929, at the age of fifty-two.[33]

ARTHUR W. PAGE, who served with Blankenhorn's field propaganda team, was a vice president for publicity and a corporate director for AT&T. Page brought science to publicity. As historian Roland Marchand wrote, he pursued "every avenue of possible measurement, from monitoring free long-distance phone calls at the company's fair exhibits for information on consumer preferences to subscribing to the Psychological Corporation's emerging project of public opinion polling." Page has been called the father of corporate public relations. The man who brought Page to AT&T was its president, WALTER S. GIFFORD, who had been director of the Council of National Defense during the war.[34]

ERNEST POOLE, along with PAUL KENNADAY and ARTHUR LIVINGSTON, who worked under him in the Foreign Press Bureau, created the Foreign Press Service. The short-lived nonprofit news service aimed to interpret the United States to the world and vice versa. Poole continued to write novels, but none of them were equal to *His Family,* the volume that in 1918 brought him the first Pulitzer Prize given for fiction. HAMILTON OWENS, editor in chief of the Poole Service, became editor of the *Baltimore Sun.*[35]

JOHN RATHOM, the Australian-born *Providence Journal* editor who helped the British expose German intrigue, became an embarrassment to the administration after the United States went to war. Like Joseph McCarthy in his wild claims of conspiracy, Rathom said that the War Department was full of German pacifists and that the Justice Department ignored his warnings about sabotage. When Attorney General Gregory threaten legal action, he confessed that many of his stories were false and promised not to repeat them. His signed confession was kept secret until 1920, when it was released to refute charges that he made against Franklin Roosevelt, who was running for vice president on the Cox ticket. "Little by little," commented the *Nation* about the Rathom revelations, "the truth about the war prevails." Rathom died in 1923. He is buried in an unmarked grave in Providence.[36]

JOSEPHINE ROCHE was a lifelong progressive. As president of the Rocky Mountain Fuel Company, which her father founded, she invited the United Mine Workers of America to organize employees. After Roche ran unsuccessfully for governor of Colorado in 1934, Franklin Roosevelt named her assistant secretary of the Treasury. There she helped write the Social Security Act, oversaw an expansion of the US Public Health Service, and developed a national health plan that paved the way for Medicare, which Congress passed in 1965.[37]

WALTER ROGERS, who led the way to American government broadcasting overseas, established the Institute of Current World Affairs with funds from his patron, Charles Crane. It gave traveling fellowships to promising young men and women who wanted to understand the world. Rogers was executive director for thirty-four years, until his retirement in 1959.[38]

Pioneering sociologist EDWARD ALSWORTH ROSS shifted his thinking about public opinion around the time of the Bolshevik revolution (on which his views were shaped by a nudge from his "A-1 friend" Raymond Robins). He now saw public opinion molding as a highly competitive field filled with many who were not concerned with the public interest. "Sooner or later the alert, well-led elements organize in order to mold social requirements to their wishes," he wrote in a 1936 memoir. "Control devices will be employed that the Past never dreamt of." In 1940, he became chairman of the American Civil Liberties Union, created after the war in response to Attorney General Palmer's over-the-top attacks on supposed Red subversives.[39]

In the next world war, EDGAR SISSON joined the Office of War Information. An OWI colleague remembered him as "a wizened minor propagandist, . . . still buttonholing people to convince them of the authenticity of his documents" showing German-Bolshevik conspiracy in the Great War.[40]

JOHN SPARGO, the pro-war socialist who went to work for the CPI's front group, the American Alliance for Labor and Democracy, became a member of the Republican Party and supported Barry Goldwater for president.[41]

HENRY SUYDAM, who headed CPI offices in London and Amsterdam, became special assistant for public relations to HOMER CUMMINGS, attorney general under Franklin Roosevelt. Suydam helped FBI director J. Edgar Hoover develop his outsized crime-fighting image. When legislators became annoyed over his salary, the highest among Cummings's special assistants, they barred the hiring of any Justice Department "special assistant" who did not have a law degree, to wit, Suydam. Cummings circumvented this by appointing him a "special executive assistant."[42]

ARTHUR SWEETSER worked for the League of Nations in Geneva and joined the United Nations staff at its inception. He thought of himself as "the world's longest serving international civil servant, certainly so of American nationality."[43]

In retirement from the army, RALPH VAN DEMAN complied 125,000 dossiers on labor and civil rights activists, actors, professors, and ordinary citizens who exhibited subversive tendencies. He had a national network of informants who used code names. Van Deman made these available to federal agencies, police departments, and conservative politicians, who continued to use the files after his death in 1952.[44]

GEORGE SYLVESTER VIERECK became an apostle of Adolf Hitler. He was imprisoned from 1942 to 1947 for failing to report his propagandizing for the German government. "Propaganda will play an ever increasing part in human relations," he wrote in *Spreading Germs of Hate* (1930), for which House wrote an introduction. "The world is defenseless against propaganda hiding under such virtuous cloaks as respectability, prosperity, humanity, and patriotism. We can legislate against its most obvious abuses, but no lawgiver can ensnare its more subtle manifestations."[45]

EMANUEL VOSKA settled on a farm in his native Bohemia after the war. In 1939 he was imprisoned by the Nazis, who remembered his counterespionage work against Franz von Papen in the United States. He was released on grounds of ill health and linked up with the Office of War Information. A secret mission to Turkey led him to his old pastime of stealing enemy documents. After the Communists took over Czechoslovakia in 1948, they tried Voska for treason. He was imprisoned and died shortly after being freed in 1960. Before World War II, WILL IRWIN helped him write his autobiography, *Spy and Counterspy*.[46]

WALTER WANGER, who became acquainted with filmmaking as a propagandist in Italy, went on to be one of Hollywood's most successful producers. His last motion picture was *Cleopatra* with Elizabeth Taylor, Richard Burton, and Rex Harrison. Looking back on his CPI experience, he said, "There is little difference between politics and show business or between statesmanship and show business."[47]

In 1921 VIRA WHITEHOUSE purchased the Buchan-Murphy Manufacturing Company, which she renamed the Whitehouse Leather Products Company. She hired a colleague from the women's suffrage movement as her vice president. Whitehouse was attracted to business because, she told a reporter, it brought "one more into contact with the problems of the modern world." She intended to "do the work as well as possible and as a measure of success to make as much money as I can." She supported unionization and reduced her employees' workweek from forty-eight to forty-four hours. Whitehouse sold the company before the stock market crash. During World War II, Whitehouse was national chairman of the Women's Action Committee for Victory and Lasting Peace.[48]

ROBERT W. WOOLLEY practiced law and was determined to remain active in Democratic politics "until the bugle's blast." In retirement, he lived in a spacious Washington, DC, apartment on Connecticut Avenue, NW, where he was visited by his grandchildren. One of them was Charles Robb, who married President Lyndon Johnson's daughter and became governor of Virginia and a US senator. Woolley, Robb recalled, "was always properly dressed, with a three-piece suit, even in August, a pocket watch with a watch fob across his vest, and a hat, to protect his bald head! He looked like a slightly slimmer version of Alfred Hitchcock and always had a twinkle in his eye."[49]

The NAVY LIBRARY, where the CPI started out, became the site of press conferences under Presidents Harry Truman and Dwight Eisenhower. Reporters called it the "Cupid Room" because of the cherubs in the corners, one of which symbolized "Liberty."

Acknowledgments

Mark Twain once commented that a particular book was good history if one does not care much about facts. This book took longer than expected because the CPI's activities were diffuse and often obscure. Then, too, the writing coincided with the unanticipated proliferation of fake news, which has dragged our democracy into Dante's eighth circle of hell with its falsifiers and sowers of discord. This development heightened the relevance of the CPI's story, which offers a usable past if one can discern exactly what happened afterward, up to the present, regarding government propaganda.

I have written elsewhere on the triteness of book acknowledgments that say the obvious, "The mistakes here are my own." It is a pleasurable obligation to repay with thanks those who led me to records and helped me make sense of them.

This list of thank-yous begins with two colleagues. Meghan Menard McCune's involvement with this book spans nearly the entire period of research and writing. The epitome of what a doctoral student should be, she tackled difficult research problems with industry and insight. Together we wrote articles on topics that came out of our research. Renee Pierce, a friend of many years, was unstintingly helpful in the organization, preservation, and use of the massive number of documents collected from various archives. She patiently solved the numerous computer problems that arose when I worked far from the university and helped prepare illustrations for publication. This book owes a great deal to both of these women.

Among other graduate students who helped, Elisabeth Fondren was indispensable in locating and using German archival material and in offering insights generally. Christina Georgacopoulos came in at the end to help polish the manuscript, a task she did with intelligence and verve. I appreciate the assistance of Hillary Aikers, Charlotte Bellotte, Kaylyn Blosser, Mallory Knutson, Jane Nevins, Lindsay M. McCluskey, Lacey Sanchez, and Lauren West.

Gaines Foster, Suzanne Marchand, Bob Mong, and Michael Schneider—all experts in subject matter relating to this book—generously read and commented in detail on the entire manuscript. I thank them for that considerable work. I frequently consulted Rob Rehg on questions that arose in approaching this story fairly. Len Apcar, Peter Finn, James T. Hamilton, Maxwell Hamilton, Regina Hamilton, John Lansing, Katherine Marshall, Tom Rosenstiel, Peter Shepherd, Heidi J. S. Tworek, and Amy Whitehead helpfully commented on portions of the book. As always, Angela Fleming assisted and encouraged.

I am grateful to John Milton Cooper for his guidance on Wilson and to Kevin Kosar on legislative and legal issues surrounding government information. It helped enormously to work with the latter to produce a report on contemporary government information policy.

An early meeting with Harold Relyea, retired from the Congressional Research Service, helped set my research course. So did historians Patricia O'Toole and Richard John as well as a number of public affairs officers with the army and navy, especially Admirals Frank Thorp and John Kirby. Toward the end of the writing, I had invaluable guidance from the staff of the US Government Accountability Office. They exemplify the importance of highly principled, nonpartisan institutions in our democracy. Former GAO comptroller general Charles Bowsher facilitated those GAO meetings. I thank Robert Mann for suggesting this book and for allowing me to use research materials he collected. Tara Yglesias, deputy executive secretary of the Harry S. Truman Scholarship Foundation, which is housed in the original CPI building across from the White House at 712 Jackson Place (the address today), generously showed me around the premises. Courtney Cooper similarly arranged for me to visit the CPI's original offices in the Eisenhower Executive Office Building, formerly the State, War, and Navy Building.

It cannot be said that every archive offered a delightful interpersonal experience. Unsurpassed in a positive way was the Manuscript Division of the Library of Congress and its chief, Jeffery Flannery. Mitchell Yockelson helped me unearth materials I would have missed at the National Archives. As so many times before, I thank Valerie Komar and her staff at the Associated Press Corporate Archives for going out of their way to help.

I am grateful to LSU Press, which maintains a reverence for book crafting at a time of declining publishing standards. I especially thank MaryKatherine Callaway for wanting this book, Alisa Plant for letting me tell the full story no matter the word count, George Roupe for his careful editing, Catherine Kadair for her patience with my rewriting, and Laura Gleason for superb book design. My friend of fifty years, Charlie McCarthy, suggested improvements, which I made.

I had significant material support and genuine encouragement from the Woodrow Wilson Center for International Scholars, where I am a fellow, and its vice president Michael Van Dusen. The LSU Foundation has for years supported my research with the Hopkins P. Breazeale LSU Foundation Professorship. Without that I could not have written this book. I am deeply appreciative.

John Maxwell Hamilton
Washington, DC
May 2020

Notes

PROLOGUE

1. Robert Hodieme, Army/Times.Com, March 8, 2003. Andrew Buncombe, "Pentagon Press Centre Gets Hollywood Glitz," *Independent,* March 17, 2003, https://www.independent.co.uk/news/world/americas/pentagon-press-centre-gets-hollywood-glitz-123104.html.

2. Michael Isikoff and David Corn, *Hubris: The Inside Story of Spin, Scandal, and the Selling of the Iraq War* (New York: Three Rivers, 2006), 48. See also Peter J. Boyer, "The New War Machine," New Yorker.com, June 30, 2003. Michael R. Gordon and Bernard E. Trainor, *Cobra II: The Inside Story of the Invasion and Occupation of Iraq* (New York: Vintage, 2007), 293. Susan A. Brewer, *Why America Fights: Patriotism and War Propaganda from the Philippines to Iraq* (New York: Oxford University Press, 2009), 248. Author interviews with Frank Thorp, November 15 and 29, 2013, and Jim Wilkerson, August 26, 2013.

3. Centcom briefings, April 28, April 5, and March 23, 2003, http:/www.globalsecurity.org/military/ops/iraqi-freedom briefs 2002-2003.htm.

4. Centcom briefing, March 26, 2003.

5. This and other unattributed background details on Building 406 are from author interviews with military personnel who spoke on background during 2012 and 2013.

INTRODUCTION

1. Edward Lilly, "Government Information before June 1942: 'Confusion Confused,'" chapter 1, p. 21, draft MS, box 26, EPL. Lilly was a predominant government expert on the subject of propaganda and its trajectory following the Great War.

2. Walter Lippmann, *Public Opinion* (1922; reprint, New York: Free Press, 1965), 158.

3. Edmund S. Morgan, *Benjamin Franklin* (New Haven, CT: Yale University Press, 2002), 143. On sedition laws, Geoffrey R. Stone, *Perilous Times: Free Speech in Wartime* (New York: W. W. Norton, 2004), chapter 1 passim. On Lincoln, Menahem Blondheim, *News over the Wires: The Telegraph and the Flow of Public Information in America, 1844–1897* (Cambridge, MA: Harvard University Press, 1994), 133; David T. Z. Mindich, *Just the Facts: How "Objectivity" Came to Define American Journalism* (New York: New York University Press, 1998), 79–80. On McKinley, Robert C. Hilderbrand, *Power and the People: Executive Management of Public Opinion in Foreign Affairs, 1897–1921* (Chapel Hill: University of North Carolina Press, 1981), 31.

4. David Greenberg, *Republic of Spin: An Inside History of the American Presidency* (New York: W. W. Norton, 2016), 68–69. James L. McCamy, *Government Publicity: Its Practice in Federal Administration* (Chicago: University of Chicago Press, 1939), 6. *Congressional Record,* September 6, 1913, 4409.

5. Executive Order 2594, April 14, 1917.

6. *HWAA,* 5.

7. H. G. Wells, *War and the Future: Italy, France and Britain at War* (London: Cassell, 1917), 134. Gary S. Messinger, *British Propaganda and the State in the First World War* (Manchester: Manchester University Press, 1992), 197. Walter von Hofmann, "Organisation von Presse und Propaganda in Frankreich, England und Italien," 1918, MSG2-15139, BArch-MA. Jean-Jacques Becker, *The Great War and the French People,* trans. Arnold Pomerans (Providence, RI: Berg, 1993), 7.

8. Edward L. Bernays, "The Marketing of National Policies," *Journal of Marketing* 6 (January 1942): 240.

9. *Cincinnati Times-Star,* May 1, 1918. Irwin Cobb, unidentified clipping [1920?], box OV8, GC. *Congressional Record,* April 9, 1918, 4827.

10. Hofmann, "Organisation von Presse und Propaganda in Frankreich, England und Italien." Paul G. Harvey and Philip Goff, *The Columbia Documentary History of Religion in American since 1945* (New York: Columbia University Press, 2005), 23.

11. *Hearing,* 24.

12. Robert Edwards Annin, *Woodrow Wilson: A Character Study* (New York: Dodd, Mead, 1924), 282.

13. Philip M. Taylor, "The Foreign Office and British Propaganda during the First World War," *Historical Journal* 23 (December 1980): 897. Alexander Watson, *Ring of Steel: Germany and Austria-Hungary in World War I* (New York: Basic Books, 2014), 5.

14. *New York Times,* November 9, 2015. John Maxwell Hamilton, "Wilson's Long Shadow over Obama's White House," *Conversation,* November 7, 2014. David Samuels, "The Storyteller and the President," *New York Times Magazine,* May 8, 2016, 44.

15. George Creel, "The Man Hunt," *McClure's,* November 1916, 34. Richard Hofstadter, *The Age of Reform* (New York: Vintage, 1955), 186.

16. "Wichita Beacon Wins Gold Medal," *Editor & Publisher,* November 23, 1918, 2.

17. Carl Ackerman to Edward M. House, December 20, 1917, box 1, EMH.

18. Maurice Low, *Woodrow Wilson: An Interpretation* (Boston: Little, Brown, 1918), 181.

19. Thomas A. Bailey, *Woodrow Wilson and the Lost Peace* (Chicago: Quadrangle, 1944), 107.

20. John Yoo, "Assassination or Targeted Killings after 9/11," *New York Law School Law Review* 56 (2011/12): 62. Walter Russell Mead, "The Big Shift," *Foreign Affairs,* May/June 2018, 19.

1. A SECTOR OF THE BATTLE FRONT

1. Christopher Clark, *The Sleepwalkers: How Europe Went to War in 1914* (New York: HarperCollins, 2013), 291–92, 394–96.

2. Edward Berenson, *The Trial of Madame Caillaux* (Berkeley: University of California Press, 1992), 2. See also Wythe Williams, *Dusk of Empire* (New York: Charles Scribner's Sons, 1937), 39; Emmet Crozier, *American Reporters on the Western Front: 1914–1918* (New York: Oxford University Press, 1959), 6.

3. "French Justice," *Literary Digest,* August 8, 1914, 221–22. Berenson, *The Trial of Madame Caillaux,* 18, 209, 218.

4. Richard M. Harnett and Billy G. Ferguson, *UNIPRESS* (Golden, CO: Fulcrum, 2003), 50. Crozier, *American Reporters,* 6. Clark, *Sleepwalkers,* 406. See also Michael Emery, *On the Front Lines: Following America's Foreign Correspondents across the Twentieth Century* (Washington, DC: American University Press, 1995), 6. The most prescient item in the *Daily News* at this time was not

a news report but a letter to the editor that foresaw "a serious European aspect" of the assassination as a result of interlocking alliances. *Chicago Daily News,* July 14. 1914.

5. Mark Sullivan, *Our Times, 1900–1925,* vol. 5, *Over Here, 1914–1918* (New York: Charles Scribner's Sons, 1936), 65.

6. *New York Times,* September 9, 1914.

7. Robert Darnton, *Poetry and the Police: Communication Networks in Eighteenth-Century Paris* (Cambridge, MA: Harvard University Press, 2010), 133–34. James Van Horn Melton, *The Rise of the Public in Enlightenment Europe* (Cambridge: Cambridge University Press, 2001), 56.

8. Darnton, *Poetry and the Police,* 131.

9. Gabriel de Tarde, *On Communication and Social Influence,* ed. Terry N. Clark (Chicago: University of Chicago Press, 2010), 304, 315. David Vincent, *The Culture of Secrecy: Britain, 1832–1998* (Oxford: Oxford University Press, 1998), 68, 117. Marco Althaus, "The Weimar Republic's 'Press Parliament,'" *Journalism History* 44 (Winter 2019): 209. The number of British newspapers (not counting Ireland) increased from 221 in 1836 to 2,064 in 1892; magazines increased from 557 to 2,097. Nicholas Wilkinson, *Secrecy and the Media: The Official History of the United Kingdom's D-Notice System* (New York: Routledge, 2009), 7–8. Melton, *The Rise of the Public in Enlightenment Europe,* 31–32, 62, 160, 197, 241. David Welch, *Germany, Propaganda and Total War, 1914–1918* (London: Athlone, 2000), 29. Berenson, *The Trial of Madame Caillaux,* 209, 234.

10. Berenson, *The Trial of Madame Caillaux,* 154, 165–66. Clark, *Sleepwalkers,* 230. M. B. Hayne, *The French Foreign Office and the Origins of the First World War: 1898–1914* (Oxford: Clarendon, 1993), 43.

11. Jack Beatty, *The Lost History of 1914: Reconsidering the Year the Great War Began* (New York: Walker, 2012), 234–35. Oron James Hale, *Publicity and Diplomacy with Special Reference to England and Germany, 1890–1914* (1940; reprint, Gloucester, MA: Peter Smith, 1964), 447–48. Clark, *Sleepwalkers,* 227.

12. Berenson, *The Trial of Madame Caillaux,* 51.

13. Berenson, *The Trial of Madame Caillaux,* 43, 119, 203, 236–37. Benjamin F. Martin, *The Hypocrisy of Justice in the Belle Epoque* (Baton Rouge: Louisiana State University, 1884), 206 and passim for the politics behind the trial.

14. Sean McMeekin, *July 1914: Countdown to War* (New York: Basic Books, 2013), 322, 385. Williams, *Dusk of Empire,* 118. For examples of similar views on the political consequences of the trial see Beatty, *The Lost History of 1914,* 204, 304. Berenson, *The Trial of Madame Caillaux,* 243.

15. Clark, *Sleepwalkers,* 170. Becker, *The Great War and the French People,* 48–63.

16. Bernadotte E. Schmitt, "France and the Outbreak of the World War," *Foreign Affairs,* April 1937, 516.

17. Jonathan Reed Winkler, *Nexus: Strategic Communications and American Security in World War I* (Cambridge, MA: Harvard University Press, 2008), 6–7, 22.

18. Paul M. Kennedy, "Imperial Cable Communications and Strategy, 1870–1914," *English Historical Review* 86 (1971): 740, 743. Winkler, *Nexus,* 15–16. "Historical Sketch of the Cable Censorship from Its Establishment on the 2nd of August 1914 to the End of 1916," January 1917, WO 32/4895.

19. Jonathan Reed Winkler, "Information Warfare in World War I," *Journal of Military History* 73 (July 2009): 845–67. Heidi J. S. Evans, "'The Path to Freedom'? Transocean and German Wireless Telegraphy, 1914–1922," *Historical Social Research* 35 (2010): 215–17.

20. British chargé d'affaires to secretary of state, August 4, 1914, and executive order of August 5, 1914, in *Papers Relating to the Foreign Relations of the United States, 1914 Supplement, The World War*

(Washington, DC: Government Printing Office, 1928), 667–68. Susan J. Douglas, *Inventing American Broadcasting, 1988–1922* (Baltimore: Johns Hopkins University Press, 1987), 268–70. Welch, *Germany, Propaganda and Total War,* 23. David Paull Nickles, *Under the Wire: How the Telegraph Changed Diplomacy* (Cambridge, MA: Harvard University Press, 2003), 140–41. Thomas Boghardt, *The Zimmermann Telegram: Intelligence, Diplomacy, and America's Entry into World War I* (Annapolis, MD: Naval Institute Press, 2012), chapter 6.

    21. Winkler, "Information Warfare in World War I," 858. Winkler, *Nexus,* 12.

    22. Ralph O. Nafziger, "World War Correspondents and Censorship of the Belligerents," *Journalism Quarterly* 14 (September 1937): 241. H. Schuyler Foster Jr., "How America Became Belligerent: A Quantitative Study of War News, 1914–17," *American Journal of Sociology* 40 (January 1935): 464–75. Other studies confirm this tilt in the news: Edwin Costrell, *How Maine Viewed the War, 1914–1917* (Orono, ME: University Press, 1940); Cedric C. Cummins, *Indiana Public Opinion and the World War: 1914–1917* (Indianapolis: Indiana Historical Bureau, 1945). See also Foster's dissertation, "Studies in America's News of the European War" (PhD diss., University of Chicago, 1932). Perry Arnold to Carl W. Ackerman, April 27, 1915, and Ackerman to John F. Ackerman, April 30, 1915, box 14, CWA. *The Mails as a German War Weapon: Memorandum of the Censorship of Mails Carried by Neutral Ships* (London: Eyre and Spottiswoode, 1916), 8, FO 395/155. This report was apparently printed for public consumption at the behest of the government.

    23. Report A.N. 16673, Transocean GmbH, received December 14, 1916, written by Zimmermann, BArch-MA. German embassy to Bethmann-Hollweg, August 16, 1914, R 901-80825, BArch.

    24. Carl W. Ackerman, "The War and Our Next Election," typescript, circa 1914, 3–4, 7, box 192, CWA. This is one of several documents in Ackerman's papers that informed his book, which is also quoted here: Carl W. Ackerman, *Germany, The Next Republic?* (New York: George H. Doran, 1917), 20. Background on his coverage of the belligerent embassies is in "Uncle Sam and the War," typescript, 1915, chapter 4. This was written in London en route to Germany.

    25. Alice Goldfarb Marquis, "Words as Weapons: Propaganda in Britain and Germany during the First World War," *Journal of Contemporary History* 13 (July 1978): 472, 481. This article provided background as does Welch, *Germany, Propaganda and Total War,* 14–15, 20–23, 31, 34, 254.

    26. Welch, *Germany, Propaganda and Total War,* 22–23. Harold D. Lasswell, *Propaganda Technique in the World War* (1927; reprint, Cambridge, MA: MIT Press, 1971), 22–23. Max Hastings, *Catastrophe 1914* (New York: Knopf, 2013), 435. Reinhard R. Doerries, *Imperial Challenge: Ambassador Count Bernstorff and German-American Relations, 1908–1917,* trans. Christa D Shannon (Chapel Hill: University of North Carolina Press, 1989), 40–41, 49–50.

    27. Arthur S. Link, *Wilson,* vol. 3, *The Struggle for Neutrality: 1914–1915* (Princeton, NJ: Princeton University Press, 1960), 57. "American Sympathies in the War," *Literary Digest,* November 14, 1914, 939–42.

    28. Robert E. Park, *The Immigrant Press and Its Control* (New York: Harper and Brothers, 1922), 319, 413. Link, *The Struggle for Neutrality,* 20–24.

    29. For discussion of German press activities see Doerries, *Imperial Challenge,* 51–76. H. C. Peterson, *Propaganda for War: The Campaign against American Neutrality: 1914–1917* (Norman: University of Oklahoma Press, 1939), 137–40. Link, *The Struggle for Neutrality,* 32. Steward Halsey Ross, *Propaganda for War: How the United States Was Conditioned to Fight the Great War of 1914–1918* (Joshua Tree, CA: Progressive, 1996), 136–42. Frank Luther Mott, *American Journalism: A History of Newspapers in the United States through 250 Years* (New York: Macmillan, 1947), 616. Chalmers M. Roberts, *The Washington Post: The First 100 Years* (Boston: Houghton Mifflin, 1977), 125–26, 146. On Dernburg see "Bernhard Dernburg: The German Whose Presence Here Has Aroused British Apprehensions," *Current Opinion,* January 1915, 401, and Gerhard Ritter, "Dernburg, Bernhard

Jakob Ludwig," in *Neue Deutsche Biographie* (Berlin: Duncker and Humblot, 1957), 3:607–8.

30. Felice A. Bonadio, "The Failure of German Propaganda in the United States, 1914–1917," *Mid-America: An Historical Quarterly* 41 (January 1959): 43, 55–56. Link, *The Struggle for Neutrality,* 20–21.

31. Phyllis Keller, "George Sylvester Viereck: The Psychology of a German-American Militant," *Journal of Interdisciplinary History* 2 (Summer 1971): 59–108. Tom Reiss, "The First Conservative," *New Yorker,* October 24, 2005, 38–47. "Believes He Is a Genius," *Saturday Evening Post,* August 31, 1907, 19.

32. Ralph Martin, *Cissy: The Extraordinary Life of Eleanor Medill Patterson* (New York: Simon and Shuster, 1979), 136–51. Also see Robert Lansing, *War Memoirs of Robert Lansing* (Indianapolis: Bobbs-Merrill, 1935), 357. Doerries, *Imperial Challenge,* 15, which is rich in information on Bernstorff's history and activities. George Sylvester Viereck, "Notes on Colonel House," October 14, 1929, box 4, GSV.

33. Nickles, *Under the Wire,* 141. Boghardt, *The Zimmermann Telegram,* 96. For the tone of the Bernstorff-Wilson conversation see Link, *The Struggle for Neutrality,* 412. Wilson's agreement with the Germans was temporary in the beginning but was continued.

34. Ernest R. May, *The World War and American Isolation, 1914–1917* (Chicago, IL: Quadrangle, 1966), 62. Arthur S. Link, *Woodrow Wilson and the Progressive Era, 1910–1917* (New York: Harper, 1963), 146–48. Evans, "'The Path to Freedom,'" 216–20.

35. Isabel V. Hull, *A Scrap of Paper: Breaking and Making International Law during the Great War* (Ithaca, NY: Cornell University Press, 2014), 185; see also 144–45, 169, 177. May, *The World War and American Isolation* 25, 45, 48, 54–71. Watson, *Ring of Steel,* 341.

36. M. Ryan Floyd, *Abandoning American Neutrality* (New York: Palgrave Macmillan, 2013), 124. Link, *The Struggle for Neutrality,* 51, 411. A. Scott Berg, *Wilson* (New York: G. P. Putnam, 2013), 43.

37. Lansing diary, July 11, 1915.

38. Thomas A. Bailey, "The United States and the Blacklist during the Great War," *Journal of Modern History* 6 (March 1934): 14, 21. Bailey notes that that these acts came close to the breaking point in Anglo-American relations, but as House noted, the German submarine warfare was worse. Hull, *A Scrap of Paper,* 212–13. Link, *The Struggle for Neutrality,* 323. May, *The World War and American Isolation,* 131–32. Niall Ferguson, *The War of the World: Twentieth-Century Conflict and the Descent of the West* (London: Penguin, 2006), 114.

39. Sullivan, *Our Times,* 5:76.

40. Doerries, *Imperial Challenge,* 52, 79, 122. George Sylvester Viereck, *Spreading Germs of Hate* (New York: Horace Liveright, 1939), 56, 81.

41. Frederic William Wile, *The Assault: Germany before the Outbreak and England in War-Time; a Personal Narrative* (Indianapolis: Bobbs-Merrill, 1916), 221. For background on Boy-Ed see Frederic William Wile, *News Is Where You Find It: Forty Years' Reporting at Home and Abroad* (Indianapolis: Bobbs-Merrill, 1939), 132, 336–37. Doerries, *Imperial Challenge,* 180, 188–89. The bombings are discussed at length in Jules Witcover, *Sabotage at Black Tom: Imperial Germany's Secret War in America, 1914–1917* (Chapel Hill, NC: Algonquin Books, 1989). Peterson, *Propaganda for War,* 148. Hubert Montgomery, minute, January 10, 1917, FO 395/70.

42. Doerries, *Imperial Challenge,* 143. May, *The World War and American Isolation,* 177. Jörg Nagler, "German Imperial Propaganda and the American Homefront in World War I: A Response to Reinhard R. Doerries," in *Confrontation and Cooperation: Germany and the United States in the Era of World War I, 1900–1924,* ed. Hans-Jürgen Schröde (Providence, RI: Berg, 1993), 170.

43. This often-told story is recounted in William G. McAdoo, *Crowded Years: The Reminiscences*

of William G. McAdoo (New York: Houghton Mifflin, 1931), 321–30. McAdoo quotes the Secret Service agent at length. See also Lansing, *War Memoirs,* 77. Other versions of this episode say Albert fell asleep on the train. See Viereck, *Spreading Germs of Hate,* 68–74.

44. *New York World,* August 15 and 17, 1915.

45. McAdoo, *Crowded Years,* 328. McAdoo claimed, "I am morally convinced that the Allies were doing the same thing, but we had no documentary proof" (329). Edward M. House to Woodrow Wilson, August 10, 1915, box 120, EMH. Viereck, "Notes on Colonel House."

46. Messinger, *British Propaganda and the State in the First World War,* 69. For background on Wellington House see James Duane Squires, *British Propaganda at Home and in the United States from 1914 to 1917* (Cambridge, MA: Harvard University Press, 1935), chapter 2; M. L. Sanders and Philip M. Taylor, *British Propaganda during the First World War, 1914–18* (London: Palgrave Macmillan, 1982), chapters 1 and 2.

47. Florence Emily Hardy, *The Later Years of Thomas Hardy, 1892–1928* (New York: Macmillan, 1930), 163. Messinger, *British Propaganda,* 35–36. D. G. Wright, "The Great War, Government Propaganda and English 'Men of Letters,'" *Literature and History* 7 (1978): 72.

48. Messinger, *British Propaganda,* 12–13.

49. Squires, *British Propaganda,* 30. Eric Hopkins, *Charles Masterman (1873-1927), Politician and Journalist: The Splendid Failure* (Lewiston, NY: Edwin Mellen, 1999), 114.

50. Philip M. Taylor, "The Foreign Office and British Propaganda during the First World War," *Historical Journal* 23 (December 1980): 896. Hale, *Publicity and Diplomacy,* 36. Sanders and Taylor, *British Propaganda,* 41–42. "British Propaganda during the War: 1914–1918," n.d., INF 4/4A.

51. Messinger, *British Propaganda,* 62. Ivor Nicholson, "An Aspect of British Official Wartime Propaganda," *Cornhill Magazine,* May 1931, 594–97. Nicholson headed the pictorial division. Ferris Greenslet, *Under the Bridge: An Autobiography* (London: Collins, 1943), 113.

52. Sanders and Taylor, *British Propaganda,* 36–37. Peter Putnis, "Share 999: British Government Control of Reuters during World War I," *Media History* 14 (2008): 154. John Buchan, "Propaganda—A Department of Information," memorandum, February 3, 1917, CAB 21/37.

53. Messinger, *British Propaganda,* 30. Testimony of W. M. Dixon, "Report of Proceedings at Wellington House on November 19, 1917," INF 4/7.

54. M. L. Sanders, "Wellington House and British Propaganda in the First World War," *Historical Journal* 18 (March 1975): 131. Messinger, *British Propaganda,* 59–62.

55. Willard Straight to Gilbert Parker, June 15, 1916, FO 395/6.

56. Arthur Willert, *The Road to Safety: A Study in Anglo-American Relations* (New York: Frederick A. Praeger, 1953), 1. Willert, *Washington and Other Memories* (Boston: Houghton Mifflin, 1972), 53, 65, 73–74, 90–93. Gaunt inaccurately said he, not Wiseman, headed the Intelligence Service in the United States. His mission, he said, "was to enlist . . . sympathy and support" and urge American entrance into the war. Guy Gaunt, *The Yield of the Years: A Story of Adventure Afloat and Ashore* (London: Hutchinson, 1940), 5, 108, 209, 234, 240. The three men had good connections. Eleanor Roosevelt was godmother to Willert's eldest granddaughter. Indicative of the attitudes of Willert's editors is a cable to him from Geoffrey Robinson, urging him to "go slow" on the Ireland question lest he "seriously prejudice AngloAmerican relations." May 4, 1916, box 2, AW.

57. Willert, *The Road to Safety,* 26–27. Arthur Willert to Geoffrey Robinson, September 21, 1914, box 2, AW. Robert Donald, "Report on Propaganda Arrangements," January 9, 1917, INF 4/8b.

58. Donald, "Report on Propaganda Arrangements." Denis Mack Smith, *Mazzini* (New Haven, CT: Yale University Press, 1994), 41–43. F. B. Smith, "British Post Office Espionage, 1844," *Australian Historical Studies* 14 (April 1970): 195, 197.

59. Vincent, *The Culture of Secrecy,* 134–35, 141.

60. Edward Cook, *The Press in War-Time, with Some account of the Official Press Bureau; an Essay* (New York: Macmillan, 1920), 32, 37. Sanders and Taylor, *British Propaganda,* 19–20, 23.

61. Charles E. Kloeber to Melville E. Stone, "Report of the News Department," September 7, 1914, AP. Ackerman, *Germany,* 220. On Ackerman being a spy see Boy-Ed to Foreign Office, October 21, 1916, R 121617, PA. Author interview with Henry Ackerman, September 7, 2016, and Henry Ackerman to author, September 12, 2016. Wile, *The Assault,* 272. Sanders and Taylor, *British Propaganda,* 30; Crozier, *American Reporters,* 71, 94–97.

62. Sanders and Taylor, *British Propaganda,* 29.

63. Cook, *The Press in War-Time,* 25, 43, 51, 58. E. A. Swettenham and E. T. Cook, "The Official Press Bureau," March 16, 1917, CAB 21/93. Press Bureau Notices to the Press, August 7, 1915, HO 139/43, and January 2, 1917, HO 139/45.

64. For an example of mail monitoring see "Daily Review of the Foreign Press," December 30, 1916, FO 395/72. P.O.G., "The Hearst Situation Here," February 21, 1917, FO 395/70. See also David Nasaw, *The Chief: The Life of William Randolph Hearst* (New York: Mariner, 2001), 241–44, 247. *New York American,* June 3, 1916. British grievances are outlined in "International News Service," unsigned memorandum, October 18, 1916, FO 395/8.

65. Robert Cecil, minute, October 12, 1916, and R. M. Coulter, "Notice for Insertion in the Canada Gazette," November 11, 1916, FO 395/8. W. H. Hearst to Gilbert Parker, February n.d., in Charles F. G. Masterman, "Second Report of the Work Conducted for the Government at Wellington House," February 1, 1916, FO 4/5. Robert Cecil to Herbert Samuel, October 6, 1916, FO 395/9. Peterson, *Propaganda for War,* 237. Edward Grey to Ambassador Walter Hines Page, message, March 6, 1917, and Louis Botha, telegram to Foreign Office, November 27, 1916, FO 395/70; Victor Cavandish, Duke of Devonshire, to Walter Long, May 16, 1917, FO 395/71.

66. Edward T. Cook, minute, August 15, 1917, FO 395/57. On American correspondents' protest see *Chicago Tribune,* August 3, 1916. H. Montgomery to Edward Cook, August 17, 1916, FO 395/57. Transcription of letter from Melville Stone to Robert Collins is in FO 395/159. Robert Cecil, "British Propaganda in Allied and Neutral Countries," January 1917, INF 4/1B.

67. Another example of using German propaganda against the Germans occurred in September 1914, when the Foreign Office published dispatches from its ambassador to Berlin describing German efforts to pollute opinion in "neutral countries." Foreign Secretary Edward Grey ordered "wide and immediate publicity" for the report. *Despatches from His Majesty's Ambassador at Berlin Respecting an Official German Organization for Influencing the Press of Other Countries* (London: Harrison and Sons, 1914), FO 115/1836.

68. Ackerman, *Germany,* 77. Sanders and Taylor, *British Propaganda,* 130–31. The book on German medals was G. F. Hill, *The Commemorative Medal in the Service of Germany* (London: Longmans, Green, 1917). Hill noted, "Whether the issue of these medals, which appear as the product of artists working on their own account or for private firms, has been actually organized, as some have supposed, by the German Government or not is a matter of indifference. They express the popular feeling in the same way and are doubtless under the same sort of control, as the German Press" (9). Donald, "Report on Propaganda Arrangements."

69. John Horne and Alan Kramer, *German Atrocities, 1914: A History of Denial* (New Haven, CT.: Yale University Press, 2001), 234, as well as general discussion on 232–37, 254–55.

70. Edward Price Bell, "A Free Europe," in Viscount Brace, ed., *The War of Democracy: The Allies' Statement* (Garden City, NY: Doubleday, Page, 1917), 41.

71. Frederic William Wile, *London Daily Mail,* October 31, 1914. Wile, *News Is Where You Find*

It, 345. Wile, *London Daily Mail,* April 16, 1917. On Masterman see Janet Adam Smith, *John Buchan* (London: Rupert Hart-Davis, 1965), 201. The bogus cadaver story is discussed in Arthur Ponsonby, *Falsehood in War-Time, Containing an Assortment of Lies Circulated throughout the Nations during the Great War* (London: Garland, 1928), chapter 17.

72. Frederic William Wile, *The German-American Plot* (London: Arthur Pearson, 1915), 8, 65. The "spewing crater" comment is from an undated article in Wile's scrapbook 7, FWW.

73. Sanders and Taylor, *British Propaganda,* 182. House diary, March 10, 1916. Cecil, "British Propaganda in Allied and Neutral Countries." For more on Gaunt see George Patey, memorandum, September 1916, FO 371/2795; Peterson, *Propaganda for War,* 153. Sanders and Taylor, *British Propaganda,* 178–82. Walter Millis, *Road to War: America, 1914–1917* (Boston: Houghton Mifflin, 1935), 75, 206–10. On Rathom see Garrett D. Byrnes and Charles H. Spilman, *The Providence Journal, 150 Years* (Providence, RI: Providence Journal, 1980), 267. Gaunt, *The Yield of the Years,* 132–33.

74. The "'well-kept' secret" is from Oulahan's unpublished, unpaginated memoir, "Presidents and Publicity," chapter 25, RVO.

75. *New York Times,* May 8 and 12, 1915. *Washington Post,* May 13, 1917. The ship carried gun powder, 1,250 cases of artillery shells, and 4,200 cases of rifle ammunition. Eric Larson, *Dead Wake: The Last Crossing of the Lusitania* (New York, Crown, 2015), 182–83. Gaunt, *The Yield of the Years,* 132–33. Doerries, *Imperial Challenge,* 43. Link, *The Struggle for Neutrality,* 378–79.

76. Peterson, *Propaganda for War,* 156–57; Doerries, *Imperial Challenge,* 142–43. Cummins, *Indiana Public Opinion and the World War,* 140. The Metropolitan Club recommendation for von Papen was from Blanton Winship, who later became the army's judge advocate general. Winship to Board of Governors, Metropolitan Club, January 29, 1914, MC. Gilbert Parker, "The United States," in Charles F. G. Masterman, "First Report of the Work Conducted for the Government at Wellington House," June 7, 1915, FO 4/5.

77. Buchan, "Propaganda—a Department of Information."

78. Edward Grey, minute, "Dependence of this Country on the United States," October 4, 1916, FO 371/2795. Arthur S. Link, *Wilson,* vol. 5, *Campaigns for Progressivism and Peace, 1916–1917* (Princeton, NJ: Princeton University Press, 1965), 67. E. T. Cook, memorandum with attached instruction, October 5, 1916, FO 395/6.

2. HE KEPT US OUT OF WAR

1. Henry Morgenthau, *All in a Life-Time* (New York: Doubleday, Page, 1922), 234.

2. House diary, April 15, 1916.

3. Robert Woolley to Edward M. House, August 19, 1915, and September 21, 1915, EMH. Also see the chapter "Ploughing the Ground for 1916," in Woolley's autobiography, PIH, which is invaluable. The manuscript, with the working title "Politics Is Hell," is unfinished. I have cited chapter titles and page numbers within chapters. Stories prepared by the Inter-Departmental Committee can be found in box 27, RWW. Woolley to House, November 24 and December 14, 1915, box 7, RWW.

4. *New York Evening Mail* clipping, n.d., attached to Norman E. Mack to William McAdoo, July 18, 1916, box 163, WGM.

5. *WWLL: 1915–1917,* 232. John Milton Cooper Jr., *Woodrow Wilson: A Biography* (New York: Alfred A. Knopf, 2009), 361. Link, *Woodrow Wilson and the Progressive Era,* 64–65, 144.

6. Woolley, "How T.R. Slaughtered Perkins's Bull Moose," PIH, 1. Roosevelt to O. K. Davis, June 23, 1915, GL. Robert Woolley to Edward M. House, April 1, 1916, box 7, RWW.

7. Robert Woolley to Edward M. House, December 14, 1915, RWW. "The Story of How the

Hughes Boom Was Started," from Martin Glynn to House, n.d., box 49, EMH. Woolley does not say who led the Hughes boom, but it was Frank H. Hitchcock, chairman of the Republican National Committee in 1908–9. Hitchcock had excellent relations with the press. Daniel C. Roper, "A Political History of the United States," unpublished manuscript, no date, box 30, DCR. Merlo J. Pusey, *Charles Evans Hughes* (New York: Macmillan, 1951), 326.

8. *New York Sun,* February 10, 1907.

9. Woolley, for instance, is absent from Greenberg's *Republic of Spin,* a history that focuses on presidential communications in elections and governance. Two monographs have been written on this election, S. D. Lovell, *The Presidential Election of 1916* (Carbondale: Southern Illinois University Press, 1980), and Lewis L. Gould, *The First Modern Clash over Federal Power* (Lawrence: University Press of Kansas, 2016). Both have little to say about Woolley.

10. Buchan, "Propaganda—a Department of Information."

11. Morgenthau, *All in a Life-Time,* 83.

12. Pusey, *Charles Evans Hughes,* 217 and chapter 19 on Hughes's legislative accomplishments. Anonymous note, "Governor on the Bench: Charles Evans Hughes as Associate Justice," *Harvard Law Review* 89 (March 1976): 961–97.

13. Pusey, *Charles Evans Hughes,* 330–32. For an example how journalists accepted his "determined purpose to let the office seek the man," see Henry L. Stoddard, *As I Knew Them: Presidents and Politics from Grant to Coolidge* (New York: Harper and Brothers, 1927), 439.

14. *New York Times,* June 18, 1916, which provides these general details on the first days of the campaign.

15. Pusey, *Charles Evans Hughes,* 316. James R. Garfield to Lawrence O. Murray, July 10, 1916, box 161; James R. Garfield to Matthew Hale, June 24, 1916, box 98, JRG. Garfield diary, June 12, 1916. For background on Garfield see Edmund Morris, *Theodore Rex* (New York: Random House, 2001), 209, 246, 514; Doris Kearns Goodwin, *The Bully Pulpit: Theodore Roosevelt and the Golden Age of Journalism* (New York: Simon and Schuster, 2013), 252, 347, 437–42.

16. Woolley, "He Kept Us Out of War?," PIH, 1. *Official Report of the Proceedings of the Democratic National Convention,* compiled by J. Bruce Kremer, 1916, 14–41. Link, *Campaigns for Progressivism and Peace,* 48. In preparing his biography of Wilson, Ray Stannard Baker asked many participants in the campaign about the origin of the slogan but never received a satisfactory answer. Josephus Daniels said the slogan was "developed" by Tom Pence, a Democratic National Committee stalwart, who died on March 28, 1916, before the platform was written. He had come to Washington as a correspondent for Daniels' newspaper. Josephus Daniels, "Wilson and the Newspaper Men," n.d., box 731, JD. Newton Baker, who handled Wilson's platform in St. Louis, believed someone on the Resolutions Committee put it in. Newton Baker to Ray Stannard Baker, August 6, 1918, box 100, RSB.

17. Morgenthau, *All in a Life-Time,* 238. Woolley, "Ploughing the Ground for 1916," PIH, passim. Woolley to House, March 2, 1916, EMH. House diary, January 8, 1916. Wile, *News Is Where You Find It,* 368–69. Frederic William Wile to Robert Woolley, October 26, 1914, box 33, RWW; Robert Woolley to Edward M. House, November 8, 1915, EMH.

18. Cooper, *Woodrow Wilson,* 185. For a reference to Woolley as a possible chair see Robert Woolley to Edward M. House, May 30, 1916, box 7, RWW. Woodrow Wilson to House, May 29, 1916, box 121, EMH. Link, *Campaigns for Progressivism and Peace,* 8–10. For a description of McCormick see Homer S. Cummings, memo, August 7, 1916, box 87, RSB. Vance McCormick and Michael Barton, eds., *Citizen Extraordinaire: The Diplomatic Diaries of Vance McCormick in London and Paris, 1917–1919* (Mechanicsburg, PA.: Stackpole Books, 2004), 7. *WWLL: 1915–1917,* 265.

19. Woolley, "Bid Kentucky Adieu," PIH, 9. Woolley's autobiography has much detail and color on his journalism adventures. *Country Life* is described in Frank Luther Mott, *A History of American Magazines,* vol. 4, *1885–1905* (Cambridge, MA: Harvard University Press, 1957), 338.

20. Robert Woolley to Vance McCormick (his report on work of the Publicity Bureau during the campaign), March 1, 1917, box 12, RWW. Hereafter this is cited as Woolley Report. Joseph Tumulty to Vance McCormick, July 7, 1916, box 21, RWW. Frank Polk to Edward M. House, July 17, 1916, box 8, FLP. John M. Blum, *Joe Tumulty and the Wilson Era* (Cambridge, MA: Houghton Mifflin, 1951), 117–18. Edward McChesney Sait, *American Politics and Elections* (New York: Century, 1927), 494. Michael McGerr, *The Decline of Popular Politics: The American North, 1865–1928* (New York: Oxford University Press, 1986), 72. Nasaw, *The Chief,* 250.

21. No author, but almost certainly Woolley, "Bureau of Publicity," no date, box 34, RWW. Joe A. Jackson, "How the Press Agent Puts It over Papers," *Editor & Publisher,* April 7, 1917, 26.

22. *Rebel,* 148. George Creel, *Rocky Mountain News,* July 7, 192. Creel, "Our 'Visionary' President," *Century,* December 1914, 192. Tarbell suggested Creel's appointment to John Dunlap, editor of *Industrial Management,* who passed the suggestion along to Wilson. Ida Tarbell to Porter Dunlap, April 10, 1916; Dunlap to George Creel, July 3, 1918, entry 1, CPI. Howe made his suggestion to McAdoo. June 13, 1918, box 161, WGM.

23. Homer Cummings to Vance McCormick, December 7, 1916, box 45, HSC. Homer Cummings, "The Conduct of a National Political Campaign," speech, February 4, 1917, box 210, HSC. Daniel C. Roper, *Fifty Years of Public Life* (Durham, NC: Duke University Press, 1941), 147, 150, 153.

24. William McAdoo to Vance McCormick, July 8, 1916, box 13, RWW.

25. Woolley Report.

26. The editors, "The Hughes Acceptance," *New Republic,* August 5, 1916, 4–5. Woolley, "He Kept US Out of War?," PIH, 6–7. Woolley Report. Working the same trick, McCormick asked the Wilson Business Men's National League to press Hughes on similarly awkward financial questions. See letter from League Secretary to Breckenridge Long, October 19, 1916, box 22, BL.

27. Theodore G. Joslin to James T. Williams, August 2, 1916, box 27, JTW. Paul R. Boller Jr., *Presidential Campaigns from George Washington to George W. Bush* (New York: Oxford University Press, 1996), 207. *New York Times,* August 12, 1916.

28. Theodore Roosevelt to W. A. Wadsworth, June 23, 1916, TR. Garfield diary, August 8, 1916.

29. Dexter Perkins, *Charles Evans Hughes and American Democratic Statesmanship* (Boston: Little, Brown, 1956), 10. T. G. Joslin to James Williams, July [n.d.] 1916, box 27, and Joslin to Williams, September 19, 1916, box 28, JTW. Pusey, *Charles Evans Hughes,* 339. Melville E. Stone, *Fifty Years a Journalist* (Garden City, NY: Doubleday, Page, 1921), 243–44. Vance McCormick to Charles Evans Hughes, October 2, 1916, box 147, CEH.

30. Donald A. Ritchie, *Press Gallery: Congress and the Washington Correspondents* (Cambridge, MA: Harvard University Press, 1991), 172, 181–82. W. Y. Morgan to James T. Williams, September 6, 1916, box 28, JTW. Tanner oral history, 235.

31. Perkins, *Charles Evans Hughes,* 55. Clarence Phelps Dodge to Harold Ickes, October 18, 1916, box 31, and Harold Ickes to William R. Willcox, October 10, 1916, box 41, HLI.

32. Tanner oral history, 228. George W. Perkins to State [Progressive Party] Chairman, June 30, 1916, box 37, HLI. James R. Garfield to Theodore Roosevelt, September 25, 1916, box 119, JRG.

33. William R. Willcox to William H. Crocker, July 18 and 30, 1916, box 147, CEH. Tanner oral history, 234. Harold Ickes to Chester H. Rowell, August 17, 1916, box 39, HLI.

34. Pusey, *Charles Evans Hughes,* chapter 32. Spencer C. Olin, *California's Prodigal Sons: Hiram Johnson and the Progressives, 1911–1917* (Berkeley: University of California Press, 1968), 136–38.

Hiram Johnson to James R. Garfield, July 5, 1916, box 161, JRG. George E. Mowry, *The California Progressives* (New York: Quadrangle, 1963), 267.

35. Robert Woolley telegram, August 1, 1916, box 33, RWW. Woolley, "Making the Mare Go and Maine Elections," PIH, 3. Bainbridge Colby to Ray Stannard Baker, May 23, 1931, box 103, RSB.

36. Milton A. McRae, *Forty Years in Newspaperdom: The Autobiography of a Newspaper Man* (New York: Brentano's, 1924), 399–402. Robert Woolley to Edward M. House, September 6, 1916, box 7, RWW. James F. Simon, *FDR and Chief Justice Hughes: The President, the Supreme Court, and the Epic Battle over the New Deal* (New York: Simon and Schuster, 2012), 102.

37. Woolley, "He Kept Us Out of War?," PIH, 10. J. Leonard Bates and Vanette M. Schwartz, "Golden Special Campaign Train," *Montana: The Magazine of Western History* 37 (Summer 1987): 26–35. Harold Ickes, *The Autobiography of a Curmudgeon* (Chicago: Quadrangle, 1969), 180. Tanner oral history, 718.

38. Woolley, "Women's Special and the Whirlwind," PIH, 4. F. B. Alexander to William Kent, November 7, 1916, box 25, WKF.

39. Link, *Campaigns for Progressivism and Peace,* 106–10. *Rebel,* 107. For an example of Wilson's use of "peace with honor" see *New York Times,* January 30, 1916. Robert Woolley to Ray Stannard Baker, November 21, 1928, box 117, RSB. Woolley, "Making the Mare Go and Maine Elections," PIH, 2. Also see Woolley to Carter Glass, January 16, 1936, box 5, RWW. *Workers' Manual,* 5, copy in box 36, ASB. McCormick thought the slogan originated with the publicity department. Vance McCormick to Ray Stannard Baker, July 12, 1928, box 111, RSB. John Milton Cooper (*Woodrow Wilson,* 322) argues the slogan referred chiefly to averting war with Mexico, but my own research shows that campaign staff clearly had the war in Europe more mind.

40. Cecil Spring Rice to Edward Grey, October 20, 1916, FO 371/2796. Peterson, *Propaganda for War,* 231–32, 238–39.

41. Theodore Roosevelt to James R. Garfield, September 28, 1916, box 119, JRG. Frederick C. Luebke, *Bonds of Loyalty: German Americans and World War I* (DeKalb: Northern Illinois University Press), 140–41. Lovell, *Presidential Election of 1916,* 33. Link, *Campaigns for Progressivism and Peace,* 139–40. Viereck, *Spreading Germs of Hate,* 252–53.

42. Viereck, *Spreading Germs of Hate,* 245–46. Link, *Campaigns for Progressivism and Peace,* 137. Cooper, *Woodrow Wilson,* 342. Will R. MacDonald and Carl E. Schmidt, "Dear Sir," October 11, 1916, box 14, FLP. How this letter ended up in Frank Polk's hands is unclear, but it illustrates the Democrats' intelligence gathering capability. For more on Republican internecine fighting see Ickes, *Autobiography,* 186–88.

43. *New York Times,* October 11, 1916. Woolley, "Viereck's Hyphenates Exposed," PIH, 1–2, 7. Link says the origin of these documents was a former congressman, Robert J. Bulkley. Link, *Campaigns for Progressivism and Peace,* 138, and House diary, October 20, 1916. House conferred with McCormick and Woolley about making them public.

44. *New York Times,* October 23 and 25, 1916. Garfield diary, October 25, 1916. Hughes later did say, "I don't want the support of any one to whom the interest of the nation is not supreme," but this was still less forceful than Wilson's statement and came late. "Mr. Hughes on the Stump," *World's Work,* October 1916, 606. "Mr. Hughes and Divided Allegiance," *Nation,* October 26, 1916, 390.

45. Link, *Campaigns for Progressivism and Peace,* 104–5, 135. Homer Cummings to Vance McCormick, December 7, 1917, HSC. Woolley Report. Cummings to Calvin McNab, August 23, 1916; memorandum to Department Heads, General Order no. 1, August 21, 1916, and Assistant Secretary Democratic State Central Committee of Wilson to Thomas J. Walsh, September 23, 1916, box 168;

Norman Hapgood to Walsh, October 26, 1916, and Walsh to Norman Hapgood, October 27, 1916, box 170, TJW.

46. Breckenridge Long to W. R. Hollister, September 29, 1916, box 24, BL. Link, *Campaigns for Progressivism and Peace,* 136. On meetings with German-Americans, see Woolley, "Viereck's Hyphenates Exposed," PIH, 4–6; Viereck, *Spreading Germs of Hate,* 241–42; Ray Stannard Baker interview with Albert Burleson, March 17–19, 1927, box 102, RSB. *New York Times,* October 25, 1916.

47. Woolley Report. The Texas incident is discussed in Woolley, "A Virtue of Necessity," PIH, passim. W. Y. Morgan to James T. Williams, September 16 and 26, 1916, box 28, JTW. Williams's work for Taft is discussed in background submitted for his membership in the Metropolitan Club, MC. David S. Barry to James T. Williams, October 22, 1916, box 28, JTW.

48. Joseph Tumulty to Robert Woolley, August 12, 1916, box 21, RWW. Woolley, "Woodrow Wilson and the Peck Letters," PIH, 6–8.

49. Breckinridge Long, "Is Mr. Hughes A 'Natural Born Citizen' within the Meaning of the Constitution?," speech, October 21, 1916, box 170, BL. Long queried Burleson on the validly of his case; Burleson referred the letter to the State Department, which indicated he had no case. Breckinridge Long to Albert S. Burleson, October 13, 1916, and Burleson to Long, October 19, 1916, box 22, BL. See also John Maxwell Hamilton and Meghan Menard, "One Hundred Years of 'Birther' Arguments," *The Conversation,* March 15, 2016.

50. Woolley Report. Fred Essary to Robert Woolley, August 20, 1916, box 5, RWW. See also, Joseph Tumulty to Robert Lansing, August 24, 1916, box 20, RL. Essary is described in Harold A. Williams, *The Baltimore Sun: 1837–1987* (Baltimore: Johns Hopkins Press, 1987), 270–71. Essary was one of the reporters Wilson held in high regard. Josephus Daniels, "Wilson and the Newspaper Men," n.d., box 731, JD. Dale E. Zacher, *The Scripps Newspapers Go to War, 1914–18* (Urbana: University of Illinois Press, 2008), 99–105.

51. George Creel, *Wilson and the Issues* (New York: Century, 1916), 29, 60–62.

52. Creel, *Wilson and the Issues,* 153. James Kerney, *The Political Education of Woodrow Wilson* (New York: Century, 1926), 409.

53. Ray Stannard Baker interview with Vance C. McCormick, July 15, 1928, box 111, RSB.

54. A. Howard Meneely interview with Robert Woolley, February 2, 1929, box 117, RSB. Baker interview with McCormick. Woodrow Wilson to Vance McCormick, August 21, 1916, box 3, VCM. Robert Woolley to Wilson, August 23, 1916, box 23, RWW.

55. Lansing, *War Memoirs,* 165. Blum, *Tumulty,* 106. A. W. McLean to Josephus Daniels, September 20, 1916, box 671, JD.

56. *New York Evening Post,* October 17, 1916. Pusey, *Charles Evans Hughes,* 351–52. James R. Garfield to F. J. Ham, September 25, 1916, box 161, JRG. Lovell, *Presidential Election of 1916,* 152. Cecil Spring Rice to Edward Grey, September 15, 1916, FO 371/2795. Pusey, *Charles Evans Hughes,* 351.

57. James K. Pollock Jr., *Party Campaign Funds* (New York: Alfred A. Knopf, 1926), 28. Breckenridge Long to Henry Morgenthau, November 8, 1916, box 24, BL. Woolley, "Making the Mare Go and Maine Elections," PIH, 6–7. Link, *Woodrow Wilson and the Progressive Era,* 247. Garfield diary, October 14 and November 2, 1916.

58. Woolley Report. Homer Cummings to Vance McCormick, November 4, 1916, box 68, HSC. Baker interview with McCormick. Link, *Campaigns for Progressivism and Peace,* 148.

59. Woolley Report.

60. Homer S. Cummings, testimony, August 30, 1920, US Congress. Senate Subcommittee of the Committee on Privileges and Elections, *Presidential Campaign Expenses,* 66th Cong., 2d Sess.,

1921, 1:1178. He and others estimated the deficit to be about $650,000 (1:1158). Link, *Campaigns for Progressivism and Peace*, 111. *New York Sun*, November 6, 1916.

61. Woolley, "Making the Mare Go and Maine Elections," PIH, 4–5. *Rebel*, 155. Martin Glynn to Edward M. House, October 15, 1918, box 49, EMH. G. B. Blaine and W. H. Weeker to Charles Evans Hughes, October 30, 1916, box 148, CEH. *New York Times*, October 23, 1916. Woolley, "Election Night: Photofinish," PIH, 1. Edith B. Wilson, *My Memoir* (Indianapolis: Bobbs-Merrill, 1939), 115.

62. Garfield diary, November 7, 1916.

63. Pusey, *Charles Evans Hughes*, 360–61. E. J. Kahn Jr., *The World of Swope* (New York: Simon and Schuster, 1965), 180–81.

64. Unless otherwise noted, the election night and aftermath are from Woolley's perspective, "Election Night: Photofinish," PIH, passim. Roper, *Fifty Years of Public Life*, 158. Ray Stannard Baker interview with Robert Woolley, November 12, 1925, box 117, RSB.

65. Woolley, "Election Night: Photofinish," PIH, 8. *Rebel*, 156. Roper confirms the criticism of Woolley. Roper, *Fifty Years of Public Life*, 159.

66. *New York Evening Mail*, November 8, 1916. Woolley, "Election Night: Photofinish," PIH.

67. On the odds the day after the election see note inserted in Woolley, PIH.

68. Pusey, *Charles Evans Hughes*, 362. Among those who do not believe the Hotel Virginia incident cost Hughes the election is Mowry, *The California Progressives*, 267. F.P.A., "Plutarch Lights of History: Charles Evans Hughes," *Harpers Weekly*, February 19, 1916, 179. Wilson's first attorney general, William C. Redfield, was "the last important public man to wear side whiskers." Link, *Woodrow Wilson and the Progressive Era*, 31. James R. Garfield to Will H. Hays, December 12, 1916, box 161, JRG. New York Democrats to Theodore Roosevelt, telegram, November 10, 1916, box 148, CEH. Viereck, *Spreading Germs of Hate*, 254. Gibson Gardner, *Lusty Scripps—The Life of E. W. Scripps* (New York: Vanguard, 1932), 193. Zacher, *The Scripps Newspapers Go to War*, 248. Edward M. House to Woodrow Wilson, December 31, 1916, box 121, EMH. Scripps commented on his part in the election: "New York was lost to Wilson. It turned out that it required to off-set this huge loss, that Ohio, California, and the State of Washington should all choose Wilson electors. These happen to be the three states in which the Scripps papers had, in one a dominating position, and in the other two, strategic positions. So close was the election in California, that it appears that had our people put forth less energy than they did, even by a small percentage, Mr. Wilson would have been defeated." E. W. Scripps to Ben Lindsey, November 20, 1917, box 56, BBL.

69. Pusey, *Charles Evans Hughes*, 248–49. Walter Lippmann, *New Republic*, September 30, 1916, 211. David J. Danelski and Joseph S. Tulchin, eds., *The Autobiographical Notes of Charles Evans Hughes* (Cambridge, MA: Harvard University Press, 1973), 184. Harold Ickes to Will H. Hays, December 12, 1916, box 32, HLI.

70. Wilbur W. Marsh, testimony, September 1, 1920, Subcommittee of the Committee on Privileges and Elections, *Presidential Campaign Expenses*, 1525. Baker interview with McCormick. See also Vance C. McCormick et al., telegram to Mrs. R. W. Woolley, November 8, 1916, box 25, RWW. On Woolley's prowess at propaganda see Pollock, *Party Campaign Funds*, 146.

71. *Atlanta Journal*, November 8, 1916. [Gifford Pinchot], "A Plan for Publicity," box 701, GP. Pinchot did not sign this document, but its tone, the background on the Forest Service, and its existence in his papers make it highly likely he is the author.

72. Frank Polk to Robert Woolley, November 10, 1916, box 28, RWW. Other congratulations can be found in this file. Woolley, "Election Night: Photofinish," PIH, 12.

73. McGerr, *The Decline of Popular Politics*, 145–51, 159. Adam Sheingate, *Building a Business of*

Politics: The Rise of Political Consulting and the Transformation of American Democracy (New York: Oxford University Press, 2015), chapter 3 passim. Independent newspapers reached large numbers of people. In the fifty largest cities, 23 newspapers could be called independent in 1870; by 1900 152 qualified as nonpartisan. The circulation of independent papers was larger than for all Republican and Democratic papers combined in 1900. James T. Hamilton, *All the News That's Fit to Sell: How the Market Transforms Information into News* (Princeton, NJ: Princeton University Press, 2004), 48, 53, 57. *Wall Street Journal,* November 9, 1916.

74. Steven A. Seidman, *Posters, Propaganda, and Persuasion in Election Campaigns around the World and through History* (New York: Peter Land, 2008), 54. Lovell, *Presidential Election of 1916,* 98. Josh Glick, "Wilson and the War Effort," in *Film and the American Presidency,* ed. Jeff Meene and Christian B. Long (New York: Routledge, 2015), 75. Artist C. R. Macauley had produced the cartoon film *The Old Way and the New* in 1912. Woolley Report. Meneely interview with Woolley. N. M. Ledbetter to R. W. Woolley, August 22, 1916, box 28, RWW. McGerr, *The Decline of Popular Politics,* 164-67.

75. Sidney Blumenthal, *The Permanent Campaign: Inside the World of Elite Political Operatives* (Boston: Beacon, 1980), especially the introduction, which elaborates the ties between professional campaign staff and progressive ideals. Years after writing this book, Blumenthal became a modern-day Woolley in the Clinton White House, where he specialized in communications and stout defenses of the president. "Money to Nominate," *New Republic,* April 14, 1920, 198.

76. Ray Stannard Baker interview with Vance McCormick, September 12, 1930, box 111, RSB. Roper, *Fifty Years of Public Life,* 152. Robert Woolley to Edward M. House, February 6, 1917, box 7, RWW.

77. Two draft documents, neither of which are signed and only one of which is dated (May 21, 1917), are in box 42, HM-LC. Morgenthau incorrectly says the committee's recommendations led to the creation of the CPI. Morgenthau, *All in a Life-Time,* 252-53.

78. House diary, May 21, 1917.

79. Ray Stannard Baker interview with George Creel, May 23, 1932, box 103, RSB.

3. A MATURED PUBLIC OPINION

1. Arthur Sweetser, unpaginated typescript marked "AP Days," July 27, 1916, box 3, AS. Sweetser's notes and recollections from this period are often scraps of paper mixed into correspondence and articles. Some are not titled. The description of the room is by D. Harold Oliver, n.d., box 2, EMH-LC. Robert C. Hilderbrand, *Power and the People: Executive Management of Public Opinion in Foreign Affairs, 1897-1921* (Chapel Hill: University of North Carolina Press, 1981), 103. *WWLL: 1915-1917,* 326.

2. Arthur Sweetser, *Roadside Glimpses of the Great War* (New York: Macmillan, 1916), 148-50.

3. *New York Times,* November 20, 1916.

4. *WWLL: 1915-1917,* 258, 288. Tanner oral history, 186. Baker interview with McCormick, September 12, 1930.

5. *PWW,* 31:342. Link, *Campaigns for Progressivism and Peace,* 26. Cooper, *Woodrow Wilson,* 327-28.

6. *WWLL: 1915-1917,* 386. Wilson, *My Memoir,* 123.

7. Arthur Sweetser, "Peace," typescript note on Lansing meeting, n.d., box 3, AS.

8. Ackerman, *Germany,* 157. George G. Bruntz, *Allied Propaganda and the Collapse of the Ger-*

man Empire in 1918 (Stanford, CA: Stanford University Press, 1938), 161. For a discussion of German thinking on peace at the time see Link, *Campaigns for Progressivism and Peace,* 210–11.

9. *PWW,* 40:264, 272. Arthur Sweetser, untitled, unpaginated typescript note, box 3, AS. *New York Times,* December 19, 1916.

10. On House's and Lansing's objections see Cooper, *Woodrow Wilson,* 362–63. Link, *Campaigns for Progressivism and Peace,* 193.

11. Sweetser, "Lansing's Conference." n.d., box 3, AS. This entire section, unless otherwise noted, draws from this note. Blum, *Tumulty,* 128.

12. *PWW,* 40:306.

13. *PWW,* 40:308.

14. Lansing, *War Memoirs,* 187, 208–9, 356. On Bernstorff's support for the peace initiative see Doerries, *Imperial Challenge,* 191–92. Arthur Sweetser, untitled note, n.d., box 3, AS. The significance of Lansing's efforts to thwart Wilson's peace note is discussed in Link, *Campaigns for Progressivism and Peace,* 220–37. *PWW,* 40:319.

15. Edward Alsworth Ross, *Seventy Years of It: An Autobiography* (New York: D. Appleton-Century, 1936), 50, 56. Bernhard J. Stern, ed., "The Ward-Ross Correspondence, 1891–1896," *American Sociological Review* 3 (June 1938): 390. Richard L. McCormick, *The Party Period and Public Policy: American Politics from the Age of Jackson to the Progressive Era* (New York: Oxford University Press, 1986), 283. For a discussion of Ross's significance see William L. Kolb, "The Sociological Theories of Edward Alsworth Ross," in *An Introduction to the History of Sociology,* ed. Harry Elmer Barnes (Chicago: University of Chicago Press, 1948).

16. Edward Alsworth Ross, *Social Control: A Survey of the Foundations of Order* (1901; reprint, Cleveland: Press of Case Western Reserve University, 1969), 47, 51–52.

17. Edward Alsworth Ross, "Freedom of Communication and the Struggle for Right," *Publications of the American Philosophical Society* 9 (1915): 1. Ross, *Social Control,* 104.

18. Jeremy Bentham, "Of Publicity," in *The Works of Jeremy Bentham* (New York: Russell and Russell, 1962), 2:311. Ross, *Social Control,* 46. Ross offered a lengthy discussion of the press's shortcomings in Edward Alsworth Ross, *Changing America: Studies in Contemporary Society* (New York: Century, 1912), chapter 7.

19. Theodore Roosevelt to Edward Alsworth Ross, September 19, 1907, TR. Sheingate, *Building a Business of Politics,* 20. *New York Times,* February 17, 1903. Melvin D. Urofsky, *Louis D. Brandeis: A Life* (New York: Pantheon, 2009), 87. Louis D. Brandeis, "What Publicity Can Do," *Harper's Weekly,* December 20, 1913, 10.

20. *Congressional Record,* August 28, 1917, 6392. Charles Postel, *The Populist Vision* (New York: Oxford University Press, 2007), 47. On increases in the number of publications see Harold S. Wilson, *McClure's Magazine and the Muckrakers* (Princeton, NJ: Princeton University Press, 1970), 28–32; Mott, *A History of American Magazines,* vol. 3, *1865–1885* (Cambridge, MA: Harvard University Press, 1967), 5; and Mott, *A History of American Magazines,* 4:11. William Allen White to John S. Phillips, May 25, 1908, WAW.

21. Louis Filler, *The Muckrakers* (1939; reprint, Stanford, CA: Stanford University Press, 1993), 252–53. Michael McGerr, *A Fierce Discontent: The Rise and Fall of the Progressive Movement in America* (New York: Oxford University Press, 2005), 280. Mott, *A History of American Magazines,* 4:208–9. Wilson, *McClure's Magazine and the Muckrakers,* 29. Ross, *Changing America,* 15.

22. Mark Sullivan, *The Education of an American* (New York: Doubleday, Doran, 1938), 165–66. *Independent,* August 25, 1905, 8. The argument as to who started muckraking is discussed in Filler,

The Muckrakers, chapter 5 and 82–83; and Peter Lyon, *Success Story: The Life and Times of S. S. Mc-Clure* (New York: Scribner's, 1963), 204.

23. Ross, *Social Control,* 10. Robert E. Park, "The Blood Money of the Congo," *Everybody's,* January 1907, 60–70. George Creel, "The Press and Patent Medicines," *Harper's Weekly,* February 13, 1915, 157–58. Ray Stannard Baker, "Railroads on Trial: How Railroads Make Public Opinion," *McClure's,* March 1906, 535–36.

24. Fred H. Matthews, *Quest for an American Sociology: Robert E. Park and the Chicago School* (Montreal: McGill-Queen's University Press, 1977), 146–47. Rollo Ogden, "Some Aspects of Journalism," *Atlantic Monthly,* July 1906, 15. Baker diary, February 3, 1917. For a discussion of this mystical belief in publicity, see Robert H. Wiebe, *The Search for Order, 1877–1920* (New York: Hill and Wang, 1967), 162. Ross put it this way: "The muck-rakers, despite the sensationalists and liars-for-profit that follow in their wake, deserve the credit of having roused a great many dozing jurors," by which he meant members of the public who had been absorbed in petty local interests. Ross, "Freedom of Communication and the Struggle for Right," 1–2.

25. J. O. Hertzler, "Edward Alsworth Ross: Sociological Pioneer and Interpreter," *American Sociological Review* 15 (October 1951): 598. Ross, *Seventy Years of It,* 180. Julius Weinberg, Gisela J. Hinkle, and Rosce C. Hinkle, introduction to Ross, *Social Control,* xvii. Louis Menand, *The Metaphysical Club* (New York: Farrar, Straus and Giroux, 2001), 411–12. Edward Alsworth Ross, *Sin and Society: An Analysis of Latter-Day Iniquity, with a Letter from President Roosevelt* (New York: Harper and Row, 1973), 15–16.

26. Cooper, *Woodrow Wilson,* 122–23. Blum, *Tumulty,* 21–22

27. Woodrow Wilson, "The Study of Administration," *Political Science Quarterly* 2 (June 1887): 208. Ralph Waldo Emerson, "Worship," in *The Conduct of Life* (1876; reprint, New York: AMS Press, 1968), 224. For examples of Wilson's use of this phrase see *WWLL: 1910–1913,* 98, 103. Woodrow Wilson, *Constitutional Government in the United States* (New York: Columbia University Press, 1908), 68.

28. Hester Eloise Hosford, *Woodrow Wilson: His Career, His Statesmanship and His Public Policies* (New York: G. P. Putnam's Sons, 1912), 93. *Day Book,* March 19, 1914. *New York Times,* August 12, 1916. *Literary Digest,* March 3, 1917, 3.

29. "'Pitiless Publicity' Again," *San Francisco Call,* June 8, 1913. Irving Shuman to Carl Vrooman, November 3, 1915, in McAdoo file, box 22, RWW.

30. House diary, January 4 and 11, 1917.

31. Cooper, *Woodrow Wilson,* 5, 193. For other character sketches of Wilson see Arthur S. Link, *Wilson: The New Freedom* (Princeton, NJ: Princeton University Press, 1956), 76–78; Link, *Woodrow Wilson and the Progressive Era,* 9. Anne Wintermute Lame and Louise Herrick Wall, eds., *The Letters of Franklin K. Lane* (Cambridge, MA: Houghton Mifflin, 1922), 175. Lansing, *War Memoirs,* 221.

32. *WWLL: 1915–1917,* 33. John Milton Cooper calls Wilson "one of the few great political scientists his nation has produced." Cooper, "Few and Mostly Far Between: Reflections on Intellectuals as Presidents," *Presidential Studies Quarterly* 47 (December 2017): 794.

33. *WWLL: 1915–1917,* 236.

34. Cooper, *Woodrow Wilson,* 214.

35. Discussion of the German and Allied responses can be found in May, *The World War and American Isolation,* 368–69; and Link, *Campaigns for Progressivism and Peace,* 232–39.

36. Woodrow Wilson, Address to Senate, January 22, 1917, in *PPWW:ND,* 2:269–70. Link, *Campaigns for Progressivism and Peace,* 269–71.

37. Ackerman, *Germany*, 289–90. Ackerman, "The War and Our Next Election," 2.

38. John Morton Blum, *Woodrow Wilson and the Politics of Morality* (Boston: Little, Brown, 1956), 19. Frederic C. Howe, *The Confessions of a Reformer* (New York: Charles Scribner's Sons, 1925), 35. Ray Stannard Baker interview with Charles Swem, July 16, 1925, box 115, RSB. See also Link, *The New Freedom*, 75; and Blum, *Tumulty*, 59. House diary, November 6, 1916.

39. *Washington Post*, March 21, 1914. *Philadelphia Record*, January 9, 1902. Woodrow Wilson, remarks, typescript, box 15, GCR. For a discussion of Roosevelt's press relations see George Juergens, *News from the White House: The Presidential-Press Relationship in the Progressive Era* (Chicago: University of Chicago Press, 1981), chapter 2; and Hilderbrand, *Power and the People*, chapter 3.

40. *WWLL: 1910–1913*, 369. Link, *The New Freedom*, 83.

41. Blum, *Tumulty*, 2–3. *PWW*, 27:210–12. Oulahan, "Presidents and Publicity," chapter 11.

42. Wilbur Forrest, *Behind the Front Page: Stories of Newspaper Stories in the Making* (New York: D. Appleton-Century, 1934), 11. *PWW*, 31:63. House diary, February 14, 1913, and November 6, 1914. Gould, *The First Modern Clash over Federal Power*, 8, 57–58. Kerney, *The Political Education of Woodrow Wilson*, 344.

43. Woodrow Wilson to Charles W. Eliot, June 1, 1914, WW-LC. Ray Stannard Baker observed the "project became a reality" with the creation of the CPI. *WWLL: 1913–1914*, 234–35.

44. Joseph P. Tumulty, *Woodrow Wilson as I Know Him* (Garden City, NY: Doubleday, Page 1921), 255. Woodrow Wilson, Address to Congress, February 3, 1917, *PPWW:ND*, 2:425. Arthur Sweetser, "Severance of Relations with Germany," n.d., box 3, AS.

45. Many accounts of this episode—with differing details—exist. Among the more well known is Barbara W. Tuchman's *The Zimmermann Telegram* (New York: Ballantine, 1985), 112. I have relied chiefly on Thomas Boghardt's more recent *The Zimmermann Telegram: Intelligence, Diplomacy, and America's Entry into World War I* (Annapolis, MD: Naval Institute Press, 2012); its details on interception of the telegram benefit from better access to archival material than Tuchman enjoyed. Also useful is Joachim von zur Gathen, "Zimmermann Telegram: The Original Draft," *Crytologia* 31 (2007): 19–20.

46. Boghardt, *The Zimmermann Telegram*, 28–30, 66–67, 143. von zur Gathen, "Zimmermann Telegram," 26. Sweetser, "Lansing's Conference." "Edwin Hood Is Daddy of All at Capital," *Fourth Estate*, February 18, 1922, 12. Hood's papers contain many references to his close relationship with officials, for instance, Robert Lansing to Hood's wife, August 11, 1923, and Gridiron Club memorial, n.d., by his colleagues, EMH-LC. Richard Pyle, "World War I: A Circuit to Anywhere," in *Breaking News* (New York: Princeton Architectural Press, 2007), 48–49. Lansing, *War Memoirs*, 228–29. In his recollection of Hood, Sweetser noted that Hood was disappointed not to be allowed to write the story. See Sweetser, "Hood Papers," June 18, 1962, box 2, EMH-LC. Following the AP's scoop, Melville Stone wrote to Polk that he wanted to "withdraw the rather ungracious remark that I made to you the other day to the effect that the Administration did not discriminate between newspapers as carefully as I thought it should. I deeply appreciate the opportunity given us last night to do a distinguished service." March 1, 1917, box 1, FLP.

47. George Sylvester Viereck to Albert S. Burleson, telegram, March 1, 1917, box 18, ASB. Nickles, *Under the Wire*, 159. Link, *Campaigns for Progressivism and Peace*, 356. Tuchman, *The Zimmermann Telegram*, 183. *Berliner Tageblatt*, March 3, 1917. Lansing, *War Memoirs*, 231. Arthur Sweetser, note, untitled, n.d., first line begins, "March 28 proved," box 3, AS. "The Disclosure in the United States," unsigned report, n.d., HW 3/180.

48. Arthur Sweetser, "Correspondents to Be Barred," n.d., box 3, AS. Link, *Campaigns for Progressivism and Peace*, 309. *Philadelphia Public Ledger*, February 18, 1917. Millis, *Road to War*, 412.

49. *PWW,* 40: 474. Charles Merz, "Letter Number 6, January 15 [1917]," box 20, WL. Arthur Sweetser, "Wilson's Second Move," n.d., box 3, AS. This section draws from this account.

50. *Washington Times,* January 13, 1917. Sweetser notes Polk's role in withholding information is in "Wilson's Second Move." Sweetser, "Correspondents to Be Barred."

51. George Creel, "General MacArthur," *Collier's,* May 15, 1948, 58. D. Clayton James, *The Years of MacArthur,* vol. 1. *1880 to 1941* (Boston: Houghton Mifflin, 1970), 130–31. Arthur Herman, *Douglas MacArthur: American Warrior* (New York: Random House, 2017), 91–92. *New York Times,* June 30, 1916. Rupert Hughes, "Activities of the Censorship Section—M.I.10," n.d., chief military censor, Military Intelligence Division, WDGS.

52. Harold Edgar and Benno C. Schmidt Jr., "The Espionage Statutes and Publication of Defense Information," *Columbia Law Review* 73 (May 1973): 939–41. H.R. 20757, 64th Cong., 2d Sess., "A Bill to Define and Punish Espionage," February 5, 1917. James R. Mock, *Censorship 1917* (Princeton, NJ: Princeton University Press, 1941), 41–42.

53. Untitled editorial comment, *New Republic,* March 3, 1917, 118.

54. On Scripps see Oliver Knight, ed., *I Protest: Selected Disquisitions of E. W. Scripps* (Madison: University of Wisconsin Press, 1966), 450; Zacher, *Scripps Newspapers Go to War,* 33–35, 54, 68. The Interior official was W. I. Swanton. "A Government Bureau of Information," n.d., but likely late 1915 or early 1916, box 31, RWW. An iteration of this plan, which ended up in CPI files, is in W. I. Swanton to Frederick Cleveland, White House Chief of the Bureau of Municipal Research, October 29, 1910, entry 1, CPI. Swanton prepared a chart on the government bureaucracy for the CPI's *Official Bulletin,* December 1, 1917.

55. Memorandum, n.d., apparently from Herbert B. Brougham of the *Public Ledger,* box 18, EMH. Also, *PWW,* 40:243, House diary, March 11, 1917. On Willcox, Edward M. House to Woodrow Wilson, February 8, 1917, box 121, EMH. F. W. Kellogg to William McAdoo, March 28, 1917, box 176, WGM.

56. Arthur Bullard, *The Diplomacy of the Great War* (New York: Macmillan, 1916), 211. Arthur Bullard to Edward M. House, August 21, 1915, July 17, 1916, February 23 and March 15, 1917, box 9, AB. Bullard to House, November 11, 1915, and March 31, 1916, box 21, EMH. House diary, March 19, 1917. Arthur Bullard, "Censorship Memorandum," July 1916, box 9, AB. The general staff statement, reported in the *New York Times,* July 7, 1916, was based on a War College study, *The Proper Relationship between the Army and the Press in War* (Washington, DC: Government Printing Office, 1916). The War College requested military attachés overseas to collect information on censorship practices of the Allies as well as Germany and Austria. James G. Randall, "Censorship during the Great War," 1918, box 2, JGR. Randall, a historian who worked with the CPI, wrote this paper after the CPI asked him to review War College files. The details of the War College study were reported in the *New York Times,* May 28, 1916.

57. Edward M. House to Walter Page, July 18, 1918, box 86, EMH. Herbert Croly, "The New Republic Idea," *New Republic,* December 6, 1922, 3. Bliven oral history, 35. Walter Lippmann, *A Preface to Politics* (1913; reprint, Ann Arbor: University of Michigan Press, 1962), 229.

58. House diary, March 4, 1917. *PWW,* 40:360. Walter Lippmann to Woodrow Wilson, February 6, 1917, box 33, WL. Link discusses Lane's leaking in *The New Freedom,* 126. See also Ray Stannard Baker interview with Newton Baker, March 26, 1918, box 100, RSB.

59. *PWW,* 40:445, 448–49, 474. "Editors, Though Ignored by Government Will Observe Censorship Regulations," *Editor & Publisher,* March 24, 1917, 6. *New York Times,* March 18 and 25, 1917.

60. George Creel to Josephus Daniels, March 19, 1917, JD.

61. George Creel, *New York World*, March 25, 1916. Creel, *Wilson and the Issues*, 37. Examples of Daniels's distribution of the Creel article can be found in boxes 171 and 420, JD. Creel told Daniels he wanted to write "an assertion of your patriotic and intelligent handling of delicate and critical matters." George Creel to Josephus Daniels, March 4, 1916, box 203, JD-UNC.

62. Inaugural invitation to Creel is in box 7, GC. Creel's angling for a Wilson interview is in George Creel to William McAdoo, November 13, 1916, box 169, WGM. George Creel, "The Next Four Years," *Everybody's*, February 1917, 138. At the outbreak of the war, Creel expressed support for Wilson's neutrality. George Creel, "The Ghastly Swindle," *Harper's Weekly*, August 29, 1914, 1197.

63. George Creel to Josephus Daniels, March 28, 1917, box 73, JD.

64. *PWW*, 42:557–58.

65. Woodrow Wilson, "A Memorandum," in Cooper, *Woodrow Wilson*, 391, also 39.

66. Walter S. Gifford to Grosvenor B. Clarkson, March 17, 1917, box 27; Grosvenor B. Clarkson, "A Memorandum on the Past and Future Functions of the Council of National Defense," March 22, 1918, box 31, CND. Mock, *Censorship 1917*, 44. Crozier, *American Reporters*, 28. Gibson Gardner to Josephus Daniels, April 9, 1917, JD. Daniels diary, April 3 and 6, 1917.

67. Arthur Bullard, "Democracy and Diplomacy," *Atlantic Monthly*, Aril 1917, 492. For a discussion of Bullard's thinking see Stephen L. Vaughn, "Arthur Bullard and the Creation of the Committee on Public Information," *New Jersey History* 97 (Spring 1979): 45–53. Arthur Bullard, *Mobilizing America* (New York: Macmillan, 1917), 40, 58.

68. *PWW*, 42:39–41. George Creel to Josephus Daniels, April 4, 1917, box 73, JD.

69. Baker diary, April 5, 1917. George Creel to Josephus Daniels, April 4, 1917, box 73, JD. A conflict exists between Baker's diary entry, which says the meeting occurred on April 4, and Creel's letter, which indicates the meeting occurred the evening before. Baker's diary makes no mention of an April 3 gathering. The best explanation is that Creel, who wrote another letter to Daniels dated April 4, misdated this one. The invitation to Lippmann to attend the April 4 dinner is Jesse Lynch Williams et al. to Walter Lippmann, March 26, 1917, box 27, WL.

70. Arthur Bullard to Edward M. House, "Sunday," n.d., box 21, EMH. Walter Lippmann to George Creel, February 3, 1915; Creel to Lippmann, March 27, 1915; Lippmann to Creel, March 24 and March 29, 1915, box 7, WL. [Paul Kellogg], "Editorials," *Survey*, October 10, 1914, 53–55. George Creel, "How 'Tainted' Money Taints," *Pearson's*, March 1915, 295. "Paul Kellogg Muckraked," *New Republic*, February 20, 1915, 61. Creel wrote a rebuttal, "George Creel Replies," *New Republic*, March 27, 1915, 210–11. The episode is discussed in Shelton Stomquist, "Class Wars," in *Labor Histories: Class, Politics, and the Working-Class Experience,* ed. Eric Arnesen, Julie Greene, and Bruce Laurie (Urbana: University of Illinois Press, 1998), chapter 4.

71. House diary, April 11, 1917. Walter Lippmann to Edward M. House, April 12, 1917, box 14, and Lippmann to Charles Merz, April 11, 1917, box 20; Lippmann to Franklin Lane, April 11, 1917, box 17, WL. Vance McCormick to Robert Woolley, April 6, 1917, box 12, RWW.

72. Josephus Daniels to Gibson Gardner, April 6, 1917, box 14, JD-D. Daniels diary, April 6 and 9, 1917. *PWW*, 42:39, 43. For an example of Daniels reaching out to Baker on press management see Josephus Daniels to Ray Stannard Baker, March 29, 1917, box 14, JD-D. Daniels knew about Lippmann's proposal. A note in his diary on April 13 reads: "Littmann [*sic*] & School of Journalism." As will be discussed later, Lippmann's plan involved Columbia's journalism school.

73. *PWW*, 42:52–59, 71. *Rebel*, 158.

74. *PWW*, 42:71.

75. *Rebel*, 158. Histories of the CPI sometimes date the order to April 13, but it is recorded in

government records as April 14. That also was the day the announcement was made. Both Daniels's diary of April 13, 1917, and the diary of Wilson's assistant, Thomas Brahany (April 15, 1917; found at PWW, 42: 71) indicate the order was signed on April 13.

76. Mitchel A. Sollenberger and Mark J. Rozell, *The President's Czars: Undermining Congress and the Constitution* (Lawrence: University Press of Kansas, 2012), 19 and, for background discussion, chapters 1 and 2.

77. Wiebe, *The Search for Order,* xiv.

4. A NEW DEFINITION OF NEWS

1. This section draws from George Creel, "The Truth Shall Make You Free," *Collier's,* November 1, 1941, 17ff. It is difficult to overstate the ubiquity of feeling on the part of CPI staff that nothing was established as to what it "should do or how it was to perform," as William Chenery put it. *APD,* 8.

2. John Milton Cooper Jr., *Breaking the Heart of the World: Woodrow Wilson and the Fight for the League of Nations* (Cambridge: Cambridge University Press, 2001), 416. The originator of the phrase "war to end war" may have been A. D. Lindsay, a British scholar who wrote a propaganda pamphlet called *The War to End War.* Kate Haste, *Keep the Home Fires Burning* (London: Allen Lane, 1977), 26–27.

3. Cooper Union brochure, April 11, 1915, box 7, GC.

4. *Rebel,* 17. Undated newspaper articles reporting the School Board incident can be found in box OV4, GC. Ivan H. Epperson, "Missourians Abroad, No. 3—George Creel," *Missouri Historical Review* 20 (January 1918): 101.

5. *Rebel,* 74–76. The goals of the *Independent* were outlined its maiden issue, March 11, 1899. *Newsbook* lasted from March 7 to June 20, 1908. Edward Alsworth Ross, "The Suppression of Important News," *Atlantic Monthly,* March 1910, 309. George Creel, "The Great Conspiracy," *Newsbook,* March 28, 1908. In both *Newsbook* and the *Independent,* Creel satirized other newspapers. A regular feature was "The Daily Slush."

6. Creel's local celebrity, including his service as a coal oil inspector, is chronicled in clips, mostly undated and without name of publication, found in box OV4, GC. See description of Creel in "The Stung Club," box 7, GC. He is referred to in this club document as "Coal Oil" Creel.

7. Gene Fowler, *Timber Line: A Story of Bonfils and Tammen* (New York: Garden City, 1933), 276. For details on Creel's work in Denver with the *Post* see chapter 24. Meatpacking magnate J. Ogden Armour was a silent partner in the purchase of the *Kansas City Post. Rebel,* 86.

8. P. C. MacFarlane, "The Fortunes of Citizen Creel," *Collier's,* July 19, 1913, 6.

9. Charles Larsen, *The Good Fight* (Chicago: Quadrangle, 1972), 177. For examples of Creel reporting on himself see *Rocky Mountain Daily News,* August 20, 1912, and his story on vice, September 15, 1912. Creel's resolution is in box 7, GC. *Rocky Mountain News,* January 31, February 2, 3, 16, and May 18, 1913.

10. Creel, "George Creel Replies," 209.

11. Donald Wilhelm, "Our Uncensorious Censor," *Independent,* January 5, 1918, 21. George Creel, "Four Million Citizen Defenders," *Everybody's,* May 1917, 551. Also see Creel, "Military Training for Our Youth," *Century,* May 1916, and Creel, "Universal Training and the Democratic Ideal," read at a meeting of Academy of Political Science, May 18, 1919.

12. George Creel to [?] White, April 30, 1916, NYW. The article appeared in the *World* on April 17. Other newspaper accounts indicate that a near riot did ensue. Creel alone probably did not

provoke it, but his comments certainly contributed to what the *New York Times* called "disturbing scenes."

13. Thomas Fleming, "Propagandist George Creel's Drumbeat for America's Persuaders," *Military History,* December 1995, 26. *Rebel,* 20. MacFarlane, "The Fortunes of Citizen Creel," 5. No author, no title, *Bang,* July 23, 1917, 1–7.

14. *PWW,* 38:14–15. *Rebel,* 141. Creel took a more positive attitude on his wife's independence, years earlier, in "I Married an Electric Light," *Cosmopolitan,* July 1924, 42. He scarcely mentions his wife in his memoir. Author interview with Georgia Bates Creel, Creel's granddaughter, July 24, 2012. Bates's wit is apparent in this comment on her first marriage, to a cavalry officer, which lasted four weeks: "At this period of my life I seem to have had a fad for brief engagements." H. L. Kleinfild, "Blanche Bates," in *Notable American Women: A Biographical Dictionary,* ed. Edward T. James, Janel Wilson James, and Paul S. Boyer (Cambridge, MA: Harvard University Press, 1971), 1:113–14. Lillian Russell, "Lillian Russell's Autobiography," *Cosmopolitan,* August 1922, 81.

15. "Creel: An Announcement," *Everybody's,* January 1919, 25. SWW, 9. Ralph Block, *New York Tribune,* March 20, 1918. Robert Woolley to Edward M. House, April 15, 1917, box 124, EMH. "George Creel," *Editor & Publisher,* April 21, 1917, 28. Stone, *Fifty Years a Journalist,* 326. *New York Times,* April 16, 1917. H. H. Tammen to William G. McAdoo, April 17, 1917, box 178, WGM.

16. *Hearing,* 4.

17. Garfield diary, April 3, 1917. Louis W. Koenig, *Bryan: A Political Biography of William Jennings Bryan* (New York: G. P. Putnam's, 1971), 569. Neil M. Johnson, *George Sylvester Viereck, German-American Propagandist* (Urbana: University of Illinois Press, 1972), 59. In January Viereck said, "Before I am a German sympathizer, I am an American citizen and a citizen of the world. As such I will do everything in my power to aid the President in his noble endeavor to restore peace and sanity to the world." George Sylvester Viereck to Albert Burleson, January 20, 1917, box 18, ASB. On the offer of services see William Churchill to E. J. Wheeler, January 28, 1918, entry 1, CPI.

18. John A. Thompson, *Reformers and War: American Progressive Publicists and the First World War* (New York: Cambridge University Press, 1987), 103–5. George Creel, "The Ghastly Swindle," *Harper's Weekly,* August 29, 1914, 197. Ernest Poole, *The Bridge: My Own Story* (New York: Macmillan, 1940), 263–64.

19. Ralph Bourne, "Twilight of Idols," *Seven Arts,* October 1917, 688–702. Ernest Freeberg, *Democracy's Prisoner: Eugene V. Debs, the Great War, and the Right to Dissent* (Cambridge, MA: Harvard University Press, 2008) 44. *Portland Oregonian,* April 7, 1917.

20. Joseph Tumulty to Woodrow Wilson, May 31, 1917, box 48, JPT. Shotwell oral history, 61.

21. Hew Strachan, *The First World War* (New York: Viking, 2004), 228, 247. Sanders and Taylor, *British Propaganda,* 189. Arthur Willert to Eustace Perry, February 14, 1917, box 3, AW. For an example of British worry over money and men see M. Dixon, testimony, "Report on Proceedings of Wellington House," November 19, 1917, INF/411.

22. Lansing, *War Memoirs,* 279. Gilbert Parker, "The United States and the War," *Harper's Magazine,* March 1918, 522–23. Geoffrey Butler to John Buchan, June 27 and July 9, 1917, FO 395/75. Louis Tracy, *Who's Who in the British War Mission to the United States of America* (New York: Edward J. Clode, 1917), xii. "British Propaganda during the War, 1914–1918," INF 4/4A. Lord Northcliffe to C. J. Phillips, August 23, 1917, box 6, AW. Sanders and Taylor, *British Propaganda,* 190–97. On Northcliffe's fear of assassination, Paul Ferris, *The House of Northcliffe: A Biography of an Empire* (New York: World, 1972), 202.

23. Russell Buchanan, "American Editors Examine American War Aims and Plans in April 1917,"

Pacific Historical Review 9 (September 1940): 263. *Chicago Daily News,* April 24, 1917. On Scripps, Knight, *I Protest,* 495, 570; and Josephus Daniels to Woodrow Wilson, May 28, 1917, WW-LC.

24. Herbert Croly to Edward M. House, April 10, 1917, box 31, EMH. *New York Times,* March 24, 1917. House diary, April 3, 1917. Nathan A. Haverstock, *Fifty Year at the Front* (Washington, DC: Brassey's, 1996), 195. Robert Miraldi, *The Pen is Mightier: The Muckraking Life of Charles Edward Russell* (New York: Palgrave Macmillan, 2003), 247. Palmer described his press operation in "Memorandum on Censorship and Public Information of the A.E.F.," n.d., box 1, NDB, and "Memorandum of My Activities as a War Correspondent Prepared for the Institute of Current World Affairs," February 1945, FP. House suggested to Wilson that Palmer would be a good choice. *PWW,* 41:555.

25. Filler, *The Muckrakers,* 375. A list of these early government appointments can be found in an undated newspaper article, "Newspaper Men's Talents Recognized in War Work," box OV6, GC. For an example of *Editor & Publisher* lists see "Newspaper Men Quick to Heed Colors' Call," June 30, 1917, 3. Charles E. Kloeber to Melvin E. Stone, September 22, 1917, AP. For a story on the staff shortage problem see, "Newspaper Men Needed Badly in Washington," *Editor & Publisher,* September 15, 1917, 18.

26. *New York Morning Telegraph,* April 16, 1917. *Chicago Daily News,* April 16, 1917. For Creel's early comments in this regard see "Special Message to Amer. Newspapers through *The Editor & Publisher,*" typescript, April 17, 1917, box 5, GC.

27. Daniels diary, April 17, 1917.

28. Messenger, *British Propaganda and the State in the First World War,* 106. This is usefully discussed in Edward P. Lilly, "Psychological Warfare," unpublished MS, chapter 1, box 58, EPL. Kendall Banning to George Creel, June 4, 1917, entry 163, WDGS. Lansing diary, May 3, 1917, RL. Lansing made meticulous notes in his diary of everyone he saw during the day along with subject discussed. Cook, *The Press in War-Time,* 99.

29. Josephus Daniels to Ray Stannard Baker, August 8, 1927, box 103, RSB. Josephus Daniels, *The Wilson Era: Years of War and After, 1917–1923* (Chapel Hill: University of North Carolina Press, 1946), 222. Lansing diary, April 17, 1917. Graham H. Stuart, *The Department of State: A History of Its Organization, Procedure and Personnel* (New York: Macmillan, 1949), 243. *Hearing,* 14. The Division of Foreign Intelligence was also supposed to undertake other CPI work, as with universities, but this does not seem to have happened to any degree. Arthur Sweetser, untitled, n.d., note, first line begins, "March 28 proved," box 3, AS. On Patchin see Robert Cecil, "British Propaganda in Allied and Neutral Countries," January 1917, INF 4/1B. *Service Bulletin of the Associated Press,* February 15, 1918, 7.

30. *HWAA,* 70.

31. "Report of the Cartoon Division," September 9, 1918, entry 13, CPI.

32. *HFIL,* 32, 194. *Hearing,* 10, 34, 136. *Report,* 12. *Hearing,* 2177. Baker designated Pew "my personal representative in the matter of publicity" in 1918. CPI press release, May 10, 1918, box 5, NDB.

33. *HWAA,* 74. *Hearing,* 47–48, 53. Frank Hardee Allen, "Government Influence on News in the United States during the World War" (PhD diss., University of Illinois, 1934), 92.

34. Jesse Lynch Williams, "Writers, Mobilize and Write!" *Bulletin of the Authors' League of America,* April 1917, 1–5. Creel's column started in early 1918 and ended that May, when he found them "a drain upon my time and energy." Hamilton Holt to George Creel, January 25, 1918, and Creel to Karl V. S. Holland, May 1, 1918, entry 1, CPI.

35. *HWAA,* 224–26. *Hearing,* 132. Allen, "Government Influence on News in the United States during the World War," 90. On British authors see Sanders and Taylor, *British Propaganda,* 39; Haste, *Keep the Home Fires Burning,* 25–26; and Peterson, *Propaganda for War,* 17–18. Other first-

rank authors helped. Arthur Conan Doyle and G. K. Chesterton sold the war in novels and pamphlets. In 1915 humorist P. G. Wodehouse lampooned American unpreparedness in a short story about a German and Japanese invasion thwarted by the Boy Scouts. The invasion, he said, was ably covered by Ernest Poole and Mary Roberts Rinehart. P. G. Wodehouse, *The Swoop! or, How Clarence Saved England & The Military Invasion of America* (New York: Overlook, 2013), 135. It was the same in other countries. Peterson notes, "Practically every well known writer in France was engaged in propaganda of one sort or another."

36. Wilson, *Constitutional Government,* 126. Woodrow Wilson to George Creel, April 27, 1917; Wilson to Joseph Tumulty, undated but July 1917, WW-LC. Creel to Representative Henry A. Barnhart, September 5, 1918, entry 1, CPI. See also Creel's untitled speech in Indianapolis, probably January 1918, box 5, GC; *Report of the Director of the Official U.S. Bulletin to the Chairman of the Committee on Public Information* (Washington, DC: Government Printing Office, 1918), 11–12; and "Facts Concerning Official Bulletin," n.d., entry 98, CPI.

37. *Official Bulletin,* October 15, 1918, 10. "Official Bulletin No Longer Free," *Editor & Publisher,* October 26, 1918, 22. *HWAA,* 211.

38. Mock, *Censorship 1917,* 80. "Stopping the Leaks," *Philadelphia Public Ledger,* clipping, n.d., box OV7, GC. A majority of the cable traffic in either direction involved news dispatches.

39. Department of Justice, *Annual Report of the Attorney General 1918* (Washington, DC: Government Printing Office, 1918), 16–17. Jane Addams, Statement to the House, Committee on the Judiciary, *Espionage and Interference with Neutrality,* Hearings, April 9, 1917, 51. A good discussion of censorship measures is in Stone, *Perilous Times,* 147–53.

40. T. W. Waring to Josephus Daniels, March 20, 1917, box 573, JD. P. H. Whaley to Josephus Daniels, n.d., box 573, JD. The proposed bill was read into the Senate debate, *Congressional Record,* April 18, 1917, 788–89. The proposal from the four editors was forwarded to Daniels; see C. Van Anda to R. V. Oulahan, telegram, April 12, 1917, box 573, JD. Van Anda was the editor of the *Times* and Oulahan the *Times*'s Washington bureau chief. *Chicago Daily News,* April 4, 1917.

41. *Philadelphia Public Ledger,* May 28, 1917. *New York Times,* April 20 and 24 and May 24 and 28, 1917. Oulahan, "Presidents and Publicity," chapter 22, which has a good discussion of the censorship clause. A similarly useful discussion of press opposition is in Allen, "Government Influence on News in the United States during the World War," chapter 2. Paul L. Murphy, *World War I and the Origins of Civil Liberties in the United States* (New York: W. W. Norton, 1979), 78. *New York Evening Post,* June 1, 1917.

42. *Congressional Record,* April 30, 1917, 1590–91. *Chicago Daily News,* April 19, 1917.

43. Arthur Brisbane to Woodrow Wilson, April 20, 1917; Wilson to Brisbane, April 25, 1917, WW-LC.

44. *Congressional Record,* May 11, 1917, 2098, and May 4, 1917, 155. Joseph Tumulty to Woodrow Wilson, May 8, 1917, box 48, JPT. *Congressional Record,* May 3, 1917, 1768. Daniels, *The Wilson Era: Years of War and After, 1917–1923,* 225–26. *The Proper Relationship between the Army and the Press in War,* 12–13.

45. *HFIL,* 330. Arthur Bullard to L. L. S. Bagg, May 1, 1917, box 8, AB. *New York Times,* April 15 and 20, 1917.

46. Robert Lansing to Edward Smith, May 14, 1917, box 27, RL. *New York Times,* May 8, 1917. "Lansing Muzzles All Department Employees," *Editor & Publisher,* May 12, 1917, 6. Lansing diary, May 9, 1917. Unsigned editorial [Sweetser], *New Republic,* May 12, 1917, 32. (Sweetser draft is in box 3, AS.) *New York Tribune,* May 9, 1917.

47. Woodrow Wilson to George Creel, May 17, 1917, with his edited "Preliminary Statement

to the Press" attached, box 1, GC. *HWAA,* 18–19. *Philadelphia Public Ledger,* May 28, 1917. *Chicago Daily News,* May 23, 1917. Woodrow Wilson to Edwin Webb, May 22, 1917, WW-LC. Wilson to Frank Cobb, May 23, 1917, box 8, WW-P. Oulahan, "Presidents and Publicity," chapter 22.

48. David Lawrence to Woodrow Wilson, May 24, 1917; Wilson to Lawrence, May 25, 1917, WW-LC.

49. *HWAA,* 20. George Creel, "Remarks of Mr. George Creel," n.d., but almost certainly May 25, 1917, box 5, GC. The transcript was made public on May 28, and a story was published the next day in the *New York Times.* Committee on Public Information, *Preliminary Statement to the Press of the United States* (Washington, DC: Government Printing Office, 1917).

50. Wilkinson, *Secrecy and the Media,* 490.

51. *New York Times,* May 28, 1917. *New York Globe,* May 29, 2917. A *New York World* editorial decried Lansing's addendum to Creel's guidelines. "Nothing could be less in harmony with the spirit of every word the President himself has spoken." *New York World,* May 29, 1917. Unsigned editorial, *New Republic,* June 2, 1917, 119. *Indianapolis News,* May 24, 1917. Seward W. Livermore, *Woodrow Wilson and the War Congress, 1916–1918* (Seattle: University of Washington Press, 1966), 36. Arthur Bullard to Edward M. House, May 24, 1917, box 9, AB.

52. *New York Evening Post,* June 1, 1917.

53. Stone, *Perilous Times,* 149. *PWW,* 43:247. *New York Times,* May 31, 1917. Burleson's interest in legislation is found in Burleson letters to two congressional leaders on the bill, George Chamberlain and Edwin Webb, both April 9, 1917, entry 2, PO. Thomas F. Carroll, "Freedom of Speech and of the Press in War Times: The Espionage Act," *Michigan Law Review* 17 (June 1919): 645.

54. *Congressional Record,* May 3, 1917, 1767. *New York World,* May 29, 1917.

55. Baker interview with Creel, May 23, 1932, box 103, RSB.

56. The Editor [George Harvey], "Fair Play for the Government and Whole Truth for the People," *North American Review,* June 1917, 823–24. Frank Cobb to Woodrow Wilson, May 22, 1917. David Lawrence in the *New York Evening Post,* July 6, 1917. Carl Ackerman to Edward M. House, May 24, 1917, box 1, EMH. "Publicity Bureau Plans Urged upon President," *Editor & Publisher,* July 7, 1917, 32. See House diary, May 20, 1917, in which he noted "Robert Adamson came to talk about the publicity plan we have in hand with Willcox." Details of joint proposal are in box 42, HM-LC. Oulahan, "Presidents and Publicity," chapter 22.

57. Stephen E. Ponder, "Executive Publicity and Congressional Resistance, 1905–1913: Congress and the Roosevelt Administration's PR Men," *Congress & the Presidency* 13 (1986): 178, 182–83. *Congressional Record,* May 24, 1917, 5420, and May 25, 1918, 7054.

58. George Creel, "The Limits of Censorship," *Public Opinion Quarterly* 6 (Spring 1942): 9. *HWAA,* 20. Copies of the War College bill may be found in box 573, JD. For a comment on the US military's interest in DORA see "Congress to Provide Adequate Censorship," *Editor & Publisher,* March 17, 1917, 27. Herbert Corey, *Cincinnati Times-Star,* undated story in box OV6, GC. Also see *New York Times,* August 12, 1917, and "Comedy of Errors in Censorship of News," *Editor & Publisher,* June 30, 1917, 6. The *Army and Navy Register,* a service newspaper, denounced Creel's July Fourth "elaboration," "Creel Criticized by Service Paper," *Fourth Estate,* July 21, 1917, 8.

59. *HWAA,* 28–29. More detail can be gleaned from *New York Times,* June 29, July 6 and 8, 1917; *Chicago Tribune,* July 5, 1917; *New York Morning Telegraph,* July 4, 6, and 7, 1917; and "Confidential Notice to the Press" July 5, 1917, entry 5, CPI. Creel denies Baker temporarily withdrew his authority. *New York Times,* July 6, 1917.

60. Gus Karger, *Cincinnati Times-Star,* May 14, 1917. Karger was chairman of the Standing Committee of Washington Correspondents, which regulated the portals to the Capitol Hill press galleries. *New York Evening Post,* May 24, 1917.

61. *Washington Herald,* May 23, 24, and 25, 1917. Creel's statement can be found in entry 2-A1, CND. *Indianapolis News,* May 24, 1917.

62. The cables are reproduced in Walton E. Bean, "The Accuracy of Creel Committee News, 1917–1919: An Examination of Cases," *Journalism Quarterly* 18 (September 1941): 264. *New York Times,* July 7, 1917. *Official Bulletin,* July 5, 1917, 1.

63. *New York Evening Telegram,* July 6, 1917, which describes Creel's reaction and his admission of how he wrote his statement. When Daniels asked the AP to kill the story, it dutifully sent out a message to that end, but it was too late. Stone, *Fifty Years a Journalist,* 327. A good summary of what went wrong with the AP report is Melville E. Stone to George Creel, April 17, 1918, and J. R. P. Pringle to Commander US Naval Forces Operating in European Waters, August 3, 1917, entry 1, CPI. Pringle concluded the AP reporter was "more sinned against that sinning."

64. Boies Penrose, "Activities of Committee on Public Information," *Congressional Record,* July 24, 1917, 5415 and 5416. For a portrait of Penrose see Anonymous [C. W. Gilbert], *The Mirrors of Washington* (New York: G. P. Putnam's, 1921), 229–41, and Paul Beers, *Pennsylvania Politics Today and Yesterday* (University Park: Pennsylvania State University, 1980), 49. *New York Evening Telegraph,* July 4, 1917. *New York World,* August 2, 1917. The navy report and a discussion of the incident is found in *Hearing,* 25–30.

65. *New York Globe,* August 1, 1917. *Washington Post,* July 29, 1917.

66. "What the Government Asks of the Press," press release, July 30, 1917, entry 5, CPI. "New War Rules Are Issued," *Fourth Estate,* August 4, 1917, 6. *Boston Globe,* July 29, 1917. *New York Times,* July 31 and August 1, 1917.

67. *New York Sun,* August 5, 1917. *New York Times,* August 7, 1917. The *Sun* reported the criticism by army officers who said Creel emphasized favorable news. For an example of efforts to establish a workable relationship with the army see "Memorandum for the Secretary of War," July 7, 1919, entry 6, CPI. This is unsigned and on War Department stationery.

68. David Lawrence, "'Not for Publication,'" *Saturday Evening Post,* December 1, 1917, 101. On Williams monitoring the CPI see James Williams to Theodore G. Joslin, October 8 and October 15, 1917, box 30, JTW. *Evening Transcript* article, n.d., box OV7, GC.

69. *New York Times,* August 7, 1917.

70. Frank Cobb to Edward M. House, August 2, 1917, box 28; Robert Woolley to House, July 11, 1917, box 124, EMH. Also, Vance McCormick to Woolley, April 18, 1917; Woolley to McCormick, August 29, 1917, box 12, RWW.

71. Walter Williams to Josephus Daniels, July 10, 1917, box 573, JD. R. G. Rhett communication to White House, September 1, 1917, WW-LC.

72. *New York Sun,* July 30, 1917.

73. Blum, *Tumulty,* 133–34. Joseph Tumulty to Woodrow Wilson, July 12 and October 19, 1917, January 21, 1918, box 5, JPT. Years later, *New York Times* Washington correspondent Delbert Clark wrote that Creel created the "institutions of the government press agent and the handout.... When the war ended and with it this voluntary censorship, the value of the press agent and the handout had become so apparent to the Executive Branch of the government that they were never discarded." Clark, *Washington Dateline* (New York: Frederick A. Stokes, 1941), 119.

74. *New York Sun,* August 5, 1917. *New York Times,* August 31, 1917. *HFIL,* 323. George Creel, speech, typescript, [Indianapolis, 1918], box 5, GC. James Williams to L. Ames Brown, July 9, 1917, box 29, JTW. Rochester, *Report of the Director of the Official U.S. Bulletin to the Chairman of the Committee on Public Information,* 3.

75. Allen, "Government Influence on News in the United States during the World War," 159–61. George Creel to Woodrow Wilson, December 26, 1917; Wilson to Creel, December 31, 1917, WW-

LC. *Third Annual Report of the United States Council of National Defense* (Washington, DC: Government Printing Office, 1919), 59.

76. David Lawrence to Oswald Garrison Villard, July 25, 1917, box 134, DL. Creel to US Representative Henry A. Barnhart, September 5, 1918, entry 1, CPI. Wilson also objected to curtailing the amount of handout material because he did not want to rile legislators who saw personal advantage in sending out "practically everything the government publishes." Woodrow Wilson to George Creel, December 31, 1917, WW-LC. "Government Publicity," *Editor & Publisher,* June 15, 1918, 22.

77. *Washington Herald,* November 29, 1918. Correspondents to CPI, September 28, 1918, entry 6, box 5 CPI. Arthur Sweetser, "Lansing Gags State Department," undated note, box 3, AS. "Newspapers of the Country Are Flooded with Publicity Copy from Washington," *Editor & Publisher,* March 16, 1918, 7.

78. Stone, *Perilous Times,* 137. Donald Johnson, "Wilson, Burleson, and Censorship in the First World War," *Journal of Southern History* 28 (February 1962), 48, 50. Unsigned editorial, *New Republic,* July 21, 1917, 316.

79. *New York Evening Post,* June 1, 1917.

80. Daniels's mailbox overflowing with letters from contrite journalists can be found in box 573, JD. Charles E. Kloeber to Melvin Stone, September 22, 1917, 3, AP. *New York Times,* July 31, 1917. *Los Angeles Times,* June 15, 1917. Oulahan, "Presidents and Publicity," chapter 22.

81. George Creel, "Remarks of Mr. George Creel," *HWAA,* 17. George Creel to Woodrow Wilson, November 28, 1917, box 3, GC.

5. ALL MEN MUST HARKEN TO MY MESSAGE

1. *Rebel,* 97. Harvey O'Higgins to George Creel, November 4, 1918, entry 1, CPI.

2. Will Irwin, *The Making of a Reporter* (New York: G. P. Putnam, 1942), 354. Irwin, *Propaganda and the News; or, What Makes You Think So?* (New York: Whittlesey House, 1936), 184. History on the buildings can be found in Benjamin Ogle Tayloe, *Our Neighbors on La Fayette Square: Anecdotes and Reminiscences; Selections from in Memoriam* (Washington, DC: privately printed 1872 and reprinted Junior League of Washington, n.d.); Lonnie J. Hovey, *Lafayette Square* (Charleston, SC: Arcadia, 2014). The CPI-related photo on page 51 of Hovey's book is almost certainly misdated.

3. Caleb Stephens, *Worst Seat in the House: Henry Rathbone's Front Row View of the Lincoln Assassination* (Fredericksburg, VA: Willow Manor, 2014), passim. *HWAA,* 71.

4. Ralph Hayes to Newton Baker, September 20, 1917, box 255, NDB. Details on the appearance of the CPI headquarters and on his encounter with Creel is in SWW, 8–9. See also *Hearing,* 140; Zoe Beckley, *Indianapolis News,* November 11, 1917; EKE [E. K. Ellsworth] to Walter S. Gifford, February 5, 1917, entry 2-A1, CND; and Guy Stanton Ford, "America's Fight for Public Opinion," *Minnesota History Bulletin* 3 (February 1919): 11. The contents of Creel's office are listed in "Inventory of Furniture and Fixtures in Executive Office," n.d., entry 1, CPI.

5. SWW, 14.

6. SWW, 14, 34.

7. Background on the Chicago origins of the organization is in *The Four Minute Men of Chicago* (Chicago: History Committee of the Four Minute Men, 1919), passim.

8. Wayne Alfred Nicholas, "Crossroads Oratory: A Study of the Four Minute Men of World War I" (PhD diss., Columbia University, 1953), 64.

9. Nicholas, "Crossroads Oratory," 65.

10. McGerr, *The Decline of Popular Politics,* 25. Homer Cummings to Woodrow Wilson, De-

cember 12, 1916, box 68, HSC. Lisa Mastrangelo, "World War I, Public Intellectuals, and the Four Minute Men: Convergent Ideals of Public Speaking and Civic Participation," *Rhetoric & Public Affairs* 12 (2009): 607.

11. *HWAA*, 84–85.

12. Detail on the beginnings of the Four Minute Men is in *Four Minute Men News,* Edition F, Historical, December 24, 1918, and a companion supplement. The *News,* as I shall refer to it hereafter, and the *Four Minute Men Bulletin,* which is shortened in this chapter to *Bulletin,* are scattered throughout CPI files and organized in WMB. Alfred E. Cornebise, *War as Advertised: The Four Minute Men and America's Crusade, 1917–1918* (Philadelphia: American Philosophical Society, 1984), 7.

13. Harvey O'Higgins, n.d., in farewell note on Blair's departure. WMB. Gundlach's skills are discussed in Ford oral history, 393. Blair's organizational abilities were highly praised when he resigned to join the military. See letters in WMB.

14. *WWW,* 115. Report on the Organization and Activities of the State Councils of Defense, June 18, 1917, box 65, EMH. Newton Baker to Woodrow Wilson, July 24, 1918, box 8, NDB. G. B. Clarkson, Field Division report, October 1, 1918, entry 18A-B3, CND. *News,* Edition F, Supplement; William J. Breen, *Uncle Sam at Home: Civilian Mobilization, Wartime Federalism, and the Council of National Defense, 1917–1919* (Westport, CT: Greenwood, 1984), xvi, 34–35. Baker was chairman of the Council of National Defense.

15. *WWW,* 118. *News,* Edition F, Historical.

16. *News,* Edition B, January [n.d.] 1917. On Clark's advice to the Democrats, see Donald L. Morrill to Thomas J. Walsh, October 6, 1917, and Walsh to Morrill, October 7, 1916, box 173, TJW. For background on advisors, see Nicholas, "Crossroads Oratory," 111–14. Biographical data on Martin is in finding aid, Mac Martin Adverting Agency Papers, Minnesota Historical Society.

17. George Creel to Josephus Daniels, June 21, 1917, box 73, JD. Nicholas, "Crossroads Oratory," 96–97. William McCormick Blair to Harvey O'Higgins, June 24, 1918, entry 49, CPI.

18. "Excerpts from Speeches," *News,* Edition B.

19. William McCormick Blair to Arthur Bestor and John Pettijohn, May 16, 198, entry 49, CPI.

20. *Tennessean,* July 24, 1917. Breen, *Uncle Sam at Home,* 99. For background on Dunlap and state politics see "History of Tennessee State Treasurers (1836–Present)," Tennessee Department of Treasury; *Tennessean,* May 30 and November 15, 1914, January 7, 1915, October 22, 1916, and January 25, 1917; *Tennessee Blue Book, 1937–1938* (Nashville: A. B. Broadbent, 1938), 112; and Dewey W. Grantham, "Tennessee and Twentieth-Century American Politics," *Tennessee History Quarterly* 54 (1995): 211. The recollection of Dunlap's tenure as state treasurer is from his obituary in the *Tennessean,* February 8, 1954.

21. Henry Atwater to Porter Dunlap, August 2, 1917, and William McCormick Blair to chairmen, August 25, 1917, TFMM. Blair to Dunlap, December 7, 1917, TFMM.

22. *News,* Edition B.

23. William McCormick Blair to chairmen, November 8, 1917, TFMM.

24. *WWW,* 113. *Report,* 29. William McCormick Blair to chairmen, October 12, 1917, TFMM. Cornebise, *War as Advertised,* 50. Nicholas, "Crossroads Oratory," 251.

25. Porter Dunlap to William McCormick Blair, May 19, 1918, TFMM. *News,* Edition E.

26. *News,* Edition F, Historical.

27. *News,* Edition B. *The Four Minute Men of Chicago,* 17–18M. Guy Bishop, "Strong Voices and 100 Per Cent Patriotism: The Four-Minute Men of Los Angeles County, 1917–1918," *Southern California Quarterly* 77 (Fall 1992): 200.

28. *HWAA,* 94. *Bulletin,* no. 7.

29. *Bulletin,* nos. 7 and 7a. Nicholas, "Crossroads Oratory," 148.

30. *Bulletin,* nos. 17 and 7a.

31. *Bulletin,* nos. 16, 29, and 34. *News,* Edition D.

32. Wm. H. Ingersoll, "The Body," in George William Poole and Johnathan John Buzell, *Letters That Make Good: A Desk Book for Business Men* (Boston, American Business Book Co., 1915), 50–51. *Bulletin,* nos. 3 and 30. *News,* Edition E, October 1, 1918.

33. William McCormick Blair to Porter Dunlap, December 27, 1917, TFMM. Nicholas, "Crossroads Oratory," 218. *Tennessean,* August 1, 1918.

34. *Bulletin,* no. 7a.

35. "Four Minute Men," report from State Councils of Defense, September 21, 1917, entry 15-C1, CND. According to 1920 US Census data, Tennessee had an illiteracy rate of 10 percent, versus 8 percent nationally. *News,* Edition B. Porter Dunlap to William McCormick Blair, March 29, 1918; Dunlap to local chairs, May 2, 1918, TFMM. *Tennessean,* December 6, 1918.

36. W. Curtis Nicholson to Porter Dunlap, April 19, 1918, TFMM.

37. Nicholas, "Crossroads Oratory," 72, 117, 119. *Tennessean,* May 2, August 26, and October 9, 1918.

38. W. Curtis Nicholson to Porter Dunlap, April 19, 1918, TFMM. *Tennessean,* November 3, 1918. Cornebise, "War as Advertised," 23. Nicholas, "Crossroads Oratory," 72, 74. *Tennessean,* September 30, 1917; May 31 and July 4 and 14, 1918.

39. *News,* Edition F, Supplement. *Tennessean,* January 19, 1918. Daniel C. Roper to Chambers of Commerce and other organizations, March 5, 1918, TFMM.

40. *School Bulletin,* nos. 1 and 3. *News,* Edition F, Supplement.

41. Glenn N. Merry, "National Defense and Public Speaking," *Quarterly Journal of Speech Education* 4 (1918): 57. Mary Yost, "Training Four Minute Men at Vassar," *Quarterly Journal of Speech Education* 5 (May 1919): 246, 151.

42. Cornebise, "War as Advertised," 32. Richard Melzer, "Stage Soldiers of the Southwest: New Mexico's Four Minute Men of World War I," *Military History of the Southwest* 20 (Spring 1990), 31. *HWAA,* 93. *Bulletin,* no. 38.

43. *Bulletin,* no. 17, Supplement. *News,* Edition E.

44. *New Orleans Times-Picayune,* October 22, 1917. O. A. Nicklaus to William McCormick Blair, February 26, 1918; Blair to Nicklaus, March 4, 1918, entry 13J-A3, CND. Martha Evans Martin to Mrs. Sumner B. Pearmain, April 9, 1918, entry 13J-A1, CND. "Report of the Fourteen Minute Women Speakers Bureau for the First Six Months of Its Organization," July 12, 1918, entry 13J-A1, CND. Nicholas, "Crossroads Oratory," 214.

45. Fred A. Wirth, "The Four Minute Men," *Quarterly Journal of Speech Education* 5 (January–October 1919): 61–62.

46. In an undated [1917], untitled memorandum, Bestor outlined the problem of having so many speakers. Also see "Records of the First Meeting Conference on Speakers," n.d. [1918]; "League to Enforce Peace," October 12, 1917, entry 79, CPI.

47. Committee to George Creel, September 6, 1917, and "Plan of Organization of Speaking Division," n.d., entry 82; Ford to Bestor, September 14, 1917, entry 79, CPI. See also Secretary of Conference to George Creel, September 5, 1917, entry 13, CPI.

48. "Free Speech Issue, Climax to Bestor Talk," *City Club Bulletin,* Chicago, n.d. [1917], box 124, AEB. In July 1917, Chautauqua hosted an NSL training camp for volunteer speakers involved in "Patriotic Service." Creel, Solomon Clark, and Ryerson also spoke.

49. For a summary of coordination of these groups see untitled, typewritten report, n.d. [1917], no doubt written by Bestor, entry 79, CPI; and Nicholas, "Crossroads Oratory," 133–38.

50. Arthur Bestor to John H. Patterson, February 27, 1918, entry 75; Bestor to George Creel, May 13, 1918, entry 79, CPI. Arthur E. Bestor, "The War and the Making of Public Opinion," Philadelphia, December 18, 1917, used by the Publicity Department of the Committee of Public Safety for the Commonweal of Pennsylvania, box 124, AEB.

51. "Meetings Addressed by Private Raymond Guyette" and "Schedule of Dates of Iowa Pershing Soldiers," n.d., entry 89, CPI. [?] to George Creel, June 15, 1918, entry 89, CPI. [?] Klein to Leonard Omerad, May 22, 1918, entry 89; Arthur Bestor to Guy Stanton Ford, May 28, 1918, entry 28, CPI. *Nashville Banner,* May 25 and 26, 1918. See "Blue Devils," May 14, 1918, entry 89, CPI.

52. Walter Gifford, "A National Picture Puzzle," *Independent,* May 5, 1917, 237. Donald Wilhelm, "The Mobilizer-in-Chief," *Independent,* May 5, 1917, 236. "Speakers Campaigns Inaugurated," report, October 4, 1917, entry 15-C1, CND. *Official Bulletin,* March 2, 1918. Arthur Bestor to William McCormick Blair, May 25, 1918, entry 67, CPI.

53. Nicholas, "Crossroads Oratory," 138. *News,* Edition F, Historical. The CPI's listing of war conferences does not include one in Tennessee, but as noted below, the CND had a longer list. *Report,* 36. The Tennessee Women's Committee of the Council of National Defense held a war conference in May 1918; see Isabelle Wilson, "Report of Educational Propaganda," n.d., entry 13J-A2, CND. William F. Saunders to Arthur Bestor, April 3, 1918, entry 82, CPI.

54. Transcript of Council of National Defense state speakers' bureaus, Chicago, Illinois, November 17, 1917, entry 82, CPI. On grading "patriotic citizens," typewritten report, no title, n.d., entry 79, CPI. Typescript drafts of tip sheets for speakers can be found in entry 67, CPI. Advisory Committee meeting, November 26, 1917, entry 82, CPI.

55. Byron Shimp to Joseph G. Brown, May 23, 1918, entry 88, CPI. Arthur Bestor to Guy Stanton Ford, May 28, 1918, entry 28, CPI. [?] to Shimp, May 22, 1918; "The Report of the Activities of the Fifty Returned Pershing Soldiers," July 2, 1918, entry 88, CPI.

56. Blair hoped to leave earlier, but Ingersoll was reluctant to take over. After Ingersoll agreed, concerns arose about Justice Department litigation over price fixing of dollar watches, but he ended up being appointed. William McCormick Blair to Donald Ryerson, August 20, 1918, WMB. Frederick Allen to Arthur Fleming, July 13, 1918, entry 15-C1, CND. Allen to his mother, July 14, 1917, box 27, FLA. Bestor thought the merger unwise. See Arthur Bestor to John Pettijohn, July 23, 1918, entry 49, CPI.

57. Allen, "draft letter to Major Smith," August 1918, entry 15-C1, CND. Pettijohn worked on university war mobilization before coming to the CPI. Frederick Allen to Arthur Fleming, July 15, 1918, entry 15-C1, CND. John Pettijohn to H. H. Weir, October 22, 1918, entry 75, CPI.

58. Frederick Allen to Grosvenor B. Clarkson, October 11, 1918, entry 18A-B3, CND. *HWAA,* 150. "Publicity Material on Aviation Tour," n.d., entry 82, CPI.

59. SWW, 35. Thomas J. Mahon to Shimp, November 16, 1917, and other letters of praise for Russel's oratorical prowess, box 8, CER. Harold Ickes to Arthur Bestor, April 4, 1918, entry 82, CPI. *HWAA,* 152. *News,* Edition F, Historical.

60. E. H. West to Porter Dunlap, April 2, 1918, TFMM.

61. W. Curtis Nicholson to Porter Dunlap, April 11, 1918, and Dunlap to Nicholson, May 1, 1918, TFMM. On state government funding see Mable [?] to Martha Evans Martin, August 1, 1918, entry 2-A1, CND. Dunlap's letter asking local chairs for money is May 2, 1918, TFMM. *News,* Edition B. Nicholas, "Crossroads Oratory," 141. About twenty-six hundred chairs had franking privileges, *News,* Edition F, Historical.

62. Lafayette Young, "Memorandum Relative to Four-Minute-Men," September 18, 1917, entry 15-C1, CND. Nicholas Marcus Loew to George Creel, January 31, 1918, entry 1, CPI.

63. The comment on the speaker and the "sweet little gal" was made by Frederick J. Haskin, a syndicated writer, in the *Tennessean*, November 19, 1917. Cards for Purvis and Farrow are in entry 64, CPI. Nicholas, "Crossroads Oratory," 106. John M. Barry, *The Great Influenza* (New York: Penguin, 2004), 344, 347, 359, 397.

64. Porter Dunlap to William McCormick Blair, May 24, 1918, TFMM. *News,* Edition D.

65. Unless otherwise noted, statistics reported here are from *News,* Edition F, Historical. The number of chairmen is derived by adding those in lodges with total immediately above it on page 5.

66. Data on speakers are on cards in entry 64, CPI. Nicholas, "Crossroads Oratory," 189.

67. Melzer, "Stage Soldiers of the Southwest," 31. Nicholas, "Crossroads Oratory," 127, 232. Edward Clifford, "Selling the First Installment of the Liberty Loan," report of the Seventh Federal Reserve District, 1917, 10. *News,* Edition F, Historical. W. H. Lambeth, to George Creel, April 30, 1918, entry 1, CPI; *Tennessean,* October 11, 1918.

68. Daniel Okrent, *Last Call: The Rise and Fall of Prohibition* (New York: Scribner, 2010), 79.

69. Greenberg, *Republic of Spin,* 192. The point on Four Minute Men prefiguring FDR's radio speeches is from Elmer E. Cornwell, "Wilson, Creel, and the Presidency," *Public Opinion* 23 (Summer 1959): 195.

70. *Tennessean,* December 6, 1917.

6. YOU'VE GOT TO CHANGE THEIR ENVIRONMENT

1. *Richmond Times-Dispatch,* January 13 and 14, 1918. *HWAA,* 153–54. On the marriage of Marquis de Polignac see *Washington Times,* October 24, 1917. Charles Edward Russell to George Creel, January 22, 1918, entry 1, CPI.

2. Poole, *The Bridge,* 267–68.

3. Irwin, *Propaganda and the News,* 195–96. Frederick Allen to H., July 4, 1918, box 1, FLA.

4. Carl Byoir to Executive Committee, YMCA, May 17, 1918, entry 5, CPI. George Creel, speech, typescript, [July 29, 1918], box 5, GC.

5. Fowler, *Timber Line,* 324. Wilhelm, "Our Uncensorious Censor," 43.

6. Robert Jackall and Janice M. Hirota, *Image Makers: Advertising, Public Relations, and the Ethos of Advocacy* (Chicago: University of Chicago Press, 2000), 32.

7. *HWAA,* 4. Arthur E. Bestor, "How to Advertise a War Rally," n.d., typescript, entry 49, and Bestor form letter to Rotary Clubs, n.d., entry 79, CPI. Nicholas, "Crossroads Oratory," 283. William Ingersoll to Arthur Bestor, November 2, 1917, entry 75, CPI. Ingersoll had been president of the Advertising Men's League of New York. On Ingersoll's background see *Four Minute Men News,* Edition E.

8. *Report,* 40. Scott M. Cutlip, *The Unseen Power: Public Relations, a History* (Hillside, NJ: Lawrence Erlbaum, 1994), 28 and passim for the early years of publicity. Reichenbach spelled out his idea for Loyalty Day in communication to Will Irwin, June 4, 1918, entry 1, CPI. Terry Ramsaye, *A Million and One Nights: A History of the Motion Picture through 1925* (London: Frank Cass, 1954), 626. David Freedman, "In Conclusion," in Harry Reichenbach, *Phantom Fame: The Anatomy of Ballyhoo* (New York: Simon and Schuster, 1931), 256–58. In his book, Reichenbach describes his stint in Montevideo, 119–22. See also *Fourth Estate,* August 26, 1916, 29. A third pioneer in public relations was Ivy Lee. Lee represented John D. Rockefeller, who brutally broke a strike in his Colorado mines—a cause in which Creel was on the strikers' side. But as publicity advisor to the American Red Cross,

Lee worked with the CPI. See, for instance, Ivy Lee to George Creel, January 4, 1918, entry 1, and Lee to F. D. Casey, October 29, 1917, entry 5, CPI. In addition to the ad executives mentioned in this and the previous chapter, the associate editor of the *Four Minute Men Bulletin* was Charles Henry Mackintoch, who had a Duluth advertising agency and was president of the Direct Mail Advertising Association. Cornebise, *War as Advertised,* 15.

9. Larry Tye, *The Father of Spin: Edward L. Bernays and the Birth of Public Relations* (New York: Crown, 1998), 12–18. Edward Bernays, *New York Evening Post Magazine,* July 21, 1917. Poole, *The Bridge,* 335. Edward Bernays, *Biography of an Idea* (New York: Simon and Schuster, 1965), 157.

10. Byoir wrote a partial autobiography that unfortunately has been lost along with his papers. My profile of him comes largely from a master's thesis that drew from this material, Robert J. Bennett, "Carl Byoir; Public Relations Pioneer" (master's thesis, University of Wisconsin, 1968). I also draw from Cutlip, *The Unseen Power,* chapter 17 and 586.

11. "Possible War and the Advertising Idea in America," *Advertising & Selling,* March 1916, 7. *HFIL,* 142.

12. Samuel Hopkins Adams, "The New World of Trade: The Art of Advertising," *Collier's,* May 22, 1909, 15. George Creel, "Quacks and Quackery," *Independent,* August 11, 1906. For background on the emergence of professional advertising see Billy I. Ross and Jef I. Richards, *A Century of Advertising Education* (New York: American Academy of Advertising, 2008); John Gunther, *Taken at the Flood: The Story of Albert D. Lasker* (New York: Harper, 1960), 42. Stephen Fox, *The Mirror Makers: A History of American Advertising and Its Creators* (Urbana: University of Illinois Press, 1997), 68.

13. David M. Potter, *People of Plenty: Economic Abundance and the American Character* (Chicago: University of Chicago Press, 1954), 169. William Leach, *Land of Desire: Economic Abundance and the American Character* (New York: Random House, 1993), 61. James Fraser, *The American Billboard: 100 Years* (New York: Harry N. Abrams, 1991), 8–14.

14. Edd Applegate, *The Rise of Advertising in the United States: A History of Innovation to 1960* (Lanham, MD: Roman and Littlefield, 2012), 37. A good discussion of the mania of professionalism is in Sidney Ralph Bernstein, typescript history of J. Walter Thompson, n.d., IV, 14–19, Sidney Ralph Bernstein Company History Files, box 10, JWT. On chaotic ad placement see "President Praises Division of Advertising for Splendid Work in War Campaigns," *Editor & Publisher,* May 11, 1918, 9–10ff. A good summary of the board's work in the early Liberty Loan campaigns is in Herbert S. Houston to William McAdoo, January 21, 1917, entry 5, CPI. Woolley put in a good word for Houston with the CPI. Robert Woolley to George Creel, April 18, 1917, box 4, RWW. As soon as the war began, the Associated Advertising Clubs wired McAdoo to say it wanted to be the "advertising arm of the Government." Houston to McAdoo, April 3, 1917, box 176, 1917, WGM.

15. For an example of views in favor of paid-for advertising see W. C. D'Arcy, "Advertising Needed to Unify Country's Mind," *Editor & Publisher,* September 15, 1917, 6. An editorial in the same issue notes that many in the press agreed with D'Arcy. See also "The Greatest Selling Task in the World's History," *Editor & Publisher,* April 28, 1917, 28; "Put an End to Bungling in the Great Bond Sale," *Editor & Publisher,* May 19, 1917, 18; "Woolley Admits That Congress Made Error," *Editor & Publisher,* June 23, 1917, 14; "Bond Advertising Now Up to Senate," *Editor & Publisher,* September 8, 1917, 30; "Benjamin Strong Urges Preparation for Next Government Issue," *Financier,* June 23, 1917, 1741; and "Liberty Loan Publicity Report," Liberty Loan Committee, Second Federal Reserve District, July 1917, 22–23, box 5, LLCR. For the government view see "Guy Emerson Raises Objections to Paid Advertising Policy," *Editor & Publisher,* March 2, 1917, 8. See also *HFIL,* 141–48, and *HWAA,* 156–57. *Congressional Record,* September 6, 1917, 1917, 6698.

16. James O'Shaughnessy to "Dear Member," February 9, 1918, entry 97A, CPI. George Creel

to Ivy Lee, January 23, 1918, entry 1, CPI. "Plan for a Patriotic Demonstration of Advertisers," *Printers' Ink,* November 22, 1917, 88. For an example of McClary's previous activism see *Chicago Tribune,* January 24, 1917.

17. George Creel to Herbert S. Houston, December 1, 1917; Houston to Creel, November 21 and December 8, 1917, entry 1, CPI. "National Advertisers in Convention Name Men to Aid Government Win War," *Editor & Publisher,* December 8, 1917, 7–8ff.

18. George Creel to William Johns, December 21, 1917, entry 4, CPI. For relevant articles during this time see "Uncle Sam Forms an Official Advertising Department," *Advertising & Selling,* January 1918; "Ad Division for Government," and "Specials to Aid Patriotic Ads," *Fourth Estate,* December 22, 1917, and January 12, 1918; and "Advertised Business in War to Be Discussed by A.N.A.," *Printers' Ink,* December 13, 1917. John Sullivan, secretary-treasurer of the ANA, said his organization was responsible for the division. "This is the whole Truth, and nothing but the Truth," he asserted in an article, "The Truth about the Division of Advertising," *Advertising News,* July 20, 1918. His account of the meeting with McClary purposely does not name the executive who asked her to see Creel. His account is reprised in a subsequent unsigned article, "Credit to Whom Credit Is Due," *Advertising News,* July 27, 1918. William C. D'Arcy, president of the Associated Advertising Clubs of the World, insisted his clubs were "the sole progenitors of the Division of Advertising." William C. D'Arcy, "The Achievements of Advertising in a Year," *Printers' Ink,* July 11, 1918, 18.

19. Eula McClary to Carl Byoir, January 21, 1918, entry 4, CPI. Rankin's disappointment over not being selected is in his letter to Byoir, February 23, 1918, entry 5, CPI. For example, of how much a seat on the board meant to the prestige of advertisers see Thomas Cusack to William D'Arcy, July 27, 1917, entry 97A, CPI.

20. William McAdoo to George Creel, January 5 and 8, 1918; Creel to McAdoo, January 11, 1918, entry 1, CPI. In his letter, Creel reminded McAdoo that he had opposed the CPI's organization of the film industry, speakers, and artists, "but today all three of these bodies are among your most valuable assets." *Hearing,* 87.

21. William Johns to William D'Arcy, January 2, 1918, entry 97A; and Johns to Carl Byoir, telegram [January 1918], entry 99, CPI. "Purpose and Scope of the Work of the Division of Advertising," Division of Advertising, Bulletin no. 1, June 1, 1918, 2. Although this bulletin puts the date of recognition as January 20, a press release indicates the date was the day before. Both can be found in entry 98, CPI. George Creel to William McAdoo, December 22, 1917, entry 1, CPI. This letter includes a list of the other officials to whom it was sent.

22. Lewis B. Jones to Carl Byoir, April 9, 1918, entry 99, CPI. William Johns to George Creel, February 27, 1918, entry 4, CPI. Jackall and Hirota, *Image Makers,* 34. Cusack's and Neal's lobbying for a role is seen in their correspondence in entry 4, CPI.

23. "Purely Personal," *Fourth Estate,* March 23, 1918, 19. James O'Shaughnessy, Member Bulletin no. 6, December 24, 1917; O'Shaughnessy, letter to members, January 23, 1918; Minutes of the Executive Board of AAAA, October 8, 1918, AAAA.

24. H.A.L. to Frank Presbrey Company, February 26, 1918, entry 97A, CPI. For free services by printers see C.A.H. to Jesse H. Neal, May 24, 1918, entry 97A, CPI.

25. "Memorandum for Mr. Jones," March 6, 1918; P. S. Florea to Terrell Marston, October 1, 1918, entry 97A, CPI. "Purpose and Scope of the Work of the Division of Advertising," 3. George Creel to Augustine Longergan, January 4, 1918, entry 1 CPI. Creel to Edward Percy Hoard, editor of *American Press,* January 2, 1918, entry 99, CPI.

26. William Johns to R. F. Ayers, February 11, 1918, entry 97A, CPI. On wanting the privilege of running patriotic ads see Adv. Mgr. to George Creel, July 2, 1918, as well as, for example, J. A. Van Buren, *New Orleans Times-Picayune,* to CPI, August 27, 1918, entry 97A, CPI. *Editor & Publisher*

remained vocal in is objections to the government paying for advertising space; see for instance "Editorial," *Editor & Publisher,* May 25, 1918, 24. *HWAA,* 159.

27. *New York Times,* January 20, 1918. William Johns to William D'Arcy, February 7, 1918, entry 97A, CPI. Meeting notices can be found in entry 97A.

28. William Johns to George Creel, December 24, 1918, entry 1, CPI. Lewis Jones to Carl Byoir, April 17, 1918, entry 99, CPI. *Editor & Publisher,* March 1, 1919, 9.

29. Carl Byoir to William Johns, January 26, 1918, entry 99, CPI. George Creel to Charles Gibson, April 17, 1917, entry 163, WDGS. Eric Van Schaack, "The Division of Pictorial Publicity in World War I," *Design Issues* 22 (Winter 2006): 33. *WWW,* 101. Creel to Gibson, November 8, 1917, entry 1, CPI.

30. Gibson asked for official presidential sanction for the division so that it could make the claim it was "truly national." Charles Gibson to George Creel, January 28, 1918, entry 1, CPI. Creel to Gibson, January 31, 1918, entry 1, CPI. *Philadelphia Record,* January 27, 1918.

31. *New York Times,* January 20, 1918; George L. Vogt, "When Posters Went to War: How America's Best Commercial Artists Helped Win World War I," *Wisconsin Magazine of History* 84 (Winter 2000): 47. Susan E. Meyer, *James Montgomery Flagg* (New York: Watson-Guptill, 1974). 37. Some details on Gibson's division can be found in a program prepared to celebrate its work at the end of the war. Cass Gilbert, "Division of Pictorial Publicity," no publisher, 1919, no page numbers.

32. *Milwaukee Journal,* August 18, 1918. The Madonna theme was picked up by others, including artist Harrison Fisher. Wilmot Lippincott, *Outdoor Advertising* (New York: McGraw-Hill, 1923), 233.

33. William Johns to George Creel, November 20, 1918, entry 100, box 2, CPI. A list of publications can be found in box 1 of that entry. *WWW,* 106, 161. Gibson's subsequent reports to Creel showed a sharp increase in output. His report on work accomplished from October 1917 through February 1918 was twice the length of the first one, which covered a slightly longer period. Gibson, Reports, October 1, 1917, and March 1, 1918, entry 5, CPI.

34. "Government Advertising Foundation Is Laid," *Editor & Publisher,* December 30, 30ff. Jackall and Hirota, *Image Makers,* 23. Schaack, "The Division of Pictorial Publicity in World War I," 22. *New York Times,* January 20, 1918. William Johns to George Creel, October 15, 1918, entry 100, box 1, CPI.

35. Bliven oral history, 19. Bruce Bliven to George Creel, June 27, 1918, entry 4, CPI. *HWAA,* 165.

36. Roland Marchand, *Advertising the American Dream* (Berkeley: University of California Press, 1985), 6. Jackson Lears, *Fables of Abundance: A Cultural History of Advertising in America* (New York: Basic Books, 1994), 221.

37. William H. Johns et al., *Government War Advertising: Report of the Division of Advertising* (Washington, DC: Government Printing Office, 1918), CPI.

38. Leach, *Land of Desire,* 41. E. W. Lightner, *Pittsburgh Dispatch,* November 16, 1919.

39. Richard Butsch, *The Making of American Audiences* (New York: Cambridge University Press, 2000), 146–48. Richard Koszarski, *An Evening's Entertainment* (New York: Charles Scribner's Sons, 1990), 12.

40. Welch, *Germany, Propaganda and Total War,* 46. Ian F. W. Beckett, *The Making of the First World War* (New Haven, CT: Yale University Press, 2012), 91.

41. Welch, *Germany, Propaganda and Total War,* 57. Harry Kessler, *Journey to the Abyss,* trans. Laird M. Easton (New York: Alfred A. Knopf, 2011), 753. Beckett, *The Making of the First World War,* 100. Hastings, *Catastrophe 1914,* 435.

42. Larry Wayne Ward, *The Motion Picture Goes to War: The U.S. Government Film Effort dur-*

ing World War I (Ann Arbor: UMI Research, 1885), 29, 33–34. Ward's treatment of the CPI's film activities is the best available. Welch, *Germany, Propaganda and Total War,* 53. Such a British film map is dated December 1917, WO 153/1348. By early 1917, British films had been sent to forty countries. John Buchan, memorandum, "Propaganda—a Department of Information," February 3, 1917, CAB 21/37. In July 1917, the New York office reported its films were in thirty cities. Geoffrey Butler to Herbert Montgomery, July 17, 1917, INF 395/75. Luke McKernan, "Propaganda, Patriotism and Profit: Charles Urban and British Official War Films in America during the First World War," *Film History* 14 (2002): 383.

43. *Rebel,* 133–39. Details on the Lindsey film are found in box 217, BBL. *Washington Times,* July 19, 1918. Creel, *Denver Post,* November 14, 1909.

44. "A Publicity Campaign about the Constructive Work of the Wilson Administration," n.d., box 12, RWW. It is unclear who wrote this, but the author probably was Woolley or D. H. MacAdam, who assisted Woolley. MacAdam had been the *St. Louis Post* correspondent in Washington before joining the administration.

45. Ward, *The Motion Picture Goes to War,* 18. Ramsaye, *A Million and One Nights,* 728.

46. Ward, *The Motion Picture Goes to War,* 24.

47. Leslie Midkiff DeBauche, *Reel Patriotism: The Movies and World War I* (Madison: University of Wisconsin Press, 1997), xvii. Brady had been one of those who proposed film assistance in Wilson's reelection. "Liberty Loan Publicity Report," 5. Ward, *The Motion Picture Goes to War,* 49–50. Kendall Banning to Frederick H. Elliott, May 19, 1917; Elliott to Banning, and Banning to Elliott, May 23, 1917; Banning to Elliott, May 29, 1917, entry 163, WDGS. Banning, a poet and magazine editor, also helped Woolley in this endeavor. Banning to Louis Fancher, May 19, 1917, entry 163, WDGS. William Brady to Joseph Tumulty, June 22, 1917, and George Creel to Tumulty, June 22, 1917, WW-LC. See also Creel to Josephus Daniels, May 18 and July 31, 1917, box 73, JD, and Ward, *The Motion Picture Goes to War,* 49–52.

48. Woodrow Wilson to George Creel, August 10, 1917; Wilson to William Brady, June 28, 1917, WW-LC.

49. *Official Bulletin,* July 19 and 30, 1917. The CPI used Clark in a film for overseas audiences. George Creel to Woodrow Wilson, October 17, 1917, WW-LC.

50. The resignation letter is Louis Mack to George Creel, April 8, 1918, entry 1, CPI. Ward, *The Motion Picture Goes to War,* 85–87.

51. Ward, *The Motion Picture Goes to War,* 96–97. Rufus Steele, "Progress Report of the Department of Scenarios an Outside Production," August 10, 1918, entry 13, CPI.

52. Sanders, "Wellington House and British Propaganda in the First World War," 138. Ward, *The Motion Picture Goes to War,* 84, 97.

53. Ward, *The Motion Picture Goes to War,* 106–7. *Hearing,* 74.

54. Ward, *The Motion Picture Goes to War,* 108–9. *Hearing,* 77.

55. James W. Castellan, Ron van Dopperen, and Cooper C. Graham, *American Cinematographers in the Great War, 1914–1918* (Herts, UK: John Libbey, 2014), 260.

56. David Mould, "Washington's War on Film: Government Film Production and Distribution, 1917–18," *Journal of the University Film Association* 32 (Summer 1918): 24.

57. *Hearing,* 8. [Elliott M. Sanger?] to Lawrence Rubel, May 1, 1918, entry 13, CPI. *WWW,* 155. George T. Blakey, *Historians on the Homefront: American Propagandists for the Great War* (Lexington: University Press of Kentucky, 1970), 68, 86.

58. W. H. Rankin, memorandum, August 8, 1918, entry 1, CPI. The number of visitors is from "Winning the World's Mind," *Chicago Commerce,* September 19, 1918, 1. Creel estimated two mil-

lion. *HWAA*, 145. "Plan of the U.S. Government War Exhibitions at the State Fairs in 1918," n.d., entry 6, box 5, CPI.

59. "The War Zone in America," *Outlook*, October 31, 1917, 321–22. *WWW*, 108. Michael T. Coventry, "'Editorials at a Glance': Cultural Policy, Gender, and Modernity in World War I Bureau of Cartoons," *Review of Policy Research* 24 (2007): 101.

60. Ramsaye, *A Million and One Nights*, 784. *HWAA*, 125. Ward, *The Motion Picture Goes to War*, 105.

61. George Creel to William McAdoo, May 23, 1918, entry 1, CPI.

62. Ford oral history, 370–71. I have drawn on his account to describe this episode and Ford's early involvement with the CPI. Ford discusses his letter to superintendents in letters to Waldo G. Leland, May 3 and May 4, 1917, box 1, NBHS.

63. Carol S. Gruber, *Mars and Minerva: World War I and the Uses of the Higher Learning in America* (Baton Rouge: Louisiana State University Press, 1975), 100, 226, 229. Robert A. McCaughey, *Stand, Columbia: A History of Columbia University in the City of New York, 1754–2004* (New York: Columbia University Press, 2003), 253. *Columbia's War Work* (New York: Alumni Federation of Columbia University, 1918), 3, 8, 21, 27, 30. This Columbia list, for instance, did not include Pitkin and Keppel. On the photography school see *New York World*, January 9, 1918.

64. Walter Lippmann to Charles Merz, April 11, and to House, April 12, 1917, box 14, EMH. James Boylan, *Pulitzer's School: Columbia University's School of Journalism, 1903–2003* (New York: Columbia University Press, 2003), 50–52. Walter B. Pitkin, "How Columbia University Can Serve the Country," February 8, 1917, box 666, CU. "Journalism Students Turn to War Service," *Editor & Publisher*, April 28, 1917, 46. Walter Pitkin to Nicholas Butler, April 10, 1917, box 666, CU.

65. Nicholas Butler to Walter Pitkin, May 21, 1917, box 666, CU. Pitkin's proposals can be found in these files. For Lippmann's continuing interest in Pitkin's scheme see Walter Lippmann to Pitkin, April 25, 1917, box 24, WL. For Pitkin's association with CND see Ferris Greenslet to James Shotwell, July 27, 1917, box 2, NBHS.

66. Gruber, *Mars and Minerva*, 103.

67. Roger L. Geiger, *The History of American Education: Learning and Culture from the Founding to World War II* (Princeton, NJ: Princeton University Press, 2015), 429. McCaughey, *Stand, Columbia*, 237. Thomas D. Snyder, ed., *120 Years of American Education: A Statistical Portrait* (Washington, DC: National Center for Education Statistics, 1993), passim.

68. Blakey, *Historians on the Homefront*, 4, 7. James Gray, *The University of Minnesota, 1851–1951* (Minneapolis: University of Minnesota Press, 1951), 182–85. This volume has a profile of Ford's personality. Applegate, *The Rise of Advertising in the United States*, 151. Edward Alsworth Ross, "The Diseases of Social Structure," *American Journal of Sociology* 24 (September 1918): 148. Nicholas Butler to Sir Gilbert Parker, December 26, 1917, FO 395/70. Some nine thousand Americans studied in Germany from 1820 to 1920. Gruber, *Mars and Minerva*, 17.

69. Squires, *British Propaganda*, 17. Gruber, *Mars and Minerva*, 66, 120–21. For an example of American scholars' appreciation of the Oxford approach see H. D. Foster to Waldo G. Leland, May 5, 1917, box 1, NBHS. J. F. Jameson to Guy Stanton Ford, April 19, 1917, box 34, GSF. Blakey, *Historians on the Homefront*, 16. Waldo G. Leland, "The National Board for Historical Service," in *Annual Report of the American Historical Association for the Year 1919* (Washington, DC: Government Printing Office, 1923), 1:162. As this report notes, the University of Wisconsin Department of History independently suggested that a "bureau of historical information" be established under the CPI. Shotwell oral history, 69. For examples how the NBHS referred to its intimate relationship with the CPI see Waldo G. Leland to J. Franklin Jameson, June 1, 1917, box 2; [?] to J. J. Pettijohn, September 18, 1917, box 3; [?] to Frank J. Klingberg, October 9, 1917, box 2, NBHS.

70. James Shotwell to F. C. Ensign, June 4, 1917, box 1, NBHS. Ford oral history, 371–72, 377–79; Guy Stanton Ford to Grace Ford, September 10, 1917, box 35, GSF. On Shotwell-Pitkin collaboration see Walter Lippmann to Walter Pitkin, April 25, 1917, box 25, WL; Pitkin to Shotwell, April 30 and June 11, 1917 (two letters this date); Shotwell to Pitkin, June 11, 1917, box 3, NBHS; C. H. Hull, to Pitkin, n.d., box 2, NBHS.

71. Leland, "The National Board for Historical Service," 180. C.H.H. to Butler, October 6, 1917; Geoffrey G. Butler to James Shotwell, July 6, 1917; [Dana C. Munro?] to Woodrow Wilson, January 15, 1918; C.H.H. to Ulrich B. Phillips, April 6, 1918, box 20, NBHS. Harold Josephson, "History for Victory: Board for Historical Service," *Mid-America: A Historical Review* 52 (July 1917): 221. J. Franklin Jameson to Robert Woodward, January 7, 1918, box 121, JFJ. Guy Stanton Ford to Waldo G. Leland, October 20, 1919, box 1, NBHS. The director of the service was Victor S. Clark, who described the intelligence gleaned from the German press (but does not mention the existence of the Enemy-Press Intelligence Service) in "The German Press and German Opinion," *Atlantic Monthly,* July 1918, 1–9. After the war he was more forthcoming in "The German Press and the War," *Historical Outlook,* November 1919, 425–28.

72. Ford oral history, 372–74. This story is not told the same way in *HWAA,* 101–2. *Report,* 15. Blakey, *Historians on the Homefront,* 39.

73. G. S. Ford, Circular no. 4, May 13, 1917, box 16, NBHS. *Report,* 15. The division was later renamed the Division of Civic and Educational Publications. See also Donald Wilhelm, "The Government's Own Publicity Work," *Review of Reviews,* November 1917, 510; Ford oral history, 372–75; *WWW,* 159; *HFIL,* 100; and William E. Connelley, "J. W. Searson," in *A Standard History of Kansas and Kansans* (Topeka, KS: Lewis, 1918), 228. Donald Wilhelm, "The Government's Own Publicity Work," *Review of Reviews,* November 1917, 510. *WWW,* 159. *HFIL,* 100.

74. *Hearing,* 100–103. *WWW,* 162–64.

75. *National Service Handbook* (Washington, DC: Government Printing Office, 1917), 1–2. *WWW,* 171. Guy Stanton Ford to "Dear Sir," July 13, 1917, entry 37, CPI. Frederic L. Paxson, Edward S. Corwin, Samuel B. Harding, and Guy Stanton Ford, eds., *War Cyclopedia: A Handbook for Ready Reference on the Great War* (Washington, DC: Government Printing Office, 1918), 66, 84.

76. Guy Stanton Ford to "Dear Sir," February 20, 1918, entry 37, CPI. See other correspondence in entry 28, CPI, and the related plea made in *The History Teachers' Magazine,* box 3, NBHS. *WWW,* 171, 181. Gruber, *Mars and Minerva,* 131. Blakey, *Historians on the Homefront,* 116–18.

77. *HFIL,* 99–101. Blakey, *Historians on the Homefront,* 106–7. A discussion of the need to reach such students is in minutes of the NBHS executive committee, on which Ford served, November 9, 1917, box 16, NBHS. O. L. Davis Jr., "The National School Service and American Schools during World War I," *Journal of the Midwest History of Education Society* 23 (1996): 66. Also Ford, "America's Fight for Public Opinion," 3–26. Creel had a lower estimate of the number of teachers reached, 520,000. *Report,* 19. *HFIL,* 99, 293. Vaughn shows how this publication was a prime example of progressive reformist literature.

78. *Report,* 15–18. For a discussion of the difficulty of arriving at the total number of publications see *HFIL,* 42. Executive chairman, Department of Educational Propaganda, to Annie E. Shelland, February 20, 1918, entry 13J-A2, CND.

79. *The Kaiserite in America: One Hundred and One German Lies* (Washington, DC: Committee on Public Information, 1918), 3, 13. *WWW,* 159, 162, 176, 185. *HWAA,* 110. Frederick Lewis Allen wrote O'Higgins, March 18, 1918, to suggest using commercial travelers. entry 5, CPI.

80. Nicholas Butler to Arthur Bullard, May 7, 1917, entry 29, CPI. *The Activities of the Committee on Public Information* (Washington, DC: Government Printing Office, 1918), 15. *WWW,* 131–32.

81. Gruber, *Mars and Minerva*, 103, 124. The list of scholars, undated, with a note from Ford that begins, "List of academic men," box 34, GSF. *HWAA*, 101.

82. SWW, 35.

83. P. S. Florea to Clarence A. Hope, February 9, 1918, entry 97A, CPI. For examples of services rendered by the division see secretary of Division of Advertising to P. S. Florea, April 22, 1918; and to William Johns, March 7, 1918; and "Memorandum for Mr. Jones," February 18, 1918, entry 97A, CPI. Florea was the executive manager of the Associated Advertising Clubs of the World. Jackall and Hirota, *Image Makers*, 25. In a letter to his wife, Ford said that he "did one good job last week in getting conference on speakers to put their recommendations up to Creel" so the CPI could take the lead. September 10, 1917, box 35, GSF. Ford oral history, 376, 392.

84. Adams, "The New World of Trade," 13. David M. Kennedy, *Over Here: The First World War and American Society* (New York: Oxford University Press, 1980), 106. Sung Won Kang and Hugh Rockoff, "Capitalizing Patriotism: The Liberty Loans of World War I," *Financial History Review* 22 (April 2015): 69–74. The model $1,000 bond is equivalent to about $20,000 today, and smaller denominations of $50 were still pricey at about $1,000 in 2020 buying power. The $4.12 War Savings Certificates alone accounted for about 3.5 percent of the outstanding government debt at the end of the war. More striking is a survey that found families with annual incomes at or below $1,000 spent about 2 percent of their income on war loans.

85. *National Service Handbook*, 15. HFIL, 103. "Rural Press Delivery Plan," n.d., entry 5, CPI.

86. Carl Byoir, "Influencing Public Opinion," lecture, Army War College, October 7, 1935, AWC. Guy Stanton Ford, "A New Educational Agency," *Addresses and Proceeding of National Education Association of the United States* 56 (1918): 207. A typescript, dated July 13, 1918, is in box 35, GSF.

7. A TEST OF LOYALTY

1. Samuel Hopkins Adams, *Common Cause* (Boston: Houghton Mifflin, 1919), 457–59.

2. "Liberty Loan Publicity Report," 17–18. "Fourth Loan Advertising Suggestions," August 10, 1918, box 15, LLCR. *New York Times*, January 20, 1918.

3. J. Harry Welling to Martin Egan, March 20, 1917, ME. Joan M. Jensen, *The Price of Vigilance* (Chicago: Rand McNally, 1968), 17. Ralph H. Van Deman, *The Final Memoranda: Major General Ralph H. Van Deman, USA ret., 1865–1952, Father of the U.S. Military Intelligence* (Wilmington, DC: Scholarly Resources, 1984), 30.

4. H. C. Peterson and Gilbert C. Fite, *Opponents of War, 1917–1918* (Seattle: University of Washington Press, 1957), 142–43, 152, 196–202. Christopher Capozzola, *Uncle Sam Wants You: World War I and the Making of the Modern American Citizen* (New York: Oxford University Press, 2008), 149. Elmer Gertz, *Odyssey of a Barbarian: The Biography of George Sylvester Viereck* (New York: Prometheus, 1978), 147. Johnson, *George Sylvester Viereck*, 65. George Creel to W. H. Lamar, February 27, 1918, entry 1, CPI.

5. *PPWW:ND*, 1:423. *PPWW:WP*, 1:66–67.

6. *Official Bulletin*, June 14, 1917. George Creel to Thomas Gregory, December 20, 1917, entry 1, CPI.

7. George Creel, "Public Opinion as a War Measure," *National Marine*, June 1918, 32. For another example of his claim that the CPI did not do propaganda see his letter to the editor, "Caras y Caretas," August 16, 1918, entry 1, CPI. Guy Stanton Ford, "America's Fight for Public Opinion," address to Minnesota Historical Society, St. Paul, January 20, 1919, box OV1, GC.

8. *Rebel*, 196.

9. Samuel Hopkins Adams to Ferris Greenslet, September 5, 1917, box 2, HM.

10. *Four Minute Men Bulletin*, no. 17, 6.

11. *The Activities of the Committee on Public Information*, 17. *HWAA*, 223. Details on Service Bureau found here and in *Report*, 67–71. "Monthly Report of the Service Bureau," July 31, 1918, entry 13, CPI. *Official Bulletin*, July 1, 1918. The growth in the size of government is apparent in a summary of war agencies issued by the National Archives after the war, *Handbook of Federal War Agencies and Their Records, 1917–1918* (Washington, DC: Government Printing Office, 1943). It ran 666 pages.

12. Harvey O'Higgins, "The Official Facts," n.d., entry 9, CPI. Examples of CPI releases can be found in entries 17 and 45, CPI. For a good discussion of the content of the *Official Bulletin* see Robert A. Emery, "The *Official Bulletin*, 1917–1919: A Proto-Federal Register," *Law Library Journal* 102 (June 2010): 441–48.

13. George Creel, "Public Opinion in War Time," *Annals of the American Academy of Political and Social Science* 78 (July 1918): 187. *HWAA*, 100. Robert Jackall and Janice M. Hirota, "America's First Propaganda Ministry," in *Propaganda,* ed. Robert Jackall (New York: New York University Press, 1995), 158. Harvey O'Higgins to Ben Lindsey, January 31, 1919, box 60, BBL.

14. Pitkin, "How Columbia University Can Serve the Country." Ackerman, *Germany,* 275.

15. Josephson, "History for Victory," 215–16.

16. Gruber, *Mars and Minerva,* 132.

17. Paxson et al., *War Cyclopedia,* 85.

18. *The President's Flag Day Address with Evidence of Germany's Plans* (Washington, DC: Government Printing Office, 1917), 13.

19. John Higham, *Strangers in the Land* (New York: Atheneum, 1978), 208. *The President's Flag Day Address,* 6. George Creel to Woodrow Wilson, December 1, 1917, WW-LC. Henry Atwater, Report on Distribution, January 1918, entry 13, CPI.

20. Wallace Notestein to George Burton Adams, November 27, 1917; Adams to Notestein, December 4, 1917, box 18, GBA. Blakey, *Historians on the Homefront,* 44–45. Guy Stanton Ford, foreword to *Conquest and Kultur: Aims of the German in Their Own Words* (Washington, DC: Government Printing Office, 1918), 7. Ford, "America's Fight for Public Opinion," address to Minnesota Historical Society.

21. Blakey, *Historians on the Homefront,* 46. George Winfield Scott and James Wilford Garner, *The German War Code Contrasted with the War Manuals of the United States, Great Britain and France* (Washington, DC: Committee on Public Information, 1918), 2.

22. Wallace Notestein and Elmer E. Stoll, *Conquest and Kultur: Aims of the Germans in Their Own Words* (Washington, DC: Committee on Public Information, 1918), 5. Joseph Schaefer to R. A. Brand, box 5, NBHS.

23. Gray, *The University of Minnesota,* 247. Justus D. Doenecke, *Nothing Less Than War: A New History of America's Entry into World War I* (Lexington: University Press of Kentucky, 2011), 22.

24. Blakey, *Historians on the Homefront,* 60. Guy Stanton Ford to George Creel, July 24, 1918, entry 28, CPI. Ford's trip is described in a book by one of the people who went with him, James A. B. Scherer, *The Nation at War* (New York, George H. Doran, 1918), chapter 8. Scherer was president of Throop College, the forerunner of the California Institute of Technology, and a field representative for the Council of National Defense.

25. Robert Lansing to Woodrow Wilson, June 9, 1917, box 28, RL.

26. Kennedy, *Over Here,* 101, 151, 167. McAdoo, *Crowded Years,* 374. Robert Lansing to Woodrow Wilson, May 31, 1917, box 28, JPT. Robert Woolley to Edward M. House, August 24, 1917, box 7, RWW.

27. *Four Minute Men News,* June 29, 1918, 17. *HFIL,* 126. *Four Minute Men Bulletin,* no. 29, 15. Cyrus Kerr to W. T. Kennerly, [Carl Byoir?] to Kennerly, May 10, 1918, entry 5, CPI. Edward Robb Ellis, *Echoes of Distant Thunder: Life in the United States, 1914–1918* (1975; repr. New York: Kodansha International, 1996), 423. Mould, "Washington's War on Film," 22. Creel, "Public Opinion in War Time," 186, 191.

28. Harold J. Laski, "The Two Candidates," *Dial,* October 19, 1916, 306. George Creel, "The Commoner," *Harper's Weekly,* June 26, 1915, 604. Creel, "Public Opinion as a War Measure," 38.

29. George J. Hecht, *The War in Cartoons* (New York: E. P. Dutton, 1919), 3. Hecht's introduction gives a brief description of the bureau's origins. *Philadelphia Public Record,* January 27, 1918. Writing in *McClure's* about the work of Gibson's artists, a leader of the Vigilantes observed, "When you are walking along the street or riding in a car, and in passing catch sight of a poster, you should have to think hardly at all. The thinking has already been done by the artist. It is your part merely to react to his appeal—to feel impelled to do the thing that poster urges." Julian Street, "Our Fighting Posters," *McClure's,* July 1918, 13.

30. Ward, *The Motion Picture Goes to War,* 95. *New York Times,* July 30, 1918.

31. Merle Curti, "The Changing Concept of 'Human Nature,'" *Business History Review* 41 (Winter 1967): 350.

32. Hecht, *The War in Cartoons,* 75, 143.

33. Kennedy, *Over Here,* 12. Garfield diary, March 19, 1917.

34. Edward Alsworth Ross, *The Old World in the New* (New York: Century, 1914), 51. John A. Garraty, *Henry Cabot Lodge: A Biography* (New York: Alfred A. Knopf, 1953), 39.

35. Okrent, *Last Call,* 102–3. Higham, *Strangers in the Land,* 195–96.

36. Edward A. Ross, "Why It Is a 'Liberty Bond,'" *Independent,* September 28, 1918, 42. Creel later claimed the "Bachelor of Atrocities" ad was written in the Treasury Department; CPI staff were supposed to vet copy, he said, but neglected to do so in this case. He also said the ad was used in one small paper. In fact, it was widely used. Walton E. Bean, "George Creel and His Critics: A Study of the Attitudes of the Committee on Public Information, 1917–1919" (PhD diss., University of California, 1941), 201.

37. SWW, 26.

38. Paxson et al., *War Cyclopedia,* 23, 104.

39. "Creel, "Public Opinion as a War Measure," 36. "Address by Mr. Arthur Bestor," n.d., typescript, entry 75, CPI.

40. Examples of advertisements can be seen in entry 100, CPI.

41. Henry Butterfield to "The Publisher," form letter, n.d. This and other details on syndication can be found in entry 5, CPI.

42. Horne and Kramer, *German Atrocities,* 297–301. See also Sanders and Taylor, *British Propaganda,* 176–77, 195, 264; Messinger, *British Propaganda and the State in the First World War,* 92; Willert, *Washington and Other Memories,* 73; George Allison to E. Gowers, December 5, 1916; Neville Foster to T. O. Wilson, April 17, 1917; G.S.A. to Masterman, minute, April 18, 1917; and Foreign Office note, April 23, 1917, FO 395/77. Wilson said he admired Raemaekers's work. *WWLL: 1917–1918,* 242. The text with the depiction of German slitting of babies' throats read, in part, "This cartoon is not the least allegorical, and it is far less terrible than the reality." Louis Raemaekers, *Kultur in Cartoons* (New York: Century, 1917), 2.

43. George Creel, "Raemaekers—Man and Artist," *Century,* June 1917, 256–59. Grosvenor B. Clarkson to George Creel, August 14, 1917, entry 10A–A2, CND.

44. Louis Raemaekers, *America in the War* (New York: Century, 1918), 106.

45. Robert Woolley to Hans Rieg, September 11, 1918, box 17, RWW. "Great Bond Issue to Be Widely Advertised," *Editor & Publisher,* May 12, 1917, 16. Rieg was controversial. In the cited letter, Woolley wrote, "I take pardonable pride in having placed you in your present position and fought successfully on at least one occasion to keep you there." When Woolley's successor considered letting Rieg go, Woolley intervened with McAdoo. Woolley to William McAdoo, June 27, 1917, box 14, 1917, RWW.

46. Allen, "Government Influence on News in the United States during the World War," 197.

47. Hans Rieg to Louis Hammerling, July 19, 1917, entry 4, CPI.

48. On the publications Hammerling's agency serviced see his letter to Byoir, March 1, 1918, entry 4, CPI. Louis Hammerling to William H. Johns, February 13, 1918, entry 97A, CPI. Hammerling to Carl Byoir, May 13, 1918, entry 4, CPI.

49. L. E. Rubel, "Copy for Letter to School Teachers," March 7, 1918, entry 99, CPI. "Suggestions for Brief Speeches on the Liberty Loans Proposed by Four Minute Men," Bureau of Speakers and Meeting, 2nd Federal Reserve district, box 9, LLCR.

50. Flyer, n.d., box 15, LLCR. Meirion Harries and Susie Harries, *The Last Days of Innocence: America at War, 1917–1918* (New York: Vintage 1997), 302.

51. Adams, "Invaded America," *Everybody's,* February 1918, 30.

52. *Washington Post,* April 5, 1918. See also *Washington Herald,* April 5–6, 1918; *Evening Star,* April 4–5, 1918. The staff member who fractured his skull was William Churchill. His obituary published by his alma mater recounted the spy story as if true. "William Churchill," *Obituary Record of Yale Graduates, 1919–1920* (New Haven, CT: Yale University, 1920), 1426.

53. Meneely interview with Woolley. Higham, *Strangers in the Land,* 220. Minutes, Advisory Committee Speaking Division, November 7, 1917, entry 82, CPI.

54. Jensen, *Price of Vigilance,* 78, 99. "America Infested with German Spies," *Literary Digest,* October 6, 1917, 1. *Nashville Banner,* July 27, 1917. John Gurda, *The Making of Milwaukee* (Milwaukee: Milwaukee County Historical Society, 1999), 224–25. Florence Finch Kelly, *What America Did: A Record of Achievement in the Prosecution of the War* (New York: E. P. Dutton, 1919), 239, 398.

55. Executive Order 2587A, April 7, 1917. Murphy, *World War I and the Origin of Civil Liberties,* 74. Long diary, March 16, 1917.

56. *New York Morning Telegraph,* July 7, 1917. William McAdoo to Woodrow Wilson, April 16, 1917, box 521, WGM. Thomas Gregory to Francis H. Weston, August 10, 1917, box 1, TWG.

57. For an example of the word *surveillance* being used by CPI staff see William Churchill to A. F. Kovarik, November 15, 1917, entry 32, CPI. James Shotwell to Philip Patchin, July 25, 1917, box 3, NBHS. Guy Stanton Ford to H. E. Bourne, May 18, 1917, entry 32, CPI. Arthur Bullard to George Creel, June 9, 1917, entry 1, CPI. The list of professors, undated, is in entry 32, CPI. Laurence Larson to Ford, September 13, 1917, box 1, LML. Creel speech reprinted in *Editor & Publisher,* August 17, 1918, 6. Ford to Laurence Larson, January 7, 1918, box 1, LML.

58. Cornebise, *War as Advertised,* 46–47. HFIL, 203. SWW, 22.

59. Walter Lippmann to Ralph Hayes, November 19, 1917, box 77, WL. The anonymously written article was "Blood Rent for the Trenches," *Pearson's,* December 1917, 246. *Four Minute Men Bulletin,* no. 15.

60. Ford, "America's Fight for Public Opinion," 13. Scott and Garner, *The German War Code,* 12. Herbert S. Houston to Will Irwin, June 18, 1918, entry 97A, CPI.

61. SWW, 23.

62. Harvey O'Higgins, "The Daily German Lie," *Berkeley Daily Gazette,* June 20, 1918. Harvey

O'Higgins, *The German Whisper* (Washington, DC: Committee on Public Information, 1918), 27. [O'Higgins?], typescript, n.d., entry 16, CPI.

63. "Typical Speech B2 for last 10 Days," *Four Minute Men Bulletin,* no. 17, 11.

64. Emerson Hough, *The Web* (Chicago: Reilly and Lee, 1919), 62. For an example of advertisements see *American Paint and Oil Dealer,* July 1918, copy in entry 97A, CPI. The "invisible host of spies" slogan is on a list prepared by the CPI, which is in entry 6, CPI.

65. Lewis Jones to Carl Byoir, April 25, 1918, entry 99, CPI.

66. *Four Minute Men Bulletin,* no. 35, 2–3. Cornebise, *War as Advertised,* 126. *Tennessean,* October 11, 1918.

67. *Hearing,* 134.

68. Samuel V. Kennedy, *Samuel Hopkins Adams and the Business of Writing* (Syracuse, NY: Syracuse University Press, 1999), 3–5.

69. Samuel Hopkins Adams to Roger L. Scaife, May 24, 1918, box 2, HM. Samuel Hopkins Adams, "Common Cause," *Saturday Evening Post,* July 27, 1918, 5–8ff. It was on the strength of his story that he was commissioned to write the novel, which he expected to appear before the war concluded.

70. Samuel Hopkins Adams, "The Orator of the Day," *Collier's,* May 25, 1918, 9. "The Dodger Trail," *Collier's,* October 5 and 12, 1918. Kennedy, *Samuel Hopkins Adams,* 115–17. *Washington Post,* April 19, 1918.

71. Samuel Hopkins Adams, "Invaded America," *Everybody's,* December 1917, 10, 13, 86. The series ran monthly through March 1918.

72. Samuel Hopkins Adams to Ferris Greenslet, November 2, 1918, box 2, HM.

73. Kennedy, *Samuel Hopkins Adams,* 116–19. O'Higgins, "The Issue," *Century,* January 1917, 407.

74. Harvey O'Higgins to Phelps Stokes, January 24, 1918, JGPS. Although the authorship of *The Kaiserite* is sometimes described as uncertain, see *HFIL,* 78. Creel also credited O'Higgins. *HWAA,* 458. O'Higgins, *The German Whisper,* 3.

75. Harvey O'Higgins, "The Daily German Lie," *The Indicator,* October 21, 1918, 326. For a discussion of O'Higgins and his column see Michael S. Sweeney, "Harvey O'Higgins and 'The Daily German Lie,'" *American Journalism* 23 (Summer 2006): 9–28. Copies of the "Daily German Lie" can be found in entry 16, CPI. For names of publications that received the column see entry 9, CPI.

76. Harvey O'Higgins to Roy Caldwell, July 5, 1918, entry 8, CPI.

77. D. E. Isaac to Ray Stannard Baker, December 20, 1917, and George Creel to Baker, December 26, 1917, entry 1, CPI.

78. *Rebel,* 196.

79. Albert Bushnell Hard and Arthur Lovejoy, eds., *Handbook of the War for Public Speakers* (NY: National Security League, 1917). *New York Morning Telegraph,* June 25, 1917. Robert M. McElroy, *Annual Report upon the Educational Work of the National Security League* (New York: National Security League, 1918). The appointment of McElroy was passed to Creel for approval. Arthur Bestor to Guy Stanton Ford, October 22, 1917, entry 71, CPI. Blakey, *Historians on the Homefront,* 30, 78.

80. Porter Emerson Browne, "The Vigilantes," *Outlook,* May 8, 1918, 67–69. Hermann Hagedorn, "What Is the 'Vigilantes?,'" n.d., box 31, HH-Y. Eugenie M. Fryer, "The Vigilantes," *Book News Monthly,* January 1918, 150. For a discussion how Vigilantes sent out material see Charles J. Rosebault to Martin Egan, May 17, 1917, ME, and "the Authors and Illustrators Lend a Hand," *Red Cross Maga-*

zine, September 1918, 409. On Vigilante poetry see Mark W. Van Wienen, *Partisans and Poets: The Political Work of American Poetry in the Great War* (Cambridge: Cambridge University Press, 1997), 154–64. The author makes the point that the Vigilante's poets seemed to be spontaneous and autonomous, but it was a hierarchal organization whose "enforced discipline" led poets to write rapidly on patriotic themes for mass distribution.

81. Discussion of Woolley as Vigilante: E. L. Harvey to Robert Woolley and Woolley to Harvey, August 24 and 27, 1917, box 7, RWW. Hermann Hagedorn to Ernest Poole, April 29, 1918, box 2, HH.

82. Robert Murray to H. D. Craig, September 11, 1918, entry 105, CPI.

83. [?], Memorandum, October 13, 1917, box 9, ADS. Jensen, *Price of Vigilance,* 96.

84. George Creel to Clarence S. Thompson, July 31, 1918, entry 1, CPI. *Indianapolis Star,* May 26, 1917.

85. Fryer, "The Vigilantes," 150. Isaac F. Marcosson, "German Poison," *Saturday Evening Post,* March 23, 1918, 84. Isaac F. Marcosson to George Creel, January 10, 1918, entry 1, CPI. The letter was misdated as 1917.

86. Edward Bell to Leland Harrison, January 9, 1918, Classified Case Files of Edward Bell, entry A1-350, GRDS.

87. *Official Bulletin,* January 16, 1918. *New York Times,* January 17, 1918. The information was sent to Washington by Edward Bell in the American embassy in London, January 9, 1918, Classified Case Files of Edward Bell, 1917–19, entry A1-350, GRDS. For background on this Caillaux episode, see Beatty, *The Lost History of 1914,* 304–6; Strachan, *The First World War,* 180.

88. Entry 11, CPI, contains correspondence O'Higgins received. Guy Stanton Ford to Frank Polk, January 11, 1918, box 4, FLP. Ford to George Creel, with attachment, June 17, 1918, entry 1, CPI.

89. *HWAA,* 225. Kennedy, *Samuel Hopkins Adams,* 103, 114. *New York Times,* September 23, 1917. Creel briefed Lansing on the article on September 10. Lansing diary of that date. *Official Bulletin,* September 27, 1917. The Brooklyn editor's comment is in "Newspapers of the Country Are Flooded with Publicity Copy from Washington," *Editor & Publisher,* March 16, 1918, 7.

90. Arthur E. Bestor, address, "America and the Great War," Patriotism through Education series, no. 15, page 7, issued by National Security League, box 124, AEB.

91. George Creel to Charles Gibson, October 21, 1918, entry 1, CPI. *Rebel,* 196. Joseph Pennell, *Joseph Pennell's Liberty Loan Poster* (Philadelphia: J. B. Lippincott, 1918), 9, 14. Pennell explicitly thanked H. Devitt Welsh, who was based at the CPI offices on Lafayette Square and served as a liaison with the Division of Pictorial Publicity office in New York. *HWAA,* 134. Cass Gilbert, "Division of Pictorial Publicity." "Winning the World's Mind," *Chicago Commerce,* September 19, 1918, 8–9. Byoir said Liberty Loan posters were an exception, but as noted here, they were an exception that had exceptions. The Advertising Division did ads for many agencies, even those with their own publicity bureaus, and heavily supported Treasury publicists promoting Liberty Loans. Untitled report on war bond activities, with cover memorandum, August 5, 1918, box 552, WGM.

92. Blum, *Tumulty,* 102. Creel, speech to North Carolina Press Association, Minutes of the Forty-Sixth Annual Convention, Ashville, NC, July 24–25, 1918, box 5, GC.

93. Peterson and Fite, *Opponents of War,* 182. Luebke, *Bonds of Loyalty,* 245. William McAdoo to Thomas Gregory, June 2, 1917, WW-LC. Jensen, *Price of Vigilance,* 94.

94. G. J. A. O'Toole, *Honorable Treachery: A History of U.S. Intelligence, Espionage, and Covert Action from the American Revolution to the CIA* (New York: Atlantic Monthly Press, 1991), chapter 22. Henry Landau, *The Enemy Within; the Inside Story of German Sabotage in America* (New York:

G. P. Putnam, 1937), chapter 12. David Jimenez, "Black Chamber," in *Spies, Wiretaps and Secret Operatives,* ed. Glenn P. Hastedt (Santa Barbara, CA: ABC-CLIO, 2011), 90–92.

8. WORKING FROM THE INSIDE

1. Byoir, "Influencing Public Opinion."

2. Karen Falk, "Public Opinion in Wisconsin in World War I," *Wisconsin Magazine of History* 25 (June 1942): 404. George F. Kull form letter to newspapers in the state, February 1919, box 2, HM. The Loyalty League also worked with the American Alliance for Labor and Democracy. W. R. Gaylord to Phelps Stokes, January 14, 1918, box 29, JGPS.

3. *HWAA,* 184. Creel, "The Truth Shall Make You Free," 27.

4. Creel, "Prisoners of Public Opinion," *Harper's Weekly,* November 7, 1914, 438. A second article in the series, under the same title, ran on November 14, 1914, 955–56. In a third article Creel attacked Billy Sunday for being used by "Special Privilege" in Colorado. Creel, "Salvation Circus," *Harper's Weekly,* June 19, 1915, 580–82. For the *Survey* counterattack on Creel see "Letting George Do It," *Survey,* February 13, 1915, 541–42.

5. Samuel Hopkins Adams, "The Dodger Trail," *Collier's,* October 12, 1918, 30.

6. Baker, "Railroads on Trial," 539.

7. T. W. Gregory, "Woodrow Wilson and the League of Nations," address, April 24, 1926, box 2, TWG. For other details see *HWAA,* 200–207; *Washington Post,* July 4–5, 1918. Frederick Lewis Allen to H., July 4, 1918, box 1, FLA.

8. *New York Times,* July 5, 1918. *Washington Post,* July 4–5, 1918. *Harrisburg (PA) Telegraph,* July 5, 1918. *San Francisco Chronicle,* July 5, 1918.

9. Creel discussed Loyalty Day in *HWAA,* chapter 16; *Report,* 80–84; and *Rebel,* 240–41. John Firman Coar to George Creel, May 9, 1918; Creel to Coar, May 16, 1918, entry 1, CPI. Robert Bender to Creel, June 25, 1918, entry 1, CPI. The *New York Times* editorial board questioned the wisdom of highlighting diversity. Byoir wrote to the publisher, Adolph Ochs, to complain that this attitude would play into the hands of German propagandists, who would discredit efforts to build patriotic sentiment among the foreign-born. Carl Byoir to Adolph Ochs, June 7, 1918, entry 5, CPI. Working in concert with the CND, the CPI helped mobilize local support for the foreign-born demonstrations. But it wanted those groups to make "necessary arrangements with Mayors and other authorities in charge of the parades, meetings etc. in their respective cities." Antonio Stella to Byoir, June 30, 1918, entry 110; George Creel to Frank Gates, August 8, 1918, entry 1, CPI.

10. Will Irwin to J. J. Freschi, April 30, 1918, entry 112, CPI. Irwin, *Propaganda and the News,* 195–96. *Official Bulletin,* May 25, 1918, 7. Some accounts assert, incorrectly, that Byoir arranged the petition through the League of Oppressed Nations, which he was said to have been particularly proud of inventing. In one telling, "This was the name given by the CPI to the central organization representing all the various ethnic loyalty groups in this country." Bennett, "Carl Byoir," 55. It will be recalled that Bennett had access to Byoir's papers, which have since been lost. His interpretation is endorsed by Robert Jackall, who interviewed a business associate of Byoir's. Jackall and Hirota, *Image Makers,* 30, 243; Jackson and Hirota, "America's First Propaganda Ministry," 155, 168. See also Cutlip, *The Unseen Power,* 585–86. But the league—as its name suggests—was not a CPI umbrella group for organizing its work with loyalty groups. Byoir's recollections, passed down by others, likely referred to a later event, a mass meeting of the Oppressed Nations at Independence Hall, Philadelphia, on October 26, 1918, when Tomáš Masaryk issued a Czech Declaration of In-

dependence. *HWAA*, 203; George Creel to Woodrow Wilson, June 25, 1918; Wilson to Creel, June 26, 1917, box 4, GC.

11. Byoir, "Influencing Public Opinion." Julius Koettgen to George Creel, February 18, 1918, entry 1, CPI.

12. Alexander Konta to George Creel, January 15 and 16, 1918, entry 1, CPI. A discussion of the organization of the Hungarian league is in US Congress, Senate, Subcommittee on the Judiciary, *Brewing and Liquor Interests and German and Bolshevik Propaganda*, Hearing and Report, 66th Cong., 1st Sess., 1919, 650, 1:726–27. Creel to Konta, January 14, 1918, entry 1, CPI. Hans Rieg to Creel, July 10, 1918, entry 1, CPI. Harold Ickes, who worked with foreign-born groups in Chicago and cooperated with the CPI, was equally uninformed. Harold Ickes to Konta, April 12, 1918, entry 112, CPI.

13. *New York Times*, February 16–17, 1918. See also coverage in *New York World, Tribune, Sun*, and *Christian Science Monitor*, February 15–18, 1918. George Creel to Thomas Gregory, February 20, 1918; Creel to William Phillips, January 4, 1918, entry 1, CPI. Creel told Gregory, "Everything it [Friends of German Democracy] does is done under my direction."

14. Bennett, "Carl Byoir," 53. *WWW*, 218. Julius Koettgen to Carl Byoir, October 3, 1918; Byoir to Koettgen, October 4, 1918, entry 112, CPI.

15. Konta spelled out his success through the end of July 1918 in a letter to Creel, July 26, 1918, entry 112, CPI. Alexander Konta to Carl Byoir, telegram, June 6, 1918, entry 112, CPI. Konta to Byoir, June 10, 1918, and Byoir to Konta, August 8, 1918, entry 5, CPI. On Hungarian contributions see, for instance, *Perth Amboy Evening News*, July 15, 1918.

16. Louis Hammerling to William H. Johns, February 13, 1918, entry 97A, CPI. Park, *The Immigrant Press and Its Control*, 392. On the publications Hammerling served see his letter to Carl Byoir, March 1, 1918, entry 4, CPI. Hammerling to Byoir, May 27 and August 29, 1918, entry 4, CPI. In this letter, Hammerling writes, "I was appointed by your Committee, as per identification card you furnished me, and designated as you told me, Assistant Director."

17. Robyn Muncy, *Relentless Reformer: Josephine Roche and Progressivism in Twentieth-Century America* (Princeton, NJ: Princeton University Press, 2015), 27, 46–54. George Creel, "Josephine Roche of the Denver Police," *Woman's Journal*, July 12, 1913, 218.

18. Muncy, *Relentless Reformer*, 87, 89. Ben Lindsey to Geoffrey Butler, October 8, 1918, Lindsey to Creel, October 30, 1918, box 59, BBL; Larsen, *The Good Fight*, 141. On his return, Lindsey traveled for two months in the United States promoting Liberty bonds and for the War Camp Community Service. Lindsey estimated he reached half a million people, not counting the large audiences he had in England and Italy.

19. Creel, "Public Opinion as a War Measure," 35. George Creel, "The Hopes of the Hyphenated," *Century*, January 1916, 350, 351.

20. Breen, *Uncle Sam at Home*, 164–65. Muncy, *Relentless Reformer*, 65. Higham, *Strangers in the Land*, 239–50.

21. Creel, "Public Opinion as a War Measure," 35. Americanization Survey, June 10, 1918, entry 112, CPI. Muncy, *Relentless Reformer*, 91. George Creel to Woodrow Wilson, August 6, 1918, WW-LC. Creel did call on public librarians to give immigrant patrons "Americanization Registration Cards," which read, in part, "Americanization means the use of a common language for the entire nation. The desire of all peoples in America to unite in a common citizenship under one flag." Wayne A. Wiegand, *"An Active Instrument for Propaganda": The American Public Library during World War I* (New York: Greenwood, 1989), 120–21.

22. Laurence Larson to E. B. Greene, January 22, 1918, box 2, 1918, NBHS. Larson was elected

president of the American Historical Association in 1938. His letter to Greene, the NBHS chair, made its way to the CPI and eventually to Edwin Bjorkman, who got the job. Edwin Bjorkman to Greene, February 20, 1918, box 1, LML.

23. *Report,* 81. I have drawn on Roche's summary of the division's activities in *Report,* 80–98. Higham, *Strangers in the Land,* 248.

24. Allen, "Government Influence on News in the United States during the World War," 95. *WWW,* 228. For an example of playing up enemy setbacks see *Official Bulletin,* January 5, 1918, 12. *Report,* 90–91.

25. Background on Bjorkman is found among his papers at the University of North Carolina and in a biography that accompanies the finding aid for those papers. As an example of his patriotism, Bjorkman answered the call from the navy to donate optical instruments. F. D. Roosevelt to Edwin Bjorkman, March 21, 1918, box 2, EB. C. H. Mair to Bjorkman, October 23, 1918, box 1, EB. On the *Daily Telegraph* see John M. Le Sage to Bjorkman, July 11, 1916, box 2, EB. Sanders and Taylor, *British Propaganda,* 113–14. The authors misidentify Bjorkman as "S. Bjorkmann." Bjorkman to Mair, June 29, 1917, box 2, EB.

26. George Creel to Edwin Bjorkman, January 15, 1918; Creel to Bjorkman, December 11 and 20, 1917; Bjorkman to Creel, January 3, 1918; Creel to Bjorkman, January 10, 1918, box 2, EB. Bjorkman to Creel, January 3, 1918, entry 1, CPI. Bjorkman to Laurence Larson, February 20, 1918, box 1, LML. Bjorkman speech quoted in the *Moline (IL) Daily Dispatch,* n.d., box 20, EB.

27. *Report,* 85. Edwin Bjorkman to George Creel, July 17, 1918, entry 1, CPI. Creel later described the proclamation in his "Our 'Aliens'—Were They Loyal or Disloyal?," *Everybody's,* March 1919, 36.

28. These details are found in a valuable report, Robert E. Lee to Josephine Roche, [1919?], box 2, EB. Lee was Bjorkman's assistant. Edwin Bjorkman to George Creel, July 17, 1918; Bjorkman to Editors, April 26, 1918, entry 1, CPI.

29. Lee report to Roche.

30. Edwin Bjorkman, address to Lincoln Liberty League, November 11, 1918, box 20, EB. On the desire to work quietly among Scandinavians see *WWW,* 226.

31. William McCormick Blair to state chairmen, June 18, 1918, TFMM. "Memorandum for Mr. Byoir," May 14, 1918, entry 5; George Creel to Frederick Keppel, April 9, 1918, entry 1, CPI. Emmett J. Scott, *Scott's Official History of the American Negro in the World War* (Chicago: Homewood, 1919), 347.

32. Carl Byoir to Emmett Scott, August 14, 1918, entry 5, CPI. Thomas Winter, "The Training of Colored Troops," in *Hollywood's World War I Motion Picture Images,* ed. Peter C. Rollins and John E. O'Connor (Bowling Green, OH: Bowling Green State University Popular Press, 1977), 15–16. Harold Nicolson to Porter Dunlap, April 19, 1918, TFMM. *Hearing,* 119–20.

33. Emmett Scott to George Creel, June 3, 1918, entry 5, CPI. Scott to Woodrow Wilson, June 27, 1918, *PWW,* 48:452. On military intelligence's interest in this conference see Roy Talbert Jr., *Negative Intelligence: The Army and the American Left, 1917–1941* (Jackson: University Press of Mississippi, 1991), 119–23. Wilson to Creel, June 18, 1918; Creel to Wilson June 17, 1918, box 2, GC. The CPI put out a news release saying Wilson was "greatly pleased" by the conference; the release, n.d., can be found in entry 5, CPI. Ralph Tyler to Carl Byoir, October 9, 1918, EJS. Tyler provided his credentials to Byoir in a letter of July 25, 1918. entry 5, CPI. For background see Jinx Coleman Broussard, *African American Foreign Correspondents: A History* (Baton Rouge: Louisiana State University Press, 2013), chapter 3. As Broussard notes, one other black reporter covered the war, Roscoe Conkling Simmons of the *Chicago Defender,* but he "remained encamped in Paris, distracted by its allure and its women" (51). John Maxwell Hamilton, *Journalism's Roving Eye: A History of Ameri-*

can Foreign Reporting (Baton Rouge: Louisiana State University Press, 2009), 335. Tyler to Emmett Scott, November 5, 1918, EJS.

34. Henry Atkinson et al., to Sidney L. Gulick, April 23, 1918, box 221, CRIA. Frederick Lynch to George Creel, December 19, 1917; Creel to Lynch, January 7, 1918, entry 1, CPI. Roland Marchand, *The American Peace Movement and Social Reform, 1898–1918* (Princeton, NJ: Princeton University Press, 1972), 366. Kate Hallgren, *Toward Peace with Justice: One Hundred Years of the Carnegie Council* (New York: Carnegie Council for Ethics in International Affairs, 2014), 21–24. When it received a letter suggesting it was not fully supportive of the war, a member of the CPU responded, "Please note the red lines at the end of this letterhead." Mary Breed to Sidney L. Gulick, February 12, 1918; Gulick to Breed, February 15, 1918, box 221, CRIA.

35. *WWW,* 219.

36. George Creel to Vance McCormick, December 4, 1918, entry 6, CPI.

37. *Report,* 9, 17 33. There is another brief mention of the Alliance: "The American Alliance for Labor and Democracy were [*sic*] furnished many speakers, but most of the engagements were made direct" (38). *HWAA* does not mention of Maisel or the two labor divisions; an appendix in HWAA listing publications produced by the CPI includes six for the Alliance, 458.

38. Lewis L. Lorwin, *The American Federation of Labor: History, Policies, and Prospects* (Washington, DC: Brookings Institution, 1933), 159–61. The *Republic* cartoon was reprinted in the *Literary Digest,* August 18, 1917, 12. George Creel to Samuel Gompers, July 26, 1917, in *The Samuel Gompers Papers,* ed. Peter J. Albert and Grace Palladino (Urbana: University of Illinois Press, 2007), 156.

39. SWW, 14. Lorwin, *American Federation of Labor,* 167. *Report,* 249.

40. Roger Babson to William McAdoo, August 3, 1916, box 163, WGM. Roger W. Babson, *Actions and Reactions: An Autobiography of Roger W. Babson* (New York: Harper, 1950), 172, 178. Also "Remarks by Roger W. Babson," typescript, n.d., entry 4, CPI. Before joining the CPI, Babson helped establish the United States Employment Service, which sought to funnel workers to war industries.

41. Published in *Survey,* July 7, 1917, 328. Roger Babson to George Creel, January 4, 1918, entry 4, CPI. Babson evidently believed he could make this a self-financing operation by selling the booklets. In his letter, he indicated a willingness to work on a commission basis, although he said he preferred having a salary. Babson to Carl Byoir, January 5, 1918, entry 5, CPI.

42. *WWW,* 192–93. This book does an excellent job of piecing together the CPI's relationship with labor. Roger W. Babson, *Human Bait* (Washington, DC: Committee on Public Information, n.d.). This can be found in entry 4, CPI. CND Report shows its dates as February 16 to March 15, 1918.

43. *WWW,* 192–93. Babson, *Actions and Reactions,* 179–80. George Creel to Woodrow Wilson, March 12, 1918; Wilson to Creel, March 22, 1918, WW-LC. *Hearing,* 54. Creel to William Chenery, May 31, 1918, entry 1, CPI. Roger W. Babson, *W. B. Wilson and the Department of Labor* (New York: Brentano's, 1919) 219–20. *APD,* 8. *Hearing,* 10–11, 122–24.

44. George Creel to Samuel Gompers, July 26, 1917, entry 1, CPI. Creel also wrote in this letter, "Out of my knowledge of you, and the men associated with you, I have the conviction that it is not necessary to explain that such efforts, in order to have this support, must be open and above board." In light of the CPI's veiled role and the alliance's efforts to disguise its work from time to time, it is difficult to know what Creel meant. A good discussion of the founding of the AALD and its secrecy is in John Reinertson, "Colonel House, Woodrow Wilson and European Socialism, 1917–1919" (PhD diss., University of Wisconsin, 1971), 210–39. Gompers form letter, January 21, 1918, box 30–

31, JGPS. The AALD was on the advisory group to Bestor's Speaking Division as though it were an independent organization. Arthur Bestor to George Creel, April 1, 1918, entry 7, CPI.

45. Bernard Mandel, *Samuel Gompers: A Biography* (Yellow Springs, OH: Antioch, 1963), 88, 169–70, 491. Frank L. Grubbs, *The Struggle for Labor Loyalty: Gompers, the A. F. of L., and the Pacifists, 1917–1920* (Durham, NC: Duke University Press, 1968), 146. Rowland Hill Harvey, *Samuel Gompers, Champion of the Toiling Masses* (Palo Alto, CA: Stanford University Press, 1935), 249. Samuel Gompers, *Seventy Years of Life and Labor* (New York: E. P. Dutton, 1925), 1:380. Albert and Palladino, *Gompers Papers*, 156–57.

46. Markku Ruotsila, *John Spargo and American Socialism* (New York: Palgrave Macmillan, 2006), 1. Spargo oral history, 242 263–66. Grubbs, *Struggle for Labor Loyalty*, 41. Both Spargo and Stokes would have quotes in Louis Raemaekers, *America in the War* (New York: Century, 1918), 120, 192.

47. Ronald Radosh, *American Labor and United States Foreign Policy* (New York: Random House, 1969), 66. *Rebel*, 49. For background on Walsh see Harry Haskell, *Boss-Busters & Sin Hounds: Kansas City and Its Star* (Columbia: University of Missouri Press, 2007), 91–92, 97, 136, 168–70. Jessie James appears to have been innocent. The story is told in L. A. Little, ed., *The Trial of Jesse James, Jr.: The Son of an Outlaw Stands Accused* (Kansas City: Vintage Antique Classics Publishing, 2012). *Independent*, March 11, 1899. Judy Ancel, "Frank P. Walsh—Labor's Tribune," paper, Institute for Labor Studies, n.d., derived from a talk in October 1992. Joseph A. McCartin, *Labor's Great War: The Struggle for Industrial Democracy and the Origins of Modern American Labor Relations, 1912–1921* (Chapel Hill: University of North Carolina Press, 1997), 66–67. Frank Walsh to H. L. Fagin, June 19, 1917, FPW.

48. WWW, 193–208. Chester Wright to George Creel, July 20, 1918, entry 5, CPI.

49. Grubbs, *Struggle for Labor Loyalty*, 22–23, 37. Radosh, *American Labor and United States Foreign Policy*, 55.

50. Grubbs, *Struggle for Labor Loyalty*, 37, 45, 71, and 55–69 for Minneapolis meeting. Spargo oral history, 271–72.

51. Marchand, *American Peace Movement and Social Reform*, 316. John R. Commons, "Why Workingmen Support the War," *Bulletin of the University of Wisconsin* 1 (January 1918): 5. This was published under the alliance's auspices.

52. Gustavus Myers, *The German Myth: The Falsity of Germany's "Social Progress" Claims* (New York: Boni and Liveright, 1918), 13. Frank L. Grubbs Jr., "Council and Alliance Labor Propaganda: 1917–1918," *Labor History* 7 (Spring 1966): 163–67. Examples of Wright's stories can be found in box 35, JGPS. Wright's journalism experience included an association with Scripps's Newspaper Enterprise Association. George Creel to Julius Koettgen, February 22, 1918, entry 1; Chester Wright to Creel, July 20, 1918, entry 5, CPI.

53. Grubbs, *Struggle for Labor Loyalty*, 72. Chester Wright to George Creel, September 27, 1918, entry 1, CPI. *WWW*, 209–10.

54. SWW, 17. For a discussion of Creel's involvement with the commission see Haskell, *Boss-Busters & Sin Hounds*, 144–45. *Rebel*, 144. *WWW*, 198–206, 212. For other examples of Creel's caution see Grubbs, *Struggle for Labor Loyalty*, 97, 100.

55. Radosh, *American Labor and United States Foreign Policy*, 58–59. Wilson told Spargo he had the money to fund propaganda with labor. Spargo oral history, 266. Albert and Palladino, *Gompers Papers*, 161. Grubbs, *Struggle for Labor Loyalty*, 65; Radosh, *American Labor and United States Foreign Policy*, 61. Robert Maisel to Carl Byoir, March 27, 1918, entry 5, CPI; George Creel to Maisel,

March 26 and July 5, 1918, entry 1, CPI. For examples of Byoir paying attention to details see Maisel's letter to him, July 29, 1918, and other correspondence, entry 6, CPI. Some alliance reports are found entry 13, CPI.

56. Grubbs, *The Struggle for Labor Loyalty*, 67. Peterson and Fite, *Opponents of War*, 76. For Spargo's belief in free speech see John Spargo to Samuel Gompers, July 30, 1917; and Albert and Palladino, *Gompers Papers*, 159–60. George Creel to Frank Walsh, September 1, 1917, FPW. Radosh, *American Labor and United States Foreign Policy*, 64.

57. Lorwin, *American Federation of Labor*, 149–50. George Creel to Frank Walsh, September 10, 1917, FPW. Radosh, *American Labor and United States Foreign Policy*, 66.

58. Mandel, *Samuel Gompers*, 396. Radosh, *American Labor and United States Foreign Policy*, 62. Chester Wright to George Creel, July 20, 1918, and Robert Maisel to Executive Committee of AALD, February 20, 1918, entry 5, CPI. Estimates of the number of locals varied. In his February 1918 report, Maisel claimed there were 126 locals in thirty-nine states. Grubbs, *Struggle for Labor Loyalty*, 78.

59. Lorwin, *American Federation of Labor*, 150. Robert Maisel to J. G. Phelps Stokes, March 28, 1918, box 30–31, JGPS. *Report of Proceedings of the Thirty-Seventh Annual Convention of the American Federation of Labor* (Washington, DC: Law Reporter Printing, 1917), 283, 285.

60. Albert and Palladino, *Gompers Papers*, 240–41. Simeon Larson, *Labor and Foreign Policy* (Rutherford, NJ: Fairleigh Dickinson University Press, 1975), 41–42, 142–43. Elizabeth McKillen, *Chicago Labor and the Quest for a Democratic Diplomacy, 1914–1924* (Ithaca, NY: Cornell University Press, 1995), 46–49, 81–85. Resistance was also found in South Bend, Indiana. R. S. Pridemore to Samuel Gompers, September 8, 1917, vol. 238, AFLR.

61. Grubbs, *Struggle for Labor Loyalty*, 42.

62. Albert and Palladino, *Gompers Papers*, 227. John Spargo to Samuel Gompers, October 9, 1917, vol. 239, AFLR. Spargo to Chester M. Wright, October 12, 1917; and Spargo to Robert Maisel, October 10, 1917, box 28, JGPS. Lorwin, *American Federation of Labor*, 151.

63. Chester Wright to George Creel, July 20, 1918, entry 5, CPI. Minutes of Executive Council, AALD, February 21, 1918, box 30–31, JGPS. Samuel Gompers to Robert Maisel, March 14, 1918, vol. 244, AFLR. Grubbs, *Struggle for Labor Loyalty*, 76. J. G. Phelps Stokes to Maisel, March 22, 1918, box 30, JGPS. Byoir to Maisel, March 25, 1918, entry 6, CPI.

64. George Creel to Samuel Gompers, July 26, 1918; Gompers to J. G. Phelps Stokes, August 26, 1918, vol. 249, AFLR. Lorwin, *American Federation of Labor*, 150–51. Robert Maisel to Executive Committee of AALD, February 20, 1918, entry 5, CPI. Grubbs, *Struggle for Labor Loyalty*, 104–6. See boxes 30–31, JGPS, for lists of contributions.

65. Albert and Palladino, *Gompers Papers*, 495–96, 498. George Creel to Samuel Gompers, July 17, 1918; Creel to Roger Babson, July 17, 1918, entry 1, CPI. Grubbs, *Struggle for Labor Loyalty*, 76, 118–19, 122–23. Gompers adamantly opposed taking money from Babson but apparently reversed himself. Babson to Creel, April 6, 1918, entry 5, CPI. Albert and Palladino, *Gompers Papers*, 496. In September the CPI also underwrote an alliance event in Chicago to welcome Gompers on his return from a labor mission abroad.

66. *WWW*, 206–7. Grubbs, *Struggle for Labor Loyalty*, 123–24. For a discussion of Creel's frustrations see George Creel to Stephen Wise, October 15, 1918, entry 1, CPI.

67. Samuel Gompers to Woodrow Wilson, July 18, 1918; Gompers to Wilson, July 30, 1918; Gompers to George Creel, August 6, 1918, vol. 249, AFLR. This letter was cryptic. At this time Wilson received a report from Baker on German propaganda in Mexico. Wilson to Creel, July 31, 1918; Wilson to Creel, August 2, 1918, box 4, GC. Albert and Palladino, *Gompers Papers*, 498–99. A good

discussion of the decision to create and fund *El Obrero Pan-Americano* is in Sinclair Snow, "Samuel Gompers and the Pan-American Federation of Labor" (PhD diss., University of Virginia, 1960).

68. Samuel Gompers to Woodrow Wilson, July 30, 1918; Gompers to George Creel, August 6, 1918, vol. 249, AFLR. Wilson did not accept Gompers's proposition that funding should go to "three trustees named by you" and supervised by the AFL. The paper was edited by a labor organizer and journalist in Latin America, John Murray. Gompers and Creel met with Murray on August 12, 1918, and told him to start immediately. John Murray to J. G. Phelps Stokes, August 26, 1918; Chester Wright to Stokes, September 12, 1918, box 30–31, JGPS. Grubbs, *Struggle for Labor Loyalty,* 119–20.

69. McCartin, *Labor's Great War,* 194. Grubbs, *Struggle for Labor Loyalty,* 132, 144–45. On Maisel's departure see Matthew Woll to Robert Maisel, July 14, 1919, box 30–31, JGPS.

70. Grubbs, *Struggle for Labor Loyalty,* 83, 127–28, 144. The union shared space with the American Civil Liberties Union.

71. Radosh, *American Labor and United States Foreign Policy,* 71.

9. NAIL UP THE DAMN THING

1. Hans Krabbendam, *The Model Man: A Life of Edward William Bok, 1863–1930* (Amsterdam: Editions Rodopi B.V., 2001), 146. George Creel to R. L. Maddox, April 5, 1918, entry 1, CPI.

2. Walter S. Rogers to George Creel, September 23 and 28, 1918; James M. Tuohy to *New York World,* September 24, 1918, entry 1, CPI. Tuohy was the *World* bureau chief in London, and the correspondence cited here is the story he cabled home.

3. Cass Gilbert to Charles Gibson, February 23, 1918; Gibson to George Creel, February 27, 1918; Creel to Gilbert, February 28, 1918, entry 1, CPI.

4. Reginald Wright Kauffman, "The News Embargo," *North American Review,* November 1918, 831. H. B. Bristol to Walter Sweeney, n.d. [May 1918?], entry 221, AEF.

5. Frederick Palmer, *With My Own Eyes: A Personal Story of Battle Years* (Indianapolis: Bobbs-Merrill, 1932), 340.

6. George Creel, "Public Opinion in War Time," *Annals of the American Academy of Political and Social Science* 78 (July 1918): 187. *New York Tribune,* June 28, 1917. *Der Deutsche Correspondent,* August 3, 1917. Maurice Bourgeois, quoted in *Living Age,* February 23, 1924, 342.

7. Mark Sullivan, "Creel—Censor," *Collier's,* November 10, 1917, 14.

8. Frank Irving Cobb, *Cobb of "The World," A Leader of Liberalism,* ed. John L. Heaton (New York: E. P. Dutton, 1924), 268–70. This quote is sometimes disputed, but considerable opinion weighs it as true, even if the date of the meeting in Cobb's book is probably incorrect. See Cooper, *Woodrow Wilson,* 642. Arthur S. Meyers, *Democracy in the Making: The Open Forum Lecture Movement* (Lanham, MD: University Press of America, 2012), 39–43. George Creel to Woodrow Wilson, November 4, 1917; Wilson to Creel, November 5, 1917, WW-LC.

9. Woodrow Wilson to Thomas Gregory, August 27, 1917, box 1, TWG. George Creel to Wilson, August 24, 1917, WW-LC. The article, which was published August 12, 1917, and the Justice Department's analysis are attached to this letter.

10. Minute, "Proposed Reinstatement of the International News Service," n.d. [circa June 25, 1917], FO 395/70. The idea of restoring privileges had been around for a while (e.g., Geoffrey Robinson to Arthur Willert, February 8, 1917, box 2, AW). *PWW,* 43:132–33. Polk covered for Lansing by saying Lansing had discussed the matter with the British but never really suggested they restore privileges. British Foreign Office files have much correspondence on what to do about Hearst, for instance, Walter H. Long to Victor Cavandish, Duke of Devonshire, May 16, 1917; Hubert Mont-

gomery to F. M. Gunther, June 23, 1917; Montgomery to William Wiseman, August 31, 1917 with memo, "Mr. Hearst and the International News Service," FO 395/71. Cecil Spring-Rice to Foreign Office, cable, June 13, 1917, FO 395.

11. George Creel to Ernest Chambers, February 22, 1918, entry 1, CPI. The *New York Times* reported Lansing was the agent of change. *New York Times,* February 15, 1918. House diary, January 21, 1919. Censorship Board Minutes, March 20, 1918, entry 53, CPI. The Wiseman Papers have rich detail on the unwinding of the Hearst ban. See especially "Mr. Hearst and the International News Service," n.d.; and William Wiseman to Eric Drummond, June 16, 1918, box 5, WW-Y. When news of the lifting of the ban came out, Creel said he had nothing to do with it. *New York Tribune,* May 1, 1918.

12. The affidavit is J. Earl Clauson, June 4, 1918, entry 1, CPI. George L. Darte to Chief, Military Intelligence Branch, July 16, 1918, entry 165, WDGS. Nasaw, *The Chief,* 261.

13. On Gregory's warning see *New York Times,* April 7, 1917. Ray Stannard Baker interview with Albert Burleson, March 17, 1927, box 102, RSB. Albert Burleson to Woodrow Wilson, July 16, 1917, box 24, ASB. Background is in Peterson and Fite, *Opponents of War,* 96–97; Cooper, *Woodrow Wilson,* 398; Capozzola, *Uncle Sam Wants You,* 151; and Jensen, *Price of Vigilance,* 15–16.

14. Merrill Rogers to Commission on International Justice and Good-Will, May 3, 1917, box 221, CRIA.

15. "Address of Hon. A. S. Burleson to the Annual Convention of the National Hardware Association," Atlantic City, NJ, October 15, 1919, box 24; Albert Burleson, no title, typewritten draft, box 23, ASB. Albert Burleson to Arthur Brisbane, September 25, 1917, entry 2, PO. For another example of Burleson's defensiveness, see Burleson to Gilson Gardner, July 24, 1917, entry 40, PO. *Editor & Publisher* to Burleson, telegram, [January 1920]. Burleson, draft statement, January 3, 1920, box 25, ASB.

16. *Official Bulletin,* April 16, 1918, 2. There were newspaper editorials in support of Gregory's argument. "Stronger Curb on Enemies at Home," *Literary Digest,* May 4, 1918, 19.

17. Department of Justice, *Annual Report of the Attorney General 1918,* 18. Murphy, *World War I and the Origins of Civil Liberties,* 83.

18. Zechariah Chafee Jr., *Free Speech in the United States* (New York: Atheneum, 1969), 14–15. David M. Rabban disputes Chafee's claim that the First Amendment had little judicial scrutiny before World War I but does not disagree that the courts were unsympathetic to free speech claims and their decisions "doctrinally sparse." Rabban, "The First Amendment in Its Forgotten Years," *Yale Law Journal* 90 (January 1981): 523. Paxson et al., *War Cyclopedia,* 101. For background on common understanding of the law see Stone, *Perilous Times,* 158–60. "Address of Hon. A. S. Burleson to the Annual Convention of the National Hardware Association."

19. Capozzola, *Uncle Sam Wants You,* 9–10, 17. Edward E. Bok, *The Americanization of Edward Bok: The Autobiography of a Dutch Boy Fifty Years After* (Chicago: R. R Donnelley, 2000), 378, 391.

20. *Washington Post,* July 1, 1918. *New York Tribune,* September 16, 23, 30, 1917. The first article in the series appeared the same day that Adams's unsigned analysis of the purloined von Igel documents ran in the *New York Tribune;* both appeared on the front page. Regarding another anti-Hearst series in the *Tribune* see Nasaw, *The Chief,* 268–69. Ben Procter, *William Randolph Hearst: The Later Years, 1911–1951* (New York: Oxford University Press, 2007), 54–55.

21. Cornebise, *War as Advertised,* 126. Lafayette Young, *Fifteen Patriotic Editorials: From the Des Moines Capital* (Des Moines, IA: Des Moines Capital, n.d.), 2–3. Lafayette Young to Carl Byoir, January 22, 1918; Jason Rogers, "An Invitation to A Patriotic Service," May 15, 1918; Jason Rogers to Byoir, May 27, 1918; Byoir to Rogers, n.d., entry 5, CPI.

22. "After Alien Enemies," *Editor & Publisher*, April 14, 1917, 6. *Official Bulletin*, May 12, 1917, 4. Thomas Ewing Dabney to Josephus Daniels, March 29, 1917, box 573, JD.

23. Minna Lewinson and Henry Beetle Hough, *A History of the Services Rendered to the Public by the American Press during the Year 1917* (New York: Columbia University Press, 1918), 4. The prize was in the category of Newspaper History, which was never given again. "Censorship," *Editor & Publisher*, April 14, 1917, 32. "The 'Joke' Is on the Kaiser," *Editor & Publisher*, September 29, 1917, 18. "'Standing by the President,'" *Editor & Publisher*, March 17, 1917, 24.

24. "Geo Creel Outlines Censorship Policy," *Editor & Publisher*, April 21, 1917, 18. Committee on Public Information, *Preliminary Statement to the Press*, 10.

25. Sullivan, "Creel—Censor," 14. For an example of Creel expressing disapproval of the censorship clause see George Creel, Address to the Economic Club, Hotel Astor, April 4, 1918, box 5, GC. Bullard's comments were reported in *New York Evening Post*, May 29, 1917. Mock, *Censorship 1917*, 43.

26. George Creel to Louise Bryan Reed, September 20, 1918, entry 1, CPI.

27. *Editor & Publisher*, May 18, 1918, 32. Stephen Vaughn has an excellent analysis of CPI attitudes toward free speech: "First Amendment Liberties and the Committee on Public Information," *American Journal of Legal History* 23 (April 1979): 115. Harvey O'Higgins, "Freedom of Speech," *Century*, December 1917, 303. Samuel Hopkins Adams, "Invaded America," *Everybody's*, January 1918, 82. Bullard, "Censorship Memorandum."

28. *HWAA*, 4. *HFIL*, 330. Office of Naval Intelligence, *Cable Censorship Digest* (Washington, DC: Government Printing Office, 1933), 48. Office of the Chief Cable Censor, *CCC List: Issued as Index No. 6* (Washington, DC: Government Printing Office, February 6, 1919), R7. *United States Cable Censorship: Instructions* (New York: Navy Mobilization Bureau, 1918), 87. This can be found in Records Kept by Leland Harrison, entry A1-349, GRDS. *Official Bulletin*, February 4, 1918, 13. On Creel's involvement with hiring see his letter to Daniels, December 10, 1917, box 73, JD. For an example of communication with the British see Edgar Sisson to Cecil Spring-Rice, July 17, 1917, and related correspondence in the same file, FO 115/2191. "Notice to the Press," Serial D 584, August 30, 1917, HO 139/45.

29. George Creel, note, typewritten, n.d., box 573, JD. Creel to David W. Todd, August 6, 1917, entry 5, CPI.

30. Committee on Public Information, *Preliminary Statement to the Press*, 8.

31. Bean, "George Creel and His Critics," 90.

32. [George Creel?] to Arthur B. Hoff, July 24, 1917, entry 5, CPI.

33. Memorandum to Chief Cable Censor, October 8, 1917; "Press Censorship Regulations," October 17, 1917, entry 5, CPI.

34. George Creel to Woodrow Wilson, May 9, 1918; Wilson to Creel, May 10, 1918, box 2, GC.

35. *New York Evening Post*, December 31, 1917. *Official Bulletin*, December 31, 1917, 10. "Confidential to Editors," August 24, 1917, entry 5, CPI.

36. George Creel, "The American Newspaper," *Everybody's*, April 1919, 40. *New York Sun*, July 30, 1917. Richard Barry, "'Freedom' of the Press?," *North American Review*, October 1918, 704. Lawrence, "'Not for Publication,'" 101. For a discussion on newsprint issues see Jeff Nichols, "Propaganda, Chicago Newspapers, and the Political Economy of Newsprint during the First World War," *Journalism History* 43 (Spring 2017): 21–31.

37. *Alien Property Custodian Report* (Washington, DC: Government Printing Office, 1919), 152. *HFIL*, 324–25.

38. Ward, *The Motion Picture Goes to War*, 116. *HFIL*, 211. For an army directive on procedures

see adjutant general to all commanders, October 20, 1917, entry 164, WDGS. Review of applications to take pictures can be found in these files. Kendall Banning to Cranston Bronton, May 17, 1917, entry 163, WDGS. Daily Film Report, National Board of Review, March 21, 1918, entry 164, WDGS.

39. *WWW,* 148–50. Office of Chief Signal Officer, September 7, 1917, entry 5, CPI. *New York World,* June 23, 1918.

40. William A. Brady, statement, July 12, 1918, entry 1, CPI. Ward, *The Motion Picture Goes to War,* 121, 128. Mock, *Censorship 1917,* 177–78. George Creel to Ernest J. Chambers, February 6, 1918, entry 1, CPI.

41. Ward, *The Motion Picture Goes to War,* 10, 123, 127–29. *WWW,* 157. Creel to H. A. Garfield, May 23, 1918; Creel to William McAdoo, May 23, 1918; Creel to Charles Hart, June 6, 1918, entry 1, CPI. *The Dramatic Mirror,* June 22, 1918.

42. *Hearing,* 129. *WWW,* 153.

43. Ward, *The Motion Picture Goes to War,* 118. George Creel to M. L. C. Funkhouser, May 22, 1918, entry 1, CPI. "An Old Exhibitor," *Dramatic Mirror,* May 18, 1918.

44. "Caillaux Case Made into Photoplay," *Motography,* April 27, 1918, 795. Winfield Sheehan to L. M. Rubel, telegram, April 30, 1918; George J. Hecht to Rubel, May 8, 1918; Philip Patchin to George Creel, August 7, August 9, and September 5, 1918; J. W. McBride to Creel, August 28, 1918; Creel to Fox Film Corporation, August 8, 1918; Louis Aubert to Creel, August 2, 1918, entry 1, CPI.

45. John Tuerk to George Creel, November 25, 1918, entry 1, CPI. Creel to Blair Coan, July 5 and July 15, 1918; George J. Hecht to Lawrence Rubel, May 2, 1918; K. K. Kawakami to G. K. Kimball, May 31, 1918, entry 1, CPI.

46. Irwin, *Propaganda and the News,* 198.

47. William Churchill, "Memorandum for the Chief of Staff," August 5, 1918, entry 150, WDGS.

48. William Churchill to Blaine Walker, October 25, 1918, entry 164, WDGS. Newton D. Baker to George Creel, June 27, 1918, entry 1, CPI, discusses problems with permits. "Memorandum for Major Hughes," September 27, 1918, entry 150, WDGS. "Situation Summary, for week ending October 29, 1918"; "Situation Summary, for week ending September 25, 1918"; "Situation Summary, for week ending August 24, 1918," entry 150, WDGS.

49. Minutes of the Censorship Board, April 17 and May 29, 1918, entry 1, CPI. "U.S. Cable Censorship Digest: Representative of Chief Cable Censor, New Orleans, La.," which is found in "Summaries of Activities of Cable and Post Censor (1917–1918)," n.d., entry 108, CNO. For a description of the duties of each agency at the station level see Censorship Board to "All Censorship Stations," Circulation no. 90, "Rules and Regulations for the Operation and Conduct of United States Postal Censorship Stations," n.d., entry 154, WDGS.

50. W. H. Lamar to George Creel, March 6, 1918, entry 44, PO. See also Creel to Lamar, March 8, 1918; Lamar to Creel, March 19, 1918; and Creel to Lamar, April 3, 1918, entry 44, PO. Lamar summed up his attitude this way: "If the speaker or writer wants his country to win the war, if he feels that his country must win the war, if he be determined, so far as he himself is personally concerned, that it shall win the war, he cannot offend." William H. Lamar, "The Government's Attitude Toward the Press," *Printers' Ink,* August 8, 1918, 135.

51. Minutes of the Censorship Board, October 24, 1918, entry 1, CPI. William Churchill to W. H. Lamar, November 7, 1817, entry 44, PO. George Creel to Robert L. Maddox, December 12, 1917, entry 1, CPI.

52. Minutes of the Censorship Board, April 3, 1918, and George Creel to R. L. Maddox, April 3, 1918, entry 1, CPI.

53. Minutes of the Censorship Board, April 3, 1918. *New York Times,* February 21, 1918. Brooks Shepard to Marlborough Churchill, June 26, 1918, entry 150, WDGS.

54. Minutes of the Censorship Board, September 5 and October 24, 1918, entry 1, CPI.

55. Donald Johnson, *The Challenge to American Freedoms: World War I and the Rise of the American Civil Liberties Union* (Lexington: University Press of Kentucky, 1963), 59. Albert Burleson to Champ Clark, November 18, 1918, entry 40, PO.

56. *Spy Glass,* July 25, 1918, 2. For a discussion of this tradition see Daniel Patrick Moynihan, *Secrecy: The American Experience* (New Haven, CT: Yale University Press, 1998), chapter 2.

57. Harry C. Shriver and Cedric Larson, "Mars with a Blue Pencil: The U.S. Censorship Board of 1917–18," *Bill of Rights Review* 1 (Winter 1941): 302. Mock, *Censorship 1917,* 69.

58. William C. Bullitt to editor, *Philadelphia Public Ledger,* n.d.; George Creel to John J. Spurgeon, November 14, 1917; Creel to Robert Bender, June 5, 1918, entry 1, CPI. Mock, *Censorship 1917,* 139. The story can be found in *Washington Herald,* June 3, 1918.

59. Newton D. Baker to Woodrow Wilson, May 28, 1918, box 4, NDB; H. P. McCain to John Pershing, June 21, 1917, entry 240, AEF. Crozier, *American Reporters,* 126–27. Frederick Palmer to John Buchan, July 28, 1917, entry 240, AEF.

60. George Creel to Mark Sullivan, August 10, 1917, entry 1, CPI. For an instance of Creel helping with letters see Creel to Frederick Palmer, September 7, 1917; and A. L. James to McCabe, July 11, 1918, entry 221, AEF. Bean, "George Creel and His Critics," 85. Walter Campbell Sweeney, *Military Intelligence, a New Weapon in War* (New York: Frederick A. Stokes, 1924), 118. Sweeney headed the AEF Censorship and Press Section of the AEF.

61. George Creel to Woodrow Wilson, March 16, 1918, WW-LC. *HWAA,* 76–78. Ralph Hayes to Frank McIntyre, January 22 and February 5, 1918, entry 150, WDGS. Wilson to George Barr Baker, August 210. 1918, box 6, GBB. Creel to George Barr Baker, August 15, 1918, entry 1, CPI. Creel to Wilson, August 14, 1918, WW-LC. Amos Pinchot to Creel, November 14, 1917, box 25, AP-LC.

62. Mock, *Censorship 1917,* 190–91. George Creel to P. Collins, June 24, 1918; Creel to Joseph Tumulty, September 27, 1918, entry 1, CPI. Vaughn, "First Amendment Liberties and the Committee on Public Information," 110. Rupert Hughes, Memorandum on the Activities of the Book Subsection of the Censorship Section, October 18, 1918, entry 150, WDGS.

63. George Creel, untitled, undated typewritten note; Woodrow Wilson to George Creel, n.d., box 4, GC. *Rebel,* 199.

64. Johnson, *The Challenge to American Freedoms,* 93. George Creel to Roger Baldwin, December 2, 1920, entry 1, CPI. Creel to Harry Weinberger, February 14, 1921, box 1, HW-Y. The list of signatories to the appeal is in box 3, HW-Y. Frederick Pollock, "The Results of Spy Mania," *La Follette's Magazine,* December 1920, 189.

65. Vaughn, "First Amendment Liberties and the Committee on Public Information," 113. Arthur Bestor to George Creel, March 16, 1918; and Creel to William Ingersoll, October 31, 1918, entry 1, CPI. SWW, 19.

66. Office of Naval Intelligence, *Cable Censorship Digest,* 46. Chief Cable Censor, *CCC List,* R7.

67. William Churchill to Assistant Chief of Staff, G-2, October 22, 1918, entry 243, AEF. Broussard, *African American Foreign Correspondents,* 49.

68. Bean, "George Creel and His Critics," 82. George Barr Baker to George Creel, March 20, 1918; R. H. Van Deman to Creel, May 9, 1918, entry 1, CPI. H. L. Haas to William Churchill, September 5, 1918; Office of Military Intelligence to Director, Division of Military Intelligence, September 10, 1918, entry 150, WDGS.

69. A. B. Bielaski to George Creel, May 27, 1918; Creel to W. H. Lamar, October 23, 1918; Creel to Thomas Gregory, July 8, 1918; Creel to John Lord O'Brian, August 15, 1918, entry 1, CPI. Bean, "George Creel and His Critics," 104–5.

70. John Lord O'Brian to George Creel, January 11, 1918; Creel to O'Brian, November 26, 1918, entry 1, CPI.

71. George Creel to Frederick H. Elliott, May 22, 1918, entry 1, CPI. Bean, "George Creel and His Critics," 105–6. Wiegand, *"An Active Instrument for Propaganda,"* 101. Robert Murray to Creel, March 22, 1918, entry 17, CPI.

72. E. Meredith to George Creel, n.d.; Creel to International Film Service, December 28, 1918, entry 164, WDGS. The photograph appeared on December 22, 1917. Mock, *Censorship 1917,* 154, 191. Harvey O'Higgins to editor, July 12, 1918, entry 8, CPI.

73. Blakey, *Historians on the Homefront,* 89. Guy Stanton Ford to George Creel, June 25, 1918; Ford to Albert Shaw, July 3, 1918, entry 1, CPI. *Two Thousand Questions and Answers about the War* (New York: Review of Reviews, 1918), 325.

74. Jeffrey A. Keshen, *Propaganda and Censorship during Canada's Great War* (Edmonton: University of Alberta Press, 1996), 79, and for background on Chambers, 70–73. Ernest J. Chambers to George Creel, December 8, 1917; Creel to Herbert Putnam, December 12 and 14, 1917; Chambers to Creel, January 7, April 22, May 5, and September 18, 1918; Creel to Editor, *Harvard Lampoon,* November 10, 1917; Creel to Editor, *Boston Record,* November 10, 1917; Chambers to Creel, November 7, 1917, entry 1, CPI. To buttress his complaint about stories on Canadians, Creel quoted from Robert E. Sherwood, the future playwright, who had quit Harvard to join the Canadian Black Watch (at six feet eight he was too tall for the US military). Sherwood was director of Franklin Roosevelt's Office of War Information in World War II.

75. Arthur Bullard to George Creel, June 8, 1917, entry 13; Bullard to Creel, June 9, 1917, entry 1, CPI.

76. For CPI staff views on foreign press counter to Bullard's see, for instance, J. W. McConaghy to Edgar Sisson, June 18, 1917, entry 31, CPI. Guy Stanton Ford to Laurence Larson, July 12, September 13, and October 3, 1917, box 1, LML. Larson to Ford, August 25, 1917, entry 27, CPI. Larson to E. B. Greene, January 22, 1918, box 2, NBHS. Edwin Bjorkman to George Creel, April 17, 1918, entry 1; Bjorkman to Carl Byoir, April 18, 1918, entry 105, CPI.

77. Carl Wittke, *The German-Language Press in America* (Lexington: University Press of Kentucky, 1957), 266, and for background, chapter 13. Park, *The Immigrant Press and Its Control,* chapter 27. Luebke, *Bonds of Loyalty,* 228–29.

78. Park, *The Immigrant Press and Its Control,* table 17, following page 318. Paul Finkleman, "The War on German Language and Culture, 1917–1925," in Schroder, *Confrontation and Cooperation,* 193.

79. Julius Koettgen to George Creel, October 7, 1918; Julius Koettgen's reports to Creel, March 18 and November 22, 1918, entry 13, CPI.

80. Gregor Dallas, *At the Heart of a Tiger: Clemenceau and His World, 1841–1928* (New York: Carroll and Graf, 1993), 439. A summary of Clemenceau's efforts to thwart the press can be found in Robert A. Burnett, *"L'Homme Libre—L'Homme Enchaîné:* How a Journalist Handled the Press," *Journalism Quarterly* 50 (Winter 1973): 708–15.

81. Herbert Adams Gibbons, "The Caillaux Case," *Century,* February 1920, 476. *Christian Science Monitor* quoted in Sisley Huddleston, *In My Time: An Observer of War and Peace* (New York: E. P. Dutton, 1938), 58.

82. *Annual Report of the Postmaster General 1918* (Washington, DC: Government Printing Of-

fice, 1919), 12. For a list of publications being stopped see "A list of Newspapers and Other Publications Declared Unamiable," May 10, 1918, entry 154, WDGS. It totaled over three hundred publications. Department of Justice, *Annual Report of the Attorney General 1918,* 47. Stone, *Perilous Times,* 174.

83. Capozzola, *Uncle Sam Wants You,* 157. Ernest Freeberg, *Democracy's Prisoner: Eugene V. Debs, the Great War, and the Right to Dissent* (Cambridge, MA: Harvard University Press, 2008), 58. Pollock, "The Results of Spy Mania," 189. Stone, *Perilous Times,* 230–31.

84. Merrill Rogers to Commission on International Justice and Good-Will, May 3, 1917, box 221, CRIA. Park, *The Immigrant Press and Its Control,* 426. J. Frederick Essary, *Covering Washington: Government Reflected to the Public in the Press, 1822–1926* (Boston: Houghton Mifflin, 1927), 221.

85. *New York Times,* August 267, 1918. Ford, "America's Fight for Public Opinion," 10. *Washington Post,* April 12, 1918. Bruce W. Bidwell, *History of the Intelligence Division, Department of Army General Staff: 1775–1941* (Frederick, MD: University Publications of America, 1986), 200. On the *Post*'s violations of guidelines see *WWW,* 86–88. The AEF general staff concluded, "Almost all American correspondents can be fully trusted." *Reports of the Commander-in-Chief, staff Sections and Service: United States Army in the World War, 1917–1919* (Washington, DC: Center of Military History, 1991), 116.

86. George Creel, speech to City Editors' Association, Columbus, Ohio, January 19, 1918, box 5, GC. As an example of self-policing by journalists, Roy Howard, head of United Press, wrote an angry telegram to Daniels complaining about the AP's dispatch reporting troop landings in late July 1917. "In name of our papers throughout country we file most vigorous protest against action of associated press," Howard wrote, adding, "Request reply by wire to what steps are being taken to protect those who keep faith." Roy Howard to Josephus Daniels, July 28, 1917, box 573, JD.

87. Bean, "George Creel and His Critics," 113. Guy Stanton Ford to George Creel, August 10, 1918 (with editorial appended); Creel to editor, August 15, 1918, entry 1, CPI. The *Commercial-News* editorial was reprinted in the *Chicago Tribune,* August 6, 1918.

10. OFFICIALS OF DOUBTFUL STATUS

1. "Inventory of Furniture and Fixtures in Executive Office," n.d., entry 1, CPI. *The Activities of the Committee on Public Information,* 4–5. Creel's report was transmitted to Wilson on January 7, 1918. Wilson endorsed it on January 14, 1918. Wilson's comment on American harmony was to Ambassador Spring-Rice, *WWLL: 1917–1918,* 447.

2. A. L. James to Dennis Nolan, June 9, 1918, entry 235, AEF. Woodrow Wilson to Frank Marion, November 14, 1917, WW-LC.

3. Caitlín Marie Thérèse Jeffrey, "Journey through Unfamiliar Territory: American Reporters and the First World War" (PhD diss., University of California, Irvine, 2007), 145–46. Frank Marion to George Creel, January 15, 1918, entry 1, CPI.

4. David Lawrence to Woodrow Wilson, April 8, 1917; Lawrence to Robert Lansing, April 7, 1917, WW-LC. Frederic William Wile to Dennis Nolan, June 18, 1917, box 6185, AEF. Frederic William Wile, "General Outline of Scheme for 'Discovering America' for the Benefit of the British Public," n.d., box 86, EMH. Walter Page to Edward M. House, n.d. [April 1917?], box 86, EMH. John Milton Cooper, *Walter Hines Page: The Southerner as American, 1855–1918* (Chapel Hill: University of North Carolina Press, 1977), 381. Proceedings, "Propaganda Inquiry," November 19, 1917, INF 4/11. From the beginning, Bullard advocated foreign publicity. "The British, having sent over to us Prof. Murray and so many propagandists, could hardly object if we returned the compliment.

... The President or Mr. Lansing could in similar way lay our intentions directly before the people of Europe." Arthur Bullard to House, July 18, 1916, box 9, AB. Other suggestions came in. The first week Creel was on the job, H. B. Brougham of the *Philadelphia Public Ledger* suggested his work should stretch to Europe right away. Raymond Graham Swing, a young Paris correspondent with the *Chicago Daily News,* advised House that the United States needed to "reinstate her prestige with the European people" after having taken so long to get into the war. Herbert B. Brougham to House, April; 16, 1917, box 18; Raymond Graham Swing to House, via State Department cable, June 13, 1917, box 108, EMH.

5. Felix Frankfurter to Newton Baker, August 7, 1917, box 45, EMH. In September, Henry Morgenthau returned from Europe with a similar thought. "French affairs are now subject to petty political differences, schemes and counter-schemes of those who are in power and men like Caillaux." A publicity commission was needed "to make Frenchmen forget at this critical juncture all their petty strifes." Henry Morgenthau to Woodrow Wilson, September 15, 1917, box 8, HM-LC. For a glimpse of the swirl of rumors on Caillaux see Gibson diary, June 8, 1918.

6. Arthur Bullard to Edward M. House, July 18, 1916, box 9; Bullard to George Creel, November 17, 1917, box 6, AB. Woodrow Wilson to Creel, January 16 and March 22, 1918, WW-LC. Arthur Bestor to Creel, October 22, 1917; Bestor to John Pettijohn, May 24, 1918; Bestor, "Memorandum to Mr. Pettijohn," June 3, 1918, entry 70, CPI. *HWAA,* 244. Creel's strong interest in propaganda in friendly countries was noted in T. P. O'Connor to Charles Edward Russell, September 4, 1917, box 8, CER. On Wiseman, see Willert, *The Road to Safety,* 94. Creel to Edgar Sisson, August 21, 1918, entry 105, CPI

7. *Foreign Relations of the United States: Lansing Papers, 1914–1920* (Washington, DC: Government Printing Office, 1940), 2:326. *Foreign Relations of the United States: Public Diplomacy, World War I* (Washington, DC: Government Printing Office, 2014), 7. Washburn oral history, 120–21. Russell, who was on the mission, was eager for more to be done immediately by way of publicity and disappointed it was not. The mission distributed half a million copies of Wilson's Flag Day speech, which emphasized German aggression.

8. Robert A. Krantz Jr., "Edgar Sisson's Mission to Russia, 1917–1918" (PhD diss., University of Wichita, 1957), 25–27. See also Richard Leopold, *Elihu Root and the Conservative Tradition* (Boston: Little, Brown, 1954), 119–20. George Creel to Woodrow Wilson, December 27, 1917; Wilson to Creel, December 29, 1917, WW-LC. Creel told his friend Gus Karger that he supported Root's suggestion and thought Root should have gone ahead with his plan when he was in Russia, as it would "never have been repudiated." The idea, Creel said, was "kicked around in the State Department and no one took action." Gus Karger to William Howard Taft, February 28, 1918, WHT.

9. George Creel to Woodrow Wilson, November 15, 1917, WW-LC.

10. Jonathan Fenby, *The International News Services* (New York: Shocken, 1986), 36–39. Walter S. Rogers, "Tinted and Tainted News," *Saturday Evening Post,* July 21, 1917, 82. Walter S. Rogers to Edward M. House, November 20, 1916, box 95, EMH. *PWW,* 43:456–59. Charles R. Crane, "The Life and Letters of Charles R. Crane," ed. Edgar Snow, typescript, n.d., in possession of author, part VI, chapter 6. For discussion of Crane's news ventures see part IV, chapter 7. Another version of the manuscript can be found in the Hoover Institution Archives, Stanford University. One of those whom Rogers urged to do more abroad was Roy Howard. See Rogers to House, December 2, 1916, box 63, EMH. Howard was in touch with Creel, e.g., Roy Howard to George Creel, October 1, 1917, box 63, EMH.

11. Office of Naval Intelligence, *Cable Censorship Digest,* 50–51. *HWAA,* 251. For examples of the news service see entries 135, 138, 179, CPI. *Report,* 117.

12. Poole, *The Bridge*, 267–68, 332. Ernest Poole to George Creel, December 3, 1917, entry 105, CPI. *Report*, 127–40. Owens oral history, 25.

13. Strachan, *The First World War*, 248, 255. Paul Fussell, *The Great War and Modern Memory* (New York: Oxford University Press, 2000), 9, 241. Adam Hochschild, *To End All Wars: A Story of Loyalty and Rebellion, 1914–1918* (New York: Houghton Mifflin Harcourt, 2011), 303. "Confidential Report on the Need and Form of British Propaganda in France," n.d., INF 4/6. Wilkinson, *Secrecy and the Media*, 73. Gibson diary, April 30, 1918.

14. Creel, "A Memorandum for an American Bureau of Public Information in Europe," January 31, 1918, in *PWW*, 46:201.

15. Carl Crow, "The Great War on the China Front," typescript, 3, folder 48, CC. Hamilton, *Journalism's Roving Eye*, 111–12. Paul French, *Carl Crow—A Tough Old China Hand: The Life, Times, and Adventures of an American in Shanghai* (Hong Kong: Hong Kong University Press, 2006), 50–51, 71–72. Nelson Trusler Johnson to Robert Lansing, September 28, 1918; Carl Crow to Johnson, with attached plan for the minister, August 12, 1918; and Harry Rickey to William Phillips, January 3, 1918 [1919], Central Decimal File, 1910–29, box 735, GRDS.

16. Barry D. Karl, *Charles E. Merriam and the Study of Politics* (Chicago: University of Chicago Press, 1974), 12, 45. Daniela Rossini, *Woodrow Wilson and the American Myth in Italy: Culture, Diplomacy, and War Propaganda* (Cambridge, MA: Harvard University Press, 2008), 114.

17. Creel, "A Memorandum for an American Bureau of Public Information in Europe." Kerney, *The Political Education of Woodrow Wilson*, 415. Woodrow Wilson to George Creel, January 2, 1918, WW-LC. Whitehouse, *A Year as a Government Agent*, 80–81. *WWW*, 292. Creel to Wilson, July 31, 1918, box 4, GC. Creel discusses the criticism of Kerney, leveled by Hugh Gibson and Arthur Frazier, in an undated note in box 4, GC.

18. George Creel to James Kerney, May 8, 1918, entry 1, CPI. *HWAA*, 365 and 368. *Report*, 279, 284. Stefan Rinke, *Latin America and the First World War* (Cambridge: Cambridge University Press, 2017), 162. Peter MacQueen, "The Empire of the Children of the Sun," *National Magazine*, July 1914, 570. On the growth of military attachés see James L. Gilbert, *World War I and the Origins of U.S. Military Intelligence* (Lanham, MD: Roman and Littlefield, 2015), 107. *Foreign Relations of the United States: Public Diplomacy*, 50.

19. *Report*, 137. CND Report, subsection 1. State Department to American Embassy, London, telegram, copy, March 24, 1918, entry 159, CPI. A CPI distribution list, n.d., can be found in entry 107, CPI. For CPI listings of overseas offices see distribution list, n.d., in entry 107 and memoranda in entry 105, CPI. For discussion of the difficulty of identifying CPI representatives abroad see *WWW*, 243–45.

20. *HWAA*, 247. Irwin, *The Making of a Reporter*, 352. Vira B. Whitehouse to James Kerney, October 1, 1918, entry 184–86, CPI. Will Irwin, "Report on Foreign Propaganda," n.d., entry 105, CPI. (This report constituted Irwin's plan for managing work overseas.) Russell diary, June 14, 18, 20, and 27, 1918. Russell's frustrations with the British had several dimensions. The British, he thought, did not do enough to support CPI materials; he believed they were suspicious of his intentions on account of his socialist leanings; he disliked their assiduous propagandizing of Americans to further their imperial interests. On this see Russell, typescript on British propaganda, 1925, box 37, CER. He also had complaints about the CPI not responding to his queries and the nature of the work. He thought that he would be explaining America to the British and vice versa, but he found his brief much narrower. See Charles Edward Russell to Will Irwin, June 11, 1918, box 9, CER.

21. Frank Marion to Will Irwin, April 2, 1918, entry 110, CPI. "GAD" to George Creel, May 13, 1918, entry 110, CPI. Vira B. Whitehouse to Edgar Sisson, September 30, 1918, entry 184–86, CPI.

22. Creel to Vira B. Whitehouse, December 31, 1917, VBW.

23. French, *Carl Crow*, 72. Crow, "The Great War on the China Front," 22, 25. For a discussion of diplomats' elitist attitudes see Martin Weil, *A Pretty Good Club: The Founding Fathers of the U.S. Foreign Service* (New York: W. W. Norton, 1978). Carl Crow, "President Wilson's Eyes & Ears," typescript, 1, folder 46, CC.

24. The story of the Gibson martini is told in Perrin C. Galpin, ed., *Hugh Gibson, 1883–1954: Extracts from His Letters and Anecdotes from His Friends* (New York: Belgian American Education Foundation, 1956), 28–29. For more detail on Gibson's role with this salubrious beverage see Lowell Edmunds, *Martini, Straight Up: The Classic American Cocktail* (Baltimore: Johns Hopkins University Press, 1998), 141. Charles Dana Gibson, also associated with the CPI, is sometimes credited with the martini invention. The homage paid to Gibson by Galpin suggests the deep friendships he made with Herbert Hoover and many others who enjoyed his clever humor and respected his professional work. Yet he created another set of memories, as noted in Robert M. Crunden, *A Hero in Spite of Himself: Brand Whitlock in Art, Politics and War* (New York: Alfred A. Knopf, 1969), 365.

25. William Sharp to embassy, Rome, March 11, 1918, entry 166, CPI. Sharp, March 6, 1918, inserted in Gibson diary, April 28, 1918. Creel to Will Irwin, May 4, 1918, entry 110, CPI.

26. Hugh Gibson to Will Irwin, May 21, 1918, box 46, HSG. Gibson to Philip Patchin, June 22, 1918, box 56, HSG. Vira Whitehouse also thought Gibson wanted his job. Gibson diary, October 3, 1918. Charles Merriam to George Creel, May 7, 1918, entry 110, CPI.

27. Gibson's suggestions are attached to Hugh Gibson to Martin Egan, June 20, 1918, ME. Gibson diary, April 13 and 14, 1918. Irwin, possibly on advice from Gibson, turned down Kerney's proposal with the argument that the money for it was needed elsewhere. Will Irwin to James Kerney, April 20, 1918, entry 107, CPI.

28. Hugh Gibson, note, June 6, 1918, box 83; Gibson to Philip Patchin, May 30, 1918, box 56, HSG. Gibson diary, April 30, 1918. Hugh Frazier, a senior diplomat who worked closely with Gibson, wrote to Lansing and House about what was wrong with propaganda in Europe, noting that Gibson wanted to keep his views unattributed: "Gibson is as much alive to the situation as I am, but his position precludes him from expressing his views with the same frankness." Jackson Alfred Giddens, "American Foreign Propaganda in World War I" (PhD diss., Tufts University, 1966), 330.

29. Weil, *A Pretty Good Club*, 46–47.

30. *New York Times*, April 5, 1908. *San Francisco Examiner*, July 19, 1903. The clippings in VBW are full of similar comments. *Wall Street Journal*, December 13, 1926. Gregg Wolper, "Woodrow Wilson's New Diplomacy," *Prologue*, Fall 1992, 228.

31. *New York Times*, August 19, 1915, December 1 and 12, 1918, April 12, 1957. *New York Evening Post*, November 21, 1916. Vira B. Whitehouse to Alice Paul, July 9, 1917, boxes 50–51, NAWSA. Doris Daniels, "Building a Winning Coalition: The Suffrage Fight in New York State," *New York History* 60 (January 1979): 79.

32. Vira B. Whitehouse, *A Year as a Government Agent* (New York: Harper, 1920), 2–4, 289. Vira Whitehouse, "Report of Mrs. Norman de R. Whitehouse," n.d.; George Creel to Vira B. Whitehouse, December 31, 1917, VBW.

33. *New York World*, December 31, 1917, January 10, 1918. *New York Times*, December 31, 1917, January 9 and 10, 1918.

34. Frank Polk to Embassy Paris, telegram, January 22, VBW. The wording for the denial was from George Creel to Frank Polk, January 21, 1918, box 4, FLP. "Paraphrase of Telegram Received from Department of State dated January 26 [1918]," VBW.

35. Hugh R. Wilson, *Diplomat between Wars* (New York: Longmans, Green, 1941), 17. White-house handwritten note on "Copy Telegram," [January 1918], VBW. Whitehouse, *A Year as a Government Agent,* 28–29. Hugh Wilson to secretary of state, cable, February 8, 1918, VBW. Vira B. Whitehouse to George Creel, February 11, 1918, entry 1, CPI.

36. Stephen Kinzer, *The Brothers: John Foster Dulles, Allen Dulles, and Their Secret World War* (New York: Henry Holt, 2013), 22–23. Pleasant Alexander Stovall, *Switzerland and the World War* (Savannah, GA: Mason, 1939), 178. Vira B. Whitehouse to George Creel, February 24, 1918, entry 1, CPI. Allen Dulles to Robert Lansing, February 11, 1918, box 37, AWD.

37. House diary, May 29, 1917. Charles Seymour, ed., *The Intimate Papers of Colonel House* (Boston, MA: Houghton Mifflin, 1928), 3:132–35. Walter S. Rogers to Edward M. House, May 14, 1917, box 95, EMH. Carl Ackerman, *Washington Evening Star,* June 24, 1917. Carl W. Ackerman, "The War of Words," *Saturday Evening Post,* September 8, 1917, 8. Carl Ackerman, "Robert VanderHoof Ackerman," unpublished manuscript, n.d., chapter 3, page 6, CA. House diary, October 4, 1917. Ackerman, Memorandum to Library of Congress, June 21, 1962, box 158, CWA. Carl W. Ackerman, "Fighting for a Free Press," *Saturday Evening Post,* April 16, 1918, 145. Ackerman to House, December 20, 1917, box 1, EMH. Ackerman told House that he would go to London or Italy if he could be of service there. Ackerman to House, February 4, 1918, box 1, EMH. On the *Post* being aware of the arrangement see Paul Abelson to Mrs. Carl Ackerman, box 143, CWA. Hugh Wilson to Lansing, February 11, 1918, Central Decimal File, 1910–29, box 736, GRDS.

38. Carl Ackerman to Edward M. House, January 7 and April 29, 1918, box 1, EMH. Ackerman to House, February 9, 1918, Central Decimal File, 1910–29, box 736, GRDS. Whitehouse, *A Year as a Government Agent,* 104–5. For an example of Ackerman taking on assignments for Hugh Wilson see Hugh Wilson to State Department, January 30, 1918, box 1, EMH. For an example of Ackerman offering views on other correspondents see Carl Ackerman to Edward M. House, January 26, 1918, box 1, EMH. Ackerman wrote a long memorandum to Hugh Wilson spelling out why propaganda needed to be disguised and carried out through seemingly independent news agencies as the French and British did. Ackerman to Wilson, February 12, 1918, Central Decimal File, 1910–29, box 736, GRDS. On his demeanor see Ackerman, "Robert VanderHoof Ackerman," chapter 2, page 4. While a United Press correspondent in Berlin, his neighbors cautioned him to lower his voice when he told his wife about the day's doings.

39. Hugh Wilson to secretary of state, February 8, 1918, VBW. Vira B. Whitehouse to Woodrow Wilson, January 30, 1918, entry 1, CPI. Creel's note to Whitehouse on Wilson's approval is in Robert Lansing to Bern legation, February 16, 1918, VBW. Gregg Wolper, "The Origins of Public Diplomacy: Woodrow Wilson, George Creel, and the Committee on Public Information" (PhD diss., University of Chicago, 1991,) 34–35.

40. Allen Dulles to Robert Lansing, August 13, 1917, box 30, RL. Arthur Hugh Frazier to Edward M. House, April 4, 1918, box 45, EMH. Wilson, *Diplomat between Wars,* 11–12. Peter Grose, *Gentleman Spy: The Life of Allen Dulles* (Boston: Houghton Mifflin, 1994), 28–29. Gibson noted in his diary that Stovall returned to Bern "in a much more amenable state of mind. . . . Anything that is done and submitted to him he approves." Gibson diary, April 20, 1918. Vira Whitehouse to Pleasant Stovall, March 9, 1918, entry 110, CPI.

41. Robert Lansing to Embassy Paris, March 15, 1918; Vira B. Whitehouse to George Creel, March 18, 1918, VBW.

42. Robert Lansing to Embassy Paris, March 22, 1918, VBW. Creel told Wilson that he wanted to avoid open conflict with the legation. George Creel to Woodrow Wilson, March 26, 1918,

WW-LC. Whitehouse, *A Year as a Government Agent*, 88. *Baton Rouge State Times Advocate*, April 16, 1918; story appears with a photo of Whitehouse. The *New York World* story is by Herbert Bayard Swope, March 29, 1918. Creel to Vira B. Whitehouse, via Navintel, March 23, 1918, VBW.

43. Whitehouse, *A Year as a Government Agent*, 98–100.

44. Carl Ackerman to Edward M. House, 12 April 1918, box 1, EMH. Pleasant Stovall to Woodrow Wilson, March 27, 1918, and Stovall to Robert Lansing, May 8, 1918, Central Decimal File, 1910–29, box 736, GRDS. "Introductory Note" to Stovall, *Switzerland and the World War*, 7. Gibson diary, April 21 and 22, 1918.

45. Hugh Gibson to Will Irwin, April 24, 1918, entry 110, CPI. Hugh Wilson to Irwin, April 25, 1918, Central Decimal File, 1910-29, box 732, GRDS. Gibson diary, April 20, 1918. Gibson to Irwin, paraphrase of telegram, April 24, 1918, ME. Gibson said Charles Grasty had "promised [Ackerman] the representation in Switzerland of the New York Times." Grasty, who had been treasurer of the *New York Times*, was at the time a war correspondent for the paper. In his book on the war, he called Switzerland a "beehive of German propagandism." Charles Grasty, *Flashes form the Front* (New York: Century, 1918), 179. George Creel to Norman de R. Whitehouse, April 12, 1918, entry 1, CPI. Woodrow Wilson to George Creel, March 27, 1918, WW-LC.

46. Woodrow Wilson to George Creel, April 19, 1918, WW-LC. Creel to Charles Hart, May 20, 1918, entry 1, CPI. Vira B. Whitehouse to Joseph Tumulty, April 27, 1918, attached to Wilson to Tumulty, May 8, 1918, WW-LC. Philip Patchin to Hugh Gibson, May 27, 1918, box 56, HSG.

47. Woodrow Wilson to Vira B. Whitehouse, May 23, 1918; Wilson to Pleasant Stovall, May 23, 1918, WW-LC. Wilson also told Lansing that Whitehouse went "with his approval." Wilson to Robert Lansing, May 23, 1918, WW-LC.

48. Whitehouse, *A Year as a Government Agent*, 112–15, 121–23. Gibson diary, July 14, 1918. Vira B. Whitehouse to Paul Kennaday, July 17, 1918, entry 183; Whitehouse to James Kerney, August 5, 1918, entry 148, CPI.

49. John Pershing to Newton Baker, November 15, 1917, box 20, JJP. Herbert Corey, "Perfectly Irresponsible," chapter 11, page 108, unpublished manuscript, HC. Walter von Hofmann, "Organisation der feindlichen Propaganda: Vereinigte Staaten von Amerika," MSG2-15139, 1918, BArch-MA. Earl H. Smith to Dennis Nolan, March 16, 1918, entry 239, AEF. Vira B. Whitehouse to James Kerney, July 22, 1918, entry 148, CPI.

50. Alfred Erich Senn, *Diplomacy and Revolution: The Soviet Mission to Switzerland, 1918* (Notre Dame, IN: University of Notre Dame Press, 1974), 111. Vira B. Whitehouse to W. F. H. Godson, September 24, 1918, entry 183, CPI.

51. Harry Kessler, *Journey to the Abyss: The Diaries of Count Harry Kessler, 1880–1918* (New York: Vintage, 2013), 748, 831. Vira B. Whitehouse to W. F. H. Godson, September 24, 1918, entry 183, CPI. J. C. O'Laughlin to Dennis Nolan, August 10, 1918, entry 235, AEF. This is an illuminating report on propaganda in Switzerland and reactions to Whitehouse.

52. Vira B. Whitehouse to Paul Kennaday, August 5, 1918, entry 183, CPI. Whitehouse, "Report of Mrs. Norman de R. Whitehouse." Wolper, "Woodrow Wilson's New Diplomacy," 46.

53. Whitehouse, *A Year as a Government Agent*, 132. Vira B. Whitehouse to W. F. H. Godson, August 7 and September 24, 1918; Whitehouse to Walter S. Rogers, September 3, 1918, entry 183, CPI. Whitehouse, "Report of Mrs. Norman de R. Whitehouse."

54. Kessler, *Journey to the Abyss*, 753. Louis Ador to Vira B. Whitehouse, August 24, 1918, entry 188, CPI. Whitehouse to George Creel, June 14, 1918; Whitehouse to William Jury, June 19 and July 20, 1918; Jury to Whitehouse, June 25, 1918, entry 186, CPI. The genesis of the plan is laid out

in F. N. Bates to Whitehouse, February 6 and 16, 1918, entry 186, CPI. "Telegram sent June 30, 1918, for Creel from Whitehouse," entry 186, CPI.

55. Ward, *The Motion Picture Goes to War,* 120. An example of the export agreement is in entry 1, CPI. Whitehouse, *A Year as a Government Agent,* 151–55.

56. Vira B. Whitehouse to Walter S. Rogers, September 3, 1918, entry 183, CPI.

57. Whitehouse, "Report of Mrs. Norman de R. Whitehouse." Vira B. Whitehouse to Paul Kennaday, August 24, 1918; Kennaday to Whitehouse, October 8, 1918; Whitehouse to James Kerney, August 27, 1918, entry 183, CPI. Whitehouse to A. L. James, October 15, 1918, entry 239, AEF. Whitehouse to R. H. Van Deman, August 14, 1918; Whitehouse to A. L. James, November 4, 1918, entry 183, CPI. See telegrams, William Sharp to Legation, Bern, September 20, October 15 and 17, 1918, entries 184–86, CPI.

58. Whitehouse, *A Year as a Government Agent,* 262. Stoval's attitude toward Schwimmer is outlined in her letter to Whitehouse, December 7, 1918, RS. Details of this mission are found in Wolper, "Woodrow Wilson's New Diplomacy"; and Tibor Glant, "Against All Odds: Vira B. Whitehouse and Rosika Schwimmer in Switzerland, 1918," *American Studies International* 40 (February 2002): 34–51.

59. Vira B. Whitehouse to George Creel, October 22, 1918, entry 183, CPI. Wolper, "The Origins of Public Diplomacy," 47. Herbert Walter, the *London Times* correspondent in Bern, carried out propaganda for Northcliffe. Walter criticized Whitehouse's openness. "In this connection," an American intelligence officer reported, "it was learned that Mrs. Whitehouse requested that Mr. Walters be recalled." The intelligence officer went on to say that French and Italian reporters and Swiss editors thought her openness "advantageous as far as the Swiss people themselves are concerned." J. C. O'Laughlin to Dennis Nolan, August 10, 1918, entry 235, AEF. James Kerney to George Creel, August 20, 1918, entry 1, CPI. Allen Dulles to Robert Lansing, August 24, 1918, box 37, AWD. Whitehouse and Dulles, who was a dedicated ladies' man, seem to have reached their own entente cordiale by the time she returned to Washington to protest her circumstances. Before leaving Paris and uncertain she would return, Whitehouse wrote to Dulles, "I hope fate will be kind enough to throw us together again and let us be friends in spite of differences of age, up-bringing, ideas, ideals and everything that as a rule makes friendship an impossibility." Vira B. Whitehouse to Dulles, April 5, 1918, box 58, AWD. See also Gibson diary, June 17, 1918.

60. Whitehouse, *A Year as a Government Agent,* 219.

61. George Creel to Norman Whitehouse, November 4, 1918, VBW. Wilson, *Diplomat between Wars,* chapter 2.

62. Joseph Willard to Frank Marion, January 9, 1918; Creel to Polk, February 20, 1918; Marion to Willard, January 10, 1918; Marion to George Creel, January 17, 1918; Creel to William Churchill, August 23, 1918, entry 1, CPI. Leslie Eaton Clark, *George Bronson Rea, Propagandist: The Life and Times of a Mercenary Journalist* (Madison, NJ: Fairleigh Dickinson University Press, 2018), 132–33. *Propaganda in Its Military and Legal Aspects* (Washington, DC: Military Intelligence Branch, 1918), 36. Creel to Frank Polk, June 21, 1918, box 4, 1918; Nicholas Murray to Norman Hapgood, September 16, 1916, box 7, FLP. Woolley refers to Murray's State Department work in Robert Woolley to Edward M. House, January 24, 1917, box 124, EMH. Polk to ambassador, Mexico City, June 21, 1918, Central Decimal File, 1910–29, box 732, GRDS. On Reichenbach see R. H. Van Deman to George Creel, April 2, 1918; and Harry Rickey to Creel, November 25, 1918, entry 1, CPI; and Edward Bell to Hugh Gibson, November 6, 1918, box 14, 1918, HSG.

63. George Creel to Wrisley Brown, November 25, 1918, entry 1, CPI. Louis John Nigro Jr.,

"Propaganda, Politics, and the New Diplomacy: The Impact of Wilsonian Propaganda on Politics and Public Opinion in Italy, 1917–1918" (PhD diss., Vanderbilt University, 1979), 81. Walter Page to Woodrow Wilson, April 23, 1918; Page to Robert Lansing, January 29, 1918, box 10, TNP. Charles Merriam to Creel, April 15, 1918, entry 166, CPI.

64. Charles Merriam, "Ode to Uncivil Service and Administrative Management," n.d., box 1, CEM. Charles Merriam to Will Irwin, May 14, 1918, entry 110, CPI. John H. Hearley, "Final Report—Rome Office Activities," n.d., box 10, CEM. Walter Wanger to Merriam, May 25 and July 28, 1918, entry 170, CPI.

65. Charles Merriman to Will Irwin, May 21, 1918, entry 110, CPI. Karl, *Charles E. Merriam*, 87, 91–92. Rossini, *Woodrow Wilson and the American Myth in Italy*, 114. Charles Edward Russell to James Kerney, August 31, 1918, entry 148, CPI. Giddens, "American Foreign Propaganda in World War I," 94–97.

66. Gino Speranza, *The Diary of Gino Speranza, Italy, 1915–1919* (New York: MMS, 1966), 2:209–10. Thomas Nelson Page to Robert Lansing, September 24, 1918, box 734, and Page to Lansing, September 30, 1918, Central Decimal File 1910–29, box 535, GRDS. Rossini, *Woodrow Wilson and the American Myth in Italy*, 228. Walter Page to Arthur Hugh Frazier, October 11, box 11, TNP. Wolper, "The Origins of Public Diplomacy," 101, 106. George Creel to William Churchill, October 9, 1918, entry 1, CPI. Creel to Woodrow Wilson, January 8, 1918, WW-LC.

67. Kingsley Moses to Charles Merriam, August 7, 1918, entry 170, CPI. Kingsley Moses, "Report to Captain Merriam," n.d., entry 170, CPI. Gibson diary, June 5 and July 24, 1918. Hugh Gibson to Philip Patchin, June 22, 1918, box 56, HSG. Whitehouse, *A Year as a Government Agent*, 80. Gibson shared Whitehouse's view of Kerney's work ethic. Gibson diary, May 9 and June 2, 1918.

68. *Report*, 198. Edwin Bjorkman to Carl Byoir, July 17, 1918, entry 105, CPI. *WWW,* 229.

69. Charles E. Merriam, "American Publicity in Italy," *American Political Science Review* 13 (November 1919): 552. *Washington Post,* July 4, 1918. On the AP wires being jammed (with a whopping 16,750 words of cabled news) see Jackson Elliott to Elmer Roberts, July 8, 1918, box 2, ER-UNC. Irwin, *Propaganda and the News,* 196

70. Rossini, *Woodrow Wilson and the American Myth in Italy*, 115. Whitehouse, *A Year as a Government Agent,* 118. J. R. Mott to George Creel, February 8, 1918; Woodrow Wilson to Creel, August 2, 1918, WW-LC. Mott to Creel, September 7, 1918, entry 1, CPI. Nigro, "Propaganda, Politics, and the New Diplomacy," 107. C. Howard Hopkins, *John R. Mott, 1865–1955: A Biography* (Grand Rapids, MI: William B. Eerdmans, 1979), 524.

71. Bernays, *Biography of an Idea,* 157. *HWAA,* 367. *Report,* 136.

72. Irwin, *Propaganda and the News,* 195.

73. Norman Whitehouse to Vira B. Whitehouse, September 26, 1918, JNW. The visiting journalists' trip is chronicled in Norman Whitehouse's letters to his wife. For instance, Norman Whitehouse to Vira B. Whitehouse, October 19, 1918, JNW.

74. Daniels diary, September 10, 1918. *Report,* 205. Wolper, "The Origins of Public Diplomacy," 158. James Kerney, Second Report on Lectures, 1918, entry 1, CPI.

75. Rossini, *Woodrow Wilson and the American Myth in Italy*, 121. Nigro, "Propaganda, Politics, and the New Diplomacy," 137. Rudolph Altrocchi to Kingsley Moses, July 23 and August 2, 1918, box 3, RA. "Summary of Information Regarding Current Italian Propaganda," April 23, 1918, entry 170, CPI. George Creel, "America's Fight for World Opinion," *Everybody's,* February 1919, 15.

76. *HWAA,* 243.

77. Vira B. Whitehouse to George Creel and Edgar Sisson, July 29, 1918; Whitehouse to Creel,

June 14, 1918, entry 186, CPI. A description of Northcliffe's plan is in Campbell Stuart, *Secrets of Crewe House; The Story of a Famous Campaign* (London: Hodder and Stoughton, 1920), 99. Wolper, "The Origins of Public Diplomacy," 56.

78. Clark, *George Bronson Rea, Propagandist,* 127–29. Frank Marion to James Kerney, with accompanying report, March 16, 1918, entry 148, CPI. *WWW,* 270–71, 329. Gregg Wolper, "Wilsonian Public Diplomacy: The Committee on Public Information in Spain," *Diplomatic History* 17 (Winter 1993): 27.

79. *WWW,* 305. Edgar Ansel Mowrer, *Triumph and Turmoil: A Personal History of Our Time* (New York: Weybright and Talley, 1968), 100.

80. Grubbs, *The Struggle for Labor Loyalty,* 107–10. Rossini, *Woodrow Wilson and the American Myth in Italy,* 124. John Reinertson, "Colonel House, Woodrow Wilson and European Socialism, 1917–1918" (PhD diss., University of Wisconsin, 1971), 486. Merriam, "American Publicity in Italy," 553.

81. George Creel to Philip Patchin, May 1, 1918, entry 1, CPI. Wolper, "The Origins of Public Diplomacy," 60. Frank Bohn to Dennis Nolan, March 10, 1918, entry 235, AEF. Vira B. Whitehouse to Creel, June 16, 1918; Robert Lansing to Bern Legation, November 15, 1918, entry 186, CPI. Gibson diary, April 21, 1918. "Godson" to military staff, Washington, May 8, 1918, entry 110, CPI. Creel to Richard Crane, October 8, 1918; Creel to Julius Koettgen, November 11, 1918; Creel to Rupert Hughes, July 3, 1918, entry 1, CPI.

82. Edward Robinette, "Memorandum of Propaganda in Scandinavia," March 26, 1918, entry 110, CPI. See also American Embassy, London, to State Department, May 22, 1918, entry 195, CPI. Irwin, *Propaganda and the News,* 159–60.

83. Embassy London to Department of State, Washington, May 22, 1918, Central Decimal File, 1910–29, box 9303, GRDS. In the same file see Department of State to Paris, January 25, 1918; Department of State to Stockholm, January 29, 1918; Stockholm to Department of State, June 15, 1918. Theoden Adelsward and Otto Mannheimer, "Basis Concerning Creation of a New Press Agency in Sweden," February 18, 1918, entry 195, CPI. B. J. C. McKercher, *Esme Howard: A Diplomatic Biography* (New York: Cambridge, 1989), 185–86. Robinette report attached to Roger Welles to Will Irwin, July 17, 1918, entry 110, CPI. Attachment with Roger Welles to Leland Harrison, July 17, 1918, Records Kept by Leland Harrison, entry A1-347, GRDS.

84. Miles Bouton to AP New York, intercepted cable, June 5, 1918; Bouton to Melville Stone, June 17, 1918; Philip Patchin to Leland Harrison, n.d.; Robert Lansing to embassy, Stockholm, July 5, 1918; Irwin Laughlin to Lansing, September 27, 1918, Central Decimal File, 1910–29, box 9303, GRDS. Robert Collins to Stone, copy of letter, n.d., entry 161, CPI. Bouton's harassment by his government is chronicled in his unpublished memoir, "A Veteran Journalist Reports," chapters 16–20, box 6, SMB. Before being dismissed from the AP, Bouton was the first American correspondent in Berlin after the armistice. The State Department was anxious about this. A diplomat in Stockholm said the "dream of [Boutin's life] was to return to Germany and spend the rest of his days there." Sheldon Whitehouse to Leland Harrison, November 1918, Records Kept by Leland Harrison, entry A1-349, GRDS. Van Deman claimed Bouton had gone to Berlin to "create sentiment in United States favorable to furnish German food supply." Miles Bouton to Newton Baker, September 2, 1919, box 1, SMB.

85. Will Irwin to Harry Rickey, April 9, 1918, Central Decimal File, 1910–29, box 732, GRDS. On Robinette Navy Cross, see https://valor.militarytimes.com/hero/9990. Lord Northcliffe to Edward M. House, October 23, 1919, box 83(a), EMH.

86. Crow, "The Great War on the China Front," 15–18. French, *Carl Crow,* 78. His condemnation of the Germans for doing the same thing is mentioned in Hans Schmidt, "Democracy for China: American Propaganda and the May Fourth Movement," *Diplomatic History* 22 (Winter 1998): 28. *HWAA,* 362.

87. Crow, "The Great War on the China Front," 17–21. French, *Carl Crow,* 80–81. *HWAA,* 361. *Report,* 276.

88. R. H. Van Deman to George Creel, "Liaison between Army Intelligence and U.S. Foreign Education Campaign," February 7, 1918, entry 111, CPI. Arthur Woods to Van Deman, February 28, 1918, entry 111, CPI. Kingsley Moses to Charles Merriam, September 11, 1918, entry 170, CPI. Speranza, *The Diary of Gino Speranza,* 2:210. Wolper, "Wilsonian Public Diplomacy," 112. "The situation here while good on the surface contains very many elements of danger underneath the official surface of things," Merriam melodramatically told Creel. "I take it that the Committee wishes me to go as deeply into what is going on as is possible." Merriam to Creel, May 7, 1918, entry 110, CPI.

89. Captain Wickes, handwritten note, March 9, 1918, entry 156, AEF. George Creel to A. C. Murray, January 24, 1918, entry 1, CPI. James Kerney to Will Irwin, June 24, 1918, entry 152, CPI. Creel to Carl Hayden, July 8, 1918, entry 1, CPI.

90. Whitehouse, *A Year as a Government Agent,* 269.

91. Whitehouse, *A Year as a Government Agent,* 286.

92. Vira B. Whitehouse to George Creel and Edgar Sisson, July 29, 1918, entry 185–186, CPI.

93. Henry Suydam, "Memorandum," April 8, 1918, box 9, CER. Charles Edward Russell to Will Irwin, May 19, 1918, entry 110, CPI. *WWW,* 297–98. Egan diary, May 22, 1918. Russell diary, June 20, 1918.

94. Will Irwin to Charles Edward Russell, July 8, 1918, box 9, CER. *WWW,* 267. Edwin Bjorkman to Walter S. Rogers and Edgar Sisson, August 16, 1918, entry 105, CPI. For examples of various news stories see entry 187, CPI. Irwin to Kerney, fragment of letter, n.d., entry 107, CPI.

95. "Memorandum Regarding Foreign Press Division (Cable Service)," May 28, 1918, entry 13, CPI. Another set of statistics is found in *Report,* 122–25; see also 126, 137. For examples of Homestuff, see, September 10 and 11 and November 5, 1918, entry 137, CPI. *HWAA,* 256–57. John Russell report on mail service, August 9, 1918, box 105, CPI. John L. Balderson to Paul Kennaday, September 28, 1918, entry 1, CPI.

96. John H. Hearley, "Final Report—Rome Office Activities," n.d. [1919], box 10, CEM.

97. *Report,* 285. [US Embassy?] to George Creel, June 6, 1919, with "Report on Propaganda Work," entry 1, CPI.

98. Wolper, "Wilsonian Public Diplomacy," 17–34. Guy Croswell Smith, report, n.d. but sent with a June 1 covering letter, entry 106, CPI. Richard Wood, introduction to *Film and Propaganda in America: A Documentary History* (New York: Greenwood, 1990), 1:xxvi.

99. Erez Manela, *The Wilsonian Moment: Self-Determination and the International Origins of Anticolonial Nationalism* (New York: Oxford University Press, 2007), passim, on the impact of Wilson ideology on colonies. Nigro, "Propaganda, Politics, and the New Diplomacy," 5.

100. *Report,* 161, 276. *WWW,* 331. A discussion of journalism tours is in *HWAA,* chapter 20. Merriam arranged Italian tours and Bjorkman Scandinavian tours to the United States. Commissioners also organized tours to AEF lines. Nigro, "Propaganda, Politics, and the New Diplomacy," 79. Rossini, *Woodrow Wilson and the American Myth in Italy,* 123. Rogers, "Tinted and Tainted News," 17. On Crow also see Manela, *The Wilsonian Moment,* 100–103.

101. Harold Nicolson, *Diplomacy* (London: Oxford University Press, 1950), 168–69.

102. Richard T. Arndt, *The First Resort of Kings: American Cultural Diplomacy in the Twentieth Century* (Washington, DC: Potomac Books, 2005), 27, 512. "The consensus [is that the term was coined by] retired diplomat and Dean of the Fletcher School of Law and Diplomacy [Tufts University].... He was searching for a term other than propaganda that would be an umbrella for 'information,' 'cultural diplomacy,' and 'international broadcasting.'" Bruce Gregory to Michael Schneider, May 25, 2019, forwarded to author. Joseph S. Nye Jr., "The Future of American Power: Dominance and Decline in Perspective," *Foreign Affairs*, November–December 2010, 2.

103. Philip Patchin to Hugh Gibson, June 10, 1918, box 56, HSG. Ambassador Page advanced the same idea as a solution to his Merriam problem; see Gibson diary, August 30, 1918. The country team concept was created in 1961. In 1964 a House Foreign Affairs Committee study found that more than twenty departments and agencies were running ideological and psychological activities abroad, all of it much improved by the country team concept. Subcommittee on International Organization and Movements, *Ideological Operations and Foreign Policy* (Washington, DC: Government Printing Office, 1964), 17.

104. Lois W. Roth, "Public Diplomacy and the Past: The Search for an American Style of Propaganda (1952–1977)," *Fletcher Forum*, Summer 1984, 354. Denver Nicks, "Lawmakers Push Changes for Voice of America," *Time*, May 1, 2014, http://time.com/84965/voice-of-america-congress/.

105. Loch K. Johnson, *America's Secret Power: The CIA in a Democratic Society* (New York: Oxford University Press, 1918), 183. These activities were covered extensively in a three-part *New York Times* series, December 25, 26, 27, 1977.

106. *New York Times*, April 20, 2008.

107. Ackerman, *Germany*, 289.

11. A HAZY AFFAIR

1. *Report*, 114–15, 174. Creel gives slightly more attention to field propaganda but without indicating what actually occurred (and again misleadingly mentions the July meeting) in *HWAA*, part II, chapter 5. *WWW*, chapter 11, mentions that the AEF took over field propaganda, but again without specifics. *WWW* refers readers to Blankenhorn's account, *Adventures in Propaganda: Letters from an Intelligence Officer in France* (Boston: Houghton Mifflin, 1919), which is useful but mentions the CPI only once, in passing. Neither Creel nor Keeley appear in the book anywhere.

2. Gibson diary, August 10, 1918. Reichenbach, *Phantom Fame*, 238–39. Bruntz, *Allied Propaganda and the Collapse of the German Empire*, 45, 74. *New York Times*, February 16, 1918.

3. Viereck, *Spreading Germs of Hate*, 145. Bruntz, *Allied Propaganda and the Collapse of the German Empire*, 85. Henry Suydam to Edgar Sisson, August 12, 1918, entry 107, CPI. On German efforts to manipulate news in these countries see Elisabeth Fondren, "'Breathless Zeal and Careless Confidence': German Propaganda in World War I (1914–1918)" (PhD diss., Louisiana State University, 2018), 109, 111, 166; and Otto Hammann, Foreign Office, to Imperial Navy Press Office, August 1, 1914, RM3/10266, BArch-MA.

4. Campbell Stuart, *Secrets of Crewe House*, 169. *Report*, 175. *WWW*, 255.

5. Hugh Gibson to Will Irwin, April 17, 1918, entry 110, CPI.

6. Giddens, "American Foreign Propaganda in World War I," 306–14.

7. *WWW*, 258–59.

8. Edward M. Coffman, *The War to End All Wars: The American Military Experience in World War I* (Lexington: University Press of Kentucky, 1998), chapter 2.

9. E. Alexander Powell, *The Army behind the Army* (New York: Charles Scribner's Sons, 1919), 332. Gilbert, *World War I and the Origins of U.S. Military Intelligence,* 83. Van Deman, *The Final Memoranda,* 21–22. Messenger, *British Propaganda and the State in the First World War,* 103.

10. Stanley Washburn to Robert Lansing, April 2, 1917, box 1, SW. Peter Hart, *The Great War: A Combat History of the First World War* (New York: Oxford University Press, 2013), 412.

11. George Creel to R. H. Van Deman, March 19, 1918, entry 1. Frederic William Wile to Dennis Nolan, June 18, 1917, box 6185, AEF. Wile, *News Is Where You Find It,* 361, 374–75.

12. Gilbert J. Gall, "Heber Blankenhorn: The Publicist as Reformer," *Historian* 45 (August 1983): 515, 525.

13. Blankenhorn oral history, 76–78.

14. Giddens, "American Foreign Propaganda in World War I," 248, 253–58. Blankenhorn oral history, 79.

15. Powell, *The Army behind the Army,* 347–48. Clayton D. Laurie, "'The Chanting of Crusaders': Captain Heber Blankenhorn and AEF Combat Propaganda in World War I," *Journal of Military History* 1 (July 1995): 459–62. Blankenhorn oral history, 80–86. A report around this time noted the weakening of enemy morale by "psychological means." Unknown author, "Memorandum No. 11," February 13, 1918, entry 222, AEF.

16. Creel, "A Memorandum for an American Bureau of Public Information in Europe."

17. Frederick Palmer to Compub, telegram, April 2 and 5, 1918, Central Decimal File, 1910–29, box 732, GRDS.

18. Will Irwin to Hugh Gibson, April 8, 1917, and April 12, 1917, box 46, HSG. Irwin to Gibson, May 7, 1918, Central Decimal File, 1910–29, box 732, GRDS. *WWW,* 252. "Memorandum of Conversation with Commandant Chaix," June 13, 1918, and "Memorandum: From Pershing, June 20, 1918, paraphrase," entry 235, AEF.

19. Joseph Green to Frederick Palmer, March 12, 1918, entry 240, AEF. Hugh Gibson to Will Irwin, April 9, 1918; Gibson, memorandum, April 4, 1918, entry 110, CPI.

20. George Creel to Will Irwin, May 4, 1918, entry 110, CPI.

21. Dennis Nolan to Peyton Marsh, July 6, 1918, entry 239, AEF. "Suggested Proposal to Allied Conference," n.d., entry 225; Philip Patchin to Will Irwin, June 17, 1918, entry 235, AEF.

22. Washburn oral history, 73–76. "Memorandum by Major Stanley Washburn, Cavalry Reserve Corps, Headquarters 2th American Division," July 17, 1918, CAB 24/58/93. Stanley Washburn to Lord Northcliffe, July 30, 1918, box 1, SW. Washburn to George Creel, July 23, 1918, with attached "Memorandum: Propaganda over Enemy Lines," entry 1, CPI.

23. Gibson diary, July 17, 1918. Stanley Washburn to Edward M. House, September 10, 1917, box 116, EMH. Washburn oral history, 121–22. Washburn sent Creel a related plan, "Moral Preparedness in U.S.A. for an Offensive," to encourage correspondents to "discount" heavy losses in the final all-out battles, which would demoralize Americans and possibly erode their support for the war. N. P. A. Hankey to War Cabinet, "Propaganda by Airplane," July 22, 1918, CAB 24/58/93.

24. Giddens, "American Foreign Propaganda in World War I," 264–69. *WWW,* 245–46.

25. Blankenhorn oral history, 87. Giddens, "American Foreign Propaganda in World War I," 268. Peyton March to Dennis Nolan, June 11, 1918, entry 235, AEF.

26. Giddens, "American Foreign Propaganda in World War I," 268–72. I draw here on Blankenhorn's unpublished memoir, "A Long Look Back," chapter 3, HB.

27. It is likely that two meetings took place with Baker, the one mentioned here, in late May, when Baker may have expressed encouragement if not tentative approval, and one on June 21, when the final authorities were determined, which is mentioned later in the chapter. Blankenhorn, mem-

orandum, June 21, 1918, entry 171, WDGS. Blankenhorn oral history, 95–99, suggests that Baker gave complete approval in late May. For background on the run-up to Baker's assent see Giddens, "American Foreign Propaganda in World War I," 273–74.

28. Heber Blankenhorn, "Mr. Merz's Report," June 11, 1918; Charles Merz to Heber Blankenhorn, "Propaganda in Enemy Countries," n.d. [June 1918], entry 171, WDGS. Also see Ronald Steele, *Walter Lippmann and the American Century* (Boston: Little, Brown, 1980), 141–42; and Giddens, "American Foreign Propaganda in World War I," 279–84.

29. Heber Blankenhorn to Walter Lippmann, June 14, 1918, entry 235, AEF.

30. Walter Lippmann to Newton Baker, May 3, 1917, box 2. Lippmann to Herbert Hoover, May 15, 1917, box 14, WL.

31. Walter Lippmann to Edward M. House, June 16, 1918; House to Lippmann, June 19 and July 7, 1918, box 14, WL.

32. Giddens, "American Foreign Propaganda in World War I," 289–90. Blankenhorn, "Mr. Merz's Report"; Walter Lippmann to Heber Blankenhorn, June 19, 1918, box 4; Lippmann to Newton Baker, June 20, 1918, box 2, WL.

33. Heber Blankenhorn, memorandum, June 20, 1918, entry 171, WDGS. Heber Blankenhorn to Walter Lippmann, June 21, 1918, box 4, WL.

34. Giddens, "American Foreign Propaganda in World War I," 292–93.

35. Giddens, "American Foreign Propaganda in World War I," 295. Marlborough Churchill to R. H. Van Deman, July 12, 1918, entry 171, WDGS.

36. Ifft's background is in *Princeton Alumni Weekly*, February 4, 1975, 20.

37. Blankenhorn, *Adventures in Propaganda*, 1.

38. Forrest, *Behind the Front Page*, 186. Heber Blankenhorn to Frederick Keppel, August 2, 1918, entry 171, WDGS. Blankenhorn oral history, 4–5.

39. John Pershing to Newton Baker, August 7, 1918, box 20, JJP. Blankenhorn, *Adventures in Propaganda*, 4–6, 25. Gibson diary, July 25, 1918.

40. Blankenhorn, *Adventures in Propaganda*, 27. Keeley to family, July 14, 1918, JK. See also James Weber Linn, *James Keeley, Newspaperman* (Indianapolis: Bobbs-Merrill, 1937), 218–20; *New York Times*, June 10, 1918; and Joseph Tumulty to Woodrow Wilson, May 23, 1918, box 48, JPT. Creel had been thinking of naming Charles Edward Russell, who was the commissioner in London, as head of enemy propaganda, but Russell left. (See Russell diary, June 13, 1918.)

41. Hamilton, *Journalism's Roving Eye*, chapter 10. Gibson diary, August 20, 1918.

42. Walter Lippmann to Hugh Gibson, August 11, 1918, inserted in Gibson diary.

43. Marlborough Churchill to Will Irwin, July 10, 1918; Irwin to Churchill, July 12, 1918, entry 105, CPI.

44. Newton Baker to John Pershing, July 2, 1918, entry 235, AEF. Blankenhorn, "What Was Attempted," n.d., entry 171, WDGS. Marlborough Churchill to Heber Blankenhorn, September 14, 1918, entry 163, WDGS; D.E.N. [Dennis E. Nolan], memorandum, July 29, 1918, entry 235, AEF. The Noland memorandum expresses wonderment at what Baker wanted to achieve.

45. John M. Dunn to Heber Blankenhorn, September 4, 1918, entry 235, AEF. Colonel Dunn headed what was called the "positive section," which assessed enemy intentions and capabilities. Edgar Sisson to Marlborough Churchill, July 25, 1918, entry 105, CPI. This was signed by Creel and countersigned by Churchill and was returned by Churchill on July 30. The gist of the agreement is in Sisson to James Kerney, August 30, 1918, entry 154, CPI. This is discussed in Giddens, "American Foreign Propaganda in World War I," 308–11.

46. On Creel meeting with Wilson see George Creel to Woodrow Wilson, July 11, 1918, WW-

LC. On the army taking over press duties see "Situation Summary, for week ending August 17, 1918," entry 150, WDGS. On September 1, 1918, for instance, the military assumed responsibility for reviewing pictures.

47. Blankenhorn, "What Was Attempted." "H.B. W.L. J.K., agreement," August 17, 1918, entry 163, CPI.

48. James Keeley to George Creel and Edgar Sisson, telegram, August 9, 1918, Central Decimal File, 1910–29, box 733, GRDS. Heber Blankenhorn and Walter Lippmann to Dennis Nolan, August 8, 1918, entry 235, AEF. Stuart, *Secrets of Crewe House,* 170. Russell diary, June 13, 1918.

49. [Heber Blankenhorn?], "Memorandum for the Secretary of War," n.d., entry 235, AEF. Robert Lansing to Woodrow Wilson, with attached memorandum, September 4, 1918, *PWW,* 49:432–33. G. H. Edgell to Edgar Sisson, August 27, 1918, Central Decimal File, 1910-29, box 733, GRDS.

50. Blankenhorn, *Adventures in Propaganda,* 47.

51. Heber Blankenhorn to Marlborough Churchill, August 27, entry 171, WDGS. Laurie, "'The Chanting of Crusaders,'" 467. Blankenhorn oral history, 121.

52. Walter Lippmann to Edward M. House, August 9 and 15 and September 2, 1918, box 70, EMH. Walter Lippmann, "For a Department of State," *New Republic,* September 17, 1919, 195.

53. Arthur Hugh Frazier to Edward M. House, September 5, 1918, box 45, EMH. Giddens, "American Foreign Propaganda in World War I," 331–32. Wilson, *Diplomat between Wars,* 53.

54. George Creel to Woodrow Wilson, August 26, 1918; Creel to Wilson, November 28, 1917; Wilson to Creel, November 30, 1917, WW-LC. Two days later Sisson suggested the CPI should take over the War Department's propaganda budget, since the AEF was "falling down on the mechanical side of its distribution program for enemy propaganda." Giddens, "American Foreign Propaganda in World War I," 339. Steele, *Walter Lippmann and the American Century,* 146. Wilson to Edward M. House, August 31, 1918; House to Wilson, September 3, 1918, box 121, EMH. Giddens comments on how Wilson became aware of Lippmann's complaints. Giddens, "American Foreign Propaganda in World War I," 334–36.

55. *PWW,* 49:449.

56. Woodrow Wilson to Benedict Crowell and Crowell to Wilson, both September 8, 1918, are in *PWW,* 49:487–88. Crowell to Newton Baker, September 8, 1918, entry 235, AEF. Giddens, "American Foreign Propaganda in World War I," 341. Marlborough Churchill to attachés, September 9, 1918, entry 1, CPI. Edward M. House to Walter Lippmann, September 6, 1918, box 70, EMH.

57. John Pershing to Newton Baker, August 7, 1918, box 22, JJP. Pershing to chief of staff, August 10, 1918; Baker to Robert Lansing, August 12, 1918, box 6, NDB. Baker to Pershing, August 22, 1918, entry 235, AEF. Gibson diary, July 1 and October 24, 1918. Giddens, "American Foreign Propaganda in World War I," 331. Reinertson, "Colonel House, Woodrow Wilson and European Socialism," 507.

58. Dennis Nolan to Wilbur Marsh, September 10, 1918, entry 235, AEF. Heber Blankenhorn to Marlborough Churchill, December 6, 1918, entry 171, WDGS.

59. Blankenhorn oral history, 107–8, 111.

60. Bruntz, *Allied Propaganda and the Collapse of the German Empire,* 189. Heber Blankenhorn to Marlborough Churchill, September 20, 1918, entry 163, WDGS. Blankenhorn to Dennis Nolan, "Final Report on Propaganda Against the Enemy," November 14, 1918, entry 235, AEF. (Another useful summary is "Relating with Committee on Public Information in Regard to Propaganda in Enemy Countries," n.d., entry 235, AEF.) *Reports of the Commander-in-Chief, Staff Sections and Service: United States Army in the World War, 1917–1919* (Washington, DC: Center of Military History, 1991), 13:119, 122. AEF censorship of soldiers' mail served a similar purpose of gaining insights on their morale. Blankenhorn to Marlborough Churchill, September 20, 1918.

61. Blankenhorn, *Adventures in Propaganda*, 53. Giddens, "American Foreign Propaganda in World War I," 317, 331.

62. Giddens, "American Foreign Propaganda in World War I," 343–48. Heber Blankenhorn to Frederick Keppel, October 19, 1918, entry 171, WDGS. The Lippmann "Memorandum for the Secretary of War" is in box 6, NDB.

63. Gibson diary, October 17, 1918; Cable, "For Secretary of War," October 19, 1918; John Pershing to Newton Baker, October 19, 1918; Baker to G-2-D, November 1, 1918, entry 171, WDGS. Keeley to family, November 9 and 21, 1918, JK.

64. Heber Blankenhorn to Marlborough Churchill, December 6, 1918; Heber Blankenhorn, "Addendum to Final Report on Propaganda against the Enemy," n.d., entry 171, WDGS. Woodrow Wilson, fourth Liberty Loan speech, September 27, 1918, in *PPWW:WP*, 1:255. *Reports of the Commander-in-Chief*, 13:122.

65. *Boston Evening Record*, March 12, 1919. Dennis Nolan to Heber Blankenhorn, April 1, 1919, entry 171, WDGS.

66. Heber Blankenhorn to Dennis Nolan, October 14, 1918, entry 171, WDGS. Heber Blankenhorn, "Memorandum by Captain Blankenhorn," n.d., entry 171, WDGS. Sanders and Taylor, *British Propaganda*, 212. For more on German concern with propaganda used against its troops see Bruntz, *Allied Propaganda and the Collapse of the German Empire*, 194–98; and *Reports of the Commander-in-Chief*, 13:126.

67. Carl Ackerman, "When Von Hindenburg Whistles," *Saturday Evening Post*, August 31, 1918, 50. See also Heber Blankenhorn to Marlborough Churchill, September 20, 1918.

68. J. Keith Torbert, "Let Us Forgather: The Biography of Martin Egan," unpublished, chapter titled "No 'Doctor of Publicity,'" ME.

69. Torbert, "Let Us Forgather," chapter titled "Supplementing the Diary," ME.

70. John Pershing to Martin Egan, February 22, 1918. Egan diary, April 29, 1918.

71. Harry A. Franck, "Memorandum for Mr. Kerney," n.d., entry 240, AEF. Torbert, "Supplementing the Diary." Mark Watson to E. R. W. McCabe, June 1, 1918, entry 228, AEF. On commissioners pleading for a service from the front see Henry Suydam to Will Irwin, April 18, 1918, entry 110, CPI. Egan diary, April 22, 28, 29, 1918. George Creel to Martin Egan, March 30, 1918, ME. Creel to Marlin Pew, November 1, 1918, entry 1, CPI. William Sharp to State Department, for Walter S. Rogers from Henry Arnold, September 27, 1918, entry 152, CPI.

72. *WWW*, 273.

73. Hugh Gibson to Philip Patchin, July 3, 1918, box 56, HSG. Gibson diary, June 19, 1918. Egan diary, April 28, 1918. Martin Egan to George Creel, May 11, 1918, entry 105, CPI.

74. Heber Blankenhorn, "The Morale of War," *Harper's*, September 1919, 510.

75. Robert J. Kodosky, *Psychological Operations American Style: The Joint United States Public Affairs Office, Vietnam and Beyond* (Lanham, MD: Lexington, 2007), 69. Laurie, "'The Chanting of Crusaders,'" 457. Edward Lilly, "12 March 1951—PW—Organization in U.S. 1917–1945," box 58, EPL. EPL is a useful collection of papers on the origins of psychological warfare. *APD*, 45–46. Blankenhorn talks about Mason and his World War II experience in chapter 20 and "Heber Blankenhorn, Lt. Col., M.I.," a chapter in his unpublished memoir, HB.

76. Laurie, "'The Chanting of Crusaders,'" 479–80. Department of Defense, *Information Operations Roadmap*, October 30, 2003, 4, 26, accessed at https://www.gwu.edu/~nsarchiv/NSAEBB/NSAEBB177/info_ops_roadmap.pdf. Carl von Clausewitz, *On War*, trans. J. J. Graham (London: N. Trübner, 1873), 38.77. D.E.N. memorandum, July 29, 1918.

78. Talbert, *Negative Intelligence*, 8–9. Van Deman, *The Final Memoranda*, 21.

79. Emblematic of the confusion that existed are Wilson's initial instructions to Pershing. Pershing's only meeting with the president before leaving for Europe was reminiscent of Wilson's meeting in April 1917 with Creel to outline his duties. The president told Pershing that he had his "full support" and offered no comment on looming questions such as to how Pershing should combine his forces with the Allies forces—questions that had political as well as military significance. Pershing and his chief of staff prepared their own instructions, which Newton Baker supplemented in a second letter given them as they boarded ship for France. Coffman, *The War to End All Wars,* 49.

80. Sweeney, *Military Intelligence,* 7. Sweeney's book is a thoughtful, largely democratic reflection on intelligence that deserves to be remembered.

81. Gilbert, *World War I and the Origins of U.S. Military Intelligence,* 106. Bidwell, *History of the Intelligence Division,* 158. Gibson diary, August 21, 1918. Giddens, "American Foreign Propaganda in World War I," 342. Lippmann had a low opinion of other colleagues; for instance, he said Monty Woolley was of "no use except that he did speak German." Lippmann oral history, 107.

82. A, L. James to Walter Lippmann, November 10, 1918, box 40, WL. Thomas M. Johnson, *Without Censor: New Light on Our Greatest World War Battles* (Indianapolis: Bobbs-Merrill, 1928), 292. Lippmann, "For a Department of State," 196.

83. On praise for Rogers's service see, for example, *Use of Naval Radio Stations for Commercial Purposes,* Hearing of Subcommittee of Committee on Naval Affairs (Washington, DC: Government Printing Office, 1919), 185–86.

84. Creel gave almost as little attention to Gibson, saying only that he "was loaned to the committee for a part of the time by the State department" *Report,* 167. Lippmann almost never mentioned his work with the AEF in anything he subsequently wrote.

85. Whitehouse, *A Year as a Government Agent,* 59.

12. ACRIMONIOUS CONTENTION

1. Ford oral history, 401.

2. This account is drawn from *New York World,* which estimated a thousand attended, as well as the *New York Herald, New York Times, New York Tribune, New York American,* and *New York Evening Post,* whose stories appeared during the week of May 13, 1918. Also, *New York Times,* March 11 and April 16, 1918. The newspaper reporters sometimes recorded a slightly different "slumming" quote, but the differences were immaterial. The one used here is from *New York World,* May 13, 1918.

3. George Creel, speech, City Editors' Association, Columbus, Ohio, January 19, 1918, box 5, GC. *Rebel,* 56.

4. Susan E. Tifft and Alex S. Jones, *The Trust: The Private and Powerful Family behind the New York Times* (Boston: Little, Brown, 1999), 89. Murdock Pemberton to George Baker, May 17, 1918, box 9, GBB.

5. Daniels diary, May 16, 1917. *Congressional Record,* May 13, 1918, 6469. *New York Sun* and *New York Tribune,* May 14, 1918.

6. George Creel to Stephen Wise, May 23, 1918; Creel to Frank C. Dean, May 20, 1918, entry 1, CPI.

7. Harvey O'Higgins, "You and Josephus Daniels," typescript, n.d., entry 17, CPI.

8. *New York Tribune* and *New York Times,* May 19, 1918.

9. The menu signed by Hoover and the seating chart is in box 19, GCR. *Washington Herald,* December 9, 1917, which with other clippings can be found in box 92, GCR. The skit script is in box 19.

10. Woodrow Wilson to Robert Lansing, September 5, 1918, in *PWW,* 49:447. Baker interview with Creel.

11. Sullivan, *Our Times,* 5:367–69. Herbert Swoop to Ray Stannard Baker, August 30, 1932, box 115, RSB. Kahn, *The World of Swope,* 188–89.

12. Bakhmeteff oral history, 302, 346–51. One CPI view on recognition that may have counted was Arthur Bullard's. He was in Russia working with Sisson and was highly respected. Bullard suggested withholding recognition in a message to Creel that was given to Lansing, who worked with Wilson on a strategy for implementing the nonrecognition policy. George F. Kennan, *Russia Leaves the War: Soviet-American Relations, 1917–1920* (Princeton, NJ: Princeton University Press, 1956), chapter 8.

13. Daniels, *The Wilson Era: Years of War and After, 1917–1923,* 222. Palmer, *With My Own Eyes,* 367. "Ministers of Propaganda," *Notes and Clippings,* August 15, 1918. (This is an Ivy Lee publication.) Kerney, *Political Education of Woodrow Wilson,* 409.

14. Glick, "Wilson and the War Effort," 78. Woodrow Wilson to George Creel, May 14, 1917, WW-LC.

15. Howe, *Confessions of a Reformer,* 289.

16. George Creel to Woodrow Wilson, February 19, March 29, May 2, and June 20, 1917, box 1, GC. Creel appended a note to this box describing how he often helped Wilson digest material.

17. Sullivan, *Our Times,* 5:439. Gibson diary, October 24, 1918. Woodrow Wilson to Frank Polk, August 2, 1918; Wilson to George Creel, January 14, 1918, WW-LC.

18. George Creel to George Bates Creel (his son), March 21, 1931, box 1, GC. See also Ronald H. Carpenter, "Woodrow Wilson as Speechwriter for George Creel: Presidential Style in Discourse as an Index of Personality." *Presidential Studies Quarterly* 19 (Winter 1989): 117–26. As an example of toning down hyperbole see Woodrow Wilson to Creel, January 3, 1918, WW-LC. Creel said he consulted Wilson "almost to the point of annoyance" *Hearing,* 160.

19. Gibson diary, May 26, 1918.

20. *Hearing,* 73–76, 141. *Report,* 111.

21. "William Churchill," *Obituary Record of Yale Graduates, 1919–1920* (New Haven, CT: Yale University, 1920), 1425–27.

22. Martin Egan to George Creel, December 27, 1917, ME. Sullivan, *Our Times,* 5:425. *New York Times,* September 3, 1918.

23. Edward L. Bernays, "The Marketing of National Policies: A Study of War Propaganda," *Journal of Marketing* 6 (January 1941): 239. Bernays, *Biography of an Idea,* 156. Harvey O'Higgins, "Incredible Mr. Creel," *New Yorker,* July 4, 1925, 8.

24. Babson, *Actions and Reactions,* 178. SWW, 11. Guy Stanton Ford to Grace Ford, "Saturday, 3. P.M.," [August 1918?], box 35, GSF. Cable censor, New York, to chief cable censor, Washington, DC, "Attention Mr. George Creel," May 2, 1918; Ernest Poole to George Creel, December 24, 1918, entry 1, CPI.

25. Bernays, "The Marketing of National Policies," 240. Owens oral history, 25.

26. Irwin, "Report on Foreign Propaganda." Robert V. Hudson, *The Writing Game: A Biography of Will Irwin* (Ames: Iowa State University Press, 1982), 109–12. Will Irwin to Martin Egan, March 13, 1918, ME. Irwin discussed the "stormy" meeting in Irwin to Marlborough Churchill, n.d., entry 105, CPI. Gibson diary, May 26, 1918. "P" to Brand Whitlock, May 1, 1918, box 37, BW. On the "stormy" meeting, John Dunn to Heber Blankenhorn, September 4, 1918, entry 235, AEF. Reinertson, "Colonel House, Woodrow Wilson and European Socialism, 1917–1918," 516. Gibson diary, October 3, 1918.

27. Ford oral history, 381–82, 388, 401.

28. Maurice F. Lyons to George Draper, May 29, 1918, entry 1, CPI. Carl Byoir to W. P. Freeman, June 13, 1918, entry 4, CPI.

29. Guy Stanton Ford to Grace Ford, June 24, 1918, box 35, GSF.

30. J. Franklin Jameson to Frederick H. Gillett, June 27, 1918, box 73, JFJ. Shotwell oral history, 75–75. Wallace Notestein to E. B. Greene, May 8, 1918, box 8, NBHS.

31. Baker interview with Creel. Daniels, *The Wilson Era: Years of War and After, 1917–1923,* 221–22. *Rebel,* 154.

32. William L. Chenery, *So It Seemed* (New York: Harcourt Brace, 1952), 120.

33. George Creel to Woodrow Wilson, August 15, 1917, WW-LC. Creel to Brand Whitlock, August 24, 1917, box 36, BW. Wilson to Robert Lansing, August 16, 1917, box 30, RL. Lansing told Whitlock he liked the articles when they came out but did not support the idea of a movie on the book; the president also disagreed with Lansing on the movie. Lansing to Whitlock, March 25, 1918, box 37; Whitlock to Curtis Brown, October 1, 1918, box 38, BW. More details in Brand Whitlock, *The Letters and Journal of Brand Whitlock,* ed. Allan Nevins (New York: D. Appleton-Century, 1936), 1:242–50, and 2:445–46. *Report,* 163.

34. For Long's involvement with publicity see his diary, July 26, August 2, and September 13 and 14, 1918. Charles Merz to Walter Lippmann, March 14, 1917, box 20, WL. Breckenridge Long to Woodrow Wilson, with memorandum, November 19, 1917; Wilson to Long, November 20, 1917; Long to Wilson, December 15, 1917; Wilson to Long, December 19, 1917, box 30, BL.

35. Philip Patchin to Hugh Gibson, June 10, 1918, box 56, HSG.

36. James D. Startt, "Colonel Edward M. House and the Journalists," *American Journalism* 27 (Summer 2010): 32. Seymour, *The Intimate Papers of Colonel House,* 3:141. How House viewed himself in his press role is clear from his entry in this diary entry, August 5, 1917: "I gave [Lincoln] Colcord and [Herbert] Brougham a talk concerning a world-wide press organization for the purpose of creating international comity. Something should be done to stop the loose talk of nations by one another." He asked an AP manager going abroad to "get the people of South America to understand our point of view." House diary, June 8, 1918.

37. Giddens, "American Foreign Propaganda in World War I," 177–85 and chapter 4. Giddens does an excellent job of describing and analyzing the Maugham-Voska scheme, as well as others House toyed with. Woodrow Wilson to Edward M. House, July 21, 1918, box 121, EMH. Seymour, *The Intimate Papers of Colonel House,* 3:142–48.

38. *PPWW:WP,* 1:155–62.

39. Charles A. Beard and Mary R. Beard, *The Rise of American Civilization* (New York: Macmillan, 1954), 651. William Appleman Williams, *American Russian Relations, 1781–1947* (New York: Rinehard, 1952), 12. Claude E. Fike, "The Influence of the Creel Committee and the American Red Cross on Russian-American Relations, 1917–1919," *Journal of Modern History* 31 (June 1959): 97. Mark Sullivan tells the story as Creel saw it, with Wilson asking for House's help *after* Creel suggested the speech. Sullivan, *Our Times,* 5:445–46. Sisson cablegram to Creel, January 3, 1918, entry 106, CPI. Creel, "Note," n.d., box 1, GC. *Rebel,* 168. Edgar Sisson, *One Hundred Red Days: A Personal Chronicle of the Bolshevik Revolution* (New Haven, CT: Yale University Press, 1931), 206.

40. Joseph Tumulty to Woodrow Wilson, January 4, 1918; George Creel to Wilson, January 5, 1918, WW-LC. On the preparation for Wilson's speech see Cooper, *Woodrow Wilson,* 419–24; Lippmann oral history, 108.

41. Kennan, *Russia Leaves the War,* 251–52 and chapter 12 passim. *Report,* 217.

42. George Creel to Edward M. House, June 7, 1916, March 8 and September 25, 1918, box 31, EMH. By way of example, Arthur Woods consulted House on going to work for the CPI, and Will Irwin dropped by to brief the colonel. House diary, January 12 and May 14, 1918.

43. Creel, "The Break between Wilson and House," *Collier's,* May 22, 1926, 7–8ff. Baker inter-

view with Creel. House diary, December 18, 1917. George Sylvester Viereck, "Scraps from Conversations with House (Unpublished Material)," 1929, box 4, GSV. Blankenhorn said Creel was "bitterly hostile" to House. According to House biographer Arthur D. Howden Smith, Creel complained about "Mr. House's extra-official position in the Administration." Smith recounted an unspecified occasion when House asked him to attend a speech by Creel "and challenge him if he made certain statements." Smith implausibly believed Creel suppressed his 1918 biography of House. Arthur D. Howden Smith, *Mr. House of Texas* (New York: Funk and Wagnalls, 1940), 271, 315. Giddens, "American Foreign Propaganda in World War I," 189–90.

44. Irwin, *Propaganda and the News,* 184. Edward M. House to Arthur Frazier, cable, September 5, 1918, box 45; House to Woodrow Wilson, February 17, 1918, box 121, EMH.

45. Giddens, "American Foreign Propaganda in World War I," 175–76. Baker interview with McCormick, July 15, 1928. Charles E. Neu, *Colonel House: A Biography of Woodrow Wilson's Silent Partner* (New York: Oxford University Press, 2015), 248–49. House diary, May 17, 1918.

46. George Creel to Edward M. House, June 5, 1918, box 31; House to Creel, December 14, 1918, box 31, EMH.

47. George Creel, "Beware the Superpatriots," *American Mercury,* September 1940, 35.

48. Phyllis Keller, *States of Belonging* (Cambridge, MA: Harvard University Press, 1979), 235–36. Hagedorn's files are full of his complaints about Creel. For instance, Hermann Hagedorn to Governor Moses Alexander, July 8, 1918, and Hagedorn to Reginald Wright Kauffman, June 25, 1918, box 2, HH.

49. *New York Sun,* September 12, 1918. Blakey, *Historians on the Homefront,* 92–97. George Creel to National Security League, September 12, 1918, entry 1, CPI.

50. Peterson and Fite, *Opponents of War,* 64–65, 191–92. Herbert Earle Gaston, *The Nonpartisan League* (New York: Harcourt, Brace, and Howe, 1920), 249–51. George Creel to Woodrow Wilson, February 19, 1918, WW-LC. Livermore, *Wilson and the War Congress,* 156.

51. George Creel to Bruce Bielaski, January 28, January 30, and February 14, 1918, entry 1, CPI. Creel made the same confidential admission on the Friends of German Democracy to John J. Spurgeon of the *Public Ledger,* when that paper wrote unfavorably about the organization, January 28, 1918, entry 1, CPI.

52. M. Scheitzer, *Transatlantic Broadway: The Infrastructural Politics of Global Performance* (New York: Palgrave Macmillan, 2015), 184. R. H. Van Deman to George Creel, April 10, 1918; Alexander Konta to Creel, September 23, 1918; and Memorandum for Mr. Bielaski, April 14, 1918, entry 1, CPI. *WWW,* 222. *New York Tribune,* October 10, 1918. *HWAA,* 187.

53. George Creel to A. Bruce Bielaski, March 16, 1918; Creel to Edwin Bjorkman, June 28, 1918, entry 1, CPI. Garet Garrett to Creel, November 191, 1917; R. H. Van Deman to Ralph Hayes, January 21, 1918, entry 11, CPI. Ackerman encountered Niebuhr in Berlin in 1915 when he was with the United Press and wrote the story on his return in 1917 for the *New York Tribune.* Niebuhr claimed he was on a reporting mission to counteract German propaganda in the United States. *HWAA,* 119, 187.

54. *APD,* 17. R. H. Van Deman to "Whom It May Concern," April 22, 1918, box III-6, ELB. Other letters or recommendation can be found in the same location. George Creel to Vira B. Whitehouse, January 2, 1918, entry 1, CPI. On Whitehouse being a spy see Hugh Gibson to Philip Patchin, June 22, 1918, box 56, HSG.

55. Military Intelligence Branch, "Report on the Committee on Public Information," May 1918, entry 1, CPI.

56. George Creel to Marlborough Churchill, July 8, 1918; Creel to Ralph Easley, July 9, 1918;

and copy of undated, unsigned letter to Easley, entry 1, CPI. Irwin, *The Making of a Reporter*, 355.

57. Reginald Wright Kauffman, *Victorious* (Indianapolis: Bobbs-Merrill, 1919), 5, 49, 176. Kauffman's book received tepid reviews for having been written too hastily and being a little heavy on sex.

58. Kauffman, *Victorious*, 389. Kauffman was a member of the Publicity Committee of the American Defense Society, a group that was keen to suppress dissent. His novel on white slavery, *The House of Bondage*, is considered the best of its time, and his wartime book *Our Navy Army Work* was a paean to "The Yankee Fleet in French Waters." See attachment to Richard M. Hurd to Chas. S. Davison, September 5, 1917, box 1, ADS. Filler, *Muckrakers*, 290–91.

59. *American Press*, February 9, 1918.

60. Harry Tammen to George Creel, July 30, 1918, entry 1, CPI; also see Frederick Bonfils to James Reed, September 22, 1917, WW-LC. "Pitiless Publicity," *Goodwin's Weekly*, December 15, 1917, 6–8.

61. Amos Pinchot to George Creel, November 14, 1917, box 26, AP-LC.

62. "Common Sense Censorship," *Associated Press Service Bulletin*, no. 48, 1918. Walter S. Rogers to George Creel, March 27, 1918; cable censor, New York, to chief cable censor, Washington, DC, "Attention Mr. George Creel," May 2, 1918, entry 5, CPI.

63. Frederick Palmer, "Memorandum on Inquiries by Mr. J. N. Lee," n.d., entry 1, CPI. United Press correspondent Lowell Mellett wrote in his diary, December 2, 1917, "One glaring case which all correspondents with the army relate was the refusal to allow them to watch and afterward describe the moving of the first American unit into the trenches. Another was the secrecy about the burial of the first American victims, a ceremony that was dramatic in itself, even if the circumstances had not made it so." "Mellette Diary," transcribed for censorship, December 15, 1917, entry 239, AEF. Wythe Williams to Charles Grasty, October 25, 1918, box 50, EMH. Wythe Williams, "The Sins of the Censor," *Collier's*, January 12, 1918, 7. Crozier, *American Reporters*, 171–72, 192–93.

64. Lawrence, *New York Evening Post*, July 6, 1917. Carl Ackerman to Edward M. House, May 24, 1917, box 1, EMH. *Baltimore Sun*, August 2, 1917. Crozier, *American Reporters*, 177. Reginald Wright Kauffman, "The News Embargo," *North American Review*, November 1918, 842.

65. Kauffman, "The News Embargo," 840. "Notes on the Mobilization of the American Press," appended to Norman Hapgood to Frank Polk, January 28, 1918, box 7, FLP. John F. Bass to "Tommy," December 8, 1917, entry 239, AEF. Bass to Vance McCormick, December 6, 1917, box 4, VCM. Crozier, *American Reporters*, 203. Crozier says Hapgood's brother, Hutchins, was the president, a mistake that he may have picked up from Kauffman's article. Norman Hapgood, *The Advancing Hour* (New York: Boni and Liveright, 1920), 21–22.

66. George Creel to Ray Stannard Baker, February 25, 1918, entry 1, CPI. Creel to James Kerney, March 22, 1918, Central Decimal File, 1910–29, box 732, GRDS. Dennis Nolan to Peyton March, March 8, 1918; Nolan to Wythe Williams, May 30, 1918, entry 221, AEF. Williams to Charles Grasty, October 25, 1918, box 50, EMH.

67. George Creel to Ray Stannard Baker, August 26, 1918, entry 1, CPI. George Creel, "Aid and Comfort the Enemy," *Independent*, March 16, 1918, 446–47. *New York Tribune*, March 15, 1918.

68. Wilhelm, "Our Uncensorious Censor," 20. John Barry, *San Francisco Bulletin*, n.d., box OV-6, GC. One account of the flight is in an article mentioning congressional criticism of Creel. "Creel's Removal Demanded," *Fourth Estate*, April 13, 1918, 12. See also undated news clips in box OV 6, GC; Wilson, *My Memoir*, 153.

69. *Cherokee Republican*, July 19, 1918. Arthur Brisbane to George Creel, May 4, 1918, entry

1, CPI. *Washington Post,* October 7, 1917. *Virginian Pilot,* clipping, n.d., box OV 7, GC. *Muskogee Phoenix,* clipping, n.d., box OV 7, GC.

70. SWW, 30–31. George Creel to David Lawrence; Creel to Clinton Brainard, August 30, 1918, entry 1, CPI.

71. *New York Times,* April 16, 1918. Creel's speech and AP feelings are reprised in "Minutes of the Board and Annual Meeting. Verbatim Minutes," April 25, 1918, AP. See also Melville Stone to George Creel, January 31, 1918, and Creel to Stone, February 5, 1918, entry 1, CPI.

72. Reginald Wright Kauffman, *New York Tribune,* September 23, 1918. Kauffman's letter is dated September 17. George Creel to Garet Garrett, October 25, 1918; Reginald Wright Kauffman to Creel, October 28, 29, and 31, 1918; Creel to Kauffman, October 29, 1918, entry 1, CPI.

73. George Creel to Walter S. Rogers, May 4, 1918; Perry Arnold, "Memo for Mr. Rogers," n.d., entry 1, CPI. "The Pride and Fall of George Creel," *Chronicle,* May 1918, 1. A photo of Mrs. William Jay, the matron, is in *New York Times,* September 15, 1918.

74. George Creel to Jason Rogers, April 11, 1918, entry 1; Rogers to Creel, April 16, 1918, entry 5, CPI.

75. *PWW,* 43:333. *New York Times,* April 11, 1918.

76. *New York Times,* April 28, 1918.

77. Frank Glass to Woodrow Wilson, May 24, 1918, WW-LC. George Creel to Edward J. Gallagher, May 4, 1918, entry 1, CPI. *PWW,* 48:177–78.

78. Corey, "Perfectly Irresponsible," chapter 16, 152–53.

79. "Conference Representing Delays in Censorship and Transmission of Press Dispatches from the Western Front to the United States," transcript, October 11, 1918, box 9, GBB.

80. For example, Congress was annoyed over the creation of the Food Administration. Livermore, *Wilson and the War Congress,* 51.

81. *Christian Science Monitor,* February 20, 1918. *New York Morning Telegraph,* July 11, 1917.

82. *Philadelphia Public Ledger,* July 26, 1917. *Congressional Record,* May 25, 1917, 2852. *New York Times,* February 5, 1918.

83. Edward Pou to George Creel, September 19, 1918, entry 1, CPI. Livermore, *Wilson and the War Congress,* 67–68.

84. *Congressional Record,* April 9, 1918, 4827. Ford oral history, 389.

85. *Congressional Record,* March 29, 1918, 4255. Bean, "George Creel and His Critics," 161–69.

86. *Congressional Record,* April 12, 1918, 5000. *Evansville Journal News,* August 25, 1918. Livermore, *Wilson and the War Congress,* 99. HFIL, 213. Creel devoted an entire chapter of *HWAA* to the aircraft controversy. Bean, "George Creel and His Critics," 169–70.

87. George Creel, "What about Hiram Johnson of California?," *Everybody's,* October 1914, 460. *HWAA,* 57. Lincoln Steffens, *The Letters of Lincoln Steffens,* ed. Ella Winter and Granville Hicks (New York: Harcourt, Brace, 1938), 346.

88. *Congressional Record,* June 17, 1918, 7912. *Washington Evening Star,* April 5, 1918. *Congressional Record,* April 4, 1918, 4567.

89. Robert Woolley to Edward M. House, July 11, 1917, box 124, EMH. Also, Vance McCormick to Woolley, April 18, 1917; and Woolley to McCormick, August 29, 1917, box 12, RWW. "Full Publicity by Congress," *Editor & Publisher,* December 22, 1917, 4.

90. *New York Times,* April 19, 1918. *New York Evening Post,* April 16, 1918.

91. *Berkshire Eagle,* February 17, 1917. *Washington Herald,* April 11, 1918. *Congressional Record,* April 11, 1918, 4975–78. *New York Times,* April 21, 1918.

92. *Congressional Record,* May 14, 1918, 6526. Daniels, *The Wilson Era: Years of War and After, 1917–1923,* 227. Baker interview with Creel, April 5, 1926, box 103, RSB. The secretary-treasurer of the American Fair Trade League told Wilson that he had it on good authority that Creel was not worried about a congressional investigation of him. Creel supposedly said the president "will go to the Capitol as my attorney." *PWW,* 48:17. Before the slumming comment Wilson told his cabinet that if the "House cited George Creel for contempt he would go up the House as his attorney & say 'It's me you are after. Here I am. Be brave enough to go after me.[']" Daniels diary, April 12, 1918.

93. Allen Treadway, House Resolution 347, May 14, 1918. Daniels, *The Wilson Era: Years of War and After, 1917–1923,* 228. *New York Times,* May 18, 1918. *Congressional Record,* June 17, 1918, 7917.

94. *Washington Herald,* June 2, 1918. Also see Edward Pou to George Creel, May 24, 1918; and Creel to Pou, May 20, 1918, in *Hearing,* 145–46.

95. Woodrow Wilson to George Creel, May 24, 1918; Wilson to Creel, June 5, 1918; Creel to Wilson, June 10, 1918, WW-LC. McAdoo to Speaker of the House, June 12, 1918, House document no. 1168, 65th Congress, 2d Sess. On the bottom of Wilson's June 5 letter is a note, written in longhand, saying the budget is for "information within the United States." The possibility of an investigation was still being discussed in early June. *Philadelphia Public Ledger,* June 2, 1918.

96. *New York Times,* June 12, 1918. *Congressional Record,* June 17, 1918, 7903. Guy Stanton Ford to Grace Ford, June 12, 1918, box 35, GSF.

97. Ford oral history, 404. *Hearing,* 143, 151.

98. *Hearing,* 152, 156, 166.

99. *Congressional Record,* June 17, 1918, 7908. *New York Times,* June 14, 1918. Ford oral history, 404.

100. *Congressional Record,* June 17, 1918, 7904.

101. George Creel to Woodrow Wilson, June 17, 1918; Wilson to Creel, June 18, 1918, WW-LC.

102. Guy Stanton Ford to Grace Ford, June 12, 1918. *Congressional Record,* June 17, 1918, 7912, 7915. Edward Pou to George Creel, September 19, 1918, entry 1, CPI.

103. Messenger, *British Propaganda and the State in the First World War,* 10–20. On the number of different propaganda offices see Hans Haeften, "Propaganda im Inland," R121341, January 1–October 31, 1918, PA. For a good discussion of this see Fondren, "'Breathless Zeal and Careless Confidence,'" chapter 6.

104. Hubert Montgomery to John Buchan, October 24, 1917, CAB 21/37. Pembroke Wicks to Edward Carson, October 20, 1917, CAB 21/27. Robert Donald, "Report on Propaganda Arrangements," January 9, 1917, INF 4/8b. Squires, *British Propaganda,* 36. Wilkinson, *Secrecy and the Media,* 71.

105. Whitehouse, *A Year as a Government Agent,* 107.

106. George Creel to Samuel Gompers, July 17, 1918, entry 1, CPI. *Hearing,* 122–24. *WWW,* 111. Creel to Henry Barnhart, September 5, 1918; Guy Stanton Ford to Creel, October 22, 1918, entry 1 CPI.

107. *Hearing,* 119–21. *New York Tribune,* July 28, 1918. *New York Tribune,* August 27, 1918. George Creel to James Baker, July 18, 1918, entry 1, CPI. *Chicago Tribune,* July 11, 1918. Taylor was called "the Emma McChesney of the war," a reference to a silent movie in which a redoubtable saleswoman by that name (played by Ethel Barrymore) saves a department store.

108. Translation from *Vossische Zeitung,* published April 28, 1918, entry 1, CPI. George Creel to George Moore, October 10, 1918, entry 1, CPI.

109. Steffens, *The Letters of Lincoln Steffens,* 425. Eula McClary to Josephus Daniels, August 2, 1918, box 73, JD. Creel's description of the "slumming" imbroglio cannot be taken at face value. He

stated, for instance, that newspapers only focused on that comment in reporting on his talk. There also is no support for his claim that it was his suggestion to shift domestic funding from Wilson's war fund to congressional appropriation. *HWAA,* 61–63.

110. *Hearing,* 125.

111. *New York Times,* July 14, 1918. *Evansville Courier,* June 30, 1918.

112. George Creel to Vira B. Whitehouse, August 9, 1918, entry 1, CPI. *New York Times,* June 28 and 29, 1918. *Congressional Record,* July 12, 1918, 8990.

113. *Hearing,* 160.

114. Hapgood, *The Advancing Hour,* 102–3.

13. THE SISSON DOCUMENTS

1. Edgar Sisson to Dixie Ladd Sisson (intended to be shown to Creel), serial letter January 9 and 13, 1918, entry 110, CPI. Sisson, *One Hundred Red Days,* 206–8. The description of the Smolny Institute is from John Reed, *Ten Days That Shook the World* (New York: Penguin, 1978), 54–55.

2. Arthur Bullard, *The Russian Pendulum* (New York: Macmillan, 1919), 1. Radical journalist John Reed had much the same thing to say: Lenin was "a strange popular leader—and leader purely by virtue of intellect; colorless, humourless, uncompromising and detached, without picturesque idiosyncrasies." Reed, *Ten Days That Shook the World,* 128. Sisson, *One Hundred Red Days,* 209.

3. Kennan, *Russia Leaves the War,* 135.

4. Catherine Merridale, *Lenin on the Train* (New York: Henry Holt, 2017), 62. Sisson, *One Hundred Red Days,* 208. Dmitri Volkogonov, *Trotsky: The Eternal Revolutionary* (New York: Free Press, 1996), 14.

5. Edgar Sisson, "Report of Edgar Sisson on Installation of Committee on Public Information Service in Russia," May 29, 1918, entry 235, AEF. Sisson cable, January 13, 1918, attached to George Creel to Woodrow Wilson, January 15, 1918, WW-LC. George Kennan, *The Decision to Intervene: Soviet-American Relations, 1917–1920* (Princeton, NJ: Princeton University Press, 1958), 193.

6. Edgar Sisson serial letter January 9 and 13, 1918. Merridale, *Lenin on the Train,* 212.

7. Edgar Sisson serial letter, January 9 and 13, 1918. Sisson, *One Hundred Red Days,* 214. Sisson claims he did not put his reservations about Lenin in his letter to his wife, who was supposed to share it with Creel, because he was afraid Creel would pass it around. The tenor of the letter, however, suggests he did not believe at the time that Lenin was an agent.

8. Woodrow Wilson to George Creel, September 4, 1917, WW-LC. *WWW,* 304. Krantz, "Edgar Sisson's Mission to Russia, 1917–1918," 35. This chapter uses the Georgian calendar, which dates the revolution on November 7. Under the Julian calendar, used by the Russians at the time, the revolution occurred on October 25.

9. David A. Langbart, "Spare No Expense: The Department of State and the Search for Information about Bolshevik Russia, November 1917–September 1918," *Intelligence and National Security* 4 (April 1989): 318. Z. A. B. Zeman, ed., *Germany and the Revolution in Russia, 1915–1918* (London: Oxford University Press, 1958), 138. Bullard, "The Breakdown of Europe's News Services," *Our World,* May 1924, 15.

10. *PWW,* 44:434. Frank Luther Mott, *A History of American Magazines,* 4:497.

11. For example of this impression of being secretive see Butler Wright to Basil Miles, July 17, 1919, Sisson Documents, 1917–21, entry 1120, GRDS. Kennan, *Russia Leaves the War,* 53–54. Sisson, *One Hundred Red Days,* 11, 37. George F. Kennan, "Random Notes on Conversation with Mr. Norman Armour," November 3, 1953, box 244, GFK.

12. Kennan, *Russia Leaves the War,* 49. Ford oral history, 382. For a sketch of Bullard see "A War Correspondent at Home," *Outlook,* August 16, 1914, 883–84.

13. Arthur Bullard to George Creel, October 19 and November 1, 1917, box 6; George Creel to Edgar Sisson, January 28, 1931, box 1, AB. Ernest Poole, "Arthur Bullard in Russia during the War," n.d., box 1, AB. The exact arrangement with the consulate is unclear. Creel describes it as "giving unpaid help."

14. Richard Pipes, *The Russian Revolution* (New York: Knopf, 1990), 419. Strachan, *The First World War,* 261. Arthur Bullard to J. Butler Wright, October 11, 1917, box 6; Bullard to George Creel, December 7, 1918, box 7, AB. Bullard also suggested his "Fulbright" scheme to Breckenridge Long, who recorded the conversation in a memorandum, May 2, 1919, box 185, BL.

15. Arthur Bullard, "America as a Belligerent in the World War," Letter Six, n.d., typescript, box 6, AB.

16. Arthur Bullard, "General Preliminary Report," in Arthur Bullard to George Creel, May 1918, box 6; Bullard to Creel, January 12, 1918; Bullard to Creel, January 13/26, 1918, box 6, AB. William Adams Brown Jr., *The Groping Giant* (New Haven, CT: Yale University Press, 1920), 101. Sisson, "Report of Edgar Sisson." James D. Startt, "American Film Propaganda in Revolutionary Russia," *Prologue,* Fall 1998, 166–79.

17. Poole oral history, 208–9. This oral history is the basis for an edited volume: DeWitt Clinton Poole, *An American Diplomat in Bolshevik Russia* (Madison: University of Wisconsin Pres, 2014). Davis oral history, 43. Fike, "The Influence of the Creel Committee and the American Red Cross on Russian-American Relations," 95. Sisson serial letter, January 9 and 13, 1918.

18. Robert Lansing, memorandum, December 4, 1917; Woodrow Wilson to Lansing, March 10, 1918, box 2, RL-P. Kennan, *Russia Leaves the War,* 125.

19. *Papers Relating to the Foreign Relations of the United States, 1918, Russia* (Washington, DC: Government Printing Office, 1931), 1:215. David Francis to Robert Lansing, December 15, 1917, Central Decimal File, 1910–29, box 731, GRDS. Kennan, *Russia Leaves the War,* 129. Sisson, *One Hundred Red Days,* 30.

20. Woodrow Wilson to Edgar Sisson, October 24, 1917, WW-LC.

21. George Creel to Edgar Sisson, December 14, 1917, Central Decimal File, 1910–29, box 736, GRDS. The CPI's continued use of poor ciphers in Russia eventually led military intelligence to complain to the State Department. H. O. Yardley to Leland Harrison, July 8, 1918, Records Kept by Leland Harrison, entry A1-346, GRDS. Creel to Woodrow Wilson, December 27, 1917, WW-LC. Sisson, *One Hundred Red Days,* 94.

22. Robert Singerman, "The American Career of the Protocols of the Elders of Zion," *American Jewish History* 71 (September 1981): 48–78. Richard S. Levy, introduction to Benjamin W. Segel, *A Lie and a Libel: The History of the Protocols of the Elders of Zion* (Lincoln: University of Nebraska Press, 1995), 6–17. *Philadelphia Public Ledger,* October 27 and 28, 1919. Carl Ackerman to John Spurgeon, November 25, 1919, box 131, CWA. In Ackerman's letter to his editor, Spurgeon, he maintained, "The information I was given showed that [the *Protocols*] were the result of or intimately related to the inner council of the Bolshevist government." Two years later, British journalist Philip Graves exposed the *Protocols of the Elders of Zion* as a forgery. Ackerman's papers at the Library of Congress contain no other explanation for his report. For a discussion on Ackerman as a conduit for leaks see Meghan Menard McCune and John Maxwell Hamilton, "'My Object Is to Be of Service to You': Carl Ackerman and the Wilson Administration during WWI," *Intelligence and National Security Intelligence and National Security* 32 (October 2017): 743–57.

23. Strachan, *The First World War,* 255. Sean McMeekin, *The Berlin-Baghdad Express: He Ot-*

toman Empire and Germany's Bid for World Power (Cambridge, MA: Harvard University Press, 2010), 221–22.

24. Charles Roetter, *Psychological Warfare* (London: B. T. Batsford, 1974), 74–75.

25. Irwin, *Propaganda and the News,* 173–74. Peter G. Filene, *Americans and the Soviet Experiment, 1917–1933* (Cambridge, MA: Harvard University Press, 1967), 46. Elihu Root cable to Robert Lansing, June 17, 1917, box 192, ER.

26. Douglas Smith, *Rasputin* (New York: Farrar, Straus and Giroux, 2016), chapter 57. Merridale, *Lenin on the Train,* 43. Zeman, *Germany and the Revolution in Russia,* 35–40. Dimitri Volkogonov *Lenin: A New Biography* (New York: Free Press, 1994), 117–18.

27. Merridale, *Lenin on the Train,* 248. Volkogonov, *Trotsky,* 121. Charles L. Robertson, *The International Herald Tribune: The First Hundred Years* (New York: Columbia University Press, 1987), 99.

28. Alexandra Becquet and Clair Davison-Pégen, *Ford Madox Ford's Cosmopolis: Psycho-Geography, Flânerie and the Culture of Paris* (Leiden, Netherlands: Brill/Rodopi, 2016), 77. George Kennan, "The Sisson Documents," *Journal of Modern History* 28 (June 1956): 143. Lothar Deeg, *Kunst and Albers Vladivostok: The History of a German Trading Company in the Russian Far East 1864–1924,* trans. Sarah Bohnet (Berlin: Druck and Verlag, 2013), 334–35. Sisson, *One Hundred Red Days,* 372–73.

29. Details of Sisson's actions and surrounding events are, unless otherwise noted, drawn from Sisson, *One Hundred Red Days,* passim; Kennan, *Russia Leaves the War,* chapters 21–22; and Kennan, "The Sisson Documents," 130–54. See also Helena M. Stone, "Another Look at the Sisson Forgeries and Their Background," *Soviet Studies* 37 (January 1985): 90–102.

30. Kennan, "The Sisson Documents," 130.

31. David Francis to Robert Lansing, March 20, 1918, box 2, RL-P. *Papers Relating to the Foreign Relations of the United States, 1918, Russia,* 1:381–82. Kennan, *Russia Leaves the War,* 417–18.

32. Sisson, *One Hundred Red Days,* 356.

33. Kennan, "The Sisson Documents," 138.

34. Kennan, *Russia Leaves the War,* 454. R. Kühlmann to Wilhelm von Mirbach, May 18, 1918, in Zeman, *Germany and the Revolution in Russia,* 128.

35. Robert Service, *Lenin: A Biography* (Cambridge, MA: Harvard University Press, 2000), 294. Volkogonov, *Trotsky,* 111. Document 25, in Richard Pipes, ed., *The Unknown Lenin: From the Secret Archive* (New Haven, CT: Yale University Press, 1988), 53.

36. Historian Richard Pipes disagrees with Kennan and Service. He makes his argument on a technicality: "As late as August 1918, three months before Germany's surrender, [Lenin] badgered Belin for money to carry out anti-French and British—that is, pro-German—propaganda in western Europe though his agent in neutral Switzerland. This surely qualified him as a German agent in the strict meaning of the word." Pipes, *The Unknown Lenin,* 12.

37. Zimmermann telegram to foreign ministry liaison office at general headquarters, March 23, 1917, in Zeman, *Germany and the Revolution in Russia,* x. Volkogonov, *Trotsky,* 117. Service, *Lenin,* 330.

38. Arthur Bullard, "Excerpt from Report to George Creel on Committee of Public Information Work," November 17, 1917, box 6, AB. A similar letter to House is December 12, 1917, box 9, AB. Bullard, *The Russian Pendulum,* 102. Arthur Bullard to Edgar Sisson, n.d. [early 1919?], box 10, AB. Bullard describes his involvement with the documents in a memorandum, May 20, 1921, box 61, SNH.

39. Kennan, *Russia Leaves the War,* 47. Inaba Chiharu, commentary in Motojirō Akashi, *Rakka*

Ryūsui: Colonel Akashi's Report on His Secret Cooperation with the Russian Revolutionary Parties during the Russo-Japanese War, ed. Olavi K. Fält and Antti Kujala, Studia Historica 31 (Helsinki: HSH, 1988), 14–20. Michael Futrell, "Colonel Akashi and Japanese Contacts with Russian Revolutionaries in 1904–5," *St. Antony's Papers* 20, *Far Eastern Affairs* 4 (London, 1967): 7–22. After the Russo-Japanese War, which led to the Russia's astonishing defeat, Akashi was awarded the third Order of the Golden Kite and rose to the rank of general and baron. Bullard, *The Russian Pendulum,* 98.

40. George Creel to Edgar Sisson, May 7, 1918, entry 1, CPI.

41. *WWW,* 308.

42. Arthur Bullard to George Creel, May 9, 1918, box 6; Bullard to Edgar Sisson, May 12, 1918, box 6, AB. Bullard was furious, too, over the delay in receiving Irwin's message. It was sent to the embassy, which had relocated to a provincial city. He had to take a train from Moscow to get it. Bullard to Creel, May 3, 1918, entry 1, CPI. Bullard to Creel, May 6, 1918; Bullard to Compub, May 11, 1918, entry 222, CPI.

43. Edgar Sisson to Arthur Bullard, March 20, 1918, box 1, AB. George Creel to Ernest Chambers, May 9, 1918, entry 1, CPI. Creel to Woodrow Wilson, May 9, 1918, box 4, GC.

44. Leland Harrison, memorandum, September 10, 1919, Sisson Documents, 1917–21, entry 1120, GRDS. The meeting is recorded in Lansing's diary as "Creel and Sisson on Trotsky. Will see latter again," May 9, 1918, RL. It is unclear when a second meeting took place, if it did. Philip Patchin to William Phillips, May 11, 1918, Central Decimal File, 1910–29, box 732, GRDS.

45. George Creel to Woodrow Wilson, May 30, 1918, WW-LC.

46. David W. McFadden, *Alternative Paths: Soviets and Americans, 1917–1920* (New York: Oxford University Press 1993), 54. George Creel to Woodrow Wilson, December 31, 1917, WW-LC.

47. *Papers Relating to the Foreign Relations of the United States, 1918, Russia,* 1:382. Arthur Bullard to Edward M. House, March 7, 1918, box 9, AB; Bullard, "German Gold in Russia," was attached to this letter.

48. R. Graham to Lord Reading, April 25, 1918, FO 371/3229. Leland Harrison to Robert Lansing, June 2, 1918; Allen Carter, "So-Called 'Sisson' Documents and Similar Series in the Possession of the Department," December 1920; Harrison, memorandum, September 10, 1919, Sisson Documents, 1917–21, entry 1120, GRDS.

49. *Rebel,* 183.

50. Edgar Sisson, no title, May 31, 1918, box 21, AB. "American Events Week Ending October 5, 1918," entry 107, CPI. US postal censorship report, index no. 34298, May 28, 1918; Sisson to Allen Carter, December 16, 1920, Sisson Documents, 1917–21, entry 1120, GRDS.

51. *Rebel,* 183.

52. "This Week," *Nation,* September 7, 1918, 1. *Papers Relating to the Foreign Relations of the United States, 1918, Russia,* 2:288. DeWitt Clinton Poole, *An American Diplomat in Bolshevik Russia* (Madison: University of Wisconsin Press, 2014), 143. *PPWW:WP,* 1:130.

53. Sisson, no title, May 31, 1918, box 21, ASB.

54. For a study of this see Carl J. Richard, *When the United States Invaded Russia: Woodrow Wilson's Siberian Disaster* (Lanham, MD: Roman and Littlefield, 2013), 23. Patchin drafted the letter. Lansing diary, September 14, 1918.

55. Lansing diary, August 30, 1918. *Foreign Relations of the United States: Lansing Papers* (Washington, DC: Government Printing Office, 1940), 2:384–85. Lansing sent a copy of Sisson's letter to Wilson, September 16, 1918, WW-LC. Long diary, September 15, 1918.

56. Robert Bender to George Creel, September 13, 1918, entry 1, CPI.

57. *Evansville Journal News,* September 15, 1918. *Boston Evening Transcript,* September 16, 1918.

Philadelphia Inquirer, September 15, 1918. "Lenine and Trotzky German Agents," *Current History,* November 1918, 291. *New York Times,* September 16, 1918.

58. *Report,* 207–8. Henry Suydam to Paul V. Perry, n.d., entry 195, CPI. Examples of cables sent out with Sisson documents can be found in this entry. Vira B. Whitehouse to Edgar Sisson, September 24, 1918, entry 185–86, CPI.

59. *Call,* November 14, 1918. Louise Bryant to George Creel, September 20, 1918; Creel to Bryant, September 20, 1918, entry 1, CPI.

60. Robert A. Rosenstone, *Romantic Revolutionary: A Biography of John Reed* (New York: Random House, 1975), 270, 315–17, 330, 335. Sisson, *One Hundred Red Days,* 286–87. Francis also wanted Reed's appointment rescinded; Robins apparently delivered that message for him through Gumberg, the same person Sisson claimed to have used. Kennan, *Russia Leaves the War,* 408.

61. John Reed, "On Intervention," *Liberator,* November 1918, 14. John Reed, *The Sisson Documents* (New York: Liberator, 1918). George Creel to Frank Polk, January 14, 1918, box 4, FLP. Creel to Thomas Gregory, October 28, 1918, entry 1, CPI. Edgar Sisson to Allen Carter, April 17, 1920, Sisson Documents, 1917–21, entry 1120, GRDS.

62. George Creel to *New Yorker Volkszeitung,* October 2, 1918, entry 1, CPI.

63. William Bullitt to Edward M. House, September 24, 1918, box 21, EMH. *WWW,* 319–20. Bullard describes his involvement with the documents in a memorandum, May 20, 1921, box 61, SNH. Bullitt's views on Creel and the Sisson documents can be found in "Notes on Thomas Woodrow Wilson," box 148, WCB. When the Franklin Roosevelt administration recognized the Soviet Union diplomatically, Bullitt became the first ambassador.

64. Kennan, *Russia Leaves the War,* 405. Christopher Lasch, *The American Liberals and the Russian Revolution* (New York: McGraw-Hill, 1962), 74. See also Edward Alsworth Ross, *Russia in Upheaval* (London: T. Fisher Unwin, 1919), 334–36. Ross, *The Russian Bolshevik Revolution* (New York: Century, 1921), chapter 16. Ross, *The Russian Soviet Republic* (New York: Century, 1923), 140. Richard Polenberg, *Faithing Faiths: The Abrams Case, the Supreme Court, and Free Speech* (New York: Viking, 1987), 111–12. *New York Tribune,* September 22, 1918, deemed the *Evening Post* the only establishment newspaper dissenter. I can find no evidence to the contrary. The *Post's* correspondent in Russia strongly supported Robins's views. Kennan, *Russia Leaves the War,* 386.

65. Oswald Garrison Villard, *Fighting Years: Memoirs of a Liberal Editor* (New York: Harcourt, Brace, 1939), 311–15. Oswald Garrison Villard to David Lawrence, December 7, 1917, box 134, DL.

66. Oswald Garrison Villard, *The Disappearing Daily: Chapters in American Newspaper Evolution* (New York: Knopf, 1944), 246–47. Nevins oral history, 54. Herman Hagedorn, *The Magnate: William Boyce Thompson and His Time, 1869–1930* (New York: John Day, 1935), 252–56. Lamont pledged not to intervene in the newspaper's coverage, but as his grandson noted, he did. Edward M. Lamont, *The Ambassador from Wall Street: The Story of Thomas W. Lamont, J. P. Morgan's Chief Executive* (Lanham, MD: Madison Books, 1994), 100–102. Thomas Lamont, *Across World Frontiers* (New York: Harcourt, Brace, 1951), 91, 95. Kennan, *Russia Leaves the War,* 449. For an example of Robins's efforts to discredit the documents see his message to Ambassador Francis in C. K. Cumming and Walter W. Pettit, eds., *Russian-American Relations, March 1917–March 1920* (New York: Harcourt, Brace and Howe, 1920), 117.

67. *New York Evening Post,* September 16, 1918. *New York Times,* September 24, 1918. *Boston Daily Globe,* September 22, 1918.

68. George Creel to Thomas Lamont, September 27, 1918; Creel to Rollo Ogden, September 30, 1918; Creel to Lamont, October 8, 1918, entry 1, CPI. The *Evening Post* published the letter on October 2, 1918. Tifft and Jones, *The Trust,* 174. *New York Evening Post,* October 2, 1918.

69. "This Week," *Nation,* October 5, 1918, 357. *New Republic,* September 21, 1918, 209. McFadden, *Alternative Paths,* 170.

70. "Civil Liberty Dead," and "The Thing Needful," *Nation,* September 14, 1918, 292, 283. George Creel to Herbert Croly, October 2, 1918; Croly to Creel, October 4, 1918; Creel to Croly, October 9, 1918, entry 1, CPI.

71. Paul A. Goble, "Sisson Documents," in *The Modern Encyclopedia of Russian and Soviet History,* ed. Joseph L. Wieczynski (Gulf Breeze, FL: Academic International, 1983), 35:51. Vira B. Whitehouse to Fritz Wieser, November 1, 1918, entry 183, CPI. Wilmot H. Lewis to Paul V. Perry, October 25, 1918, entry 148, CPI. Davis oral history, 56.

72. Hubert Montgomery, September 18, 1918; Paul V. Perry to Alfred Balfour, September 20, 1918; JW, HM, LBN, memorandum, September 23, 1918; Irwin Laughlin to Balfour, September 24, 1918, FO 371/4367.

73. Geoffrey Dawson to Arthur Willert, October 9, 1918; Willert to Dawson, September 20, 1918; Willert, "News Notes from the United States for the Week September 13–19, 1918," box 2; and Willert to Arthur Murray, October 4, 1918, box 3, AW. Willert, *Washington and Other Memories,* 111.

74. Sanders and Taylor, *British Propaganda,* 201–2. Daniel John Homick, "The Despicable Degenerate of Lucre and the State Department Investigation of the Sisson Documents, 1918–1921" (master's thesis, John Carroll University, 1971), 41. "Publicity of Bolshevik documents in the Press," September 26, 1918, FO 371/4367. The episode is well described in Krantz, "Edgar Sisson's Mission to Russia," 227–32.

75. George Creel to Joseph Schaefer, October 16, 1918; Franklin Jameson to Robert H. Lord, October 19, 1918; Lord to Jameson, October 22, 1918; Samuel N. Harper to Jameson, October 19, 1918, box 19, NBHS. *Christian Science Monitor,* September 26, 1918. The invitation to Harper was similar. Jameson to Harper, October 18, 1918, box 6, SNH.

76. *The German-Bolshevik Conspiracy* (Washington, DC: CPI, 1918), 29–30. Ford oral history, 390–91. Samuel N. Harper to Richard W. Hale, November 25, 1918; Harper to Franklin Jameson, November 27, 1918, box 19, NBHS. Privately Harper admitted the sloppy translation "tended to make one skeptical." Harper to Roger Williams, October 27, 1918, box 6, SNH.

77. Samuel N. Harper, "The Bolshevik Documents: What Do They Prove?," confidential not published, [1918?], box 61, SNH. Harper's analysis is along the lines of those who saw the Bolsheviks taking advantage of the opportunities the Germans offered them. Samuel N. Harper, *The Russia I Believe In,* ed. Paul V. Harper (Chicago: University of Chicago Press, 1945), 112. Franklin Jameson to Samuel N. Harper, November 5, 1918, box 19, NBHS. Jameson to Harper, October 20 and November 5, 1918, box 19, NBHS.

78. Samuel N. Harper, memoir, draft, n.p., box 75, SNH. This passage was likely excised by his brother, who edited the volume. Harper said the same thing at the time to Guy Stanton Ford. Samuel N. Harper to Ford, November 15, 1918, box 6, SNH.

79. *New York Evening Post,* November 11, 1918. "The Sisson Documents," *Nation,* November 23, 1918, 616.

80. Franklin Jameson to Samuel N. Harper, November 18, 1918, box 61, SNH. Michael Wreszin, *Oswald Garrison Villard: Pacifist at War* (Bloomington: University of Indiana Press, 1965), 77.

81. "Proof of Russia's Betrayal," *Literary Digest,* September 20, 1918, 18.

82. David Lawrence to Oswald Garrison Villard, April 29, 1918, box 134, DL.

83. House diary, September 24, 1918. Among the others who considered it a declaration of war was Wythe Williams. Williams, *Dust of Empire: The Decline of Europe and the Rise of the United States* (New York, Scribner's, 1937), 177.

84. Kennan, *Russia Leaves the War,* 49. Kennan, *The Decision to Intervene,* 205. Despite their quarrels, Sisson had an equally high opinion of Bullard's abilities. Sisson, "Report of Edgar Sisson." Arthur Bullard, "Excerpt from Report to George Creel on Committee of Public Information Work," November 17, 1917, box 6, AB.

85. *WWW,* 312. Harvey O'Higgins, "The Czechoslovak Crusade," release, August 25, 1918, entry 138, CPI.

86. *PWW,* 44:557–58.

87. Powell, *The Army behind the Army,* 358–59. *Philadelphia Public Ledger,* October 28, 1919.

88. Brown, *The Groping Giant,* 194.

89. *Providence Journal,* September 17, 1918. *Chicago Daily News,* September 15, 1918. Williams, *American-Russian Relations, 1781–1947* (New York: Rinehart, 1952), 154.

90. Henry Weinberger, the defense attorney, is quoted in an undated, unidentified news clipping, box OV7, GC. Chafee, *Free Speech in the United States,* 118. Stone, *Perilous Times,* 206. Williams, *American-Russian Relations,* 155–57. *New York Tribune,* October 8, 1918. Harry Weinberger to George Creel, October 17, 1918, box 1, HW-Y.

91. Nick Fischer, *Spider Web: The Birth of American Anticommunism* (Urbana: University of Illinois Press, 2016), 99–113. *Brewing and Liquor Interests and German Propaganda: Report of the Subcommittee on the Judiciary* . . . (Washington, DC: Government Printing Office, 1919), 2729, also 2393–94, 2701, 2704. For background on the hearings see McFadden, *Alternative Paths,* 174. Years later, Stevenson advised the Special Committee to Investigate Un-American Activities.

92. *Congressional Record,* December 12, 1918, 344.

93. McFadden, *Alternative Paths,* 172–74, 298–300. Senate Subcommittee of the Committee on the Judiciary, *Bolshevik Propaganda* (Washington, DC: Government Printing Office, 1919), 393, 942.

94. Edgar Sisson to Edward M. House, December 29, 1918, box 103, EMH. Sisson, *One Hundred Red Days,* 435.

95. Edgar Sisson to Basil Miles, June 17, 1919; Allen Carter to Butler Wright, July 22, 1920; Arthur Bullard to Wright, February 20, 1920; Bullard to Sisson, February 20, 1912; Sisson to Carter, March 22, 1921; Sisson, "Analysis of Bischoff Pamphlet," December 4, 1920, Sisson Documents, 1917–21, entry 1120, GRDS.

96. Edward Bell to Leland Harrison, November 18, 1918, Sisson Documents, 1917–21, entry 1120, GRDS. Carter, "So-Called 'Sisson' Documents."

97. Arthur Bullard to Basil Thomson, August 31, 1920; Edgar Sisson to Allen Carter, March 26, 1920; W. F. H. Godson to director, MID, February 28, 1921; Herbert Hoover to Carter, March 15, 1921, Sisson Documents, 1917–21, entry 1120, GRDS. McFadden, *Alternative Paths,* 313–15.

98. [Allen Carter?] to William L. Hurley, February 23, 1921, Sisson Documents, 1917–21, entry 1120, GRDS.

99. Kennan, *Russia Leaves the War,* 451–54.

100. *An Answer to Father Coughlin's Critics* (Royal Oak, MI: Radio League of Little Flower, 1940), 72.

101. Volkogonov, *Lenin,* 189. Merridale, *Lenin on the Train,* 250–52. R. C. Elwood, review of Volkogonov, *Lenin,* in *Slavic and East European Review* 74 (April 1996): 332–34.

102. *Rebel,* 179.

103. Howard Becker, "The Nature and Consequences of Black Propaganda," *American Sociological Review* 14 (April 1949): 226. George Creel to Philip Patchin, September 20, 1918, entry 1, CPI.

104. Kennan, *Russia Leaves the War,* 456. The documents, Christopher Lasch similarly argued,

perpetuated the dangerous delusion "that the Bolsheviks did not have to be reckoned with as a political force in their own right." *American Liberals and the Russian Revolution,* 117. See also Zeman, *Germany and the Revolution in Russia,* x.

105. Isikoff and Corn, *Hubris,* 49.

14. GETTING READY TO GET OUT OF BUSINESS

1. *Hearing,* 90.

2. Harvey O'Higgins to Ben Lindsey, October 31, 1917; George Creel to Lindsey, November 9, 1918, box 59, BBL.

3. "Demobilizing the Committee on Public Information," *Printers' Ink,* November 14, 1918, 12.

4. R. Maddox to Carl Ackerman, November 16, 1918, box 14, CWA. Office of Naval Intelligence, *Cable Censorship Digest,* 52–53. See *Official Bulletin,* November 13, 14, and 15, 1918, for announcements. Censorship of exported film ended December 9, 1918. *Official Bulletin,* November 30, 1918, 1.

5. *Washington Herald,* November 29, 1918. *New York Times,* November 15, 1918.

6. *Indianapolis News,* December 3, 1918.

7. *Congressional Record,* November 21, 1918, 11616.

8. [?] to C. A. Prosser, October 23, 1918, entry 1, CPI. *WWW,* 312. *Foreign Relations of the United States: Public Diplomacy,* 78. Edgar Sisson to James Keeley, October 30, 1918, Central Decimal File, 1910–29, box 735, GRDS.

9. Peterson and Fite, *Opponents of War,* 286. *Official Bulletin,* December 9, 1918. Marlborough Churchill to Marlin Pew, November 22, 1918, entry 150, WDGS.

10. John Tuerk to George Creel, November 25, 1918, entry 1, CPI. *Foreign Relations of the United States: Public Diplomacy,* 87. Ernest Poole to Ben Lindsey, February 25, 1919, box 60, BBL. "German Propaganda Still Rife in U.S., Says Creel," *Editor & Publisher,* November 23, 1918, 42.

11. George Creel to Clayton D. Lee, November 21, 1918, entry 16, CPI.

12. George Creel to Charles Hart, November 14, 1918; Edward Rochester to Creel, November 20, 1918, entry 1, CPI. Creel to Woodrow Wilson, November 16, 1918; Creel to Joseph Tumulty, November 27, 1918, WW-LC.

13. *Handbook of Federal War Agencies,* 512. O. L. Davis Jr., "The National School Service and American Schools during World War I," *Journal of the Midwest History of Education Society* 23 (1996): 67.

14. Muncy, *Relentless Reformer,* 97–103. Park, *The Immigrant Press and Its Control,* 459–63.

15. "To All Four Minute Men of the Committee on Public Information," November 29, 1918, entry 1, CPI. George Creel to Clayton D. Lee, November 21, 1918, entry 14, CPI. Justin Nordstrom, "Beyond 'The Bleak and Dismal Shore,': The Wartime and Postwar Experiences of American Four Minute Men, 1917–1927," *First World War Studies* 5 (2014): 313–14. George W. Coleman, "Salvaging the Four Minute Men," *Survey,* March 29, 1919, 324.

16. Edward Hungerford, "The Peace Treaty—a Failure in Advertising," *Advertising and Selling,* November 29, 1919, 1.

17. *New York World,* December 24, 1918.

18. Gibson diary, November 16, 1918. Wolper, "The Origins of Public Diplomacy," 310. *New York Evening Post,* November 25, 1918. Blum, *Tumulty,* 170.

19. *New York Times,* November 19, 1918. *Chicago Tribune,* November 22, 1918.

20. *New York World,* November 21, 1918.

21. *New York World,* November 27, 1918, *New York Herald,* November 28, 1918, and clippings in box OV8, GC.

22. George Creel to Paul V. Perry, November 25, 1918, entry 1, CPI. Bean, "George Creel and His Critics," 121. *New York American,* December 5, 1918. *New York Sun,* December 6, 1918.

23. *New York Times,* December 6, 1918. *HWAA,* 406–7.

24. George Creel to Paul V. Perry, cable, November 25, 1918; Creel to Harry N. Rickey, November 22, 1918, entry 1, CPI. Bernays, *Biography of an Idea,* 160. Creel's general letter of introduction for Sisson, November 16, 1918, entry 105, CPI.

25. Bernays, *Biography of an Idea,* 160–67.

26. *HWAA,* 411.

27. Unidentified clipping, n.d., box OV8, GC.

28. *PWW,* 53:349, 376. See also Westermann diary, December 10, 1918.

29. W. O. Waters, "Memorandum to General Parker," December 28, 1918, entry 241, AEF. Hudson, *The Writing Game,* 119.

30. House diary, December 16, 1918. *PWW,* 54:394. *Kansas City Post,* December 29, 1918.

31. Gilbert Close to Helen Close, December 6, 1918, box 1, GFC. Wolper, "The Origins of Public Diplomacy," 312. House diary, December 14, 1918.

32. George Creel to Woodrow Wilson, December 24, 1918, WW-LC. Baker comments on reasons for Creel going to Italy in notes he wrote, box 130, RSB. The "huff" comment was Tumulty's characterization of press reports. Joseph Tumulty to Cary Grayson, December 28, 1919, WW-LC.

33. *Rebel,* 207. Wolper, "The Origins of Public Diplomacy," 317. *PWW,* 51:637–38. The only thorough study of this event that I have found is in the Wolper's doctoral dissertation, "The Origins of Public Diplomacy." Wolper pieced together the facts of the mission by diligently searching government papers and translating local newspaper articles written at the time. I have leaned on him for this section.

34. Wolper, "The Origins of Public Diplomacy," 318.

35. Wolper, "The Origins of Public Diplomacy," 316. Gibson diary, July 10, 1918.

36. Sanders and Taylor, *British Propaganda,* 200. Willert, *The Road to Safety,* 24. Emanuel Voska and Will Irwin, *Spy and Counterspy* (Garden City, NY: Doubleday, Doran, 1943), vi–xii, chapters 2, 4, 5, 11, and 13.

37. *HWAA,* 418–20. Voska and Irwin, *Spy and Counterspy,* 299. Wolper, "The Origins of Public Diplomacy," 321–22. *Papers Relating to the Foreign Relations of the United States, The Paris Peace Conference, 1919* (Washington, DC: Government Printing Office, 1942), 11:17.

38. Edgar Sisson to Edward M. House, February 11, 1919, box 103, EMH. In his memoir, Voska claimed the impetus for this Bohemian episode came from General Bliss. Voska and Irwin, *Spy and Counterspy,* 300.

39. Wolper, "The Origins of Public Diplomacy," 326. For background on the Teschen controversy see Piotr S. Wandycz, *France and Her Eastern Allies, 1919–1925* (Minneapolis: University of Minnesota Press, 1962), 83; and D. Perman, *The Shaping of the Czechoslovak State: Diplomatic History of the Boundaries of Czechoslovakia, 1914–1920* (Leiden: E. J. Brill, 1962), 108–9. *Papers Relating to the Foreign Relations of the United States, The Paris Peace Conference,* 11:73. Joseph Grew to Tasker Bliss, February 24, 1919, and Emanuel Voska memorandum to Bliss, February 25, 1919, box 247, THB.

40. *Rebel,* 211. Wolper, "The Origins of Public Diplomacy," 323–29. Wandycz, *France and Her Eastern Allies,* 159. Nicholas Roosevelt, *A Front Row Seat* (Norman: University of Oklahoma Press, 1953), 100. Teschen was a matter of regular discussion among the American commissioners; see for

instance Henry White's papers, box 23, HW-LC. Those papers make no mention to Creel's mediation.

41. Wolper, "The Origins of Public Diplomacy," 329. *Papers Relating to the Foreign Relations of the United States, The Paris Peace Conference,* 11:80. "Notes of a Conversation between General T. H. Bliss and Captain Emanuel Voska, February 24, 1919," box 247, THB.

42. Emanuel Voska to Edgar Sisson, February 25, 1919, box 247, THB. Voska and Irwin offer a slightly different interpretation in *Spy and Counterspy,* chapter 1, namely that Voska's theory and the standard one of a Serb assassination were both correct. A Serb did murder the archduke, the book argues, but a bomb thrown a few minutes before, which missed its mark, was "a Hungarian job."

43. *New York Tribune,* March 28, 1919.

44. Wolper, "The Origins of Public Diplomacy," 337. *Papers Relating to the Foreign Relations of the United States, The Paris Peace Conference, 1919,* 11:34. *PWW,* 54:471. Peter Pastor, *Hungary between Wilson and Lenin* (New York, Columbia University Press, 1976), 102–3. *New York Times,* March 25, 1919.

45. Edgar Sisson to Allen Carter, August 18, 1920, Sisson Documents, 1917–21, entry 1120, GRDS. "Minutes of the Daily Meetings of the Commissioners Plenipotentiary," February 27, 1919, box 80, HW-LC.

46. Edgar Sisson to Eric Palme, February 3, 1919, entry 152, CPI. *WWW,* 313.

47. Kingsley Moses to John H. Hearley, February 19, 1919, entry 170, CPI. Consulate in Irkutsk to State Department, March 7, 1919, Central Decimal File, 1910–29, box 735, GRDS. Phil Norton to Harry Rickey, February 10, 1919, entry 221, CPI. *Report,* 213.

48. Crow, "President Wilson's Eyes & Ears." Sisson's comments on closedown are in *Report,* 213. On March 31, 1919, Paul Kennaday asked Clayton Lee in the CPI business office, "Can you tell me whether Carl Crow is, *1st,* still working for Compub., and *2nd,* whether he is still in China, and *3rd,* if not, where he is?" (entry 105, CPI.) The American legation was unclear what should be done with the CPI funds, as per legation cable to E. H. Hobbs, at the CND, August 19, 1919, Central Decimal File, 1910–29, box 736, GRDS.

49. Whitlock, *The Letters and Journal of Brand Whitlock,* 2:551–52.

50. *Rebel,* 214.

51. House diary, February 28, 1919. George Creel to Woodrow Wilson, March 1, 1919; Wilson to Creel, March 20, 1919, box 2, GC.

52. *Sundry Civil Bill, 1920* (Washington, DC: Government Printing Office, 1919), part II, 1747. Josephine Roche to Ben Lindsey, March 5, 1919, box 61, BBL. *HWAA,* 428. Creel gave other dates for his resignation, including March 15, 1919.

53. John Spencer Walters, *U.S. Government Publication* (Lanham, MD: Scarecrow Press, 2005), 104. US Congress, Joint Committee on Printing, *Official U.S. Bulletin: Hearing before the Joint Committee on Printing,* 66th Cong., 1st Sess. August 12, 1919, 21.

54. US Congress, Senate, Committee on Printing, 66th Cong., 1st Sess., 1920, *Report of the Joint Committee on Printing on Government Periodicals and Field Printing* (Senate Document 66-265), 13. John Walters, "The *Monthly Labor Review,*" *Government Publications Review,* 18 (May–June 1991): 258.

55. *Report of the Joint Committee on Printing,* 19–20, 92.

56. Frederick Palmer to George Creel, March 22, 1918, entry 1, CPI. John Walters, "The Official Bulletin of the United States: America's First Official Gazette," *Government Publications Review* 19 (May/June 1992): 247.

57. *Official U.S. Bulletin: Hearing,* 33; anonymous informant statement is in appendix I, 45. Walters, "The Official Bulletin of the United States," 250.

58. *Official U.S. Bulletin: Hearing,* 21, 31.

59. *New York Times,* April 13, 1920. *Report of the Joint Committee on Printing,* 22, 25. Walters, *U.S. Government Publication,* 103. *New York Times,* April 17 and 28, 1920. Frederick Palmer to George Creel, March 22, 1919; Roger Babson to Reed Smoot, April 17, 1920; and Edward Rochester to Smoot, April 18, 1920, entry 1, CPI.

60. Walters, "The Official Bulletin of the United States," 251. *WWW,* 95–96.

61. Walters, *U.S. Government Publication,* 120. *Congressional Record,* April 12, 1920, 5563, and April 26, 1922, 6027.

62. LeRoy Charles Merritt, *The United States Government as Publisher* (Chicago: University of Chicago Press, 1943), 1.

63. Emery, "The Official Bulletin," 443–44. "A Research Guide to the Federal Register and the Code of Federal Regulations," Law Librarians' Society of Washington, DC, https://www.llsdc.org/ fr-cfr-research-guide.

64. *Report of the Joint Committee on Printing,* 14.

65. Executive Order 3154, August 21, 1919. Press release, Council of National Defense, October 30, 1919, entry 1, CPI. Emmons K. Ellsworth to George Creel, January 12, 1920, entry 1, CPI. Gertrude Gocheler, who worked on the CPI books and stayed around in 1919, said the boxes were delivered to the Fuel Administration building in "perfect order." Gertrude Gocheler to Creel, November 10, 1919, entry 1, CPI.

66. *Sundry Civil Appropriation Bill, 1922* (Washington, DC: Government Printing Office, 1920), part I, 420. *Third Annual Report of the United States Council of National Defense* (Washington, DC: Government Printing Office, 1919), 20. George Creel to Woodrow Wilson, November 8, 1918, WW-LC. Wilson also held the impression that the CND was closely aligned to the Republican Party. Woodrow Wilson to Newton Baker, November 16, 1918, box 8, NDB.

67. "British Propaganda during the War, 1914–1918," n.d., p. 31, INF 4/4a. "The Activities of Wellington House during the Great War 1914–18," INF 4/1b. Janet Adam Smith, *John Buchan: A Biography* (London: Rupert Hart-Davis, 1965), 215.

68. The CND reported receiving a total of 789 file drawers. CND Report, 6.

69. George Creel to Ethel Bullard, February 26, 1930, box 1, AB. These details are found in Frank Hardee Allen, "Classification Scheme Records of the Committee on Public Information, 1917–1919," National Archives and Records Administration, 1938, xii. This document can be found at the archives.

70. *Official Bulletin,* November 27, 1918, 4.

71. In October 1918, Creel pressed Democratic senator Overman, chair of the appropriations committee, to undertake hearings on the topic as soon as possible, but Overman declined due to the upcoming congressional elections. George Creel to Senator Lee Overman, October 21, 1918; Overman to Creel, October 22, 1918; Edward Rochester to Creel, April 18, 1920, entry 1, CPI. Gibson diary, June 2, 1918. Arthur Bullard to Creel, March 5, 1918, box 6, AB. Similar concerns in Russia came from Graham Taylor to Bullard, February 1, 1919, entry 107, CPI.

72. Emmons K. Ellsworth to George Creel, January 6, 1920, entry 1, CPI.

73. Edgar Sisson to Emmons K. Ellsworth, March 10, 1920; Ellsworth to George Creel, March 11, 1920. entry 1, CPI. Entry 22, CPI, contains a draft agreement, with Creel as Wilson's "authorized agent," that gave $1 million to the YMCA for entertainment for servicemen and "and other persons engaged in any allied line of the United States of America." Ellsworth to Creel, February 4, 1920, entry 1, CPI.

74. Emmons K. Ellsworth to Nicholas Murray, March 19, 1921; George Creel to Ellsworth, February 8, 1921, entry 1, CPI.

75. Emmons K. Ellsworth to Francis E. Warren, October 23, 1919, entry 1, CPI.

76. *Washington Post,* November 2, 1919.

77. Newton Baker to George Creel, November 4, 1919; press release, Council of National Defense, October 30, 1919; statement by George Creel, for release November 1, 1919; Creel to N. Baker, November 7, 1919; Creel to Josephus Daniels, December 31, 1919, entry 1, CPI. *New York Times,* November 1, 1919.

78. George Creel to Josephus Daniels, March 10, 1920, entry 1, CPI. *Congressional Record,* March 5, 1920, 3906. Frederick Lewis Allen to Grosvenor B. Clarkson, October 11, 1918, entry 18A-B3, CND.

79. George Creel to Woodrow Wilson, October 21, 1920, WW-LC. The advertisement is in *McClure's,* January 18, 1920, 7.

80. *Lowell Courier-Citizen,* July 31, 1920.

81. George Creel to Newton Baker, November 7, 1919; Creel to Josephus Daniels, December 31, 1919; Daniels and Baker to Creel, January 3, 1920, entry 1, CPI.

82. *Sundry Civil Appropriation Bill, 1922,* 424. Emmons K. Ellsworth to George Creel, March 24, 1921, entry 1, CPI.

83. The need for fairness is discussed in Henry N. Stenton of CND, "Notes on Informal Conversation," April 15, 1910, entry 22, CPI. On Creel's speech to the advertising group see clipping, n.d., in box OV 8, GC. CND Report, 5–9. *HWAA,* 13. Other reductions in the cost to taxpayers involved the sale of CPI equipment. *WWW,* 67, uses the totals in Creel's report. To a small extent the differences in the various reports may be explained by the fact that they were written at different points in time.

84. Cedric E. A. Larson and James R, Mock, "Found: Records of the Committee on Public Information," *Public Opinion Quarterly* 1 (January 1939): 116–18.

85. Among the lost records were a directory of government agencies prepared by the CPI's Service Bureau; files pertaining to the Women's War Work Division; and various correspondence, daily reports, and press releases. *Handbook of Federal War World War Agencies and Their Records, 1917–1921* (Washington, DC: Government Printing Office, 1943), 95, 512. The archives summary is in Allen, "Classification Scheme Records of the Committee on Public Information."

86. *New York Times,* February 9, 1919. Unidentified newspaper clippings, box OV 8, GC. *Tennessean,* December 20, 1918.

87. Remarks of Gus J. Karger and guest list, box 4, GC. Carl Byoir to William Johns, November 14, 1918, entry 99, CPI.

88. Ralph Van Deman to Vira B. Whitehouse, November 11, 1918; Whitehouse to Van Deman, November 22, 1918, entry 183, CPI.

89. Ernest Poole to George Creel, November 15, 1917, entry 5, CPI. Robert Woolley to Creel, November 20, 1918, entry 1, CPI.

90. H. G. Wells, *In the Fourth Year* (New York: Macmillan, 1918), vi, 152.

15. MORE IMPORTANT NOW THAN EVER

1. Homer Cummings, "Memorandum Made November 21, 1928," box 103, RSB.

2. Vance McCormick to Robert S. Bright, February 6, 1919, box 1, VCM. Homer Cummings, "Confidential Memorandum," October 11, 1918, box 68; Cummings, "Memorandum for Mr. Kane," n.d.; McCormick to Cummings, August 8, 1918; McCormick to Edward M. House, October 19, 1918, box 47, HSC.

3. *WWLL: 1918,* 513. Cummings urged the president to link the elections with the negotiations. Homer Cummings to Woodrow Wilson, October 22, 1918, box 68, HSC.

4. *Democratic Campaign Manual 1918* (Washington, DC: Democratic National Committee, 1918), box 27, RWW. Woolley, "'Dear Theodore' and 'Dear Cabot' Get Revenge," PIH, 8.

5. *WWLL: 1918,* 514. Will H. Hays, *The Memoirs of Will H. Hays* (New York: Doubleday, 1955), 176. Will H. Hays to James T. Williams, November 2, 1918, box 32, JTW. Sweetser diary, December 4, 1921. Williams urged senators to reach out to the public before Wilson did. (Albert J. Beveridge to Medill McCormick, June 19, 1919, box 6, HMF.) The Democrats did their best to show that it was common to call for unity at a time of crisis, but the message was drowned out by the Republicans. The Democrats' historical case for such a partisan call is spelled out in Tumulty to Cuyahoga County Republic Committee, October 27, 1918, box 11, JPT.

6. Jeffrey L. Cruikshank and Arthur W. Schultz, *The Man Who Sold America* (Cambridge, MA: Harvard Business Review Press, 2010), chapter 11. Gunther, *Taken at the Flood,* 62, 95, 100–103.

7. Gould, *The First Modern Clash over Federal Power,* 77. Livermore, *Wilson and the War Congress,* 44. James McLachlan, October 22 and November 1, 1918, FO 371/3428. Ben Lindsey to George Creel, November 9, 1918, box 59, BBL. For an example of the priority Hays gave to starting early see Will H. Hays to Medill McCormick, February 14, 1917, box 5, HMF.

8. George Creel to Mark Sullivan, November 28, 1922, box 6, MS. George Creel, *The War, the World and Wilson* (New York: Harper, 1920), 146. Frederick Lewis Allen to Grosvenor Clarkson, October 11, 1918, 18A-B3-CND. Many of Wilson's advisors agreed the letter was a great mistake: see Ray Stannard Baker interviews with Albert Burleson, March 17, 1927; Homer Cummings, November 21, 1928; Josephus Daniels, August 8, 1936; and Vance McCormick, July 15, 1928, and September 12, 1930, RSB.

9. Woolley, "'Dear Theodore' and 'Dear Cabot' Get Revenge," 9. Baker interview with Woolley.

10. Cobb, *Cobb of "The World,"* 226. Gus Karger to William Taft, November 8, 1918, WHT.

11. David Lawrence to Ray Stannard Baker, November 26, 1937, box 110, RSB.

12. Douglas B. Craig, *Progressives at War: William G. McAdoo and Newton D. Baker, 1863–1941* (Baltimore: Johns Hopkins University Press, 2013), 170. Stanley Coben, *A. Mitchell Palmer: Politician* (New York: Columbia University Press, 1963), 131–32. For an example of German plots uncovered by Palmer see *Official Bulletin,* October 19, 1918, 2, which reports German efforts to control highly explosive materials. Palmer was attuned to the importance of campaign publicity as well. In 1915, when he was chairman of Executive Campaign Committee of the Democratic National Committee, Palmer appealed for funds for a national publicity campaign leading up to the next election. A. Mitchell Palmer, broadside letter, March 30, 1915, box 34, RWW.

13. "C. B. Gibson's Committee for Patriotic Posters," *New York News Magazine,* January 1918.

14. Ford oral history, 388. *Censor,* June 21, 1917. *Report of the Joint Committee on Printing,* 26. The great communication advantage given a president is implicit in a proposed congressional resolution during the treaty fight. Since Wilson had a travel fund of $25,000 when he stumped for the peace pact, the resolution argued, senators who hit the road to argue against him should be provided with $15,000. Berg, *Wilson,* 624.

15. Walter S. Rogers to George Creel, May 30, 1918, entry 1, CPI. *Hearing,* 41. A summary of the staff's political affiliations can be found in "Creel Answers Pou's Charges of Partisanship and Error," *Editor & Publisher,* June 8, 1918, 18. Occasionally a Republican legislator echoed Creel's claim that CPI materials were impartial in that they came without comment (*Congressional Record,* June 17, 1918, 7910), but this was not a common view.

16. Nicholas, "Crossroads Oratory," 190. Elmer E. Cornwell Jr., *Presidential Leadership of Public*

Opinion (Bloomington: University of Indiana Press, 1965), 52. "Typical Speech No. 3," *Four Minute Men Bulletin* no. 16, September 24, 1917, 7.

17. Harvey O'Higgins to Ben Lindsey, October 29, 1918, box 59, BBL. With regard to O'Higgins's article on Daniels see his "YOU and Josephus Daniels," typescript, n.d., entry 17, CPI. It is unclear if the article was published. In his diary, November 8, 1917, Daniels said Creel and O'Higgins came to dinner to discuss the article and criticism of him. Hapgood, *The Advancing Hour,* 35. Arthur Willert to William Wiseman, August 8, 1918, box 5, AW.

18. "Put the Blame Where It Belongs," *Metropolitan,* March 1918, 71–72. Creel, "The Case for Mr. Garfield," *Independent,* March 9, 1918, 408–9. *New York Times,* March 9, 1918. *New York Evening Post,* reprinted in *Washington Times,* April 15, 1918. Wilson, who was slow to promote women's suffrage, endorsed an idea presented by several editors to play down embarrassing news of suffragist picketers at the White House in 1917. There is evidence that Creel helped with this. Sally Hunter Graham, "Woodrow Wilson, Alice Paul, and the Woman Suffrage Movement," *Political Science Quarterly* 96 (Winter 1983–84): 673. Among other things, navy censors of outgoing news dispatches were instructed to "suppress all references to Women' Suffrage pickets at the White House." Office of the Censor, August 23, 1918, box 5, AW.

19. *Official Bulletin,* November 30, 1918, 4. Frank Marion to George Creel, March 15, 1918, entry 148, CPI. *HWAA, 347.*

20. These can be found in undated, unidentified clips in box OV8, GC. *Los Angeles Times,* 29, 1918.

21. *New York Tribune,* October 31, 1918. *New York Sun,* October 31, 1918. "Political Slides a Boomerang," *Motion Picture News,* November 9, 1918, 2838. Undated clippings, box OV6, GC.

22. *New York Times,* October 30, 1918. Hays, *The Memoirs of Will H. Hays,* 179. On the betting odds see *New York World,* November 20, 1918.

23. Theodore Roosevelt, *Kansas City Star,* November 26, 1918.

24. Elmer Roberts, private memorandum, December 1917, box 1, ER-UNC. "Confidential Memorandum Dictated by Ms. Shoecraft, January 2, 1919," Classified Case Files of Edward Bell, 1918–1919, entry A1-350, GRDS. Arthur Willert told Lord Northcliffe that the election "was a great blow to the Democrats and especially to the President's personal prestige." Willert to Northcliffe, November 8, 1918, box 3, AW.

25. Viereck, *Spreading Germs of Hate,* 211. Thomas A. Bailey, *Woodrow Wilson and the Great Betrayal* (Chicago: Quadrangle, 1945), 23.

26. Oswald Garrison Villard to Joseph Tumulty, November 8, 1918, *PWW,* 51:646. George Creel to Woodrow Wilson, November 8, 1918, WW-LC.

27. Creel, "America's Fight for World Opinion," 10.

28. Creel, *The War, the World and Wilson,* 163. Bailey, *Wilson and the Lost Peace,* 27. Ray Stannard Baker interview with Walter Lippmann, December 9 and 10, 1927, box 110, RSB.

29. Joseph Tumulty to Woodrow Wilson, April 25, 1919, box 49, JPT. For other examples see Herbert Bruce Brougham to Wilson, December 16, 1918, *PWW,* 53:407.

30. George Creel to Woodrow Wilson, October 18, 1918, box 2, GC. Creel to Wilson, November 8, 1918, WW-LC.

31. Frank Cobb, memorandum, November 6, 1918, *PWW,* 51:615. Vance McCormick, draft letter, n.d., box 3, VCM.

32. Woodrow Wilson to David Lawrence, October 5, 1917, box 110, RSB. Henry Cabot Lodge to Elihu Root, January 3, 1919, box 161, ER.

33. Igna Floto, *Colonel House in Paris: A Study of American Policy at the Paris Peace Conference*

1919 (Princeton, NJ: Princeton University Press, 1973), 69–70. David Lawrence mentions the possibility of Cobb's appointment in a story written before Wilson left for France, undated *New York Evening Post* clipping in box OV8, GC. Edward M. House to Woodrow Wilson, October 22, 1918, *PWW,* 51:406–8. "Memorandum on the Inquiry," October 26, 1918; "Memorandum on Press Correspondents," n.d., box 38, WL. Ray Stannard Baker to Arthur Krock, October 14, 1927, box 17, AK.

34. Woodrow Wilson to Joseph Tumulty, December 19, 1918, box 48, JPT. *HWAA,* 413. Baker interview with Creel, May 23, 1932. Baker diary, December 16, 1918. Diary entries during war also may be found in Ray Stannard Baker, *A Journalist's Diplomatic Mission: Ray Stannard Baker's World War I Diary,* ed. John Maxwell Hamilton and Robert Mann (Baton Rouge: Louisiana State University Press, 2012).

35. Creel, *The War, the World and Wilson,* 168–71. Hilderbrand, *Power and the People,* 188. George Creel to Walter S. Rogers, January 6, 1919 (two letters), entry 1, CPI. Rogers to Clayton D. Lee, January 21, 1919, Central Decimal File, 1910–29, box 735, GRDS.

36. Filler, *The Muckrakers,* 87. Baker diary, February 8, 1918.

37. Ray Stannard Baker to Frank Polk, February 17, 1918, box 1, FLP. Baker diary, February 19, 1918. Polk to Baker, February 15, 1918, box 1, RSB-P. Baker's letters to Polk can be found in box 3, RSB-P.

38. *WWWS,* 127–28.

39. Arthur Sweetser to Herbert Croly, n.d., box 3, AS. On Sweetser's move to the Military Intelligence Branch see Heber Blankenhorn to Chief, G-2-D, September 1, 1918, entry 235, AEF.

40. *WWWS,* 106.

41. *WWWS,* 119–20. The amounts allotted to individual newspapers were small—on one day, for instance, 222 words to the *New York Sun* and 189 to the *Detroit News.* For details see entry 156, CPI.

42. *WWWS,* 127, 130. Hilderbrand, *Power and the People,* 172; *Papers Relating to the Foreign Relations of the United States, The Paris Peace Conference,* 1:220.

43. Unsigned note, n.d., box 4, RSB-P.

44. Ray Stannard Baker to Norman Hapgood, October 6, 1921, box 9, NH. See also Baker's comments to the press, Baker diary, December 21, 1918. For a discussion on serving two masters see Daniel C. Hallin, ed., *The President, the Press, and the People* (San Diego: University of California, San Diego Press, 1992), chapter 2.

45. *WWWS,* 133. For a discussion of Baker at the conference see Oulahan, "Presidents and Publicity," unpublished memoir, chapter 6, RVO.

46. Simeon Strunsky, "The Peace-Makers," *Atlantic Monthly,* April 1919, 528.

47. *Service Bulletin of the Associated Press,* June 14, 1919, 21.

48. Cobb and Lippmann's suggestion is in Edward M. House to Woodrow Wilson, telegram, October 29, 1918, and Wilson to House, October 30, 1918, *Papers Relating to the Foreign Relations of the United States, 1918, Supplement 1, The World War* (Washington, DC: Government Printing Office, 1933), 1:405, 421. Wilson did offer some clarification in a memorandum to the Senate, but this was hardly enough to make an impression. *WWWS,* 127. William Wiseman, "Notes of an Interview with the President in the White House," October 14, 1918, box 1, WW-Y. Walter Lippmann, "Managed News," *Newsweek,* April 15, 1963, 23. Wiseman's personal papers show him in a dual advisory role, and Willert recognized this to be the case. At one point, Wiseman suggested that Wilson give a statement to the *Times* of London and then drafted it for him. Willert, *The Road to Safety,* 178.

49. Bailey, *Woodrow Wilson and the Lost Peace,* 127–33. Bayard Swope and others to Woodrow Wilson, January 14, 1919, *PWW,* 54:60; Hankey's Notes of a Meeting of the Council of Ten, January

16, 1919, *PWW,* 64:96–99. For background see James D. Startt, *Woodrow Wilson, the Great War, and the Fourth Estate* (College Station: Texas A&M University Press, 2017), chapter 13.

50. Charles T. Thompson, *The Peace Conference Day by Day: A Presidential Pilgrimage, Leading to the Discovery of Europe* (New York: Brentano's, 1920), 112. Strunsky, "The Peace-Makers," 532.

51. Startt, *Woodrow Wilson, the Great War, and the Fourth Estate,* 267.

52. Bayard Swope to Woodrow Wilson, n.d., HBS. It is unclear if the letter was sent. No copy of it appears in Wilson's papers.

53. Hugh Gibson, *The Road to Foreign Policy* (Garden City, NY: Doubleday, Doran, 1944), 78. Wilson, "The Study of Administration," 208.

54. Bailey, *Woodrow Wilson and the Lost Peace,* 189–90.

55. Baker diary, March 8, 1919.

56. *WWWS,* 151. See chapters 7 and 8 for Baker's discussion of publicity. David Lawrence, *The True Story of Woodrow Wilson* (New York: George H. Doran, 1924), 348.

57. Woodrow Wilson to Robert Lansing, December 17, 1918, box 40, RL. Lansing to John Davis, January 4, 1919, box 3, RL-P. *WWWS,* 131, 417.

58. Alden Hatch, *Edith Bolling Wilson, First Lady Extraordinary* (New York: Dodd, Mead, 1961), 161–62.

59. Joseph Tumulty to Cary Grayson, December 16 and 17, 1918, WW-LC. *PWW,* 53:447–48. Hilderbrand, *Power and the People,* 168–69, 190. Hood diary, March 30, 1919.

60. Robert Lansing to Charles W. Valentine, February 13, 1919, box 3, RL-P. Arthur Sweetser, unpublished article, 1919, box 3, AS. William Allen White, *The Autobiography of William Allen White* (New York: Macmillan, 1946), 555. Edward Hungerford, "The Peace Treaty—a Failure in Advertising," *Advertising and Selling,* November 29, 1919, 3.

61. Hilderbrand, *Power and the People,* 178. Hamilton, *Journalism's Roving Eye,* 147–48. *New York American,* n.d.; story from *Washington Post-Public Ledger* correspondent, n.d., box OV8, GC. Ray Stannard Baker, *American Chronicle: The Autobiography of Ray Stannard Baker* (New York: Charles Scribner's Sons, 1945), 397.

62. Frazier Hunt, *One American and His Attempt at Education* (New York: Simon and Schuster, 1938), 168–71. Ritchie, *Press Gallery,* 208. "Opening of the Sixty-Sixth Congress," *Current History,* July 1919, 54. Hilderbrand, *Power and the People,* 186. *Congressional Record,* June 9, 1919, 782, 786. Gus Karger to William Howard Taft, June 10, 1919, WHT.

63. Walter Lippmann to Edward M. House, March 18, 1919, box 70, EMH.

64. Gilbert Close to Helen Close, May 29, 1919, box 1, GFC.

65. George Creel to Woodrow Wilson, February 3, 1919, WW-LC. Ray Stannard Baker to Wilson, March 6, 1919, box 4, RSB-P. Cooper, *Breaking the Heart of the World,* 54. Baker diary, April 25, 1919. Baker was more forgiving of Wilson publicly. *WWWS,* 317.

66. Bullard, *The Diplomacy of the Great War,* 215–16.

67. Baker diary May 31, 1919. In a note to Balfour, Wiseman relates how confident Wilson was that he would prevail. William Wiseman to Alfred Balfour, July 18, 1919, box 1, WW-Y.

68. "Nation-Wide Press-Poll on the League of Nations," *Literary Digest,* April 5, 1919, 13–16ff. Stephen Bonsal, *Unfinished Business* (Garden City, NY: Doubleday, Doran, 1944), 48. Robert Woolley to Vance McCormick, August 1, 1919, box 12, RWW. Woolley to Edward M. House, August 14, 1919, box 124, EMH.

69. Oswald Garrison Villard, "The Truth about the Peace Conference," *Nation,* April 26, 1919, 647. Steele, *Walter Lippmann and the American Century,* 163. Lippmann told Norman Hapgood, "The President's negotiations seem to me to have been based upon a fundamental miscalculation:

namely, on the idea that he must purchase assent to the League by accepting the program of Imperialism." Lippmann to Hapgood, July 28, 1919, box 10, NH.

70. Ruhl F. Bartlett, *The League to Enforce Peace* (Chapel Hill: University of North Carolina Press, 1944), 114–16, 131. Cooper, *Breaking the Heart of the World,* 58. Subcommittee of the Committee on Privileges and Elections, *Presidential Campaign Expenses,* 2593–98. The extension secretary was Tom Jones Meek; see minutes of the Emergency Campaign Committee, December 16, 1918, box 124, HAG.

71. Livermore, *Woodrow Wilson and the War Congress,* 114. Joseph R. Hayden, *Negotiating in the Press: American Journalism and Diplomacy, 1918–1919* (Baton Rouge: Louisiana State University Press, 2010), 195–96. Walters, *U.S. Government Publications,* 106.

72. Hays, *The Memoirs of Will H. Hays,* 182. *Cincinnati Times-Star,* June 30, 1919.

73. Arthur S. Link, *Woodrow Wilson: Revolution, War, and Peace* (Chichester: Wiley-Blackwell, 1985), 110.

74. Hays, *The Memoirs of Will H. Hays,* 202, 205. Thomas J. Knock, *To End All Wars: Woodrow Wilson and the Quest for a New World Order* (Princeton, NJ: Princeton University Press, 1992), 176. Remarks to Members of the Democratic National Committee, *PWW,* 55:323.

75. Bartlett, *The League to Enforce Peace,* 143–46. In the 1916 election, Taft had such "contempt" for Wilson he could not hold himself back from making speeches that personally attacked the president. William Howard Taft to Charles Hillis, July 27, 1916, box 122, CDH.

76. Breckenridge Long, "The Fight for the League of Nations," n.d., box 110, RSB. Henry Morgenthau to Woodrow Wilson, November 26, 1917, box 8, HM-LC. Long's pamphlet came about as follows: In early 1919, Wilson warned Long off giving pro-League speeches as he doubted "the time has come for a systematic campaign on this subject." Wilson did permit him to meet with Tumulty to discuss what else might be done. The resulting pamphlet, "The League of Nations," aimed to simulate community discussion and promote organized public opinion. It was sent out on May 5, 1919. The first printing of 100,000 copies went mostly to teachers and members of the Democratic Party organization.

77. Joseph Tumulty to Woodrow Wilson, April 25, 1919, box 49, JPT. A plea to keep Roche's committee alive came from John Palmer Gavit to Tumulty, April 9, 1919, box 11, JPT. Gavit saw the committee as having special value in heading off "Bolshevism." Cass Gilbert, "Division of Pictorial Publicity," no publisher, 1919, no page number. A similar quotation is in *HWAA,* 136.

78. Nordstrom, "Beyond 'The Bleak and Dismal Shore,'" 311–14. *Tennessean,* August 9, 1918. C. F. Reisner to Ben Lindsey, November 8, 1918, box 59, BBL. Reisner told Lindsey speakers would "receive every two weeks a 'talk' sheet similar to that being used by the Government." George W. Coleman, "Salvaging the Four Minute Men," *Survey,* March 29, 1919, 324.

79. Douglas MacArthur to Vance McCormick, April 16, 1917, box 2; McCormick to Woodrow Wilson, June 28, 1917, box 3; McCormick to Gavin McNab, September 9, 1924, box 1, VCM. Vance McCormick, *Citizen Extraordinaire,* 156. *Citizen Extraordinaire* is McCormick's diary in Paris and is useful in showing his attitudes on publicity and his intimacy with Wilson. George Creel to Herbert Houston, April 17, 1917, box 8, RWW.

80. Hungerford, "The Peace Treaty—a Failure in Advertising," 4. Bailey, *Wilson and the Lost Peace,* 127.

81. *WWLL: 1915–1917,* 264. *PWW,* 51:408. *HWAA,* 416. Creel, "Why the Peace Treaty Was Not Advertised," *Advertising & Selling,* December 34, 1919, 32.

82. Link, *Woodrow Wilson,* 113.

83. Cooper, *Woodrow Wilson,* 521. Blum, *Tumulty,* 209. Baker, *American Chronicle,* 462–65.

84. *Address of President Wilson,* Senate document 120 (Washington, DC: Government Printing Office, 1919), 351.

85. Baker, *American Chronicle,* 462. Livermore, *Woodrow Wilson and the War Congress,* 209.

86. Hays, *The Memoirs of Will H. Hays,* 208.

87. Bailey, *Wilson and the Great Betrayal,* 201. Hays, *The Memoirs of Will H. Hays,* 213.

88. Frank Cobb to William Howard Taft, November 12, 1919, WHT. The ad is attached to W. H. Short, memorandum, November 26, 1919, WHT.

89. Cooper, *Breaking the Heart of the World,* 377.

90. Cooper, *Woodrow Wilson,* 426. Link, *Woodrow Wilson,* 126. Arthur Willert to Lady Astor, December 19, 1919, box 1, AW.

91. Robert Woolley to Woodrow Wilson, November 7, 1918, and November 3, 1920, box 23, RWW. Charles Edward Russell to Stephen Bonsal, November 15, 1920, box 5, SB.

92. Robert Woolley to Daniel Roper, August 19, 1920, box 18; Woolley to George Creel, September 14, 1920, box 4, RWW. Woolley, "Harding—'In a Smoke-Filled Room,'" PIH, passim. Blum, *Tumulty,* 254. *New York Times,* October 12, 1918. *Presidential Campaign Expenses,* 2342.

93. Hays, *The Memoirs of Will H. Hays,* 217. Randolph C. Downes, *The Rise of Warren Gamaliel Harding, 1865–1920* (Columbus: Ohio State University Press, 1970), 490–92. John A. Morello, *Selling the President, 1920: Albert D. Lasker, Advertising, and the Election of Warren G. Harding* (Westport, CT: Praeger, 2001), 46.

94. Downes, *The Rise of Warren Gamaliel Harding,* 477–81.

95. Bailey, *Wilson and the Great Betrayal,* 338, 344.

96. Arthur Sweetser, memorandum of conversation with Hughes, March 25, 1922, box 1, AS.

97. Knock, *To End All Wars,* 33.

98. Margaret MacMillan, *Paris 1919: Six Months That Changed the World* (New York: Random House, 2001), 493. Crow, "President Wilson's Eyes & Ears," typescript, 1–2, folder 46, CC.

99. Palmer, *With My Own Eyes,* 380. Robert Lansing, "Making the Treaty," n.d., box 10, RL-P. Frederic C. Howe, "Where Are the Pre-War Radicals?" *Survey,* March 1926, 50.

100. Gilbert Close to Helen Close, March 16, 1919, box 1, GFC.

101. Kerney, *The Political Education of Woodrow Wilson,* 346.

102. Baker diary, March 8, 1919.

103. Cooper, "The Historical Presidency: Few and Mostly Far Between: Reflections on Intellectuals as Presidents." Viereck, *Spreading Germs of Hate,* 168.

104. Bernays, *Biography of an Idea,* 177. SWW, 45.

105. Stephen C. Schlesinger, *Act of Creation* (Cambridge, MA: Westview, 2003), 54–57. Knock, *To End All Wars,* 13.

106. Arthur Bullard to Edward M. House, July 7, 1916, box 9, AB. Woodrow Wilson to George Creel, January 19, 1923, box 2, GC.

107. Cooper, *Breaking the Heart of the World,* 409.

108. Author interview with John Milton Cooper, March 5, 2019.

109. Ray Stannard Baker to Louis Brandeis, November 11, 1931, box 1, RSB-P.

16. THE QUESTION

1. Matthew C. Naylor, "The Last One Down: Henry Gunther," in program for *World War I Armistice Day Centennial Sacred Service,* November 11, 2018, Washington National Cathedral.

2. Hugh Chisholm, "Editorial Preface," and P.C.M., "Propaganda," *Encyclopaedia Britannica* (London: Encyclopaedia Britannica, 1922), 30:vii, x, xii, and 32:176. Guy Stanton Ford wrote a sturdy entry for "Censorship," a subject also missing from the prior edition. The previous edition had a heading for "Censor," but this discussed officials who oversaw the census in the Roman Empire around the time of Christ. For a discussion of the word *propaganda* over time see Erwin W. Fellow, "'Propaganda': History of a Word," *American Speech* 34 (October 1959): 182–89. The word "public opinion" did not appear in *Merriam-Webster's Dictionary* until 1920. Eric F. Goldman, *Two-Way Street: The Emergence of the Public Relations* (Boston: Bellman, 1948), 13.

3. This claim that only the enemy does propaganda was made time and again. For instance, "This fight for public opinion is the business of the Committee on Public Information. We do not call it propaganda, for that work, in the German hands, has come to be associated with lies, secrecies and shameful corruptions. Our work is educational and informative, for we have such confidence in our case that we feel this is needed no more than fair presentation of its facts to win the war." George Creel, "Public Opinion as a War Measure," 32. Vira Whitehouse informed Creel, "*Propaganda* is a word that must never be said in Switzerland. The Germans have made it mean all sorts of illegal, dark, sneaky things." Vira B. Whitehouse to George Creel, January 30, 1918, entry 1, CPI. French historian Georges Weill said: "There was a very strange psychological phenomenon: Each of the warring nations persuaded itself that its government had neglected propaganda, where as the enemy, on the contrary, had been most effective." Becker, *The Great War and the French People*, 59.

4. *HFIL*, 34, 194–95. Allen, "Government Influence on News in the United States during the World War," 92. Harvey O'Higgins to George Creel, n.d., entry 1, CPI.

5. *WWW*, 72. "Items" include news stories, editorials, letters to the editor, photos, short fillers, and advertisements in which the CPI is mentioned. The results are derived from a search of Newspapers.com. By way of comparison, the *Hartford Courant* ran thirty releases, images, or advertisements related to the CPI in 1918.

6. Gilbert, "Division of Pictorial Publicity," no page number. *WWW*, 72.

7. *WWW*, 191.

8. Jerry Israel, *Progressivism and the Open Door: America and China, 1905–1921* (Pittsburgh: University of Pittsburgh Press, 1971), 160.

9. Edgar Sisson, "Method for Military Intelligence," June 25, 1918, entry 235, AEF.

10. Muncy, *Relentless Reformer*, 89. *WWW*, 71.

11. *New York Evening Post*, reprinted in *Washington Times*, April 15, 1918. For a discussion of emotional levels in World War I exceeding those in World War II, see Ernst Kris and Nathan Letes, "Trends in Twentieth Century Propaganda," *Psychoanalysis and the Social Sciences* 1 (1947): 393–409.

12. William Johns to [Carl Byoir], July 4, 1918, entry 97A, CPI.

13. Will Irwin, "The Age of Lies," *Sunset*, December 1919, 54.

14. Wilkinson, *Secrecy and the Media*, 119.

15. *Hearing*, 88, 141. *HWAA*, 165, 212. Ernest Poole to George Creel, November 20, December 29, 1917, and January 22, 1918; Creel to Poole, November 21, 1917; Ford to A. B. Jewett, January 10, 1918, entry 1, CPI. Jules Brulatour to James Kerney, February 16, 1918, entry 148, CPI. Hamilton, *Journalism's Roving Eye*, 335. James Montgomery Flagg, whose "I want you" recruiting poster became an American icon, was incensed when an artist at one of Gibson's meeting said they should be paid for their government work. "Balls!" he exclaimed when he took the floor. The single word, he said later, "summed up the feelings of all present." James Montgomery Flagg, *Roses and Buckshot* (New York: G. P. Putnam, 1946), 157.

16. This was Public Law 181, passed July 1, 1918, described in *Congressional Record*, July 1, 1918,

646. A useful definition of a "czar" is: "An executive branch official who is not confirmed by the Senate and is exercising final decision-making authority that often entails controlling budgetary programs, administering/coordinating a policy area, or otherwise promulgating rules, regulations, and orders that bind either government officials and/or the private sector." Sollenberger and Rozell, *The President's Czars,* 7, as well as 39–48, which offers a broader discussion of Wilson's circumvention of Congress and the Constitution. Another discussion of this phenomena can be found in Edward Samuel Corwin, *Total War and the Constitution: Five Lectures Delivered on the William W. Cook Foundation at the University of Michigan, March 1946* (Freeport, NY: Books for Libraries, 1947), 50–55. A 1918 act gave Wilson authority to reorganize existing agencies already established by law and create new ones relating only to airplane production. The law did not cover the CPI, the War Industries Board, or the National War Labor Board.

17. For instance, nine days after the 2001 terrorist attacks on the United States, President Bush announced the creation of a cabinet-level Office of Homeland Security to coordinate government communications and policy. His executive order detailed its director's duties. After congressional complaints, Bush sought approval for a Department of Homeland Security. Sollenberger and Rozell, *The President's Czars,* 136. For a discussion of the impact of war on the imperial presidency see Arthur M. Schlesinger Jr., *The Imperial Presidency* (Boston: Houghton Mifflin, 1973), ix.

18. This point is made in Peter Buitenhuis, "The Selling of the Great War," *Canadian Review of American Studies* 7 (Fall 1976): 139–41.

19. Wilson, *Constitutional Government,* 68. Baker diary, March 8, 1919.

20. Ray Stannard Baker interview with George Creel, April 5, 1926. *PWW,* 64:81; *PWW,* 67:231.

21. Zechariah Chafee, "Charles Evans Hughes," *Proceedings of the American Philosophical Society* 93 (June 10, 1949): 270–71.

22. One of Woolley's crafty ideas during the war was straight out the 1916 campaign, namely, to discredit Lord Lansdowne, who had called for a negotiated peace. Perhaps, Woolley said to Polk, Scotland Yard had intercepted communication between Lansdowne and the kaiser, with whom he was personally familiar. This is not the sort of scheme Creel would have thought up. He was a clever wit, but not crafty. Robert Woolley to Frank Polk, November 30, 1917, box 16, RWW.

23. Frank Cobb to Grosvenor B. Clarkson, September 4, 1917, entry 1, CPI. Irwin, *The Making of a Reporter,* 357–58.

24. Warren I. Cohen, *The American Revisionists: The Lessons of Intervention in World War I* (Chicago: University of Chicago Press, 1967), 35. This study provides an excellent survey of the change in attitude among American thinkers. Hadley Cantril, ed., *Public Opinion, 1935–1946* (Princeton, NJ: Princeton University Press, 1951), 201.

25. Cohen, *The American Revisionists,* 110. Viereck, *Spreading Germs of Hate,* 210.

26. Corey, "Perfectly Irresponsible," chapter 11, 103. The code, called the Canon of Journalism, was approved by the American Society of Newspaper Editors.

27. Baker, "Railroads on Trial," 535–36.

28. Frederic William Wile, "Government by Propaganda," *Outlook,* December 26, 1928, 1388. Cobb, *Cobb of "The World,"* 322, 344. The speech was also reprinted in Frank I. Cobb, "The Press and Public Opinion," *New Republic,* December 31, 1919. William Allen White, "Where Are the Pre-War Radicals?," *Survey,* February 1926, 557.

29. Walter Lippmann to Ellery Sedgwick, April 7, 1919, box 1, WL.

30. Lippmann, *Public Opinion,* 31, 158. The term "manufacture of consent" does not originate with Lippmann as some suggest. It can be found, for instance, in Max Sherover, *Fakes in American Journalism* (Brooklyn, NY: Free Press League, 1914), 22.

31. Arthur Bullard, memorandum, February 6, 1920, box 5, AB. Ernest Poole, *Blind: The Story of These Times* (New York: Macmillan, 1920), 353.

32. Ford, "America's Fight for Public Opinion," address to Minnesota Historical Society. SWW, 44–45. *APD*, 9. For his part, Creel said, "I am not sure that, if the war had to come, it did not come at the right time for preservation and reinterpretation of American ideals. . . . Coming when it did, it found us ready to respond with the self-abandon of youth to great visions and to direct our policies and weigh our actions with the ripened wisdom of maturity." *HWAA*, 105.

33. Bennett, "Carl Byoir; Public Relations Pioneer," 63.

34. Bernays oral history, 59. Edward L. Bernays, *Propaganda* (1928; reprint, Brooklyn, NY: IG, 2005), 110. Bernays, *Biography of an Idea*, 288. Also see Edward L. Bernays to Myron S. Blumenthal, October 6, 1919, box II-1, ELB. Many struggled for a better word than press agent. "Some word," said public relations pioneer Ivy Lee in 1918, "ought to be coined, not as a reproach but as an honor, which would describe the conscious effort to present to the minds of men facts and arguments designed to lead them to a given conclusion." Lee, "Ministers of Propaganda," *Notes and Clippings*, August 15, 1918. Martin Egan abhorred the idea of publicity, as it smacked of theater agents. He called what he did for J. P. Morgan "public relationships." Torbert, "Let Us Forgather," chapter titled "No 'Doctor of Publicity,'" ME. Even after *public relations* became the common term, the search for euphemisms continued. Al Golin, who helped propel McDonald's into the forefront of fast food, was said to coin the term "trust strategist." *New York Times*, April 16, 2017. The term *public relations* was not utterly new when Bernays used it, but he may not have been aware of this. The American Bankers Association created a Department of Public Relations in 1915. Marcus Cayce Myers, "Revising the Narrative of Early U.S. Public Relations History: An Analysis of the Depictions of PR Practice and Professionals in the Popular Press, 1770–1918" (PhD diss., University of Georgia, 2014), 9.

35. Carl Ackerman, "Public Opinion and the Press," *Vital Speeches of the Day*, June 15, 1937, 521. Bernays widely publicized that he was teaching the NYU PR course. See, for instance, *Boston Transcript*, February 2, 1923; *New York Journal*, February 3, 1923; *New York Herald*, February 1, 1923; and *New York Times*, February 1, 1923. Norman Hapgood made a speech at the Church of the Ascension, the same place Creel gave his infamous "slumming" speech, in which he signaled how the press had become wary of government: "A generation ago we did not expect from the Press what we do now." Norman Hapgood, "The Public and the Press," n.d., box 14, NH.

36. Walter von Hofmann, "Organisation von Presse und Propaganda in Franchfreich, England and Italien"; Directive, "Über en amtlichen Pressedienst," November 12, 1918, R 121428, PA. On emulating the British model see Hofmann, "Vorschläge für eine inensivere Austaltung unserver Propaganda," MSG2-15137, 1490154, BArch-MA.

37. Lasswell, *Propaganda Technique in the World War*, 34. The enduring value of the book is discussed in Ralph Haswell Lutz, "Studies of World War Propaganda, 1914–33," *Journal of Modern History* 5 (December 1933): 496. On the use of *Propaganda Technique* by revisionists see Cohen, *The American Revisionists*, 111.

38. *New York Times*, April 5, 1923. Lucy Maynard Salmon, *The Newspaper and Authority* (New York: Oxford University Press, 1923), 312. Edward Lilly, "OWI History," unpublished MS, chapter 1, box 26, EPL. Creel, "The Truth Shall Make You Free," 28ff. Lilly's chapter is good at explaining what FDR created. The Office of War Information created a Victory Speakers program that explicitly drew from the Four Minute Men. Nicholas, "Crossroads Oratory," 291.

39. Stone, *Perilous Times*, 154.

40. Walters, *U.S. Government Publication*, 18. Merritt, *The United States Government as Publisher*, 2.

41. Mordecai Lee, *Congress vs. the Bureaucracy: Muzzling Agency Public Relations* (Norman: University of Oklahoma Press, 2011), 93, 125, 129, 170. For a general discussion of these issues see John Maxwell Hamilton and Kevin R. Kosar, "Government Information and Propaganda: How to Draw a Line?," R Street Policy Study, 2016. There are other categories of proscribed communications besides "purely partisan materials": "covert propaganda" (that is, communications that do not acknowledge they emanate from the government) and "self-aggrandizement (that is, communication that tends to advertise the importance of an agency, which is another restriction that is difficult to enforce since the materials can be presented as informational). Another law bans materials that urge citizens to lobby Congress on behalf of the administration. For a discussion of these restrictions see *Principles of Federal Appropriations Law,* 4th ed., 2017 rev., GAO-16-464SP (Washington, DC: March 2016), chapter 3, 235–305. The partisan nature of congressional control over information is discussed in the excellent, if dated, book Francis E. Rourke, *Secrecy and Publicity: Dilemmas of Democracy* (Baltimore: Johns Hopkins Press, 1961), 186 and passim. As the author notes, government information is the "Promethean gift" (14). For a study of contemporary citizens' attitudes toward government information—and their tendency to view it through a partisan lens as politicians do—see Michael Henderson and John Maxwell Hamilton, "Public Service or Propaganda? How Americans Evaluate Political Advocacy by Executive Agencies," *Social Science Quarterly* 101 (January 2020): 144–60.

42. J. William Fulbright, *The Pentagon Propaganda Machine* (New York: Liveright, 1970), 20. Author interview with Linda Koontz, October 24, 2012. I had extensive conversations with current GAO officials, whose insights were helpful. Lee, *Congress vs. the Bureaucracy,* 231.

43. On the GAO study see Heather Krause to Senator Mike Enzi, September 30, 2016, https://www.gao.gov/assets/690/680183.pdf, referencing GAO-16-877R, "Public Relations Spending." This study was prompted in part by Hamilton and Kosar, "Government Information and Propaganda"; and Hamilton and Kosar, "How the American Government Is Trying to Control What You Think," *Washington Post,* September 24, 2015. One of the first serious scholarly studies of government publicity pointed out the problem of identifying who was doing publicity work. The author blamed Congress for this, arguing that its resistance to executive branch publicity led to efforts to hide it. McCamy, *Government Publicity,* chapter 5. On military bands see Jessica T. Mathews, "America's Indefensible Defense Budget," *New York Review of Books,* July 18, 2019, 23.

44. Author interviews with Brian Cullen, October 11, 2012, and Steven H. Warren, January 14, 2013. Hohenberg, *The News Media: A Journalist Looks at His Profession* (New York: Holt, Rinehart, and Winston, 1968), 116. George Michael, *Handout* (New York: G. P. Putnam, 1935), 237. George Michael was a pseudonym.

45. Myers, "Revising the Narrative of Early U.S. Public Relations History," 137. Blakey, *Historians on the Homefront,* 26.

46. Goldman, *Two-Way Street,* 13. "Foreword," editorial, *Public Opinion Quarterly* 1 (January 1937): 3.

47. George Creel, speech to the Wilmette Club, Chicago, February 20, 1921, box 5, GC. P.C.M., "Propaganda," 176.

48. The Roosevelt administration created the Press Intelligence Service under the National Emergency Council, a New Deal coordinating agency, to assess news coverage. Stories were categorized as "favorable" or "unfavorable" and by the political leaning of the newspaper in which they appeared. The results were not made public. McCamy, *Government Publicity,* 150–51.

49. Charles Merriam to Walter S. Rogers, July 15, 1918, box 21, CEM. Sasha Issenberg, *The Victory Lab: The Secret Science of Winning Campaigns* (New York: Crown, 2012), chapter 1. Charles

E. Merriam, *Civic Education in the United States* (New York: Charles Scribner's Sons, 1934), 126.

50. *Washington Post,* June 26, 2015.

51. Sarah Stillman, "Good Behavior," *New Yorker,* January 23, 1917, 46. Sharon Weinberger, "Still in the Lead?" *Nature,* January 2008, 390–93. Author interview with Read Montague, August 22, 2013.

52. Salmon, *The Newspaper and Authority,* 361. *Chilling Effects: NSA Surveillance Drives U.S. Writers to Self-Censor* (New York, PEN American Center, 2013). Information Security Oversight Office, *2017 Report to the President* (2018), 4, 9. https://www.archives.gov/files/isoo/reports/2017-annual-report.pdf. Steven Aftergood to author, January 20, 2020. On EPA budget see https://www.epa.gov/planandbudget/budget.

53. Michael, *Handout,* 219. Leonard Downie Jr., *The Obama Administration and the Press,* Report by the Committee to Protect Journalists, October 10, 2013. *New York Times,* April 22, 2014. *Washington Post,* January 24, 2017, and June 8, 2019. "Every administration learns from the previous administration," television journalist Bob Schieffer said, quoted in Downie. "They become more secretive and put tighter clamps on information." In his first year, Obama held eleven solo news conferences. Eisenhower held about twenty-three a year and Kennedy held twenty-six a year. Jill Colvin, "In Trump Era, the Death of the White House Press Conference," AP News, April 30, 2018, https://apnews.com/f29a23df19214466b226e2cbdec78cbd; Martha Joynt Kumar, "*Source Material:* Presidential Press Conferences: The Importance and Evolution of an Enduring Forum," *Presidential Studies Quarterly* 35 (March 2005): 166–92.

54. Amos Pinchot, speech, typescript, February 16, 1914, box 90, AP-LC.

55. Howe, *Confessions of a Reformer,* 282. Cohen, *The American Revisionists,* 57.

56. Lasswell, *Propaganda Technique in the World War,* 3.

57. Hannah Arendt, *Crises of the Republic* (New York: Harcourt and Brace, 1969), 34–35.

58. Vira B. Whitehouse to George Creel, January 30, 1918, entry 1, CPI.

59. This 17 percent figure includes those who "always" or "most of the time" trust Washington. "Public Trust in Government: 1958–2019," Pew Research Center, Washington, DC, April 11, 2019, https://www.people-press.org/2019/04/11/public-trust-in-government-1958-2019/. Frank Cobb to Grosvenor B. Clarkson, September 4, 1917, entry 1, CPI.

60. David Cole," The Path of Greatest Resistance," *New York Review of Books,* February 7, 2019, 22.

61. Innumerable studies show the decline in the number of journalists. For instance, between 2009 and 2014, the number of Washington, DC–based reporters for local newspaper accredited by the Senate to cover Congress declined by 11 percent. In twenty-one states, none of the newspapers have their own reporter on Capitol Hill. Kristine Lu and Jesse Holcomb, Pew Research Center, January 7, 2016.

62. Simon, *FDR and Chief Justice Hughes,* 340. This was a familiar theme for Hughes, who said on another occasion, "We may well wonder in view of the precedents now established whether constitutional government as hitherto maintained in this Republic could survive another great war even victoriously waged." Charles Evans Hughes, *Two Addresses Delivered before the Alumni of Harvard Law School at Cambridge, June 21, 1929* (Boston: Harvard Law School Association, n.d.), 23.

63. Jackson Giddens, introduction to "American Foreign Propaganda in World War I." *APD,* 4–5.

64. Baker diary, entry date unclear. The statement appears on page 127 of his diary, during the period after the treaty negotiations.

65. George Creel, typescript speech [1918], box 5, GC. Hugh Chisholm, "Editorial Preface," ix.

EPILOGUE

1. Ackerman, *Germany,* 20. Ackerman, "How Free Is American Press," *Vital Speeches of the Day,* June 15, 1941, 543. Also see Hollington K. Tong, *China and the World Press* (Nanking, China: n.p., 1948), 277; William J. Donovan to Carl Ackerman, July 5, 1945, CA; Boylan, *Pulitzer's School,* 96; Ackerman, "Robert VanderHoof Ackerman," chapter 8. On corporate image building see Roland Marchand, *Creating the Corporate Soul: The Rise of Public Relations and Corporate Imagery in American Big Business* (Berkeley: University of California Press, 1998), 139 and passim.

2. *Sauk Country Democrat,* n.d., box 2, HM. Kennedy, *Samuel Hopkins Adams,* 130–31.

3. Background on Baker's postwar work can be found in box 2, GBB.

4. George Creel to Edith Bolling Wilson, March 23, 1920, WW-LC. Merrill D. Peterson, *The President and His Biographer: Woodrow Wilson and Ray Stannard Baker* (Charlottesville: University of Virginia Press, 2007), 206. Baker, *American Chronicle,* 508, 514. Creel thought he would be the executor of Wilson's papers. George Creel to Arthur Krock, October 2, 1922, box 23, AK. Baker, *American Chronicle,* 377.

5. Bernays, *Propaganda,* 48.

6. Heinrich von Bernstorff to Frank Polk, February 13, 1917, box 2, FLP. Doerries, *Imperial Challenge,* 11. *New York Times,* September 16, 1930, and October 15, 1941.

7. "Biographical Information," Bjorkman Finding Aid, EB. Warren I. Kuehl and Lynne Dunn, *Keeping the Covenant: American Internationalists and the League of Nations* (Kent, OH: Kent State University Press, 1977), 77.

8. *Diamond of Psi Upsilon,* November 1932, 53–54. *Chicago Tribune,* July 1932.

9. Gilbert J. Gall, "Heber Blankenhorn, the Lafollette Committee, and the Irony of Industrial Repression," *Journal of Labor History* 23 (Spring 1982): 252–53. Laurie, "'The Chanting of Crusaders,'" 479. Blankenhorn, unpublished memoir, chapter 6, HB.

10. Katherine Adams, *Progressive Politics and the Training of American Persuaders* (Mahwah, NJ: Lawrence Erlbaum, 1999), 128. Cruikshank and Schultz, *The Man Who Sold America,* 261.

11. Roland Morris to Arthur Bullard, August 4, 1920, box 1. Bullard to Charles O. Bauer, August 31, 1925, box 8, AB. Ernest Poole, "Arthur Bullard in Russia During the War," n.d., box 1, AB. Ethel Bullard to Edward M. House, October 26, 1929, box 21, EMH.

12. Donald Johnson, "Wilson, Burleson, and Censorship in the First World War," *Journal of Southern History* 28 (February 1962): 56–58. Adele S. Burleson, *Every Politian and His Wife* (Philadelphia: Dorrance, 1921), 173, 176.

13. Cutlip, *The Unseen Power,* 531, 580. Tong, *China and the World Press,* 111–12. Bennett, "Carl Byoir; Public Relations Pioneer," 74–78. Keller, "George Sylvester Viereck," 98.

14. Martin, *The Hypocrisy of Justice in the Belle Epoque,* 218–91. Berenson, *The Trial of Madame Caillaux,* 225. Beatty, *The Lost History of 1914,* 237–38, 305–6.

15. The *Collier's* billing is found in blurb, box 4, and George Creel, "McCarthyism," n.d., typescript, box 6, GC. Kathryn S. Olmsted, *Right Out of California: The 1930s and the Big Business Roots of Modern Conservatism* (New York: New Press, 2015), 65–67. His "bleeding heart" comment was in *San Francisco Call-Bulletin,* October 23, 1952. Creel had one other trip abroad for Wilson. In 1920, Wilson sent him on an unofficial mission to Mexico. News reports that Creel was traveling as a writer and under a false name led to observations that "Creel's Adventures in Mexico Resemble Plot of Comic Opera." He came back recommending diplomatic recognition of the Mexican government. When recognition was given over the objections of the State Department, the *Evening Post* reported, "George Creel has put one over on another Secretary of State." *New York Evening*

Post, November 1, 1920; also see *Washington Herald,* October 10, 1920; *Washington Post,* October 14, 1920; *Philadelphia Public Ledger,* October 16 and October 25, 1920; *New York Herald,* October 30, 1920. William L. Chenery, responsible for labor news at the CPI, became editor and later publisher of *Collier's,* for which Creel was Washington correspondent after the war.

16. Crow, "President Wilson's Eyes & Ears," 15. Carl Crow, *400 Million Customers: The Experiences, Some Happy, Some Sad, of an American in China, and What They Taught Him* (New York: Harper, 1937), 32, 41, 189.

17. William Bullitt believed that the Sisson documents infuriated Durant and drove him to the Soviet side. William Bullitt to R. Walton Moore, February 22, 1936, box 3, RWM.

18. Galpin, *Hugh Gibson,* 58–61. Gibson, *The Road to Foreign Policy,* 59.

19. Samuel N. Harper, draft memoir, n.p, box 75, SNH. This anecdote did not make it into the published version of his memoir. It also was probably dropped by his brother, who edited the book after Samuel died.

20. George Sylvester Viereck, *The Strangest Friendship in History: Woodrow Wilson and Colonel House* (New York: Liveright, 1932), xiv. Creel, *The War, the World and Wilson,* 32–33.

21. Chafee, "Charles Evans Hughes," 281. Perkins, *Charles Evans Hughes and American Democratic Statesmanship,* 139. Wile, *News Is Where You Find It,* 426.

22. Irwin, *Propaganda and the News,* 206. Hudson, *The Writing Game,* 136, 149, and passim.

23. Minutes of the executive board, October 8, 1918, box AF2, AAAA. The Ad Council's link with business interests can be as benign as preventing automobile accidents, which lowers insurance losses.

24. James Keeley to family, November 9, 1918, JK. Linn, *James Keeley,* 253–58.

25. Lansing, *War Memoirs of Robert Lansing,* 322–33. Creel, *The War, the World and Wilson,* 32, 67.

26. Gunther, *Taken at the Flood,* 194, 297.

27. *United States Daily,* March 4, 1926. David Lawrence, speech, November 12, 1968, box 113, DL.

28. Lippmann, unidentified clipping, July 3, 1920, box OV2, GC. Dominique Trudel, "Revisiting the Origins of Communication Research: Walter Lippmann's World War II Adventure in Propaganda and Psychological Warfare," *International Journal of Communication* 11 (2017): 371–73.

29. Rebecca Erbelding, *Rescue Board* (New York: Doubleday, 2018), 55–54. Also see Gregory J. Wallace, *America's Soul in the Balance: The Holocaust, FDR's State Department, and the Moral Disgrace of an American Aristocracy* (Austin, TX: Greenleaf, 2012), 169–73.

30. Edwin M. Hood et al. to Newton Baker, April 4, 1917, box 255, NDB. George Weller, *First into Nagasaki: The Censored Eyewitness Dispatches on Post-Atomic Japan and Its Prisoners of War,* ed. Anthony Weller (New York: Crown, 2006), 275–76.

31. John Buchan, *Pilgrim's Way: An Essay in Recollection* (Boston: Houghton Mifflin, 1940), 169. *Times,* November 18, 1927. Wilkinson, *Secrecy and the Media,* 70.

32. Charles E. Merriam, "Taming Big Bill," autobiographical fragment, typescript, 4, box 3, CEM. Raymond Seidelman and Edward Harpham, *Disenchanted Realists: Political Science and the American Crisis* (New York: State University of New York Press, 2015), 109. "Summary of Discussion and Action," Document no. 90, Commission on Freedom of the Press, January 27–29, 1946, box 127, CEM. Merriam, *Civic Education in the United States,* ix.

33. Harvey O'Higgins and Edward H. Reede, *The American Mind in Action* (New York: Harper and Brothers, 1924), 25.

34. Marchand, *Creating the Corporate Soul,* 84. Noel L. Griese, *Arthur W. Page: Publisher, Public Relations Pioneer, Patriot* (Atlanta: Anvil, 2001), 2, 121–24.

35. "Foreign Contacts," *Survey,* January 3, 1920, 1.

36. Jensen, *Price of Vigilance,* 99–100. "Faked Spy Revelations Exposed," *Issues and Events,* February 23, 1918, 148. Byrnes and Spilman, *Providence Journal,* 295–301. *New York Times,* October 28, 1920, carried a story on Roosevelt's claim of libel. "More Thrilling Than Fiction," *Nation,* November 10, 1920, 522.

37. Muncy, *Relentless Reformer,* 1–3.

38. Peter Bird Martin, "A Brief History of the Institute of Current World Affairs," https://www.icwa.org/about/history/.

39. Ross, *Seventy Years of It,* 96, 248.

40. William Harlan Hale, "When the Red Storm Broke," *American Heritage,* February 1961, 103.

41. Ruotsila, *John Spargo and American Socialism,* 234–35.

42. Lee, *Congress vs. the Bureaucracy,* 149–51.

43. Sweetser biographical sketch, typescript, n.d., box 2, AS.

44. *New York Times,* September 7, 1971. Alfred W. McCoy, *Policing America's Empire: The United States, the Philippines, and the Rise of the Surveillance State* (Madison: University of Wisconsin Press, 2009), 343–45. "Ralph Van Deman," *Encyclopaedia Britannica,* https://www.britannica.com/biography/Ralph-Van-Deman.

45. Viereck, *Spreading Germs of Hate,* 295–96.

46. Two short undated biographies of Voska can be found in the slim folder of his papers at the Library of Congress. One is by his daughter and the other by an author identified as Egon Hostovský. See also CJA to Elmer David, October 31, 1953, EVV. Also, Voska and Irwin, *Spy and Counterspy,* 314–21.

47. *APD,* 21.

48. *Sacramento Union,* December 25, 1921. *New York Times,* November 9, 1926, and April 12, 1957.

49. "Au Revoir?," PIH, 2. Charles Robb to author, May 7, 2015.

A Note on Sources

The Committee on Public Information presents challenges to historians.

Not all of the CPI's files made it into National Archives. Some of those that did were later discarded, and the surviving portions are in many places untidy. It does not help that the CPI was continually in flux. Some units existed for a fleeting moment or their names changed. Chapter 14 describes the organization's haphazard dissolution. If the records were neat and intact, however, they would not tell the full story any more than a box score tells the full story of a baseball game. As the rewards of looking elsewhere became apparent, I turned over every promising archival stone I could find.

Another difficulty is George Creel's articles, books, speeches, and letters. They are indispensable *and* unreliable. This requires elaboration. Some of Creel's false claims (e.g., "We do not touch censorship at any point") are explicable. He was a propagandist. But Creel also misled when he had no reason to do so. By way of illustration, he inaccurately claimed in his autobiography that African-American opinion was never "a cause of concern for the Committee." Creel was, as he told President Wilson, engaged in "the negro problem." An unsigned memo in the CPI files, probably written by Creel, directed the *Official Bulletin* to make as much use as possible of material prepared by Emmett Scott, the African-American advising Secretary of War Baker on race issues: "I am very anxious to cooperate in every way possible with the important work among negros that Mr. Scott is doing." Only one black American correspondent was accredited to the AEF in France. To Creel's credit, the CPI arranged that in order to improve news to African-American readers.

How can this be explained? Creel was impulsive. His exuberance carried him away. He wrote and spoke with blinding speed. He had little time in his hyperkinetic life for reflection. He prized clever turns of phrase. He was more interested in making an impression than in literal accuracy. In the case of his statement on African-Americans, Creel probably wanted to make the point that the CPI did not spend as much time on that segment of the population as it did on immigrant groups. "Creel was a crusader," said journalist and propagandist Stanley Washburn. "He didn't tell the truth." Harold Ickes, a progressive Republican who worked for Charles Evans Hughes's 1916 presidential race and cooperated with Creel at the CPI, confided to a mutual friend, "Mr. Creel has never been notable for accuracy or objectivity."

After reading reams of Creel's writing, I have concluded that he believed what he wrote—when he wrote it. It is worth noting, too, that while he overlooked facts that did not suit him at the moment, he was an open book. Privately he made fun of himself. These qualities won him loyal friends. He seems to have done little or nothing to weed out unflattering comments from the personal papers he donated to the Library of Congress. I have done my best to check Creel's statements against other records while making his propaganda *about* the CPI part of the history told in this book.

Two useful histories have been written on the CPI. *How Words Won the War,* by James R. Mock and Cedric Larson, was published in 1939. It drew from CPI archives, although without citations. (Mock wrote a useful book on censorship—*Censorship 1917*—that also employed CPI archival material.) Stephen L. Vaughn focused on the CPI's domestic operations in *Holding Fast the Inner Lines,* published forty years ago. It points to the value of going beyond the CPI's official files. These books made the writing of this book easier.

Several doctoral dissertations and a thesis deserve to be singled out:

Frank Hardee Allen. "Government Influence on News in the United States during the World War." PhD diss., University of Illinois, 1934.

Walton E. Bean. "George Creel and His Critics: A Study of the Attacks on the Committee on Public Information, 1917–1919." PhD diss., University of California, Berkeley, 1941.

Robert J. Bennett. "Carl Byoir; Public Relations Pioneer." Master's thesis, University of Wisconsin, 1968.

Elisabeth Fondren. "'Breathless Zeal and Careless Confidence': German Propaganda in World War I (1914–1918)." PhD diss., Louisiana State University, 2018.

Jackson Alfred Giddens. "American Foreign Propaganda in World War I." PhD diss., Tufts University, 1966.

Robert A. Krantz Jr. "Edgar Sisson's Mission to Russia, 1917–1918." PhD diss., University of Wichita, 1957.

Wayne Alfred Nicholas. "Crossroads Oratory: A Study of the Four Minute Men of World War I." PhD diss., Columbia University, 1953.

Louis John Nigro Jr. "Propaganda, Politics, and the New Diplomacy: The Impact of
   Wilsonian Propaganda on Politics and Public Opinion in Italy, 1917–1918." PhD
   diss., Vanderbilt University, 1979.
Gregg Wolper. "The Origins of Public Diplomacy: Woodrow Wilson, George Creel,
   and the Committee on Public Information." PhD diss., University of Chicago,
   1991.

I have used shorthand references for frequently cited publications, manuscripts,
and diaries, and for archival collections. These are elaborated below.

PUBLICATIONS AND MANUSCRIPTS

APD   Robert F. Delaney and John S. Gibson, eds. *American Public Diplomacy:
           The Perspective of Fifty Years.* Medford, MA: Edward R. Murrow Center
           of Public Diplomacy, Tufts University, 1967.
CND Report   Director, Council of National Defense, "A Report Concerning Papers,
           Files, Records, Public Property, Assets and Liabilities, etc. of the Commit-
           tee on Public Information," transmitted June 9, 1920, entry 22, CPI.
Hearing US Congress, House, Subcommittee of House Committee on Appropri-
           ations. *Sundry Civil Bill for 1919, Hearing.* Part III. 65th Cong., 2d Sess.,
           1918.
HFIL   Stephen Vaughn. *Hold Fast the Inner Lines: Democracy, Nationalism, and
           the Committee on Public Information.* Chapel Hill: University of North
           Carolina Press, 1980.
HWAA   George Creel. *How We Advertised America.* New York: Harper and Broth-
           ers, 1920.
PIH   Robert W. Woolley. "Politics is Hell." Unpublished autobiography, circa
           1946, boxes 44–45, Robert Wickliffe Woolley Papers, Library of Congress.
PPWW   Ray Stannard Baker and William E. Dodd, eds., *The Public Papers of Wood-
           row Wilson.* Two two-volume sets, *The New Democracy* and *War and Peace.*
           Cited as *PPWW* followed by *ND* or *WP,* volume number and page (e.g.,
           PPWW:WP, 2:324).
PWW   Arthur S. Link, ed. *The Papers of Woodrow Wilson* (Princeton, NJ: Prince-
           ton University Press), 69 vols. Cited as *PWW* followed by volume and
           page number (e.g., *PWW,* 45:465).
Rebel   George Creel. *Rebel at Large: Recollections of Fifty Crowded Years.* New
           York: G. P. Putnam, 1947.
Report   George Creel, *Complete Report of the Chairman of the Committee on Public
           Information.* Washington, DC: Government Printing Office, 1920.

SWW   Harvey O'Higgins. "Selling the World War." Typescript, n.d., box 6,
          George Creel Papers, Library of Congress. (This was a draft for an article
          that appeared in much shorter form as "Incredible Mr. Creel, *New Yorker,*
          July 4, 1925, 7–8.)
WWLL   Ray Stannard Baker. *Woodrow Wilson: Life and Letters.* New York: Charles
          Scribner's Sons, 1946. 8 vols. Cited as WWLL followed by time period
          covered in volume and page number (e.g., *WWLL: 1917–1918,* 447).
WWW   James R. Mock and Cedric Larson. *Words That Won the War: The Story of
          the Committee on Public Information, 1917–1919.* Princeton, NJ: Princeton
          University Press, 1939.
WWWS   Ray Stannard Baker. *Woodrow Wilson and World Settlement.* Vol. 1. Gar-
          den City, NY: Doubleday, Page, 1923.

ARCHIVAL COLLECTIONS

ASSOCIATED PRESS CORPORATE ARCHIVES, NEW YORK, NEW YORK

AP   Associated Press

BOSTON UNIVERSITY, HOWARD GOTLIEB ARCHIVAL RESEARCH CENTER, BOSTON, MASSACHUSETTS

HBS   Herbert Bayard Swope Papers

UNIVERSITY OF CHICAGO, SPECIAL COLLECTIONS RESEARCH CENTER, CHICAGO, ILLINOIS

RA   Rudolph Altrocchi Papers
CEM   Charles E. Merriam Papers
SNH   Samuel N. Harper Papers

GERMAN FEDERAL ARCHIVES

BArch   Bundesarchiv, Berlin-Lichterfelde
BArch-MA Militärarchiv, Freiburg
PA   Politisches Archiv-Auswärtiges Amt, Berlin

FRANKLIN D. ROOSEVELT PRESIDENTIAL LIBRARY AND MUSEUM, HYDE PARK, NEW YORK

RWM   R. Walton Moore Papers

COLUMBIA UNIVERSITY, RARE BOOK AND MANUSCRIPT LIBRARY, NEW YORK, NEW YORK

CRIA   Council on Religion and International Affairs
CU   Office of the President, Columbia University, Central Files

JGPS	James Graham Phelps Stokes Papers
WLW	William Linn Westermann Papers
NYW	[New York] *World* Records

LIBRARY OF CONGRESS, MANUSCRIPT DIVISION, WASHINGTON, DC

AFLR	American Federation of Labor Records
AP-LC	Amos Pinchot Papers
AS	Arthur Sweetser Papers
ASB	Albert Sidney Burleson Papers
BBL	Ben B. Lindsey Papers
BL	Breckenridge Long Papers
BW	Brand Whitlock Papers
CEH	Charles Evans Hughes Papers
CER	Charles Edward Russell Papers
CWA	Carl W. Ackerman Papers
ELB	Edward L. Bernays Papers
EMH-LC	Edwin Milton Hood Papers
ER	Elihu Root Papers
EVV	Emanuel Victor Voska Papers
FLA	Frederick Lewis Allen Papers
FWW	Frederic William Wile Scrapbooks
GC	George Creel Papers
GCR	Gridiron Club Records
GP	Gifford Pinchot Papers
HAG	Harry Augustus Garfield Papers
HC	Herbert Corey Papers
HH	Hermann Hagedorn Papers
HLI	Harold L. Ickes Papers
HMF	Hanna-McCormick Family Papers
HM-LC	Henry Morgenthau Papers
HW-LC	Henry White Papers
JD	Josephus Daniels Papers
JFJ	J. Franklin Jameson Papers
JJP	John J. Pershing Papers
JPT	Joseph P. Tumulty Papers
JRG	James R. Garfield Papers
NAWSA	National American Woman Suffrage Association Records
NBHS	National Board for Historical Service Records
NDB	Newton D. Baker Papers
NH	Norman Hapgood and Elizabeth Reynolds Hapgood Papers

RL   Robert Lansing Papers
RSB   Ray Stannard Baker Papers
RWW   Robert Wickliffe Woolley Papers
SB   Stephen Bonsal Papers
SW   Stanley Washburn Papers
THB   Tasker Howard Bliss Papers
TJW   Thomas James Walsh and John Edward Erickson Papers
TR   Theodore Roosevelt Papers
TWG   Thomas Watt Gregory Papers
WAW   William Allen White Papers
WGM   W. G. McAdoo Papers
WHT   William Howard Taft Papers
WW-LC   Woodrow Wilson Papers

DUKE UNIVERSITY, DAVID M. RUBENSTEIN RARE
BOOK & MANUSCRIPT LIBRARY, DURHAM, NORTH CAROLINA

AAAA   American Association of Advertising Agency Records
DCR   Daniel C. Roper Papers
JD-D   Josephus Daniels Papers
JWT   J. Walter Thompson Company, Sidney Ralph Bernstein Company History
              Files
JTW   James T. Williams Papers
TNP   Thomas Nelson Page Papers

DWIGHT D. EISENHOWER LIBRARY, ABILENE, KANSAS

EPL   Edward P. Lilly Papers

HARVARD UNIVERSITY, HOUGHTON LIBRARY,
CAMBRIDGE, MASSACHUSETTS

HM   Houghton Mifflin Papers

HARVARD UNIVERSITY, SCHLESINGER LIBRARY, RADCLIFFE
INSTITUTE FOR ADVANCED STUDY, CAMBRIDGE, MASSACHUSETTS

VBW   Vira Boarman Whitehouse Papers

HERBERT HOOVER PRESIDENTIAL LIBRARY, WESTBRANCH, IOWA

RVO   Richard V. Oulahan Papers

UNIVERSITY OF ILLINOIS, ARCHIVES, UNIVERSITY
LIBRARY, URBANA-CHAMPAIGN, ILLINOIS

AEB   Arthur E. Bestor Papers

JGR   James G. Randall Papers
LML   Laurence M. Larson Papers

METROPOLITAN CLUB, ARCHIVES, WASHINGTON, D.C.

MC   Metropolitan Club Records

UNIVERSITY OF MINNESOTA, ELMER L. ANDERSON LIBRARY, MINNEAPOLIS, MINNESOTA

GSF   Guy Stanton Ford Papers

MORGAN STATE UNIVERSITY, BEULAH DAVIS RESEARCH CENTER, BALTIMORE, MARYLAND

EJS   Emmett J. Scott Papers

STATE HISTORICAL SOCIETY OF MISSOURI, COLUMBIA, MISSOURI

CC   Carl Crow Papers

NATIONAL ARCHIVES AND RECORDS ADMINISTRATION, COLLEGE PARK, MARYLAND, AND WASHINGTON, DC

AEF   American Expeditionary Forces, Record Group 120
CND   Council of National Defense, Record Group 62
CNO   Chief of Naval Operations, Record Group 38
CPI   Committee on Public Information, Record Group 63
GRDS   General Records of the Department of State, Record Group 59
PO   Post Office Department, Record Group 28
WDGS   War Department General and Special Staffs, Record Group 165

NEW YORK HISTORICAL SOCIETY, NEW YORK, NEW YORK

ADS   American Defense Society Records
GL   Gilder Lehrman Collection
JNW   James Norman Whitehouse Papers

NEW YORK PUBLIC LIBRARY, MANUSCRIPT AND ARCHIVES DIVISION

FPW   Frank P. Walsh Papers

UNIVERSITY OF NORTH CAROLINA, LOUIS ROUND WILSON SPECIAL COLLECTIONS LIBRARY, CHAPEL HILL, NORTH CAROLINA

EB   Edwin Bjorkman Papers
ER-UNC   Elmer Roberts Papers
JD-UNC   Josephus Daniels Papers

PIERPONT MORGAN LIBRARY, NEW YORK

ME   Martin Egan Papers

PRINCETON UNIVERSITY, NEW JERSEY SEELEY G. MUDD
MANUSCRIPT LIBRARY, PRINCETON, NEW JERSEY

AB   Arthur Bullard Papers
AK   Arthur Krock Papers
AWD   Allen W. Dulles Papers
DL   David Lawrence Papers
GFC   Gilbert F. Close Papers
GFK   George F. Kennan Papers
LLCR   Liberty Loan Committee Records
RL-P   Robert Lansing Papers
RSB-P   Ray Stannard Baker Papers
WW-P   Woodrow Wilson Collection

PRITZKER MILITARY MUSEUM & LIBRARY
ARCHIVAL COLLECTIONS, CHICAGO, ILLINOIS

WMB   William McCormick Blair Collection

STANFORD UNIVERSITY, HOOVER INSTITUTION, STANFORD, CALIFORNIA

GBB   George Barr Baker Papers
HSG   Hugh S. Gibson Papers
MS   Mark Sullivan Papers
RS   Rosika Schwimmer Papers
SMB   Stephen Miles Bouton Papers

US ARMY MILITARY HISTORY INSTITUTE,
CARLISLE BARRACKS, PENNSYLVANIA

AWC   Army War College Curricular Archives

UNIVERSITY OF VIRGINIA, ALBERT AND SHIRLEY SMALL SPECIAL COL-
LECTIONS LIBRARY, CHARLOTTESVILLE, VIRGINIA

HSC   Homer Stille Cummings Papers

WAYNE STATE UNIVERSITY, WALTER E. REUTHER LIBRARY,
ARCHIVES OF LABOR HISTORY AND URBAN AFFAIRS, DETROIT, MICHIGAN

HB   Heber Blankenhorn Papers

YALE UNIVERSITY, BEINECKE RARE BOOK AND
MANUSCRIPT LIBRARY, NEW HAVEN, CONNECTICUT

HH-Y   Hermann Hagedorn Papers

YALE UNIVERSITY, MANUSCRIPTS AND ARCHIVES,
STERLING MEMORIAL LIBRARY, NEW HAVEN, CONNECTICUT

AW   Arthur Willert Papers
CDH   Charles D. Hillis Papers
EMH   Edward Mandell House Papers
FLP   Frank Lyon Polk Papers
GBA   George Burton Adams Papers
GSV   George Sylvester Viereck Papers
HW-Y   Harry Weinberger Papers
VCM   Vance C. McCormick Papers
WCB   William C. Bullitt Papers
WKF   William Kent Family Papers
WL   Walter Lippmann Papers
WW-Y   William Wiseman Papers

TENNESSEE STATE LIBRARY AND ARCHIVES, NASHVILLE, TENNESSEE

TFMM   Tennessee Four Minute Men Association, 1917–1918

UNITED KINGDOM, NATIONAL ARCHIVES, KEW, SURREY

CAB   Cabinet Office
FO   Foreign Office
HO   Home Office
HW   Government Communications Headquarters
INF   Ministry of Information
WO   War Office

FILES HELD PRIVATELY

CA   Papers of Carl Ackerman, held by Henry Ackerman
FP   Papers of Frederick Palmer, held by Bertrand Bell III
JK   Papers of James Keeley, held by Julie Potter

DIARIES

Diaries are found in collections noted and cited as, for example, "Baker diary, June 10, 1918."

Ray Stannard Baker, RSB
Josephus Daniels, JD-UNC
Martin Egan, ME
James R. Garfield, JRG
Hugh S. Gibson, HSG
Edwin Milton Hood, EMH-LC
Edward Mandel House, EMH
Robert Lansing, RL
Breckenridge Long, BL
Arthur Sweetser, AS
Charles Edward Russell, CER
William Linn Westermann, WLW

ORAL HISTORY RESEARCH OFFICE, COLUMBIA UNIVERSITY

Oral histories are cited, for example, as "Bakhmeteff oral history," followed by page number.

"The Reminiscences of Boris A. Bakhmeteff," 1950
"The Reminiscences of Edward M. Bernays," 1971
"The Reminiscences of Bruce Ormsby Bliven," 1970
"The Reminiscences of Heber Blankenhorn," 1955
"The Reminiscences of Malcom Waters Davis," 1950
"The Reminiscences of Guy Stanton Ford," 1955
"The Reminiscences of Walter Lippmann," 1950
"The Reminiscences of Allan Nevins," 1963
"The Reminiscences of Hamilton Owens," 1958
"The Reminiscences of Dewitt Clinton Poole," 1952
"The Reminiscences of James Thompson Shotwell," 1952
"The Reminiscences of John Spargo," 1950
"Oral History of Frederick C. Tanner," 1960
"The Reminiscences of Stanley Washburn," 1950

Index

Note: Page numbers in italic refer to figures and tables.

About the Author

John Maxwell Hamilton is the Hopkins P. Breazeale LSU Foundation Professor of Journalism at Louisiana State University and a Senior Scholar at the Woodrow Wilson International Center in Washington, DC.

Hamilton began his journalism career with the *Milwaukee Journal.* He has written on domestic and foreign affairs for the *New York Times,* the *Washington Post,* the *Christian Science Monitor,* the *Nation, Foreign Affairs,* and other newspapers and magazines. He reported abroad for ABC Radio and was a longtime commentator on public radio's *Marketplace.*

Hamilton served in the Agency for International Development during the Carter administration and on the staffs of the House of Representatives Foreign Affairs Committee and the World Bank. In the 1970s he followed the intelligence community, then the subject of House and Senate investigations, for US Representative Michael Harrington.

At LSU Hamilton was the founding dean of the Manship School of Mass Communication and the university's executive vice chancellor and provost.

Hamilton has been a fellow at Harvard University's Shorenstein Center on Press, Politics, and Public Policy and is on the board of directors of the International Center for Journalists. With support from the Ford Foundation and the Carnegie Corporation, Hamilton carried out a project in the 1980s to improve reporting on developing countries. The *National Review* said he probably did "more than any other single journalist" to shape public opinion about the complexity of US–Third World relations.

Hamilton is the author or coauthor of six other books and editor of the LSU Book series From Our Own Correspondent. His book *Journalism's Roving Eye: A History of American Foreign Reporting* won the Goldsmith Prize and the Tankard Book Award and was named Book of the Year by the American Journalism Historians Association.

Milton Keynes UK
Ingram Content Group UK Ltd.
UKHW012116250124
436597UK00015B/323